Environment, Climate, and Social Justice

Devendraraj Madhanagopal ·
Christopher Todd Beer · Bala Raju Nikku ·
André J. Pelser
Editors

Environment, Climate, and Social Justice

Perspectives and Practices from the Global South

Editors
Devendraraj Madhanagopal
School of Sustainability
XIM University
Bhubaneswar, Odisha, India

Bala Raju Nikku
Faculty of Education and Social Work
Thompson Rivers University
Kamloops, BC, Canada

Christopher Todd Beer
Sociology and Anthropology
Lake Forest College
Lake Forest, IL, USA

André J. Pelser
Department of Sociology
University of the Free State
Bloemfontein, Free State, South Africa

ISBN 978-981-19-1986-2   ISBN 978-981-19-1987-9 (eBook)
https://doi.org/10.1007/978-981-19-1987-9

© The Editor(s) (if applicable) and The Author(s), under exclusive license to Springer Nature Singapore Pte Ltd. 2022
This work is subject to copyright. All rights are solely and exclusively licensed by the Publisher, whether the whole or part of the material is concerned, specifically the rights of translation, reprinting, reuse of illustrations, recitation, broadcasting, reproduction on microfilms or in any other physical way, and transmission or information storage and retrieval, electronic adaptation, computer software, or by similar or dissimilar methodology now known or hereafter developed.
The use of general descriptive names, registered names, trademarks, service marks, etc. in this publication does not imply, even in the absence of a specific statement, that such names are exempt from the relevant protective laws and regulations and therefore free for general use.
The publisher, the authors, and the editors are safe to assume that the advice and information in this book are believed to be true and accurate at the date of publication. Neither the publisher nor the authors or the editors give a warranty, expressed or implied, with respect to the material contained herein or for any errors or omissions that may have been made. The publisher remains neutral with regard to jurisdictional claims in published maps and institutional affiliations.

This Springer imprint is published by the registered company Springer Nature Singapore Pte Ltd.
The registered company address is: 152 Beach Road, #21-01/04 Gateway East, Singapore 189721, Singapore

Preface

The initial thoughts to produce this book originated during the discussions between the two editors (Devendraraj Madhanagopal and Bala Raju Nikku) in October 2020. We recognized a compelling need to produce a book that provides a comprehensive and holistic overview of Environment, Climate, and Social Justice. Initially, we thought of writing this book with an exclusive focus on South Asia. Over the period, we realized that the exclusive focus on South Asia would not be sufficient, and there is a need to focus on the entire Global South, especially to discuss climate justice challenges. Along with him, I put together our thoughts and invited Christopher Todd Beer and André J. Pelser to join us as the co-editors to produce this book. They shared a great interest in working on this book and offered valuable insights and support to produce it throughout the process. I am thankful to Christopher Todd Beer, Bala Raju Nikku, and André J. Pelser for their valuable support and motivation.

In late 2020, I approached some potential scholars in different regions of the world who could contribute chapters for this book. I received an overwhelming response from them. A few potential scholars could not contribute chapters due to their work schedules; however, they shared their best wishes and noted the imperatives of producing such a comprehensive edited volume, focusing on the Global South. I thank all our contributing authors for their support and commitment throughout the process.

As the themes and regional focus of the chapters are highly diversified, it was expected to face certain challenges in identifying reviewers. Nevertheless, thankfully, we found a good number of potential senior and emerging scholars, educators, and practitioners in different regions of the world who could provide peer reviews to our submitted manuscripts. I sincerely thank all our reviewers for supporting us to maintain the quality of the manuscripts by sharing their valuable insights and suggestions.

I thankfully acknowledge Nupoor Singh, the Editor at Springer Nature, for her continuous support and constant guidance to make this project successful. I thank Fermine Shaly, Ashok Kumar, Daniel Joseph Glarance, Jayanthi Narayanaswamy, and the entire Springer Nature team for producing this book.

Along with my co-editors, I happily thank our families, friends, colleagues, and the academic institutions (XIM University, Odisha, India; Lake Forest College, IL, USA; Thompson Rivers University, Kamloops, Canada; University of the Free State, South Africa) that we belong to for their support in various ways throughout the making of this book.

Odisha, India   Devendraraj Madhanagopal
March 2022

Acknowledgements

The editors wish to specially thank our external reviewers

- Ariel Salleh (Ph.D.), Honorary Associate Professor in Political Economy, University of Sydney, Australia.
- C.R. Bijoy, Independent Researcher, Tamil Nadu, India.
- Carmen G. Gonzalez, Morris I. Leibman Professor of Law, Loyola University Chicago School of Law, USA.
- Lochner Marais (Ph.D.), Professor, Centre for Development Support, University of the Free State, Bloemfontein, South Africa.
- Louis Nyahunda (Ph.D.), Research Associate, The Department of Research and Administration, University of Limpopo, South Africa.
- Md. Abdul Awal Khan (Ph.D.), Associate Professor, Department of Law, Independent University, Bangladesh.
- Michael Spacek, Ph.D. Candidate, Department of Political Science, Carleton University, Ottawa, Canada.
- Neera Singh (Ph.D.), Associate Professor, Department of Geography and Planning, University of Toronto St. George, Canada.
- Pamela Towela Sambo (Ph.D.), University of Zambia, School of Law, Zambia.
- Pushpa Kumar Lakshmanan (Ph.D.), Faculty of Law, University of Delhi, India.
- Roelf Reyneke (Ph.D.), Adjunct Professor, Department of Social Work, University of the Free State, Bloemfontein, South Africa.
- Sairam Bhat (Ph.D.), Professor of Law & Centre Coordinator, Centre for Environmental Law Education, Research and Advocacy (CEERA), National Law School of India University, Bengaluru, India.
- Sethulego Matebesi (Ph.D.), Senior Lecturer, Department of Sociology, University of the Free State, Bloemfontein, South Africa.
- Shangrila Joshi (Ph.D.), Environmental Studies and Geography, Member of the Faculty, Climate Justice, The Evergreen State College, USA.
- Suratha Kumar Malik (Ph.D.), Assistant Professor of Political Science, Vidyasagar University, West Bengal, India.

- Tanzim Afroz (Ph.D.), Lecturer, School of Business and Law, Edith Cowan University, Australia.
- Tattwamasi Paltasingh (Ph.D.), Professor & Head , P.G. Department of Sociology, Sambalpur University, Odisha, India.

Contents

Environment, Climate, and Social Justice: Interdisciplinary Voices from the Global South 1
Devendraraj Madhanagopal, Christopher Todd Beer, Bala Raju Nikku, and André J. Pelser

Climate and Social Justice: Role for Social Work

The Social and Economic Implications of Environmental Justice for the Elderly: A Case for Social Work Interventions in the Caribbean 17
Debra D. Joseph and Roshnie A. Doon

The Human-Nature Nexus: A Sustainability Framework for Social Work? 45
Antoinette Lombard

Disaster Injustice in the Coastal Region of Bangladesh: In Quest of Local Actors-Driven Recovery Intervention 61
Rabiul Islam

Governance, Policy Advocacy and Legal Activisms in the Global South

Advancing Climate Justice in Africa: A Survey of Civil Society Capacities, Geopolitical Trust, and Policy Advocacy 81
Christopher Todd Beer and Mithika Joseph M. Mwenda

Development of Community-Owned Renewable Energy (CORE) in South Africa 99
Meron Okbandrias

The Impact of Climate Change on the Gender Security of Indigenous Women in Latin America 117
Úrsula Oswald-Spring

Reflections of the Climate Justice Framework in Public Policies:
The Bangladesh Perspective 143
S. M. Kamrul Hassan, Niaz Ahmed Khan, and Nashmiya Khanam

Climate Risks in an Unequal Society: The Question of Climate
Justice in India 161
Devendraraj Madhanagopal and Vidya Ann Jacob

Litigating for Climate Justice–Chasing a Chimera? 189
M. K. Ramesh and Vidya Ann Jacob

Protected Areas as a Catalyst for Environmental Sustainability,
Social Justice, and Human Development: Lessons from South
Africa 207
André J. Pelser

Critical and Social Movement Perspectives from the Global South

Indigenous Environmental Movements of Eastern India: Seeing
Through Henri Lefebvre's Spatial Lens 229
Tanaya Mohanty and Devendraraj Madhanagopal

Can the Global South Count on the U.S. Climate Movement?
Support for Compensatory Climate Justice Among U.S. Climate
Change Protesters 255
Christopher Todd Beer

Eco-Feminisms in Theory and Practice in the Global South: India,
South Africa, and Ecuador 275
Devendraraj Madhanagopal, Patrick Bond, and Manuel Bayón Jiménez

Hydraulic Fracturing as an Environmental and Social Justice
Issue in South Africa 297
Wade Goodrick and Nola Redelinghuys

Land Acquisition and a Question of "Justice": Voices
of the Unheard Marginal Groups in the Interior Odisha, India 323
Mohon Kumar Naik and Devendraraj Madhanagopal

Climate Change, Conflict, and Prosocial Behavior in Southwestern
Bangladesh: Implications for Environmental Justice 349
Tuhin Roy, Md Kamrul Hasan, and M. M. Abdullah Al Mamun Sony

Ecological Justice in Post-COVID-19 Politics: The Role of Affective
Ecologies and Amazonian Indigenous Ontologies 371
Maria Fernanda Gebara

Editors and Contributors

About the Editors

Devendraraj Madhanagopal (Ph.D.) is an Assistant Professor (II) in the School of Sustainability at XIM University (Odisha, India). He holds a Ph.D. in Sociology from the Department of Humanities and Social Sciences, Indian Institute of Technology Bombay (Mumbai, India). He is the recipient of several international travel grants/fellowships. His works appear in Environment, Development and Sustainability & Metropolitics journals. He is the corresponding editor of the forthcoming edited books: i. Social Work and Climate Justice: International perspectives (Routledge, UK). ii. Climate Change and Risk in South and Southeast Asia: Sociopolitical Perspectives (Routledge, UK).

Christopher Todd Beer (Ph.D.) is an Associate Professor at Lake Forest College (Lake Forest, IL, USA) in the Department of Sociology and Anthropology. His research and teaching interests include environmental sociology, climate justice, racial justice, social movements, and globalization. His previous published work examines support for climate justice among Kenyan environmental NGOs, the rationale of early adopters of fossil fuel divestment in the US, the pathways that connect world society actors to domestic actors, and the support for a radical shift away from capitalism among US climate change protestors. His work appears in *Sociological Perspectives*, *The Sociological Quarterly*, *The Journal of the Global South*, and *The International Journal of Sustainability in Higher Education.*

Bala Raju Nikku (Ph.D.) is currently serving as an Assistant Professor of social work at Thompson Rivers University, Kamloops, Canada. Bala served as the founding director of the Nepal School of Social work from 2005 to 2011 and held international teaching positions in Malaysia, India, and Thailand until before joining TRU in 2018. Dr. Nikku's research focuses on race and racialization of politics and policy, human mobility, and displacement choices during and after disasters and pandemics.

André J. Pelser (Ph.D.) is a professor emeritus and research fellow at the Department of Sociology, University of the Free State (South Africa). His research interests and expertise fall within the multi-reciprocal interface of population, environment and development and includes applied social and policy research, social ecology, and the implications of demographic changes for human development and the environment. In an academic and research career spanning almost 40 years he has produced more than 120 publications in the form of books, chapters in books, scholarly articles and commissioned research reports. Besides consulting extensively for national agencies and private companies, he has also served as research and technical advisor to, amongst others, the *United Nations Population Fund*, the *International Foundation of Science* (Sweden), the *Research Council of Norway* and the *African Climate Change Fellowship Programme* (Tanzania).

Contributors

M. M. Abdullah Al Mamun Sony is a Doctoral Student of Géza Marton Doctoral School of Legal Studies, University of Debrecen, Hungary. His research interest includes transgender, legal studies, society 5.0, change in people's livelihood, and disaster management.

Patrick Bond (Ph.D.) studied economic geography at Johns Hopkins University in Baltimore. After Ph.D. research in Zimbabwe, during the early 1990s he lived in Johannesburg and worked within South Africa's urban social movements. In 1994 and 1996, Patrick was a policy drafter in President Nelson Mandela's office, responsible for the first White Paper. He has authored or edited four books on climate change, and hosted South Africa's civil society meetings during the 2011 UN climate summit in Durban. He has worked at the Universities of KwaZulu-Natal, Witwatersrand, Western Cape and Johannesburg where he is presently a Professor of Sociology.

Dr. Roshnie A. Doon is an independent researcher in the field of Labour Economics. She holds a PhD. in Economic Development Policy, MSc. Economics, and BSc. Economics from the University of the West Indies St. Augustine, Trinidad. She has completed a PhD. Master Class in International Business from the Henley School of Business at the University of Reading, U.K., and is currently an affiliate of the Global Labor Organization (GLO), Essen Germany. Her academic interests are focused on Applied and Empirical Economics, in the areas of Labour, Gender, and Education Economics. Here she has published on a wide range of areas, which includes Higher Education Instruction, Economic implications of Covid-19, Returns to Schooling, Educational Mismatch, STEM Education, Wage Inequality, Gender Wage Gaps, and Economic Development Policy.

Maria Fernanda Gebara (Ph.D.) is a social anthropologist who spent the past two decades working with different traditional communities in the Brazilian Amazon. Fernanda's research focuses on the challenges of changing anthropocentric attitudes from diverse perspectives investigating local practices, traditional knowledge, policies, networks, and media to understand alternative configurations between human and other-than-human beings. Most of her writings and scientific publications can be found on her personal page: www.forestless.net.

Wade Goodrick (Ph.D.) is a lecturer in the Department of Sociology at the University of the Free State (UFS), Bloemfontein in South Africa. He completed his doctoral studies at the University of the Free State, Bloemfontein in South Africa, in 2021. His research is focused on the social construction of the perception of risk associated with hydraulic fracturing, renewable energy and climate change adaptation in South Africa and the global south.

Md Kamrul Hasan (Ph.D.) is an Adjunct Research Fellow at the Bangladesh Institute of Social Research Trust (BISRT) and a staff member at Western Sydney University, Australia. He held positions at BRAC University in Bangladesh and at Chiang Mai University, Thailand. He holds a Ph.D. from UNSW Sydney. His research interests encompass masculinities and men's health, disasters, climate change, disability, ICT and healthcare, international development and gender.

S. M. Kamrul Hassan is currently working as an Assistant Professor at the Department of Disaster Science and Climate Resilience, University of Dhaka. He has completed MA in Economics from Colorado State University as a Fulbright scholar. His main research interest includes the issues of disaster economics, environmental valuation, cost benefit analysis, disaster governance etc. He has published research papers in several impact factor journals. In addition to teaching, he has been involved with different research projects of the Government of Bangladesh as well as several other national and international development organizations.

Rabiul Islam (Ph.D.) is a Professor at the Department of Social Work, University of Rajshahi, Bangladesh. He received his Ph.D. from the Macquarie University, Australia. He completed his M.Sc. degree in Disaster Management from the Asian Institute of Technology (AIT), Thailand and both the Bachelor and Masters in Social Welfare from the University of Dhaka. Professor Islam is an honorary fellow at the Macquarie School of Social Sciences, Macquarie University, Australia, and an international fellow at the Brown University, USA. His research interests are—social capital and disaster resilience, community-based disaster risk reduction, climate change adaptation, and gender and development.

Vidya Ann Jacob is an Assistant Professor at School of Law, Christ University, Bangalore, Karnataka (India) and has been associated with the law school for the past eight years. Her research interests include Human Rights, Urban Development Law, Environmental Law and Climate Change Law and Policy. She has been a part of research projects funded by the Karnataka Government and National Law School of India University, Bengaluru. Ms. Vidya Ann Jacob was a Fulbright-Kalam Climate Doctoral Fellow between 2019 and 2020 at Lewis and Clark Law School, Portland Oregon (USA). Her research focused on how the USA has adopted different climate resilience mechanisms to address climate challenges.

Manuel Bayón Jiménez is a heterodox critical geographer with 10 years of experience working in the Ecuadorian Amazon, he works on issues of urbanisation, territorialisation, gender and extractivism. Geographer from the University of Valladolid with a Master's degree in Human Rights from UNED and in Urban Studies from FLACSO. He is a member of the Critical Geography Collective of Ecuador and a Ph.D. candidate at the University of Leipzig. He has published on the Ecuadorian Amazon in some of the most widely read scientific journals, and is co-author of three books, on urban megaprojects, the anti-oil struggle in Yasuní and the links between bodies, territories and feminisms.

Debra D. Joseph (Ph.D.) is a Lecturer in Social Work and Coordinator of the Social Work Programme at the University of the West Indies, Cave Hill. Dr. Joseph holds a Bachelor of Science Degree in Social Work with a minor in Psychology with First Class Honours and a Master of Social Work (Clinical) from the University of the West Indies, St. Augustine, Trinidad. Dr. Joseph also holds a Ph.D. in Social Work (Human and Health Sciences) from the University of Huddersfield, United Kingdom. She is also a clinical social worker who has been working with individuals and families for over fourteen years. Her research interests have been in the field of HIV/AIDS, environmental justice and sustainability, natural disasters, domestic violence, and women in fisheries. Her current publications include: HIV/AIDS, environmental justice and sustainability, natural disasters and domestic violence. She was recently awarded the 2019 Jeremy Collymore Award for Research in Humanitarian Response and Disaster Risk Management from The Caribbean Disaster Emergency Management Agency (CEDEMA).

Niaz Ahmed Khan (Ph.D.) is currently Pro Vice Chancellor, Independent University, Bangladesh (IUB). His other positions include Professor (Grade 1) and former Chairman at the Department of Development Studies, University of Dhaka; Senior Academic Adviser, National Defence College (NDC), and Senior Academic Adviser, BRAC Institute of Governance and Development(BIGD). He pursued higher education and research in the University of Oxford, University of Wales Swansea, and Asian Institute of Technology. His career reflects a rich blend of academic and practicing development management experiences gained in Bangladesh, Thailand, and the UK. He has published prolifically (more than 160 refereed publications including some 45 in Web of Science and/or Scopus indexed journals).

Nashmiya Khanam has completed her bachelor's degree program in economics from University of Chittagong. Currently she is pursuing the graduate program of economics in the same school. Nashmiya is an enthusiastic young researcher and has worked in several research projects during her undergraduate career. She is mainly interested in the time series analysis and forecasting, good governance, policy analysis and contemporary issues of climate change research. She aspires to pursue further study and research in economics.

Antoinette Lombard (Ph.D.) is a professor in social work and head of the Department of Social Work and Criminology at the University of Pretoria, South Africa. She is a leading scholar in developmental social work and social development.

In her research, she endeavours to contribute to social change and a sustainable world by advocating for social, economic, environmental and ecological justice. She is a rated researcher at the National Research Foundation in South Africa. She represents the International Schools of Social Work (IASSW) on the Global Taskforce in co-designing and facilitating the *Global Agenda for Social Work and Social Development*.

Tanaya Mohanty (Ph.D.) is Assistant Professor of Sociology at Utkal University. Having completed her Masters from the University of Hyderabad, She went on to complete her Ph.D. from Jawaharlal Nehru University, New Delhi. She was awarded with Endeavour fellowship and completed her post-doctoral studies from the University of Sydney in 2015. She has taught post-graduate students for more than 13 years. Her areas of interests are Sociology of Popular Culture and Media, Gender Studies, and Identity Studies. Her ongoing research in identity studies made her realize the importance of ecology in strengthening community-based identity, triggering her interest in environmental studies. She has worked on projects on Media in Odisha, and Manual Scavengers. She has published research articles and book reviews in various national and international journals, and authored books themed on Identity issues.

Mithika Joseph M. Mwenda (Ph.D.) currently serves as the Executive Director of the Pan African Climate Justice Alliance and the Chair of the Institutional Collaboration Platform for Climate Research for Development in Africa (CR4D). He has extensive experience in climate change policy advocacy and has worked to catalyze transformative change in communities, civil society and other sectors for more than 20 years. In 2019, Dr. Mwenda was named by Apolitical as one of the most influential people in the world on climate policy, the Sierra Club nominated him for their most prestigious Earthcare Award, and Pan African Magazine, L'Afrique, named Dr. Mwenda among the top 50 African Intellectuals for his contributions to climate policy discourse. Dr. Mwenda represents the African civil society in the Participants' Committee of the Forest Carbon Partnership Facility (FCPF) of the World Bank and the Climate for Development in Africa (ClimDev-Africa) Program. His area of research at the University of Witwatersrand, South Africa where he is pursuing his Ph.D. seeks to understand the deeper meaning of climate justice through African perspectives. He holds a Master of Science in Public Policy Analysis from Jomo Kenyatta University of Agriculture and Technology in Kenya, a certificate in Globalization and Social Transformation from Chulalongkorn University in Thailand, among other qualifications. Dr. Mwenda is widely published on the area of climate justice and climate change.

Mohon Kumar Naik is a doctoral scholar in the Department of Humanities and Social Sciences at the Indian Institute of Technology Bombay, India. He was associated with Foundation for Ecological Security (Odisha, India) for around two years in project-related positions. Along with that, he has had associations with community-level organizations in Odisha. His research interests span common property resources, resettlement and rehabilitation of project-affected people, and developmental issues of marginal communities. He has recently published a part of his doctoral work in The Oriental Anthropologist (SAGE Journal).

Meron Okbandrias (Ph.D.) received Ph.D. in public policy and Masters in Public Administration and Management from the University of Kwa-Zulu Natal (UKZN). He is currently teaching Public Administration and Management at the University of the Western Cape. A strong advocate for innovative solutions for governance problems and ethical leadership, he is involved in Smart Cities, Renewable Energy and Public Policy research. His previous research activities focus on Migration and Cooperatives. He serves as a postgraduate coordinator for the School of Government and is a member of the South African Association for Public Administration and Management (SAAPAM).

Úrsula Oswald-Spring (Ph.D.) is a full time professor at the National Autonomous University of Mexico-Regional Multidisciplinary Research Centre. She has studied medicine, psychology, philosophy, modern languages, anthropology and ecology in Madagascar, Paris, Zurich and México and has a Ph.D. form the University of Zurich. She is the first MRF-Chair on Social Vulnerability at United National University Institute for Environment and Human Security (UNU-EHS); a lead author of the IPCC and taskforce of IIASA. Between 2002 and 2006, she was General Secretary of Latin-American Council for Peace Research. She was also the first General Attorney for Environment and Minister of Environment and Development in the state of Morelos. She has written 70 books and more than 402 scientific articles and book chapters.

M. K. Ramesh (Ph.D.) has been a Professor at the National Law School of India University since June 1992 and also served as the University Vice Chancellor between August 1, 2019 and September 25, 2019. He has teaching experience of over 40 years and has worked for over two years as a Commercial Tax Officer in the Government of Karnataka. His areas of specialization include International Law, Human Rights Law, Environmental Law and Natural Resources Management Law (Land, Water, Forests, Wildlife, Biodiversity and Agriculture). He founded three Centers of Excellence at NLSIU: Centre for Environmental Law Education Research and Advocacy (CEERA) (1997); Commons Cell (2009) and Environmental Law Clinic (2012). He was a Senior Fulbright Fellow in the US (2005–2006) and an Environmental Law Fellow, 2006, Environmental Law Institute, Washington D.C. He is the Founder Editor of Indian Journal of Environmental Law (IJEL) and has published about 60 research articles and five books.

Nola Redelinghuys (Ph.D.) is an independent business development consultant and a research fellow in the Department of Sociology, University of the Free State (UFS), Bloemfontein, South Africa. She holds a Ph.D. in Sociology from this university. Before venturing into the private sector, she was a senior lecturer in Sociology at the UFS, specialising in Environmental Sociology. Her current research focuses on the socio-economic aspects of unconventional oil and gas development.

Tuhin Roy (Ph.D.) is a professor of the Sociology Discipline of the Khulna University of Bangladesh. He obtained his Ph.D. degree from the Institute of Disaster Management and Vulnerability Studies of the University of Dhaka. His research interest's climate change adaption, environmental politics, coastal risk management, disaster management, public health, sustainable development, population, and societal vulnerability and their livelihoods.

Contributors

M. M. Abdullah Al Mamun Sony University of Debrecen, Debrecen, Hungary

Christopher Todd Beer Sociology and Anthropology, Lake Forest College, Lake Forest, USA

Patrick Bond Department of Sociology, University of Johannesburg, Johannesburg, South Africa

Roshnie A. Doon Global Labor Organization (GLO), Essen, Germany

Maria Fernanda Gebara Independent Scholar, London, United Kingdom

Wade Goodrick Department of Sociology, University of the Free State (UFS), Bloemfontein, South Africa

Md Kamrul Hasan Western Sydney University, Sydney, Australia;
Bangladesh Institute of Social Research Trust, Dhaka, Bangladesh

S. M. Kamrul Hassan Department of Disaster Science and Climate Resilience, University of Dhaka, Dhaka, Bangladesh

Rabiul Islam Department of Social Work, University of Rajshahi, Rajshahi, Bangladesh

Vidya Ann Jacob Christ University, Bangalore, Karnataka, India

Manuel Bayón Jiménez University of Leipzig, Leipzig, Germany

Debra D. Joseph The Department of Government, Sociology, Social Work and Psychology, The University of the West Indies, Cave Hill, Barbados

Niaz Ahmed Khan Independent University, Bangladesh (IUB), Dhaka, Bangladesh

Nashmiya Khanam Department of Economics, University of Chittagong, Chittagong, Bangladesh

Antoinette Lombard Professor in Social Work and Head of the Department of Social Work and Criminology, University of Pretoria, Pretoria, South Africa

Devendraraj Madhanagopal School of Sustainability, XIM University, Odisha, India

Tanaya Mohanty Department of Sociology, Utkal University, Bhubaneswar, Odisha, India

Mithika Joseph M. Mwenda Pan African Climate Justice Alliance, Nairobi, Kenya

Mohon Kumar Naik Department of Humanities and Social Sciences, Indian Institute of Technology Bombay, Mumbai, India

Bala Raju Nikku Faculty of Education and Social Work, Thompson Rivers University, Kamloops, BC, Canada

Meron Okbandrias School of Government (SOG), Faculty of Economic and Management Science, University of the Western Cape (UWC), Cape Town, South Africa

Úrsula Oswald-Spring Regional Centre for Multidisciplinary Studies, National Autonomous University of Mexico (CRIM-UNAM), Cuernavaca, Morelos, Mexico

André J. Pelser Department of Sociology, University of the Free State, Bloemfontein, Free State, South Africa

M. K. Ramesh National Law School of India University, Bengaluru, India

Nola Redelinghuys Department of Sociology, University of the Free State (UFS), Bloemfontein, South Africa

Tuhin Roy Khulna University, Khulna, Bangladesh

Environment, Climate, and Social Justice: Interdisciplinary Voices from the Global South

Devendraraj Madhanagopal, Christopher Todd Beer, Bala Raju Nikku, and André J. Pelser

Since the seminal work of Robert Bullard's *"Dumping in Dixie: Race, Class and Environmental Quality"* (Bullard, 1990), there has been increasing attention to and academic research on environmental justice and its corresponding social movements across the world. Similar to looking through a justice lens at environmental problems more broadly, looking at climate change through a lens of justice reveals various socially constructed racial-ethnic, geopolitical, cultural, social, and economic inequalities. Because of these inequalities, the many social, environmental, economic, and environmental effects of climate change are not only disproportionately impacting the poor and marginalized communities of the world, but they also affect lower income, less resilient developing countries and regions to a far greater extent than their more affluent counterparts in industrialized countries. UN Secretary-General, António Guterres, warned that "Climate change is the defining challenge of our time, yet it is still accelerating faster than our efforts to address it" (UN, 2018).

As this book goes to press in early 2022, the world stands at a crossroads with time running out to avoid an average global temperature increase of more than 1.5 °C and make progress toward net-zero emission by 2050. The last 7 years were the hottest on record (Copernicus Climate Change Service, 2022). The second largest emitter

---

D. Madhanagopal (✉)
School of Sustainability, XIM University, Bhubaneswar, Odisha, India
e-mail: devendraraj.mm@gmail.com

C. T. Beer
Sociology and Anthropology, Lake Forest College, Lake Forest, USA
e-mail: beer@lakeforest.edu

B. R. Nikku
Faculty of Education and Social Work, Thompson Rivers University, Kamloops, BC, Canada
e-mail: bnikku@tru.ca

A. J. Pelser
Department of Sociology, University of the Free State, Bloemfontein, Free State, South Africa
e-mail: pelseraj@ufs.ac.za

© The Author(s), under exclusive license to Springer Nature Singapore Pte Ltd. 2022
D. Madhanagopal et al. (eds.), *Environment, Climate, and Social Justice*,
https://doi.org/10.1007/978-981-19-1987-9_1

in the world, the US, has still failed to pass significant climate mitigation legislation at the national level. Climate change threatens the well-being of billions of people across the globe, and it is widely accepted as one of, if not the greatest, challenges of our time (UN, 2017). We already witness the effects of climate change in our lives, livelihoods, and ecosystems. Climate change is expected to be an unprecedented challenge for humankind for the foreseeable future. Unless addressed, the harms done by climate change and environmental crises will continue to align with nations and the world's existing social inequalities. There is a broad consensus that environmental and climate injustices share historical roots with global and local social injustices and their multiple facets within the social sciences. The recent and growing scientific evidence strongly emphasizes that climate change will continue to impact the livelihoods of millions of individuals in the twenty-first century, but it will do so unequally. Less and least developed nations, Small Island Developing States (SIDS), global climate change hotspot nations, landlocked nations, and post-conflict transition nations are widely recognized as more vulnerable to the adverse effects of climate change. Most of these nations are in the Global South. Current research concludes that most of the nations of the Global South are not equipped to sufficiently counter the increasing challenges of climate change and associated extreme weather events. Climate crises and the resulting threats and uncertainties create multiple burdens and risks for millions of people in these nations, generating new challenges and exacerbating existing challenges for the vulnerable populations.

Globally, the environmental movement has taken on leaps and bounds in recent years. However, in many developing countries, large segments of the population are still caught up in daily battles for economic survival. In many cases, environmental concerns are featured low on the agenda of authorities and marginalized communities, as the daily struggle for resources and human development take first priority in the poor countries of the Global South. As a result, an issue like environmental justice is often brushed aside and excluded from education programs and development initiatives. In recent years, there has been a growing body of research examining environmental and climate justice activism and movements across the world (Hicks & Fabricant, 2016; Kluttz & Walter, 2018; Martiskainen et al., 2020; Schlosberg & Collins, 2014; Tokar, 2014; Tramel, 2018; Tormo-Aponte & Garcia-Lopez, 2018).

Nevertheless, many social, cultural, and ethical complications of climate change and associated environmental and social justice in the Global South remain under-explored. Despite the growing and varied attention to environmental and climate [in]justices cutting across legal and policy frameworks in the recent decades, a dearth of Global-South-focused scholarship remains, particularly that which draws upon and integrates perspectives from disciplines such as sociology, social work, governance, and education. What is mostly missing, however, is a comprehensive approach to environmental, climate, and social justice. Such integrated knowledge gaps are exceptionally high in the Global South. Glaring knowledge gaps exist in the research regarding the growing diversity and complexity of the environmental movements in the low-income and socially marginalized regions outside Europe and North America, or the "Global South" as it's often referred to. Among the existing literature, social work knowledge to address environmental and climate injustices and disasters remains limited. Some exceptions include contributions by Dominelli, 2011; Dominelli, 2012; Gray et al., 2013; Dominelli & Ioakimidis, 2015; and Erikson, 2018. Despite some noted contributions (Desai, 2007; Mathbor, 2007), the voice of social work research focused on the interface between environmental justice and climate change, particularly in the Global South, is largely underrepresented.

Our aim then with this volume is to contribute meaningfully to filling that gap through an inter-disciplinary focus. It addresses key aspects of the existing knowledge gaps in the themes highlighted above by bringing together contributions across various social science disciplines. This volume gives much-needed additional attention to "equity" and "justice" claims in climate change and environmental scholarship. The selection of chapters contributes to a better and deeper understanding of the interrelated challenges of climate change, environmental crises, and social justice. Given the increasing recognition that climate change impacts are potentially catastrophic and have unequal physical, social, and human consequences, there is a strong need to advance and expand the research on environmental and climate justice that is strongly linked to social justice—both in theory and practice.

Collectively, the chapters of this book have a broad scope as they invoke both conceptual and empirical-based discussions through a variety of fieldwork, practice, activism, advocacy, and policy-oriented discourses. Broadly, this book carries two aims: one is to expand the scope of environmental justice by exploring the resistance of different stakeholders to climate and social injustices through indigenous, democratic, decentralized, local-ecological, feminist, and other climate-related movements from the Global South; the other aim of this book is to contribute certain novel insights on social work knowledge and practice in reducing environmental, climate, and social injustices from the perspectives of the Global South. We believe that practicing social workers, policymakers, social movement advocates, and academics will find value in this volume.

More than a great deal of the existing literature, this book focuses on the voice, people, communities, practices, and movements of the Global South through the lens of environmental and climate [in]justices and inequalities. At the core of this volume are the people, communities, and nations that have contributed the least to climate change but are and will likely continue to bear the brunt of the negative consequences. From eco-feminist perspectives in South Africa to vulnerable tribal populations in India, to indigenous cultures of the Amazon, to the plight of the elderly in the Caribbean, we turn to those who have been harmed by climate injustice, environmentally destructive extractivism, and social inequality. This is not just a collection of research written *about* climate, environmental, and social justice in the Global South. Nearly every chapter is *written by* authors from the Global South, those with not only academic but also lived experiences on the front lines of climate change, environmental crisis, and global social inequality. Authors in this volume are from or conduct research in India, Bangladesh, Kenya, South Africa, Brazil, Barbados, Mexico, Trinidad, Canada, and the U.S.

We examine environmental movements and climate change activism as the response of people and communities to long-standing social injustices, structural inequalities, and historical exploitation. Environmental activism, including climate change activism and environmental concerns, is not confined to a certain race, social class, or nation. However, highly visible climate change movements and their leadership across the world are still largely homogenous in their race, class, and gender (Park, 2009). Environmental and climate activists the world over seek justice for the loss of their communities, culture, and ecosystems.

The selection of chapters in this book, however, shows that being a basic human right, environment, and climate justice cannot be separated from social justice, and the two often go hand in hand. As such, this book speaks to three main groups of the population in the Global South: students, practitioners, and policymakers. It alerts these groups to the fact that environmental justice and social justice are flipsides of the same coin that enshrines basic human rights, and as such, everybody—and particularly those in the Global South who often find themselves alienated from their basic human rights—should be allowed to actively partake and influence decisions that impact their livelihoods, environments, and living conditions in one way or another. Many of the chapters in this book demonstrate that in the absence of environmental justice, communities often fall victim to the development plans and policy interventions of authorities and practitioners who supposedly act in the best interest of such communities. The selection of case studies and best practices in this book will re-emphasize to its reader that oppression, discrimination, marginalization, and environmental ignorance in policies and development plans all interlock to trigger and unleash numerous negative social issues for all stakeholders involved.

While this book centers around voices and experiences of the Global South, it is not just for readers and practitioners of the Global South. Implementing climate justice will require cooperation and a political will from the vast populations and powerful policymakers of the Global North. Academics of the Global North need to have a broad view of the consequences of climate change, engage in and make public the ethical debates about climate justice, use their positions of privilege to amplify the voices of those who are infrequently heard, and educate their students across disciplines about climate justice. Funders and administrators of international development, social work, and environmental conservation from the Global North need to consider the complexities of climate justice in order to focus the impact of their work on the most vulnerable. Policymakers from the Global North need to realize that their seemingly very local decisions can have global implications when it comes to climate change. Social movements of the Global North should serve as allies to those unjustly harmed in the Global South, using their mobilizing resources and power to steer politicians to act with climate justice at the forefront. So, while the chapters of this book largely focus on cases, perspectives, and efforts in the Global South, the causes of climate change disproportionately emanate from the heavily industrialized and high-consuming Global North. Subsequently, this book is applicable no matter where you live or work.

1 Organization and Summary of the Chapters

This book focuses on environmental, climate, and social justice in the Global South in three thematic sections: i. Climate and Social Justice: Role for Social Work. ii. Governance, Policy Advocacy, and Legal Activisms in the Global South, and iii. Critical and Social Movement Perspectives from the Global South. What follows is a brief overview of the chapter-specific contents and what the reader may expect to find in each of the chapters in terms of core focus and arguments.

Part I of this volume, **"Climate and Social Justice: Role for Social Work,"** contains three chapters. As pointed out earlier, environmental changes impact differentially on various segments and sub-populations in society, and marginalized communities and groups usually suffer disproportionately from the consequences of such changes. This brings the question of environmental rights and justice for vulnerable groups such as the poor, the elderly, and indigenous women into the spotlight. In their chapter entitled, "The social and economic implications of Environmental Justice for the elderly: A case for social work interventions in the Caribbean," Debra D. Joseph and Roshnie A. Doon point out that by 2050 approximately 80% of all older people will be residing in low- and middle-income countries. The social and economic implications of such rapid aging call for the implementation of social work programs and interventions with an environmental justice theme in the field of gerontology, as well as the role that the social worker might play in the care of the elderly. Against this context, the authors examine the multifaceted nature of environmental injustice that the elderly population of many countries in the Caribbean region faces. The chapter further argues that some areas in the Caribbean have created a haven for the elderly, which strives to meet the social, physiological, environmental, and ecological needs of the latter. Within these four contexts, the social worker plays a crucial role in maintaining the human rights of the elderly population, not only by acting as an advocate and mediator in environmental justice issues but also to ensure that the elderly are treated with dignity and respect.

The chapter entitled "The Human-Nature Nexus: A Sustainability Framework for Social Work?" by Antoinette Lombard of this section offers conceptual discussions linking the social work profession and practice with not only environmental justice but also ecological justice in the background of the sustainability framework. She argues that there is a need to redefine sustainability and the sustainable framework in the social work profession to accommodate the interconnectivity between humans and the nature paradigm and advocates that social justice in the social work profession needs to clearly be articulated and linked with the natural environment that we live in, and this can only be achieved through the lens of ecological justice, environmental justice, and climate justice. This chapter also makes the readers engage with the scholarly discussions on ecology and deep ecology and argues that the social work profession will only be accomplished if it embraces the natural environment and is lined with ecological justice. To bolster conceptual discussions, at the end of this chapter, Antoinette also provides a brief review of three case studies from Africa and another one from India to show the interventions of social workers in promoting environmental justice and in the formation of sustainable and just communities.

Rabiul Islam's chapter entitled "Disaster injustice in the coastal region of Bangladesh: In quest of local actors-driven recovery intervention" unravels the multiple facets of disaster-led injustice led by the local actors, including the local leaders and NGO staff to coastal Bangladesh's cyclone-affected communities. Though this chapter is focused on a few selected coastal villages of Bangladesh, the rich insights backed with field narratives of the disaster victims makes the readers think and reflect on the nuances, politics, bribery, and nepotism of local actors-driven disaster recovery intervention processes of other regions of Bangladesh and in other parts of the Global South. After providing a careful review of disaster justice, and an outline of methods adopted to conduct this research at the field sites of Bangladesh, this chapter critically discusses the deprivation and injustices faced by the cyclone-affected communities in receiving their disaster recovery and rehabilitation support from the local actors. The coastal regions of Bangladesh are among the most vulnerable areas to climate risks and coastal hazards not just in South Asia but also in the entire world. These regions are also home to millions of marginalized coastal communities. They are primarily dependent on the aids, assistance, and support of the state and NGOs to recover from disasters and climate risks. Bribery, nepotism, and the resulting unequal distribution of the post-disaster recovery support further marginalizes the coastal communities. It makes them more vulnerable and deprives them of their rights and livelihoods. Highlighting its seriousness, Rabiul Islam also offers some suggestions to be followed in the post-disaster recovery support of the local actors at the policy levels in the coastal areas of Bangladesh.

Part II, "Governance, Policy Advocacy, and Legal Activisms in the Global South," contains seven chapters examining topics as diverse as the democratization of power generation in South Africa to gender security among indigenous women in Latin America to disaster politics in Bangladesh to climate litigation in India and more.

Civil society actors continue to play a role in influencing and implementing global-level negotiations and policies. African climate-justice-focused civil society organizations (CJO) are diverse in many ways, including the geographical scope of their work, the types of communities they serve, and the issues on which they focus. The chapter entitled "Advancing Climate Justice in Africa: A Survey of Civil Society Capacities, Geopolitical Trust, and Policy Advocacy" by Christopher Todd Beer and Mithika Joseph M. Mwenda provides an in-depth empirical descriptive analysis of the capacity, geopolitical trust, and policy advocacy of African climate justice civil society by analyzing responses from 121 organizational members of the Pan African Climate Justice Alliance (PACJA). The results show that climate injustices amplify existing vulnerabilities. Most African CJOs have integrated climate change programming into numerous other issues that are challenging to their communities. In addition to climate change issues, education and literacy issues were also addressed by two-thirds of CJOs surveyed. The survey results show that China and the US were afforded the least amount of trust by African CJOs regarding country commitments to meet the climate justice targets, with a majority of CJOs expressing either very little trust or no trust in either nation. Four out of ten (41.5%) organizations from the sample indicated that they trusted their own nations a great deal to reduce emissions to limit warming to 1.5 degrees Celsius. Climate adaptation plans are largely state-driven and top-down in approach. Hence, this chapter argues for an active role for African CJOs in climate advocacy. Climate change is mainly experienced by the local communities and can only be effectively addressed by engaging local groups and institutions. The chapter entitled "Development of community-owned renewable energy (CORE) in South Africa" by Meron Okbandrias analyzes the decentralization and democratization of power generation in South Africa in the last decade (2010–2020). The development of community-owned renewable energy (core) projects in South Africa plays a critical role in seeking environmental justice for rural communities. The author argues that though the projects are supposed to be owned and managed by the communities, the fact on the ground is that these communities do not own the renewable projects in their truest sense. There is an infiltration of solar power generation by the private companies in many African countries where supply is erratic, and communities are weak in terms of resources and technical skills.

Another contribution to socio-environmental vulnerability is the chapter by Úrsula Oswald-Spring, "The impact of climate change on the gender security of indigenous women in Latin America," that explores the impact of climate change on the gender security of indigenous women in Latin America. This chapter argues that a top-down adaptation strategy led by the national government is not enough to deal with climate change and that important lessons can be learned from the traditional cosmovision of indigenous women that offers a decentralized and culturally diverse alternative to deal with unknown climate threats. Although 5% of indigenous people count among the poorest in the world, they protect up to 80% of the biodiversity on the planet. Women are especially active in environmental care and ecosystem restoration, but in Central America and Mexico, poor indigenous women are disproportionately affected by climate change—a situation which is aggravated by their limited capacity for adaptation and a lack of governmental support. The author continues to explain how the indigenous Aymaras in the Andes have developed remarkable resilience and new ways to overcome pandemics, disasters, and poverty through their indigenous cosmovision of "living well." Also, in Colombia and Chile, social movements are challenging the conventional model of neoliberal mass consumption and force national governments to reconsider their neoliberal agenda of development and move toward alternatives in production and consumption. An emerging philosophy of living well, solidarity, and care of people and nature synthesizes these diverse efforts.

How are the three components of climate justice reflected in climate change policy documents and action plans, and how do those documents differ from one other in delivering the different components of climate justice? In the chapter entitled "Reflections of the Climate Justice Framework in Public Policies: The Bangladesh Perspective," S M Kamrul Hassan, Niaz Ahmed Khan, and Nashmiya Khanam address these questions by analyzing the climate change policy documents of Bangladesh. By adopting secondary literature review, documentary research, and discourse analysis, the authors offer conceptual discussions of climate justice, and a careful review and analysis of three major climate change policy documents of Bangladesh, and discuss how the three components of climate justice, compensatory, distributive, and procedural justice, are being reflected in those policy documents. At the end of the chapter, the authors also caution the limits of discourse analysis to understand the reality of delivery of the principles of climate justice to the climate change victims and the general public. Rather the practical actions, efforts, dedication, and other resources of the state and governance actors only determine the successes of the delivery of climate justice. However, this chapter reveals the stark knowledge gaps on the different components of climate justice in the public policies of Bangladesh. How does climate governance at any level protect the most vulnerable? How do policies and climate action plans account for variations in the risks of different vulnerable groups?

In the chapter, "Climate risks in an unequal society: the question of climate justice in India," Devendraraj Madhanagopal and Vidya Ann Jacob examine the climate action plans of two Indian states, Kerala and Odisha, both known for their decentralized governance. While the two states have a reputation for their positive response to climate change, the authors find that their climate action plans lack sufficiently specific policies for two of the most vulnerable populations, the Scheduled Caste and Scheduled Tribes. The authors argue that in order to increase the justice of the two climate action plans, they should be based on climate justice principles rather than a science and technology approach. Not all groups are equally vulnerable to the risks and damage of climate change, but a binary view of "vulnerable" and "not vulnerable" is also insufficient for the implementation of climate justice. Rather the authors encourage greater nuance in identifying and designing policy for the "vulnerable among the vulnerable." Such consideration will provide more effective and more just responses to climate disasters. Climate justice policies should not be developed with a "one-size-fits-all" mentality.

Efforts to address climate change take many forms, including legal action. Throughout the world, legal challenges have been brought before the courts at every level in an effort to force actors to mitigate with greater speed and magnitude, compensate victims of loss and damage due to climate change, and hold state actors accountable for their responsibilities regarding climate change and the protection of their citizenry. In their chapter, "Litigating for Climate Justice: Chasing a Chimera?" authors M.K. Ramesh and Vidya Ann Jacob examine the legal space and actors in the Indian judiciary. Their analysis is preceded by a valuable review of the capacity and action of courts in the United States, the United Kingdom, Netherlands, Philippines, South Africa, and Pakistan to address climate litigation. Ramesh and Jacob find that Indian courts are insufficiently equipped to address climate change litigation, especially from a climate justice standpoint. The authors argue that while the Indian National Green Tribunal has begun to introduce the feasibility of climate litigation, the courts in India need to be better prepared to not only consider climate change's place in the law and enforcement by the courts but to do so through more of a holistic human rights-based approach. This approach will empower the court to deliver climate justice to people internally displaced by climate disaster, refugees seeking protection in India, and other vulnerable groups seeking justice through litigation. To be a more viable avenue, the judiciary must be trained to better understand the science of global and local climate change, as well as the unequal consequences of climate disasters. Only through this sort of capacity building, the authors argue, will the courts in India be able to serve as a venue of climate justice.

Boillat et al. (2018) argued that equity had become a major concern in conserving nature. However, in the Global South, inequitable social impacts of conservation largely prevail. The chapter entitled "Protected areas as a catalyst for environmental sustainability, social justice and human development: Lessons from South Africa" by André J Pelser provides evidence and hope for the environmental justice movement. In this chapter, he argues that given South Africa's turbulent political and socio-economic history, restoring the environmental and social injustices of the apartheid era—including injustices committed under the banner of conservation—has become an essential point on the post-apartheid agenda. Integrating conservation with human development at South African National Parks is vital for achieving environmental equity for communities. This chapter argues the need to strike a balance between the two polarized interests of conservation and development groups as a key strategy to achieve progress and justice for communities living in and around protected conservation areas. Overcoming the impediments in implementing any benefit-sharing program and supporting the livelihoods of neighboring communities in an environmentally sustainable way are crucial in securing environmental justice for these communities.

The third and final section of this volume, **"Critical and Social Movement Perspectives from the Global South,"** contains seven rich chapters that examine a range of movements and ideologies around environmental and climate justice, including eco-feminism in India, South Africa, and Ecuador; anti-fracking movements in South Africa; indigenous movements in India and Amazonia; mass mobilized protestors in the US; and more.

What is the nature of space, and how does the capitalist state define space in contrast to indigenous perspectives? Tanaya Mohanty and Devendraraj Madhanagopal examine these questions through Henri Lefebvre's theories in their chapter, "Indigenous Environmental Movements of Eastern India: Seeing Through Henri Lefebvre's Spatial Lens." Using Lefebvre's concept of abstract and absolute space, among others, the authors propose that indigenous movements are able to challenge the capitalist state's hegemonic development discourse through a discourse of sacredness and natural rights. The claims of the state and those indigenous movements are in conflict, and the indigenous efforts to redefine or reestablish the meaning of ecosystem spaces are a form of resistance against an ecologically and culturally destructive modern state. Examining two cases of indigenous population resistance in eastern India, the authors make an in-depth case for using Lefebvre's work to better understand the forms of resistance to capitalism and the state's effort to control space to transform all of life into commodities for extraction and profit maximization.

In the chapter, "Can the Global South count on the U.S. climate movement? Support for Compensatory Climate Justice among U.S. climate change protesters" by Christopher Todd Beer examines the support for compensatory justice to the Global South [including developing and under-developed nations] among the active climate justice protest participants in the U.S. To examine this, he conducted empirical research in the two largest climate change mobilizations in the US—the People's Climate March in New York City in 2014 and the March for Jobs, Justice, and the Climate in Washington, DC, and Chicago in 2017. This chapter is backed with rich empirical data on the views of climate justice protestors on providing large-scale monetary support to the Global South nations as a part of transnational compensatory climate justice. Christopher Todd Beer pertinently chose to conduct this least researched but most essential topic with the active climate justice protestors of the United States. Based on the careful quantitative analysis on the association between the social backgrounds and political ideology of the protestors with their views on transnational climate justice, he offers interesting insights. This chapter also provides a comprehensive review and critical discussions on compensatory climate justice. At the end of this chapter, he also cautions against generalizing these findings to more passive bystanders of the climate justice movement as the respondents of this research were active protest participants, and he underscores the areas of climate justice that need to be explored in the future to have a better understanding of views of climate justice supporters in providing transnational compensatory justice for climate harm.

In Devendraraj Madhanagopal, Patrick Bond, and Manuel Bayón Jiménez's chapter, "Eco-feminisms in theory and practice in the Global South: India, South Africa, and Ecuador," they look at the development of the complexities of eco-feminism and the ways that environmental and climate movements are integrating and could better integrate eco-feminist principles in the three countries. The authors argue that eco-feminism has much to offer the climate movement. This includes the eco-feminist challenge to not only patriarchy but also capitalism for its role in ecological destruction and social domination. The eco-feminist perspective also recognizes the extended timeframe of ecological processes that would help the climate movement fully recognize and confront the "slower" consequences of climate change like mass specifies extinction and sea level rise. As evident in many environmental and indigenous movements in the Global South, the authors argue that the climate movement would benefit from more female leadership and participation. After establishing some of the basic debates within eco-feminism, the authors provide a rich examination into the complexities, opportunities, and existing practices of integrating the eco-feminist perspective into fights for environmental and climate justice within the cultural, historical, and political contexts of India, South Africa, and Ecuador. Eco-feminism is neither fixed nor singular. This chapter demonstrates both the complexities and the shared visions and practices of eco-feminism that we would benefit from giving more attention to.

Extensive research over the last decade globally has demonstrated that communities that live near hydraulic fracturing wells and their associated infrastructure are at risk of a variety of health problems and often denied justice. Wade Goodrick and Nola Redelinghuys in their chapter entitled "Hydraulic fracturing as an environmental and social justice issue in South Africa" discussed the politics and why the South African government has committed to making use of the hydraulic fracturing technology to extract non-renewable natural gas, despite the controversies. Their work further unravels how the South African government and local communities have navigated and perceived issues surrounding decision-making, community participation, responsibility, and the distribution of risk as a result of the potentially serious environmental and societal implications associated with hydraulic fracturing. And how the use of such a controversial technology potentially harms not only the current but also the future generations of South Africans by hindering the transition from non-renewable energy types to renewable energy systems. One way is to analyze the complex issue from a justice framework. The distributive environmental justice sees *who bears the risks* of living near wells. Similarly, ensuring procedural environmental justice deems *who participates* in decisions about wells. If the communities that bear the risks can participate in the decisions made, then perhaps environmental justice could be ensured. The authors conclude that, "to invoke a justice-defined system that effectively incorporates the local communities surrounding and within the energy project, the initiative and process of fracking should be one where the community is considered a defining mechanism of the project's entire process from beginning to end" (Goodrick, 2020; Marlin-Tackie et al., 2020).

Land expropriation and the forced relocation of communities for various development-related purposes has always been a burning issue in many countries, but particularly in the developing nations of the global south. In their chapter on land acquisition practices (Land acquisition and a question of "justice": Voices of the unheard marginal groups in the interior Odisha, India) in Odisha, India, Mohon Kumar Naik and Devendraraj Madhanagopal discuss the weaknesses and inadequacies of current policies to ensure social and environmental justice to marginalized communities who often fall victim to land acquisition by the authorities. Land and common property resources are of great cultural and economic importance for the survival of marginal populations, but in many developing countries, such communities have a long history of being deprived of their ancestral lands in the interest of large-scale economic developments. This chapter outlines some of the social and environmental consequences and injustices of the state's land acquisition process for the marginalized communities in Odisha, India, and argues that contemporary policies have failed these communities and caused extensive social and environmental injustices, as well as environmental destruction in many cases. Subsequently, many displaced people are compelled to live in resource-poor and substandard conditions. The chapter concludes by recommending that the current development model in India needs to be reconceptualized to allow for the recognition of individual and community rights of the local people who are affected by such development initiatives.

Does climate change affect inter- and intragroup behaviors, interpersonal relationships, family, and kinship relationships, and does it impact their overall social bonds and community relationships? The case study conducted by Tuhin Roy, Kamrul Hasan, and M.M. Abdullah Al Mamun Sony in selected Southwestern Bangladesh villages (Climate change, conflict, and pro-social behavior in Southwestern Bangladesh: Implications for environmental justice) brings novel insights into how climate change negatively aggravated human relationships and weakens social bonds among the communities and the ways in which climate change generated inter-group conflicts and livelihood vulnerabilities in both short and long run. With a special focus on the changes of relationships among and within the communities and social groups in the aftermath of the disastrous hit of the 2009 cyclone Aila, the authors reveal the direct and indirect impacts of climate change and risks. This includes the disruption of traditional community relationships, social bonds, traditional local decision-making systems, and the resulting rise of individuality, inter-group conflicts, self-interest, and competition for resources, which overall have pushed the community to face social and economic marginalization in multiple ways. The disruption of social bonds within and among the communities also, directly and indirectly, impacts environmental justice. The authors, through field narratives, argue that a rising sense of individuality and loss of cooperation weaken the communities and enfeeble their collective voices and actions to respond to climate change and make them more prone to environmental injustices.

Extensive ecological destruction and environmental injustice clearly demonstrate the need for humanity to deeply rethink our very relationship with non-human species, our way of being in relation, rather than just a few new regulatory policies here and there. As we enter into a potential fifth mass extinction, driven this time by far-reaching and seemingly insatiable human impact, Maria Fernanda Gebara challenges us, through a multifaceted cultural critique, to examine indigenous Amazonian ontologies and affective ecologies to reset our relationships with other species and ecosystems. In her chapter entitled "Ecological justice in post-COVID politics: the role of affective ecologies and Amazonian indigenous ontologies" she examines indigenous beliefs and influence in Brazil, Bolivia, and Ecuador, this chapter presents ways that different relations, shifting away from a stark human-nature dichotomy, could be put into political practice. Examples include the constitution of Ecuador acknowledging the rights of nature or a Bolivian statute granting rights to "Mother Earth." Key to such shifts includes an affective ecology that generates collaboration, connection, and commitment through an ethics of care for the more expansive community of nature.

These contributions from the Global South academics and activists show that though there is not a single, united, coherent global environmental justice movement that shares common goals, frames, and forms of mobilization while seeking justice, global communities and the justice movements do share similar struggles, strategies, and forms of contestations with power, further testifying to the need for stronger coalitions and advocacy movements for environmental justice for all.

References

Boillat, S., Gerber, J.D., Oberlack, C., Zaehringer, J.G., Ifejika Speranza, C., & Rist, S. (2018). Distant interactions, power, and environmental justice in protected area governance: A telecoupling perspective. *Sustainability, 10*(11), 3954 https://doi.org/10.3390/su10113954

Bullard, R. (1990). *Dumping on Dixie: Race, Class, and Environmental Quality.* Westview Press

Copernicus Climate Change Service. (2022, January 10). Copernicus: Globally, the seven hottest years on record were the last seven; carbon dioxide and methane concentrations continue to rise. Retrieved January 14, 2022, from https://climate.copernicus.eu/copernicus-globally-seven-hottest-years-record-were-last-seven

Desai, A. (2007) Disaster and social work responses. In: L. Dominelli (Ed.) *Revitalising Communities in a Globalizing World.* Ashgate 213–297

Dominelli, L. (2011). Climate change: Social workers' roles and contributions to policy debates and interventions. *International Journal of Social Welfare 20*(4), 430 - 438. https://doi.org/10.1111/j.1468-2397.2011.00795.x

Dominelli, L. (2012). *Green Social Work: From Environmental Crises to Environmental Justice.* Cambridge, Polity Press.

Dominelli, L., & Ioakimidis, V. (2015). Social work on the frontline in addressing disasters, social problems and marginalization. *International Social Work 58*(1), 3–6. https://doi.org/10.1177/0020872814561402

Erickson, C.L. (2018). *Environmental Justice as Social Work Practice.* Oxford University Press

Goodrick, W.F. (2020). *The Social Construction of the Perception of Risk Associated with Unconventional Gas Development in South Africa.* Doctoral Thesis: University of the Free State.

Gray, M., Coates, J., & Hetherington, T. (Eds.) (2013). *Environmental social work.* Routledge.

Hicks, K., & Fabricant. N. (2016). The Bolivian climate justice movement: Mobilizing indigeneity in climate change negotiations. *Latin American Perspectives, 43*(4), 87–104. https://doi.org/10.1177/0094582X16630308.

Kluttz, J., & Walter, P. (2018). Conceptualizing Learning in the Climate Justice Movement. *Adult Education Quarterly, 68*(2), 91–107. https://doi.org/10.1177/0741713617751043.

Marlin-Tackie, F.A., Polunci, S.A., & Smith, J.M. (2020) Fracking controversies: Enhancing public trust in local government through energy justice. *Energy Research and Social Science, 65*, 101440 https://doi.org/10.1016/j.erss.2020.101440

Martiskainen, M., Axon, S., Sovacool, B.K., Sareen, S., Furszyfer, Del Rio, D.F., & Axon, K. (2020). Contextualizing climate justice activism: Knowledge, emotions, motivations, and actions among climate strikers in six cities, *Global Environmental Change, 65*, 102180. https://doi.org/10.1016/j.gloenvcha.2020.102180.

Mathbor, G. (2007). Enhancement of community preparedness for natural disasters: The role of social work in building social capital for sustainable disaster relief and management. *International Social Work 50*(3), 357–369 https://doi.org/10.1177/0020872807076049

Park, A. (2009). *Everybody's Movement: Environmental Justice and Climate Change.* Environmental Support Center. Retrieved December 10, 2021, from https://kresge.org/sites/default/files/Everybodys-movement-climate-social-justice.pdf.

Schlosberg, D., & Collins, L.B. (2014). From environmental to climate justice: Climate change and the discourse of environmental justice. *Wires Climate Change 5*(3), 359–374 https://doi.org/10.1002/wcc.275

Tokar, B. (2014). *Toward Climate Justice: Perspectives on the Climate Crisis and Social Change.* New Compass Press.

Tormos-Aponte, F. & Garcia-Lopez, G.A. (2018). Polycentric struggles: The experience of the global climate justice movement. *Environmental Policy and Governance 28* (4), 284–294 https://doi.org/10.1002/eet.1815

Tramel, S. (2018). Convergence as political strategy: Social justice movements, natural resources and climate change. *Third World Quarterly, 39*(7), 1290–1307. https://doi.org/10.1080/01436597.2018.1460196

UN (2017). UN Climate Change ANNUAL REPORT 2017. United Nations Framework Convention on Climate Change (UNFCCC). Retrieved December 10, 2021, from http://www.indiaenvironmentportal.org.in/files/file/UNClimateChange_annualreport2017_final.pdf.

UN (2018, September 10). Secretary-General's remarks on Climate Change [as delivered]. Retrieved January 14, 2022, from https://www.un.org/sg/en/content/sg/statement/2018-09-10/secretary-generalsremarks-climate-change-delivered

Climate and Social Justice: Role for Social Work

The Social and Economic Implications of Environmental Justice for the Elderly: A Case for Social Work Interventions in the Caribbean

Debra D. Joseph and Roshnie A. Doon

1 Introduction

According to the Environmental Protection Agency (EPA, 2021), environmental justice (EJ) refers to the equitable treatment of all persons, regardless of their social and economic background, regarding the implementation of environmental legislation. Within the EJ literature, there are a host of terms used to describe the inequalities that vulnerable communities and individuals are likely to experience, such as environmental racism, environmentalism of the poor, environmental injustice, and gentrification. The most important of these are those which concerns environmental injustice and its linkages to social justice, equity, and the quality of human life (Agyeman et al., 2002; Martinez-Alier et al., 2016).

Environmental injustice refers to the unfair treatment of vulnerable persons and marginalized communities in response to environmental hazards. These groups tend to bear the economic costs of being exposed to negative environmental consequences such as air pollution, poor transit, and toxic facilities, rather than the economic benefits that accrue to the creators of such hazards, namely businesses operating within the public or private sector (Agyeman, 2007; Agyeman et al., 2016). Most of the world's individuals who live in poverty are not producers of environmental hazards, as these are created by highly industrialized and high-income countries. However, vulnerable groups are the most negatively impacted (Agyeman et al., 2002). As a result, this led to creating a specific type of environmental injustice, known as environmental racism (Brulle & Pellow, 2006). The latter, according to Mohai et al.

D. D. Joseph (✉)
The Department of Government, Sociology, Social Work and Psychology, The University of the West Indies, Cave Hill, Barbados
e-mail: debra.joseph@cavehill.uwi.edu

R. A. Doon
Global Labor Organization (GLO), Essen, Germany

© The Author(s), under exclusive license to Springer Nature Singapore Pte Ltd. 2022
D. Madhanagopal et al. (eds.), *Environment, Climate, and Social Justice*,
https://doi.org/10.1007/978-981-19-1987-9_2

(2009), has sustained the environmental injustice literature over many decades for three main reasons:

- First, environmental movements tend to ignore social justice and equity issues that the vulnerable in society may experience.
- Second, it is often challenging to document and measure the impact of environmental hazards on vulnerable groups because environmental injustices tend to vary according to the communities' level of development and affluence.
- Third, there is a lack of studies on mitigation measures concerning environmental justice. For this reason, even though it is common knowledge as to how the problem of environmental injustice is caused, there is very little information on how to treat such issues.

The EJ literature has generally focused on the injustices experienced by different groups based on their racial background, as persons are often marginalized based on their ethnicity, spatial location, and household income (Banzhaf et al., 2019; Bullard et al., 2020). There remains, however, a dearth of research on the environmental injustices experienced by the elderly within the Caribbean region. One of the reasons for this may be because the concept of age is hardly discussed within the EJ literature, as elderly persons are often considered to be a part of the economically vulnerable segment of the population (Day, 2010). The EPA (2014) acknowledges the importance of the elderly in EJ issues, as they are more vulnerable to environmental stressors. According to the World Health Organization (WHO, 2021), the social and economic resources needed by the elderly to make healthy choices are indeed limited and must be covered to ensure that they are present in society and communities. Given the importance of this topic to the EJ literature, this chapter made use of a literature review-type methodology to not only examine the social and economic implications of EJ for the elderly but to also design a specific social and economic blueprint for social work interventions to cater for the needs of the Caribbean's elderly population affected by EJ issues.

2 Social Implications for Environment Justice

According to the Environmental Protection Agency (EPA), environmental justice seeks to provide fair action when dealing with environmental issues (EPA, 2021). This goal is achieved when everyone enjoys equal access and protection from health hazards and decision-making to access an environment in which they can live and grow. Most persons, according to the WHO (2021), are expected to live beyond their 60 s, and their numbers are projected to be around 2 billion by 2050. Presently, 125 million people are aged 80 years or older, and by 2050, 80% of these persons are expected to be living in low- and middle-income countries. These statistics raise critical EJ and health concerns for the elderly, and thus more attention to the plight of the elderly through environmental gerontology and the practice of green social work.

Dominelli (2012) explains that "green social work" integrates two practices, namely social work and environmental protection, with the aim to simultaneously address socio-economic and environmental issues. She adds that people need not only a sense of place and belonging but also to have a say in society, to respect and value the environment. If this is not accomplished, then alienation of the elderly can occur quite easily. Social workers can play a critical role in EJ issues by influencing policymakers to affect change that impacts the elderly by practicing green social work. The latter respects and values the physical and natural environment of the elderly as a social construct and makes the relationship between the people and their notion of space interdependent and symbiotic (Domenelli, 2012). Added to this, green social work decries the unequal distribution of goods, services, and natural resources, as it is deemed political and builds on the insights of radical and anti-oppressive practice, but also provides opportunities for innovation and encourages a holistic approach to sustainable development.

Given that social work is a practice-based profession and an academic discipline that promotes social change, development, social cohesion, and the empowerment and liberation of people, the principles of social justice, human rights, collective responsibility, and respect for diversities are central to the field (IFSW, 2018). Underpinned by theories of social work, social sciences, and humanities, experts in the fieldwork towards engaging people and structures to address life challenges and enhance the well-being of all persons. When the social worker considers EJ, social justice, human rights, and social change in the context of the elderly, the role of the social worker in gerontology changes to one where she/he assists older adults with challenges in living and accessing essential services, concrete roles such as being an enabler, that is, actively listening to the elderly, a broker who links individuals and groups with community services, and an advocate who acts on their behalf, all contribute to designing a framework for EJ for the elderly.

3 The Soroptimist International (SI) Barbados-Village and Hildegarde Activity Centre

This chapter looks at the needs of the elderly in terms of environmental gerontology and justice in the Caribbean, with the focus being placed on the social implications for this vulnerable group. To do this, an elderly project managed by Soroptimist International (SI)-Barbados is used as a case study example of good environmental gerontology in the Caribbean. SI is a non-governmental organization (NGO) with direct access to the United Nations (UN). Founded in 1921, SI is a global volunteer movement with a network of around 72,000 club members in 121 countries. This organization advocates for human rights and gender equality, whose main thrust is its advocacy work across eight UN centers, where UN representatives ensure that the voices of women and girls are heard. The membership work on grassroots projects that help women and girls achieve their individual and collective potential to realize aspirations, and have an equal voice in communities worldwide (Soroptimist Village & Hildegarde Activity Centre, 2020).

The Soroptimist Senior Citizen's Village and Hildegarde Activity Centre is located on 2.4 acres of land in the Caribbean Island of Barbados. The Village is situated in a scenic environment amidst trees and shrubbery with proximity to the necessary amenities in the community. The Village consists of 24 living units (duplexes) that cater to the elderly of 60 years and older and foster independent living. Each unit consists of one bedroom and a self-contained bathroom and kitchen in the space of 900 square feet. There is a laundromat on site that provides support for washing and drying for residents. Situated on the compound is the Hildegarde Activity Centre. This consists of a large hall, foyer, administrative office, board room, sickbay, bathroom facilities, and a fully furnished kitchen for the preparation of meals for the seniors. This center is available to both the on-site residents and seniors in the community 3 days a week from 9 am to 3 pm. The center provides a lot of activities for the seniors, such as games, exercise to music, singing, dancing, and other recreational undertakings.

4 Environmental Gerontology in Latin America and the Caribbean

Sánchez-González and Rodríguez-Rodríguez (2016) purport that by 2005–2010, the total fertility rate had declined in all major regions. Still, the reduction had been most rapid in Asia and Latin America and the Caribbean. Their total fertility levels had dropped by at least 3.5 children per woman in each region leading to a low total fertility rate of 2.3 children per woman in both regions. Given their rapid reduction of fertility, the populations of Asia, Latin America, and the Caribbean are aging faster than the population of Europe did before 1950. In Latin America and the Caribbean, female survivorship probability stood at 84 and 80% for Asia. In both regions, the numbers of older persons total about 40 million, with 8.6 million of them aged 80 or older. This number increased 11-fold between 1950 and 2010 in Latin America and the Caribbean. The percentage of women over the age of 80 is higher than among those aged over 65 because men continue to die earlier than women as they age. Europe had the second largest population of persons aged 65 or over. By 2100 Africa and Latin America, and the Caribbean are projected to surpass it.

5 Environment and Aging

According to Leeson (2017), the world is rapidly aging, and as such, the growing population is posing quite a challenge for countries to manage. On the other hand, it should also be regarded as a success story as more persons can live longer and able lives. As this global affair continues, Latin America and the Caribbean, with their history, culture, and traditions, continue to grapple with these challenges (Brea, 2003).

Society constructs age being matched with certain roles (Hagestad & Uhlenberg, 2005). However, despite biases and stereotypes, older adults should still have the right to have access to resources and take part in meaningful activities (Angus & Reeve, 2006). The aging population needs to be involved in community initiatives, especially environmental initiatives that foster participation and involvement in the decision-making process to enhance their lives (Riche, 2019). This was stated in 2005 and is still supported today. As explained below, ageism can contribute to the treatment of the elderly as less than the average human being.

According to Riche (2019), symbolic interactionism demonstrates how biases and stereotypes tend to affect how others view the elderly in a way that reduces their value and visibility to others. This may inadvertently reduce their contribution to society and to matters that directly impact their well-being. Seniors' knowledge of the environment and the vulnerabilities therein can prepare them for adverse weather events related to climate change. They can play an important role in the mitigation of the same (Haq & Gutman, 2014). The creation of partnerships with environmental organizations and the community will ensure civic participation and reduce the likelihood of ageism (Riche, 2019).

6 Physical and Social Adjustments to Environmental Change

Elderly persons in developing countries are exposed to the risks associated with climate change, and this is predicted to rise in the twenty-first century (IPCC, 2007). Members of the scientific community are warning governments that whenever a natural disaster occurs, the community which is most likely to be affected is the elderly (Loke et al., 2012). This is made worse by the fact that only 1% of human-itarian aid is allocated to the elderly (HelpAge, 2007). Another study conducted by HelpAge (2011) during 2010–2011 found that elderly persons are more susceptible to environmental shocks and can suffer greater exclusion and challenges during the disaster recovery period, as they face mobility challenges and access to essential services such as health care. Elderly women living alone with mobility and social exclusion issues are even more vulnerable (Smith & Lindley, 2009; Walsh et al., 2017; WHO, 2021).

In climate emergencies, the elderly can become displaced due to inadequate, informal social support, and damages to both personal and public housing and infras-tructures such as roads, bridges, walkways, drainage, and sewerage. In addition, the disruption of these basic services such as water and electricity and public resources such as health and transportation and support from humanitarian efforts is also nega-tively impacted during natural disasters (Shultz et al., 2005). There is a need to include the elderly in participation and planning for these inclement weather events by ensuring that knowledge of their physical and social environments is safe and reliable (HelpAge, 2007). Being familiar with their environment is critical for the safety of the elderly, as this is where difficulties arise in emergencies that may adversely affect their vulnerability and resilience to natural events (Danziger & Chaudhury, 2009). In recent years, there has been an increased focus on resilience, i.e., skills, strategies, and assets, that the elderly must anticipate recovering from a disaster experience (Sanchez-Gonzales & Egea, 2011). In the context of this discussion, resilience refers to the coping ability of the elderly concerning extreme events and their ability to adapt (Wood et al., 2010).

Byrnes et al. (2007) state that environmental gerontology has paid little attention to the study of environments impacted by climate change and its consequences to the elderly. The sheer lack of knowledge about disasters in the physical and social environments contributes to the morbidity and mortality of the elderly. Harvision et al. (2011) add that knowledge of the aging environment's attributes and functions can help improve risk management and, in turn, improve the capacity to cope on behalf of the elderly and to adapt to climate change, where coping can be referred to as "the action or process of overcoming a problem or difficulty," or "managing or enduring a stressful situation or condition," and adapting as "rendering suitable, modifying one's actions or behaviors" (OED, 1989). Coping is linked to resilience (Wood et al., 2010).

7 Areas of the Social Sphere that Impacts Elderly Persons

There are many areas of the social spheres that impact the elderly and impinge on EJ. Broadly categorized, these areas are related to accessibility, safety, control, privacy, simulation, and maintenance discussed briefly below. The Soroptimist Village and Hildegarde Activity Centre are used as a case study for the following social spheres, as it is managed by an administrator who also provides a supportive role in the field of social work. Both the village and center are governed by a working committee, chairwoman, and president, which is comprised of at least eleven members of Soroptimist International (SI) Barbados. The chairwoman has primary training in social work, which is integral to intervention with the elderly from a micro, meso, and macro perspective. Further to this, social work students at the University of the West Indies (UWI) Cave Hill, Barbados campus also volunteer at the center during planned days of activities to interact with the elderly. This has since been curtailed because of the Covid-19 pandemic.

7.1 Accessibility

At the Soroptimist Village and Hildegarde Activity Centre, there is easy access to roads, transport, and telephone services. Each resident has at least two guarantors listed to be contacted in case of emergencies. A clinic is less than half an hour away and facilitates the elderly in the instance that any should become ill. If there is a further need for health intervention, they are taken to the main hospital by ambulance. Proximity to friends and relatives is an asset. This favors relationships and informal help (Sánchez-González, 2009). Accessibility reduces fears and creates an atmosphere of mobility and assistance. Accessibility is critical for the elderly. It takes into consideration how they will access a service, resources, and formal support during a crisis despite their abilities. If this is not present, it makes them more vulnerable to what is taking place. Easy access and means to manage a crisis are very important for their safety (Tolea et al., 2012).

7.2 Safety

Safety refers to the absence of danger. Security is very important for the residents of the Soroptimist Village. So much so, a report was tabled on the required safety and security measures needed on the compound as feeling insecure and unsafe raises anxiety levels of the elderly. Even though they have each other on the compound, they live alone in their units, which can cause concern. Lighting is important to ensure that they can get to their homes safely. The knowledge of their spatial environment and details in their memory favors their orientation to their space, autonomy, and privacy (Rowles & Bernard, 2013). There is a main gate attached to the compound that is closed at night. External lights to housing units are periodically changed once repairs are needed, as maintenance is key to ensure the safety of tenants.

7.3 Control

Control is attributed to safety and refers to the environmental conditions that may improve or reduce the ability of autonomy. This impinges on their ability to achieve personal changes, needs, and goals (Rowles & Bernard, 2013). The ability to control one's space helps to reduce helplessness and hopelessness in times of danger is crucial for seniors. It also reduces anxiety and fear and supports the coping ability needed in a crisis. Control could also improve resilience and the ability to cope in adverse circumstances.

7.4 Privacy

Privacy refers to the ability to have a personal space where one will not be disturbed (Wahl & Gitin, 2007). Even though the residents live in duplexes, they have their unit that fosters privacy for living. Andersson (2011) states that separated rooms and spaces increase this attribute and are linked to residential satisfaction, as this can influence their health. It should be noted that the elderly may perceive a loss of privacy in the homes of their relatives, and this can negatively impact their welfare and self-esteem (Lok & Akin, 2013; Robinson & Rosher, 2001).

7.5 Stimulation

This refers to physical–social functions that assist the elderly to engage in activities and, as a result, improve their ability to cope with environmental pressures (Wahl & Gitin, 2007). Environments should foster creativity, freedom of expression, and perform activities that improve autonomy and well-being. The degree of stimulation depends on the individual. The resident seniors and those from the community congregate 3 days per week at the Activity Centre, and each day consists of devotions, music, games, dancercise, and any other activity conducive to active living.

Recently, the center partnered with an environmental agency to do a workshop on vertical gardening and salad gardening, where seniors were given seeds and plant containers with soil. They were told what to do, and in 3 days, everyone saw the seedlings sprout. These containers were placed next to their kitchen sinks for ease of watering and the joy of seeing them grow. The seniors propagated the vertical garden, and they found that activity quite enjoyable and provided intrinsic value. The vertical planting and salad gardening gave the seniors an added activity, which provided them with a fresh supply of organic vegetables and fruits while reducing the food bill of the center. While other fruit trees were planted, the activity contributed to the elderly's sense of self and raised their self-esteem, as growing their food contributed to their livelihoods in a meaningful way. These activities contribute to the physical and emotional health and well-being of the elderly.

7.6 Maintenance

Maintenance refers to the physical and social environmental function that suggests changes to and upkeep of the elderly's living area, which in turn helps their ability to lead their lives independently (Rowles & Bernard, 2013). Awareness of this attribute is important as physical activity can decrease. The physical environment of the center and village is maintained by different organizations that usually offer their services for free. The trees are trimmed, and there are benches under the trees for the elderly residents to sit and socialize. There are plans to have a time capsule buried and a tranquil garden developed in the surrounding areas. The units are maintained regularly via painting, electrical, and plumbing repairs, as well as the servicing of alarms; however, the elderly residents must pay bills for their electricity and telephone and the servicing of fire extinguishers. In addition, information on fire and weather preparedness during the hurricane season is provided to residents on an ongoing basis to ensure that they are aware of current information in the event of an imminent meteorological event such as depressions, storms, and hurricanes, or any adverse weather.

The physical and social implications for EJ weigh heavily on stakeholders for attention and action to not only bring greater awareness but to reduce ageism and invisibility of the elderly. Subsequently, attention is placed on the areas that can enhance their quality of life, where one such example is the Soroptimist Senior Village and Hildegarde Activity Centre that caters to the social and physical needs of the elderly. Some goals of social workers outlined by the National Association of Social Work (NASW, 2010) which is also the aim of the village and center, is to enhance the problem-solving and coping abilities of people while linking people to systems that provide them with services, resources, and opportunities to fulfill their needs and promote the effectiveness and humane operations of systems. That being said, a few social work interventions that support EJ from a social perspective, as stated by the World Bank (2020), include the following:

- The use of pertinent and appropriate methodologies for social protection (SP) of the elderly. This includes case management, where assessments, interventions, and follow-up are done with individuals and families to access services and resources for improved living. Community intervention includes raising awareness and resolving issues that may impede the security and livelihoods of the elderly and family accompaniment, i.e., building ties with family members to support elderly interventions.
- Many countries in the Caribbean have qualified social workers who can assist in SP. As such, social workers should have Disaster Risk Management (DRM) training in crisis intervention. They should be able to manage shelters, help to evacuate vulnerable groups, assist seniors, and assess the needs of a household affected by disasters, as in the case of Jamaica.
- Risk assessment and communication can be undertaken as part of the training and role of the social worker to support SP and EJ. Social workers must be familiar with risk assessments and situations where the elderly can be exposed and be able to make them aware of such risks.
- Risk Reduction through family accompaniment. Social workers can provide education to promote actions and practices in families and the community to assist the elderly.
- Preparedness of the elderly by social workers who can work with families to prepare contingency plans in case of adverse weather events to ensure their vulnerability concerns are included.
- Resilience reconstruction in the aftermath of a natural disaster. Social workers can help assess the magnitude of damage and loss in the post-disaster period.

8 The Economic Implications of Environmental Justice Issues

The importance of the elderly in EJ issues is linked to behavioral and physiological changes in the elderly population by their defend against environmental stressors (EPA, 2014; Parrado et al., 2019). This much is ascertained as environmental determinants such as private sector development, urbanization, and mass transport, can all influence modifiable risk factors of the elderly population through their diet, socialization, and physical activity, as discussed earlier (Hospedales, 2017). Before embarking on the discussion, for clarification, the term "environmental hazards" refers to man-made environmental threats created by companies/industries, while the term "elderly" is a part of the vulnerable population of a country. Bearing in mind these interpretations, from the perspective of the Caribbean, this section aims to first highlight the economic consequences that the elderly may experience because of EJ issues, second to examine the current legislation and social protection programs implemented to protect the elderly, and third to put forward ways in which the social worker can ensure EJ for the elderly which in effect becomes a way forward for social work interventions in this regard.

9 Inequity/Inequality

The problem of environmental injustice is complex, as it can be a source of several negative production externalities. When the circumstances of the elderly in the Caribbean are considered, one of the first externalities encountered is inequity. In the EJ context, legislative equity occurs when there is no bias in favor of either the elderly or the owners of companies who wish to locate in rural communities (Bullard, 2008). If, however, there is legal inequity present, then companies producing environmental hazards may be given more leeway during evaluation exercises. This may, in turn, hurt the human rights of elderly persons, leading to feelings of ill-will and discontent. One example of such inequity is reflected in the proposed construction of the Aluminium Smelter Complex in La Brea Trinidad, where the persons most affected by the plant's construction are those who are economically and socially disadvantaged (ELAW, 2007). Even though companies may have public consultations with various communities, if they do not cater to the specific needs of the elderly, by having flexible meeting times, one-on-one discussions, using printed materials, and including persons with disabilities, then this can lead to a more autocratic type of discussion being held amongst stakeholders. This is important as this type of leadership style is one that ignores group communication, as facilitators are more likely to be giving information rather than encouraging discussion and feedback. For this reason, the elderly may not view themselves as active players in the changes taking place in their community (Day, 2010).

10 Location and Proximity

Often persons experiencing moderate to severe forms of environmental injustice through pollution, and dumping of poisonous waste, reside close to these hazards (Bullard, 2008). This can produce negative externalities as the concerns of elderly persons living in remote areas may not be effectively represented during community consultations due to the high cost of hiring legal representatives. Thus, becoming even more vulnerable to land-use decisions concerning the relocation of homes and residential facilities being made without their input. Without a voice to speak on their behalf, such as a social worker, or community representatives, the elderly who are already financially at-risk may encounter added costs of relocation and may become homeless. In the Caribbean and Latin American communities such as Puerto Rico, the Dominican Republic, and Haiti, the long-term use of toxic substances such as mercury, according to Foley et al. (2020), can cause significant cognitive decline in the elderly leading to the early onset of Alzheimer's disease in the elderly. Notwithstanding the use of toxic pollutants for personal use, the ritualistic use of chemicals such as mercury has not been addressed in the Caribbean region.

11 Social Inequity

Social equity refers to the features of elderly persons' lifestyles, such as their race, culture, class, ethnicity, religion, buying habits, and education level, that may influence the environmental decision-making process of companies (Bullard, 2008; GPI, 2021). Social inequity tends to occur when businesses choose to either locate or dump industrial waste close to at-risk communities. Based on these social factors, low-income elderly persons living in rural districts may be afforded a different level of environmental protection and representation by government officials then another elderly person with a higher social status living in a wealthier urbanized area. This difference in representation may lead to the lack of social and EJ for some segments of the elderly population. Landfills and garbage dumps are the most common means of disposing of waste materials in the Caribbean. However, there have been a few instances as in the case of some countries such as Jamaica, St. Maarten, and Puerto Rico, where these landfills, having reached their legal limit, have led to the illegal burying and dumping of waste in open lots and gullies, which can contaminate sources of groundwater (Planning Institute of Jamaica, 2007). Although there are legal mandates against such acts, poor capacity building and implementation by the security and environmental bodies is one reason why illegal dumping persists in the Caribbean region.

12 Zoning, Land Use, and Gentrification

Depending on the type of area in which companies choose to locate and the intensity to which environmental hazards are taking place, the market value of properties can change through adjustments in the regulation of real estate and housing legislation. Zoning is one of the most frequent tools used by the government to regulate land use. However, it can also become an economic constraint to the elderly.

12.1 Zoning and Rezoning

In the first case, exclusionary zoning, and rezoning of land, using government and institutional authority can encourage discriminatory practices (Bullard, 2008). As a result, elderly persons of different social statuses, when making renovations to their homes, can become victims of land-use discrimination, as changes in zoning restrictions may lead to variations in the size of residential lots, the heights of buildings, the number of houses on a specific parcel of land, and deed restrictions. Thus, depending on the type of restriction, the elderly may incur additional costs when making real estate purchases, undertaking home renovations to comply with the land-use limits while protecting their environmental interests. The subtle differences in the zoning of land can lead to environmental racism. In that, any policy implemented, whether deliberate or not, which concerns a specific group of persons, influenced by their political affiliations/representation, ethnicity, and community type, i.e., rural or urban areas, may be related to environmental racism (Martinez-Alier et al., 2016). In this instance, land use and zoning decisions are likely to be synonymous with either that of the government or companies located in communities and not necessarily that of elderly residents. One such example of this occurred in Barbuda, where their government has focused on generating external capital and entrepreneurship, creating national parks, and developing private lands (Gould & Lewis, 2018).

12.2 Land Use and Gentrification

A second case in which the exposure to the environmental hazard is linked to housing costs and real estate is that of gentrification. Specifically, improvements made to a community through beautification and development projects can also influence the demand for housing in different locations throughout a country (Banzhaf et al., 2019). A significant consequence of such behavior can lead to changes in the price of housing, where the rising cost of houses in a richer or affluent community may contribute to the gentrification of the district. Although these environmental improvements tend to create positive production externalities for improving the quality of life and value of housing real estate, they also play a role in the pricing out or exclusion of real estate made available for low-income households, favoring wealthier housing clients. This, too, contributes to environmental injustice, as housing facilities may be distributed unevenly across communities (BCNUEJ, 2021). Such inequality may encourage poorer persons to choose inferior or less developed communities to reside in.

Simply put, the gentrification of communities, also known as the "Starbucks Effects", that is, the rising cost of property value, and rental of real estate in response to a cleaner environment, can become an added burden to the elderly. In the first case, a rise in the rental value of properties may enhance the cost of public goods such as electricity, water, and amenities in these communities. As a result, if elderly persons are unable to meet these costs, then they are more likely to become displaced (Banzhaf, 2010). Furthermore, a change in the demographics of the environment can lead to a change in the provision and cost of retail goods and services. In the Caribbean, the gentrification of many communities is a widespread issue. Countries in the Latin American and Caribbean region such as Mexico, Argentina, and Brazil, spanning the period 2003–2013, have found significant evidence to support the existence of gentrification, not only through the rise in property prices and land values but also the consumption of durable goods and transportation((Galiani & Schargrodsky, 2010; Gonzalez-Navarro & Quintana-Domeque, 2016).

Given that the elderly may have a limited income, the rising cost of goods and services can put this segment of the community at risk of entering poverty as they may no longer be able to afford necessities, even if the level of environmental hazards in the communities is small. This then contributes to the disseminating of poverty traps amongst the elderly. As explained by Banzhaf (2010), even though the elderly may be opposed to environmental hazards in their community, since the demand for housing tends to drop in environmentally unsafe areas, so too would the real estate values, thus leading to a cheaper form of housing. This now encourages poor elderly persons who cannot afford housing in an environmentally safe area, to seek permanent housing in these communities.

12.3 Health and Well-Being

The fifth area of concern, which is related to environmental racism, and the restrictions implemented to accommodate companies located in rural districts, is its impact on the health and well-being of elderly residents and their families (Bryne et al., 2002). Where land restrictions exist, the elderly may have reduced access to recreational activities in their communities, where the distance to recreational parks is long, and the quality of walking pathways and road infrastructure are poor (Agyeman, 2007; Boone et al., 2009). Given that environmental "goods" such as recreational parks, quality green, and play spaces have a positive impact on the physical and mental health of persons, as it forms a place of physical activity and social interaction with community members, less access to such facilities may not only cause the elderly to become more isolated but also become more susceptible to developing non-communicable diseases, such as cardiovascular diseases, diabetes, obesity, and stress (Malin & Ryder, 2018). This creates an added cost to both the elderly and the health system, as the uncontrolled pollution of rural and urban districts through the dumping of waste matter and the burning of biomass can not only reduce the quality of air in these communities but also contaminate watercourses. Furthermore, this can also increase the elderly risk of developing chronic respiratory diseases and lead poisoning due to weakening immune systems, which, together with the previously mentioned health issues, may see a rise in governments expenditure on healthcare facilities, to treat the outcome of these environmental hazards (Brulle & Powell, 2006).

To treat such issues, the creation of green spaces such as parks, in both rural and urban areas, can not only encourage the elderly with bad self-rated health care to visit these parks but also help them to better integrate themselves into the social networks of younger, older persons, and social workers in their communities (Enssle & Kabisch, 2020). The creation of this social network is likely to increase socio-EJ, as it allows the elderly, together with persons from their community, to change the EJ narrative enforced by the government by forming their own cohesive and robust social network (Falcone et al., 2020). This community-based approach can now lead to the appropriate changes being made, such as one which focuses on the linkage between issues such as health and well-being of the elderly, as well as the structural disparities and inequities that they experience (King et al., 2021).

12.4 Environmental and Social Exclusion

As recognized by many countries around the world, the sixth concern is the connection between the economic consequences of environmental and social segregation with that of environmental and economic degradation (Agyeman et al., 2002). This intersection, together with the presence of environmental injustices, can also exacerbate the economic impact of natural disasters on the elderly. When the elderly reside in communities more prone to natural hazards such as flooding and where toxic waste is produced, then a natural disaster such as storms and hurricanes can make them more vulnerable to toxic leakages (Sherwin, 2019).

In addition to this, because most elderly persons come from low-income households, they may also be discriminated against during the post-storm recovery efforts, as, unlike more affluent communities, the elderly in rural communities may be unable to relocate out of flood zones due to the high cost of real estate in more environmentally safe areas. An example of such discrimination occurred in Texas after the passage of hurricanes before 2018, where the inequitable distribution of relief aid led to more help being given to residents in high-income communities and less towards low-income communities. Further to this, one prominent example of social exclusion resulting from environmental injustice is the privatization of communal goods such as water in Columbian communities. Where the privatization of water resources and the transition of land use for agricultural type industries through state licenses has led to the collapse of indigenous fishing practices, reduced access to a clean supply of water by rural communities, and the appropriation of land by companies (Arango et al., 2021). These problems all contribute to the worsening situation of social exclusion of not only vulnerable communities but also the elderly members of native communities.

12.5 Employment

The seventh and final area of concern in which EJ can indeed impact the elderly is that of employment. In that, the uneven distribution of environmental hazards discussed previously may encourage senior employees to retire early due to pollution-related health issues. According to Banzhaf et al. (2019), depending on the type of company located in the elder community, the trade-off between the environmental protection offered to the elderly and the associated environmental policies implemented in the communities can impact the level of job creation in the area. In an instance where there is little job creation, and economic activity taking place, companies may be likely to engage in greater site pollution. This, as the low cost of land, labor, and transport facilities, typically reflects that the economic conditions of the community have degraded, consequently creating the perfect conditions for companies to exploit the environment and its community members.

Social workers should endeavor to reduce risks in the environment inhabited by the elderly and with groups and communities that support this population (Willers, 1996). This could be done by the attention given to policy areas and areas of teaching such as more social work programs with an emphasis on the elderly, research that focuses on the lives and livelihoods of the elderly, and practice in terms of the involvement of social workers in their communities. The consequence is to decrease vulnerabilities and foster resilience with the elderly. Attention to intervention processes that involve raising awareness, lobbying, mobilizing, researching issues, and training is a move on the right path for keeping the elderly in focus. It encompasses the physical, social, and economic spheres as each impacts the other and gives the elderly a front seat on issues that affect their quality of life.

13 The Protection of the Elderly Through Caribbean Legislation

Before going into the details of the legislative arrangements for the elderly in the Caribbean, we should briefly look at the two international declarations which influence the policies on aging in the Caribbean, i.e., the Madrid International Plan of Action on Aging (MIPAA) (2002), and the San Jose Charter on the Rights of Older Persons in Latin America and the Caribbean (2012).

14 The Madrid International Plan of Action on Aging (MIPAA) (2002)

Implemented in 2002, the MIPAA is a comprehensive action plan to address the growth of the world's aging population. The plan focuses on three areas, i.e., the health and well-being of the elderly, the creation and sustaining of a supportive environment, and the development of the elderly (UN, 2002). Under each area of concern, recommendations for action are made, which ranges from creating opportunities for the elderly to continue to contribute to their society through the mentorship of young adults, the recognition of the elderly in the socio-economic and cultural development of their country, to their effective integration and participation of the elderly in the decision-making process of a country's development towards the achievement of the Millennium Development Goals (MGDs) (UN, 2002). These recommendations, when guided by the three previously mentioned areas of concern, allow the governments of countries to dedicate resources to several different aspects of an aging society, such as the integration and participation of the elderly, the impact that it has on their respective labor markets, and their quality of life (UNECE, 2002).

Even though the MIPAA policy is one of the most recent and modern approaches to ensuring the development of an aging society, it is noted that while 44 countries have responded on how the implementation of the MIPAA have improved the human rights conditions of the elderly in their countries, there is a noticeable absence of responses on the implementation of the MIPAA by ministerial bodies, human rights institutions, civil society organizations, and academic institutions in the Caribbean region (OHCHR, 2021). One of the main reasons behind the slow implementation of the MIPAA in the Caribbean is the lack of age-aggregated data for the elderly and an inability to effectively develop the MIPAA monitoring toolkit of Active Aging Index Indicators, which observes the employment, social participation, health, and well-being, as well as the capacity for an empowering environment for the elderly (Zaidi, 2018). Further to this, even though some Caribbean nations have developed social protection programs for their elderly population, there continues to be a divergence between the implementation and practices of these policies because of inadequate funding and limited ministerial support (Quashie et al., 2018).

15 San Jose Charter on the Rights of Older Persons in Latin America and the Caribbean (2012)

The second international declaration that informs the social protection of the elderly in the Caribbean is the San Jose Charter on the Rights of Older persons in Latin America and the Caribbean. It was during the Third Regional Intergovernmental Conference on Aging in Latin America and the Caribbean in 2012 that governments expressed a concern over the rights and protection of older persons, considering the limitations faced when implementing social protection programs as previously mentioned (UN, 2012). Under this Charter, governments agree to improve their social protection programs to realistically meet the social security requirements, health needs, and the need for social services by the elderly. However, even though ministerial and non-ministerial bodies have acknowledged the importance of a human rights approach to aging in the Caribbean, only 12 countries have designed specific policies on aging (Quashie et al., 2018).

Notwithstanding the challenges that many Caribbean nations experience in bringing greater social protection to their elderly, two of the top high-income countries in the Caribbean, that is, Barbados as well as Trinidad and Tobago, have made significant progress regarding the implementation of social policies in the MIPAA, and the San Jose Charter, as reflected by Table 1 below. In the case of Barbados, their social protection program includes the non-contributory old-age pension, national assistance program, and the home care program (Morlachetti, 2015). Whereas in Trinidad and Tobago, there is the contributory old-age pension, the non-contributory old-age pension, health coverage program, home and care facilities, and the elderly and differently able mobile facilities (Ministry of Social Development & Family Services, 2020a; UN, 2017).

16 Legislation Governing Social Protection Programmes for the Elderly in Barbados and Trinidad and Tobago

The social protection, and care of the elderly population of the Caribbean, through the provision of the previously mentioned programs, are influenced by several pieces of legislation, which varies from country to country, as in the case of Barbados and Trinidad and Tobago. For purposes of this chapter, due to the expansive nature of the literature, emphasis will be placed on the two latter countries. Beginning with Barbados, the pieces of legislation which is linked to the protection and the basic human rights of the elderly include the Constitution of Barbados, the National Assistance Regulations Act (1969), the National Insurance and Social Security Act (1966), and the National Policy on Aging (2012) (Morlachetti, 2015; Ministry of People Empowerment & Elder Affairs, 2012; Parliament of Barbados, 2002; ILO, 2014a, 2014b).

In the case of Trinidad and Tobago, persons who are aged 60 years and older are part of the elderly population. To raise awareness and create initiatives that focus on the aging population, the Division of Aging (DOA) was created in 2003 and approved in 2006, followed closely by the National Policy on Aging (2007) (Ministry of Social Development & Family Services, 2020a; Rouse, 2017). Like many Caribbean countries, even though in Trinidad and Tobago, there has not been any formulation of policy and legislation specific to the elderly. There are a few important parts of the legislation that influences their rights and protection. These include the Constitution Accords (1976), which concerns the universal rights of all citizens, the Aging Policy (2007), the Homes for Older Persons Act (2000), the

Senior Citizens Pension Act (1939), and the National Insurance Act (1971) (The 2016b; Ministry of Social Development, 2007; Republic of Trinidad & Tobago, 2007; The Republic of Trinidad & Tobago, 2016a).

17 Economic Interventions for Caribbean Environmental Injustice Issues Faced by the Elderly

Bearing in mind the economic implications of environmental injustice faced by elderly persons and vulnerable groups, despite the legislation which governs the social protection programs accessed by the elderly in the Caribbean, there remain several issues that may hinder their rights to social protection and EJ. In this regard, there are several possible roles that the social worker may play in the alleviation and reduction of such economic consequences of environmental injustice to the elderly.

17.1 Legislative Equity

Given that elderly persons are amongst the most vulnerable when it comes to environmental injustice issues in the Caribbean, it is noted that in environmental law cases that often the victims of such hazards cannot afford proper legal representation (ELAW, 2007). This is an important concern, as environmental law cases, either against the state or private industrial companies can take quite a long time to be resolved, thus becoming even more costly over time. Bearing this in mind, to ensure legislative equity for the elderly in environmental injustice matters, the social worker can provide the elderly with information regarding access to free legal counseling, support, and representation. Across the Caribbean, the social worker can turn to many government-based legal departments for information to support their elderly clients. These include the Legal Aid and Advisory Authority (LAAA) in Trinidad and Tobago, the Community Legal Services Offices in Barbados, which is mandated by the Community Legal Services Act (1981–33) to provide legal services to persons who are finally unable to afford legal services from their resources, and the Legal Aid Clinic in Jamaica which provides legal services at a subsidized cost to persons who find that their civil rights are being infringed upon (LAAA, 2021; Ministry of Justice, 2021; The Barbados Parliament, 2018). While these legal bodies are known to assist persons in a range of issues such as the drafting of wills, transfers, probates, and civil matters, it is not known how much legal representation is afforded to private/public environmental injustice cases for vulnerable populations in the Caribbean.

The Social and Economic Implications … 35

17.2 Collaborative Work with Environmental Statutory Bodies

Furthermore, given those vulnerable populations, i.e., inclusive of the elderly segment of the Caribbean populace, are also at risk to environmental man-made hazards if residing near landfills, industrial parks, and illegal dumping sites, the social worker assigned to the elderly in these specific communities have a responsibility to ensure the protection of these persons. Bearing this in mind, apart from the provision of information regarding legal representation discussed above, the social worker can also partner with the relevant environmental management authorities such as the Environmental Management Authority (EMA) in Trinidad and Tobago, the Ministry of Environment and National Beautification (MENB) in Barbados, and the National Environmental Protection Agency (NEPA) in Jamaica to help the elderly in EJ issues in a variety of ways (EMA, 2021; MENB, 2020; NEPA, 2021). These strategies include:

- Making recommendations for the inclusion of the elderly population in national environmental policies that complement the social and economic agenda of the relevant ministerial bodies.
- Developing programs with the previously mentioned environmental protection/management bodies to highlight and promote the connection that elderly communities in the Caribbean have with their physical environment.
- Assisting in the creation of environmental standards, which are in line with the recommendations for the national aging policies in Caribbean islands such as Barbados and Trinidad and Tobago.
- Ensuring that all stakeholders, particularly the elderly population, are included in consultations with industrial companies and that they continue to play a significant role in helping the elderly adopt a healthier and environmentally friendly lifestyle, one which sees them making great use of green spaces, such as recreational parks and boardwalks. From this perspective, the social worker can become a strong advocate for the health care of the elderly in environmental injustice cases where air, land, water, and noise pollution pose a high risk to the elderly.

17.3 Social Equity

Additionally, the social worker also plays an important role in ensuring social equity for the elderly, i.e., ensuring that their need for impartiality, fairness, and justice in environmental injustice matters are met. It is important to look at the social equity for the elderly in this regard, as assistance is provided based on their needs. The social worker can help to improve the social equity needs of the elderly in environmental injustice issues by creating formal and informal networks of environmental agents such as ministerial bodies, non-governmental organizations, legal representatives, and stakeholders, i.e., community members, that can safeguard the interests of the older heads of households are acknowledged in environmental injustice matters (ICMA, 2021). In doing so, the social worker would have ensured that not only would the elderly have access to EJ resources but also promoted greater inclusiveness through the engagement of the community, thus enriching further the lives of the elderly. Such activities geared towards social equity also improve the dialogue between environmental authorities across the Caribbean, which in turn can advance the decision-making process, with the input of the elderly playing a crucial role (Carpentieri et al., 2020).

17.4 Rebranding of Housing Properties

Moreover, bearing in mind the changes in land use, zoning, and the gentrification of communities, the social worker can also play an important role in the rebranding of housing properties. Specifically, the work that the social worker does for the elderly in the communities includes improving their quality of life through better access to community services. This can be done by encouraging them to take a more active role in their communities and by helping them to better cope with problems such as those related to environmental injustice (Dhavaleshwar, 2016; FSU, 2020; HSE, 2021). Some of the tools that can be used by social workers who practice from a community development or organization perspective are their understanding of power dynamics and social relations between the community and the managers of industrial companies, building community capacity, creating collaborations/alliances, identifying community leaders, and providing education for the elderly, to achieve greater social and EJ for the former group, through structural change. These activities can not only change the image of the elderly's community, particularly that located in rural districts but also encourage de-gentrification of communities, where residential areas now become affordable to the poor.

17.5 Cultural and Environmental Inclusion

Besides the areas mentioned above, the social worker can ensure that the cultural practices of the elderly indigenous groups in the Caribbean are passed down to the younger generation. This is especially important as indigenous communities tend to experience several human rights violations such as environmental destruction, inadequate access to public utilities such as health care, water, and electricity, land disposition, and resettlement (Ford et al., 2020; Thompson et al., 2021). In the case of the indigenous Caribs of northeastern St. Vincent, climate change injustices such as extreme weather events like hurricanes and droughts tend to expose these vulnerable groups to further socio-economic hardships, as they may suffer from economic neglect and marginalization (Smith & Rhiney, 2016). These issues may cause the most susceptible of the group, i.e., indigenous elderly members, to be further neglected, as they tend to have a heavy reliance on land-based resources for their survival.

With this in mind, the role of the social worker becomes important in not only ensuring that the farming practices of these groups are passed on through the mentorship of younger community members but their customs are also preserved through the creation of community museums and grassroots civic forums, which promotes the shared narratives of the experiences of elderly community heads (Mei-Fang & Sheng-Chun, 2020). In addition to this, given that indigenous communities have strong cultural practices, this provides the social worker with the opportunity to learn how these ancestral traditions can become aids to helping them to keep their principles, values, and customs while ensuring that their human rights needs are met (Mooney et al., 2020).

18 Conclusion

The environmental injustice that the elderly segment of the population of many countries in the Caribbean region suffers is a multifaceted one, which becomes more crucial as the populace continues to age at a rapid pace. Given the exponential growth of the Caribbean's elderly residents, it is noted within the literature that they are deemed to be the most vulnerable to environmental injustice issues that may arise from the development of private and public sector business enterprises. This much as ascertained from their limited legal representation in environmental justice cases, their corroding socialization, and inclusion in the decision-making process within their communities, as well as their declining physical and mental health through the exposure to toxic pollutants. All of which contributes to the elderly facing more instances of inequality and exclusion in terms of access to resources, the inequitable valuation of properties, as well as the social and environmental injustice within their communities. Despite this, some areas in countries such as Barbados, as reflected through the creation of the Soroptimist Senior Citizen's Village and Hildegarde Activity Centre, have created a haven for their elderly population, which strives to meet the social, physiological, environmental, and ecological needs of the elderly. It is within these four contexts that the social worker plays a crucial role in maintaining the human rights of the elderly in the Caribbean, to not only act as an advocate and mediator in EJ issues but also to ensure that they are treated with dignity and respect.

Conflict of Interest The authors have no conflict of interest.

References

Agyeman, J. (2007). Environmental Justice and Sustainability. In G. Atkinson, S. Dietz, & E. Neumayer (Eds.). *Handbook of sustainable development* (pp. 171–188). Edward Elgar Publishing Limited. http://www.communita.com.br/assets/handbookofsustainabledevelopment.pdf.

Agyeman, J., Bullard, R., & Evans, B. (2002). Exploring the nexus: Bringing together sustainability, environmental justice and equality. *Space and Polity, 6*(1), 77–90. https://doi.org/10.1080/135625 70220137907

Agyeman, J., Schlosberg, D., Craven, L., & Matthews, C. (2016). Trends and directions in environmental justice: From inequality to everyday life, community, and just sustainabilities. *Annual Review of Environment and Resources, 41*, 321–340. https://doi.org/10.1146/annurev-environ-110615-090052

Andersson, J. E. (2011). Architecture for the silver generation: Exploring the meaning of appropriate space for ageing in a Swedish municipality. *Health and Place, 17*(2), 572–587. https://doi.org/10.1016/j.healthplace.2010.12.015

Angus, J., & Reeve, P. (2006). Ageism: A threat to "Aging Well" in the 21st century. *The Journal of Applied Gerontology, 25*(2), 137–152. https://doi.org/10.1177/0733464805285745

Arango, J., Senent-De Frutos, J., & Molina, E. (2021). Murky waters: The impact of privatizing water use on environmental degradation and the exclusion of local communities in the Caribbean, *International Journal of Water Resources Development*, 1–21. https://doi.org/10.1080/07900627.2021.1931052

Banzhaf, S. (2010). *Regulatory impact analyses of environmental justice effects.* National Centre for Environmental Economics (NCEE). Environmental Protection Agency National Center for Environmental Economics. Retrieved October 27, 2021, from https://www.epa.gov/sites/default/files/2014-12/documents/regulatory_impact_analyses_of_environmental_justice_effects.pdf.

Banzhaf, S., Ma, L., & Timmins, C. (2019). Environmental justice: The economics of race, place, and pollution. *Journal of Economic Perspectives, 33*(1), 185–208. https://doi.org/10.1257/jep.33.1.185

Barcelona Lab for Urban Environmental Justice and Sustainability (BCNUEJ). (2021). *Critical sustainable studies.* Retrieved February 2, 2021, from http://www.bcnuej.org/green-gentrification/

Boone, C., Buckley, G., Grove, M., & Sister, C. (2009). Parks and people: An environmental justice inquiry in Baltimore, Maryland. *Annals of the Association of American Geographers, 99*(4), 767–787. https://doi.org/10.1080/00045600903102949

Brea, J. A. (2003). Population dynamics in Latin America. *Population Bulletin 58*(1). https://www.prb.org/wp-content/uploads/2020/11/Population-Bulletin-2003-58.1-PopulDynamicsLatinAmer.pdf.

Brulle, R., & Pellow, D. (2006). Environmental justice: Human health and environmental inequalities. *Annual Review of Public Health, 27*, 103–124. https://doi.org/10.1146/annurev.publhealth.27.021405.102124

Bullard, R., Patterson, J., & Thomas, S. (2020). Roundtable on the pandemics of racism, environmental injustice, and covid-19 in America. *Environmental Justice, 13*(3), 56–64. https://doi.org/10.1089/env.2020.0019

Bullard, R. (15 Nov 2008). *Environmental Justice in the 21st Century.* Retrieved February 7, 2021, from https://uwosh.edu/sirt/wp-content/uploads/sites/86/2017/08/Bullard_Environmental-Justice-in-the-21st-Century.pdf.

Byrnes, M., Peter, L., & Lysack, C. (2007). Environmental press, aging in place, and residential satisfaction of urban older adults. *Journal of Applied Social Science, 23*(2), 50–77. https://doi.org/10.1177/19367244062300204

Bryne, J., Martinez, C., & Glover, L. (2002). A brief on environmental justice. *Discourses in International Political Economy*, pp. 3–17. Retrieved February 1, 2021, from https://www.researchgate.net/profile/John-Byrne-14/publication/280075782_A_Brief_on_Environmental_Justice/links/5cb3841c299bf12097665041/A-Brief-on-Environmental-Justice.pdf.

Carpentieri, G., Guida, C., & Masoumi, H. (2020). Multimodal accessibility to primary health services for the elderly: A case study of Naples Italy. *Sustainability, 12*, 781. https://doi.org/10.3390/su12030781

Danziger, S., & Chaudhury, H. (2009). Older adults' use of adaptable design features in housing units: An exploratory study. *Journal of Housing for the Elderly, 23*(3), 134–148.

Day, R. (2010). Environmental Justice and older age: Consideration of a qualitative neighbourhood-based study. *Environmentl and Planning a: Economy and Space, 42*(11), 2658–2673. https://doi.org/10.1068/a43109

Dhavaleshwar, C. (2016). The role of social worker in community development. *International Research Journal of Social Sciences, 5*(10), 61–63. http://www.isca.in/IJSS/Archive/v5/i10/10.ISCA-IRJSS-2016-063.pdf.

Domenelli, L. (2012). *Green Social Work: From Environmental Crisis to Environmental Justice.* Polity Press.

Enssle, F., & Kabisch, N. (2020). Urban green spaces for the social interaction, health, and well-being of older people—An integrated view of urban ecosystem services and socio-environmental justice. *Environmental Science and Policy, 109*, 36–44. https://doi.org/10.1016/j.envsci.2020.04.008

Environmental Law Alliance Worldwide (ELAW). (29 Jun 2007). Trinidad and Tobago— Smelta Karavan v. The Environmental Management Authority (2007). *The High Court of Justice (Petition for Judicial Review).* Retrieved August 8, 2021, from https://www.elaw.org/caribbean/cases.

Environmental Management Authority (EMA). (2021). *What We Do?* Retrieved August 2, 2021, from https://www.ema.co.tt/about/what-we-do/.

Environmental Protection Agency (EPA). (2014). *Guidelines for Preparing Economic Analysis.* Retrieved August 12, 2021, from https://www.epa.gov/sites/production/files/2017-09/documents/ee-0568-10.pdf.

Environmental Protection Agency (EPA). (2021). *Eenvironmental Justice. The United States Environmental Protection Agency (EPA).* Retrieved August 2, 2021, from https://www.epa.gov/environmentaljustice.

Falcone, P., D'Alisa, G., Germani, A., & Morone, P. (2020). When all seemed lost: A social network analysis of the waste-related environmental movement in Campania Italy. *Political Geography, 77*, 102114. https://doi.org/10.1016/j.polgeo.2019.102114

Florida State University (FSU). (27 Jul 2020). *The Social Worker Role and Impact on the Community.* Retrieved October 27, 2021, from https://onlinemsw.fsu.edu/blog/social-worker-role.

Foley, M., Seidel, I., Sevier, J., Wendt, J., & Kogan, M. (2020). One man's swordfish story: The link between Alzheimer's disease and mercury exposure. *Complementary Therapies in Medicine, 52*(1), 102499. https://doi.org/10.1016/j.ctim.2020.102499

Ford, J., King, N., Galappaththi, E., Pearce, T., McDowell, G., & Harper, S. (2020). The resilience of indigenous peoples to environmental change. *One Earth, 2*(6), 532–543. https://doi.org/10.1016/j.oneear.2020.05.014

Galiani, S., & Schargrodsky, E. (2010). Property rights for the poor: Effects of land titling. *Journal of Public Economics, 94*(9–10), 700–729. https://doi.org/10.1016/j.jpubeco.2010.06.002

Global Partners International (GPI). (9 Jun 2021). *Cultural, Political and Social Factors Influence the Meaning of Translations.* Global Partners International (GPI). Retrieved October 27, 2021, from https://www.globalizationpartners.com/2016/06/09/cultural-political-and-social-factors-influence-the-meaning-of-translations/.

González-Navarro, M., & Quintana-Domeque, C. (2016). Paving streets for the poor: Experimental analysis of infrastructure effects. *Review of Economics and Statistics 98*(2), 254–267. https://doi.org/10.1162/REST_a_00553.

Gould, K., & Lewis, T. (2018). Green gentrification and disaster capitalism in Barbuda. *NACLA Report on the Americas, 50*(2), 148–153. https://doi.org/10.1080/10714839.2018.1479466

Hagestad, G., & Uhlenberg, P. (2005). The social separation of old and young: A root of ageism. *Journal of Social Issues, 61*(2), 343–360. https://doi.org/10.1111/j.1540-4560.2005.00409.x

Haq, G., & Gutman, G. (2014). Climate gerontology: Meeting the challenge of population ageing and climate change. *Zeitschrift Für Gerontologie + Geriatrie, 47*(6), 462–467. https://doi.org/10.1007/s00391-014-0677-y

Harvison, N., Newman, R., & Judd, B (2011). *Ageing, the Built Environment and Adaptation to Climate Change* (Discussion Paper, Node 3). Sydney: University of New South Wales. Retrieved October 27, 2021 from https://www.accarnsi.unsw.edu.au/sites/accarnsi/files/uploads/PDF/Discussion/Ageing%20the%20Built%20Environmnet%20and%20Climate%20Change.pdf.

HelpAge International. (2007). *Personas Mayores En Desastres y Crisis Humanitarias: Líneas Directrices Para la Mejor Práctica.* HelpAge International, UNHCR, United Nations. Retrieved October 27, 2021 from https://www.helpage.org/silo/files/personas-mayores-en-desastres-y-crisis-humanitarias-lneas-directrices-para-la-mejor-prctica.pdf.

HelpAge International. (2011). *Insights on Ageing: A Survey Report*, 2010. Retrieved October 27, 2021 from https://www.helpage.org/silo/files/insights-on-ageing-a-survey-report.pdf.

Hospedales, C. J. (2017). *The Caribbean Chronic Disease Epidemic: What We Know and What We Need to Know.* Pan American Health Organization (PAHO). Retrieved October 27, 2021, from https://www.healthycaribbean.org/wp-ontent/uploads/2017/05/Hospedales_to_C HIRS_Oct_08_What_we_know_about_NCDs_in_Caribbean.pdf.

Human Services Education (HSE). (2021). *Social Work Career and Licensure Exploration.* Retrieved August 12, 2021, from https://www.humanservicesedu.org/social-work/

International County Management Association (ICMA). (11 Jun 2021). *Three Strategies for Advancing Social Equity and Increasing Community Sustainability.* Retrieved October 27, 2021, https://icma.org/articles/article/three-strategies-advancing-social-equity-and-increasing-community-sustainability.

International Federation of Social Workers (IFSW). (2018). *Global Social Work Statement of ethical Principles.* Retrieved October 27, 2021, from https://www.ifsw.org/global-social-work-statement-of-ethical-principles/.

International Labour Organization (ILO). (2014a). *Barbados-Database of national labour, social security, and related human rights legislation.* Retrieved July 27, 2021, from https://www.ilo.org/dyn/natlex/natlex4.detail?p_lang=&p_isn=105424.

International Labour Organization. (2014b). *Barbados-Database of national labour, social security, and related human rights legislation.* Retrieved July 27, 2021, from https://www.ilo.org/dyn/natlex/natlex4.detail?p_lang=en&p_isn=52132.

Intergovernmental Panel on Climate Change (IPCC). (2007). *Impacts, Adaptation and Vulnerability, Contribution of Working Group II to the Fourth Assessment Report of the Intergovernmental Panel on Climate Change.* Cambridge University Press. Retrieved October 27, 2021 from https://www.ipcc.ch/site/assets/uploads/2018/03/ar4_wg2_full_report.pdf.

King, A. C., Odunitan-Wayas, F. A., Chaudhury, M., Rubio, M. A., Baiocchi, M., Kolbe-Alexander, T., Montes, F., Banchoff, A., Sarmiento, O. L., Bälter, K., Hinckson, E., Chastin, S., Lambert, E. V., González, S. A., Guerra, A. M., Gelius, P., Zha, C., Sarabu, C., Kakar, P. A., … Gardiner, P. A. (2021). Community-based approaches to reducing health inequities and fostering EJ through global youth-engaged citizen science. *International Journal of Environmental Research and Public Health, 18*(3), 1–29. https://doi.org/10.3390/ijerph18030892

Legal Aid Advisory Authority (LAAA). (2021). *Services Provided by the LAAA.* Retrieved August 2, 2021, from https://laaa.org.tt/index.php/services.

Leeson, G. W. (2017). Realizing the potentials of ageing. *Population Ageing, 10,* 315–321. https://doi.org/10.1007/s12062-017-9207-1.

Lok, N., & Akin, B. (2013). Domestic environmental risk factors associated with falling in elderly. *Iranian Journal Public Health 42*(2), 120–128. Retrieved October 27, 2021, from https://www.ncbi.nlm.nih.gov/pmc/articles/PMC3595650/.

Loke, A., Yuen, L., Claudia, K. Y., & Fung, O. (2012). At-home disaster preparedness of elderly people in Hong Kong. *Geriatrics and Gerontology International, 12*(3), 524–531. https://doi.org/10.1111/j.1447-0594.2011.00778.x

Malin, S., & Ryder, S. (2018). Developing deeply intersectional environmental Justice scholarship. *Environmental Sociology, 4*(1), 1–7. https://doi.org/10.1080/23251042.2018.1446711

Martinez-Alier, J., Temper, L., Del Bene, D., & Schiedel, A. (2016). Is there a global environmental justice movement? *The Journal of Peasant Studies, 43*(3), 731–755. https://doi.org/10.1080/03066150.2016.1141198.

Mei-Fang, F., & Sheng-Chun, S. (2020). Indigenous political participation in the deliberative systems: The long-term care service controversy in Taiwan. *Policy Studies.* https://doi.org/10.1080/01442872.2020.1760233

Ministry of Environment and National Beautification (MENB). (2020). Report for NBSAP and Biodiversity Policy. *Ministry of Environment and National Beautification.* Retrieved October 27, 2021. https://biodiversity.gov.bb/page/2/.

Ministry of Justice. (2021). *Legal Aid Clinic.* Retrieved October 27, 2021, from https://moj.gov.jm/legal-aid-clinic.

Ministry of People Empowerment and Elder Affairs. (2012). *National Policy on Ageing for Barbados, Towards a Society for all Ages.* Retrieved October 27, 2021, from https://conferenciaenvejecimiento.cepal.org/4/sites/envejecimiento4/files/barbados2.pdf.

Ministry of Social Development and Family Services. (2020a). *Support for Older Persons.* Retrieved October 27, 2021, from http://www.social.gov.tt/support-for-older-persons/.

Ministry of Social Development. (2007). *National Policy on Aging for Trinidad and Tobago.* Division of Aging, Port-of-Spain. Retrieved October 27, 2021, from http://www.social.gov.tt/division-of-ageing/.

Mohai, P., Pellows, D., & Roberts, T. (2009). Environmental justice. *Annual Review of Environment and Resources, 34*, 405–430. https://doi.org/10.1146/annurev-environ-082508-094348

Mooney, H., Watson, A., Ruwhiu, P., & Hollis-English, A. (2020). Māori social work and māori mental health in Aotearoa New Zealand. In R. Ow & A. Poon (Eds.), *Mental Health and Social Work* (pp. 1–21). Springer.

Morlachetti, A. (2015). *The Current State of Social Protection Legislation in Barbados and the Organization of Eastern Caribbean States from a Human Rights perspeCtive.* Retrieved July 23, 2021, from http://www.fao.org/3/i4688e/i4688e.pdf.

National Association of Social Workers (NASW). (2010). NASW for Social Work Practice:Family Caregivers of Older Adults. Retrieved October 27, 2021, from https://www.socialworkers.org/Practice/Practice-Standards-Guidelines.

National Environmental Protection Agency (NEPA). (2021). *History and Development.* Retrieved August 12, 2021, from https://www.nepa.gov.jm/index.php/agency-profile.

Office of the High Commissioner of Human Rights (OHCHR). (2021). *Madrid International Plan of Action on Aging.* Retrieved August 8, 2021, from https://www.ohchr.org/en/issues/olderpersons/ie/pages/mipaa.aspx.

Parliament of Barbados. (2002). *The Constitution of Barbados.* Retrieved August 8, 2021, from https://www.oas.org/dil/the_constitution_of_barbados.pdf.

Parrado, C., Mercado-Saenz, S., Perez-Davo, A., Gilaberte, Y., Gonzalez, S., & Juarranz, A. (2019). Environmental stressors on skin aging. Mechanistic insights. *Frontiers in Pharmacology, 10.* https://doi.org/10.3389/fphar.2019.00759.

Planning Institute of Jamaica. (2007). Management of Hazardous and Solid Wastes in Jamaica. Sustainable Development and Regional Planning Division. Retrieved August 8, 2021, from http://extwprlegs1.fao.org/docs/pdf/jam175968.pdf.

Quashie, N., Jones, F., Geny, L., & Abdulkadri, A. (2018). Population aging and sustainable development in the Caribbean: Where are we 15 years post MIPAA? *International Journal on Aging in Developing Countries, 2*(2),128–148. https://www.inia.org.mt/wp-content/uploads/2018/07/2.2-7-Quashie-FINAL.pdf.

Republic of Trinidad and Tobago. (2007). *Homes for Older Persons Act, 2000.* Retrieved July 23, 2021, from http://www.ttparliament.org/legislations/a2007-20.pdf

Republic of Trinidad and Tobago. (2016a). *Senior Citizens Pension Act.* Retrieved July 23, 2021, from https://rgd.legalaffairs.gov.tt/laws2/Alphabetical_List/lawspdfs/32.02.pdf.

Republic of Trinidad and Tobago. (2016b). *National Insurance Act.* https://rgd.legalaffairs.gov.tt/laws2/alphabetical_list/lawspdfs/32.01.pdf.

Riche, M. (2019). Creating change: Finding older adults role in local environmental issues. *Community Engagement Student Work, 24,.* Retrieved October 27, 2021, from https://scholarworks.merrimack.edu/soe_student_ce/24

Robinson, S. B., & Rosher, R. B. (2001). Effect of the "half-full aging simulation experience": Medical students' attitudes. *Gerontology and Geriatrics Education, 21*(3), 3–12.

Rouse, J. (2017). *Protection of the Rights of Older Persons in the Framework of the San Jose Chapter.* The UNECLAC Caribbean Preparatory Meeting for the 4th Regional Intergovernmental Conference on Ageing and the Rights of Older Persons in Latin America and the Caribbean. Port of Spain: Trinidad. Retrieved on August 9, 2021, from https://www.cepal.org/sites/default/files/presentations/trinidad_and_tobago.pdf.

Rowles, G. D., & Bernard, M. (2013). The meaning and significance of place in old age. In G. D. Rowles & M. Bernard (Eds.), *Environmental gerontology: Making meaningful places in old age* (pp. 3–24). Springer Publishing Company.

Sánchez-González, D. (2009). Environmental context and spatial experience of aging in place: The case of Granada. *Papeles De Población, 15*(60), 175–213.

Sánchez-González, D., & Rodríguez-Rodríguez, V. (2016). Introduction to Environmental Gerontology in Latin America and Europe, in Diego Sánchez-González, Vicente Rodríguez-Rodríguez, *Environmental Gerontology in Europe and Latin America Policies and Perspectives on Environment and Aging,* pp. 1–10. Retrieved November 09, 2021 from https://link.springer.com/book/https://doi.org/10.1007/978-3-319-21419-1.

Sánchez-González, D., & Egea, C. (2011). Social vulnerability approach to investigate the social and environmental disadvantages. Its application in the study of elderly people. *Papeles de Población 27*(69): 151–185.

Sherwin, B. (2019). After the Storm: The importance of acknowledging environmental justice in sustainable development and disaster preparedness. *Environmental Law and Policy, 29*(2), 273–300. https://scholarship.law.duke.edu/delpf/vol29/iss2/2.

Shultz, J., Russell, J. & Espinel, Z. (2005). Epidemiology of tropical cyclones: The dynamics of disaster, disease, and development. *Epidemiologic Reviews* 27(1), 21–35. Retrieved October 27, 2021 from https://doi.org/10.1093/epirev/mxi011.

Smith, J., & Lindley, R. (2009). The assessment of fraility in older adults in acute care. *Australasian Journal of Ageing, 28*(3), 170–170. https://doi.org/10.1111/j.1741-6612.2009.00405.x

Smith, R. J., & Rhiney, K. (2016). Climate (in)justice, vulnerability, and livelihoods in the Caribbean: The case of the indigenous Caribs in northeastern St Vincent. *Geoforum, 73,* 22–31. https://doi.org/10.1016/j.geoforum.2015.11.008

Soroptimist Village and Hildegarde Activity Centre (2020). *Soroptimist International Could Receive Government Assistance.* Retrieved October 27, 2021 from https://gisbarbados.gov.bb/blog/soroptimist-international-could-receive-government-assistance/

The Barbados Parliament. (2018). *Barbados, Chapter 112A. Community Legal Services, 1981–33.* Retrieved July 23, 2021, from http://104.238.85.55/en/ShowPdf/112A.pdf.

The Oxford English Dictionary (OED). (1989):. Oxford, UK.

Thompson, K., Harpring, J., & Whitegoat, W. (2021). Indigenous world views and social work field practice: Reflections from social workers advancing through grounded education program (SAGE) educators. *Journal of Human Rights and Social Work, 6,* 49–53. https://link.springer.com/article/https://doi.org/10.1007/s41134-020-00144-y.

Tolea, M. I., Ferrucci, L., Costa, P. T., Faulkner, K., Rosano, K., Satterfield, S., Ayunayon, H. L., & Simonsick, E. M. (2012). Personality and reduced incidence of walking limitation in late life: Findings from the health, aging, and body composition study. *The Journals of Gerontology Series B: Psychological Sciences and Social Sciences, 67*(6), 712–719. https://doi.org/10.1093/geronb/gbs001

The Social and Economic Implications ... 43

United Nations (UN). (2002). *Political Declaration and Madrid International Plan of Action on Aging.* Retrieved July 23, 2021, from https://www.un.org/esa/socdev/documents/ageing/MIPAA/political-declaration-en.pdf.

United Nations (UN). (2012*). San Jose Charter on the Rights of Older persons in Latin America and the Caribbean.* Retrieved July 23, 2021, from https://repositorio.cepal.org/bitstream/handle/11362/21535/1/S2012897_en.pdf.

United Nations (UN). (2017). *Guiding Questions to Facilitate the Open-Ended Working Group on Aging.* Retrieved July 23, 2021, from https://social.un.org/ageing-working-group/documents/eighth/Inputs%20Member%20States/Trinidad&Tobago.pdf.

United Nations Economic Commission for Europe (UNECE). (2002). *Regional Implementation Strategy for the Madrid International Plan of Action on Aging, 2002* .Retrieved, July 23, 2021 from https://unece.org/DAM/pau/RIS.pdf.

Wahl, H.W., and Gitlin. L.N. (2007). Environmental Gerontology. In *Encyclopedia of Gerontology*, pp. 494–501. Economic Press.

Walsh, K., Scharf, T., & Keating, N. (2017). Social exclusion of older persons: A scoping review and conceptual framework. *European Journal of Ageing, 14*, 81–98. https://doi.org/10.1007/s10433-016-0398-8

Wood, N., Burton, J., & Cutter, S. (2010). Community variations in social vulnerability to Cascadia-related tsunamis in the U.S. Pacific Northwest. *Natural Hazards, 52*(2), 369–389. https://doi.org/10.1007/s11069-009-9376-1

World Health Organisation (WHO). (2021). *Decade of Healthy Aging.* Retrieved October 27, 2021 from https://www.who.int/initiatives/decade-of-healthy-ageing#:~:text=The%20United%20Nations%20Decade%20of,improve%20the%20lives%20of%20older.

Willers, H. (1996). Environmental injustice: Evidence and economic implications. *University Avenue Undergraduate Journal of Economics, 1*(1), 1–16. http://digitalcommons.iwu.edu/uauje/vol1/iss1/4.

Zaidi, A. (29 Jan 2018). *Implementing the Madrid Plan of Action on Aging: What have we learned? And where do we go from here?* Retrieved July 23, 2021, from http://hdr.undp.org/en/content/implementing-madrid-plan-action-ned-and-where-do-we-go-here.

The Human-Nature Nexus: A Sustainability Framework for Social Work?

Antoinette Lombard ⓘ

1 Introduction

In the earlier Holocene, there were far fewer people, and they lived in balance with the natural world, an existence that was sustainable (Attenborough, 2020, p. 125). Humans' options increased with the advent of farming, both agriculture and animal husbandry, but these subsistence patterns changed their relationship with nature, as people came "to regard the wild world as something to tame, to subdue and use" (Attenborough, 2020, p. 125). Consequently, people shifted from being "a part of nature to being apart from nature" (Attenborough, 2020, p. 125). Today, faced with accelerating climate change, the natural environment and human beings are in a crisis—what in this chapter refer to as the human-nature crisis. Humans and nature are interdependent, and their fate is therefore intertwined. That makes this crisis everyone's crisis, also that of social work. In the twenty-first century, humanity, including social work practitioners, must face the question of whether the planet can survive (Besthorn, 2012), and we must all take steps to help it to do so, for its own sake and for that of humanity. As Hawkins (2010) remarks: "The greatest challenge facing humanity in the twenty-first century is to address the resultant ecological calamity before we destroy the very environment that sustains us" (p. 68).

Social work's involvement with environmental issues and advocacy for environmental equality for all people can be traced back to its foundational years, but the profession was more widely identified with a dual focus on the person and environment which was known as the person-in-environment (PIE) approach (Norton, 2012). This approach focuses exclusively on the *social* environment. Nevertheless, this focus took a turn toward the end of the twentieth century when the emphasis shifted to including the natural (physical) environment (Besthorn, 2012). Great strides have

---

A. Lombard (✉)
Professor in Social Work and Head of the Department of Social Work and Criminology, University of Pretoria, Pretoria, South Africa
e-mail: antoinette.lombard@up.ac.za

© The Author(s), under exclusive license to Springer Nature Singapore Pte Ltd. 2022
D. Madhanagopal et al. (eds.), *Environment, Climate, and Social Justice*,
https://doi.org/10.1007/978-981-19-1987-9_3

been made, but Coates and Gray's remark (2012), almost a decade ago, that the pace was still too slow for social work to claim that it was meaningfully represented in the environmental crisis discourse, is still applicable. At that time, Besthorn (2012) concurred that social work had yet to embrace the natural world in ways involving more than linking social and environmental justice, and Heinsch (2012) called for a new language to explain humans' relationship with nature.

To embrace our interconnectivity with the natural environment, it is important to understand how humans fit into the planet. One key aspect of the human-nature crisis is encapsulated in the statement in the United Nations' (UN's) *Report of the World Commission on Environment and Development [WCED]: Our common future* that "[t]he earth is one but the world is not" (UN, 1987, p. 39). Although they are part of the earth's biodiversity, and humans depend on the biosphere to sustain their lives (Attenborough, 2020), the humans that make up the "world" continue to make war, impoverish each other and exploit nature and one another. The biosphere draws on the planet's biodiversity (the variety of all life functioning in the world). It encapsulates millions of species (animals, plants, fungi and micro-organisms such as bacteria) and billions of individuals with trillions of different characteristics (Attenborough, 2020). As a profession embedded in social justice, social work already advocates for the inclusion of human diversity, but to embrace nature in human-based interventions we need a full understanding of the fact that "[t]he greater the biodiversity, the more *biosphere* is able to deal with change, maintain balance and support life" (Attenborough, 2020, p. 224 [emphasis in original]).

The Anthropocene, as the most recent part of the Holocene is now often referred to, is characterized by human activity as the "dominant influence on climate and the environment" (Attenborough, 2020, p. 223). This requires the spotlight to fall on justice in a broader sense. In the context of this book and chapter, the question is how to engage in social work that finds an inclusive way to embrace the natural world in its long-standing concern with social justice (Norton, 2012). Besthorn (2012) acknowledges the importance of social justice, but remarks that in itself this is not sufficient, warning that "[t]he natural world will not care if social workers spend their time solely focused on insuring a degree of social justice for the human species. The earth system will collapse whether social workers are successful at those efforts or not" (p. 255). As Attenborough (2020) points out, "[w]e often talk of saving the planet, but the truth is that we must do these things to save ourselves. With or without us, the wild will return" (p. 218). The evidence for this claim can be found in the ruins of Pripyat, the model city which had to be abandoned after the Chernobyl nuclear reactor disaster in 1986. Now, more than 35 years since its evacuation, the deserted city is becoming a forest: the concrete is broken up by shrubs, and the bricks are pulled apart by ivy; roofs sag from the weight of flourishing vegetation and seeds sprout in pavements; erstwhile gardens and parks host canopies of oak, pine and maple. The returning flora shelter animals, including ones being saved from extinction, hiding them from hunters. The wild has reclaimed its territory (Attenborough, 2020, p. 218). To prevent disaster to both nature and the humans who depend on nature, justice thus requires a much broader scope to restore the balance between nature and humans.

Placing the focus of justice in the context of only social *or* environmental justice, calling for unilateral redress to inequity and redistribution, is a kind of silo approach that limits the enactment of one kind of justice at the cost of other forms of justice, leaving other injustices without redress. The environmental crisis and its impact require a fundamental reconceptualization of justice, including a rethinking of social justice, even in its broadest sense, in relation to the natural world. Schlosberg's (2007) analysis of justice from different theoretical and environmental movement perspectives identifies a plurality of potential definitions of justice that fits well into a human-nature nexus approach: adopting a pluralistic view of justice will enable social work to "draw parallels between the application of notions of justice as *distribution, recognition, capability*, and *participation* in both the human and nonhuman realms" (Schlosberg, 2007, p. 6 [emphasis added]).

The goal of this conceptual chapter is to reframe the role of social work in contributing to a sustainable and just world by embracing the natural world while serving humanity and Earth. I propose that social work adopts a broader justice framework to bridge the human-nature divide in social work, that climate justice, environmental justice and social justice start with the natural environment, and that justice for the natural world and humans can only be achieved in a sustainability framework. Therefore, it is critical for social work to articulate its stance in respect of the natural environment in relation to social justice. I argue that this can be achieved through the lens of environmental justice, climate justice, ecology and deep ecology. Awareness of humans' position in the broader natural environment will enable social work to shift its focus "from anthropocentrism to a clearer ecological understanding that all living creatures are populations-at-risk or endangered species, and that Earth itself is 'at risk'" (Miller et al., 2012, p. 276). Thus far, the conventional definition of social justice has excluded the natural world in weighing up its rights and responsibilities, but as a matter of urgency, social work must link social, environmental and ecological justice with a firm understanding that "issues of sustainability and environmental justice must become a part of social work's understanding of itself and what it does" (Besthorn, 2012, p. 255).

The chapter outlines the relation of social work and justice to environmental and ecological justice and calls for broadening the scope of social justice in social work to a more inclusive view that encompasses the natural world, showing the interconnection between humanity and the natural environment. This is followed by a discussion of the relevance of climate change for social work, emphasizing how climate change affects the natural environment and humanity, and in doing so extends social work's role and responsibility to engage in activities that prevent or curb the impact of climate justice. The exposition on the sustainability framework stresses that sustainability is more than managing natural resources for current and future generations: it embraces the interconnectedness between people, the planet, prosperity, peace and partnerships as a foundational approach for social work, based on the premise that all in the human-nature nexus, both living and nonliving, have equal standing. In the section on sustainable social work, some best practice examples are shared to show how social work can become involved in human and nature activities, demonstrating their interdependence. The chapter concludes with a plea for social work to take up its responsibility toward humanity and nature in contributing to a more just, sustainable world.

2 Social Work and Justice

It is very clear that the rapid changes in our world affect both the planet and its people in different ways, and that therefore social work cannot do justice to people without embracing the natural environment. A one-sided view of justice for humans will not save them or the planet. If only one of the two will survive, it is likely to be the planet, as it can "rewild" itself if humans are out of their way, as the example of Pripyat shows (Attenborough, 2020).

That does not invalidate social work's long-standing commitment to social justice, a focus that is inherent to the social work profession (Miller et al., 2012). But it does imply that it is necessary to rethink the scope of social justice to include the natural world so that social work will truly contribute to a more just and sustainable world. In conventional social work, social justice is rooted in advocating for human rights, fairness and the equitable distribution of social goods, such as land, opportunities and wealth (Besthorn, 2012). The first step in revisioning social justice is to understand the concept of *environment* because it is the foundation for understanding the incremental shifts that social work can make toward fully embracing a human-nature approach to social work. Gray et al. (2013) refer to the environment in general terms as things that surround people and speak to a person's social environment, including the family, community, employment and relationships with people and organizations. This definition is in line with the person-in-environment (PIE) approach. A shift from the social environment to the natural world means a shift to environmental justice, which includes awareness of elements such as the air, water and minerals that surround all organisms on earth (Gray et al., 2013). Environmental justice acknowledges the need to reduce harm to the environment and equal distribution of environmental benefits or goods, for example, by protecting clean water and access to it (Besthorn, 2013).

Environmental justice extends the human rights focus of social justice to concerns of the natural environment, but with the emphasis on how it affects humans (Miller et al., 2012). Thus, although environmental justice focuses on the natural world, its priority to preserve the natural environment and its resources is in the first instance intended to benefit humans (Besthorn, 2013). Embracing environmental justice is a logical and vital shift for social work because the poor, and other marginalized and vulnerable people are the ones who are most affected by environmental degradation through pollution, deforestation and chemical contamination (Miller et al., 2012). They are also the ones most likely to have the least access to sustainable food resources (Miller et al., 2012). Environmental degradation of land and coastal ecosystems, for example, can result in the loss of livelihoods and displacement, which in turn leads to poverty and possible ill-health outcomes (McKinnon, 2008).

Prioritizing humans does not mean that nature is not valued in environmental justice, "but simply that nature has no *intrinsic* or *objective* value apart from that which the human species ascribes to it" (Besthorn, 2013, p. 36 [emphasis in original]). Thus, although environmental justice helps social work to broaden its social justice focus, the emphasis on benefiting humans only does not yet position social work to contribute toward saving the planet. Nonetheless, it is a start toward identifying ways in which the profession could shift to embrace the natural environment in social work practice (Miller et al., 2012).

Just as humans have a right to a clean, healthy and safe environment, the environment too has the right to justice; for example, not to be polluted (Hawkins, 2010). It is helpful to note a point made by the United Nations Office of the High Commissioner for Human Rights (OHCHR, 2018), namely that human rights can be impeded by environmental degradation, but conversely, human rights can be exercised to protect the environment from harm and promote sustainable development. To benefit both humanity and the planet, the roots of environmental injustices should be addressed in the nonhuman sphere, as well as in relation to human beings (Schlosberg, 2013, p. 44).

Ecological justice takes social work's focus on environmental justice further by recognizing that "the human social world does not operate in a silo separate from the rest of nature. ... instead, [it] is an inextricable part of the Earth and natural realm" (Miller et al., 2012, p. 271). Humans remain the focus in environmental justice theories in relation to natural resources, but in ecological justice theories "nature or Earth expands in scope to become the universe, with recognition that humans are one part of that universe" (Miller et al., 2012, p. 271). Such an approach acknowledges the worth of the natural world irrespective of its value to humans, and "seeks to preserve the integrity and beauty of the natural world" (Gray et al., 2013, p. 321). Furthermore, ecological justice refers to justice between humans and the rest of the natural world (Schlosberg, 2007). As the "ethical cousin" of environmental justice, ecological justice holds similar conceptualizations regarding rights, responsibilities, fairness, recognition and distributive standards in the context of environmental concerns (Besthorn, 2013, p. 36).

Ecological justice advocates argue that the world is deteriorating, despite decades of environmental justice, showing that the overly human-centered environmental justice movement is "a shallow form of justice" (Besthorn, 2013, p. 39). In adopting a more comprehensive ecological justice paradigm, social work "accepts the idea that Earth is shared by humans and nonhumans whose fate is inextricably linked" (Miller et al., 2012, p. 270).

Ecological justice helps social work to eradicate social injustice, protect vulnerable human populations and benefit from equitable distribution of the positive goods of the natural world (Besthorn, 2013). The fundamental difference between ecological justice and environmental justice is that ecological justice extends the conceptualization of environmental justice "toward a *radical egalitarian ecological* justice where nonsentient beings and natural systems are given equal moral standing" (Besthorn, 2013, p. 37 [emphasis in original]), which means that it all begins and ends with the natural world. Its "deep justice" posits the more radical environmental thinking around justice that nonhuman beings and natural systems have equal moral standing, and the argument that humans are not privileged over others (Gray et al., 2013:320). Human claims to domination are superseded by developing a "deep empathy" for nature and "ecological awareness" of the harm done to the planet led by profit and materialism (Norton, 2012, p. 304). Emphasis on human needs only causes an imbalance in the relationship between humans and nature, resulting in injustices, subordinating the interests of other elements of the natural world to humans' interests (Miller et al., 2012, p. 271).

A radical egalitarianism approach pushes the boundaries of justice to the entire natural environment, requiring a drastic change to social work's conventional ideas of justice (Besthorn, 2013). An interim step is "deep ecology," a construct developed by Norwegian philosopher Aren Naess, focusing on a deeper interrelationship between humans with the natural world by finding solutions to critical environmental concerns (Gray et al., 2013, p. 320). According to Besthorn (2012), from a deep ecological perspective, to act justly toward other beings and entities, it is important to have a broader understanding of "humanity's place in the interconnectedness of all existence" (p. 255). Deep Ecology can assist humans to let go of their "previously unexamined assumption of power *over* the natural world" (Norton, 2012, p. 303 [emphasis in original]).

In applying justice that considers the natural-human nexus, social work has to apply social justice, environmental justice and ecological justice, along with other types of justice relevant to the space and context in which social work interventions are required. A narrow focus on equity and issues of distribution is "essential but incomplete," as injustice is more than a matter of inequitable distribution—there are other explanations for some people getting more than others (Schlosberg, 2007, p. 15). Hence Schlosberg's (2007, p. 6) plea for a pluralistic view of justice is applicable to enable social work to serve the human *and* the nonhuman realms. All these conceptions of justice as *distribution, recognition, capability*, and *participation* are strongly linked, so in talking of one, we must consider the others (Schlosberg, 2007). A pluralistic approach to environmental justice recognizes relationships between natural systems and human communities, and how they function, as well as how natural systems support the functioning of human communities (Schlosberg, 2013).

A discussion on social work and justice is incomplete without an understanding of climate change and its associated environmental risks and impacts on nature and humans.

3 Climate Change and Social Work

Climate change threatens humanity (International Climate Justice Network, 2002) and the entire planet with all its species. For the purposes of this chapter, climate change refers to an increase in Earth's average temperature due to global warming; it shifts weather patterns, affecting long-term changes in the chemical composition of the atmosphere (Gray et al., 2013). Climate change is associated with natural events,

The Human-Nature Nexus: A Sustainability Framework for Social Work?   51

and human activity such as pollution, deforestation, the release of carbon dioxide (Gray et al., 2013) and other greenhouse gases, land degradation, precipitating natural disasters such as droughts, floods, mudslides and wildfires, and the exhaustion of food sources (e.g., by overfishing).

Climate change affects everyone, but the impact on impoverished indigenous peoples is disproportionate (Hawkins, 2010, p. 74). The poor are the most exposed to environmental injustices, and are often unduly blamed for their role in damaging nature, for example, for their cutting trees for firewood to cook food, or dumping waste in informal communities, where garbage is not removed by a local municipality. Jayaraman (2019) points out that we need to deal with "global warming in an unequal and unjust world" (p.16), warning that it is impossible to oppose climate change without equality and equity. Hattingh (2019) makes a plea for not leaving the poor behind in ethical terms, suggesting that "solidarity in the fight against climate change conversely means that the poor and the vulnerable cannot be left behind" (p. 29), and for their needs to be addressed and prioritized. However, as already discussed, using only an equity lens, environmental conditions may be too narrowly regarded as only another form of social injustice (Schlosberg, 2013).

Climate change adds to the layer of injustices, making it part of the human-nature justice and sustainability discourse. Environmental justice and climate justice were originally articulated in the dominant liberal discourse of distributive equity, given that some communities face disproportionally more environmental risks than others (Schlosberg, 2007, 2013). This linking of environmental justice concerns to climate change has expanded the discourse on the environment, taking the analysis of the meaning of injustice beyond inequity, and creating opportunities to adopt more multiplicitous forms of social justice (Schlosberg, 2013). The expanded discourse started when the more traditional environmental justice concerns debate on climate change and climate justice shifted to a concern with adaptation (Schlosberg, 2013). There has thus been a noticeable shift from the original narrow view, where climate change was seen "as simply another, if broader, environmental manifestation of social injustice," to a broader concept linked to environmental justice concerns (Schlosberg, 2013, p. 46). Such an extended perspective includes shifting the focus of justice from the individual to the community and broader spaces by looking at the global nature of environmental injustices, and human relationships with the nonhuman world (Schlosberg, 2013).

Supporting an appeal for integration, Hattingh (2019) advocates that the fight against climate change and all forms of injustice be presented *together*, as "two dimensions of the same agenda that are inseparably linked and need to be pursued together" (p. 29). This implies that the measures adopted to respond to climate change should simultaneously contribute to human development, to benefit both. This affirms the relevance of *capabilities justice* (Schlosberg, 2007), which Jayaraman (2019) attaches to a procedure of social-economic order related to a social justice that promotes, extends and develops human capabilities. The *Bali principles of climate justice* (International Climate Justice Network, 2002), for example, provide a set of principles aimed at giving climate change a human face, including the rights of indigenous and other affected people to represent and speak for themselves.

Climate change has interrupted people's relationship with the natural environment that they depend on for their survival and well-being, for healthy air, water, food and the other goods they consume (Isbister, 2001), but humans' role in this process must be acknowledged (Norton, 2012, p. 304). Humans and the environment both suffer the consequences of environmental and climate injustices, but it is humans who "altered the balance of nature, changed the world's climate, and threatened the sustainability of Earth itself" (Hawkins, 2010, p. 68), so humans must also play a part in righting this injustice. Social workers therefore cannot contribute to a more sustainable and just world without recognizing the environmental rights of people, *and* the rights of the physical environment (Dominelli, 2012). The challenge for social work is to advocate for people and mobilize action that contributes to sustainability for humans and nature.

4 Sustainability Framework

The sustainability framework for social work that I propose includes the people, the planet, prosperity, peace and partnerships dimensions of the *2030 Agenda for sustainable development* at the global, national and local levels to transform the world (UN, 2015). Sustainability is about the protection and care of the natural environment, and also about the quality of society in different ways (Peeters, 2012, p. 290). Sustainability must be conceptualized by "planetary boundaries," a concept and model developed by earth system scientists John Rockström and Will Steffen "in order to define a safe operating space for humanity" (in Attenborough, 2020, p. 235). They and their team defined nine factors from multiple sources that influence the stability of the Earthy system by calculating,

> "the degree to which current human activity is impacting upon those factors and established threshold, that, if crossed, may lead to potentially catastrophic change. Of these nine factors, the team identified two, that is climate change and biodiversity loss as the 'core boundaries'" (Attenborough, 2020, p. 235).

Both are affected by all the other boundaries and "could alone, if crossed, bring about the destabilisation of the planet" (Attenborough, 2020, p. 235). These scientists advised that humankind has already crossed four boundaries: climate change, biodiversity loss, land-use change and the use of nitrogen and phosphorous. This already destabilizes the earth's system (Attenborough, 2020).

Protecting natural resources in a way that can support the needs of the present and future generations requires much more than managing the physical environment (UN, 1987). The effort to achieve sustainability for humans and nature has social, economic, environmental, peace, partnerships and political dimensions. Humanity has to discover a new kind of sustainable lifestyle that could bring the "contemporary human world back into balance with nature once again" (Attenborough, 2020, p. 126). Only then can the earth rewild sufficiently for stability to return (Attenborough, 2020). A sustainability framework speaks to human-nature justice in all its dimensions. In the social sphere, a focus on human beings, their capabilities, and participation to free themselves from poverty and hunger and achieve their potential in dignity and equality in a healthy environment, can only occur by also protecting the planet and managing its natural resources. Likewise, economic, social and technological progress to ensure prosperity can only be realized in harmony with nature. Peace and development, which must be achieved together and reciprocally, can be fostered through peaceful, inclusive and just societies that take into account the natural environment as an essential part of what allows for such societies. Conversely, partnerships embedded in global solidarity, including earth, must continue to focus on the needs of the poorest and most vulnerable in collaboration with all stakeholders—it must prioritize the inclusion of people who have been left behind (UN, 2015).

Poverty and hunger must end to ensure people's right to dignity and to reach their potential in a healthy environment (UN, 2015). Poor people find themselves in a vicious downward spiral (UN, 1987). To survive, they are forced to overuse environmental resources. Then their impoverished environment not only further impoverishes them, but complicates their survival further: "A world in which poverty and inequity are endemic will always be prone to ecological and other crises" (UN, 1987, p. 54). People depend on the biosphere for sustaining their lives. It has to be protected from degradation, including through sustainable consumption and production and sustainable management of its natural resources and action on climate changes in relation to meeting current and future generations' needs (UN, 2015).

All future social and economic development depends on sustainable management of the planet's natural resources (UN, 2015). Protection of the earth and humanity includes not tolerating injustices in the social and economic world, even though the two are often played off against one another (Jayaraman, 2019). An example is an argument that factories that are polluting the environment should be shut down, ahead of any concern about what happens to the employees. Such an approach, Jayaraman (2019) explains, sharpens the question of equity and justice for humanity and nature. Hattingh (2019) points out that the opposite also occurs, where job losses and the risk of disadvantaging workers are used as an excuse for not engaging in the struggle against climate change because it is claimed that the first obligation is to make sure that people have developed opportunities to move out of poverty. Recognizing the connection between sustainability and human rights is then helpful to envision environmental sustainability that is fair and just to all (Hawkins, 2010). Human rights are clearly intertwined with the environment in which people live, and are by definition part of social work. Therefore, it is relevant for social work to articulate clearly how the concepts of human rights, environmental justice and sustainability relate to enable the profession to achieve its goal of "making the world a more just, human, and sustainable home for all life" (Hawkins, 2010, p. 68).

Networking, relationships and community-building are keys to transformative social work practice, and that "developing new social-economic relations through bottom-up economic projects is crucial for a just and sustainable future" (Peeters, 2012, p. 295). Norton (2012, p. 305) alludes to the important role that social workers should play in ensuring that social institutions, including the family, health, welfare and education on human well-being, are sensitive to human connections to the natural world. Furthermore, they can assist in making settings such as hospitals, social service organizations, long-term care, residential and psychiatric facilities and workplaces aware of humanity's deep need to be connected to nature (Norton, 2012). As Norton (2012) states, "[a]long with organization improvements, community-wide change is needed to promote sustainability" (p. 305).

Regarding the role of peace in human and environmental sustainability, the emphasis is on the reciprocal relationship between sustainable development and peace; one is a prerequisite for the other. Jayaraman (2019) makes the point that peace and security are preconditions for dealing effectively with climate-driven issues that are underpinned by social and political conditions; for example, war and armed conflict can cause migration, which means that taking effective climate action has to be aligned with social justice. Conflict over scarce resources such as water, land, food and energy can disrupt social sustainability and lead to further depletion of the available resources (McKinnon, 2008).

Peeters (2012) promotes a vision of a strong sustainable development framework which "allows the ecosystem to limit the economy and society" (p. 293) in a new paradigm or framework, where "nature can have meaning beyond economic and social interests" (p. 293). He sees social work as linking with sustainable development in that it frames social problems as "ecosocial," as only one step in recognizing the broader ecological agenda, while in the political and economic context, the real challenge for social work is transforming society. The question is then how social work can be engaged in a process of deep social change which focuses on structural and cultural social change (Peeters, 2012). Sustainable development has a political character and decisions for a just society have to be consistently made; therefore, "sustainable development must rest on political will" (UN, 1987, p. 25).

Attenborough (2020, p. 126) suggests that a "compass" for the journey to a sustainable future is already at hand in the planetary boundaries model, which has been designed to guide humanity on the right path to preserve the planet. The preferred starting point is to reverse climate change by attending to greenhouse gas emissions. Overuse of fertilizers must stop; the conversion of wild spaces for farmland, plantations and other developments must end and must be reversed. In addition, an eye has to be kept on the ozone layer, the use of freshwater, chemical pollution of land, water and air, and ocean acidification (Attenborough, 2020). Ending these human activities and their effects will slow and finally prevent biodiversity loss, which can then begin to reverse itself. This requires humans to make the right decisions, not only for the sake of nature but "since nature keeps the Earth stable, for ourselves" (Attenborough, 2020, p. 126). One of the biggest challenges is the lifestyle that the wealthiest become used to on Earth, making it "wholly unstable" (Attenborough, 2020, p. 126). For a sustainable future, humanity must learn how to live within the limited resources of the earth and planetary boundaries, and also share these resources more evenly (Attenborough, 2020).

For the purposes of creating a sustainability framework for social work, the development of an inner ring to the planetary boundaries model by Kate Raworth, an economist from the University of Oxford, is very helpful. Her Doughnut Model reinterprets the planetary boundaries model. The new ring includes the minimum

The Human-Nature Nexus: A Sustainability Framework for Social Work? 55

requirements for human well-being, namely "good housing, healthcare, clean water, safe food, access to energy, good education, an income, a political voice and justice" (Attenborough, 2020, p. 128). The Doughnut Model offers the required compass. There are two sets of boundaries: the outer ring is an ecological ceiling beyond which humanity must not go if they want to use an opportunity to maintain a stable and safe planet; the inner ring represents a social foundation above which everyone has to be raised to "enable a fair and just world" (Attenborough, 2020, p. 128).

Such a clear-cut sustainability path provides a clear vision for social work to commit to the journey for a fair and sustainable world. According to Gray and Coates (2012), as a profession bound to professional conduct, social work requires a sustainability framework underpinned by environmental ethics to anchor its responsibility to the nonhuman world. These authors use environmental ethics to indicate a new terrain of ethics in social work, capturing the emphasis on the physical environment. It is about people's relationships,

> to the natural environment, to the land and the animals and plants which graze and grow upon it. The land is not merely something shared by the human community. It supports diverse life forms, and all deserve the opportunity to thrive; whether plants, animals or humans, all have intrinsic value (Gray & Coates, 2012, p. 240).

Miller et al., (2012:273) cite the *17 Principles of the First National People of Color Environmental Leadership Summit report* (1991) as an empowering framework for environmentally sustainable social work practice to rethink ways in which humans and the social environment fit within an ecological paradigm, and in doing so provide a strong foundation for the profession as it continues to locate itself in global environmental politics.

5 Sustainable Social Work Practice

Many authors mention significant progress over the last two decades in expanding the dialogue and the literature on humanity's view of its relationship with nature (see Gray et al., 2013). The ongoing theorizing on social work and the natural world has given birth to environmental social work (Gray & Coates, 2013), green social work (Dominelli, 2012, 2018); ecological social work and deep ecology (Besthorn, 2012, 2013), and ecosocial work (Norton, 2012; Peeters, 2012), among other contributions. The literature covers the range of environmental awareness that has been discussed in this chapter, including environmental justice as an expansion of social justice, with extended environmental justice promoting the interests of the physical environment, and ecological social work and deep ecology and justice, which clarify social work's position vis-à-vis nature.

The 2010–2020 Global agenda for social work and social development (2012) has contributed strongly to creating awareness, exploration via new research and the documenting of best practices in its third theme for 2017 and 2018: *Promoting environmental and community sustainability* (cf. Jones, 2018; Rinkel & Powers, 2017).

Heinsch (2012, p. 314) contributes approaches and strategies along with a variety of readings in three categories of benefits that cut across micro, meso and macro practice to enhance human health and well-being through contact with the natural environment in social work practice. In summary, these approaches and strategies include emotional, cognitive and spiritual well-being; physical well-being; and social interaction and well-being (Heinsch, 2012, p. 314).

The Africa report of the third report of the *Global agenda for social work and social development* (Lombard & Twikirize, 2018) cites three case studies from South Africa, Malawi and Uganda of social workers' involvement in interventions that promote environmental justice and contributions to just and sustainable communities.

In the first case study, from South Africa, John G.I. Clarke, a social worker, reports on his work with the Amadiba Coastal Community on the environmentally sensitive Pondoland Wild Coast in the Eastern Cape. He highlights the social problems that mining causes among the most vulnerable and disadvantaged. He argues that the survival of the human species pivots on how nonrenewable resources are managed and develop technologies to extract these resources without prejudicing the interests of future generations. The Australian mining company in the area opposed his intervention but was defeated in court when it attempted to bring defamation suits against South Africans questioning its environmental and corporate practices. John Clarke's blog, www.icosindaba.co.za, gives more background on his initiatives, successes and struggles in the pursuit of human-nature justice and sustainability.

In Uganda, the Bamboo for Good (B4G) initiative among public and private institutions enhances livelihoods, while simultaneously protecting the environment. It is an initiative of Makerere University's Department of Social Work and Social Administration (Uganda), the Rwanda Bamboo organization, and Pacific Bamboo Resources (United States). The team leaders are all social work educators who work in partnership with local institutions to promote social, economic and environmental justice. B4G combines traditional sustainable development intentions with strategic use of the valuable bamboo plant as a catalyst for innovation to address critical humanitarian and wildlife habitat issues in East Africa, an area that includes the Bwindi Mgahinga Conservation Area (BMCA), a rain forest that is home to more than half of the world's remaining endangered mountain gorillas. The human population of neighboring communities around the area exerts high pressure on the BCMA's resources in search of their daily livelihoods, which frequently exposes community members to danger and loss of life as they seek resources, including bamboo, from the conservation area. To reduce this pressure and promote harmonious co-existence between human and animal populations, and biodiversity, B4G embarked on building the capacity of the communities to use alternative methods and resources, including the propagation and management of bamboo outside the BCMA. B4G partners with local community organizations, currently including the Mgahinga Bamboo Conservation Program (MBCP), Uganda Wildlife Authority, National Forestry Authority, district and sub-county administration and Change a Life. The program has been supported by the International Network for Bamboo and Rattan (INBAR).

In a case study of Mangochi, a district in the Eastern Region of Malawi, Christopher Ndaona states: "Our surrounding is vital to our health as such, caring for the environment means caring for our own lives" (in Lombard & Twikirize, 2018, p. 71). The case study reported by Ndaona shows a project that went wrong—it had a positive human impact but was unsustainable because of the impact on the environment. The construction of community-based childcare centers (CBCCs) has flourished, and the CBCC program incorporates a nutritional program where porridge is prepared for the children, but the price has been soil degradation (topsoil was used for bricks) and deforestation (wood was used for brick burning and roofing). Environmental degradation in Mangochi has resulted from the need for firewood (a mother support group cooked porridge, but used large amounts of firewood gathered in the area). The resulting bare land struck Ndaona as evidence that something was very wrong with their planning of activities, due to what he calls "environmental blindness" (Lombard & Twikirize, 2018, p. 72). Training with mother support groups then became part of the discussions. The women were trained in tree planting and issues of afforestation. Gradually, the community came to understand the need to conserve the environment, which has become part of life.

Agoramoorthy and Hsu (2015) have reported on how irrigation-based social work practiced by a local NGO has enhanced the livelihoods of poor farmers across the drylands of western India. The team included 20 social workers and 30 irrigation engineers. The households in the villages experienced such food shortages that farmers seasonally migrated to nearby towns and cities in search of paid employment. After lift irrigation systems had been set up by harvesting monsoon rains and the community had been taught how to manage the irrigation water, the farmers became self-sufficient in producing food grains, making seasonal migration unnecessary (Agoramoorthy & Hsu, 2015). The social workers continue to work with the communities, but a central aspect of the success of the initiative is the participation of the farming communities themselves, including women engaged in the decision-making processes of rural agriculture (Agoramoorthy & Hsu, 2015). This Indian study emphasizes the importance of participation and procedural justice in justice for humans and nature.

6 Conclusion

The pathway of expanding social work's social environment focus to a human-nature focus is embedded in a journey of justice. Social work cannot contribute to a just and sustainable world by clinging to a conventional social justice commitment. As Heinsch (2012) states, "[a]n unfortunate consequence of disregarding human-nature relationships is that it hinders social workers' capacity to help their clients" (p. 315).

The natural world is thus a "central variable in human development and well-being" (Norton, 2012, p. 304). By promoting an understanding of the "human-nature relationship as an issue of ecological justice" (Norton, 2012, p. 304), in a sustainable framework, social work can contribute to a more just world. However, it is important to remember that social work has only recently embarked on the journey of understanding that humans are part of nature.

The discussion in this chapter presents a pathway for social work to grow an understanding of the human-nature nexus, starting from expanding awareness of the environment to include the social environment in environmental justice, and finally embracing deep ecology and justice. Continuing the dialogue on climate change and the environmental crisis and its impact on humans and nature will eventually lead to a shift "to a clearer ecological understanding that all living creatures [including humanity] are populations-at-risk or endangered species, and that Earth itself is 'at risk'" (Miller et al., 2012, p. 276). By respecting the "diversity and otherness of nature for its own sake," and that "non-human entities are ends in themselves rather than instruments of human need or wealth creation," social work can embrace the right of human and nonhuman species to well-being and to an "enduring ability to thrive" (Besthorn, 2013, p. 38). It emphasizes, as a starting point for rethinking justice in social work, that "there can be no meaningful human existence, in fact, no human existence at all" without grounding justice in the natural world (Besthorn, 2013, p. 38). This shift is anchored in a sustainability framework for social work.

Ending poverty and inequity is a fundamental aspect of social work's role and contribution to a just and sustainable world. In the context of climate change and an environmental crisis facing the world, this focus on social work is critical, given that poverty is a "constant, ongoing disaster in its own right" (Dominelli, 2012, p. 3). Human-nature relationships must be protected for the well-being of both (Peeters, 2012). Cutting trees for fuel to cook food may be an immediate survival strategy, but it does not reduce poverty nor save the planet; it exacerbates the crisis for nature and humans. Raworth's Doughnut Model "incorporates the basic needs of people as a social foundation, in addition to the existing ecological ceiling, and therefore defines a safe and just space for humanity" (Attenborough, 2020, p. 128), which social workers can adopt as a human-nature justice approach to contribute to a sustainable world. We cannot stay below the planetary ceiling at the expense of the well-being of people, but the planetary boundaries act "as a framework for sustainable development" (Attenborough, 2020, p. 228). Keeping the balance of the Doughnut Model between the minimum requirements of human well-being (the social foundation ring) and the planetary ceiling affirms the relevance of a sustainable framework in social work. Attenborough (2020, p. 128) regards "[s]ustainability in all things" as the philosophy for all species, and sees the Doughnut Model as our "compass for the journey." He is of the view that the challenge to improve the lives of all people while also drastically reducing the human impact on the world is simple but vast, and suggests that all the answers needed to achieve this are available in the living world itself.

If social workers want to contribute professionally to a sustainable world and thus be part of rethinking and developing a new and common vision of a just world (Besthorn, 2012, p. 255), their task will be made easier if they first understand the human-nature nexus in relation to themselves and their clients' survival as human beings. For humans to live sustainably, they must first respect, save and guard the planet's own boundaries. This understanding is a fundamental principle that must underpin social work's commitment to promoting the well-being of people and defining a safe and just space for humanity that does not exceed planetary boundaries.

The Human-Nature Nexus: A Sustainability Framework for Social Work? 59

Inclusive social work can thus contribute to free the planet from human dominance by recognizing the value of all life on the planet (Heinsch, 2012). If social work embraces the interconnectivity between humans and nature, it would position social work as indispensable in debates, decisions and actions pertaining to the survival and well-being of humanity and nature.

References

Agoramoorthy, G., & Hsu, M. J. (2015). Irrigation-based social work relieves poverty in India's drylands. *International Social Work, 58*(1), 23–31. https://doi.org/10.1177/0020872812463106

Attenborough, D., with Hughes, J. (2020). *A Life on Our Planet. My Witness Statement and a Vision for the Future.* Penguin Random-House.

Besthorn, F. H. (2012). Deep ecology's contribution to social work: A ten-year retrospective. *International Journal of Social Welfare, 21*(3), 248–259. https://doi.org/10.1111/j.1468-2397.2011.00850.x

Besthorn, F. H. (2013). Radical equalitarian ecological justice: A social work call to action. In M. Gray, J. Coates, & T. Hetherington (Eds.), *Environmental Social Work* (pp. 31–45). Routledge.

Clarke, J. (n.d.) Icosindaba. Conversation for change. Blog. www.icosindaba.co.za.

Coates, J., & Gray, M. (2012). Guest editorial. The environment and social work: An overview and introduction. *International Journal of Social Welfare, 21*(3), 230–238. https://doi.org/10.1111/j.1468-2397.2011.00851.x

Gray, M., Coates, J., & Hetherington, T. (Eds.) (2013). *Environmental Social Work.* Routledge.

Dominelli, L. (2012). *Green Social Work: From Environmental Crises to Environmental Justice.* Polity Press.

Dominelli, L. (Ed.) (2018). *The Routledge handbook of green social work* (pp. 293–306). Routledge.

Global agenda for social work and social development. (2012). Collaboration between IASSW, IFSW, ICSW. http://www.globalsocialagenda.org.

Gray, M., & Coates, J. (2012). Environmental ethics for social work: Social work's responsibility to the non-human world. *International Journal of Social Welfare, 21*(3), 239–247. https://doi.org/10.1111/j.1468-2397.2011.00852.x

Hattingh, J. (2019). A question of international solidarity. *UNESCO Courier*, 3, July-September, The ethical challenges of climate change, pp. 28–30. https://en.unesco.org/courier/2019-3.

Hawkins, C. A. (2010). Sustainability, human rights, and environmental justice: Critical connections for contemporary social work. *Critical Social Work, 11*(3), 68–81.

Heinsch, M. (2012). Getting down to earth: Finding a place for nature in social work practice. *International Journal of Social Welfare, 21*(3), 309–318. https://doi.org/10.1111/j.1468-2397.2011.00860.x

International Climate Justice Network. (2002). *Bali Principles of Climate Justice.* https://corpwatch.org/article/bali-principles-climate-justice#:~:text=The%20principles%20were%20developed%20by,in%20Bali%20in%20June%202002.

Isbister, J. (2001). *Capitalism and Justice: Envisioning Social and Economic Fairness.* Kumarian Press.

Jayaraman, T. (2019). Climate and social justice. *UNESCO Courier*, 3, July-September, The ethical challenges of climate change, pp. 16–18. https://en.unesco.org/courier/2019-3.

Jones, D. N. (Ed.). (2018). *Global Agenda for Social Work and Social Development: Third Report.* Promoting community and environmental sustainability. IFSW.

Lombard, A., & Twikirize, L. (2018). Africa report. Promoting environmental and community sustainability. In D. N. Jones (Ed.), *Global Agenda for Social Work and Social Development: Third Report. Promoting Community and Environmental Sustainability*, pp. 50–79. IFSW, IASSW, ICSSW.

McKinnon, J. (2008). Exploring the nexus between social work and the environment. *Australian Social Work, 61*(3), 256–268. https://doi.org/10.1080/03124070802178275

Miller, S. E., Hayward, R. A., & Shaw, T. V. (2012). Environmental shifts for social work: A principles approach. *International Journal of Social Welfare, 21*(3), 270–277. https://doi.org/10.1111/j.1468-2397.2011.00848.x

Norton, C. L. (2012). Social work and the environment: An ecosocial approach. *International Journal of Social Welfare, 21*(3), 299–308. https://doi.org/10.1111/J.1468-2397.2011.00853.X

Peeters, J. (2012). The place of social work in sustainable development: Towards ecosocial practice. *International Journal of Social Welfare, 21*(3), 287–298. https://doi.org/10.1111/j.1468-2397.2011.00856.x

Rinkel, M., & Powers, M. (2017). *Social Work Promoting Community and Environmental Sustainability: A Workbook for Global Social Workers and Educators*. International Federation of Social Work. https://www.ifsw.org/product/books/social-work-promoting-community-and-environmental-sustainability/.

Schlosberg, D. (2007). *Defining environmental justice. Theories, movements, and nature.* https://doi.org/10.1093/acprof:oso/9780199286294.001.0001.

Schlosberg, D. (2013). Theorising environmental justice: The expanding sphere of a discourse. *Environmental Politics, 22*(1), 38–55. https://doi.org/10.1080/09644016.2013.755387

United Nations. (1987). *Report of the World Commission on Environment and Development [WCED]: Our Common Future.* https://sustainabledevelopment.un.org/content/documents/5987our-common-future.pdf

United Nations. (2015). *Transforming Our World, the 2030 Agenda for Sustainable Development.* Advanced unedited version. Finalized text for adoption (1 August). https://sustainabledevelopment.un.org/content/documents/21252030%20Agenda%20for%20Sustainable%20Development%2web.pdf

United Nations Educational, Scientific and Cultural Organization (UNESCO). (2021). *UNESCO Urges Making Environmental Education a Core Curriculum Component in All Countries by 2025.* Press statement. https://en.unesco.org/news/unesco-urges-making-environmental-education-core-curriculum-component-all-countries-2025.

United Nations Office for Disaster Reduction (UNDRR). (2012). *Sendai Framework for Disaster Risk Reduction 2015–2030.* https://www.undrr.org/publication/sendai-framework-disaster-risk-reduction-2015-2030.

United Nations Office of the High Commissioner for Human Rights (OHCHR). (2018). *Framework Principles of Human Rights and the environment.* https://undocs.org/en/A/HRC/37/59.

Disaster Injustice in the Coastal Region of Bangladesh: In Quest of Local Actors-Driven Recovery Intervention

Rabiul Islam

1 Introduction

Bangladesh is extremely susceptible to natural hazards because of its flat landscape, several big rivers, topographical location, and climate change (Dasgupta et al., 2014; Disaster Management Bureau, 2010). Coastal Bangladesh is experienced with frequent cyclones and storm surges, floods, riverbank erosion, and salinity (Disaster Management Bureau, 2010; Paul et al., 2012; Rotberg, 2010). These hazards make massive damage and loss, and the poverty of coastal people exacerbates the susceptibility of these areas to such catastrophes (Alam & Rahman, 2014; Uddin & Islam, 2020). To reduce these vulnerabilities and disaster risks, local actors—local government and NGOs—have taken many programs in the coastal region of Bangladesh.

Traditionally, natural disasters seriously affect human rights—the right of affected people to get recovery support without discrimination based on race, sex, religion, and political belief. Violation of disaster rights of affected people is one of the most complex challenges during relief activities at the recovery phase after a disaster. Unequal access to relief assistance and discrimination in aid provision (material and cash) are major problems that the affected people often face due to the effects of natural disasters (Refworld, 2008). Thus, an injustice is created in the disaster-affected community during the recovery phase, which leads to discontent among the disaster victims. They deprive themselves of their rights to get emergency support after a disaster.

Existing disaster literature has discussed various aspects of recovery. Masud-All-Kamal and Hassan (2018); Islam and Walkerden (2014) have examined the role of social capital in disaster recovery in the cyclone-affected communities of Bangladesh. Islam et al. (2020) argued how government and NGOs promote sustainable disaster

R. Islam (✉)
Department of Social Work, University of Rajshahi, Rajshahi, Bangladesh
e-mail: rabiul.islam@ru.ac.bd

© The Author(s), under exclusive license to Springer Nature Singapore Pte Ltd. 2022
D. Madhanagopal et al. (eds.), *Environment, Climate, and Social Justice*,
https://doi.org/10.1007/978-981-19-1987-9_4

recovery through community participation. Alam and Rahman (2019) and Islam, Ingham, et al. (2017) showed the women's role in post-disaster recovery. Islam and Abd Wahab (2020) argued that community-led intervention—community resource mobilization and leadership development, community participation and partnership, community planning, and empowerment—can promote sustainable disaster recovery in the Bangladesh coast. Islam and Wahab (2017) showed how coastal households use indigenous knowledge to protect food and drinking water sources from the impacts of cyclones in Bangladesh. Emphasizing the institutional role, Parvin and Shaw (2013) discussed the contribution of microfinance institutions to disaster response and recovery processes in the coastal areas of Bangladesh. Current disaster literature mostly focused on the institutional contribution (e.g., government, local government, NGOs, and other community-based organizations) to post-disaster support (e.g., relief, reconstruction, and rehabilitation) for recovery from disaster impacts. Some studies have discussed the role of social capital, women, indigenous knowledge, and microcredit in disaster recovery in Bangladesh. All too often, discussion of disaster justice and human rights of disaster victims are not sufficiently taken into account in disaster literature and during the intervention of local actors at the recovery phase.

Disaster rights of the affected people and injustice (e.g., corruption and favoritism during the distribution of relief and other emergency support) during recovery intervention are crucial. Therefore, Tierney and Oliver-Smith (2012) argued that post-disaster recovery depends on the quality of governance, institutional capacity, and equity of recovery aid. Islam, Walkerden, et al. (2017) showed the role of local government in disaster recovery and critically reviewed the equity and corruption during recovery support distribution. Considering the literature gap (i.e., less focus on disaster justice and rights) and the necessity of disaster rights and equity at the recovery phase, this chapter critically analyzes the contribution of local actors (local government and NGOs) to recover from a disaster and explores their exploitation while providing support to the disaster victims.

This chapter is organized in the following sections. The next section offers a brief methodology of the study. The third section describes the findings—disaster recovery intervention of local actors such as local government and NGOs. The fourth section presents a discussion based on the key arguments of the study, which are supported by the existing literature. The final section offers policy implications and conclusions for further action to protect disaster rights and strengthen the contribution of local actors to the recovery phase after a disaster, as well as provide a future research direction in this regard. This study will contribute additional knowledge to the existing body of knowledge that would overcome the limitations of local actors during the distribution of recovery support and open opportunities for further research in this field. This will also help the readers to understand disaster rights and injustice in the context of cyclone-affected communities of Bangladesh.

2 Methodology

The approach of this research is qualitative. This study was conducted in the two coastal villages (Tafalbaria and South Charduani at Patharghata sub-district under Barguna district) of Bangladesh—cyclone-prone areas and was severely affected by Cyclone Sidr in 2007. This area was also affected by Cyclone Aila and Cyclone Bijli (2009), Cyclone Mahasen (2013), Cyclone Fani (2019), Cyclone Amphan (2020), and Cyclone Yaas (2021). Enormous damage and losses occurred due to the impact of these cyclones in the study area. The present study is focused on Cyclone Sidr 2007. Data were collected from February to July 2013. Compared to the present time, the study data is a bit older; however, the post-cyclone intervention of local actors (e.g., local government and NGOs) is almost the same (i.e., the favoritism and corruption during the distribution of relief goods) in the coastal areas of Bangladesh.

Various data collection methods, such as Focus Group Discussions (FGDs), Key Informant Interviews (KIIs), and NGO workshops, were used in this study. FGDs were employed to get in-depth data for achieving study aims and to understand the real and perceived disaster rights and injustice during the recovery phase after Cyclone Sidr. Eight FGDs with the villagers were conducted through a semi-structured checklist. Each focus group consisted of eight to 10 members—including different occupational groups (e.g., fishing, farming, housewives, and students).

KIIs took place with key local leaders, including local government and NGO officials, Imams, teachers, village leaders, local journalists, volunteers, and so on. Sixteen key informants were taken from the local level. A checklist was used to conduct the interviews. These people are the key individuals in the villages and play a direct and indirect role in the community rebuilding process after a disaster. Therefore, their experience was important to include. Along with local key informants, national-level disaster practitioners and government policymakers were also included. Moreover, some key informants were taken from the national level (e.g., government policymakers and high officials of international organizations and national NGOs). Combining national and local experience enabled issues at each level to be considered to draw a conclusion on disaster rights and injustice that occurred after a cyclone (Figs. 1 and 2).

A day-long NGO workshop was arranged to obtain stakeholders' views on post-cyclone recovery. Twenty-six local NGOs participated in the workshop and shared their experiences of Cyclone Sidr and provided ideas on recovery efforts after a cyclone. Most of them have disaster risk reduction programs and experience working with post-Sidr redevelopment activities. A semi-structured checklist was used to explore the issues during the workshop. A discussion was initiated on how local NGOs contributed to post-cyclone redevelopment, what challenges they faced during recovery activities, and what community problems they identified that require further attention to develop. The NGOs also talked about post-disaster corruption and policy issues.

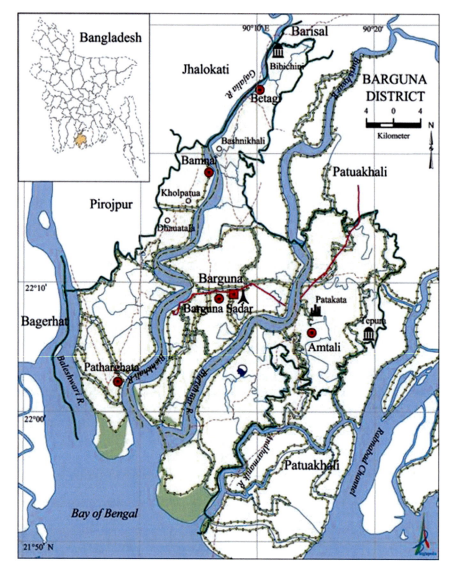

Fig. 1 Barguna district. Source: Islam & Miah, 2012

This chapter examines how local government and NGOs support the households to recover from a cyclone disaster, how they practice disaster rights, and how the cyclone-affected households are exploited during the support distribution phase.

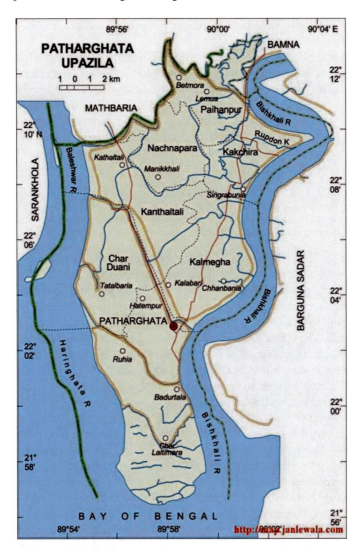

Fig. 2 Patharghata Upazila. Source: Islam & Miah, 2012

3 Results

3.1 Disaster Recovery Intervention of Local Actors

This section is designed based on the key findings of the study—how disaster-led injustice has taken place and how the cyclone-affected villagers are deprived of their rights by the local level interventions (local government (Union Parishad) and NGOs) in the coastal region of Bangladesh.

3.1.1 Local Government in the Disaster Recovery Process

Union Parishad (UP) is the lowest local government unit and rural administrative body of Bangladesh—working for maintaining law and order, implementing development programs, and providing public wellbeing services (Aminuzzaman, 2010). The UP provides the necessary support for the disaster-affected community, such as emergency relief—rice, cooking oil, dry food, drinking water, medicine, and hygiene kits (Islam et al., 2017). The UP also supports the affected people by providing cash and building materials (e.g., bamboo and tin) to repair damaged houses (FGDs and KIIs). One focus group participant said,

> I received 2500 taka from Union Parishad for repairing my partially-damaged house after cyclone. To rebuild my house after Cyclone Sidr. I bought some bamboos and other building materials (e.g., rope, fence, spade) to rebuild my house. I have benefited during the emergency; the cash support was too little than my needs in that time, though. (FGD-5)

The Union Parishad also provides support to restore the livelihoods of cyclone-affected households by distributing farming seeds and fishing nets and boats (FGDs). The FGD participants acknowledged, "We got some seeds (e.g., paddy and vegetables) and boats and nets support from the UP representatives after the Cyclone Sidr that someway helped us to resume livelihood activities such as farming and fishing" (FGD-8). The Union Parishad also did some reconstruction works of roads and culverts with the assistance of the government. Their limited contributions to reconstruction were evident after Cyclone Sidr, though (Islam et al., 2017). Despite these roles of UP after a cyclone, there are several loopholes evident in times of providing recovery support to the affected people.

Nepotism and unequal distribution were the major loopholes for UP at the post-cyclone recovery phase. The UP leaders (members and chairmen) sometimes favored their political followers and their families, friends, and relatives during the distribution of relief items after Cyclone Sidr (FGDs). FGD participants claimed, "The UP leaders favored their relatives and friends during relief works after Cyclone Sidr. A Union Parishad member gave more relief goods to his father-in-law's house compared to other affected households in the same community" (FGD-7). They also favored their political supporter during the distribution of building materials (bamboo and tin), money, and cropping seeds (FGDs and KIIs). One local key informant informed, "The UP members and chairman provided building materials, farming seeds and money to their political party-men/supporters due to their commitment during the election" (KII-2). Focus group data revealed that many non-agriculture families got farming seeds as a disaster recovery livelihood support due to nepotism. In contrast, some agro-based families were deprived of this support to restore their farming activities (FGDs). A focus group participant reported,

> As a farmer, I didn't receive any cropping seeds after a cyclone. But one of my neighbors got farming and vegetable seeds, who is not involved in agricultural activities. On the other hand, some fishermen received both the fishing and farming materials after Cyclone Sidr. (FGD-6)

Political nepotism was extreme during the distribution of post-disaster relief. The Union Parishad leaders are greatly engaged with party politics. Consequently, they cannot escape the requests of party supporters, as the party-men do hard work during an election to win them (Islam et al., 2017). Some FGD participants reported that sometimes they did not receive relief goods due to their different political ideology from the UP chairman. Due to the favor of party supporters, UP leaders failed to do good after Cyclone Sidr. Thus, mistrust between the local households and UP representatives has created, which affects their future elections (FGD-3, 8).

Favoring the own villagers was another nepotism of Union Parishad leaders after a cyclone. The UP representatives often favor their villagers (usually a Union Parishad consists of several villages) rather than other villages of the union to give recovery assistance after a cyclone. The Cyclone Sidr-affected villagers reported that the Union Parishad Chairman constructed more government-financed public housing (i.e., the government donated community house) in his native village (Tafalbaria—a study village) compared to the requirements of South Charduani (another study village) villagers (FGDs). One FGD participant commented,

> Along with their relatives and friends, members and chairman of Union Parishad are some-times biased to their native villagers to provide government-supported relief goods and other rehabilitation schemes. Due to this type of biased attitude, other villagers deprived of their rights to get government relief support equally. (FGD-1)

Uneven distribution of relief goods also happened due to households' physical location of cyclone-affected people. Key informant data showed, "Due to isolated location and bad communication, cyclone-affected households sometimes do not get relief and other recovery support equally" (KII-2). FGD participants also reported that some households in remote locations did not get necessary relief support after Cyclone Sidr as those in a good location, i.e., nearby roads (FGD-2, 4, and 8).

Corruption was also a major loophole of UP at the post-cyclone recovery phase. Union Parishad leaders often take bribes during the distribution of recovery support after disasters. As the government distributes most recovery supports through UP (FGDs and KIIs), they get this opportunity. A piece of evidence found in a study village, because of connection with post-cyclone corruption, a former Union Parishad member could not contest in an election (FGD-1). The government also distributed cash through UP to repair the damaged shelters of cyclone-affected households, which increased corruption opportunities. One key informant claimed,

> In the cyclone-affected areas, post-disaster money and material flow are larger than the pre-disaster time, mostly distributed through Union Parishad. Therefore, the UP representatives get an opportunity to misuse money and commit corruption through bribing and favoring relatives, friends, and political supporters. (KII-5)

Focus group data revealed that many affected people in study villages had to give bribes to UP members to get government donations, e.g., building materials, cash, and relief goods. FGD participants said they gave the bribe to get building materials (e.g., tin, wood, and bamboo) for repairing the damaged house and to get a new house—provided for the replacement of a fully damaged house (FGD-3, 7). Due to this bribery practice, many needy households did not get government support, as they could not pay bribe money to the UP representative. One FGD participant informed, "I was selected to receive building materials from the Union Parishad. Finally, my name was deleted from the distribution list, as I failed to pay bribe money to a UP member" (FGD-5). An alternative scenario is also found that all UP leaders are not corrupted. A few UP representatives are also at the ground—dedicated to bringing wellbeing for the cyclone-affected people (KII-4).

The cyclone-affected households of study villages were also deprived of their rights by the influence of the middleman. These village-headmen work as the middleman in the coastal areas of Bangladesh. The UP leaders greatly rely on the village-headmen because they can influence voters during an election (Islam et al., 2017). Therefore, UP representatives prepare relief distribution lists with the help of village-headmen. Taking this influence as an advantage, the village-headmen demand bribes from the affected people for putting their names on the distribution list (FGDs and KIIs). Thus, many affected households of the study villages are deprived of their rights to get government support due to the inability to pay bribes. A focus group participant said,

> I had a chat with a village headman to get taka 3000 as recovery support from Union Parishad after Cyclone Sidr. He worded me to give this amount and demanded taka 1000 as a bribe to manage this money. I couldn't give him a bribe amount. Finally, I hadn't received that support. (FGD-7)

The cyclone-affected people in study villages were also deprived of receiving a good quality of relief. The UP representatives often distribute lower quality relief goods. Focus groups reported, "In many cases, almost half of the distributed relief rice was rotten because UP representatives sometimes sell the good quality rice in secret and buy lower quality rice to distribute" (FGD-1, 8). Thus, the cyclone-affected households were also deprived of their rights to get government-provided actual relief goods. The UP representatives also distributed less quantity of goods than committed to provide. For example, after Cyclone Sidr, many villagers of the study villages heard that they would get about 30 kg of rice per household as relief from the UP; however, they finally got 10–15 kg (FGDs). A key informant (local journalist) informed,

> Initially, I heard that the UP gave below quality relief goods to the cyclone victims. I checked it and found the truth about the bad quality of rice. The political cadres of UP representatives also gave less quantity of rice than their commitment to providing. However, the UP's logic of providing less quantity was to support more victims by the less amount of rice than the needs of the villagers. (KII-3)

Thus, the cyclone victims of study villages were deprived of their rights to get government relief support with just and equity. The UP representatives could not equally distribute the relief and other rehabilitation items to the cyclone victims due to nepotism, corruption, and interference from their political cadres and village-headmen (middlemen). However, this scenario has been changed a bit due to the government monitoring, involvement of local administration (sub-district level), local civil society, Ward Disaster Management Committee (WDMC), and Union

Disaster Management Committee (UDMC) in the distribution process of relief goods (KIIs).

3.1.2 NGOs Intervention in Disaster Recovery

NGOs play a vital role in the post-disaster recovery phase in the coastal areas of Bangladesh. NGOs provide emergency relief support, including food and non-food items—rice, oil, pulses, medicine, cash, and cooking materials (FGDs and KIIs). An NGO official key informant said,

> We have provided many relief goods to the villagers after Cyclone Sidr. The relief items include rice, cooking oil, potato, pulse, cooking utensils, personal hygiene items, emergency medicine, bucket, etc. We also provided baby foods, drinking water, and education materials for children. These items were useful for the cyclone-affected villagers to manage crises after the cyclone. (KII-1)

Many Sidr-affected families of the study villages got disaster relief from NGOs; however, livelihood support (e.g., farming seeds, livestock, and poultry) was significantly less than the emergency relief (FGDs and KIIs). One FGD participant said,

> Relief items (both food and non-food) after cyclone were almost common both from the NGOs, local government, and other community-based organizations. These items were useful for us immediately after a cyclone. However, we expected to get more rehabilitation support like farming and fishing equipment (cropping seeds, fishing nets, and boats), which could help us to restore our livelihood activities after the cyclone. (FGD-6)

In addition, NGOs provided building materials to the affected households to repair damaged shelters; however, they distributed inadequate new shelters to replace those that were damaged by the impact of Cyclone Sidr (KIIs and NGO workshop). NGO officials claimed,

> Along with relief and rehabilitation support, we also provided cash and building materials for rehabilitation after Cyclone Sidr. NGOs provided taka 2500 for the partially damaged house and taka 5000 for the fully damaged house due to cyclone. However, due to our limited capacity, we couldn't provide adequate support according to the needs of the cyclone victims, as we are very much dependent on donor funds to support the victims. (NGO workshop)

The support (both relief and rehabilitation) of NGOs was useful for the Cyclone Sidr victims. However, the study found some drawbacks of NGO support after a cyclone in the study villages (FGDs and KIIs). Alike the Union Parishad, NGOs also practice favoritism. For example, NGOs usually support their members (microcredit receivers). After Cyclone Sidr, NGOs prioritized their microcredit borrowers while delivering relief goods and livelihood assistance (FGDs and KIIs). Focus group participants reported,

> After a cyclone, NGOs mostly provide support to their microcredit members through relief goods and other rehabilitation schemes. The national-level large NGOs (e.g., BRAC, Grameen Bank, and so on) have more capacity to provide this support to their members.

Local NGOs have limited capacity to do this type of job. Therefore, members of large NGOs got more support than the members of local NGOs, though all the study villages were affected almost in the same manner due to Cyclone Sidr. Thus, unhappiness was created among the borrowers of local NGOs. (FGD-3)

This type of favoritism negatively impacts society. For example, due to this favoritism, sometimes, badly cyclone-affected households did not get NGO's recovery support (KII-8). One FGD participant reported,

I'm a member of a local NGO, from where I received little emergency relief support after Cyclone Sidr. But one of my neighbors received more relief and recovery support than me, as he was a member of a large NGO like BRAC. Once my little daughter informed me that our neighbor got more relief items (food and non-food) than us. I understood, my little daughter felt deprived during that time, which struck me. (FGD-2)

Workshop data revealed that NGOs usually support their microcredit members during an emergency so that they can be able to recover soon and refund the loaned amount to the respective NGOs (NGO workshop). An NGO official key informant told,

We have to see the interest of our microcredit borrowers and to take care of them during an emergency through providing necessary goods. Because, if they live, our organization will sustain, as we provided them a loan to run income-generating activities and by which they will get back us that amount gradually. (KII-11)

Corruption is also a drawback of NGOs' activities during relief and rehabilitation work after the cyclone. NGOs sometimes take bribes at the time of distributing livelihood support, such as cattle for farming and rearing, and nets and boats for fishing (FGDs). One focus group participant said,

I had to pay taka 5000 as a bribe to an NGO official to get a calf as livelihood support after Cyclone Sidr. The market price of that calf was around taka 20,000. I gave the amount, as I thought the calf would be profitable for me. (FGD-7)

Corruption is more evident at the post-disaster level than in the pre-disaster stage because donor support (money and material flows) is higher in recovery time than in normal times (FGDs and KIIs). A few cases were found that due to corruption during the distribution of recovery support, an international NGO stopped work with a local NGO after Cyclone Sidr. Because of taking bribes from the affected households, few NGO workers were sacked from their jobs after Sidr (KII-9). The villagers reported that many of them had to pay bribes to get nets, boats, and livestock support from NGOs after Cyclone Sidr (FGDs). NGO officials claimed that some corruption complaints against NGOs were not true. A few cases of mismanagement were found due to handling a large cyclone like Sidr. They also claimed that people's expectation was high to get everything from NGOs. Due to limited resources, it was not possible; therefore, corruption issues came to light (NGO workshop).

4 Discussion

This section is designed based on the key arguments of the study, which are supported by the existing literature. The coastal region of Bangladesh frequently faces severe cyclones and storm surges that cause enormous damage and loss and create vulnerability. The coastal households are poor and have less physical and financial capital to address loss and vulnerability. Therefore, they need to seek support through local development actors, mainly from Union Parishad and NGOs, to recover from a disaster (Islam & Walkerden, 2015; Islam et al., 2017). The major concerns of this study are to explore the intervention of local government and NGOs in disaster recovery and whether they protect disaster rights and equity for affected people or not at this phase.

As a local government unit, Union Parishad provides recovery support to the cyclone-affected community through relief for tackling immediate emergency needs and restoring livelihoods after a cyclone. Islam et al. (2017) found that the UP played a crucial role in post-cyclone recovery by providing emergency relief, shelter, and livelihood support to the affected households in coastal Bangladesh. The UP also takes pre-disaster mitigation initiatives—mostly non-structural mitigation measures, for example, training, awareness campaign, workshop, and disaster drill (Aminuzzaman, 2010). This study found that UP representatives favor their political supporters, relatives, friends, and neighbors during the delivery of relief goods and other recovery supports. The existing literature supports this study's claim. For example, post-Sidr newspaper reports (New Age, 2007) and studies (Islam et al., 2017; Khan & Mozaharul, 1991; Mallick et al., 2009) acknowledged this favoritism, where the UP leaders gave priority to their political party-men during the distribution of recovery supports after Cyclone Sidr. Mallick et al. (2009) argued that this partiality creates conflicts among the community people and deprives the affected households of their rights. Due to this nepotism, UP leaders cannot play an impartial role in the recovery phase (Islam, Walkerden, et al., 2017).

This study also argues that the UP leaders are involved in corruption during the disaster recovery phase. They often took bribes at times of distributing recovery support. Existing literature found that post-disaster support distribution of UP is not transparent—rather mostly biased and corrupted by political preferences, extended family influences, personal interests, and monopolistic dominance of UP leaders (Aminuzzaman, 2014; Asian Development Bank, 2004; Islam et al., 2017; Khan, 2008; Rahman, 2019), which support the study findings. The counterargument of this finding is also found in the literature. Recognizing corruption of UP representatives as a major challenge of UP's financial management Aminuzzaman (2014) suggests increasing managerial and planning skills of the representatives through training. Mahmud and Prowse (2012) found that relief and recovery activities are generally corrupted due to a higher flow of kind and cash support at this stage. This huge cash and relief flow inspire the UP leaders to act corruptly (Islam, Walkerden, et al., 2017). Bribery during the distribution of government-provided relief materials and mismanagement of relief goods is also found during an emergency like the COVID-19 pandemic in Bangladesh, where local government leaders were involved (Ahmad, 2020). This study understands that post-disaster corruption by the UP representatives mostly occurred due to political influence and personal interest to get material benefits.

The study found, as the non-state local actor, NGOs provide emergency relief and other recovery support to the cyclone-affected households. This finding is supported by a study of ActionAid Bangladesh (2010) that pointed out that NGOs supported through food, water, sanitation, shelter, and livelihood support (e.g., farming seeds and fishing boats and nets) to the affected community.

This study claims that NGOs favored their microcredit group members at the time of distributing recovery support. Islam and Walkerden (2015), Paul (1998) found that NGOs provided relief aid to their microcredit borrowers after disasters, which supports this finding. This study understands that favoritism creates discrimination among the common households and microcredit borrowers of the study villages. Local NGOs' capacity to support borrowers was less than the big national NGOs (e.g., BRAC, Grameen Bank, and ASA). Therefore, the big national NGOs could give improved support than local NGOs due to their donor support and own financial abilities. Consequently, a "sense of deprivation" and "disappointment" were observed among the borrowers of small NGOs, as they were deprived of getting emergency support to survive after a cyclone (Islam & Walkerden, 2015).

The study found that NGOs are involved in corruption. They sometimes take bribes at the time of distributing livelihood support after a disaster. Mahmud and Prowse (2012) argued that NGO workers are one of the most active individuals involved in post-cyclone corruption in Bangladesh, which supports the study found. Islam and Walkerden (2015) found that NGO workers were involved in corruption during support distribution after a cyclone. Beck (2005) claimed that corruption is seen in the NGO sector due to the extensive flow of foreign aid. Mahmud and Prowse (2012) reported that NGO corruption is mostly found in relief activities after a disaster due to the substantial flow of resources. Therefore, transparency of procurement under foreign aid-led projects should be improved.

The study also found that relief distribution policies at the different phases of recovery promote inequality. At the early stage of the disaster (up to a week), UP and NGOs distributed lower quality and cheaper relief goods among the most affected and vulnerable households. At this stage, the intention was to support more vulnerable people with less amount of cash and kinds. In the second stage (up to a month), relatively improved quality of relief goods reach and are given to the moderately susceptible people. Finally (up to several months), the top-class relief goods come and are delivered to the least vulnerable people. Because of these relief delivery policies, the best quality of relief goods go to the least vulnerable households, and the lowest value of relief items go to the most susceptible households. The discussion of Islam and Walkerden (2015) supports this finding. This distribution policy creates conflict and unhappiness among the villagers and mistrust between cyclone-affected people and local actors (Islam & Walkerden, 2015; Islam et al., 2017).

The unequal distribution of relief and recovery assistance fosters clashes and disappointment within households (Islam & Walkerden, 2015). Aldrich (2010, 2011) claimed that unequal support delivery would interrupt disaster recovery and prolong resilience. In Bangladesh, people's relationships with NGOs and local government are close. However, the relief inequalities of local government and NGOs, lack of transparency in their works, and practice of receiving bribes from the affected people loosen this relation and create distrust between local actors and the community. This study finds that bribery plays a major role in increasing the vulnerability of cyclone-affected communities and weakening their capacities to withstand the adverse impacts of disasters. Indeed, corruption is embedded in the wider governance system of state and non-state organizations (local government and NGOs) that developed through the mal-governance practice in Bangladesh in the last couple of decades (Rahman, 2018).

This study found an important insight that most of the cyclone-affected villagers expected to get much support from local government and NGOs, as they could not recover from damage and loss due to their vulnerability, poverty, intensity and frequency of cyclones, and lack of financial and physical capital. This insight echoes the findings of Islam and Walkerden (2014), who found that cyclone-affected households were highly dependent on the support of UP and NGOs for their recovery. This finding indicates the relief-dependent attitude of cyclone-affected villagers, which impedes the speedy recovery and community resilience.

This study explores the contribution of local government and NGOs to disaster recovery in the Bangladesh coast. It investigates how their activities exploit the cyclone-affected people while providing recovery support. Both Union Parishad and NGOs provided crucial support after the cyclone by distributing emergency relief and other recovery and livelihood support to Cyclone Sidr-affected people. The Union Parishad representatives and NGOs staff were often involved in favoritism and corruption during the distribution of post-disaster support. According to the constitution of Bangladesh (Article 19), all citizens are entitled to get government opportunities and services equally. The state is committed to eliminating social and economic inequality and confirming the rightful distribution of wealth and opportunity among citizens (GoB, 2016). However, the local government and NGOs disregard the state's commitment to the citizens through their uneven distribution of resources after Cyclone Sidr. Thus, the disaster-affected coastal people of Bangladesh are deprived of their constitutional rights and suffer from injustice.

5 Policy Implications and Conclusions

From the above discussion, this study develops some recommendations to improve the contributions of local government and NGOs to disaster recovery in Bangladesh. These recommendations are related to local government and NGOs who have direct roles and to the central government and international NGOs, who support local actors through formulating policies, providing cash, kind and technical support, and designing further programs. To leverage the community's self-reliance, to reduce the community's relief dependency, and to build resilient communities, the following measures should be considered:

1. Union Parishad and NGOs should provide relief and recovery support to the disaster-affected community following both need-based and right-based approaches, where most needy people will get post-disaster recovery support. By following this approach, the local actors can avoid the faulty policy of relief distribution (discussed in Sect. 4, paragraph 8) favoritism to support the political cadre of UP representatives and microcredit members of NGOs (see Sect. 3.1.1).
2. The local actors should practice the fair distribution of relief goods. They can involve the local civil society members (teachers, religious leaders, senior citizens, social workers, freedom fighters, and journalists) in the process of distributing relief and recovery support. Such initiative can promote fair distribution of recovery support (see Sects. 3.1.1 and 3.1.2), reducing disaster injustice and upholding disaster rights of the affected people.
3. Creating alternative livelihood options and ensuring the security of existing livelihoods can reduce the relief dependency of coastal households (discussed in Sect. 4, paragraph 10). NGOs and government can create alternative job options (e.g., establishing fish processing industries, shipyards, and new sea-beach for tourism) and ensure the security of existing livelihoods through cultivating alternative crops. Moreover, income-generating training (on tailoring, poultry and livestock rearing, homestead gardening, and cottage industries) for women and vocational training for young people can increase their income and self-sufficiency, leading to building a disaster-resilient community.

The main purpose of this study was to explore the role of local actors (e.g., local government and NGOs) in disaster recovery and examine whether the local actors promote justice or injustice when distributing relief and livelihood support to cyclone-affected households in the Bangladesh coast. The Union Parishad and NGOs provided crucial support after Cyclone Sidr. They also provided livelihood support for restoring livelihoods after the cyclone.

The local government leaders favored their political followers, and NGO staff preferred their microcredit borrowers to distribute relief goods and recovery support. The distribution of recovery supports often is plagued with favoritism and bribery; for example, local government representatives and NGO staff sometimes took bribes during the distribution of these supports.

This study argues that the mismanagement of relief and recovery support creates mistrust between local actors and cyclone-affected households, deprives affected people of their rights, and promotes injustice in society.

This study suggests that local civil society members (e.g., teachers, religious leaders, senior citizens, social workers, and journalists) should work together for fair distribution of recovery support, which can reduce disaster injustice and uphold disaster rights in the coastal community of Bangladesh.

The present study makes several significant contributions. First, it provides an exploration of how the local government and NGOs contributed to the recovery phase by providing various supports. Secondly, it develops knowledge and adds

Disaster Injustice in the Coastal Region of Bangladesh ...

value to the existing knowledge on the disaster domain through exploring disaster rights and equity and their practice at the community level. Thirdly, the study is useful for future researchers who are interested in working in the field. Finally, this study will contribute to an improved understanding of disaster rights and injustice that overcomes the limitations of local actors during the distribution of recovery support and opens up opportunities for further research in this field.

This study has focused on the contribution of two formal actors (local government and NGOs) to the disaster recovery phase. Further research on the intervention of other key informal actors (such as moneylenders, sea-pirates and forest robbers, village-headmen, and local political cadres) at the disaster recovery phase would help to get a complete picture of nepotism and corruption and their impact on disaster rights and justice in the coastal areas of Bangladesh.

References

ActionAid Bangladesh (2010). *ActionAid commemorates loss of Cyclone Sidr*. Retrieved 10 April 2014 from http://www.actionaid.org/bangladesh/news/actionaid-commemorates-loss-cyclone-sidr.

Ahmad, M. M. (2020). *The COVID-19 outbreak: A testing time for NGOs in Bangladesh*. Retrieved 12 September 2021 from https://www.e-ir.info/2020/05/06/the-covid-19-outbreak-a-testing-time-for-ngos-in-bangladesh/.

Alam, K., & Rahman, M. H. (2014). Women in natural disasters: A case study from southern coastal region of Bangladesh. *International Journal of Disaster Risk Reduction, 8*(2014), 68–82. https://doi.org/10.1016/j.ijdrr.2014.01.003

Alam, K., & Rahman, M. H. (2019). Post-disaster recovery in the cyclone Aila affected coastline of Bangladesh: Women's role, challenges and opportunities. *Natural Hazards, 96*(3), 1067–1090. https://doi.org/10.1007/s11069-019-03591-7

Aldrich, D. P. (2010). The power of people: Social capital's role in recovery from the 1995 Kobe earthquake. *Natural Hazards, 56*, 595–611. https://doi.org/10.1007/s11069-010-9577-7

Aldrich, D. P. (2011). The externalities of strong social capital: Post-tsunami recovery in Southeast India. *Journal of Civil Society, 7*(1), 81–99. https://doi.org/10.1080/17448689.2011.553441.

Aminuzzaman, S. M. (2010). *Local government and development in Bangladesh: Lessons learned and challenges for improving service delivery of Union Parishad (UP)*. Dhaka: Eropean Union.

Aminuzzaman, S. M. (2014). *Democratic Local Governance Capacity and Natural Disasters – Building Community Resilience: Bangladesh Case Study* (E.-W. Center, Ed.). Hawaii: East-West Center.

Asian Development Bank. (2004). *Local governance and service delivery to the poor: Bangladesh case study*. Dhaka: Author.

Beck, T. (2005). *Learning lessons from disaster recovery: The case of Bangladesh*. Washington: The World Bank.

Dasgupta, S., Huq, M., Khan, Z. H., et al. (2014). Cyclones in a changing climate: The case of Bangladesh. *Climate and Development, 6*(2), 96–110. https://doi.org/10.1080/17565529.2013.868335.

Disaster Management Bureau. (2010). *National plan for disaster management 2010–2015*. Dhaka: Disaster Management and Relief Division, Government of the People's Republic of Bangladesh.

GoB. (2016). *The constitution of the People's Republic of Bangladesh* (Vol. 76 of 1972). Dhaka: Legislative and Parliamentary Affairs Division, Government of the People's Republic of Bangladesh.

Islam, E., Abd Wahab, H., & Benson, O. G. (2020). Structural and operational factors as determinant of meaningful community participation in sustainable disaster recovery programs: The case of Bangladesh. *International Journal of Disaster Risk Reduction, 50*(2020), 101710.

Islam, E., & Abd Wahab, H. B. (2020). The Impact of a cyclonic disaster on coastal communities in Bangladesh: Possible community-led interventions towards sustainable disaster recovery. *Global Social Welfare, 7*(4), 339–352. https://doi.org/10.1007/s40609-020-00181-5.

Islam, M. R., Ingham, V., Hicks, J., et al. (2017). The changing role of women in resilience, recovery and economic development at the intersection of recurrent disaster: A case study from Sirajgang, Bangladesh. *Journal of Asian and African Studies, 52*(1), 50–67. https://doi.org/10.1177%2F0 021909614560244.

Islam, S., & Miah, S. (2012). *Banglapedia*. Dhaka: The Asiatic Society.

Islam, R., & Wahab, G. M. A. (2017). Households' indigenous coping practices to face disaster-induced food and water challenges in coastal Bangladesh. *Folklore Journal, 8*(February 2017), 104–111.

Islam, R., & Walkerden, G. (2014). How bonding and bridging networks contribute to disaster resilience and recovery on the Bangladeshi coast. *International Journal of Disaster Risk Reduction, 10*(2014), 281–291. https://doi.org/10.1016/j.ijdrr.2014.09.016.

Islam, R., & Walkerden, G. (2015). How do links between households and NGOs promote disaster resilience and recovery? A case study of linking social networks on the Bangladeshi coast. *Natural Hazards, 78*(3), 1707–1727. https://doi.org/10.1007/s11069-015-1797-4.

Islam, R., Walkerden, G., & Amati, M. (2017). Households' experience of local government during recovery from cyclones in coastal Bangladesh: Resilience, equity, and corruption. *Natural Hazards, 85*(1), 361–378. https://doi.org/10.1007/s11069-016-2568-6.

Khan, M. I., & Mozaharul. (1991). The impact of local elites on disaster preparedness planning: the location of flood shelters in Northern Bangladesh. *Disasters, 15*(4), 340–354. https://doi.org/10.1111/j.1467-7717.1991.tb00473.x.

Khan, M. M. (2008). *Functioning of local government (Union Parishad): Legal and practical constraints*. Dhaka: D. Watch.

Mahmud, T., & Prowse, M. (2012). Corruption in cyclone preparedness and relief efforts in coastal Bangladesh: Lessons for climate adaptation? *Global Environmental Change, 22*(4), 933–943. https://doi.org/10.1016/j.gloenvcha.2012.07.003.

Mallick, B., Witte, S. M., Sarkar, R., et al. (2009). Local Adaptation strategies of a coastal community during Cyclone Sidr and their vulnerability analysis for sustainable disaster mitigation planning in Bangladesh. *Journal of Bangladesh Institute of Planners, 2*(December), 158–168.

Masud-All-Kamal, M., & Hassan, S. M. (2018). The link between social capital and disaster recovery: Evidence from coastal communities in Bangladesh. *Natural Hazards, 93*(3), 1547–1564. https://doi.org/10.1007/s11069-018-3367-z.

New Age. (2007, November 27). Relief supplies pile up while many survivors go hungry. New Age. Retrieved 10 September 2021 from http://www.bangladesh-web.com/view.php?hidRecord= 178864.

Parvin, G. A., & Shaw, R. (2013). Microfinance institutions and a coastal community's disaster risk reduction, response, and recovery process: A case study of Hatiya, Bangladesh. *Disasters, 37*(1), 165–184. https://doi.org/10.1111/j.1467-7717.2012.01292.x.

Paul, B. K. (1998). Coping with the 1996 Tornado in Tangail, Bangladesh: An analysis of field data. *The Professional Geographer, 50*(3), 287–301. https://doi.org/10.1111/0033-0124.00121.

Paul, S. K., Paul, B. K., & Routray, J. K. (2012). Post-Cyclone Sidr nutritional status of women and children in coastal Bangladesh: An empirical study. *Natural Hazards, 64*(1), 19–36. https://doi.org/10.1007/s11069-012-0223-4.

Rahman, K. (2019). *Overview of corruption and anti-corruption in Bangladesh*. Dhaka: T. International.

Rahman, M. A. (2018). Governance matters: Climate change, corruption, and livelihoods in Bangladesh. *Climatic Change, 147*(1), 313–326. https://doi.org/10.1007/s10584-018-2139-9.

Refworld. (2008). *Human rights and natural disasters: Operational guidelines and field manual on human rights protection in situations of natural disaster*. Brookings-Bern Project on Internal Displacement. Retrieved 14 May 2021 from https://www.refworld.org/pdfid/49a2b8f72.pdf.

Rotberg, F. J. (2010). Social networks and adaptation in rural Bangladesh. *Climate and Development, 2*(1), 65–72. https://doi.org/10.3763/cdev.2010.0031.

Tierney, K., & Oliver-Smith, A. (2012). Social dimensions of disaster recovery. *International Journal of Mass Emergencies and Disasters, 30*(2), 123–146.

Uddin, M. I., & Islam, R. (2020). Vulnerability and responsive measures of cyclone Aila affected households in coastal Bangladesh. *Social Science Journal, University of Rajshahi, 23*(2020), 101–116.

Governance, Policy Advocacy and Legal Activisms in the Global South

Advancing Climate Justice in Africa: A Survey of Civil Society Capacities, Geopolitical Trust, and Policy Advocacy

Christopher Todd Beer and Mithika Joseph M. Mwenda

One of the most fundamental principles of climate justice is holding nations accountable for disproportional levels of historical and per capita greenhouse gas emissions, particularly in relation to nations that have populations that are more vulnerable to the risks and harms of anthropogenic climate change (International Climate Justice Network, 2002). Sometimes this is referred to as climate debt. As the African Climate Justice Manifesto states:

> We call on developed countries to acknowledge they have already used more than a fair and sustainable share of the Earth's atmospheric space. They must repay their debt through deep domestic emission reductions and by transferring the technology and finance required to enable us to follow a less polluting pathway without compromising our development (an emissions debt). We call on developed countries to compensate us for the adverse effects of their excessive historical and current per-person emissions, which are burdening us with rising climate-related costs and damages (an adaptation debt). (Pan African Climate Justice Alliance, 2010)

Most nations of sub-Saharan Africa have contributed proportionally little to the causes of global climate change while being vulnerable to more severe consequences. Projected risk and occurring harm to African nations due to climate change include threats to food security, rising temperatures, erratic rain patterns, shifting seasons, declining fisheries, increased water stress, and amplified health vulnerabilities (Boko et al., 2007; Niang et al., 2014).

Part of the findings of this survey was presented at the 2nd World Forum on Climate Justice, which took place in September 2021 in Glasgow, Scotland. Mithika Mwenda is the Co-founder and Executive Director of PACJA.

C. T. Beer (✉)
Lake Forest College, Lake Forest, USA
e-mail: beer@lakeforest.edu

M. J. M. Mwenda
Pan African Climate Justice Alliance, Nairobi, Kenya

© The Author(s), under exclusive license to Springer Nature Singapore Pte Ltd. 2022
D. Madhanagopal et al. (eds.), *Environment, Climate, and Social Justice*,
https://doi.org/10.1007/978-981-19-1987-9_5

Literature from numerous academic disciplines has examined individual case studies of climate justice advocacy and social movement mobilization across sub-Saharan Africa (Beer, 2014; Bond, 2012, 2014; Mwenda & Bond, 2020). However, there have been few systematic accounts of climate-justice-focused civil society efforts at a continent-wide level. The lack of such systematic, continent-level accounts remains a glaring gap in the literature and ignores countless organizations and both their individual and collective efforts in sub-Saharan Africa. This chapter provides an empirical descriptive analysis of the capacity, geopolitical trust, and policy advocacy of African climate justice civil society through an analysis of the organizational members of the Pan African Climate Justice Alliance (PACJA). PACJA brings together a diversity of membership drawn from non-governmental organizations (NGOs), community-based organizations (CBOs), foundations, smallholder producers, women, youth and faith-based organizations working towards climate justice, often in conjunction with other development programming. This chapter is not a review of the work of PACJA itself but rather an analysis of the trends among the individual civil society organizational members of the Alliance. The PACJA member network serves as the closest proxy currently available for a sampling frame of organizations working on climate justice in African nations. What capacity do domestic African civil society organizations advocating for climate justice have? What types of work do they do, and what types of programming do they implement? Do African civil society organizations working on climate justice target and/or make an effort to serve their communities, their provinces, and/or their countries? What are their organizational perspectives on key climate justice issues at the level of transnational geopolitics and global negotiations? What perspectives do they hold, and what policies do they advocate for regarding climate justice?

We explore such questions using original data from a 2016 PACJA survey of member organizations throughout the continent. All respondents were recruited by email to participate in the survey. Surveys were made available in both English and French. The confidential survey was designed and implemented using the Qualtrics survey web platform and took approximately 30 minutes to complete. The response rate was 23.4%, representing 121 organizations from 36 countries out of 514 PACJA member organizations in 2016.

The analyses are presented in three thematic sections: organizational scope and capacities, the geopolitical trust gap, and policy advocacy and engagement. The section on organizational capacity and scope examines where PACJA members work and what type of programming they implement in their efforts to address climate change. The second section, "the geopolitical trust gap", examines the self-reported levels of trust that African climate justice organizations have in specific nations and regions to take sufficient action to reduce their greenhouse gas (GHG) emissions, provide sufficient levels of finance for climate change adaptation as well as loss and damage, and the transfer of technology to assist countries in development without the use of as many fossil fuels—coal, oil, and natural gas. The final section of analyses examines African climate justice organizations' participation in the United Nations Framework Convention for Climate Change (UNFCCC) annual meetings (also known as Conference of Parties or COP), their support for different policy directions, and their opinions of the use of fossil fuels for continued development.

1 A PACJA Primer

PACJA is a continent-wide coalition of civil society organizations (CSOs) founded in 2008 that aims to unify and coordinate otherwise isolated civil society efforts on climate change advocacy for a pro-poor and people-centered response in Africa. PACJA also collaborates with international partners, national governments, and regional governmental bodies to amplify African voices in international climate change negotiations and policy formation.

In 2008, in Johannesburg, South Africa, the New Partnership for Africa's Development (NEPAD) and Oxfam International facilitated a dialogue among African civil society organizations to generate collaborative opportunities to influence the international climate change regime. This collaboration and coordination of African CSOs was further facilitated by a coalition of 17 European-based development and humanitarian aid organizations. Today, PACJA has gained recognition at African continental and international levels, has forged strong partnerships with numerous key stakeholders and has observer status with the UNFCCC.

PACJA's mission is "to develop and promote pro-poor development and equity-based positions relevant for Africa in the international climate change dialogue and related processes."

Their objectives state: "PACJA aims to be an effective African CSO's platform to share information, strategize jointly, coordinate engagement with African governments and other relevant stakeholders, and advocate for fairness and justice in international climate change and sustainable development processes in order to adequately protect the climate while safeguarding human rights and pro-poor development."

2 Organizational Scope and Capacities

2.1 Present Impacts of Climate Change

The damage caused by anthropogenic climate change should no longer be seen as a concern limited to future losses. Loss and harm from climate change are occurring now. While the numerous harms are projected to get worse, maybe even catastrophic, in the coming decades and into the end of the twenty-first century, many people, communities, and nations are already experiencing the impacts. A vast majority (77.1%) of African climate justice civil society organizations (CJOs) indicate that the communities they work with are already impacted by climate change either a

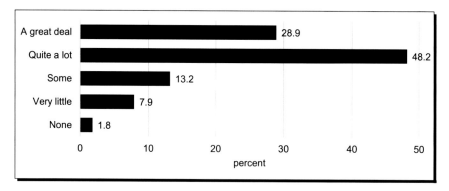

Fig. 1 How much the communities African climate justice organizations work with have been impacted by climate change ($N = 121$)

great deal or quite a lot. Only 10% said that the communities are currently impacted very little to none (see Fig. 1).

2.2 Geographic Scope

African climate-justice-focused civil society organizations are diverse in many ways, including the geographical scope of their work, the types of communities they serve, and the issues on which they focus. While a slight majority (54.2%) of CJOs are based in the large metropolitan areas (populations of more than 350,000) of their respective nations, nearly one in four (23.7%) report being based in rural areas. Larger cities tend to draw more civil society organizations with greater infrastructure, higher speed internet access, and a more educated labor force. For the majority of African CJOs in our sample, the geographic scope of their work extends beyond their immediate location. In Fig. 2, we see that over half of the African CJOs from our sample work throughout their respective countries as national organizations (45.8%) or even internationally (16.7%). A bit more than a third of the organizations work either directly with their immediate community (which could be a large city) (28.3%) or within a particular provincial or state boundary (9.2%).

Some of the gravest threats of anthropogenic climate change to human societies in Africa and elsewhere include rising sea levels and various threats to agriculture, including more erratic precipitation patterns, higher temperatures, the spread of pests, and an increased likelihood of drought (Hussein, 2011; Niang et al., 2014; Simms & Reid, 2005). Our sample of African CJOs predominantly work in agricultural (21.7%) and coastal areas (23.3%) (see Fig. 3). Those living in semi-arid and arid areas have to manage their livelihoods and meet their basic needs with very little rain, and climate change threatens to destabilize the levels of precipitation even further. Nearly one in eight African CJOs works in a semi-arid or an arid region. The remaining 20% of our

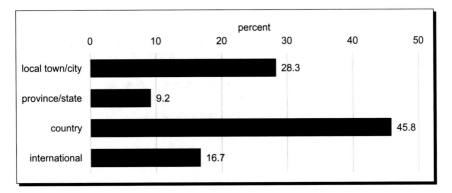

Fig. 2 Types of communities African climate justice organizations serve ($N = 121$)

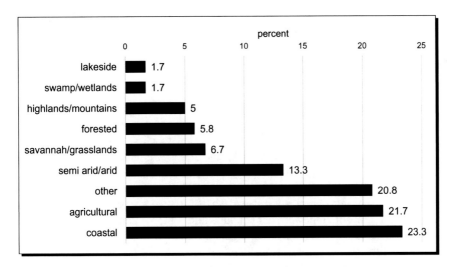

Fig. 3 Primary geographic area African climate justice organizations work ($N = 121$)

sample works in areas that are primarily forested, grasslands, mountains, wetlands, or lakeside.

2.3 Scope of Issues Addressed

Climate change is only one of many issues confronting nations and communities in Africa. Few of the African CJOs in our sample focus solely on climate change, and they are evenly split regarding climate change being their top issue priority. Exactly half of the sample indicated that climate change is their top priority and the other half indicated that it is one of many issues that they prioritize.

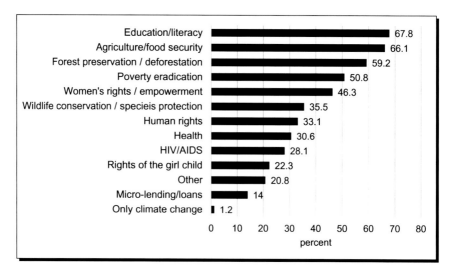

Fig. 4 Other than climate change, which issues do African climate justice organizations address in their programming ($N = 121$)

In many ways, climate change amplifies existing vulnerabilities. Most African CJOs integrate climate change programming into numerous other issues that challenge their communities (see Fig. 4). In addition to climate change, two-thirds (67.8%) of them also address education and literacy issues. Another two-thirds (66.1%) report providing programming on agriculture and food security issues. Just under 60% address forest preservation and deforestation, while half (50.8%) directly tackle poverty eradication. Nearly half (46.3%) also deliver programming on women's rights or empowerment. About a third of the organizations also address wildlife conservation (35.5%), human rights (33.1%), and/or health (30.6%). About a quarter of the organizations also address HIV/AIDS (28.1%) and/or the rights of girls (22.3%). Only 1.2% of the African CJOs in our sample report *only* addressing climate change. Clearly, climate change is both one of many issues and an issue that has been incorporated into the diverse work and programming of African CJOs.

Illustrated in Fig. 5, we see that in the 12 months prior to the survey (2016), African CJOs conducted programming on climate change across a range of topics related to mitigation, adaptation, education, and advocacy. The programming issues focused on mitigation efforts included forest preservation (79.8%), and renewable energy (49.2%), as well as recycling and waste management (26.4%), and transportation alternatives (19.2%).

Addressing climate change adaptation issues, just over two-thirds of the organizations implemented climate-related programming on agriculture and food security (67.5%). Relatedly, a third (34.7%) focused on the prevention of soil erosion and drought prevention (29.8%). Just over a quarter of the organizations focused on climate-related health issues (28.9%) and disaster preparedness/relief (28.1%). Less

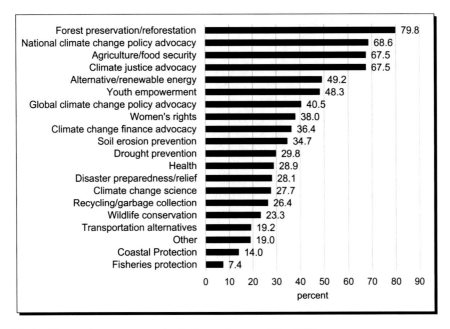

Fig. 5 Climate change programming in the previous year ($N = 121$)

than a quarter focused on adaptation issues of wildlife conservation and/or coastal and fisheries protections.

A full two-thirds of the organizations engaged in advocacy for national climate change policy (68.6%) and/or climate justice advocacy (67.5%), a good portion on global climate policy advocacy (40.5%), and a third (36.4%) on climate finance advocacy. Only 27.7% had conducted climate change science in the last 12 months. Programming also focused, on women's rights (38.0%) and youth empowerment (48.3%).

In sum, the vast majority of African CJOs report climate change is already impacting their communities quite a lot or a great deal. CJOs are primarily based in large metropolitan areas, but over half extend their work nationally or internationally. Many of the organizations are located in coastal and agriculture areas and engage in diverse areas of programming within and in addition to climate change issues.

3 The Trust Gap

Civil society organizations play an advocacy role as observers to the UNFCCC negotiating process (Allan & Hadden, 2017; Derman, 2014; Fisher, 2010; Hadden, 2015). Despite civil society efforts at both the international and domestic levels, there remains a discrepancy between the nationally determined contributions (NDCs) to reduce GHG emissions under the UNFCCC Paris Agreement and the level of reductions that the scientific community says are needed to avoid catastrophe (UNEP, 2020). The scientific research indicates reductions need to be greater in both degree and rate than the existing commitments. This discrepancy is known as the "emission gap". In its collective and collaborative efforts to reduce the impacts of climate change, the world will need to not only close the emissions gap but also an ongoing "trust gap", particularly between domestic civil society actors addressing climate change on the African continent and the advanced industrialized nations. The high per capita and historically emitting nations need to make greater commitments and show demonstrable action to reduce emissions, provide sufficient and new finance, and transfer appropriate technology. Trust between state, civil society, and market actors are imperative to foster the degree of global collective action that is necessary for humanity to successfully avoid catastrophic warming. See more details and discussion on this trust gap below.

4 Emissions Reductions

In Fig. 6, we see that a majority of African CJOs have low levels of trust for some of the high emitting nations and these nations' willingness or commitment to sufficiently reduce emissions in order to limit warming to 1.5 °C. China and the US, the two largest emitters in the world, were afforded the least amount of trust by African CJOs in our survey, with a majority expressing either very little trust or no trust in either nation. Only 16.7% of organizations expressed quite a lot or a great deal of trust in the US to reduce their emissions in order to limit global warming to 1.5 °C. Japan was afforded more trust than the US, but 43.5% of organizations still reported

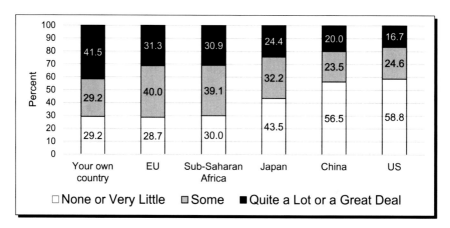

Fig. 6 Trust in nation/region to reduce their emissions in order to limit global warming to 1.5 °C ($n = 121$)

very little or no trust of the highly developed Asian nation. Comparatively, the EU, a region among the higher per capita and historical emitters, was trusted at higher levels, similar to levels of trust for Sub-Saharan Africa as a whole. Nearly a third (31.3%) of African CJOs trust the EU quite a lot of a great deal, nearly twice the rate of trust given to the US, while only 28.7% trusted the EU very little or not at all to reduce emissions sufficiently. The vast majority of the African CJOs trusted the EU at least some or greater. Four out of ten (41.5%) organizations in our sample indicated that they trusted their own nations quite a lot or a great deal to reduce emissions to limit warming to 1.5 °C—the highest rate of trust of any country or region among the choices.

5 New and Sufficient Finance

One aspect of climate justice is the transfer of financial resources from high per capita historical emitting nations to low emitting nations of the Global South as a form of compensation for emissions debt and in order to assist in both adapting to and mitigating climate change (Bond, 2012; Warlenius, 2018). This transfer of financial resources from high emitters to those suffering the harm of the emissions is known as compensatory climate justice. Not all African climate change organizations support calls for climate finance. A study of the broader field of Kenyan environmental organizations, not just climate justice-focused organizations, found that while many supported compensatory climate justice, a majority prioritized non-compensatory policies such as those that focused on emissions reductions, carbon markets, or clean energy (Beer, 2014). Among our sample for this study, Scandinavian nations (Denmark, Norway, and Sweden) are trusted quite a lot or a great deal by a majority (59.8%) of African CJOs, and another 21.4% expressed some trust for the provision of finance. Germany is also relatively trusted, with a strong majority of African CJOs expressing some (35.1%) or a great deal of trust (39.5%) (see Fig. 7). The UK, France, and Japan are all granted lower levels of trust, with about two-thirds of the sample indicating some or a great deal of trust. A majority still have very little or no trust that the US will provide sufficient finance, and only 1 in 5 indicate high levels of trust that the US will provide sufficient climate finance. It is important to note that the survey data was collected in the first quarter of 2016, prior to the election of Donald Trump as president of the US. Therefore, a lack of trust in the US by African CJOs existed prior to President Trump's efforts to both withdraw from the Paris Agreement and dismantle other climate change policy initiatives.

6 Transfers of Technology

Climate justice advocates have also called for a transfer of technology from highly industrialized nations to so-called developing nations to assist in the mitigation of

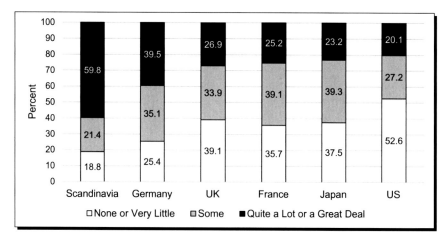

Fig. 7 Trust in other nations/regions to provide sufficient climate finance ($N = 121$)

GHG emissions and the adaptation of a warming planet. Examining the level of trust regarding the transfer of technology from highly advanced industrial nations in order to sufficiently reduce emissions, a very similar pattern of trust is evident. Again, Scandinavia is the most trusted region, with 85.4% of our sample reporting some or quite a lot of trust that Scandinavia will provide sufficient transfers of technology. The US remains a clear laggard, with only 26.1% of African CJOs affording the nation a high level of trust. More than 40% have very little to no trust in the US in this regard. Successfully addressing climate change on a global scale will and does require nations and civil society actors to collaborate in implementing mitigation and adaptation projects at every level—from the local to the transnational. The existing trust gap, especially between the African CJOs and the high-emitting US, will likely only be closed through concrete actions, sustained commitments of emissions reductions, climate finance, and the transfer of mitigating technology.

7 Policy Advocacy and Engagement

African climate justice organizations are engaged in the annual UNFCCC negotiating process, working to advance a global agreement among nations to collectively and sufficiently address climate change. However, member organizations participate in the process in different ways. On average, as of 2016, the organizations in our sample have attended three COP meetings as civil society members participating in parallel conferences and side events. On average, they have attended less than three COP meetings in a role as official civil society observers. Even fewer have participated in protests and rallies at COP meetings. On average, African CJOs have only served as part of their official national delegations during two COP meetings. By 2015, 53.5%

of our sample of organizations had a representative, in some capacity, in Paris for COP21.

At the time of our data collection, national climate action plans were in place in nations where 95.7% of our sample resides. Generally, a majority of African CJOs (60.7%) have confidence that their own nation's national climate action plans are sufficient to address climate change in their countries. Only 20.5% disagreed or strongly disagreed that their nation's climate action plan is sufficient.

While the majority find their national climate action plans sufficient, there are lower levels of trust that African national governments can effectively utilize any international climate finance from other countries. Over a third (35%) of African CJOs have very little or no trust in their national government's abilities to handle climate finance, nearly another third (30.8%) have some trust, and another third (34.2%) have quite a lot or a great deal of trust in their national governments to effectively use climate finance from international donors. A previous case study of the field of environmental organizations in Kenya points to a lack of trust in domestic governments that can hinder support for compensatory climate justice policies. Many environmental actors in Kenya thought any international compensation would either fall victim to political corruption, not be directed at assisting the most vulnerable populations or result in the nations of the Global North feeling that they had paid for the rights to keep emitting (Beer, 2014).

During early global climate negotiations, nations of the Global South were skeptical about transnational environmental treaties, seeing them as barriers to their own industrial development. There is little evidence of similar concerns among today's African CJOs. Just over three-quarters of the sampled organizations indicated that they believe addressing climate change will generate development in their countries, while just under a quarter indicated they thought it would slow development. Fears of "arrested development" are not dominant among our sample of African CJOs as international agreements push for domestic policies engaging in mitigation and adaptation efforts.

Current highly industrialized nations developed over the last century and a half with a high reliance on fossil fuels of one form or another. Figure 8 explores African CJOs level of support for the continued use of fossil fuels for the purpose of national development. We see that 45% disagree and 29.5% strongly disagree (for a total of 71.5%) that the use of fossil fuels should be their right in order to further develop. Mitigation of emissions seems to be an uncompromising priority for a strong majority of African CJOs. Just under a fifth (18.8%) agree or strongly agree that their respective nations have the right to use fossil fuels to further their development.

But what about resources discovered within one's own country? The discovery of oil or natural gas could likely help a country develop through the growth or expansion of the energy sector as well as the provision of energy to other domestic sectors. However, a generally similar pattern as above is evident when the question addresses fossil fuel resources discovered within one's national borders. Over half (59.4%) of our sample disagrees or strongly disagrees that their nations should develop any fossil fuel resources discovered within their borders. Nearly 20% agree or strongly agree that such resources should be utilized in order to help their country develop.

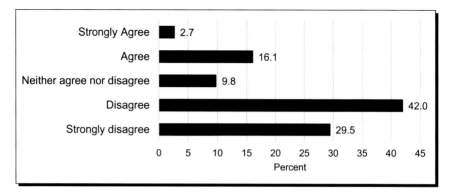

Fig. 8 Our nation has the right to further development using fossil fuels ($N = 121$)

However, when the topic of emission reduction is in competition with poverty reduction compared to the more general development, a near majority (49.5%) of respondents agree or strongly agree that emissions reductions should take a back seat to efforts to reduce poverty. Over a quarter (26.1%) *strongly* agree. That being said, over a third (34.2%) of our sample's respondents prioritized emissions reductions over poverty reduction.

8 Scope of Reform

How much economic, political, and societal change will be required to successfully address global climate change? African climate justice organizations strongly believe that a radical shift away from capitalism is the best way to address climate change. Over three quarters (77.7%) of respondents supported this position compared to less than a quarter (22.3%) who reported that global warming is best addressed within a system of capitalism. However, when forced to choose between systemic political, social, and economic changes or scientific innovation and new, more efficient technology, a smaller majority (57.5%) of this sample feels that systematic change is key to addressing global warming, while 42.5% felt that science and technology were key.

9 Fairness in Global Emissions Reductions

From the original UNFCCC agreement, individual nations' varied abilities to address and varied responsibilities for the current problems of climate change have been a consideration, albeit a source of debate, among negotiators and civil society organizations. Should developing nations be required to pursue a more sustainable path of

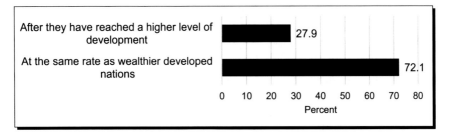

Fig. 9 A fair global agreement would require developing nations to reduce their current emissions...

development and also be required to reduce their GHG emissions at the same rate as wealthier developed nations, or should they be given access to fossil-fuel-driven development prior to committing to reductions? While this is often pitted as a North versus South disagreement, with developing nations of the Global South wanting access to development, these survey results show broad support for similar rates of emissions reductions in developing countries among African CJOs. Surprisingly, among our sample, nearly three-quarters (72.1%) report that a fair global agreement would include provisions requiring *developing* nations to cut their GHG emissions at the same rate as wealthier developed nations. Only about a quarter (27.9%) of respondents agreed that developing nations should develop more first before reducing their GHG emissions rates (see Fig. 9). This is much stronger support than was evident for prioritizing poverty reduction over emissions cuts, but it is aligned with the high rates of rejection of using fossil fuels to develop further as seen above.

Support for emissions reductions at similar rates as wealthier developed nations is also seen when asked specifically about China. A strong majority (65.2%) of African CJOs in our sample support China reducing their emissions at the same rate as wealthier nations, rather than waiting until they have reached a higher level of development. Although, it is interesting to note that the support for emissions reductions only after higher levels of development is about seven percentages points higher for China (34.8%) than it was for "developing nations" in general (27.9%) as seen above.

10 Discussion and Conclusion

In sum, African climate justice organizations in our sample overwhelmingly report that the communities that they work with have already been negatively impacted by climate change. They serve diverse geographic populations and are on the front lines of addressing climate change in their respective communities and nations. Just over half are based in large cities where internet access is more reliable and infrastructure more developed. However, for many, the scope of their service expands well beyond where they are headquartered. Almost half of the organizations serve people and communities throughout their nations, while just over a quarter of the organizations confine their work to a more local community. Coastal areas and agriculture regions are the most prominent geographic topographies where African CJOs work. Concerns about climate change causing rising sea levels and less predictable precipitation patterns, which is detrimental to food security, are imaginably influential in generating the pattern of where organizations work and the programing they implement.

Climate change is just one of many issues that developing communities face. This is reflected in half of the organizations in this sample reporting that while they address climate change, it is only one of many issues they prioritize. The other issues that receive programming attention from PACJA members include education and literacy, agriculture and food security, forest preservation, and poverty reduction. These issues were part of 50% or more of the sample's programming portfolios. African climate justice organizations have most prominently focused their climate change efforts on national policy advocacy, climate justice advocacy, alternative energy, global climate change policy advocacy, and climate change finance advocacy. Smaller numbers of members reported working on disaster preparedness, climate change science, recycling, transportation alternatives, and coastal protection.

There remains great potential for more mitigation and adaptation best practices to be distributed widely and rapidly through the existing PACJA network. Based on the diversity of communities and issues that members work on, they are a rich network of actors. As members develop successful programs in their communities, these practices could spread rapidly through the PACJA Secretariat and beyond. The scope of the network also has the potential for more international non-governmental organizations to spread knowledge and resources widely and rapidly.

Now that there is a working global climate agreement in effect, the Paris Agreement, nations and civil society need to work together to successfully implement the agreement's lofty goals, including limiting average global temperature increases to 1.5 °C and mobilizing sufficient climate finance for less wealthy nations. According to the 2021 Sixth Assessment report by the Intergovernmental Panel on Climate Change (IPCC) on the physical science of climate change, the mean global temperatures have already increased 1.1 °C compared to preindustrial levels (IPCC, 2021). The global rate of GHG accumulation in the atmosphere continues to rise, reaching a record high of 52.4 $GtCO_{2e}$ in 2019 (UNEP, 2020). One of the barriers to the cooperation necessary to reach the world's collective goal of limited warming is a lack of trust. A long history of exploitation and a more recent history of much delayed and insufficient GHG reductions by the Global North has not generated a great deal of trust between the Global South and the heavily industrialized Global North. African CJOs in our sample expressed low levels of trust that heavy emitters like the US and China would reduce their emissions in order to limit warming to 1.5 °C. According to Climate Action Tracker, after the US submitted an amended and more ambitious NDC under the Paris Agreement in April of 2021, their domestic *targets* reached the status of "almost sufficient" (up from "highly insufficient"), but their *policies* and *actions* remained "insufficient" and would lead to more than 2 °C increase in mean temperature rise relative to preindustrial levels (Climate Action Tracker, 2021).

China's current policies and actions were also deemed insufficient to keep temperatures below a 2 °C increase in mean global temperatures. Based on an analysis by Carbon Tracker, the EU's domestic targets policies and actions are "nearly sufficient" and acceptable to remain below a 2 °C temperature increase but not if the aim is a 1.5 °C increase or if their "fair share" is taken into consideration. Japan has sufficient stated targets to meet the Paris Agreement but insufficient domestic policies and actions. There remain important gaps between targets and the implementation of policies that would actually reach those targets.

Analysis of the first round of Nationally Determined Contributions (NDCs), the voluntary and self-determined commitments of each nation to reduce GHG emissions, indicate that those levels of emissions will more likely result in a 3 °C temperature rise, rather than meeting the 1.5 °C commitment made in Paris (World Resources International, 2020). In order for trust to be restored (or developed in the first place), large emitters, like the US, China, and to some extent, the EU need to show consistent, measurable progress in actually reducing GHG emissions, not just setting goals. The initial commitments made under the Paris Agreement certainly need to be met. In order to garner greater levels of trust from African CJOs, all the major emitters need to demonstrate a willingness to reduce emissions with greater ambition, and they need to commit to reductions that are aligned with what science says is necessary and the nation's respective fair shares of reductions.

PACJA members also reported little to no trust that the US would provide sufficient climate finance or transfers of technology. However, they expressed high levels of trust that Scandinavian countries, and to a lesser extent, Germany, would provide sufficient finance and transfers of technology. Generally, African CJOs were less trusting of all regions and nations to reduce emissions compared to higher levels of trust for transfers of technology and sufficient climate finance. In 2009, wealthy nations committed to mobilizing $100 billion USD in finance annually to help developing countries mitigate emissions and adapt to the climate crisis by 2020. As others have also argued, "This long-standing commitment is key to trust, and solidarity between developed and developing countries, rooted in the fact that developed nations are responsible for the majority of carbon emissions since industrialization began, and generally have a greater capacity to offer support" (Bos et al., 2021).

The Organization for Economic Cooperation and Development (OECD) reported that by 2019 only $79.6 billion had been mobilized, up only slightly from the $78.3 billion in 2018 (OECD, 2021). That's a $20 billion dollar gap in what was promised and what is yet to be delivered (2020 numbers were not released at the time this chapter went to print). A majority of the financing is directed at mitigation, although the funds for adaptation have increased more rapidly in recent years. The UN Secretary-General has called for 50% of financing to be directed toward adaptation (UNFCCC, 2021). Of the developed nations, only Australia, Belgium, Iceland, Ireland, the Netherlands, and Switzerland provide nearly 50% of their finance for adaptation (Bos et al., 2021). When export credits are excluded from the calculations, the vast majority of finance is delivered through loans ($44.5 billion in 2019) compared to grants ($16.7 billion in 2019). Of the nearly $80 billion provided, 43% went to nations and projects in Asia, 26% to African nations, and 17% to Central and South American nations. In 2019, only \$15.4 billion went to Least Developed Countries (LDCs) (OECD, 2021).

Analysis by the World Resources Institute shows that Germany, France, and Japan all contributed at least 0.25% of their gross national income (GNI) during 2016–2018, but the US only contributed 0.03% of its GNI—the lowest percentage of all the developed nations (Bos et al., 2021). The same analysis indicates that, among developed nations, the US has the largest gap in the finance it provides and what its fair share is projected to be based on its contributions to climate change and its economy. In 2021, at a speech at the UN General Assembly, US president Joe Biden committed to mobilizing \$11.4 billion a year in a variety of climate finance tools by 2024 (Colman, 2021). However, to become a reality, this pledge by the president of the US needs to also be passed by the US federal legislative bodies, the Senate, and the House of Representatives. This is far from assured. As one environmental organization in the US stated, "Showing that the U.S. will help deliver the \$100 billion per year climate finance goal will build the kind of trust that is necessary to ensure that climate summit in Glasgow (COP 26) is a success in keeping open the possibility of holding temperatures to less than 1.5 °C" (Guy & Schmidt, 2021).

African climate justice organizations are actively engaged in UNFCCC COP meetings but in diverse forms. Over half of them had a representative of their organization at COP21 in Paris. They support their domestic climate change plans but are somewhat doubtful that their governments can effectively utilize international climate finance. They are optimistic about development continuing while also addressing climate change. If the promised climate finance materializes, global and domestic mechanisms will need to be in place to ensure that planning for the funds is broadly inclusive of multiple stakeholders and the distribution of the funds is transparent. Accountability at the domestic level is equally important to ensure that finance effectively addresses the intended adaptation and mitigation efforts.

African climate justice organizations in our sample largely prioritize emissions reductions over fossil-fuel-led development, even if that means not utilizing fossil fuel resources discovered within their countries. But when asked specifically, they want poverty reduction prioritized over emissions reductions. There is a distinction between general development and poverty reduction and the relationship to climate change mitigation. That being said, the scope of change African CJOs imagine that it will take to successfully address climate change is large. The vast majority believe something as significant as a radical shift away from capitalism is needed. This is more than just a few environmental reforms under the current system. The majority see transforming the current economic, political and social systems as the key to addressing climate change. The international community can support such a focus on emissions reductions, even in developing countries, by increasing their technology transfer and support for up-scaled alternative energy.

When thinking about "common but differentiated responsibilities," African climate justice organizations seem more committed to global emissions reductions, with everyone playing a part, rather than developing countries reaching a certain level of development before reducing their GHG emissions levels. Similarly, PACJA members believe China should reduce its emissions at the same rate as developed nations. Such support for collective, global emissions reductions should be seen as a good faith effort within developing nations—an effort that should be reciprocated with similarly bold support for dramatic emissions reductions by civil society and nations states of the Global North.

This chapter presents the most thorough analysis of climate-justice-focused civil society organizations among African nations to date—next steps in the research include efforts to garner an even richer sample of organizations from across the continent. Further research should examine with more depth the specific technologies that African CJOs want their communities to have greater access to, the impacts of the Paris Agreement on CJOs participation in the UNFCCC process, the specific critiques of or concerns about capitalism that African CJOs express, and the ways that African CJOs confront the potential conflict between development and GHG mitigation, especially when their nation has oil, coal, or gas reserves.

Civil society actors continue to play a role in influencing and implementing global-level negotiations and policies. Particularly with a global problem like climate change where the implementation of mitigation and adaptation efforts will, in large part, be done by local-level actors, civil society organizations across a diversity of geographies will be necessary for success. Trust at the global, national, and community level arguably increases cooperation between actors, develops a sense of shared responsibility (albeit differentiated responsibility), and opportunities for climate justice to be realized. However, it is up to the nations of the Global North to demonstrate that they are worthy of trust from African CJOs by doing their fair share of emissions reductions, providing just levels of finance, and transferring the technology necessary to support ongoing sustainable development.

References

Allan, J. I., & Hadden, J. (2017). Exploring the framing power of NGOs in global climate politics. *Environmental Politics, 26*(4), 600–620. https://doi.org/10.1080/09644016.2017.1319017

Beer, C. T. (2014). Climate justice, the global south, and policy preferences of Kenyan environmental NGOs. *The Global South, 8*(2), 84–100. https://doi.org/10.2979/globalsouth.8.2.84

Boko, M., Niang, I., Nyong, A., Vogel, C., Githeko, A., Medany, M., Osman-Elasha, B., Tabo, R., & Yanda, P. (2007). Africa. Climate change 2007: Impacts, adaptation and vulnerability. In M. L. Parry, O. F. Canziani, J. P. Palutikof, P. J. van der Linden, & C. E. Hanson (Eds.), *Contribution of Working Group II to the Fourth Assessment Report of the Intergovernmental Panel on Climate Change* (pp. 433–467). Cambridge University Press.

Bond, P. (2012). *Politics of climate justice: Paralysis above, movement below.* University of Kwa Zulu Natal Press.

Bond, P. (2014). Climate Justice in, by, and for Africa. In M. Dietz & H. Garrelts (Eds.), *Routledge Handbook of the Climate Change Movement* (pp. 205–221). Routledge.

Bos, J., Gonzalez, L., & Thwaites, J. (2021). Are countries providing enough to the $100 billion climate finance goal? Retrieved October 4, 2021, from https://www.wri.org/insights/developed-countries-contributions-climate-finance-goal

Climate Action Tracker. Retrieved October 15, 2021, from https://climateactiontracker.org/

Colman, Z. (2021). Biden says U.S. will quadruple climate aid to poor countries. Retrieved October 15, 2021, from https://www.politico.com/news/2021/09/21/biden-united-nations-climate-aid-513414

Derman, B. B. (2014). Climate governance, justice, and transnational civil society. *Climate Policy, 14*(1), 23–41. https://doi.org/10.1080/14693062.2014.849492

Fisher, D. (2010). COP-15 in Copenhagen: How the merging of movements left civil society out in the cold. *Global Environmental Politics, 10*(2), 11–17. https://doi.org/10.1162/glep.2010.10.2.11

Guy, B., & Schmidt, J. (2021). US commits to more international climate finance. Retrieved October 15, 2021, from https://www.nrdc.org/experts/jake-schmidt/us-commits-more-international-climate-finance

Hadden, J. (2015). *Networks in contention: The divisive politics of climate change.* Cambridge University Press.

Hussein, M. A. (2011). Climate change impacts on East Africa. In W. Leal Filho (Ed.), *The economic, social and political elements of climate change* (pp. 589–601). Springer.

International Climate Justice Network. (2002). Bali Principles of Climate Justice. Retrieved October 12, 2009, from https://www.iicat.org/wp-content/uploads/2012/03/Bali-Princioples-of-Climate-Justice.pdf

IPCC. (2021). *Climate change 2021: The physical science basis. Contribution of Working Group I to the Sixth Assessment Report of the Intergovernmental Panel on Climate Change* (Masson-Delmotte, V., Zhai, P., Pirani, A., Connors, S. L., Péan, C., Berger, S., Caud, N., Chen, Y., Goldfarb, L., Gomis, M. I., Huang, M., Leitzell, K., Lonnoy, E., Matthews, J. B. R., Maycock, T. K., Waterfield, T., Yelekçi, O., Yu, R., & Zhou, B. Eds.). Cambridge University Press.

Mwenda, M., & Bond, P. (2020). African climate justice: Articulations and activism. In B. Tokar & T. Gilbertson (Eds.), *Climate justice and community renewal: Resistance and grassroots solutions* (pp. 108–127). Routledge.

Niang, I., Ruppel, O. C., Abdrabo, M. A., Essel, A., Lennard, C., Padgham, J., & Urquhart, P. (2014). Africa. In V. R. Barros, C. B. Field, D. J. Dokken, M. D. Mastrandrea, K. J. Mach, T. E. Bilir, M. Chatterjee, K. L. Ebi, Y. O. Estrada, R. C. Genova, B. Girma, E. S. Kissel, A. N. Levy, S. MacCracken, P. R. Mastrandrea & L. L. White (Eds.), *Climate Change 2014: Impacts, adaptation, and vulnerability. Part B: Regional aspects. Contribution of Working Group II to the Fifth Assessment Report of the Intergovernmental Panel on Climate Change* (pp. 1199–1265). Cambridge University Press.

OECD. (2021). Climate finance provided and mobilised by developed countries: Aggregate trends updated with 2019 data. *OECD Publishing.* https://doi.org/10.1787/03590fb7-en

Pan African Climate Justice Alliance. (2010). African climate justice manifesto. Retrieved June, 2, 2018, from http://climate-justice.info/wp-content/uploads/2011/07/African-Climate-Justice-Manifesto-PACJA-version2.pdf

Simms, A., & Reid, H. (2005). *Africa: Up in smoke?* Oxfam.

UNEP. (2020). *Emissions gap report 2020.* Nairobi.

UNFCCC. (2021). António Guterres: 50% of all climate finance needed for adaptation. Retrieved October 15, 2021, from https://unfccc.int/news/antonio-guterres-50-of-all-climate-finance-needed-for-adaptation

Warlenius, R. (2018). Decolonizing the atmosphere: The climate justice movement on climate debt. *The Journal of Environment & Development, 27*(2), 131–155. https://doi.org/10.1177/1070496517744593

World Resources International. (2020). Stepping up NDCs. Retrieved May 21, 2021, from https://www.wri.org/ndcs

Development of Community-Owned Renewable Energy (CORE) in South Africa

Meron Okbandrias

1 Introduction

Creating sustainable industrial growth for speedy economic expansion necessitates the diversification of energy potentials to various alternative energy sources such as renewable energy. Consequently, the global call to adopt renewable energy resources such as solar, wind, hydro, or geothermal as alternative energy generation and consumption sources has gained substantial momentum in recent times. Essentially, renewable energy refers to energy derived from naturally replenished resources periodically. These forms of energy are generated from sunlight, wind, rain, tides, waves, and geothermal sources (Lins et al., 2014).

The global consensus for the adoption of renewables stemmed from the deep recognition of the increasing cost of generating traditional sources of energy such as coal, oil, and natural gas, which pose severe challenges to humans and the ecosystem in general. For instance, the United Nations Development Programme (UNDP, 2019) reports that approximately 60% of the global greenhouse gases responsible for climate change are attributed to global energy production. Similarly, 3 billion people representing over 40% of the global population, rely heavily on environmentally poisoning and unhealthy fuels for daily food processing (UNDP, 2019). Therefore, there is an immediate need to move to a low-carbon economy in haste.

To address this global environmental challenge, the United Nations in 2015, initiated the Sustainable Development Goals with Goal 7 exclusively focusing on the production of "Affordable and clean energy" in all countries of the world (Franco et al., 2020; Mawla & Khan, 2020; Wang et al., 2020). The focus of Goal 7 is to speed up the expansion of infrastructure and technology upgrading that will guarantee

---

M. Okbandrias (✉)
School of Government (SOG), Faculty of Economic and Management Science,
University of the Western Cape (UWC), Cape Town, South Africa
e-mail: mokbandrias@uwc.ac.za

© The Author(s), under exclusive license to Springer Nature Singapore Pte Ltd. 2022
D. Madhanagopal et al. (eds.), *Environment, Climate, and Social Justice*,
https://doi.org/10.1007/978-981-19-1987-9_6

the provision of clean, sustainable, and more efficient energy for speedy economic growth and long-term environmental sustainability.

In response to this urgent call, many nations have formulated country-specific energy policies to produce affordable and renewable means of energy for the populace. These policy efforts are already yielding significant positive results, as evidenced in the REN21 Renewables 2020 Global Status Report. For instance, according to REN21 (2020) Renewables 2020 Global Status Report, there was a substantial 5% rise in the global production of biofuels in 2019 with a total of 15.6 GW new installed capacity yielding an overall installed capacity of 1,150 GW globally. Also, there was a 2.3% rise in global hydropower generation in 2019, leading to about 4306 TWh. The report further revealed a 12% increase in global solar PV production during 2019, yielding an aggregate of 627 GW in that same year (REN21, 2020).

In addition, there was a 19% increase in the installation of new wind power globally, which accounted for the second largest yearly increase with a total of 650 GW in 2019. The swift progression in global wind power generation was ascribed to renewable energy boots in China, the United States, and the substantial surge in Europe, following the proposed energy policy reforms in these regions (REN21, 2020). Similarly, it was established that over 55 nations had developed fully operational new wind farms, and more than 102 nations could boast of commercial wind power capacity at the end of the year 2019 (REN21, 2020).

Country-specific analysis revealed that as of 2019, about 57, 32, 29.9, and 26.4% of the electricity generation in Denmark, Ireland, Uruguay, and Portugal, respectively, was attributed to wind energy with several other nations joining the development path. There was also a recorded 11% growth in global concentrating solar thermal power (CSP) capacity in operation in 2019, yielding a total of 6.2 GW due to several emerging economies' exclusive energy policy reform efforts (REN21, 2020). Interestingly, South Africa and China also successfully introduced new energy plants into service in 2019, contributing to the all-time high of 479 gigawatts of global solar thermal capacity during the same year (REN21, 2020). In all, the report established those emerging countries outperformed their industrialized counterparts in the context of renewable energy capacity investments for the fifth consecutive year.

While there are significant developments in the renewable sector globally and South Africa, it is essential to ask to what extent communities benefit from renewable energy ownership. Community-Owned Renewable Energy has seen tremendous growth worldwide, especially in Europe. For example, European Commission estimates that by 2030 CORE in the form of cooperatives could own 17% of installed wind capacity and 21% of installed solar capacity in the European Union (Hockenos, 2021).

This book chapter explores the nature of CORE projects in South Africa, considering the last decade's drive towards renewable energy generation supported by policy support. There were several rounds of bidding to supplement power generated by ESKOM through renewable energy. Therefore, the objective is to look at several CORE projects in South Africa and explore the ownership modalities, the level of ownership, benefits for the community, and the level of decision-making in the projects. The chapter will look at the CORE models globally and in South Africa. Furthermore, it will analyze the CORE projects' development in South Africa and its shortfalls, highlighting the case of several CORE projects. Finally, it will provide policy recommendations that will ensure greater community ownership.

2 Community-Ownership Models

Community-owned social enterprises are not new. Cooperatives have been in existence for over 100 years (Altman, 2009) as social forces that can make a significant impact. Therefore, with the advent of environmental and renewable agenda, communities, especially in Europe, embraced the idea of renewable energy generation either through solar, wind, or other forms of renewables. Consequently, energy cooperatives emerged and became successful where there was a government-driven environmental protection and renewables agenda as it requires political will and resources. Baker (2017) examines community energy through the lens of *social entrepreneurship* to analyze small-scale and bottom-up energy initiatives using a tripartite framework oriented around "the purpose of the initiative, its form of organization and ownership, and its embeddedness into the local community or wider social movements." However, in resource-poor countries, bottom-up energy initiatives are far and few in between. Despite such limitations, citizens or residents should have a say on what and how services are rendered as the principle of popular sovereignty dictates (Espejo, 2011), as energy production directly impacts their health and economic welfare. Therefore, it is vital to understand the different energy community models—ownership as modes of ownership, benefits derived, and project control are relevant.

CORE projects vary in size but are often between 5 kilowatts (kW) and 5 megawatts (MW) in size, depending on where they are being implemented (Gall, 2018) and can also deploy energy storage, energy efficiency, distribution network, and district heating and cooling systems beside energy generation. A CORE project is characterized by local communities ideally owning most of the project and voting rights and control resting with a community-based organization where the benefits are therefore distributed at the local community level (IRENA Coalition for Action, 2020a). Therefore, CORE models cover the entire energy value chain: they can provide localized generation for power, heat, and energy-related services (e.g., storage, charging electric vehicles, energy trade with surrounding communities), enable efficient energy use and provide the flexibility the entire power system. Thus, they can add significant value to the traditional centralized power generation and distribution.

3 A CORE Project Usually Includes One of the Following (IRENA Coalition for Action, 2020a)

- Ownership Structure: The community can full, majority, or minority ownership. In many cases, renewable energy projects are developer-led, and communities can take partial ownership of the project. This is, in fact, the case in most South African projects. Almost all the solar projects in South Africa, for instance, are developer-led, and the community has minority ownership.
- Level of Democratic Governance: Local stakeholders have most of the voting rights concerning the decisions taken on the project. There is some level of community governance in most South African projects. However, because of the minority ownership, lack of experience, and know-how, their participation might not be effective. As Bode (2013) indicated, civil society expressed the need for referee CORE projects that would look after the interest of the communities as they lack the kind of influence required to have an impact.
- Local Distribution of Profits: Most social and economic benefits are distributed locally (e.g., jobs created locally, power supplied to the community, profits shared among individual participants to the community scheme). There are different ways that the community benefits in South Africa as in other countries. However, sharing profits is one way that the community benefits directly. There is sharing of profits in some projects. However, it is doubtful if these shared profits make significant over a short period of life. It is the sum of the benefits that are of importance.

In addition, there is also another legal form of a community-ownership business model (IRENA Coalition for Action, 2020a) (Table 1).

According to Bode (2013), the political economy of South Africa, which is neoliberal in character, is centered around transnational capital. The energy sector is not motivated by developmental objectives but to meet the energy needs of an extractive economy. Bode (2013) analysis the ownership model and types of renewable utilization in the energy sector in South Africa in the Table 2.

In addition to the CORE models, the judicial, social, and economic reasoning for the CORE is relevant in this chapter. As mentioned above, the involvement of communities is one way of ensuring popular sovereignty in the energy sector among a multitude of other services. Considering the centrality of electricity's role in our lives and the need to transition to a low-carbon economy, citizen and community participation is about energy justice in this transition. It aims to ensure that communities and societies are not held hostage by multinational companies in the value chain of energy production and utilization. Therefore, it is democratizing the energy sector. According to Leadbeater and Goss (1998), one way to attain that is through social or civic entrepreneurship, where communities define the common good and work towards achieving it. In this process, the extent to which communities control the projects and benefit from them is crucial. In communities where there is strong social capital like some European countries, civic entrepreneurship is

Development of Community-Owned Renewable Energy (CORE) …   103

Table 1 CORE models

CORE model	Description
Cooperatives	Their members jointly own cooperatives to achieve common economic, social, or cultural goals based on the democratic principle of "one member, one vote." Cooperatives could be involved across the energy value chain. However, they are primary users
Partnerships	In partnerships, individual partners own shares in the community-ownership model. The key objective of a partnership is to generate profits for the shareholders, in addition to any other benefits of the project. There is a greater chance that the communities will have a significant share of the profits and control of projects
Non-profit organizations	A non-profit organization is formed by investments from its members, who are responsible for financing the organization but do not take back any profits. Profits are reinvested in projects focused on community development. They are usually motivated by social and moral imperatives
Community trusts	Trusts use the returns from investments in community projects for specific local purposes. These benefits are also shared with people who are not able to invest directly in projects. How profits are shared, and control is exercised on the social and cultural nature of the community and trust
Housing associations	A form of non-profit, such associations offers housing to low-income families and individuals. They are primary users and their scope to get involved in the entire energy value chain is limited

(Note) - Developed from: IRENA Coalition for Action, 2020a; IRENA (2020b).

exercised with significant involvement of communities, and the benefits are equally significant (Westlund & Gawel, 2012).

The problem is primarily structural in more impoverished communities. Especially the poorer communities are often isolated from adequate resources, and there is a lack of collective action often essential to achieve development goals (Evans, 2002; Krahn et al., 2009). As the impoverished acquire and develop more capabilities, they may be able to take advantage of economic and social opportunities. Sen (1983) argued that the poor's economic well-being was best understood through their capabilities rather than through more traditional economic concepts. These conditions apply to most South African communities where CORE projects are implemented. These communities lack the capacity, either intellectual or material, to initiate such CORE projects. They are merely participants, supported by government-led programs in renewable energy projects. Even raising capital is usually beyond them. To understand the realities of the communities' participation in CORE projects, it is rather vital to look at the renewable experience of South Africa and some CORE projects that shed light on what extent the South African experience aligns with the above-mentioned models and conditions.

Table 2 Community ownership models and barriers for South Africa

Sale to utility			Sale to	Sale to Members		Offtaker	
Multiple owners	Producer cooperative	Aggregate netmetering	Multiple owners	Aggregate netmetering	Consumer cooperative	Model	
Multiple owners	Producer cooperative	Aggregate netmetering	Multiple owners	Cooperative	Cooperative	SA Legal entity	
No	No	No	Yes	No	Yes	Currency	Barriers
×	×	×	×	N/A	N/A	Lack Off-take agreements	Technical and Regulatory
×	×	×	×	×	N/A	Grid	
×	×	×	×	×	×	Cost of RE	Finance
×	×	×	×	×	×	Capital Finance	
×	×	×	×	×	×	Technological	Consumer and cultural barriers
×	×	×	×	×	×	Cultural	
×	×	×	×	×	×	Resource	
	×	×	×	×	×	Land rights	Institutional and systemic
	×	×	×	×	×	Education	

Reprinted from Bode, (2013).

4 South African CORE Experience

In recent times, there has been renewed interest in promoting infrastructure and technological advancement that will drive the speedy delivery of renewable energy in South Africa, as this is intended to supplement the nation's existing energy generation capacity. South Africa has been the destination of renewable energy (Baker, 2015). Also, the country is making conscious efforts in ensuring that all investments are channeled away from the existing traditional energy sources, which are becoming unsustainable energy-provision mechanisms. The traditional energy system in South Africa has been adjudged inefficient and environmentally unsustainable since 2008, citing the inability of the state-owned utility Eskom to provide reliable energy services for both residential consumers and business enterprises operating in the country (Lombard & Ferreira, 2015).

Eskom's is a power generation and transmission monopoly that heavily relies on mainly coal-powered aging power stations. It is the biggest energy producer in Africa and once of the biggest utility companies in the world, exporting electricity to several Southern African countries. The utility company took advantage of the abundant sources of coal in South Africa and the total monopoly it had in the country. Besides coal, it has some nuclear and few renewable sources. In the 2000s, Eskom failed to keep up with the demand for electricity and the need to transition to renewables (Bowman, 2020). As a result, the country suffered planned blackouts to manage the shortage. The two projects, Medupi and Kusile that were planned to supplement the waning generation capacity were billions over budget and years over schedule. In addition, massive corruption and maladministration plunged the utility company into 32 billion dollars debt by 2020 (Bowman, 2020). In the last 2 years, Eskom has embarked on a significant restructuring to unbundle the three functions of generation, transmission, and distribution of the utility to create three units to increase the efficiency of the utility and to restructure its debt (Mondi, 2018). In the last 12 years, there was a push to decrease the country's and Eskom's carbon footprint. Even though there were some CORE projects before 2008, almost 90% of CORE projects are the product of the 12 years effort by the government to transition to renewables.

Thus, the Renewable Energy Independent Power Producers Procurement Program (REIPPPP) in South Africa was launched in 2010 with the aim of empowering more than 92 independent power producers to generate a minimum of "6300 MW of power into the power grid, principally from solar and wind sources" (Jain & Jain, 2017). Most independent power producers are either community-initiated or have significant participation in communities. Following this energy reform, the country has reportedly achieved a significant drop in energy production costs, increasing job creation, a boost in income generation, enterprise growth, and speedy development of community infrastructures—however, the role of community ownership and how the community benefits is an essential topic of discussion. The CORE is not only about the benefit derived by the community but also the buy-in of the renewable agenda by the community. The interesting fact about these REIPPPP is that most of the renewable power projects are often situated in rural communities where there is a potential to exert significant positive effects on the host communities by way of employment generation, business development, and enhanced quality of life.

Starting from 1998, there was a recognition that coal-based power generation is unsustainable and damaging to the environment. As a result, the Mbeki government introduced the Integrated Resource Plan (IRP), with specific targets up to 2030. REIPPP is the primary mechanism for the IRP to reach "7000 MW renewable energy targets in 2020 and 17,800 MW by 2030" (Szmyd-Potapczuk, 2020). This public–private partnership mechanism provides an opportunity for independent energy producers to submit bids to develop and design large-scale renewable energy power plants. In addition, an open and periodic bidding window was meant to provide ongoing PPP projects in producing renewable energy to feed the national grid.

Eskom was not involved in the REIPPP as it was supposed to be self-sustaining in the long run as the energy generated will cover the costs. The secondary goals of REIPPP include job creation, social upliftment, and economic transformation of South African communities. The local content stipulates the involvement of communities and local companies to build some of the equipment like wind turbines. Large-scale energy generation is the primary goal of REIPPP. However, residential developments can also contribute to the national grid through an interactive grid.

Across the four REIPPP rounds of bidding, Luzuko (2020) submits a total of over 102 projects were approved, a total of 6329 MW of renewable energy has been procured to date, and 3876 MW are currently connected to the grid. As of 2020, REIPPPP has attracted over 209 billion and foreign direct investment, created over 38,000 semi-permanent and permanent jobs, over 1 billion was spent on education, over 600 bursaries were provided, over 1000 small enterprises were established, and another social-economic support was provided. More importantly, South Africans have 31% equity in projects and 48% of the total equity of the IPP projects, and communities will receive over 27 billion rands over 20 years the lifetime of the projects through the community trusts (Luzuko, 2020).

There is no doubt CORE projects have socio-economic benefits. Most CORE projects are in rural areas, supporting local communities directly through development, job creation, and improved quality of life (Jain & Jain, 2017). Wlokas et al. (2017) submitted that the aim of executing large-scale wind, solar and hydro projects in the context of South African communities is to facilitate local economic development in those communities where the projects are situated. Specifically, the crux of the REIPPPP is to create a viable avenue for energy firms to allocate part of the realized revenue as well as ownership power to local communities, as this is hoped to drive community socio-economic expansion. Community ownership usually takes one route in South Africa. Wlokas (2015) earlier noted that "local community ownership rights within the REIPPPP are usually derived through a Community Trusts." In validating Wlokas (2015) submission, the Department of Mineral Resources and Energy (DMRE, 2019) noted that local communities must hold at least 2.5% shareholding of potential projects with a total target of 5%. However, in a recent development, Muzond et al. (2021) established that local communities in South Africa now control more than the 5% overall target in renewable energy projects. To justify the earlier submission of DMRE (2018), Muzondo et al. (2021) further established that black people in local communities in South Africa now control approximately 9% shareholding of such projects.

In terms of benefit analysis, Wolkas et al. (2012) averred those projects with community shareholdings often present huge benefits to the local community throughout the project lifespan, as mentioned above. The Department of Mineral Resources and Energy (2018) argued that the benefits accrued to the local communities may be relatively low in the first 10 years in the case of a project with 20 years lifespan, while the remaining 10 years always come with huge income flows to the local communities through massive job creation, formation of new small and micro-enterprises and expansion of existing ones.

5 Exploring Community-Owned Renewable Energy Status and Implementation

Essentially, CORE refers to renewable energy projects owned and managed locally by community members to provide renewable energy sources for both household consumption and promote the development of enterprises operating in the community. Although, as noted earlier, other "shared renewable sources" are not exclusively owned or managed by the communities, the benefits are also accrued to the communities (Farrell, 2016) as governed by the REIPPPP framework.

Sequel to the limited funding capacity of the government and the failure of the state-owned energy infrastructure to provide sufficient and reliable energy services for the citizens (Baker & Wlokas, 2015), several South African communities have resorted to partnering with energy producers for the execution of renewable energy projects to enhance the provision of renewable energy to enable them to tap from the increasing benefits from global renewable energy flows. As noted earlier, the efforts have received the policy backing from the South Africa government through the implementation of the pro-poor renewable energy policy and the REIPPP initiative that empower local communities to develop and or own their renewable energy plants (Wlokas et al., 2017). Consequently, there is a growing number of community-owned renewable energy (CORE) infrastructures across various communities in South Africa, majorly based on local community trust partnerships. For instance, power technology (2017) noted that 80% of the most significant operational solar projects by installed capacity in Africa are in South Africa, with community ownership representing a significant proportion of the shareholdings.

One such notable renewable energy plant is the Steenbras hydro plant, one of the small-scale community-owned renewable energy plants situated in the "Hottentots-Holland mountains, above Gordons Bay, near Cape Town in South Africa. The 1700 m long and 28 m high dam has a total capacity of 33,517,000 m^3 which houses the hydropower project initiated in 1979. Though the dam was constructed to provide irrigation and domestic water supply to the residents, the Steenbras pumped storage was designed to provide alternative sources of electricity supply to the city of Cape

Town, especially when the demand is at its peak. The power station has a total installed capacity of 180 MW. Thus, the dam has been regarded as a "faithful supplier of water and power to the Cape Town City" (Water heritage, 2013).

The Kathu Solar Park is notable as it was regarded as the largest solar energy undertakings in Africa at that time. The solar power project is situated around the Kathu axis in the Northern Cape province of South Africa (Van-Wyngaardt, 2016) commenced operations in commercial volume in January 2019 with an installed capacity of 100 MW. The renewable energy project is currently under the shareholding of both Sishen Iron Ore Company-Community Development Trust (SIOC-CDT), the Public Investment Corporation, the Lereko Metier REIPPP Fund Trust, the Kathu Local Community Trust, Investec Bank, and Engie; a French transnational electric utility company, Engie. The solar thermal power project is built with a parabolic trough and molten salt storage technology to provide 4.5 h of thermal energy storage capacity. The Kathu Solar Park can provide renewable electricity services to over 179,000 homes in South Africa through their peak electricity demand period.

The Kathu Community Trust is part of the community trust set up by Kumba Iron to invest in the community surrounding its mines. The community trust has an 8% share in the project, with 500–1200 jobs created during the construction and 81 permanent jobs so far. It also tenders contracts to local businesses. The profit-sharing agreement will come into effect at the tail end of the project. However, despite the claim of having 42% local content claim, it is not clear the extent of the community participation in decision making through SIOC-CDT or other mechanisms.

MetroWind Van Stadens wind farm project is another renewable energy project located in Eastern Cape, South Africa. The Metrowind Community Trust collectively owns the project, holding 5% of the shares in the power project, Spilled Water Renewable Energy with 25% shareholding, Old Mutual with 35% shareholding, Basil Read Energy with 23% shareholding, and Afri-Coast Engineers with 13% shareholding (Creamer Media Reporter, 2013). In February 2014, the R550-million MetroWind Van Stadens wind farm project commenced operations with 27 MW wind power total installed capacity. Located on the farm Klein Rietfontein, in the Nelson Mandela Bay municipality, the MetroWind Van Stadens wind farm project integrates nine units of 3 MW turbines, with each of the wind turbines consisting of a 90 m high hub in addition to 3 units of 56.5 m long blades and can cut 80,000 tons of carbon dioxide annually (Creamer Media Reporter, 2013).

The wind farm is located just outside Blue Horizon Bay coastal village. Several poor communities are located close to the wind farm, and a series of development initiatives have just been developed to offer sustainable operational efficiency and effectiveness. The project is identified as a strategic regional economic development project by supplying some 80 million kWh of energy per year. It has created permanent jobs for over 50 community members. However, as indicated above, the community has only a 5% share provided by the private sector investors in the project. Besides the jobs created, the community does not benefit much from the project. Two community members sit on the project's board, consisting of one 10% of voting share in the project.

Development of Community-Owned Renewable Energy (CORE) ...

The Klipheuwel Wind Farm, situated at 5 km west of Caledon, in the Overberg region of the Western Cape, South Africa, is another Local Municipality renewable power project launched under the REIPPPP with a total installed capacity of 86,000 MWh, an output that is deemed sufficient to provide 19,000 homes with clean, renewable electrical energy demand annually (Globeleq, 2018). The Klipheuwel Wind Farm project is also known for its 24,080 tonnes annual carbon emissions reduction.

There are several benefits for the local community from the project, including the development of companies and contribution to socio-economic development, ownership of community trust, and employment opportunities. This includes enterprise and socio-economic development programs that promote access to the economy for local people, procurement, and employment opportunities that contribute funds into the local area, and the establishment of local community trust. The project subsidies the employment of teachers and educational equipment and provides a bursary program for youth from the community. Twenty percent of the Klipheuwel Wind Farm is owned by Malibongwe Women Development Trust, Ikamva Labantu Empowerment Trust & The Klipheuwel Wind Farm Community Trust who form part of the corporate entity, Fundraising. The project employs community members and uses local suppliers. However, despite a higher local content, there is not much evidence that the community has much say in decision-making.

Another notable community-owned renewable energy project under the initiative of REIPPP in South Africa is the Golden Valley Wind Energy Farm project. Launched in April 2018 (Goldwind Africa, 2018), the Wind Energy Facility is a wind energy generating project situated in the Amathole District Municipality in the heart of the Bedford town in the Eastern Cape province of South Africa. The project is under the joint ownership of The Golden Valley Wind Facility Community Trust, Letsatsi Trust, and BioTherm Energy boasts 120 MW of clean, renewable energy (electricity supply) to over "100,000 medium-sized households per annum" (MacDonald, 2018).

The communities will benefit from economic development programs during the 20-year operations period. The focus will be on education, skills development, healthcare, and local enterprise addressed through collaboration and partnership with local stakeholders and community members. It created 500 jobs during construction and 36 permanent jobs. However, there is no direct profit-sharing agreement and evidence of the role of the communities in decision-making.

In November 2012, the construction of KaXu Solar One, located in Pofadder, South Africa, commenced at the cost of $860 million under the REIPP initiative. Having been jointly funded by KaXu Community Trust with 20% shareholding, Industrial Development Corporation (IDC) with 29% shareholding, and Abengoa with 51% shareholding, respectively, the concentrated solar power (CSP) plant was commission on March 2, 2015 (Modern Power Systems, 2015), with a coverage site area about 1100 hectares (2718 acres). The energy infrastructure integrates 1200 mirrored parabolic trough CSP technology with an annual production of 320 GWh. In addition, the $860 million concentrated solar thermal energy facility stands among the most significant solar farms globally, being the foremost of its kind in the entire Sub-Saharan African region (Modern Power Systems, 2015) with a total installed capacity of 100 MW (Renewable Technology, 2017). KaXu Solar One also boasts of meeting the demand of over 80,000 South African households in addition to a significant reduction of CO_2 emissions by 315,000 tones on an annual basis. The report further revealed that the solar power plant accounted for approximately 4500 construction jobs, as well as an aggregate of 80 permanent jobs benefitted mainly by the KaXu Community (Renewable Technology, 2017). There are obviously employment and profit-sharing advantages the community shares.

The construction of Bokpoort CSP Power Plant, also known as ACWA Power Solafrica, situated in Groblershoop, Northern Cape, South Africa, also commenced with a project cost R5 billion under the REIPP arrangement (Odendaal, 2013). This project was launched in July 2013. The Bokpoort CSP Solar farm was commissioned on November 13, 2015 (Tmg Digital, 2015), with a coverage site area of about 1300 hectares (741 acres). The project is owned by the local Community Trust with 5% shareholding, LoveLife with 5% shareholding, and ACWA Solar with a sum of R5-million investment in local community development programs such as training and infrastructure provision (Kilian, 2016). The project integrates 8600 Parabolic Reflectors and can boast of the annual production of 234 GWh. In addition, the solar energy investment has a total installed capacity of 50 MWe and a storage capacity of 1300 MWht, corresponding to approximately 9.3 h daily full-load operation (Csp-World, 2013). Bokpoort CSP Power Plant also boasts of meeting the demand of over 200,000 South African households in addition to a significant reduction of CO_2 emissions by 39,100 tonnes every year (Theron, 2016). Furthermore, the solar farm project currently provides over 65 permanent jobs for the community.

These CORE projects show the nature of these projects and the level of community participation to a certain extent. The local content in these projects might be over 50%. Local content usually refers to what extent local materials, communities, investors, and businesses participated in the project. So, it hardly indicates the benefit for the community. Community ownership does not exceed more than 25% at best. Community representatives can have much say in the projects since control and financial benefits equal the ownership level. What is discouraging is that the requirement for local content in South Africa is only 2.5%. Furthermore, despite the requirement of local partnership, the local partnerships in the form of community trust have minimal decision-making influence.

6 Opportunities and Challenges in CORE Projects

Arising from the foregoing, it can be established that renewable energy projects, especially those with Community Trust's shareholding, play a significant role in developing the local community where these projects are situated. The benefits accrued to the local communities include revenue sharing rights, employment creation, development of local community infrastructures, improvement in the socio-economic well-being of the people, improvement in their quality of life through the reduction of environmentally hostile emissions rates, among others. The construction of hydropower sources provides an electricity source and boosts access to a water supply to the host community. Most importantly, the RIPPP projects have involved the communities in generating renewable energy in the last 10 years while benefiting in terms of employment and other benefits. Previously, generation benefited few communities. The decentralized nature of REIPPP and the requirement for these projects enabled communities to claim minimal ownership and gain benefits.

Nevertheless, the above discussions have revealed policy lapses in the ownership structure of these renewable energy projects. For instance, as the name implies, "community-owned" renewable energy should see the community having the larger shareholding of these projects even if they cannot be solely owned or managed by these communities. Despite the REI4P exertions to capture compulsory minimum legal capacity to encourage local community participation in the ownership and control of most renewable energy projects, none of the existing renewable energy initiatives in South Africa merits the status of "community-owned" renewable energy or "community power" projects in the truest sense. Moreover, the participation of cooperatives as the most natural and organic form of community ownership in renewables has been very minimal. This is also partly structural. Most communities in the rural areas lack the education and the capacity to participate in the policy discussion of Renewable Energy. The deep poverty and inequality that permeates the rural area and the communities that require this kind of investment don't have the requisite conditions to take advantage of the government's effort to encourage participation in renewable electricity generation. Okem (2016) concludes that challenges such as policy constraints, access to finance, and lack of technical skills are barriers to cooperatives' involvement in South Africa's renewables sector.

In addition, the 2.5–5% ownership provision is skewed to the neoliberal agenda and suggestive of undue external domination, as the bulk of the revenues generated from such projects are taken away from the community where the projects are located. In the case of foreign interest in such projects (like the Kathu Solar Park project), there are also cases of capital flights that hinder the developmental pace of the local communities. Such financial resource repatriations tend to subject the host communities to undue economic imbalances, thus leading to avoidable agitations by the members of these communities. This, therefore, calls for a more robust energy policy review that will accord more power to the local community trusts to hold a larger shareholding in the renewable energy projects located in such communities. This will hopefully boost the development of those local communities in the future long run. This must be supplemented with financing and loan support from financial institutions and the government.

A bidding process is another avenue to allow the local communities to participate in these projects fully. It will be more beneficial if the local communities are given special consideration in the entire bidding process. It is discouraging that, in the light of the current scale of the projects in South Africa and the necessities to fully participate in the bidding rounds, the tendency of the local communities to meet any or all the bidding conditions remains an illusion.

Furthermore, the level of participation of communities and the ability to exert influence on the projects seems rather superficial, and it begs the question to what extent the community benefits from these projects. It is certainly worth noting, as indicated by Okem (2016) and Wlokas (2017), that there are hardly CORE projects that are organically community-initiated either in the form of cooperatives or partnerships. It is mostly donor, government, or industry-driven initiatives where the government requirement ensures minimal community participation without sufficient share or control on the project. As a result, the benefits derived from such a project are not as much. The number of permanent jobs created by the community is not large compared to the massive capital involved. Therefore, it is very capital intensive. In addition, there are bursaries and other educational support, which is worth noting. However, for the community members to get high-paying jobs, there is a need to provide technical and high-level skills development by the companies involved.

There is also a need to effect policy changes. The idea of local content is essential. However, there must be a specific reference to the share of community ownership in the legislation above 25%, and local ownership should be over 40%. Furthermore, the Department of Trade and Industry should provide low-interest and long-term loans for cooperatives and community trusts to have a greater share in the projects. In addition, the department can set up a mechanism where a greater share in projects translates to more influence in decision-making regarding planning and operations.

7 Conclusion

The discussion of community-owned renewables is not new in Europe, North America, and Australia, where communities have taken ownership of energy generation and the entire value chain. The case is different in Africa and specifically in South Africa as the community does not own the renewable projects in its truest sense. There is a penetration of solar power generation by private companies in many African countries where supply is erratic at best. However, community involvement in power generation and the energy value chain eluded most communities in Africa. Ultimately, the problem is of resources and political will. Even in Europe, CORE was not the norm until European governments and the EU considered it a priority and put resources at the disposal of communities. Scotland, Spain, Italy, and Sweden (Cowtan, 2017) did not have significant CORE projects until the political will and support in the form of subsidies and liberalization of the energy market became available, and the number of such projects declined when the subsidies were discontinued. The same could be said about the sub-Saharan countries, including South Africa. Government policy support and subsidies can go a long way to encourage community ownership in Renewable Energy projects. Their focus has been to ensure energy security, and the traditional power generation was the tried and tested way to do so. However, the decreasing cost of solar and wind energy, in addition to environmental concerns, is increasingly providing incentives.

The same is true in South Africa. Almost all CORE projects were directly the product of the REIPPPP framework that partially liberalized the energy sector and provided a framework and resources. The challenge, however, is the extent of community participation in these CORE projects. Further liberalization of the energy market and low-interest loans would help communities in energy generation and the energy value chain. Cooperatives and active partnerships where the community has significant ownership and control of CORE projects are crucial for popular sovereignty and social entrepreneurship. The strong criticism about the REIPPPP model is flawed because it relies on community-owned renewable energy on for-profit energy companies to deliver socio-economic benefits for affected communities (McDaid et al., 2016). It is like the mining sector on which these expectations are unmet, and the same fate unavoidably awaits this sector.

References

Al-Nory, M. T. (2019). Optimal decision guidance for the electricity supply chain integration with renewable energy: Aligning smartcities research with sustainable development goals. *IEEE Access, 7*, 74996–75006. https://doi.org/10.1109/ACCESS.2019.2919408

Altman, M. (2009). History and theory of cooperatives. In H. Anheier, S. Toepler (Eds.), *International encyclopedia of civil society*. Springer.

Baker, L. (2015). The evolving role of finance in South Africa's renewable energy sector. *Geoforum, 64*, 146–156. https://doi.org/10.1016/j.geoforum.2015.06.017

Baker, L., & Wlokas, H. L. (2015). *South Africa's renewable energy procurement: A new frontier?* (ERC Research Report Series). University of Cape Town, Faculty of Engineering & the Built Environment, Energy Research Centre. Retrieved January 14, 2022, from http://hdl.handle.net/11427/13566

Baker, S. H. (2017). Unlocking the Energy Commons: Expanding Community Energy Generation. In *Law and policy for a new economy* (pp. 211–234). Edward Elgar Publishing. Retrieved January 14, 2022, from https://repository.library.northeastern.edu/files/neu:cj82rc85z/fulltext.pdf

Bode, C. C. (2013). *An analysis of collective ownership models to promote renewable energy development and climate justice in South Africa* (Doctoral dissertation, North-West University). Retrieved 15 January, 2022 from https://repository.nwu.ac.za/bitstream/handle/10394/10004/Bode_CC.pdf?sequence=1

Bowman, A. (2020). Parastatals and economic transformation in South Africa: The political economy of the Eskom crisis. *African Affairs, 119*(476), 395–431. https://doi.org/10.1093/afraf/adaa013

Cowtan, G. (2017). *Community Energy: A Guide to Community-Based Renewable-Energy Projects*. Green Books.

Creamer Media Reporter. (2013). MetroWind Van Stadens wind farm project, South Africa. *Engineering News,* Published on September 13, 2013. Retrieved May 20, from https://www.engineeringnews.co.za/article/metrowind-van-stadens-wind-farm-project-south-africa-2013-09-13

Csp-World. (2013). *Groundbreaking ceremony for Bokpoort CSP plant in South Africa has been held.* Published on September 25, 2013. Retrieved May 21,2021, from https://web.archive.org/web/20150923211633/http://www.csp-world.com/news/20130925/001189/groundbreaking-ceremony-bokpoorts-csp-plant-south-africa-has-been-held

Department of Mineral Resources and Energy (DMRE). (2019). *Integrated Resource Plan 2019*. Retrieved May 20, 2021, from http://www.energy.gov.za/files/docs/IRP%202019.pdf. Last Accessed on May 20, 2021.

Department of Minerals and Energy. (2018). *Independent Power Producers Procurement Programme (IPPPP): An overview [Quarterly report].* Retrivied 15 January,

2022 from file:///C:/Users/Admin/Downloads/20190522_IPP%20Office%20Q4_2018-19%20Overview.pdf%20(1).pdf

Espejo, P. O. (2011). *The time of popular sovereignty: Process and the democratic state.* Penn State Press.

Evans, P. (2002). Collective capabilities, culture, and Amartya Sen's development as freedom. *Studies in Comparative International Development, 37*, 54–60. https://doi.org/10.1007/BF0268 6261

Farrell, J. (2016). Beyond sharing how communities can take ownership of renewable power. *Institute for Local Self-Reliance: Energy Democracy Initiative.* Retrieved May 20, 2021, from https://ilsr.org/wp-content/uploads/2016/04/Final-Beyond-Sharing-How-Commun ities-Can-Take-Ownership-of-Renewable-Power.pdf

Franco, I. B., Power, C., & Whereat, J. (2020). SDG 7 affordable and clean energy. In *Actioning the Global Goals for Local Impact* (pp. 105–116). Springer, Singapore. https://doi.org/10.1007/ 978-981-32-9927-6_8

Gall, J. (2018). *The benefits of community-owned renewable energy projects.* University of Saskatchewan, Retrieved April 10, 2021 from https://renewableenergy.usask.ca/news-articles/ the-benefits-of-community-owned-renewableenergy-projects.php

Globeleq. (2018). *Klipheuwel Wind Farm South Africa.* Retrieved May 20, 2021, from https://www. globeleq.com/blog/power-plants/klipheuwel-wind-farm/. Last Accessed on May 20, 2021.

Goldwind Africa. (2018). *Goldwind's South African Golden Valley and excelsior projects achieved financial closures.* Published on August 7, 2018. Retrieved May 21, 2021, from http://www.gol dwindglobal.com/news/focus-article?id=2085.

Heckenos, P. (2021). Can Europe's community-owned renewables compete with Big Energy? *GreenBiz*, January 28, 2021. Retrieved 15 January, 2022 from https://www.greenbiz.com/article/ can-europes-community-owned-renewables-compete-big-energyables-compete-big-energy

IRENA Coalition for Action (2020a). Stimulating investment in community energy: Broadening the ownership of renewables, International Renewable Energy Agency, Abu Dhabi. Retrived May 21, 2021, from https://coalition.irena.org/-/media/Files/IRENA/Coalition-for-Action/IRENA_Coalit ion_Stimulating_Investment_in_Community_Energy_2020a.pdf

IRENA (2020b). Mobilising institutional capital for renewable energy, International Renewable Energy Agency, Abu Dhabi. Retrieved June 28, 2022, from https://www.irena.org/publications/ 2020/Nov/Mobilising-institutional-capital-for-renewable-energy

Jain, S., & Jain, P. K. (2017). The rise of renewable energy implementation in South Africa. *Energy Procedia, 143*, 721–726. https://doi.org/10.1016/j.egypro.2017.12.752

Kilian, A. (2016). *Bokpoort CSP officially inaugurated.* Published on March 14, 2016. Retrieved May 21, 2021, from https://www.engineeringnews.co.za/article/bokpoort-csp-officially-inaugu rated-2016-03-14

Krahn, H., Harrison, T., Haan, M., & Johnston, W. (2009). Social capital and political engagement in Canada. *International Journal of Contemporary Sociology, 46*(1), 51–76.

Leadbeater, C., & Goss, S. (1998). *Civic entrepreneurship.* Demos.

Lins, C., Williamson, L. E., Leitner, S., & Teske, S. (2014). The first decade: 2004–2014: 10 years of renewable energy progress. *Renewable Energy Policy Network for the 21st Century.* http://hdl. handle.net/10453/117208

Lombard, A., & Ferreira, S. L. (2015). The spatial distribution of renewable energy infrastructure in three particular provinces of South Africa. *Bulletin of Geography. Socio-Economic Series, 30*, 71–85. https://doi.org/10.1515/bog-2015-0036

Luzuko, N. (2020). REIPPP Comes of Age: 18 February 2020. Retrieved 14 January, 2021 from https://futuregrowth.co.za/insights/reippp-comes-ofage/#:~:text=2.,Growth%20of%20R EIPPP&text=To%20date%2C%20102%20IPP%20projects,technologies%20(see%20Figure% 202)

MacDonald, M. (2018). *Golden Valley and Excelsior wind farms reach financial close, South Africa.* Published on August 23, 2018. Retrieved 15 January, 2022 from https://www.mottmac.com/rel eases/golden-valley-and-excelsior-wind-farms-reach-financial-close-south-africa

Development of Community-Owned Renewable Energy (CORE) …

Mawla, M. R., & Khan, M. Z. R. (2020, June). A study on sustainable development goal 7: Future plan to achieve the affordable and clean energy-Bangladesh perspective. In *2020 IEEE Region 10 Symposium (TENSYMP)* (pp. 421–426). IEEE. https://doi.org/10.1109/TENSYMP50017.2020. 9230795

McDaid, L., Moran, J., & Manqele, S. (2016). *Renewable energy independent power producer procurement programme review 2016: A critique of process of implementation of socio-economic benefits including job creation.* Cape Town: AIDC. Retrieved January 15, 2022, from http://aidc. org.za/download/climate-change/Renewable-Energy-Where-are-the-Jobs.pdf

Modern Power Systems. (2015). *KaXu Solar One enters operation.* Published on April 20, 2015. Retrieved 15 January, 2022 from https://www.modernpowersystems.com/news/newskaxu-solar-one-enters-operation-4557458

Mondi, L. (2018). *State, Market and Competition-Can Eskom be rescued?* Retrieved 15 January, 2022 from https://www.cde.org.za/viewpoints-state-market-and-competition-can-eskom-be-res cued/

Muzondo, C., Bridle, R., Geddes, A., Mostafa, M., & Kühl, J. (2021). *Power by all. Alternatives to a privately owned future for renewable energy in South Africa GSI REPORT 1.* International Institute for Sustainable Development. Retrieved May 20, 2022 from https://www.iisd.org/sys tem/files/2021-04/alternatives-privately-owned-renewable-energy-south-africa.pdf

Odendaal, N. (2013). Construction starts on Bokpoort CSP plant. *Engineering News.* Published on August 2, 2013. Retrieved May 20, 2021 from https://www.engineeringnews.co.za/article/constr uction-starts-on-bokpoort-csp-plant-2013-08-02

Okem, A. E. (2016). South Africa's transition to a low-carbon economy: The role of cooperatives. *Journal of Social Sciences, 49*(3–1), 257–267. https://doi.org/10.1080/09718923.2016.11893619

REN21. (2020). *Renewables 2020 Global Status Report.* Retrieved 20 May, 2021 from https://www. ren21.net/wp-content/uploads/2019/05/gsr_2020_full_report_en.pdf

Renewable Technology (2017). KaXu Solar One, Pofadder, Northern Cape. Retrieved 21 May, 2021 from https://www.renewable-technology.com/projects/kaxu-solar-one-pofadder-northern-cape/

Sen, A. (1983). Poor, relatively speaking. *Oxford Economic Papers, 35*(2), 153–169.

Szmyd-Potapczuk, A. (2020, June 5). How REIPPP is contributing to South Africa's switch to renewable energy. *Estateliving.* Retrieved 9 February, 2022 from https://www.estate-living.co. za/news/how-reippp-is-contributing-to-south-africas-switch-to-renewable-energy/

Theron, A. (2016, March 15). *CSP plant illuminates Bokpoort community at official inaugura-tion.* Retrieved 21 May, 2021 from https://www.esi-africa.com/industry-sectors/renewable-ene rgy/csp-plant-illuminates-bokpoort-community-at-official-inauguration/

Tmg Digital (2015). One million South Africans receiving power from the world's largest storage solar farm. *Times Live.* Published on December 17, 2015. Retrieved 21 May, 2021 from https://www.timeslive.co.za/news/south-africa/2015-12-17-one-million-south-africans-rec eiving-power-from-worlds-largest-storage-solar-farm/

United Nations Development Programme (2019). *Sustainable Development Goals: Goal 7—Affordable and clean energy.* Retrieved 20 May, 2021 from https://www.ng.undp.org/content/ nigeria/en/home/sustainable-development-goals/goal-7-affordable-and-clean-energy.html#:~: text=Investing%20in%20solar%2C%20wind%20and,growth%20and%20help%20the%20envi ronment

Van-Wyngaardt, M. (2016). Construction starts on 100 MW Kathu Solar Park. *Engineering News.* Published on October 7, 2016. Retrieved 21 May, 2021, from https://www.engineeringnews.co. za/article/construction-starts-on-100-mw-kathu-solar-park-2016-10-07

Wang, R., Hsu, S. C., Zheng, S., Chen, J. H., & Li, X. I. (2020). Renewable energy microgrids: Economic evaluation and decision making for government policies to contribute to affordable and clean energy. *Applied Energy, 274*, 115287. https://doi.org/10.1016/j.apenergy.2020.115287

Water Heritage (2013). Steenbras dam—faithful supplier of water & power: Water heritage. *Water Wheel, 12*(2). 38. Published Online: 1 Jan 2013. Retrieved 15 January, 2022 from http://www. wrc.org.za/wp-content/uploads/mdocs/WaterWheel_2013_2_March.pdf

Westlund, H., & Gawell, M. (2012). Building social capital for social entrepreneurship. *Annals of Public and Cooperative Economics, 83*(1), 101–116. http://hdl.handle.net/10419/118793

Wlokas, H. L., Westoby, P., & Soal, S. (2017). Learning from the literature on community development for the implementation of community renewables in South Africa. *Journal of Energy in Southern Africa, 28*(1), 35–44. https://doi.org/10.17159/2413-3051/2017/v28i1a1592

Wlokas, H. (2015). A review of the local community development requirements in South Africa's renewable energy procurement programme. *World Wildlife Foundation Technical report, South Africa*. Retrieved 15 January, 2022 from http://awsassets.wwf.org.za/downloads/local_community_development_report_20150618.pdf

Wolkas, H. L., Boyd, A., & Andolfi, M. (2012). Challenges for local community development in private sector-led renewable energy projects in South Africa: An evolving approach. *Journal of Energy in Southern Africa, 23*, 46–51. https://doi.org/10.17159/2413-3051/2012/v23i4a3177

The Impact of Climate Change on the Gender Security of Indigenous Women in Latin America

Úrsula Oswald-Spring

1 Introduction and Aims

The present chapter questions the complex geopolitical background of the double-edged sword of neoliberal capitalism, where productivity, science, and technology have powered global growth for a small elite. The predominance of the military–industrial–scientific complex (Stiglitz, 2010) and the exploitation of human and natural resources are substantially responsible for climate change impacts (IPCC, 2021) and growing poverty in the Global South. Often forced displacement of poor people from resources-rich regions due to megaprojects, extractivism, and transnational tourism has deprived the native people of their land, forced them to migrate, and has increased extreme poverty among the human beings most in need (Stavenhagen, 2012). The limited results of the Millennium Development Goals Report (2015) are outcomes of these global neoliberal structural processes and neocolonial legal impositions, where the Bretton Woods's organisms, especially the World Bank, supported megaprojects of hydro-electrical dams and oil extraction, which have increased the foreign debts in developing countries and displaced indigenous communities.

With suddenly falling oil prices and the devaluation of the national currency, economic crises prevented governments from paying back the debt service. To avoid a total economic collapse of these countries (see Argentina, Mexico, etc.), the International Monetary Fund imposed draconic structural adjustment programs on these highly indebted countries (Strahm & Oswald-Spring, 1990). Food subsidies were forbidden, salaries collapsed, diseases increased, and life quality reduced, while debts were paid punctually often on the cost of hungry people. Additional mechanisms of extraction of surplus from the Global South were granted by the arbitraries

---

Ú. Oswald-Spring (✉)
Regional Centre for Multidisciplinary Studies, National Autonomous University of Mexico
(CRIM-UNAM), Cuernavaca, Morelos, Mexico
e-mail: uoswald@gmail.com

© The Author(s), under exclusive license to Springer Nature Singapore Pte Ltd. 2022   117
D. Madhanagopal et al. (eds.), *Environment, Climate, and Social Justice*,
https://doi.org/10.1007/978-981-19-1987-9_7

of the World Trade Organisation due to the fact that the global legal framework is based on the European justice system. The trials frequently protect corporate enterprises against southern countries, regardless of whether the consultations stipulated in the International Labour Organisation 169 were not applied or the environment was highly polluted (Arach, 2018; Centeno & Lajous, 2013).

Further, indigenous people have also suffered from internal colonialism, discrimination, and exploitation, where a dominant ethnic group has colonized these ethnic groups, considering them inferior. González (2003a) insists that generally, ethnic groups speak different languages and have other customs. Many mestizo governments had allied with the local bourgeoisie, limiting these indigenous inhabitants' economic, political, social, and educational status. This toxic alliance has enabled the dominant leadership to expropriate natural, medical, and cultural goods from ethnic societies. Indigenous people do not participate in the highest political, economic, and military offices of the central government but were colonized within their nation-state only because they belong to another race and have a telluric vision of nature and social integrity.

External control by global finances and corporate enterprises together with internal colonialism have limited in Latin America the social, economic, environmental, and human security for indigenous people. Often patriarchal behaviour from the global society further discriminates against indigenous women and girls, dispossessing them of land and other assets. Within this complex adverse context, climate change impacts are additional threats to the survival of indigenous communities. Confronted with this dual colonization, global top-down efforts are often reinforcing the dominant system of colonialism. When combined with patriarchal neoliberalism, they lead to an extreme concentration of wealth in a small elite (Oxfam, 2021). After 500 years of external and internal colonialism, indigenous people have organized against discrimination and exploitation and created resilience, enabling them to confront better national and international abuses. Their cultural integrity, based on a telluric civilization of integrating nature and society, has allowed them to conserve complex ecosystems and protect their biodiversity (UN, 2007). However, most indigenous communities are increasingly exposed to the global threats of climate change. Moreno et al. (2020) have indicated in their Report of RIOCC-ADAPT that Latin America, especially Mexico and Central America (also called Mesoamerica.[1]), is highly affected by climate disasters.

Within this context of socioeconomic discrimination and climate disasters, this chapter argues that a top-down adaptation strategy led by the national government is not enough to deal with the upcoming climate threats. Indigenous groups have learned to develop bottom-up efforts, where indigenous women play a crucial role in protecting people, culture, and ecosystems. Their traditional cosmovision and care for humans and nature offer decentralized and culturally diverse alternatives to deal with

---

[1] The term Mesoamerica was created by the Anthropologist Kirchhoff, Paul, "Mesoamérica, clasificaciones geográficas, composición étnica" [Mesoamerica, geographic classifications, ethnic composition], Mexico City, Instituto Nacional de Antropología e Historia, 1943, republished in *Dimensión Antropológica*, vol. 19, May–August, (2000), 15–32.

unknown climate threats. Their telluric understanding centres on the reproduction of people and nature, enabling a human, gender, and environmental (HUGE)—security that can overcome internal and external colonialism and the dual vulnerability of poverty and adverse natural conditions. The increase of equity in human security (HU) through processes of equality and empowerment by gender security (G) and the restoration of environment security (E) has consolidated the sustainability of nature and humankind. Among indigenous groups such as the Aymaras or Zapatistas, this bottom-up resilience-building has allowed a real redistribution of wealth. They have focused on food security with their traditional food culture, including restoring nature and its ecosystem services (Millennium Ecosystem Assessment, 2005).

The chapter first introduces gender security and then analyses climate change impacts in Latin America, focusing on the most vulnerable region, called Mesoamerica. Latin America is also the region with the highest biodiversity and with multiple indigenous people caring about these ecological hotspots. Conceptually, the chapter takes as a starting point the internal and external colonialism of indigenous societies (González, 2003a), analyses the dual vulnerability, and proposes a deepening and widening HUGE-security, instead of the dominant narrow military security centring on national sovereignty and territory. The alternative HUGE-security analyses gender security and eradicates dominant patriarchal behaviours in governments, enterprises, and families imposed through violent discrimination and exploitation. The contemporary dominant system of global military power, artificial intelligence, and intellectual–cultural control are producing further massive consumerism with dramatic emissions of greenhouse gases (IPCC, 2021).

2 Gender Security

Gender security analyses have emerged within a context of sexual violence, torture, and femicides, demonstrating and reinforcing the existing domination along gender lines (Le Masson et al., 2016). This context has included various forms of violence against women in wartime and peacetime (e.g., rape, human trafficking, forced labour). Gender security (Oswald-Spring, 2020, p. 217–254) studies holistically feminist values of respect, empowerment, care, sorority,[2] and solidarity, which are anchored in multiple societies through the unpaid care work of women (Pedrero Nieto, 2018). This approach has advocated for structural, cultural, and sustainable

---

[2] The sorority is based on the principle of human equality and equal values among everybody due to the fact that female and indigenous values were ignored by gender discrimination. There is still much androgenic thinking among women; thus, sorority shares responsibilities, and their pact exceeds social classes, economic or caste interests, cultural and even ideological diversity. Sorority promotes equality, solidarity, justice, freedom, peace, and collaboration, especially in moments of tension and social disadvantage. Sorority seeks to dismantle misogyny and promote women's empowerment, proclaiming equity among women and men.

peace to overcome male domination and its underlying prejudices. Patriarchy[3] as a historically developed concept integrates gender perspectives related to security concerns. Reardon (1985) understood the gender-related violence and war linked to the occidental male behaviour, its institutions, and its organization-building. All these processes are based on competition, discrimination, and hierarchical violence. Gender security changes the reference object from national security (the state) with its military defence of territorial integrity and sovereignty to gender and indigenous relations, including children, elders, handicapped, unemployed, and other minorities. The values at risk are equity, equality, solidarity, and resilience, and the sources of threats are patriarchal institutions such as religions, elite and authoritarian governments, exercising external and internal colonialism.

Integrated gender security (with human and environmental security, i.e., a HUGE-security) is challenging the root causes of thousands of years of violence and war based on patriarchal violence and warfare (Van Evera, 1999). It helps to understand the root causes of the present model of global capitalism with the shocking concentration of wealth, exploitation of workers (ITUC Frontlines Report, 2016), external and internal colonialism, and the destruction of the environment (Camey et al., 2020). This model has produced an increasing number of people in extreme poverty, mostly women and girls globally and in Latin America, especially indigenous people (CEPAL, 2021a). This agenda has reached its limits during the current COVID-19 pandemic in 2020,[4] where inclusive citizens in Western countries protested massively against the lack of medical services, overcrowded hospitals, and poor funeral services. Pharmaceutical corporations and occidental governments have hoarded vaccines in large quantities, thus limiting access to southern countries and poor social groups. Tedros Adhanom Ghebreyesus, head of the World Health Organization, said on 4 August 2021, "I understand the concern of all governments to protect their people from the delta variant, but we cannot accept countries that have already used most of the global supply of vaccines using even more of it, while the world's most vulnerable people remain unprotected." He also pointed out that 80% of the 4 billion COVID-19 vaccines went to wealthier countries.

---

[3] The Mexican sociologist Lagarde (1999, p. 52) argued that "...patriarchy is a generic social order of power, based on a mode of domination whose paradigm is male dominance. This order ensures the supremacy of men and the masculine over the interiorization of women and the feminine. It is also an order of domination of some men over others and enation among women. Our world is dominated by men. In it, women, to varying degrees, are expropriated and subjected to oppression in premeditated form. While they appropriated the symbolic contents, the hegemonic discourses narrate what they should be, distributing hegemonic discourses to each woman or girl a specific role to occupy, guaranteeing the traditional order of the woman, culture, and civilization. However, every time more alternative activities emerged and is emerging from the livelihood of the poor that claim, denounce, reverse or simply explain this hegemony."

[4] The management of the COVID-19 pandemic in 2020–2021 is an example of egoist interests of some industrialized countries and their transnational corporations, even though this policy has affected millions of unvaccinated people and has produced the spread of the virus by new variants (Alfa, Beta, Gamma, Delta, and Omicron) with a substantial increase of sick and dead people (Bollyky et al., 2021) also in industrialised countries.

Confronted with these selfish interests, the alternatives for the Global South, especially indigenous societies, cannot depend on the interests and goodwill of the dominant North. Ethnic communities have understood that decentralized and bottom-up efforts, such as living well (indigenous Aymara in the Andes), bolsa familia (Brazil),[5] leading obeying (Zapatistas shell indigenous model in Chiapas, Mexico), gift-giving (Vaughan, 1997, 2004), and social economy (Collin, 2020) may reinforce the resilience of vulnerable people (Oswald-Spring, 2013). The conclusion of the chapter focuses on a self-reliant climate change management by indigenous societies, where solidarity focuses on sorority, fraternity, resilience, and well-being instead of capital accumulation.

3 Climate Change Impacts in Latin America

Latin America is highly affected by climate crises due to the human impacts on the natural environment and the alteration of the physical–chemical composition of the air (IPCC, 2021; Moreno et al., 2020) and ecosystems. The Mesoamerica region is particularly exposed to extreme events that destroy power lines, roads, ports, hospitals, schools, houses, and communication infrastructures (Climate Risk Profile Mexico, 2017). These risks result from hazardous exposures, but poverty, dangerous locations (high mountain slopes, riverbeds, delta), and precarious shelters aggravate the existing socio-environmental vulnerability (Oswald-Spring, 2013). From 1970 to 2010, the subcontinent was hit by "70 climate-related disasters: 31 in Central America and Mexico, 16 in South America, and 23 in the Caribbean" (Moreno et al., 2020, p. XIII). Central America is a small strip of the continent between two warming oceans (Spalding et al., 2007), making it together with the Caribbean islands and Mexico highly exposed to extreme climate events (Moreno et al., 2020). The economic costs during this period were estimated at US$ 106,427 billion, affecting the Caribbean with US$ 21,012; Central America with US$ 17,640, and Mexico with 3754 billion dollars. Extreme precipitation has also produced floods and landslides, destroying livelihood, infrastructure, and cultivated fields (CEPAL, 2019a, 2019b). Central America is a tropical region seriously affected by climate change. To confront these threats, innovative ideas and actions should be implemented that improve the livelihoods of the populations while maintaining the economy and provisioning goods and services (Central America Regional Climate Change Project, 2018). Further, extreme droughts (idem.) are producing more and stronger wildfires on the Pacific side of Mesoamerica and in other Latin American countries such as Brazil, Chile,

---

[5] Bolsa Familia is a Brazilian social welfare program introduced by President Ignacio Lula da Silva in 2003 and converted into law in 2004. It is part of the Brazilian federal government's network of social assistance programs. It represents an income transfer program that provides financial assistance to poor families to reduce the social inequity in Brazil and allows every family to get enough food.

and Patagonia (Moreno et al., 2020). The hottest place in America was the Desert of Altar, Sonora, Mexico, with temperatures in the soil over 80 °C in 2021.[6]

Long coastlines, warm oceans in the northern part of Latin America and the Caribbean, tropical diversity, and white sand beaches have promoted national and international tourism. However, frequent extreme events have affected the tourist industry, and climate change is critical for these countries. Conservation of biodiversity, mitigation of greenhouse gases (GHG), and curbing the rate of deforestation could reduce the harmful impacts. Further, integrated water management at the basin level and in towns, together with changes in unsustainable agriculture, may allow better adaptation of exposed people. This is particularly valid for indigenous communities in risky locations. Disasters have also produced forced-climate migration from Central America through Mexico to the US. To control this massive migration flow through Mexico's southern and northern border, police and militaries are expelling migrants to Central America (Prieto Díaz, 2021), increasing their dual vulnerability. To cross these militarized borders, climate-forced migrants and many indigenous people turn to organized crime, where they often fall victim to extortion, kidnapping, and sexual abuse (Oswald-Spring, 2020).

Disaster risk reduction and management (DRR and DRM; UNISDR, 2009) and climate change adaptation (IPCC, 2014) are still incipient in Latin America. They lack an integrated multi-sectoral and inter-institutional approach. Local and state governments often ignore the existing knowledge on DRR. With early warning and preventive evacuation (Hernández, 2019), governments often could avoid human and material losses. Traditional problems of poverty, public insecurity, organized crime, corruption, and governmental inefficiency also limit efficient climate governance. Most countries lack funds for scientific research, covering the densely populated areas with meteorological stations and radars, enabling an integrated network of the weather forecast for DRR. Additional deforestation and chaotic urbanization increase the social and financial costs of disasters (Fearnside, 2000). Indigenous communities living in hilly areas are highly exposed to disasters and lack early warnings.

Furthermore, public functionaries are poorly trained in DRR with weak coordination among state and local governments. All these factors increase the threats for people who are exposed to extreme climate events, while prevention could reduce the loss of lives and livelihood (OCHA, 2020).

Confronted with increasing climate disasters, affected indigenous communities have established themselves or, with some international help, coastal management, protection of mangroves, reforestation, and climate-smart agriculture (FAO, 2013). Supplementary adaptation efforts include aquaculture and small-scale fishery among exposed communities, where different development strategies may reduce GHG emissions, sequester carbon, and increase regional food production for decreasing poverty and food insecurity (FAO, 2018a). Indigenous women (FAO, 2017) get increasingly involved in DRR (Bradshaw & Linneker, 2009). They are participating

---

[6] https://noticieros.televisa.com/ultimas-noticias/gran-desierto-altar-lugar-mas-caliente-mundo-esta-mexico/.

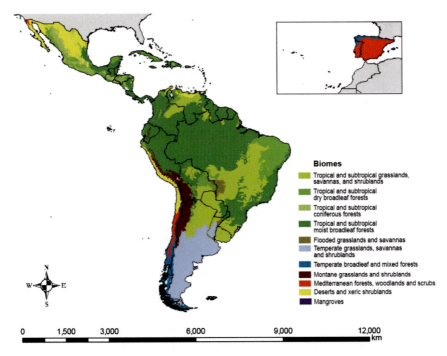

Fig. 1 Biodiversity biomes of Latin America. *Source* UNEP WCMC (2010)

in cooperatives promoting low-carbon activities, especially when they are head of households and caring about children.

3.1 Biodiversity in Latin America

Latin America is the most biodiverse region in the world. Brazil, Colombia, Mexico, Ecuador, Peru, and Venezuela belong to the 12 mega-biodiverse countries globally. Latin America house 51% of amphibians, 41% of birds, 37% of reptiles, 35% of mammals, and 29% of all seed plant species (CEPAL & Patrimonio Natural, 2013). The diversity of ecosystems includes mangroves, estuaries, marshes, seagrass beds, coral reefs, and macro-algae forests. The Amazonian rainforest[7] alone hosts about one-tenth of all plants and animals on the planet (Marengo et al., 2018). Additionally, the Orinoco River basin and the Northern Andes house large numbers of endemic plants and animals (see Fig. 1).

---

[7] The Amazonian basin covers 7.4 million km^2, including Bolivia, Brazil, Colombia, Ecuador, Peru, and Venezuela. The Amazonas river has an average precipitation of 2200 mm/year and an average discharge of 230,000 m^3 of water per second (CEPAL, 2019a, 2019b), the equivalent of one-fifth of the global continental freshwater (Marengo et al., 2013).

4 Indigenous Women in Latin America and Mesoamerica

About 370 million indigenous people (FAO, 2016), representing 5% of the world population, exist globally. These indigenous people represent 15% of the poor people (FAO, 2018a), and one-third live in rural and often hilly regions. About 5000 different ethnic groups exist in 90 countries, mostly in Asia. These indigenous communities speak about 4000 of the existing 7000 languages (FAO, 2018b). Indigenous people live on 22% of the global surface (UNDP, 2020), often in hilly regions, which are areas of high biodiversity. These indigenous communities care for about 80% of the existing biodiversity, but they are threatened by multiple development processes (Raygorodetsky, 2018). Mining, deforestation, dams, plantations of palm oil trees, soya, sorghum, and cornfields are key threats to the remaining biodiversity. "The indigenous peoples of the Amazon have proven to be the best guardians of their traditional territories. The fact that the Amazon ecosystems are as rich as they are today proof of how successful these cultures have been in living in balance with their environment" (Raygorodetsky, 2018, p. 3).

Frequently, indigenous peoples have been displaced and continue to be expelled from their traditional and native territories in the name of progress or development interests. Most governments with high biodiversity hotspots promote land-use change and mining concessions to corporate enterprises for developing their economies with low-paid jobs for native people in mining, agriculture, deforestation, and general services. Sometimes under the garb of ecotourism, the expulsion occurs not only in Latin America like Sápara from Ecuador but also in Africa and Asia. National governments justify the displacement of these ethnic societies for conservation reasons, but generally, they have produced greater biodiversity destruction (Sánchez & Urueña, 2017).[8] Worldwide vertebrate populations are estimated to have declined by 60% between 1970 and 2020. In Latin America, the Amazonas region is the most threatened by bushfires (Lehmann et al., 2014) and forest clearing for soy production, livestock, and other cash crops (Marengo et al., 2018).

Confronted with social and environmental pressure since the 1970s, indigenous groups in Latin America have got organized to protect their languages, customs, ecosystems, and cultural diversity. Mexico accounts for the greatest indigenous population, but Bolivia and Guatemala have the highest percentage of ethnic people, followed by Peru, Chile, and Ecuador. Precisely their large number has allowed them to renegotiate some political terms for recognition, and indigenous groups have achieved a certain degree of autonomy and self-determination. However, five centuries of dual colonization, exploitation, discrimination, and abuse between the Spanish conquers and later the internal colonialism of the local bourgeoisie have obliged these indigenous communities to consolidate their social organization and reinforce their demands internally (González, 2003a). These indigenous communities have established alliances with other socially discriminated and exploited groups,

---

[8] The Fourteenth Conference of the Parties held from17 to 29 November 2018 in Sharm El-Sheikh, Egypt, seriously criticized this behaviour affecting the Convention on Biodiversity.

such as Afro-Latinos, women's organizations, and peasants, building alternative cultures and caring for nature projects.

To limit the destruction of indigenous territories in Latin America, multiple ethnic associations have got collectively organized in the International Indian Treaty Council (IITC). Their key effort reinforces internal organization, sovereignty, and self-determination. The defence of their cosmovision includes the recognition and protection of their traditional culture, heritage sites, and sacred lands, often threatened by mining concessions (Arach, 2018).

Multiple indigenous organizations exist in Latin America: The Coordination of Indigenous Organizations of the Amazon River Basin (COICA), Indian Council of South America (CISA), Coordination of the Indigenous Organizations of the Brazilian Amazon (COIAB), Council of All the Mapuche Lands (CTLTM), Confederation of Indigenous Nationalities of Ecuador (CONAIE), Confederation of Indigenous People of Bolivia (CIDOB), International Mayan League, etc. These regional organizations also evolved in national movements, such as the National Indigenous Congress in Mexico (CNI), with the ongoing integration of indigenous women. These Indian women get fully involved with their partners to recognize and protect their traditional cosmovision and the right to their natural resources. Multiple international movements support these indigenous efforts, such as La Via Campesina and the Latin America Coordination of Peasant Organisations. These bottom-up associations have pressured national governments to adopt indigenous laws and allocate the committed budgets to these ethnic groups. Nevertheless, a real autonomy of these ethnic communities is still missing in Latin America.

This associative strategy made it easier to overcome the former resistance and discrimination from mestizo governments in Bolivia, Peru, and Ecuador. Indigenous movements have promoted constitutional changes, including political, cultural, social, and natural rights for Indian people with respect to nature, where women have played a crucial role. They have fought simultaneously against the lack of indigenous visibility in political and social organizations and intrafamilial violence as a result of the global patriarchal mindset. They have created an alternative political arena through wider alliances, where assignations, agendas, programs, activities, and governmental budgets slowly have emerged, and some indigenous people were appointed to governmental jobs. In Bolivia, after the military coup in 2020 against the first indigenous president Evo Morales, the election in 2021 restored the power constellation before the coup, and indigenous women and men were elected into the Plurinational Legislative Assembly.[9] However, corporate interests in mining and tourism continue to threaten these ethnic efforts by producing pollution, environmental destruction, and poverty. This dual, socio-environmental vulnerability exists not only in Bolivia. But in all Latin American countries, where corporate interests are imposing their model of extractivism (Muñoz et al., 2018).

---

[9] The active involvement of indigenous people in the electoral process brought back the constellation of former political forces with numerous representations of different ethnic groups. The interim Mestizo ex-president Jeanine Añez was arrested and was tried to murder indigenous people in the Bolivian highlands after the coup.

Indigenous women have promoted political participation, especially in Ecuador. They have understood that internal colonialism was related to the destruction of mother earth (Pacha Mama). They have reinforced their telluric social representations and developed mechanisms to prevent destruction and violence. Bolivia and Ecuador, together with Mexico, are also promoting a transversal understanding, where gender relations are integrated into their telluric cosmovision (Ibarra Sarlat, 2018). Thousands of years of patriarchal imposition, 500 years of colonial, and 200 years of internal colonialism have left social gaps among indigenous women and girls. Indigenous women in Latin America live mostly in urban contexts due to internal migration and a search for better living conditions, education, and social facilities, including reproductive health care. However, in Ecuador, 68.7% of indigenous people still live in hilly regions, similar to the south and southeast of Mexico. Most of these indigenous people have a very low income and find themselves in unstable working conditions without social security. Women, in particular, make up a disproportionate number of those trapped in extreme poverty in Latin America (CELADE & CEPAL, 2013). Most indigenous rural women also joined forces with local, national, and regional movements to fight against pollution from mining companies and development projects, which have not respected the ILO Agreement 169 (Stavenhagen, 2012). Often national governments are more interested in tax incomes than in conserving their biodiversity. They have either repressed these protests or did not address the violence from corporate enterprises against indigenous people (Muñoz et al., 2018). All these structural factors have limited gender security and increased the dual vulnerability of indigenous women and girls.

5   Dual Socio-environmental Vulnerability and Extractivism

The concept of dual vulnerability interrelates the complex nexus between social and environmental factors within climate change impacts and neoliberal globalization. This dual vulnerability (Fig. 2) is affecting especially the most biodiverse regions globally, i.e., those of Latin America and especially Mesoamerica (Moreno et al., 2020). For poor people, marginalization, discrimination, hunger, malnutrition, and privatization of public services have deteriorated their quality of life during the past three decades and affected the well-being of poor people catastrophically during the COVID-19 pandemic in the whole region (CEPAL, 2021b). In Mesoamerica, especially in the hilly regions of drug production and in the peri-urban slums, violence has dramatically increased as a result of a lack of job opportunities for the youth, who are often recruited by organized crime. The complexity of public insecurity is not only related to organized crime but also to corrupt local and national governments, drug trafficking, unsustainable urbanization developments, and ethnic discrimination, where a despotic local bourgeoisie has allied with the international capital, money laundering, paramilitary and illegal criminal groups (Yup de León, 2021).

Mexico accounts for the most serious climate impacts in Latin America (Moreno et al., 2020). When more than 70% of inhabitants belong to an ethnic community

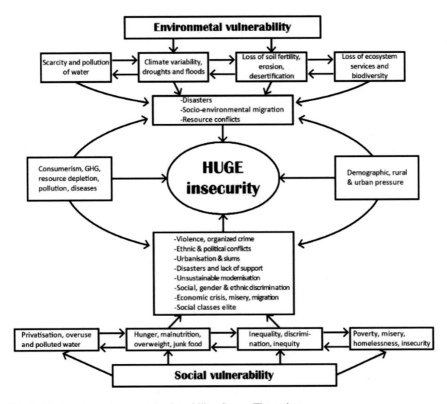

Fig. 2 Dual socio-environmental vulnerability. *Source* The author

or more than 5000 people with more than 40% of indigenous origin existing, they represent an indigenous municipality. According to the 2020 census, Mexico has a population of 16.93 million indigenous people, who represent officially 15.1% of the inhabitants. Some 7.36 million people speak one of the 68 indigenous languages (INEGI, 2021), although various languages are in the process of extinction. These indigenous people are the poorest inhabitants in Mexico: 11.9% have no income, 16.8% earn less than one minimal salary (MS),[10] 30.4% earn one to two MS, and only 30% receive more than two MS, while a family of four members currently requires about four MS to survive. Thus, by engaging in multiple activities, all indigenous family members try to get a minimal income for living, often in highly precarious conditions. Children suffer more from hunger, and their learning capacity is limited due to chronic undernourishment. Pregnant and breastfeeding women also suffer from a lack of food, and their life expectancy is shorter than that of women in the rest of the country.

---

[10] Minimal salary is established for day labor by a governmental commission. During the past 30 years of neoliberalism, the purchasing power of the minimum wage has been lost, and today it takes four minimal salaries to support a family.

These structural disadvantages are also reflected in the access to schooling, where 16.6% of indigenous women are without any education (national level 6%), 36.3% have incomplete or complete primary school training, and only 21.7% achieve an upper secondary education, compared with 40.3% at national level (INEGI, 2021). Furthermore, in 2020, 58.9% of indigenous women still cook with wood or charcoal, causing them to frequently suffer from chronic obstructive pulmonary disease. The poor living conditions are also reflected in their housing, where 13.9% live on dirt floors, precarious walls, and roofs that cannot resist extreme rainfalls or hurricanes (INEGI, 2021). These precarious living conditions not only typified indigenous people in Mexico and the whole of Mesoamerica (Ulate, 2001) as the poorest in the region, but they also suffered from a lack of public services, such as clean water, sanitation, and health facilities (CEPAL, 2020).

Besides this social vulnerability, indigenous people suffer from growing environmental exposure due to the destruction of ecosystem services, pollution of water and soil by mining activities, and illegal logging, often by organized crime. During extreme rainfalls, landslides sometimes cover entire villages. At the same time, polluted rivers resulting from mining activities have intoxicated people in different regions, thus affecting the growth and intellectual development of children and the health of all inhabitants (UNICEF-Gain, 2018).

Poor indigenous people have often constructed their shelters on slopes exposed to landslides, and deforestation increases their risks of being buried under earth masses during extreme rainfalls (Moreno et al., 2020), as has happened in Mesoamerica during the extraordinary hurricane season in 2020 and 2021. Confronted with disasters, loss of livelihood, and threats from organized crime, these ethnic families often are obliged to migrate to nearby cities or from Central America through Mexico to the US to find better living conditions. They leave behind their land, culture, ancestors, and history, but often women with children and elders while men migrate alone to improve their income (Oswald-Spring et al., 2014).

To protect the indigenous and tribal rights for greater self-determination, the conservation of their traditional knowledge, the political organization of their communities, and the free decision on concession on their historical land, the International Labour Organisation (ILO, 1989) adopted Convention 169. Most governments of Mesoamerica signed this UN Declaration on the Rights of Indigenous Peoples. It is now supporting conservation projects of most indigenous communities worldwide.[11] In addition, Bolivia and Ecuador have given nature a constitutional right similar to its citizens (UNEP, 2020).

However, these efforts are often arbitrary and violently annulated by mining and water exploitation. International tourism corporations and national governments have given long-term concessions on ethnic land and water assignments. They did not respect the right to self-determination and legal consultation of indigenous people

---

[11] For instance, Namibia promoted the Nature Conservation Amendment Act of 1996; Canada gave federal protection of the Edéhzhíe Area, Finland recognized the Havukkavaara forest in North Karelia for a community-based conservation project, where the traditional lifestyle was reinforced, while these indigenous groups are protecting the old-growth forests in the Arctic Circle (UNEP, 2020).

The Impact of Climate Change on the Gender Security … 129

ratified by the Mexican government at the Convention 169 of the International Labour Organization and other appropriate procedures. These extractivist activities have destroyed local developments of the poorest inhabitants and extinguished biodiversity and the cosmovision. Whereas the exploitation of natural resources dates back to the colonial period, the modern management of open-pit mines is destroying entire mountains, and biodiverse forests with endemic flora and fauna. It has negatively impacted millions of indigenous people (Muñoz et al., 2018).

6 Top-Down Possible Efforts to Reduce Increasing Climate Disasters

Among corporate enterprises, some more progressive leaders from the science and technology sectors, in particular, have understood the danger of climate change to Earth and humankind. They are, above all, linked to and are exploring alternative sustainable ways, such as using science and technology for the management of the Amazon forest. These modern corporations in April 2021 have offered to pay more taxes for stimulating the development of the infrastructure in the US. IRENA (2021) has published the conditions for governments and enterprises to meet the necessary reduction targets of GHG and to maintain the temperature rise by 1.5 °C by 2050. Their proposal includes a complex system of public and private activities: renewable energies (25%), energy efficiency and conservation (25%), electrification of end-users (20%), GHG capture and removal, together with reforestation (20%), and development of green hydrogen (10%). The cheapest way for sustainable development is the conservation and efficiency of all energy systems.

Photovoltaic and wind provide the expansion of renewable electric supply, while green hydrogen is a sustainable energy source. The electrification of all end-users includes complex and decentralized energy transportation and storage systems, where electricity, cars, trains, ships, planes, motorcycles, and trucks are included. Heavy pollution also results from inefficient fossil extraction. The best way to reduce pollution in extractive activities is through a global carbon tax, which will force enterprises to increase the efficiency and capture of carbon dioxide of GHG emissions. Figure 3 shows the elements for a full decarbonization process to restrict the global temperature rise to 1.5 °C. Without a doubt, human activities are altering the global climate, and only drastic actions may avoid unexpected disasters and potential tipping points in the hothouse Earth (Steffen et al., 2018). Such actions are becoming even more pressing when considering that in April 2021, the National Oceanic and Atmospheric Administration (NOAA) measured more than 420 ppm of CO_{2e}[12]—almost double the level of the preindustrial period.

However, one of the world's largest asset managers, Black Rock (Tepper, 2020), an American investment corporation, insisted that embedding environmental, social, and political governance is not the goal of corporate capitalism. Their sole interest

---

[12] CO_{2e} includes all greenhouse gases, including bio dioxides and methane.

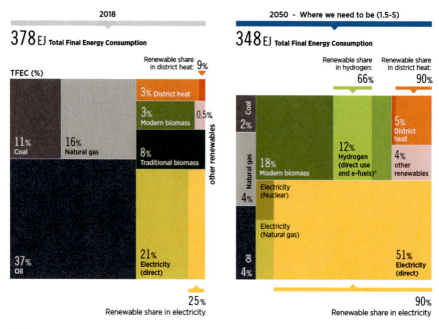

Fig. 3 Total energy consumption 2018–2050. *Source* IRENA 2021

is maximizing profits at any social and environmental costs. Thus, governments, laws, carbon taxes, and public subsidies must force these enterprises and investors to support the goal of a limit of 1.5 °C rise in the global temperature. This may produce co-benefits in the form of clean air and water, less soil pollution, better health, and recuperation of ecosystem services by mitigating climate impacts and disasters (IPCC, 2019, 2021). These actions require all countries to agree on energy efficiency and conservation, electrification of transportation, and a drastic reduction of fossil oil, gas, and carbon.

To achieve the goal of limiting global warming to 1.5 °C above preindustrial levels, the total energy consumption must be reduced from 378 to 348 EJ (Fig. 3). This implies a total change in the energy generation sector, reducing the use of fossil oil from 37 to 4% while simultaneously increasing the use of renewable energies and electricity from nuclear and gas sources (IRENA, 2021). IRENA (2021) estimates that the global investments from 2021 to 2050 for decarbonization are estimated at 4.4 billion US/year. The integration of governmental and legal adaptations, enabling technologies, market mechanisms, system operations, investment portfolios, and business models for this sustainable energy management will create three times more jobs than fossil energies. It may also reduce the electricity costs for consumers and improve their quality of life by creating a cleaner and less hazardous environment. However, as IRENA (2021) indicates, selfish corporate interests are the greatest obstacle to achieving this ambitious climate mitigation goal (Fig. 3).

7 What Is Happening with Gender Security, Especially in Indigenous Societies?

Together with Canada, Australia and the Democratic Republic of Congo, Mexico, Peru, Chile, Brazil, Bolivia, and Colombia have opened their international investments to extract and exploit natural resources (Muñoz et al., 2018). The results are rising pollution of crucial water resources, often in water-scarce regions, and the destruction of sacred traditional mountain sites. Affected people and social movements have organized collective resistance. Globally, indigenous mobilizations emerged to defend their natural resources, Earth, and telluric cosmovision. *The Observatory of Mining Conflicts in Latin America* (in Spanish OCMAL) and *the Atlas of Conflict of the Environmental Justice Project* (EJAtlas[13]) have reported increased collaboration among indigenous oppositions, environmental researchers, and non-profit organizations in quantifying the impacts of these transnational extractivist megaprojects in some of the most biodiverse regions of Latin America, including Mesoamerica.

Additionally, the National Institute on Space Studies (INPE, 2021) has reported the destruction of the rainforest in the Amazon of Brazil to its highest level since 2008, especially during the current government of President Jair Bolsonaro. INPE documented that 11,088 km^2 of tropical forest were destroyed from August 2019 to July 2020, representing an increase of 9.5% from the former year. About 99% of the bushfires were illegal during this period and have raged through vast parts of the biodiverse rainforest, clearing land for cash crops and extended cattle farming. As an outcome of this destructive development, the Amazon is rapidly drying. Risks to this unique ecosystem may transit to savannah with impacts on rainfall patterns and freshwater availability across many of South America's countries, including the recharge of aquifers. This undesirable future could also affect the water supply for the agricultural heartland and the existing megacities (São Paulo, Rio de Janeiro, and Brasilia). The bushfires are also releasing vast amounts of GHG that accelerate climate change impacts.

As explained above, these so-called development projects impact differently on ethnic groups, affecting their human, gender, and environmental security (Oswald-Spring, 2020). During the past five centuries, capitalism based on patriarchal violence and wars has penetrated all social relations and families, even in remote areas (Reardon, 1985). The accumulation of local and transnational elites has also created multiple obstacles to the empowerment and self-reliance of the most vulnerable social groups, especially indigenous women and girls. Further, human-induced climate change impacts have regained strength during the past decade, affecting above all the Global South and indigenous communities, but having economic consequences also in the Global North (IPCC, 2021). Further, the COVID-19 pandemic and initiatives to combat the financial crisis with economic stimulation projects in Europe and the USA are adding to the challenges to achieve the global goal of limiting the

---

[13] https://ejatlas.org/?translate=es.

temperature increase to 1.5 °C (IPCC, 2019). Only a broad alliance and the protection and recovery of the environment will facilitate the survival of people confronted with dual vulnerability. However, the United Nations, researchers, and the affected indigenous populations are struggling against the selfish interests of transnational corporations and their local representatives. This consciousness-raising globally questions the narrow understanding of military security, still predominant in North America, Russia, Chinese governments, and other countries. After the disintegration of the Soviet Union, researchers have explored a widened and deepened human, gender, and environmental security—a HUGE-security approach (Oswald-Spring, 2020).

8   A HUGE-Security Approach Against Climate Change

Within these alternative approaches towards a widened (Buzan et al., 1998) and deepened (Brauch et al., 2009; UNDP, 1994) security understanding, poverty, and the COVID-19 pandemic are forcing governments to place human well-being, health, economic development, and the survival of nature and humankind in the centre of political concern. A broader understanding of security to include the military–political aspect and incorporate economic, societal, and environmental security allows for a better analysis of the complex interlinks between society and nature (UNDP 2017, 2020). Complemented by a deepening focus from individuals to families, communities, nations, and global Earth, the rise of different vulnerabilities among gender, age, social classes, ethnicities, religions, and other socially constructed differences have emerged, all based on unequal social relations. As a historically constructed violent social system, patriarchy, with the male supremacy in the clan, the government, and the economy, distributes power disproportionally among men and women through means of war (Reardon, 1985). It allows men to violently accumulate wealth, prestige, and control at the expense of women, girls, powerless men, and other vulnerable people. After more than 5000 years of consolidation, patriarchy has evolved into a complex power, exploitation, control, and financial–legal–military system. Wars and repressions have created a wealth accumulation model with extreme social stratification and male leadership by corporate businesses (Oswald-Spring, 2020: 282). Although socio-psychological and cultural diversity expresses multiple regional differences, the present corporate capitalism and the exploitation of humans and nature result from these thousands of years of military–religious–ideological–political domination by small male elites.

Ecofeminists embraced both human and environmental exploitation within this patriarchal mindset and connected the domination of women with the destruction of nature (D'Eaubonne, 1974). These critical scientists interlinked the cultural and environmental critiques and developed comprehensive transgressive approaches to overcome climate change threats, social inequality, pandemics, exploitation of workers, and political discrimination. They have denounced powerful superpowers that have imposed their laws through massive destruction and economic control arms. However, climate disasters, temperature rise, and droughts are also forcing

The Impact of Climate Change on the Gender Security ...

these governments and their transnational companies to mitigate the impact of GHG in the atmosphere (IPCC, 2019) and limit global warming to levels below 2 °C (Paris Agreement negotiated in2015 among the member of COP 22 of UNFCCC). Within this feminist approach, human, gender, and environmental security have regained strength during the past decades, especially during climate disasters in regions such as Mesoamerica. Public violence, organized crime, increasing numbers of homicides, and femicides are challenging the survival of poor people (CEPAL, 2019b), but also the position of elected national and local governments (Altomonte & Sánchez, 2016).

Undoubtedly, better-educated girls and women linked to global communication networks are reinforcing the struggle against illegal extractivism, repression of environmentalists, gender-based violence, femicide, and the glass ceiling or sticky floor for women. Sexual aggression by dominant men against women has led to significant demonstrations against discrimination and violence (Camey et al., 2020). It is also pressuring for different development models, including socially responsible management of COVID-19, recovery of ecosystems, and greater social and political equity to empower discriminated women and powerless men by improving their precarious living conditions. FAO (2015) indicated that women contribute substantially to the rural and household economy. The IPCC (2019) reported that they produce half of all safe food in orchards in only 4% of the land. Women also take care of children without compensation, manage households, provide health services, promote hygiene, and fetch water and energy sources. They produce almost a third of the existing wealth globally with their unpaid household work (Pedrero Nieto, 2018). Nevertheless, women account globally only for 19% of parliamentary representation, and there is a minimal representation of women in leading positions in government and enterprises.

Global economic crises and pandemics have affected differently men and women, especially highly vulnerable groups who find themselves in informal working conditions. Therefore, mitigation, adaptation, and resilience programs with gender and ethnic perspective may reduce dual vulnerability. Such programs can particularly assist in supporting the recovery of the environment in biodiverse hotspots and improving the livelihoods of indigenous women and men. This HUGE-security approach also analyses different understandings of their cosmovision, where the indigenous Aymara in the Andes have promoted an alternative paradigm of living well (Ceceña, 2014). Confronted with high inequity, the government of Mexico has imposed gender equity at all three levels of government following the elections of 2021 despite systemic male opposition from party leaderships and gender-based violence that emerged all over the country (Serrano Oswald, 2021).

9 Resilience Among Vulnerable People: Living Well

Facing the dominant patriarchal structure and corporate neoliberalism, southern countries exposed to climate change have no tools to negotiate against global capitalism, where only three companies (Moody's Investors Service, Standard and

Poor's, & Fitch) control 95% of the worldwide credit rating business (Benmelech, 2020). These three companies have had an impact on worsening the quality of life of billions of people. Therefore, most indigenous, poor people, and women have alternative priorities. They struggle to supply safe food, water, health, shelter, and education for their communities. Their constitutional rights are frequently violated by their mestizo governments. Mesoamerica is also the most violent region globally, where drug cartels threaten the survival of especially the youth (Yup de León, 2021). In conformity in the rest of Latin America has increased social protests (e.g., Chile, Colombia, Ecuador, and Peru). Without real solutions, the Aymaras in the Andes have adopted an alternative paradigm called "living well". These Aymara indigenous understood that life quality includes social integration, dancing, moderation in eating, drinking, dignified working conditions, and creating happiness by consolidating social relations and community cohabitation. The respect for nature and the recovery of ecosystem services are crucial for alternative lifestyles and understanding the complex interrelationship between society and nature.

Their *sumaj kamaña* (living well) or *suamk kawsay* (good living). Over the past ten years, Bolivia has been able to eradicate its extreme poverty. The indigenous leadership has strengthened equity and increased sustainability equality in their indigenous regions (CEPAL, 2019a). An alternative constitution and redistribution model within a diversified cultural state has also reached the most marginalized people of the indigenous population (CEPAL, 2019b).[14] At the centre of their thoughts is "the reproduction of life as the means to understand the reproductions process as a whole and as an organizing criterion of economic issues, which could no longer be considered a divided dimension" (Ceceña, 2014, p. 11). Economic, social, and environmental activities are immersed into their traditional cosmovision, which guides their daily lives. Living well represents a telluric approach with socio-political and ecological contents oriented to ensure a decent quality of life for the most vulnerable. This social approach to well-being can mitigate dual vulnerability and reinforce HUGE-security by letting nobody behind. Several Mesoamerican indigenous groups have adopted this way of life of the Aymaras, especially in the mountains of Guatemala and Mexico.

The Maya indigenous Zapatistas in the mountains of Chiapas in Mexico have developed a participative shell governance (called *caracoles*).[15] Their consensual decision processes are reached by local debate. Women, men, young, and old are equally elected as leaders for a year and without remuneration for "leading by obeying" their communities. The whole community gets in charge of the maintenance of the family of their yearly leader. This indigenous organization is based on its historical background, the founding myths of its culture, and its cosmovision. The governance model differs from the UN system by promoting an active consensual negotiation

---

[14] The mestizo bourgeoisie in Bolivia, in collaboration with corporate enterprises, tried to destroy this social improvement with a military coup, but a legal-binding election brought back the former Indian leadership.

[15] The caracoles project "opens up new possibilities of resistance and autonomy of the indigenous peoples of Mexico and of the world, a resistance that includes social sectors fighting for democracy, freedom, and justice for all" (González, 2003b, p. 14).

The Impact of Climate Change on the Gender Security ...

through collective decision-making processes. This model of participation trains and empowers everybody, avoiding social stratification inside the community. It supports handicapped and vulnerable groups. Social inconformity and changes of authority are publicly discussed. Collective decision-makings eradicate corruption and violence. Their judicial system is a task of the whole community, and offenders collaborate with the community to remedy the damage caused. The whole community involves in preventive conflict management (Menchú, 2004). During the past three decades, no femicide has occurred in the Zapatista communities, while in Mexico, at least ten women are killed every day, primarily by their partners.

There are multiple other global efforts on the way, such as the Happiness index of Bhutan, which has promoted among its citizens a different understanding of happiness—one not based on consumerism, but as a founding principle for life and living together with solidarity and co-responsibility. In Brazil, former president Luis Ignácio Lula da Silva promoted a model called *bolsa familia* to overcome extreme poverty and has encouraged the active involvement of women in the formal school system. In synthesis, in different parts of the world, efforts of social actions and alternative economies are emerging, putting in the centre the reproduction process instead of capital accumulation (Collin, 2020). Different social groups are changing whenever multiple governments and transnational enterprises are still attached to their model of exploitation and destruction. Increasing climate disasters, also affecting the infrastructure of the Global North, will force these governments to focus more on the livelihood of their citizens, the mitigation of climate impacts, and its adaption to climate threats.

The environmental destruction continues, and corporate elites' interests are economically vital that they may force mestizo governments in Latin America to end any opposition from indigenous landowners and protectors of ecosystems. Until today, these corporate elites have no alternative exo-planet to flee to during the coming decades.

10 Conclusion

The increase in climate disasters is creating upcoming conflicts and environmental migration, thus exercising pressure against the dominant governmental policies and multinational corporations. The investments in the "corporate military–industrial–research—complex" increased in 2020 to $1981 billion, an increase of 2.6 % in real terms from 2019 (SIPRI, 2021). These expenditures limit investments in the well-being of people and combatting climate change disasters. The mismanagement of the COVID-19 pandemic in Mesoamerica with a very high death ratio, the lack of medicine, and the precarious health facilities are eroding not only human security but also gender security due to the fact that women who are basically in charge of caring for the sick are often getting infected by the virus themselves (CEPAL, 2021b; ECLAT, 2020). The hoarding of vaccines by many industrialized countries benefitted some transnational pharmaceutical enterprises and their research centres, while the lack of vaccines is spreading multiple mutagenic viruses, producing new waves of contagion (Bollyky et al., 2021). This selfish and irrational behaviour is also dominating the climate change mitigation actions.

Not only in the Global South get narrow support for vaccines against COVID-19 and adaption against climate disasters, but several governments invested in military tools, assuming unpayable debts (Stiglitz, 2007). But also, among citizens in the Global North, alternatives to deal better with future risks are limited, as indicated by the high death rate of the COVID-19 pandemic. Multiple industrialized nations can also not support their poor people and often prioritize urban middle classes, leaving indigenous and poor communities abandoned. In these unequal political conditions, ethnic groups have directed their sustainable transition towards self-sufficiency and solidarity in food, water, traditional medicine, and healing processes. Alternative educations are taking into account the self-reliant model of Freire (2005), promoting social equity among indigenous women and men, youth, and the elderly.

The realist Hobbesian power approach, based on patriarchal violence, is slowly moving away from the heavy-handed military superpowers based on sanctions and trade restrictions. People globally and in Mesoamerica, in particular, are forcing their governments to explore alternatives to the military-focused power. The president of Mexico proposed hugs instead of bullets, integrating a multidimensional systemic global change including economic, political, societal, cultural, cosmovision, and incipient environmental dimensions. The neoliberal model has dismantled democracy, and human security among most citizens increased the poverty rate with precarious working conditions for women (Jelin, 2021). Within this global discontent, an alternative HUGE-security may be an option. A humanized security approach explores new values at risk related to climate disasters and pandemics while rejecting the dominant patriarchal and violent military–political paradigm. Multiple social groups have understood that the real threats are corporate neoliberalism, financial elite, military and arms lobbies, antidemocratic-patriarchal governments, and religious dogmatism, which have exploited humans and nature for thousands of years. These patriarchal forces are predominately responsible for global environmental and climate change (Brauch et al., 2009).

The indigenous alternative paradigm with gender security in Mesoamerica focuses on gender relations, including powerless women and men, children, the elderly, the unemployed, and other minorities. Equity, social solidarity, and identity are the values at risk for these less privileged groups. The threats are directly related to the violent and exclusive system reinforced by the religious ideology of submission. The radical approach of HUGE-security addresses the survival risk of seven billion people, their quality of life and well-being, together with the sustainability of natural, agricultural and urban ecosystems. Thus, the Zapatista's struggle against the "disease called capitalism" promotes their members' social economy and sustainable agriculture. They represent decentralized efforts for alternative livelihoods in an increasing hothouse Earth. After 28 years of delinking from the Mexican government and the global neoliberal system in the hilly region of Chiapas, these Mayan indigenous people have managed to embrace an alternative way of life and improve their judicial, economic, political, environmental, and social system. They understood that global capitalism would not easily be eliminated but demonstrated that alternatives to neoliberalism are possible by delinking. The Zapatistas decided to discuss their achievements against global capitalism in Europe, organizing a trip in a precarious boat. Most of the Zapatistas passengers on the ship were women, and gender, political and social equity are central policies in their daily life. They also oppose the extractivism of mining companies and megaprojects of so-called development projects. Their local shell communities have restored forests, mountains, water, soils, and livelihood in their local shell communities. These former extremely poor indigenous people have improved nutrition and health conditions. They have better managed the pandemic COVID-19 with low infected and dead people and have developed a transparent judicial system to prevent conflicts and crimes and integrate offenders into the community. Their participative governance has increased gender security, social welfare, and political participation of women, youth, and elders.

The Zapatista philosophy took the motto of the World Social Forum, "Another World is Possible." They struggled against unsustainable development projects, corruption, a low ongoing war, paramilitaries, and selfish transnational corporation in each of their communities. Among Aymaras, indigenous women took leadership and have protested against the federal government and the failed policies of COVID-19 pandemic management in Ecuador. Similar protests have emerged in Brazil against the policy of Jair Bolsonaro. In Colombia and Chile, massive opposition forces the national governments to change their neoliberal agenda. These different social movements compel people to think about alternatives in production and consumption. Precisely decarbonization and dematerialization processes to limit GHG and environmental pollution (see Fig. 3) are global challenges of the present model of neoliberal mass consumption. Diverse activities are emerging globally, exploring ways of alternative livelihood, where primarily sustainability, environmental care, and social reproduction are producing social changes. Living well, solidarity, and care of people and nature synthesize these diverse efforts.

Within a global approach, the failure of managing the COVID-19 pandemic in many countries has awakened the affected people, and climate disasters have forced millions of people to leave their traditional homes. Oswald-Spring (2012) and Fearnside (2020) recognized that climate disasters, discrimination of women, and marginalization of indigenous people interact with other drivers of instability. Not only have they undermined livelihoods and increased vulnerability and poverty, but they have also destabilized political, social, and economic conditions locally and nationally, increasing tensions, conflicts, and violence. Thus, globally alternative movements have expressed the present crisis of civilization where most human beings are trying to survive in the present "Hothouse Earth" (Steffen et al., 2018). Alternative options include sharing their experiences, consolidating their identity through sustainable soils and water management, and anchoring their social representations (Serrano Oswald, 2009) and community belongings (Menchú, 2004). Their critique of the dominant cornucopian worldview of capitalist consumerism includes a complex, interdependent, and sustainable bio-human system of gender security, where human security is related to gift-giving (Vaughan, 2004), caring, and reproduction of equal social representations including everybody. The human and gender-centred approach is at the centre of these alternatives, often including environmental security with the restoration of ecosystem services. Education towards a sustainable, healthy, and nutritious diet may eliminate industrialized junk food and reduce health-related problems (diabetes, heart problems, strokes, and obesity). Alternative school education with collaboration and peaceful conflict resolution instead of competition may reduce violence in school, producing well-being and joy in life for children. This HUGE-security approach, based on eradicating patriarchal violence, explores an integral and diverse transition process with gender equity for a sustainable society.

Billions of human beings are under threat from the dominant corporate model. Multiple social groups, especially the youth, are pressuring their governments and promoting alternative societal behaviours for maintaining the global temperature rise at 1.5 °C, controlling especially oil and cement enterprises. However, national governments act slowly, often related to personal or group interests allied with big corporations. Therefore, it is crucial to understand that bottom-up changes are emerging besides all top-down efforts going on and the limited capacity of UN organizations to move further-such as the vaccine monopolization and the failure of COVIX have indicated. The timeframe for changing the present behaviour conditions globally is extremely short (from 2030 to 2050). Without any doubt, climate disasters, traditional wisdom, and diverse political will, together with harsher climate, health, and living conditions will motivate people and governments to explore different ways to the dominant patriarchal capitalism. Within this short time framework, the question remains: Are humans globally, but especially indigenous women and girls, able to achieve greater gender security for promoting HUGE-security? The coming decades may decide if humankind and mother Earth will get a survival change or will be destroyed by selfish corporations and neglectful governments.

References

Altomonte, H., & Sánchez, R. (2016). *Hacia una nueva gobernanza de los recursos naturales en América Latina y el Caribe*. CEPAL.

Arach, O. (2018). Like an 'Army in enemy territory. Epistemic violence in megaextractivist expansion. In Ú. Oswald-Spring & S. E. Serrano Oswald (Eds.), *Risks, violence, security and peace in Latin America* (pp. 101–112). Springer.

Benmelech, E. (2020). How credit ratings are shaping governments' responses to Covid-19? Forbes. https://www.forbes.com/sites/effibenmelech/2020/08/19/how-credit-ratings-are-shaping-government-responses-to-covid-19/?sh=b6da95a1d011.

Bollyky, T. J., Murray, C. J. L., & Reiner, R. C. (2021). Epidemiology, not geopolitics, should guide COVID-19 vaccine donations. *The Lancet, 398*(10295), 97–99. https://doi.org/10.1016/S0140-6736(21)01323-4

Bradshaw, S., & Linneker, B. (2009). Gender perspectives on disaster reconstruction in Nicaragua: Reconstructing roles and relations? In E. Enarson & P. G. Dhar Chakrabarti (Eds.), *Women, gender and disaster: Global issues and initiatives* (pp. 75–88). Sage.

Brauch, H. G., Oswald Spring, Ú., Grin, J., Mesjasz, C., Kameri-Mbote, P., Behera, N.C., Chourou, B., & Krummenacher, H. Eds. (2009). *Facing global environmental change. Environmental, human, energy, food, health, and water security concepts. Vol. 4.* Springer: Berlin.

Buzan, B., Wæver, O., Wæver, O., & De Wilde, J. (1998). *Security: A new framework for analysis.* Lynne Rienner Publishers.

Camey, I., Sabater, L., Owren, C., Boyer, A., & Wen, J. (2020). *Gender-based violence and environment linkages. The violence of inequality.* IUCN: Gland, Switzerland.

Ceceña, A. E. (2014). Del desarrollo al 'vivir bien': la subversión epistémica. In Alicia Girón (Ed.), *Del "vivir bien" al "buen vivir", entre la economía feminista, la filantropía y la migración: hacia la búsqueda de alternativas* (pp. 11–22). IIEc-UNAM.

CELADE & CEPAL. (2013). *Mujeres indígenas en América Latina: dinámicas demográficas y sociales en el marco de los derechos humanos.* CEPAL.

Centeno, M.Á., & Lajous, Á. (2013). *Challenges for Latin America in the 21st century,* Open Mind. https://www.bbvaopenmind.com/wp-content/uploads/2018/03/BBVA-OpenMind-Miguel-Angel-Centeno-Andres-Lajous-Challenges-for-Latin-America-in-the-21st-Century.pdf

Central America Regional Climate Change Project. (2018). *USAID Fact sheet,* USAID. https://www.usaid.gov/sites/default/files/documents/1862/Fact_Sheet-_Central_America_Regional_Climate_Change_Project.pdf

CEPAL & Patrimonio Natural. (2013). *Amazonia posible y sostenible.* Comisión Económica para América Latina y el Caribe (CEPAL).

CEPAL (2019a). *CEPALSTAT, Bases de Datos y Publicaciones Estadísticas.* https://estadisticas.cepal.org/cepalstat/web_cepalstat/estadisticasindicadores.asp

CEPAL (2019b). *Nudos críticos del desarrollo social inclusivo en América Latina y el Caribe: antecedentes para una agenda regional.* CEPAL.

CEPAL (2020). *Los pueblos indígenas de América Latina – Abya Yala y la Agenda 2030 para el Desarrollo Sostenible.* CEPAL.

CEPAL (2021a). *La autonomía económica de las mujeres en la recuperación sostenible y con igualdad.* CEPAL.

CEPAL (2021b). *El impacto social de la pandemia en América Latina.* CEPAL.

Climate Risk Profile Mexico. (2017). *USAID Fact sheet.* https://www.climatelinks.org/sites/default/files/asset/document/2017_USAID_Climate%20Change%20Risk%20Profile_Mexico.pdf

Collin, L. (2020). Economía local y diversa, una opción resiliente, sustentable de trabajo digno. In Ú. Oswald et al. (Eds.), Transformando al mundo y a México. Objetivos de Desarrollo Sostenible 2030 (pp. 117–140). CRIM-UNAM.

D'Eaubonne, F. (1974). *Le Féminisme ou la Mort.* Pierre Horay.

ECLAT. (2020). *Facing the challenge of COVID-19.* ECLAT.

FAO. (2013). *Climate smart agriculture. Sourcebook.* FAO.

FAO. (2015). *Status of world's soil resources.* FAO.

FAO. (2016). *Climate change and food security: Risks and responses.* FAO.

FAO. (2017). *Global Campaign for the empowerment of indigenous women for zero hunger.* FAO.

FAO. (2018a). *Ecosystem services & biodiversity (ESB),* http://www.fao.org/ecosystem-services-biodiversity/valuation/en/

FAO. (2018b). *The State of Food Security and Nutrition in the World 2018b. Building climate resilience for food security and nutrition.* FAO, IFAD, UNICEF, WFP, & WHO.

Fearnside, P. M. (2000). Global warming & tropical land-use change: Greenhouse gas emissions from biomass burning, decomposition, and soils in forest conversion, shifting cultivation and secondary vegetation. *Climatic Change, 46,* 115–158. https://doi.org/10.1023/A:1005569915357.

Tepper, T. (2020). Milton Friedman on the social responsibility of business, 50 years later. *Forbes Advisor.* https://www.forbes.com/advisor/investing/milton-friedman-social-responsibility-of-business/

Freire, P. (2005). *Pedagogy of freedom: Ethics, democracy, and civic courage.* University of Massachusetts.

González, C. P. (2003a). *Colonialismo interno. Una redefinición.* IIS-UNAM.

González, C. P. (2003b). Los 'Caracoles' zapatistas: redes de resistencia y autonomía, *Memoria, 176,* 14–19.

Hernández, A. J. F. et al. (2019). Sistemas de advertencia temprana por puntaje. Early Warning Scores (EWS). *Acta Medica Grupo Ángeles, 17*(3), 252–258.

Hernández, O. M. (2019). *Caravana de migrantes centroamericanos en Reynosa y Matamoros 2019.* El Colegio de la Frontera Norte.

Ibarra Sarlat, R. Ed. (2018). *Cambio climático y gobernanza. Una visión transdisciplinaria.* IIJ-UNAM.

ILO. (1989). *C169-indigenous and tribal peoples convention.* International Labour Organization (ILO).

INEGI. (2021). *Censo de Población y Vivienda 2020.* National Institute of Statistics and Geography (INEGI).

INPE (2021). La deforestación en la Amazonía aumentó un 21,9% en 12 meses. National Institute for Space Research (INPE). https://agenciabrasil.ebc.com.br/es/geral/noticia/2021-11/la-defore stacion-en-la-amazonia-aumento-un-219-en-12-meses.

IPCC. (2014). *Climate Change 2014: Impacts, Adaptation, and Vulnerability. Working Group II Contribution to the IPCC Fifth Assessment Report.* Cambridge University Press.

IPCC. (2019). *Special report on climate change and land.* Cambridge University Press.

IPCC. (2021). *AR6 climate change 2021: The physical science basis.* Cambridge University Press, & IPCC.

IPCC. (2019). *Global warming 1.5 °C.* Cambridge University Press, & IPCC.

IRENA. (2021). *World Energy Transition Outlook. 1.5°C.* International Renewable Energy Agency (IRENA).

ITUC Frontlines Report. (2016). *Why is the global business model in such bad shape?* https://www.ituc-csi.org/IMG/pdf/pdffrontlines_scandal_en-2.pdf

Jelin, E. (2021). Género, etnicidad/raza y ciudadanía en las sociedades de clases. *Realidades históricas, aproximaciones analíticas, Nueva Sociedad, 293,* 39–62.

Kirchhoff, P. (1943). *Mesoamérica, clasificaciones geográficas, composición étnica.* Instituto Nacional de Antropología e Historia. Republished (2000) in *Dimensión Antropológica, 19,* May–August, 15–32.

Lagarde, M. (1999). *Una mirada feminista en el umbral del milenio.* Instituto de Estudios de la Mujer, UN-San José.

Lehmann, C. E. R., Anderson, T. M., Sankaran, M., Higgins, S. I., Archibald, S., Hoffmann, W. A., Hanan, N. P., Williams, R. J., Fensham, R. J., Felfili, J., Hutley, L. B., Ratnam, J., San Jose, J., Franklin, R., Montes, D., Russell-Smith, J., Ryan, C. M., Durigan, G., Hiernaux, P., Haidar, R., Bowman, D. M. J. S. & Bond, W. J. (2014). Savanna vegetation-fire climate relationships differ among continents. *Science, 343*(6170), 548–552.

Marengo, J. A., Borma, L. S., Rodriguez, D. A., Pinho, P., Soares, W. R., & Alves, L. A. (2013). Recent extremes of drought and flooding in Amazonia: Vulnerabilities and human adaptation. *American Journal of Climate Change, 2,* 87–96. https://doi.org/10.4236/ajcc.2013.22009.

Marengo, J. A., Souza, C. A., Thonicke, K., Burton, C., Halladay, K., Betts, R., Soares, W. R. (2018a). Changes in climate and land use over the Amazon Region: Current and future variability and trends. *Frontiers in Earth Science, 6,* 228. https://doi.org/10.3389/feart.2018.00228.

Marengo, J. A., Alves, L. M., Alvala, R. Cunha, A. P., Brito, S., Moraes, O. L. (2018b). Climatic characteristics of the 2010-2016 drought in the semiarid Northeast Brazil region. *Anais da Academia Brasileira de Ciências, 90*(2), 1973–1985.

Le Masson, V., Lim, S., Budimir, M., & Podboj, J. S. (2016). *Disasters and violence against women and girls.* ODI.

Menchú, R. (2004). Culturas Indígenas, Cosmovisión y Futuro. In Ú. Oswald-Spring (Ed.), *Resolución noviolenta en sociedades indígenas y minorías* (pp. 49–62). Coltlax.

Millennium Ecosystem Assessment. (2005). *Ecosystems and the human well-being.* UNDP.

Moreno, J. M., Laguna Defior, C., Calvo Buendía, E., Marengo, J. A., & Oswald, Ú. (2020). Adaptation to climate change risks in Ibero-American countries—RIOCCADAPT Report. McGraw-Hill.

Muñoz, N. B., Sánchez, M. L., & León, F. N. (2018). Riesgos y conflictos socioambientales en Colombia y México. In Ú. Oswald, & S.E. Serrano (Eds.) Riesgos socioambientales, paz y seguridad en América Latina (pp. 123–138), CRIM-UNAM.

OCHA. (2020). *Annual report 2020*. OCHA.

Oswald-Spring, Ú., Serrano, S. E., & Estrada A., et al. (2014). *Vulnerabilidad Social y Género entre Migrantes Ambientales*. CRIM-DGAPA-UNAM.

Oswald-Spring, Ú. (2012). Vulnerabilidad social en eventos hidrometeorológicos extremos: una comparación entre los huracanes Stan y Wilma en México, *Revista Internacional de Ciencias Sociales y Humanidades. Sociotam, 22*(2), 125–145.

Oswald-Spring, Ú. (2013). Dual vulnerability among female household heads. *Acta Colombiana de Psicología, 16*(2), 19–30. https://doi.org/10.41718/ACP.2013.16.2.2

Oswald-Spring, Ú. (2020). *Earth at risk in the 21st century. Rethinking peace, environment, gender and human, water, health, food energy security, and migration*. Springer Nature Switzerland.

Oxfam. (2021). *The inequality virus. Bringing together a world torn apart by coronavirus through a fair, just and sustainable economy*. Oxfam.

Pedrero, M. (2018). *El trabajo y su medición: mis tiempos. antología de estudio sobre trabajo y género*. Universidad Nacional Autónoma de México.

Prieto Díaz, S. (2021). Reordenamientos fronterizos en el Sur de México: hacia un nuevo vórtice de (in)movilidades humanas. *Nexos, 5*. https://migracion.nexos.com.mx/2021/05/reordenamientos-fronterizos-en-el-sur-de-mexico-hacia-un-nuevo-vortice-de-inmovilidades-humanas/.

Raygorodetsky, G. (2018) Indigenous peoples defend Earth's biodiversity—but they're in danger, *National Geographic*, 16 November, https://www.nationalgeographic.com/environment/2018/11/can-indigenous-land-stewardship-protect-biodiversity-/.

Reardon, B. (1985). *Sexism and the war system*. New York.

Sánchez, B. E., & Urueña, R. (2017). Colombian Development-Induced Displacement – Considering the Impact of International Law on Domestic Policy. *Groningen Journal of International Law, 5*(1), 73–95.

Serrano Oswald, S. E. (2009). The impossibility of securitizing gender visFobe à vis 'Engendering' Security. In H. G. Brauch, et al. (Eds.), *Facing global environmental change: Environmental, human, energy, food, health and water security concepts* (pp. 1143–1156). Springer.

Serrano Oswald, S. E. (Ed.). (2021). *Diseño de una metodología triangulada de indicadores cualitativos y cuantitativos, que evalúe la prevalencia de la violencia política por razón de género en México y su impacto en el ejercicio de los derechos políticos de las candidatas a puestos de elección popular en el proceso electoral federal 2020–2021*. CRIM-UNAM-INE.

SIPRI (2021). *SIPRI Yearbook 2007: Armaments, Disarmament and International Security*. Oxford University Press.

Spalding, M. D., Fox, H. E., Allen, G. R., Davidson, N., Ferdaña, Z. A., Finlayson, M., Halpern, B. S., Jorge, M. A., Lombana, A., Lourie, S. A., Martin, K. D., McManus, E., Molnar, J., Recchia, C. A., & Robertson, J. (2007). Marine ecoregions of the world: A bioregionalization of coastal and shelf areas. *BioScience, 57*(7), 573–583. https://doi.org/10.1641/B570707

Stavenhagen, R. (2012). *Peasants, culture and indigenous peoples: Critical issues* (Vol. 4). Springer Science & Business Media.

Steffen, W., Rockström, J., Richardson, K., Lenton, T. M., Folke, C., Liverman, D., Summerhayes, C.P., Barnosky, A.D., Cornell, S.E., Crucifix, M., & Donges, J.F. (2018). Trajectories of the Earth System in the Anthropocene. *Proceedings of the National Academy of Sciences, 115*(33), 8252–8259. https://doi.org/10.1073/pnas.1810141115.

Stiglitz, J. (2007). *Globalisation and its Discontent*. Norton.

Stiglitz, J. (2010). *Freefall: America, free markets, and the sinking of the world economy*. W.W. Norton.

Strahm, R. H., & Oswald Spring, Ú. (1990). *Por Esto Somos Tan Pobres*. UNAM-CRIM.

UN. (2007). *International Expert Group Meeting on the Convention on Biological Diversity's International Regime on Access and Benefit-Sharing and Indigenous Peoples' Human Rights.* 17–19th of January, PFII/2007/WS.4/4. UN.

UNDP. (1994). *Human development report 1994.* UNDP.

UNDP. (2017). *Human development report 2017.* UNDP.

UNDP. (2020). *Human development report 2013.* UNDP.

UNEP WCMC. (2010). *State of biodiversity in Latin America and the Caribbean.* UNEP. https://www.cbd.int/gbo/gbo4/outlook-grulac-en.pdf.

UNEP. (2017) *The adaptation gap report 2017.* In A. Olhoff, H. Neufeldt, P. Naswa, & K. Dorkenoo (Eds.). UNEP.

UNEP. (2020). *Building an inclusive, sustainable and resilient future with indigenous people: A call for action.* UNEP. https://unsceb.org/building-inclusive-sustainable-and-resilient-future-indigenous-peoples-call-action.

UNICEF-Gain. (2018). Brighter futures: Protecting early brain development through salt iodization—The UNICEF-GAIN partnership project. UNICEF.

UNISDR. (2009). *Terminology of disaster risk reduction.* UNISDR.

Ulate, G. V. (2001). Las lluvias en América Central: una climatología geográfica. *Anuario de Estudios Centroamericanos,* 7–19.

Van Evera, S. (1999). *Causes of War Power and the Roots of Conflict.* Cornell University Press.

Vaughan, G. (2004). *The gift* (p. 8). Meltemi, University of Bari, New Series.

Vaughan, G. (1997). *For-giving: A feminist criticisms of exchange.* Plain View Press.

Yup de León, D. (2021). Análisis espacial de violencia homicida en la región norte de Centroamérica (2019–2020). *Revista Latinoamericana, Estudios de la Paz y el Conflicto, 2*(4), 99–114.

Zapatista. (1994). *Ejército Zapatista de Liberación Nacional (EZLN).* http://www.ezln.org.mx/

Reflections of the Climate Justice Framework in Public Policies: The Bangladesh Perspective

S. M. Kamrul Hassan, Niaz Ahmed Khan, and Nashmiya Khanam

1 Introduction

Notwithstanding the growing interest in the different aspects of justice in the realm of climate change, the concept and practice of Climate Justice (CJ) defy any universally accepted definition and standard. The idea of CJ also remains bedevilled with conceptual ramifications. Against the backdrop of strikingly limited research on the subject, especially in the context of Bangladesh, this study aims to examine the nature and characteristics of CJ by scrutinizing the key climate and relevant policy documents.

After this prologue, in what follows, the discussion is organized into five sections. The second section sets out the methodological considerations of the study. The concepts and connotations of CJ are reviewed in the third section based on the secondary literature and a desk review of official documents. The fourth section attempts to develop an analytical framework for this study that may be used to address the main objective of the research, i.e., exploring climate justice in the Bangladesh context. The fifth section contains the core of the analysis. Drawing on the analytical framework, it dissects the key relevant policy documents, namely Bangladesh Climate Change Strategy and Action Plan (BCCSAP) 2009, National Plan for Disaster Management (NPDM) 2021–2025, and Standing Orders on Disaster (SoD) 2019 in order to examine the nature and characteristics of CJ as manifested

---

S. M. K. Hassan (✉)
Department of Disaster Science and Climate Resilience, University of Dhaka, Dhaka, Bangladesh
e-mail: shikdar.kamrul@yahoo.com

N. A. Khan
Department of Development Studies, University of Dhaka, Dhaka, Bangladesh

Independent University, Bangladesh (IUB), Dhaka, Bangladesh

N. Khanam
Department of Economics, University of Chittagong, Chittagong, Bangladesh

© The Author(s), under exclusive license to Springer Nature Singapore Pte Ltd. 2022
D. Madhanagopal et al. (eds.), *Environment, Climate, and Social Justice*,
https://doi.org/10.1007/978-981-19-1987-9_8

in these documents.[1] The concluding section summarizes the main observations and arguments of the study and ends with an exhortation to further research on this relatively less explored area of study.

2 The Methodological Considerations of the Study

The major methods used in this research include secondary literature review, documentary research, and discourse analysis. A review of secondary materials is considered of primary importance for nearly all categories of academic research (Frankfort-Nachmias and Nachmias 1992). The principal sources of secondary materials for this study include relevant journal articles and book chapters. In the following May (2011), documentary research was considered useful for the purpose of this study. The rationale for the deployment of this method is as follows: the selected government documents represent the mainstay of climate and environment policy discourse in Bangladesh, and 'they can tell us a great deal about the way in which events are constructed, the reasons employed, as well as providing materials upon which to base research investigations' (May, 2011, p. 191). In scrutinizing the selected policy documents, a 'discourse analysis' was attempted based mainly on Khan (2009). Put simply, here, a 'discourse' perspective on policy refers to a way of talking about policy and conducting policy analysis, and 'a particular way of thinking and arguing' about policy' (Khan, 2009, p. 4).

This study makes the claim of being exhaustive in its treatment of all the complex dynamics and dimensions of CJ as manifested in the relevant policy documents of the operation of the projects and associated institutions. The duration of the study was short, and the resources were limited. This is intended to be an initial attempt in understanding the subject (i.e., the nature and characteristics of CJ as manifested in the key policy documents of Bangladesh) with the hope of instigating and inspiring further research on this relatively less explored area of study.

3 The Concept and Connotations of Climate Justice: An Overview

The past 20 years have observed a seismic shift in the environmental movements. More attention is given to climate change-related phenomena and their inequitable impacts on vulnerable communities (Schlosberg & Collins, 2014).Climate change is already on the agenda for many marginalized people concerned with protecting their social and economic rights (Pettit, 2004). Consequently, climate justice has taken place once ruled by the theories and concerns of environmental justice. The

---

[1] These abbreviations will be used mostly hereafter instead of the full names of those policies.

new subject matter of climate justice has experienced intense debates and discussions, which are ever-growing. The idea of CJ has played significant roles in shaping the United Nations Framework Convention on Climate Change (UNFCCC), its Kyoto Protocol, and the global treaty signed in Paris in December 2015 (Okereke & Coventry, 2016). The CJ framework is also very complicated, which involves multiple dimensions, and varies across contexts. Yet, the application of the principles of CJ is very significant for a humanity facing the consequences of climate change.

The sixth assessment report of the Intergovernmental Panel on Climate Change (IPCC) has revealed that human interventions are unequivocally responsible for the increases of the Green House Gas (GHG) concentration in the atmosphere (Intergovernmental Panel on Climate Change, 2021). It is evident that the warming from anthropogenic emissions from the pre-industrial period to the present will persist and continue to cause further long-term changes in the climate system. Paradoxically, those who contributed least to Green House Gas (GHG) emissions have become the most affected adversely by the impacts of climate change (Anderson, 2013). The ideal and moral solution to this problem was supposed to rely on differentiated burden-sharing responsibilities by the countries of the world (United Nations, 1992). This has led to the rise of the principles of equity and justice in the climate change negotiations today. But the conceptual confusion on justice, pressures from grass-root climate movements, and the presence of international climate politics have complicated the current scenario. A thorough analysis of the development of the concept of climate justice and finding out the key attributes of the climate justice framework are therefore necessary.

4 Evolution of the Concept of Climate Justice

A probe into the conceptual history reveals two major perspectives under the domain of climate justice. The theoretical/institutional aspect of CJ has developed through research, analysis, seminar, conference in academia, and research organizations. On the other hand, the empirical/political side of this concept has developed through movements and dialogues. Yet, both of them have simultaneously grown out of environmental justice during the 1970s and 1980s, and it is difficult to exactly identify which started when (Alam, 2019; Burkett, 2008; Saraswat & Kumar, 2016; Schlosberg & Collins, 2014).

The primary foundation of the concept of climate justice, both in academia and politics, was laid based upon the principle of differentiation in terms of suffering from the adverse impacts of climate change. It was apparent during the 1980s that the global temperature was rising, and the ozone layer depletion was a major proof of this change in climatic conditions. The increasing concentration of GHG in the atmosphere had led to such changes, and the developed countries were found to be responsible for the emission of higher volumes of GHG. However, it was also evident that the environmental and climatic changes had disproportionately affected the communities. This condition coincided with the existing environmental justice movement in the United States (US). The persistence of racism in American society and the disproportionate exposure of African American, Latino/a, Native American, and Asian American communities to environmental hazards had been the major focus of the US movement for environmental justice (Tokar, 2018). The principle of differentiation started to receive huge international momentum during that period. There were increasing calls for international climate justice, north–south equity, and exemplary leadership from the developed countries. The IPCC was established in 1988, and the assessment reports of the IPCC started to produce global impacts at the policy-making levels. In academic literature, E B Weiss first used the term climate justice in 1989, in a book titled 'Climate change, intergenerational equity and international law: An introductory note'. The report mainly focused on the necessity to augment international law by the principles of intergenerational equity (Alam, 2019).

During the 1990s, the references to the intersection of justice and climate reached a greater height (Schlosberg & Collins, 2014). The IPCC published a response strategy to climate change in 1990. The report mentioned that industrialized countries have specific responsibilities in climate change, and it noted that 'a major part of emissions affecting the atmosphere at present originates in industrialized countries where the scope for change is greatest' (Intergovernmental Panel on Climate & Change, 1990, p. xxvi). In 1992, the UNFCCC (the Convention) was adopted in the Rio Earth Summit by 194 countries as the basis of the global response to humanly induced climate change. The UNFCCC aimed to stabilize the GHG emissions at a safer level which will prevent dangerous human interference with the climate system (Royal Irish Academy, 2011). Article 3.1 of the convention fine-tuned the principle of differentiation with the 'Common But Differentiated Responsibility' (CBDR) principle (United Nations, 1992). Since then, the CBDR principle has been the greatest source of reference for climate justice research as well as movement. The developments following the convention, mainly the Conference of Parties (COP), have played a crucial role in shaping the principles of justice in the climate regime. The dialogues have created contentions and confusions over several articles of the UNFCCC. Scientific evidence has been accompanied by international and local climate politics in these gatherings.

In 1999, the organization Corp Watch published a report titled 'Greenhouse Gangsters and Climate Justice', which has been considered by Schlosberg and Collins (2014) and Tokar (2013) as the starting point of reference for the grass-root climate justice movement. The report was mainly an examination of the disproportionate political influence of the petroleum industry, but it also tried to define climate justice from a multifaceted approach. The main focus of the report was the impact of environmental pollution and climate change on poor communities. It emphasized that removing the causes of global warming, fostering a just transition for the low-income communities to a healthier and more just environment to work and live in, and providing assistance to communities threatened or impacted by climate change will ensure climate justice. To achieve justice, according to the report, the World Bank and the World Trade Organization should halt their funding and promotion of corporate-led fossil fuel-based globalization (Bruno et al., 1999). The principles of climate justice declared by several movements and civil society organizations were proactive in nature and demanded immediate actions by focusing on the impacts of climate change on existing poverty and inequality, vulnerable communities, and the unsustainable future path of progress. In the following years, several organizations have ramped up the movement and laid out the principles of climate justice on their own terms. The first climate justice summit at The Hague in 2000, Bali principles of climate justice in 2002, 14 principles of climate justice declaration in 2004, etc., had immediately followed the footsteps of Corp Watch. Like the COPs, a parallel development in the grass-root political conferences and declarations is also noticeable in the regime of climate justice since its inception. The political dimensions of climate justice have actually blended the concerns of people with the science of climate change. This has been accentuated by the climate justice activist Mary Robinson who said, 'Climate justice insists on a shift from a discourse on greenhouse gases and melting ice caps into a civil rights movement with the people and communities most vulnerable to climate impacts at its heart' (United Nations, 2019).

5 The Key Milestones: UNFCCC and the Climate Justice Agenda

The UNFCCC has played a pivotal role in the development of the concept of climate justice. The convention is the first global document in bringing mass attention to the scientific basis for climate change, the role of GHG emissions behind increasing temperature, and its disproportionate impact on developing counties. Different articles under the Convention have identified several principles of climate justice. Article 3.1 states that 'The Parties should protect the climate system based on equity and in accordance with their common but differentiated responsibilities and respective capabilities. The developed country Parties should take the lead in combating climate change and the adverse effects thereof' (United Nations, 1992, p. 4). The whole Convention has consistently emphasized the leadership of the developed countries and the special attention to the developing countries, especially those who are suffering from the adverse consequences of climate change. All the articles under the 3rd and 4th sections of the Convention have referred to this message. The UNFCCC entered into force in 1994, and the first COP took place in 1995 (Table 1).

Several issues of CJ came up in the annual conferences. Khan et al. (2020) identified three major regimes since the beginning of the climate talks under the UNFCCC. Similarly, we can also divide the climate justice timeline under the UNFCCC into three major clusters. They are the Kyoto Regime (1997–2008), the Copenhagen Shift (2009–2014), and Post Paris Period (2015 onwards). Each regime has produced distinct events and turning points which have influenced the principles and movements of CJ.

The Kyoto Regime (1997–2008): The Kyoto protocol was adopted in 1997. It called for the reduction of global GHG emissions by 5% below the 1990 levels during the

Table 1 Evolution of the climate justice agenda

Timeline	Key issues in the climate justice agenda
1960s and 70s	Civil rights movement Social injustice Environmental pollution
1980s	Ozone layer depletion Rising global temperature Disproportionate contribution to GHG emission Differentiated responsibility principle
1990s	Adoption of UNFCCC CBDR Principle Kyoto protocol aims to reduce the GHG emission
2000s	Ongoing debates about the emission quota Mitigation versus adaptation finance issues
2010s	Copenhagen shift Concrete financial contribution by developed countries Look up for a legally binding agreement for GHG emission reduction
2015 and onwards	Paris climate treaty Replacing CBDR with INDC Emission reduction following equity principle

Source Developed by the Authors

period from 2008 to 2012. The protocol mainly emphasized the responsibility of the developed countries in reducing global emissions. It also offered several market-based mechanisms to the developed countries to achieve compliance with their emission reduction targets. The implementation of the Kyoto protocol has been the key issue on the bargaining table since its adoption. Several funds were formed to finance the adaptation and mitigation projects during the Kyoto regime. The Global Environment Facility (GEF) was set up for funding the projects. But the developing countries were skeptical of GEF as it was donor controlled (Khan et al., 2020). This led towards the development of the Least Developed Countries Fund, Special Climate Change Fund, and Adaptation Fund in 2001. The successive conference of the parties negotiated on the implementation of the Kyoto principles and the extension of the protocol beyond 2012.

The Copenhagen Shift (2009–2014): Much hype over a new agreement for the reduction of GHG emissions during the post-Kyoto period developed in Copenhagen in 2009. But in the end, it failed to produce any significant outcomes. However, three major developments took place in Copenhagen. Firstly, Copenhagen green climate fund was set up to subsidize the adaptation and mitigation projects in developing countries with the support of developed countries. The latter promised to provide 30 billion USD for the period 2010–2012 and mobilize long-term finance of a further 100 billion USD a year by 2020 from different sources. Secondly, all of the countries recognized the need to limit the global temperature rise to 2 °C based on the science of climate change. Thirdly, the accord included some developing countries, mainly China, as the implementing party of mitigation strategies. The Copenhagen accord signalled a transformation in the climate change negotiations as well as in the principles of climate justice. Every country was held accountable with individual responsibilities to reduce GHG emissions, not only the developed countries. The CBDR principle was no longer accepted, and after 2012, no effective replacement of the Kyoto protocol took place. At the Warsaw climate change conference of 2013, a consensus was reached on the submission of Intended Nationally Determined Commitments (INDC) by all of the parties. But no other significant developments took place during this period.

Post Paris Period (2015 onwards): In 2015, the Paris agreement broke the stalemate. The agreement implicitly encompassed the concept of CJ and noted the importance of some of the components of 'climate justice' when taking actions to address climate change. The major achievement in Paris was the institutionalization of the INDC by modifying the CBDR principle. The agreement focused on the 'principle of equity and common but differentiated responsibilities and respective capabilities, in the light of different national circumstances' (United Nations, 2015, p. 1). Developing countries were also supposed to play vital roles in the fight against climate change on the basis of their respective capacities. The Paris agreement succeeded in achieving the largest possible participation by introducing enough flexibility to bring all Parties on board, but at the same time, the agreement maintained several aspects of the agreement as legally binding, especially where the process is concerned. It also introduced a new technology framework and new mechanisms as supporting actions for developing and vulnerable countries.

The climate justice agenda in the UNFCCC has been constructed and reconstructed from time to time. From the principle of differentiated responsibilities, it shifted to common but differentiated responsibilities. This has again been replaced by the principle of generalized responsibilities. The climate justice movements have also adapted to the changing circumstances. In the past 28 years, neither academia nor activists have been able to reach any consensual definition of CJ. The dynamic conditions in the ground-level reality can be implicated for such volatility of definitions of CJ. Alam (2019) has come up with an eclectic definition of CJ that integrates the changing nature of this concept as reflected in the proceedings of the COPs. It states climate justice as a vision to dissolve and alleviate the unequal burdens created by climate change. Hence, we can adopt the following definition of CJ:

> As a form of environmental justice, climate justice is the fair treatment of all the people and freedom from discrimination with the creation of policies and projects that address climate change and its systems that create climate change and perpetuate discrimination. (Alam, 2019, p. 6)

6 Exploring Climate Justice: Towards an Analytical Framework

The findings from the COPs' proceedings, analysis of the key literature, and insights from climate movements reflect several dimensions and principles of climate justice despite the absence of any accepted definition of this concept. Three major dimensions of CJ have appeared in most of the literature. The three major dimensions of climate justice are namely distributive justice, procedural justice, and compensatory justice. The purpose of this section is to briefly review these dimensions with a view to developing an analytical framework for this study that may be used to address the main objective of the research, i.e., exploring climate justice in the context of Bangladesh.

6.1 Distributive Justice

Distributive justice is mainly an outcome-based approach, where equity and fairness are considered the guiding principles of distribution (Okereke & Coventry, 2016). Most of the literature on climate finance and restrictions on GHG emissions has mainly focused on the distributive aspects of justice. Hendriks (2017) identified two main theoretical propositions that have guided the discussion of distributive justice in climate finance. The first one is the polluters pay principle. Some authors have also called it the historical responsibility approach. Under this approach, the developed countries should take full responsibility for their past actions and need to pay the affected countries for adaptation and mitigation projects. The second one can be called the carbon egalitarian approach. It emphasizes the fact that some developing countries are currently emitting more GHG than developed countries. For example, China and India were in the top five countries with the highest carbon footprint in 2020. But both the countries are in the Non-Annex II category of the UNFCCC. The carbon egalitarian approach demands the calculation of compensation on the basis of the existing records of GHG emissions.

6.2 Procedural Justice

The idea of distributive justice looks into the redistribution of the benefits as well as burdens of climate change, but the proponents of procedural justice argue that any kind of fair distribution can only be achieved if all affected parties are involved in an equitable decision-making process (Burnham et al., 2013).

The key principles of procedural justice are participation and recognition in the decision-making process. The procedural dimension of justice comes from the bottom-up principle, where people's subjective evaluation of the decision-making process is considered. The absence of participation and recognition can eventually lead to a crisis of legitimacy. Procedural injustice has also been found to be related to the violation of human rights. The domain of procedural justice is much vaster as it encompasses the environmental and social conditions that the individuals, communities, and states need to function, live, and develop (Khan et al., 2020). In the global climate justice movements, the concerns of participation of the developing countries and the recognition of the vulnerability of those countries have been repeated continuously. The principles of climate justice by Mary Robinson Foundation (2015) and the Bali principles of climate justice by the International have also brought up the local levels challenges of CJ and emphasized community participation as one of the major principles to ensure climate justice.

Distributive justice and procedural justice have been considered the building blocks to delivering climate justice. Hendriks (2017), Khan et al. (2020), and Zoffmann and Munk (2018) have emphasized ensuring both of these aspects in the climate regime. But it has been found that the thoughts on distributive justice and procedural justice mainly revolve around the mitigation and adaptation activities in the climate change negotiation process. There is also a growing concern that mitigation and adaptation policies will still not be adequate to address some of the adverse impacts of climate change (Page & Heyward, 2017). In addition, climate change policies and finances can lead towards future unavoidable problems, thus exacerbating the situation and creating future risks. Therefore, individuals and states need access to a structure that holds the international climate regime accountable, both for their past and future activities. The concept of compensatory justice, also called corrective justice, came out of these concerns.

6.3 Compensatory Justice

Compensatory justice is mainly related to concerns of future risk and uncertainty, but it stands upon the principle of democratic accountability (Hendriks, 2017). It emphasizes that people's rights have to be respected and cannot be violated through unplanned activities. If the well-being of people is hampered through climate change, then it has to be restored to what it was like before. In the UNFCCC negotiation process, these concerns were first raised in the Bali Action Plan in 2007 and subsequently led towards the development of the Warsaw International Mechanism (WIM) for Loss and Damage Associated with Climate Change Impacts. Rhaman (2016) points towards the fact that developed countries have inflicted much damage and loss by their past actions, and hence, they should pay compensation for this. However, some of the concerns under compensatory justice are also covered under the principles of distributive justice. Table 2 displays the summary of the climate justice framework. It shows the prominent principles under each of the dimensions of the climate justice framework and then breaks it down into relevant criteria. The 'scale' column shows the level of relevance of each of the dimensions. The analysis of distributive justice mostly circles around the international and national level, while

Table 2 The climate justice framework

Dimensions of climate justice	Principles of climate justice	Relevant criteria	Scale
Distributive	– Equity on the basis of historical responsibility – Equity on the basis of the individual conditions and existing capacities	– Transfer of resources to the most vulnerable in climate injustice – Ratio of mitigation versus adaptation	– Mostly international, national
Procedural	– Social and political recognition – Social and political participation	– Recognition of diversity – Inclusive and participatory decision making process	– Mostly national, local
Compensatory	– Transparency and accountability – No harm principle – Compensation for past actions	– Policy to ensure that activities do not cause harm socially and environmentally – Complaint mechanisms to address injustices – Grievance mechanisms to address inequitable or adverse impacts	– International, national, local

Source Adapted from Hendriks (2017) and Schapper (2018)

the procedural justice agenda is mainly related to national and local level contexts. The compensatory justice is, however, related to local, national, and international levels of analysis.

7 The Bangladesh Perspective: Discourse Analysis of Key Policies

The following section analyses three major policy documents of Bangladesh under the lens of the climate justice framework. The analysis will make an attempt to see if the concerns under the respective dimensions and principles of CJ have been addressed in the legal policy documents of the Government of Bangladesh (GoB). We have selected three main and relevant policies, namely BCCSAP (2009), NPDM (2021–2025), and SoD (2019), for the analysis.

Transforming the dimensions of the climate justice framework into scalable components of any policy document is a novel research idea. There is no exclusive climate justice policy in Bangladesh, and neither do the climate-change-related policies have an exclusive section on climate justice issues. But the dimensions and principles of climate justice can be broken down into relevant criteria. The selected policies will be analysed by comparing with the criteria, and the findings from this analysis can be used to measure the reflection of the climate justice framework in the selected public policies of Bangladesh. For each policy, the analysis looks into the distributive, procedural, and compensatory aspects of climate justice in serial.

7.1 BCCSAP 2009

There are not many guidelines in the BCCSAP regarding the distributive aspects of CJ from an international perspective. Bangladesh, being a developing country, contributes very little to global GHG emissions. BCCSAP recognizes this fact and emphasizes the responsibility of the western and other industrialized countries, who are the major polluters, to pay their due shares. This plan has encouraged the GoB to seek funds from different international sources in order to finance the implementation of adaptation and mitigation projects within the country. In the national context, the plan has laid out numerous guidelines that go hand in hand with the redistributive principles. First of all, it talks about the development of adaptation strategies. It has been mentioned in BCCSAP that 'Adaptation is a priority for Bangladesh in short to medium term. The country is already a world leader in the research, design, and implementation strategies, and this work will continue (Ministry of Environment and Forests, 2009, p. 3)'. The action plan has proposed 44 programs for implementation during the period 2009–2019. Among them, 6 programs are directly entitled to achieve adaptation against different types of hazards and in several productive sectors. There are adaptation projects for drought, flood, tropical cyclone, storm surge, fisheries, livestock, and health sector. Most of these adaptation programs have been included in mainly two thematic areas, namely food security, social protection and health, and infrastructure. In addition to adaptation, BCCSAP focuses on mitigation, institutional capacity building, and human development in order to achieve sustainable development in the country. Previously, the GoB has adopted different mitigation strategies for curbing the rise of global temperature. Social forestry program, plantation of coastal greenbelts, and implementation of Clean Development Mechanism (CDM) projects are some of the mitigation strategies which have been previously implemented by the government. Most of the mitigation projects in BCCSAP fall under the theme titled 'mitigation and low carbon development'. Projects under this theme mainly focus on energy efficiency, low carbon emission, waste management, and forestation-related activities.

The contents of BCCSAP also strongly reflect the principles of procedural climate justice. There have been several instructions in this plan to recognize the vulnerable groups and then about the mechanisms to ensure their participation in the programs.

Originally the report was prepared following the participatory principle. It has been mentioned in the BCCSAP that 'Programmes funded under action plan will be implemented by line ministries and agencies, with participation, as appropriate, of other stakeholder groups continue (Ministry of Environment and Forests, 2009, p. 30)'. Several terminologies, i.e., environmental refugees, poor people, women and children, migrants, slum dwellers, poor households, fishing households, etc. have been used to denote the vulnerable groups. Mapping techniques have been used to identify the hazard-prone areas of Bangladesh. It has been acknowledged in the plan that comprehensive and participatory planning can protect vulnerable groups. However, the mechanisms on the participation of the vulnerable groups in the planning and implementation of the projects are not clear.

Regarding compensatory climate justice, BCCSAP mainly walks the talk in the national context. Several projects under BCCSAP aim to reduce future risk by the development of early warning systems for flood, cyclone, and storm surge, risk management against loss of income and property, repair and maintenance of critical infrastructures like embankments, cyclone shelters, coastal polder, etc. The activities under the theme of research and knowledge management, capacity building, and institutional strengthening are also indirectly linked to reducing future risk. However, the plan does not talk about any accountability mechanism or monitoring framework for the proposed projects.

7.2 NPDM 2021–2025

The NPDM does not talk exclusively about redistributive concerns from either a domestic or international perspective. There is a small section on the Paris agreement and climate change in the plan, but there is no instruction about how to secure climate funding, deal with an emission reduction, or other relevant issues. This section states that 'strengthening the resilience and adaptive capacity of more vulnerable regions such as Bangladesh are emphasized to go with efforts to raise awareness and integrate measures into national policies and strategies (Ministry of Disaster Management and Relief, 2021, p. 18)'. Except for this indirect reference on focusing more on adaptation-related activities, there is no other discussion related to distributive climate justice.

However, the NPDM is the epitome of procedural justice. The plan is laden with clauses on the recognition of vulnerable groups as well as ensuring their participation in the implementation of different kinds of projects. It has been mentioned in the plan that 'NPDM 2016–2020 was prepared in a participatory way, having several consultations with stakeholders and established a way forward of effective partnership with organizations working at local, national and regional levels (Ministry of Disaster Management and Relief, 2021, p. 7)'. Inclusive development is one of the key strategic directions of NPDM. The key element of inclusive development is the sensitivity to gender, disability, age, and other vulnerabilities. The plan proposes 35 activities which have been divided into four priority areas. Most of these activities aim to identify the areas affected by climate change-induced hazards and the vulnerable groups which are facing the risk. Finally, the vulnerable groups are supposed to get involved in different types of risk reduction activities. Some of the prominent activities for recognition and participation of the vulnerable groups are: a review of existing multi-hazard risk assessments, conducting community-based risk assessment, implementing disaster risk reduction integrated/inclusive social safety net program, expansion of disability inclusive Disaster Risk Management (DRM), developing and implementing Risk Reduction Action Plan through Community Risk Assessment and Urban Risk Assessment, developing and implementing National DRM capacity building plan focusing on Disability inclusiveness, developing guidelines for risk-informed private sector investments, etc.

NPDM has updated mechanisms for ensuring democratic accountability and reducing future risk. The plan has various strategies like agency focal point, contingency plans, political consensus, etc., to coordinate the activities among different ministries, departments, research organizations, international donor agencies, NGOs, and the private sector. It proposes several activities, i.e., innovating models for forecasting and warning systems, the institutionalization of the Flood Preparedness Programme, etc., to reduce the losses from future risk. The plan proposes multiple activities for strengthening good governance and developing institutional capacity in the disaster management system of Bangladesh.

7.3 SOD 2019

The SoD provides limited information on the distributional aspects of climate justice at the national level. It has instructions for some ministries and departments of the GoB to follow adaptation strategies. Department of Disaster Management and Ministry of Disaster Management and Relief are ordained with the responsibility of conducting research on developing strategies for adaptation to any new hazard, impacts of climate change, and implementation of related projects. There are also some generalized guidelines for the Department of Environment and Department of Agricultural Extension to develop expertise in disaster risk reduction and climate change adaptation. SoD does not provide the details of the activities for adaptation or mitigation or any instructions about dealing with the redistributive issues of climate change impacts at the international level.

However, the contents of SoD reflect many of the aspects of procedural climate justice. The document itself has been formulated in a participatory way, and the only way for the successful implementation of SoD is through participation and coordination. Every responsible ministry has to participate in inter-ministerial meetings or coordination activities. The activities of the disaster management committees and ministries/departments/agencies of GoB emphasize the identification of physical risk and vulnerable groups. Afterward, the risk reduction and emergency response plans have to be developed in a participatory way. Even the physical risk identification process relies on participatory practice. For example, the divisional committees have to develop a list of the at-risk population with local maps based on the information received from Upazila. The short, medium, and long-term emergency response plans have to be developed by involving the local communities and vulnerable groups. The vulnerability has been identified with respect to gender, age, people with disabilities, social class, occupation, economic status, ethnicity, etc.

The ultimate objective of SoD is to promote good governance and accountability in the overall disaster management cycle of Bangladesh. It provides guidelines in order to maintain harmony between the activities of different committees and ministries during the emergency as well as normal periods. The superior committees and agencies have to look after the local level committees and agencies. The local entities also have to provide regular feedback to the national-level entities. This kind of practice helps to maintain check and balance within the government. In order to ensure accountability, every ministry is supposed to have a focal point that will smoothly coordinate the activities with other agencies. In addition, every ministry/agency needs to individually assess the impact of different hazards on its own activities. There are several guidelines in the SoD to integrate climate change issues and follow the Disaster Impact Assessment (DIA) method as well as build back better principles while preparing the development plans. The distinct aspect of SoD is that there is a specialized national-level committee for disaster damage and loss assessment. The committee regularly updates the SOS and D forms which are used to collect information on disaster damage and loss. The local-level disaster management committees and several ministries receive the updated guidelines from the national-level damage and loss assessment committee on the use of these forms. The document also mentions the necessity of providing economic and psycho-social support for disaster-affected people. Table 3 provides the summary of the findings of the discourse analysis of the policies.

The discourse analysis reveals that the principles of procedural and compensatory justice have been reflected in all of the three policies. As BCCSAP is directly related to the climate change issue, the distributive aspect of climate justice was found to be more present in this policy in comparison to the other two policies. BCCSAP focused both on the national and international issues of distributive justice. The GoB has been guided to bargain for international climate funds while implementing adaptation and mitigation projects at home. NPDM narrowly touches on this aspect of CJ, and SoD briefly talks about some of the adaptation issues in the national context. It has been evident from the analysis that the procedural aspect of climate justice is highly related to the national and local level perspectives. Recognition and participation of the vulnerable groups are the major components of ensuring procedural justice. The policy analysis has found a colossal amount of reference on the recognition, inclusion, and participation of vulnerable communities from all across the country in the matters of development project formulation as well as implementation. However, the real challenge to delivering justice, in the procedural aspect, is the actual materialization of the guidelines in the empirical context. The compensatory aspect of CJ is related to both the national as well as international context. This discourse analysis did not find any reference to the compensation issues in international context; rather, the policies have focused on national and local issues.

Reflections of the Climate Justice Framework in Public … 157

Table 3 Summary of the findings

CJ dimensions →	Distributive	Procedural	Compensatory
BCCSAP	Fund-seeking diplomacy Adaptation projects Mitigation projects	NGO and CSO involvement Physical risk assessment Vulnerability assessment	Climate monitoring and hazards forecasting Institutional capacity strengthening
NPDM	Fund-seeking diplomacy Promotes climate change adaptation	Stakeholder consultation Physical risk assessment Community-based risk assessment Gender sensitive	Accountability and monitoring framework Institutional capacity development
SoD	Sparse guidelines on adaptation Mainstreaming climate change and disaster risk reduction	Inclusive Physical risk assessment Participatory risk assessment	Good governance Damage and loss assessment Financial and psycho-social compensation Build back better

Source Developed by the Authors

Emphasis has been put on the promotion of good governance in order to ensure democratic accountability and reduce the future risk from climate change-induced hazards as well as other hazards. The SoD gave in more weight to the compensatory aspect of climate justice. NPDM and BCCSAP also had extensive clauses related to the principles of compensatory justice. Hence the comparative analysis reveals that distributive justice has mainly been marshalled in BCCSAP, procedural justice has mostly been prioritized in NPDM, and compensatory justice has been entertained in large part in SoD. Table 3 provides a quick overview of the findings from this discourse analysis.

8 Epilogue

This study aims to find out the reflections and revelations of climate justice in the major public policies of Bangladesh. The analytical framework of climate justice has fissioned the concept into scalable components. In light of the framework, we subsequently carried out the discourse analysis on the basis of the fundamental components of climate justice. There is no exclusive policy for climate justice in Bangladesh, and there has hitherto been no such scholarly venture to look for the reflections of the components of climate justice in the public policies of the country. This analysis has found the simultaneous presence of all the components, albeit in different scales and degrees, in all three policies. We cannot, however, answer whether the principles of climate justice have been delivered to the people affected by climate change-induced hazards just by looking at the outcomes of our discourse analysis. Much of the success in ensuring climate justice rests on the practical actions of the policymakers and executive branch officials of GoB. It also requires intensive advocacy by grassroot development organizations on this matter. Whether it is happening or not—can only be known by conducting further research in this novel arena; as at present, our knowledge on the subject is grossly inadequate.

References

Alam, A. (2019). *Climate justice and its impact on Bangladesh* [Doctoral thesis, University of Southern Queensland]. USQ ePrints. https://eprints.usq.edu.au/36814/

Anderson, S. (2013). *Climate justice and international development: Policy and programming* [Policy briefing]. International Institute for Environment and Development (IIED). https://pubs.iied.org/17170iied

Bruno, K., Karliner, J., & Brotsky, C. (1999). *Greenhouse gangsters versus climate justice.* Corpwatch. http://www.corpwatch.org/sites/default/files/Greenhouse%20Gangsters.pdf

Burkett, M. (2008). Just solutions to climate change: A climate justice proposal for a domestic clean development mechanism. *Buffalo Law Review, 56*(1), 169–243.

Burnham, M., Radel, C., Ma, Z., & Laudati, A. (2013). Extending a geographic lens towards climate justice, part 1: Climate change characterization and impacts. *Geography Compass, 7*(3), 239–248. https://doi.org/10.1111/gec3.12034

Frankfort-Nachmias, C., & Nachmias, D. (1992). *Research methods in the social sciences.* Martin's Press.

Hendriks, D. (2017). *Is distributive justice sufficient for a climate finance regime? A climate justice based approach to climate funds.* [Master's dissertation] Institut Barcelona d'Estudis Internacionals(IBEI). https://www.ibei.org/ibei_studentpaper41_105369.pdf

Intergovernmental Panel on Climate & Change. (1990). *Climate change: The IPCC response strategies.* [Working group III report for the first assessment report of the Intergovernmental Panel on Climate Change]. https://www.ipcc.ch/site/assets/uploads/2018/03/ipcc_far_wg_III_full_report.pdf

Intergovernmental Panel on Climate Change. (2021). *Climate change 2021: The physical science basis* [Contribution of working group I to the sixth assessment report of the Intergovernmental Panel on Climate Change]. https://www.ipcc.ch/report/ar6/wg1/downloads/report/IPCC_AR6_WGI_Full_Report.pdf

Khan, M., Robinson, S., Weikmans, R., Ciplet, D., & Roberts, J. T. (2020). Twenty-five years of adaptation finance through a climate justice lens. *Climatic Change, 161*(2), 251–269. https://doi.org/10.1007/s10584-019-02563-x

Khan, N. A. (2009). *More than meets the eye: Re-reading forest policy discourse in Bangladesh.*[Working Paper Series 177]. Queen Elizabeth House, University of Oxford. http://workingpapers.qeh.ox.ac.uk/RePEc/qeh/qehwps/qehwps177.pdf

Mary Robinson Foundation. (2015). *Principles of climate justice.* https://www.mrfcj.org/wp-content/uploads/2015/09/Principles-of-Climate-Justice.pdf

May, T. (2011). *Social research: Issues, methods and process.* Open University Press.

Ministry of Disaster Management and Relief. (2021). *National plan for disaster management (2021–2025).* Government of the People's Republic of Bangladesh. https://modmr.portal.gov.bd/sites/default/files/files/modmr.portal.gov.bd/page/a7c2b9e1_6c9d_4ecf_bb53_ec74653e6d05/NPDM%202021-2025%20Draft.pdf

Ministry of Environment and Forests. (2009). *Bangladesh climate change strategy and action plan 2009*. Government of the People's Republic of Bangladesh. https://moef.gov.bd/site/page/97b 0ae61-b74e-421b-9cae-f119f3913b5b/BCCSAP-2009

Okereke, C., & Coventry, P. (2016). Climate justice and the international regime: Before, during, and after Paris. *Wires Climate Change, 7*(6), 834–851. https://doi.org/10.1002/wcc.419

Page, E. A., & Heyward, C. (2017). Compensating for climate change loss and damage. *Political Studies, 65*(2), 356–372. https://doi.org/10.1177/0032321716647401

Pettit, J. (2004). Climate justice: A new social movement for atmospheric rights. *IDS Bulletin, 35*(3), 102–106. https://doi.org/10.1111/j.1759-5436.2004.tb00142.x

Rhaman, M. (2016). Climate justice framing in Bangladeshi newspapers, 2007–2011. *Journal of South Asia Research, 36*(2), 186–205. https://doi.org/10.1177/0262728016638717

Royal Irish Academy. (2011). *The geography of climate justice*. https://www.ria.ie/reports/geosci ences-and-geographical-sciences-committee-reports

Saraswat, C., & Kumar, P. (2016). Climate justice in lieu of climate change: A sustainable approach to respond to the climate change injustice and an awakening of the environmental movement. *Energy, Ecology and Environment, 1*(2), 67–74. https://doi.org/10.1007/s40974-015-0001-8

Schapper, A. (2018). Climate justice and human rights. *International Relations, 32*(3), 275–295. https://doi.org/10.1177/0047117818782595

Schlosberg, D., & Collins, L. B. (2014). From environmental to climate justice: Climate change and the discourse of environmental justice. *Wires Climate Change, 5*(3), 359–374. https://doi.org/10. 1002/wcc.275

Tokar, B. (2013). Movements for climate justice in the Us and worldwide. In M. Dietz & H. Garrelts (Eds.), *Routledge handbook of the climate change movement* (1st ed., pp., 131–146). Routledge. https://doi.org/10.4324/9780203773536

Tokar, B. (2018). On the evolution and continuing development of the climate justice movement. In T. Jafry, M. Mikulewicz, & K. Helwig (Eds.), *Routledge handbook of climate justice* (1st ed., pp., 13–25). Routledge. https://doi.org/10.4324/9781315537689

United Nations. (1992). *United nations framework convention on climate change*. https://unfccc. int/resource/docs/convkp/conveng.pdf

United Nations. (2015). Paris agreement. https://unfccc.int/sites/default/files/english_paris_agre ement.pdf

United Nations. (2019, May 31). Climate justice. *United Nations Sustainable Development Blogs*. https://www.un.org/sustainabledevelopment/blog/2019/05/climate-justice/

Zoffmann, M., & Munk, T. S. (2018, July 6). *Climate justice: An important component of climate adaptation projects*. Ramboll Group. https://ramboll.com/ingenuity/climate-justice

Climate Risks in an Unequal Society: The Question of Climate Justice in India

Devendraraj Madhanagopal and Vidya Ann Jacob

1 Introduction: Climate Change and Its Urgency

The continuous advancement of fossil fuel industrialization and its resulting anthropogenic activities has had a massive impact on the changing trends of Earth's climatic change (Stocker et al., 2013). Recent research has shown that the global average temperature has drastically increased due to human activities, approximately 1.5 °C since the pre-industrial period (IPCC, 2018a). With the current trends of the surge in temperatures, there will be a massive temperature rise that will reach 1.5 °C between 2030 and 2052 (IPCC, 2018b). Climate change, a global phenomenon, has had multiple implications on development and growth worldwide over the past few decades (Rosencranz et al., 2010). Though climate change is a global phenomenon, the impacts are disproportionately felt by the less developed nations and regions worldwide (Stocker et al., 2013), widening already existing socioeconomic inequities within and between countries. Climate change impacts disproportionally affect the populations of the developing and underdeveloped nations, who are more dependent on climate-sensitive resources for their livelihoods. They are already disadvantaged due to their socioeconomic status and living standards (World Social Report, 2020). To counter this, climate inequity challenges have been an essential discussion of international climate negotiations in recent years and decades (Islam & Winkel, 2017).

The global discussions on "climate justice' within the broader area of "environmental justice" promote issues and mechanisms to foster both sustainability and equity concerning climate challenges (EJnet, 2002). The growing evidence has warned that by 2030, India would lose around 34 million full-time jobs (ILO, 2019),

---

D. Madhanagopal (✉)
School of Sustainability, XIM University, Odisha, India
e-mail: devendraraj.mm@gmail.com

V. A. Jacob
School of Law, Christ University, Bangalore, Karnataka, India

© The Author(s), under exclusive license to Springer Nature Singapore Pte Ltd. 2022
D. Madhanagopal et al. (eds.), *Environment, Climate, and Social Justice*,
https://doi.org/10.1007/978-981-19-1987-9_9

resulting in tremendous setbacks in achieving poverty reduction, sustainability, and social and environmental justice. Needless to say, the poor are the most vulnerable to climate change effects, and hence, there is a strong need to ensure policy measures are taken at the local, state, and national levels to render climate justice. The major concepts of climate justice include fairness or equity, human rights, and sustainability (Chauhan, 2019).

India, one of the most densely populated developing nations in South Asia, is largely prone to the adverse effects of climate change, including heatwaves, cyclones, and droughts (Sivakumar & Stefanski, 2011; van Oldenborgh et al., 2018; Mehta et al., 2019; Krishnan et al., 2020). The global surge in temperature has caused the increased melting of the Himalayan ice sheets and glaciers, which have caused harm to the ecosystem (Tayal, 2019) and the well-being of millions of people not just in India but also in the entirety of South Asia (Wester et al., 2019). These changes negatively impact the livelihood, health conditions, and rights of the vulnerable communities, causing climate injustices (Panda, 2009). For example, heat waves affect the agricultural community and urban labor class by impacting their work, productivity, and income (ILO, 2019), pushing them to live in poor and unhealthy living spaces, and threatens their food security. All these adverse effects have a big stake in their environmental and climate justice.

In recent years, similar adverse impacts of climate change and risks are being experienced in almost all the states of India. In particular, the coastal populations of Southern India are among the front-line victims of climate injustices. The socioeconomic status and other assets, including social and political networks, have influenced these coastal populations' vulnerability to climate change and risks. For example, with hundreds of human mortalities, the Kerala floods in 2018 and cyclone Phailin in 2013 resulted in the displacement and the loss of livelihoods for millions of people. This chapter aims to critically discuss the legal regime and frameworks of climate change in India by taking the case of two recent climate extreme events. We review and highlight the problems and potential of the existing legal framework in addressing climate injustices for the marginal sections of Indian society who are already experienced socioeconomic inequalities.

This chapter provides an understanding of climate change, inequity, and climate justice by discussing two recent climate extreme events that devastatingly affected two states of India. We examine the already existing "multiple" social injustices of Indian society and highlight how those risks were amplified during and after the climate extreme events. We explore the responses of multiple actors to these climate events and discuss the need to incorporate climate justice mechanisms into the action plans of the union and state governments in responding to extreme climate events.

2 Climate Change, Inequity and Climate Justice: A Brief Account of the Global Actions and Legislations

Climate justice aims at providing social, ecological, and economic justice for all (Saraswat & Kumar, 2016). Climate change threatens the cultural identities of many social groups, particularly indigenous tribes, as well as other vulnerable social groups such as coastal and island populations, by dispossessing their territories (Heyward, 2014). One of the earliest references to climate justice can be traced back to the United Nations Conference on the Human Environment of 1972 to balance environmental needs and human development (Sohn, 1973). The Rio Declaration on Environment and Development further articulated climate justice in 1992 (United Nations Conference on Environment and Development, 1992). The Rio Principle, as it became known, emphasizes protecting people's rights by ensuring environmental protection and sustainable development (United Nations Conference on Environment and Development, 1992). The core principles of climate justice are fairness and equity (Cameron et al., 2013), which are broadly reflected in the Rio principle of "common but differentiated responsibilities and capabilities," with respect to burden-sharing of climate crises between developed and developing countries (Jean-Baptiste et al., 2017). In the contemporary period, climate justice has become an essential component of climate challenge issues, which has to be incorporated into the local, national, and international policies (Saraswat & Kumar, 2016). The United Nations Framework Convention on Climate Change (UNFCCC), 1992 in Article 3 provides for the principles of "*common but differentiated responsibilities and respective capabilities*" (CBDRRC). Developed countries are bound by international agreements to contribute more toward combating climate crises when compared to developing countries to ensure fairness and equity (Rajamani, 2015). The principles of CBDRRC require all parties to work together to meet the objectives to stabilize greenhouse gas emissions and climate crises and support differential treatment among parties (Rajamani, 2015). Besides, the principles of CBDRRC also encompass the elements of "sustainable management" and "cooperation in development" in the efforts of combating climate challenges (UNFCCC—art 4(1), 1992). For the past few decades, these principles have been core elements in climate negotiations in rendering climate justice at the international level. The Paris Agreement emphasizes these principles to ensure effective operationalization by including community participation, sustainable development, and differentiation (Huang, 2017).

While it may not be a panacea for all climate-related challenges. Still, it has incorporated certain mechanisms that possess the ability to overcome the lacunae of the earlier negotiations that resulted in climate injustices. Also, the Paris Agreement has acknowledged the importance of sustainable development for developing countries and has established capacity-building bodies to cater to facilitate their economic and social needs (Huang, 2017). One of the most evident impacts of the Paris Agreement has been the rising protection of indigenous communities around the world from climate injustice challenges. With the adoption of the Paris Agreement in 2015, the principles of significant climate justice initiatives have been introduced at the international levels. The platform for local communities and indigenous people was incorporated by parties in 2017, and the adoption of the Gender Action Plan (2017) are some of the outcomes of the Paris Agreement. The local communities and indigenous people's platform provide inclusive participation of local communities and indigenous people to work toward climate mitigation and adaptation mechanism (UNFCCC, 2017). The Gender Action Plan 2017 has been the first-ever initiative in climate negotiation that facilitates in formulating "gender-responsive climate actions" at the local and national levels (UN Women, 2017). The indigenous communities have been disproportionately affected by climate impacts as they lack "economic and political clout" in society (Abate & Warner, 2013). The geographical locations of these communities and their vulnerable nature also aggravate their chances of being climate change victims. Thus, vulnerable communities, including the indigenous population, are prone to grave climate injustices, and there is a need to ensure a rights-based approach to render justice (Pearl, 2018). Even though it is not legally binding, the Paris Agreement in 2015 incorporated the rights of indigenous communities and vulnerable people in the Preamble (UNFCCC, 2015a). By acknowledging the rights of vulnerable populations, the Paris Agreement aims to fulfill climate justice at the international level. The climate justice concept evolved from environmental justice principles that emphasize equal burden-sharing among the people for environmental betterment and enjoying environmental benefits (Huang, 2017).

One of the core components of the Paris Agreement 2015 to come into force has been the voluntary commitments and actions by countries called the Nationally Determined Contributions (NDCs) (UNFCCC, 2015b). NDCs have to be prepared by all countries according to their capability and may include features that are of most importance at the national level policy measures to reduce emissions and climate challenges (Mills-Novoa & Liverman, 2019). The concern regarding the NDCs is that countries are not setting sufficiently ambitious goals (Mills-Novoa & Liverman, 2019). The existing climate mechanisms need to be more effective to ensure justice for the current and future generations (Cameron et al., 2013).

Research conducted between 1987 and 2002 shows that climate change disproportionately harms disadvantaged communities (Galloway, 2009). Climate impacts amplify multiple inequities across countries and regions (Islam & Winkel, 2017). Vandana Shiva, one of the well-known faces of environmental activism in South Asia, argues that the working process of the global economy contributes to the climate crises, which in turn intensifies inequities among the disadvantaged communities, and makes them more prone to climate crises (Shiva, 2008). In recent decades, there has been mounting evidence growing across the world, proving that the disadvantaged communities face inequities in accessing natural resources equitably; they often face human rights violations that emanate from environmental challenges and climate

Climate Risks in an Unequal Society ... 165

change (Baird, 2008; UNDP, 2011). Adverse climate change impacts trigger financial loss, food insecurity, loss of life, and forced migration among the vulnerable communities across the world (Schneider & Lane, 2006; International Organization for Migration IOM, 2008). It also creates social unrest and conflicts among the communities and regions (Koubi, 2019).

In this context, it is important to highlight that the communities with poorly protected rights are not prepared and equipped to confront the adverse climate change impacts. Adding to this, climate change is not only an international issue but also a domestic issue where government policies and arrangements are being formulated to mitigate and adapt to the new challenges (Dubash et al., 2018). The fourth assessment report of the IPCC reports that the climatic conditions in the tropical and subtropical countries, including India, would adversely impact the weather pattern (IPCC, 2007). The Bali Action Plan parties have urged developed countries to take immediate climate actions at the domestic level to address the climate crisis. The Reducing Emissions from Deforestation and forest Degradation, plus the sustainable management of forests and the conservation and enhancement of forest carbon stocks (REDD+) of 2013, have provided for reducing emissions from deforestation (United Nations, 2013). The REDD+ has provided principles including actions in nations interest, efficient national forest governance, respect for traditional knowledge of indigenous communities, and collective participation of stakeholders including indigenous communities (Ministry of Environment, Forest and Climate Change, Government of India, 2018). India is a signatory to the international conventions on climate change, including the UNFCCC (1992) and the Paris Agreement (2015), and aims to meet the climate targets both at the domestic and international levels to reduce emissions.

3 India's Policy and Actions in Response to Natural Disasters and Climate Change

India had faced several natural disasters and extreme climate events in the 2000s, including the 2004 Indian Ocean Tsunami disaster, various flood events across the country, and the 2005 Kashmir earthquake. By recognizing the crucial need to counter natural disasters through legal and institutional frameworks at multiple levels, India, for the very first time, enacted a statute to deal with the disaster, both natural and man-made, through the Disaster Management Act, 2005. It came into effect in 2005. Consequently, the state formed the disaster management authority at the central, state, and district levels, under the name of National Disaster Management Authority (NDMA), State Disaster Management Authority (SDMA), and District Disaster Management Authority (DDMA), respectively. The role of the disaster management authorities are as follows: i. Formulate and approve policies and plans on disaster management at their respective levels. ii. Coordinate the implementation of disaster management plans. iii. Ensure the provision of funds to mitigate the disasters, prevent, prepare for, and mitigate the disasters, and take measures for capacity building (Government of India, 2005). However, this act was criticized for its weak implementation and ambiguities in classifying various disasters and deceleration of disaster-prone zones that hinder effective execution and implementation of the rules therein (Sarma & Sarkar, 2006). In 2009, the Government of India approved the National Policy on Disaster Management 2009 (NPDM). It provides clear-cut guidelines and recognizes the need to avoid ambiguities of responsibilities and implementation in all phases of disaster management. Besides that, it is in accordance with the frameworks and approaches adopted by the United Nations (National Disaster Management Authority, 2009; National Disaster Management Plan, 2016). In the era of climate change, the disaster management law needs to be strengthened to address climate impacts in India as reports show that inequities between communities have widened due to a lack of a comprehensive legal framework on climate change (Bahadur et al., 2016).

India has been an active player in the international debate on climate change from the very early stage (Sengupta, 2019). India's position in international climate negotiations can be traced back to the 1972 United Nations Conference on Human Environment in Stockholm, where the then Prime Minister Indira Gandhi gave her seminal speech:

> ...The environmental problems of developing countries are not the side effects of excessive industrialization but reflect the inadequacy of development. The rich countries may look upon development as the cause of environmental destruction, but to us it is one of the primary means of improving the environment for living, or providing food, water, sanitation and shelter; of making the deserts green and the mountains habitable... (Plenary Session of United Nations Conference on Human Environment, Stockholm, 14th June, 1972. Cited from LASU-LAWS, 2012).

Indira Gandhi's statement still resonates with India's position on climate negotiations, affirming India's objectives to eradicate poverty, ensure equity and financial assistance for the country (Saran & Jones, 2017). In 1992, India voiced her concerns about sharing the burden of climate actions and emphasized adapting the principles of *"common but differentiated responsibilities and capabilities"* (CBDRRRC) in the Rio Declaration on Environment and Development (Agarwal & Narain, 1991). The incorporation of the principle of equity in the UNFCCC was highly influenced by developing countries, including India, during the climate negotiation (Agarwal & Narain, 1991). India's position in the climate negotiations became more prominent over the years as India took a leadership role among developing countries to address climate challenges (Kapur et al., 2009). When it accepted the global goal to cut its emissions by 1.5 °C, India took a significant step in the Paris Agreement. The goals of maintaining emission targets despite the country's domestic challenges on development and poverty eradication in the face of stringent norms to reduce carbon emissions from industrial development (Dubash, 2017).

In 2008, the then union government of India introduced various policy frames, including the National Action Plan on Climate Change (hereafter, NAPCC), to address the challenges of climate change at the domestic level (Kumar & Naik, 2019). For the first time, India established the Prime Minister's Council on Climate Change (PMCCC) to formulate strategies to address climate actions. The PMCCC, with other government departments, introduced the National Action Plan on Climate Change or the NAPCC in 2008 (Pandve, 2009; Rattani, 2018). The NAPCC encompasses mechanisms, including eight missions for adopting strategies on climate action by transitioning to "clean and green" energy for a sustainable approach (Government of India, 2008). The NAPCC's core principle is based on the concept of the co-benefit approach (Dubash et al., 2013). The co-benefit approach aims to enhance the country's developmental needs sustainably by encompassing effective climate mechanisms (Government of India, 2008).

The Union Government introduced the Energy Conservation Act (2001), the National Environment Policy (2006), and the NAPCC in 2008 at the domestic levels. However, sustainable development goals and their targets are not clearly specified under the missions of the National Action Plan on Climate Change and objectives (Byravan & Rajan, 2012). Despite various efforts and actions by the union government of India, there are no comprehensive approaches that direct these initiatives to get implemented effectively (Kumar & Naik, 2019). The eight missions including the National Solar Mission, the National Mission for Enhanced Energy Efficiency, the National Mission on Sustainable Habitat, the National Water Mission, the National Mission for Sustaining the Himalayan Ecosystem, the National Mission for a Green India, the National Mission for Sustainable Agriculture, and the National Mission on Strategic Knowledge for Climate Change have been introduced to mitigation climate change impacts in India. (Government of India, 2008). In 2009, the then union government of India directed all the states to develop state-level climate action plans in tune with the strategy outlined in the National Action Plan on Climate Change (Dubash & Jogesh, 2014).

With the support of consultancies, most states developed state action plans on climate change between 2010 and 2011, and they are the products of top-down processes within the states. The action plans follow a state uniform structure in identifying the unique vulnerabilities of the state with respect to climate change and in devising an approach to respond to such vulnerabilities. Overall, the state action plans have emphasized adaptation more than mitigation directed by the union government (Gogoi, 2017). Many states have developed climate change action plans as sustainable development action plans. While developing the action plans, there have been many procedural and administrative complexities. The plans have also faced several obstacles in the implementation process. The lack of clear actions and compliance with state budgets and financial obligations, resource restrictions, and a lack of clear ideas regarding the sources of funding to implement the action plans are practical issues that plague the plans (Dubash & Jogesh, 2014; Gogoi, 2017).

The existing climate policy framework at the national level is technology-driven and raises concerns among people on the matter of justice and equity. In addition, the government has not incorporated any concrete welfare measures to deal with climate crises in policy or legislation. At the state levels, the government had notified all states and union territories to prepare action plans on climate change in 2009 (Dubash & Jogesh, 2014). The State Action Plan on Climate Change (hereafter, SAPCC) serves as an important guiding policy framework at the state levels to mitigate and adapt to climate risks (Dubash & Jogesh, 2014). However, the SAPCCs are currently confined only to state jurisdictions, overlooking the vision at the central level.

Moreover, some SAPCCs ignore cities and districts in many climate actions (Dubash & Jogesh, 2014). The original intent of the state-level action plans across states has not been achieved due to a lack of finance and the failure of interlinking departments and sectors at the local, state, and central levels. As states are revisiting their existing action plans to meet national and global commitments, there is a need to ensure that community participation of local people across the state is included. India needs to adopt the measures proposed by the IPCC, arguing that climate change impacts will be more likely to hit the water resources, densely populated coastal regions, forests and mountain ecosystems, health, and energy security of the country. The poor and the most vulnerable are expected to have the largest share of the negative implications of climate change (Youdon, 2020), which needs to be supported by strong and sensitive legal and institutional dispensations. Besides that, the past few decades in particular have seen rapidly rising global temperatures; consequently, climate extreme events are causing casualties across India that have never been encountered in history (Mohanty, 2020). Therefore, disaster management bodies need to take strong measures at executing their functions in a time with the assistance and involvement of all other allied departments, including climate action bodies of the respective states, in preventing and coping with natural disasters and extreme climate events; it would essentially help in mitigating the loss caused to the environment, people, and their livelihood.

The National REDD+ Strategy of India introduced in 2018 aims to reduce deforestation emissions to help address climate challenges. The National REDD+ Strategy aims at facilitating the country in achieving its National Determined Contribution to the UNFCCC under the Paris Agreement by creating carbon sinks through afforestation (Ministry of Environment, Forest and Climate Change, Government of India, 2018). The objectives of the National REDD+ strategy can be only met if the existing environmental laws, including the Environment (Protection) Act 1986, Biodiversity Act, 2002, and The Schedule Tribes and Other Traditional Forest Dwellers (Recognition of Forest Rights) Act, 2006 provide for provisions on mitigation and adaptation measure toward climate change.

4 The Climate Injustice of Extreme Events: Two Cases from India

Despite various policy attempts and actions by India at the state, national and international levels, the global climate risk index has ranked India to be the seventh most vulnerable country to climate change and risks (Eckstein et al., 2017). Recent climate disasters in India have caused loss of property, economy, and human rights violations to the poor, widening existing inequities (Thomas et al., 2018), resulting in climate injustices. The most visible effects of climate change are the increasing intensity and frequency of climate extreme events. The intensity, frequency, and magnitude of climate extreme events in recent years have been the brunt. According to a GermanWatch report, in 2016 India had the most fatalities of any country due to extreme climate events. India ranked sixth among all the countries affected by extreme climate events. In May 2016, India faced record-breaking high temperatures and heatwaves across North India. It was followed by an intense monsoon that devastated eastern, western, and central India. In December 2016, Chennai, one of the densely populated coastal cities in the South of India, was hit by the mighty Cyclone Vardha, which caused several fatalities and massive infrastructure and asset loss (Eckstein et al., 2017). Scientific research focused on India acknowledges climate change impacts in multiple dimensions. Between 1978 and 2015, the annual maximum precipitation and the mean and annual maximum dew point temperatures have increased in most Indian regions. In particular, across central and south India, the frequency of extreme precipitation events has risen greatly since 1982. The frequency and duration of extreme precipitation events have increased in recent decades (Mukherjee et al., 2018).

The following case studies of the 2018 Kerala floods and the 2013 Cyclone Phailin in Odisha will illustrate the various climate injustices faced by the Indian population in recent years. The state climate action plans of Kerala and Odisha have been selected to analyze the measures undertaken at the local and state levels to address climate crises. Both Kerala and Odisha have witnessed climate catastrophes in recent years, rising inequity, and climate injustices.

5 Kerala Floods: The Many Climate Injustices and the Complications of Plans and Policies

Kerala is one of the Southern States of India that consists of around 1.27% of the country's total area. The 2011 Census of India shows that the population of Kerala is about 33.3 million, and it is one of the most densely populated states in India (Census of India, 2011). Kerala has three different geographical regions that include lowlands, midlands, and highlands. Kerala is located on the Southwestern fringes of the Western Ghats Mountain range, one of the world's biodiversity hotspots spanning Kerala, Tamil Nadu, Karnataka, Goa, Maharashtra, and Gujarat. Due to its location along the Western Ghats, Kerala receives rains from two different types of monsoon patterns: southwest (June to September) and northeast (October to December); the average yearly rainfall of the Kerala region comes next to the Northeastern states of India. Also, the state is bounded by the Arabian Sea, and hence, it has a coastline of around 580 km. The lowland region of the state runs along the coast bordering the Arabian Sea. Approximately 322 km of the coastline of Kerala is prone to severe sea erosion. This state is known for its estuaries, backwaters, and wetlands. Kerala has around 44 rivers. About 50 dams of the state are distributed across the Western Ghats range (Chackacherry & Mammen, 2018; ENVIS Centre: Kerala, 2021; Government of Kerala, 2018a; Hunt & Menon, 2020; KSCSTE, 2007; Ramasamy et al., 2019).

The Western Ghats mountains range of Kerala has been under severe ecological pressure from various stakeholders due to mining, deforestation, quarrying, and land-use changes (Government of India, 2011; Ravi Raman, 2010). The influence of the Western Ghats on the climate patterns, including rainfall patterns of Peninsular India, has always been strong (Gunnell, 1997). A recent study has warned that the continuous destruction of the Western Ghats will increase the water scarcity levels of southern states of India, including Kerala (Paul et al., 2018). Similarly, recent long-term research has also found that there has been an increase in temperature in the state from 0.5 degrees Celsius to 1 degree Celsius during the past 100 years, and there is a decline in rainfall patterns and rainy days. It shows that the regions in the southern Western Ghats of Kerala have been subject to large-scale changes in climate patterns (Ramachandra & Bharath, 2019). Historically, the Western Ghats Mountain range is home to millions of tribal populations in the country. In Kerala, the Paniyas of Wayanad and the Kattunayakans of the Malabar region are well-known tribal groups who live in the dense forests of the Western Ghats. Overall, around 90% of the tribes of Kerala live in the rural regions and hilly areas; hence, their lives and livelihoods are highly interrelated with nature. Their social and economic conditions are in extreme backward conditions.

For the past few decades, the Kerala model of development has received widespread attention in India and at the international level for its social welfare schemes and the resulting human development (Devika, 2016; Kannan & Vijayamohanan Pillai, 2004; Patnaik, 1995). However, even before the two recent decades, there was criticism against the Kerala model of development for its economic stagnation, resulting in alcoholism and over-politicization (Tharamangalam, 1998). Additionally, there have also been many criticisms of the Kerala model of development in its failure to protect the forest environment, river, and coastal ecosystems, the indigenous way of life, and even its negative impact on religion, caste, and gender (Korakandy, 2000; Ravi Raman, 2010). Though Kerala is often celebrated as one of the leading states in human development, Dalits and Adivasis have largely been marginalized and left out of such development (Chathukulam & John, 2006; Devika, 2010).

Recent research on social inclusion in Kerala also shows that the Scheduled Castes and Scheduled Tribes[1] and Scheduled Tribes populations of Kerala remain largely poor. They have lower access to drinking water facilities, and they are primarily

---

[1] This chapter, we use the term "Scheduled Castes" and "Dalits" interchangeably. Likewise, we use the terms "Scheduled Castes" and "tribes" and "indigenous communities" interchangeably. Articles 366 (24) and 366 (25) of the Constitution of India have defined scheduled castes and scheduled tribes. The identification and definitions of scheduled castes and scheduled tribes are contained in articles 341 and 342 of the Constitution of India. The definitions are as follows: "Schedule" means a Schedule to the Constitution. Article 366 (24): "Scheduled Castes" mean such castes, races, or tribes or parts of or groups within castes, races, or tribes as are deemed under Article 341 of the Constitution to be the Scheduled Castes for the purposes of the Constitution. Article 366 (25): Scheduled Tribes means such tribes or tribal communities or part of or groups within such tribes or

involved in casual wage jobs (World Bank Group, 2017). In August 2018, Kerala faced torrential rains with floods for about two weeks. From August 1 to 21, 2018, Kerala experienced around 53% above average rainfall. Whereas, from June 1 to August 18 2021, the rains that Kerala experienced were about 42% above the normal average across 14 districts. This increased precipitation forced the release of excess waters from 37 dams across the entire state, which caused large-scale devastation. During this period, the state experienced approximately 341 landslides. Around 483 human mortalities occurred, as well as significant damages to the state's infrastructure, livelihoods, biodiversity, and economic conditions of millions of Keralites. The floods and landslides affected around 5.4 million people and displaced 1.4 million across 1,259 villages in all the districts of Kerala. (Mishra et al., 2018; National Dalit Watch—National Campaign on Dalit Human Rights, 2019; RGIDS, 2018). It also forced millions of people from their regions. This disaster can be attributed to the effects of climate change (Hunt & Menon, 2020).

The effects of the 2018 Kerala flood hit the marginal populations most significantly, especially the indigenous populations, persons with physical disabilities, migrant workers, aged people, children, and women. According to the 2011 census, 1.45% of the population of Kerala belongs to a scheduled tribe category, and 9.1% of the population of the state belongs to a scheduled caste category. Of them, around 18% of scheduled tribes communities are based on the Wayanad district (Census of India, 2011), one of Kerala's most ecologically fragile districts and one of the highly affected districts. Wayanad is home to almost one in every three indigenous persons in the state. Large portions of this district are already under stress due to unscientific land-use patterns, deforestation, and mining (Münster & Münster, 2012; Jisha, n.d). This district was one of the worst-hit regions by the 2018 landslides and floods, which provided brunt effects on the tribal settlements; it caused large-scale

---

tribal communities as are deemed under Article 342 to the Scheduled Tribes (STs) for the purposes of this Constitution (National Commission for Scheduled Castes Government of India, n.d).

The term "Dalits" has strictly been used to denote the ex-untouchables of Indian society. It denotes "oppressed" or "broken," and it was used in the 1930s as a Hindi and Marathi translation of "Depressed Classes" (Webster, 1999). The term "Dalits" mainly denotes the communities with social exclusion, but not to denote the economically poor ones. This term became popularized in the Indian discourse aftermath of the emergence of the Dalit Panther's movement in Maharashtra, a Western State of India, in the 1970s. Initially, the Dalit Panther movement used the term. "Dalits" denote all the oppressed sections of the society, including scheduled castes, scheduled tribes, poor, the landless peasants, and so on (Kumar, 2005). In modern parlance, scholars and Dalit writers use the term "Dalit" to denote revolution, agitation, and the symbol of change.

Sociologically, the social exclusion of the scheduled castes is entirely different than the social exclusion of the scheduled tribes. This is because the tribes were never treated as a part of the social order of India; instead, they had their independent social lives, customs, traditions, norms, values, and governance systems. Similarly, their geographical locations are primarily based on the hills and terrains (Kumar, 2005). However, it is essential to note that the tribes had faced social exclusion and oppression by the outsiders in pre-independent India. It is still continued in the contemporary period in multiple forms.

Some of the common characteristics and attributes of tribal communities of India are of the following: Geographical isolation, backwardness, distinctive culture, language and religion, and shyness of contact (Labour Bureau Government of India, n.d.).

destruction to the livelihoods of the scheduled caste and tribal populations of this district and pushed them to be permanently displaced, and the state declared their places uninhabitable (National Dalit Watch—National Campaign on Dalit Human Rights, 2019).

Around one-third of Kerala's tribal populations live in reserve forests and forest fringe areas that are highly prone to landslides and climate risk events; hence, they have been regular victims. While the 2018 Kerala floods and landslides disproportionately affected them, they also faced discrimination in rescue operations (Rajesh & Chandran, 2018). Mathrubhumi, the media, and publishing house based in Kerala, in collaboration with the Centre for Migration and Inclusive Development, provided a detailed report on how indigenous populations, Dalits, women, children, disabled people, older people, fishers, and migrant workers were largely affected during and in the aftermath of this disaster. This report also highlighted the increasing intensity and frequency of tropical cyclones in the Arabian Sea from 1979 to 2010 and pointed out the need to strengthen disaster recovery and rehabilitation measures and to address climate change impacts along with risk addition factors on vulnerable populations of the state (Thummarukudy & Peter, 2018).

The Kerala State Action Plan on Climate Change was introduced in 2014. Like climate action plans of the other states, Kerala's action plan is consistent with the National Action Plan on Climate Change while accounting for the state's unique geographic and socioeconomic context. It integrates the climate change concerns of the state with the ongoing developmental plans, schemes, and programs of the state, and it echoes the vision and mission of the state. This action plan acknowledges the vulnerabilities of marginal people, including tribals, fishers, and farmers, in the face of climate change and risks. However, it does not separately pronounce the climate change vulnerability of scheduled caste populations (Government of Kerala, 2014). In 2018, the Directorate of Environment & Climate Change of the Government of Kerala had acknowledged the loopholes of the state climate change action plan in addressing the problems of the vulnerable sections of the society and recommended that a gender and social inclusion approach and strategy be incorporated into the state action plans and its implementation processes at many levels. It has stressed the need to develop proper institutional arrangements at the local levels to address the vulnerabilities of women, children, Dalits, and tribals.

It also addresses the gender issues in agriculture, coastal regions, forestry, and among the socially excluded in the context of climate change and risks (Government of Kerala, 2018). However, it should be pointed out that this is merely a set of recommendations to ensure the well-being of the marginal populations of the society in the state climate change action plan. It is yet to be incorporated, and the state is still in the beginning stage. There are many aspects of vulnerabilities of the socially excluded sections in the context of climate change, and risks are yet to be explored and are yet to be duly incorporated in the legal and institutional dispensations of climate change.

The climate action plan of Kerala has provided for monitoring mechanism at state, local, and sectoral levels. Some of the key features of this action plan include:

i. Forests and biodiversity: The state government emphasizes integrating the conservation of forests and community participation of forest dwellers. This initiative has been aligned with the National Green India Mission; ii. Kerala Model of Health: For establishing health centers and research units to promote research and mechanism in human health and climate change; iii. Energy sector: It lays down provisions for promoting renewable energy at micro-levels; iv. Local self-governance mechanism: To coordinate activities at the municipal and panchayat levels in climate actions (Government of Kerala, 2014). Kerala has been known for implementing effective schemes and programs at the local level (Devika, 2016; George, 2006). Hence, integrating climate action at the local level to address climate action is a means to bridge climate inequities. Though the state climate change action plan has emphasized sustainable development and community participation elements, procedural and administrative lacunas exist due to the lack of a comprehensive institutional framework (Pillai & Dubash, 2021). This gap must be addressed to ensure justice by interlinking departments to deal with the issues of marginal and deprived populations.

6 Case 2: Climate Extreme Events in Odisha: Climate Action Plans and Complacency

Odisha is one of India's coastal states bounded by the Bay of Bengal on the east. It possesses rich social and cultural significance in the history of the Indian subcontinent. According to the 2011 census of India, Odisha's population is around 41.9 million, and it stood as the 11th largest state by population. About 22.8% of the total population of Odisha belongs to the scheduled tribes category, and around 17.1% belong to the scheduled caste category. The survey shows that around 86.84% of the scheduled caste and around 88.57% of scheduled tribes' households in the state are in poverty. Scheduled caste' and scheduled tribes' communities are engaged with different occupations across the state. In coastal regions, scheduled caste populations are also involved in fishing and fishing-related occupations. In general, a large proportion of scheduled caste and tribal people and the marine fishers of Odisha live off a subsistence economy (Census of India, 2011; Padhi & Sadangi, 2020). While fishing is one aspect of the people's livelihoods, Odisha's economy is based mainly on agriculture. Despite the recent advancement of urbanization, around 70% of Odisha people are still dependent on agriculture and allied occupations for their livelihoods. It is also important to note that the economic poverty status in Odisha is around 22% above the national level (Government of Odisha, 2018).

India's eastern coastal area has two regions: Kolkata–Vishakhapatnam and Vishakhapatnam–Tamil Nadu. The 480 km of the long coastline of Odisha lies in the Kolkata–Vishakhapatnam region. In India, these coastal regions of the Bay of Bengal are the most vulnerable to storms (Alam et al., 2003). Also, many perennial rivers, including Mahanadi, Brahmani, Baitarani, and various other tributaries, pass through this state. Hence, the coastal districts of Odisha are also vulnerable to flooding. About 3,54,000 ha of Odisha are prone to flooding, and 75,000 ha of the state are vulnerable to waterlogging, particularly in the delta regions (Bahinipati, 2014; Government of Odisha, 2018). The delta districts of Odisha often face problems from intense rainfalls. The complex geography of these regions prohibits excess water from being either absorbed into the groundwater table or drained into the ocean (Chittibabu et al., 2004). The weather patterns of Odisha are characterized by high temperature, high humidity, and medium to high rainfalls.

The entire coastline of Odisha is vulnerable to cyclones and flood events. In particular, the coastal regions of Kendrapara, Jagatsinghpur, Puri, Khordha, and Ganjam are mainly vulnerable to severe storm surge-related flooding; hence, these districts regularly face heavy devastation during cyclones. In 1999, a super cyclone created a monumental catastrophe across 12 districts of Odisha with ten thousand mortalities; one-third of the state's total population was affected (Roy et al., 2002). From 1965 to 2006, Odisha experienced 17 droughts, over 20 floods, and 8 cyclones, including the super cyclone in 1999. In the aftermath of the disastrous 1999 super cyclone's effects, the state administration made several initiatives to improve early warning systems, communication facilities, infrastructure, cyclone shelters, and several other disaster management measures. However, given this state's social and geographical nature, it continued to be one of the most vulnerable states in India to climate change and associated risks (Singh & Jeffries, 2013). In recent years, there has been much scientific research highlighting the vulnerability of Odisha to climate change and risks (Bahinipati, 2014; Kumar et al., 2010; Patnaik et al., 2013). Some of the major calamities, many amplified by climate change, that hit Odisha include the heatwave of 1998, 1999 Super Cyclone, 2013 very severe cyclonic storm Phailin, floods in 2001, 2003, 2005, 2008, and 2011 and severe drought in 2002, 2009, and 2015 (Government of Odisha, 2019). Every year from 1996 to 2015, almost half of the districts of Odisha were affected by natural calamities (Government of Odisha, 2017). From March to October, a large majority of the population of Odisha regularly experienced troubles from floods, cyclones, heavy rains, or heat waves. Given the high poverty levels, vulnerable geographic location, and increased dependency on natural resources, climate change exacerbates the vulnerability of the marginalized groups of the society, including scheduled caste (SC), scheduled tribes (ST), and marine fishers.

On October 12, 2013, an extremely severe cyclonic storm, "Phailin", with a wind speed of up to 220 km/hour hit the east coast of peninsular India, mainly the coasts of Odisha. Of the 30 districts of Odisha, 18 districts were severely affected by this unprecedented cyclonic storm, floods, and torrential rains. Around 13.2 million people were affected in 18,370 villages of Odisha. With 44 mortalities in the state, it caused massive devastation in Ganjam, Puri, Khordha, and the Chilika lagoon. Human mortalities in the cyclone Phailin were less than the human mortalities of the 1999 super cyclone in Odisha. However, cyclone Phailin caused a much greater loss of assets and infrastructure of the millions of farmers, fishers, and Dalits. A large proportion of the victims of this cyclone were Dalits and fishers who were already in a vulnerable state (Government of Odisha, 2018a; Mukhopadhyay et al., 2014; Singh & Jeffries, 2013).

By examining the case of the Bhadrak district of Odisha, recent research (Jaman et al., 2021) has revealed that the very low literacy rate and substandard living conditions of SC/ST people had put them in a more vulnerable state during and aftermath of the devastating strike of the cyclone Phailin. In particular, the poor education levels of SC/ST people in this district increased their social vulnerability and likelihood of experiencing climate injustices. Besides this, the prevailing caste discrimination norms against Dalits (Scheduled caste) and indigenous populations in Odisha made them suffer much. The cyclone shelters in the coastal areas of Odisha are mainly in the control of upper castes and a few powerful village elites who continue to maintain their dominance in handling access to the cyclone shelters. Caste discrimination and its adverse impacts on vulnerable populations, particularly Dalits, are not new in Odisha. Discrimination also occurred during the 2019 Cyclone Fani, the recent extremely severe cyclonic storm that caused extensive damage in 14 districts of Odisha (EPW, 2019).

An apt example was the 1999 super cyclone's adverse effects on Odisha. Large-scale human mortalities were reported in the 1999 super cyclone of Odisha. A large proportion of victims of this cyclone were Dalits. There were around 10,000 reported fatalities (most of them were Dalits) in the Erasma Block of Jagatsinghpur, a coastal district of Odisha when the super cyclone's tidal waves struck. Caste discrimination was attributed as a strong reason for these large-scale human deaths. The Dalits were not evacuated adequately to safe places, and there were no cyclone shelters in their areas. All these factors collectively exacerbated the vulnerability of Dalits and cornered them to confront the brunt effects of the super cyclone (Pattnaik, 2019). In the 1999 super cyclone, the hamlets and living places of Dalits and middle castes were first inundated by floods compared to the hamlets primarily resided by upper caste people. During and after the disasters, including cyclones, the social vulnerability of women was mediated by the complex interplay of caste, gender, and class. In the Hindu society's caste hierarchy, the women who belong to middle and lower castes are among the most vulnerable sections in cyclonic disasters (Ray-Bennett, 2009). The marginal populations of Odisha, including Dalits (particularly Dalit women) and predominately other backward caste populations, have been one of the hardest-hit communities during and after cyclonic disasters. In Odisha, around 25 Dalit families, including the Dalit women, were denied entry into the public shelters by the dominant caste people to safeguard themselves from the brunt effects of 2009 Cyclone Fani (Chari, 2019). In most cases, their living places and hamlets are in low-lying areas and/or near the sea or rivers, which naturally increases their vulnerability.

Compared to the 1999 super cyclone that hit Odisha, the well-functioned disaster risk reduction systems of the state government of Odisha, including early warning alerts and cyclone shelters, saved thousands of lives in 2013 cyclone Phailin. Around 4 lakh people who lived in low-lying areas were safely evacuated to the cyclone shelters. Despite the enormous economic and livelihoods loss, the authorities ensured the immediate safety, food, and other health needs of the evacuated people (Senapati, 2013; Singh, 2013; UNEP-GEAS, 2013). However, the question of climate justice for vulnerable populations remains unanswered. For example, a field report in some villages of the Ganjam district of Odisha, one of the most affected districts by the cyclone Phailin, revealed that caste prejudices continued to haunt the lives of Dalits in receiving the compensatory measures to rebuild their houses. There was also a sense of negation among the authorities that Dalits are disproportionately, and in fact, more affected by cyclones' adverse effects (Mangala, 2014). News outlets reported that marginal populations had trouble accessing relief materials, and they were unsure if they would receive compensation and rehabilitation measures from the authorities to rebuild their houses and livelihoods (Mohanty, 2013; Pujari, 2014; The Hindu, 2016). Odisha, in 2010, was among the first few states in India to formulate a state climate action plan for effective adaptive and mitigation measures (Jogesh & Dubash, 2014).

The Orissa[2] climate change action plan [2010–2015] identified 11 sectors to address climate change. The sectors include agriculture, coastal zones and disasters, energy, fisheries, and animal resources, forests, health, industry, mining, transport, urban planning, and water. Interestingly, the priorities identified, and strategies devised as a part of these sectoral missions are largely based on technology and are driven by "science," and the social vulnerabilities of the communities are less and limitedly discussed in the action plan. The sectors of forests and mining each briefly discuss the importance of ensuring the livelihoods of tribals and a forest-based economy. However, it has not envisaged special coping and adaptation strategies on the lines of the social vulnerabilities and challenges of different tribal groups across Odisha. Overall, the Odisha state climate change action plan has several positive visions and plans for sustainable management and ensuring climate-resilient practices in response to climate change impacts. The action plan also acknowledges that it does not emphasize meeting the demands of the tribal populations (Government of Orissa, 2010). However, the problems of the tribal communities during and after the extreme climate events have been complex. Therefore, their resilience to climate events should be explored through extensive field-based research and the consultation of various stakeholders, particularly with the participation of the tribal populations. In 2018, the state government of Odisha revised its state climate change action plan to align with the changing need of the state. The revised plan has included and emphasized the inclusion of gender-related inequalities in addressing climate risks, apart from the existing provisions addressed in the earlier action plan. In addition, a revision of budget allocation and interlinking district, local, and state action plans has been incorporated to address climate change (Government of Odisha, 2018a).

Overall, the state climate change action plan of Odisha provides a more inclusive model of climate adaptation and mitigation strategies than the erstwhile Orissa climate change action plan 2010–2015. However, the implementation of the critical priority areas does not focus on the effective participation of climate-vulnerable communities. There is a minimal pronouncement of scheduled caste and scheduled tribes, resulting in inadequate attention to ensuring the climate justice of socially excluded and marginal sections of the society. Odisha is one of the very few states in the entire Indian subcontinent where a large proportion of scheduled caste and scheduled tribes reside. They possess a long history of multiple vulnerabilities and deprivation. The recent cyclone that hit the state caused grave injustices to them,

---

[2] The name of the state, Orissa was officially altered to Odisha in 2011.

and there was severe loss of lives, livelihoods, living spaces, and territories. The climate-resilient practices and measures of the state have widely been appreciated. However, there is a strong need for these practices, measures, and actions to focus on the already existing inequity in society.

7 Conclusion

In this chapter, by taking the cases of two extreme climate events, we discuss the question of climate justice for the marginal sections of society. The historical background, geography, and demography of Kerala and Odisha are different for many reasons. However, in India, both the states are well known for responding to climate change and their efficient decentralized governance systems. Odisha recently received praise from the United Nations for providing important disaster management lessons to the world. Ms. Mami Mizutori, Special Representative of the Secretary-General for Disaster Risk Reduction and Head of UNDRR, described Odisha's disaster governance as "strengthening disaster risk governance, investing in preparedness and scenario planning while spreading a greater understanding of disaster risk" (Thakur, 2021). The Reserve Bank of India has recently praised the Kerala model of local self-government in mitigating the effects of COVID-19. It has praised the state for its effective empowerment of local self-governments and community participation across the state. The report also shows that the devolution of funds of the state government of Kerala to the local-self-governments is much higher than in any other state in the entire nation. However, we have found that the climate action plans of these two states (Government of Kerala, 2014; Government of Odisha, 2018a) show that both states do not provide clear-cut guidelines in dealing with the vulnerabilities of the socially excluded people, including the scheduled caste and scheduled tribe populations. Besides that, neither action plan has incorporated a human rights approach in dealing with the climate change problems of the most vulnerable sections of society. Instead, the action plans of both states are primarily driven by technology, science, and finance. This is more or less mainly applicable to the climate change action plans of all the states in the subcontinent.

In May 2021, Cyclone Tauktae hit the Kerala coast and caused considerable damage to life and property, resulting in the relocation of 293 families to relief camps (The New Indian Express, 2021). The families affected are mainly the fishing community and the people from the marginal sectors (Surya, 2021). At the same time, the recent experiences show that the state policies on climate change do not encompass provisions to provide capacity building and human development of the vulnerable communities for resilience and adaptation to such events (Climate Action Network South Asia, 2017), pushing the lakhs of socially excluded people to confront climate change risks. Ensuring efficient and effective rehabilitation mechanisms for the climate-vulnerable communities is a significant challenge for the state authorities who deal with the implementation processes of state climate change action plans.

In many cases, the compensation and rehabilitation mechanisms for vulnerable people, including scheduled caste, scheduled tribes, and other socially excluded sections of extreme climate events, are getting delayed or complicated as the state does not have clear-cut guidelines, procedures, or earmarked funds in its action plans at both national- and state-levels. As the chapter has shown, in India, vulnerabilities of certain sections of the society to extreme climate events cannot be merely generalized as one category, "marginal sections." This is because the levels of vulnerability and adaptation to extreme climatic events of those social groups are too complex, and vulnerability has to be understood through extensive research with the stakeholders and acknowledged in action plans, particularly in the state climate change action plans.

The vulnerability and adaptive capacity of certain social groups may not be similar across the entire state; it may vary along with several factors. For example, it may be too simplified to generalize "tribals" as a single category. Some tribal communities are more vulnerable to climate extreme events than the other tribal groups due to their deprived historical background, vulnerable geographic locations, and socioeconomic factors. There are around 75 primitive tribal groups in the entire Indian subcontinent. Among them, Odisha is the home to 13 primitive tribal groups, and Kerala is the home to 5 primitive tribal groups (Nayak, 2010; KIRTADS, n.d). A large proportion of them historically resides in the hills and interior regions with no basic transportation facilities. Also, they are primarily dependent on forest-based resources for their livelihoods. Similarly, the vulnerability and adaptation levels among the fishing communities also vary along with socioeconomic and geographic factors.

There is growing consensus that small-scale fishers along coastal India are highly sensitive and exposed to climate change impacts due to geographic and socioeconomic factors (ICSF, 2016; Jena & George, 2018; Salagrama, 2012). Given this, there is a need for acknowledgment of "vulnerables" and "vulnerables among the vulnerables" in the national and state climate change action plans rather than grouping all the "vulnerables" into a single category. We argue that making such differentiation among the "vulnerables" and providing emphasis on "vulnerables among the vulnerables" in policy and action plans will provide more institutional support to them during and after the climate shocks. It will also help them to ensure that climate justice emerges from the institutional dispensations more effectively.

Climate change and its threats are widely acknowledged as one of the greatest challenges modern humankind has ever faced (UN, 2021). Global climate negotiations and the policy responses of the states to counter climate change effects are of utmost importance in protecting natural resources and the environment (Dryzek et al., 2012). Nevertheless, those actions and measures should also consider the development and well-being of vulnerable populations across the globe (United Nations Committee for Development Policy, 2018). The climate change action plans of India's union and state governments possess this understanding and concern from the very beginning. Hence, India's climate change action plans have always been consistent with the sustainable development needs and the ongoing programs and schemes of the nation and respective states (Government of India, 2021). We argue that this aspect is one of the robust features of the climate change policy and actions. However, it is also equally essential to examine India's climate change legal framework through the lens of social vulnerability and to discuss the remedial measures of the state in addressing the challenges of vulnerable populations and socially excluded groups. As Saran and Mishra (2015) have argued, gone are the days, where "development" exclusively considered the economic and social necessity of the society, whereas the contemporary and future world requires development that is attuned to the best climate change adaptation. The world needs the "development" that enforces the response capabilities and assets of vulnerable populations to protect their fundamental human rights to life, health, and livelihoods. They can successfully adapt and mitigate climate change.

The United Nations Human Rights Commission specifies that the rights-based approach in the legal regimes, frameworks, and policy-oriented actions is essential to combat climate change effects. The rights-based approach has the potential to "analyze obligations, inequalities, and vulnerabilities" and "redress discriminatory practices and unjust distributions of power" (Saran & Mishra, 2015). Integrating human rights into climate actions and empowering the most vulnerable populations, including women, children, socially excluded people, and communities in India to participate as change-makers in the adaptation and mitigation processes will expedite the mobilization required to combat the impacts (UNFCCC, 2015a).

Conflict of Interest No potential conflict of interest was reported by the author(s).

References

Abate, R. S., & Warner, E. A. K. (2013). Commonality among unique indigenous communities: An introduction to climate change and its impacts on indigenous peoples. In R. S. Abate & E. A. K. Warner (Eds.), *Climate change and indigenous peoples: The search for legal regime* (pp. 3–8). Edward Elgar Publishing.

Agarwal, A., & Narain, S. (1991). *Global warming in an unequal world: A case of environmental colonialism.* Centre for Science and Environment.

Alam, M., Hossain, M., & Shafee, S. (2003). Frequency of Bay of Bengal cyclonic storms and depressions crossing different coastal zones. *International Journal of Climatology, 23*(9), 1119–1125. https://doi.org/10.1002/joc.927

Bahadur, A., Lovell, E., & Pichon, F. (2016). *Strengthening disaster risk management in India: A review of five start disaster management plans.* Retrieved September 21, 2021, from https://cdkn.org/wp-content/uploads/2016/07/India-disaster-management-web.pdf

Bahinipati, C. S. (2014). Assessment of vulnerability to cyclones and floods in Odisha, India: A district-level analysis. *Current Science, 107*(12), 1997–2007.

Baird, R. (2008). Climate change and minorities. In M. Ishbel (Ed.). *State of the World's minority.* Minority Rights Group International. Retrieved May 25, 2021, from https://minorityrights.org/wp-content/uploads/old-site-downloads/download-461-Climate-Change-and-Minorities.pdf

Byravan, S., & Rajan, S. C. (2012). *An evaluation of India's national action plan on climate change.* Centre for Development Finance (CDF), IFMR, and Humanities and Social Sciences, IIT Madras. Retrieved on April 23, 2021, from https://papers.ssrn.com/sol3/papers.cfm?abstract_id=2195819

Cameron, E., Shine, T., & Bevins, W. (2013). *Climate justice: Equity and justice informing a new climate agreement.* Retrieved April 3, 2021, from http://pdf.wri.org/climate_justice_equity_and_justice_informing_a_new_climate_agreement.pdf

Census of India. (2011). *Executive summary.* Office of the Registrar General & Census Commissioner, India, Ministry of Home Affairs, Government of India. Retrieved March 10, 2021, from https://www.censusindia.gov.in/2011census/PCA/PCA_Highlights/pca_highlights_file/kerala/Exevitive_Summary.pdf

Census of India. (2011). *Provisional population totals Kerala series 33.* Office of Registrar General & Census Commissioner, India. Retrieved February 12, 2021, from https://censusindia.gov.in/2011-prov-results/data_files/kerala/Final_Kerala_Paper_1_Pdf.pdf

Chackacherry, G., & Mammen, P. C. (2018). Markers of climate change in Kerala and the path ahead. In M. Thummarukudy, & B. Peter (Eds.), *Leaving no one behind: Lessons from the Kerala disasters* (pp. 209–214). Mathrubhumi Books.

Chari, M. (2019, May 13). *Cyclone fani: Dalits in puri say they were turned away from shelters at height of storm.* Scroll.in. https://scroll.in/article/923211/cyclone-fani-dalits-in-puri-say-they-wereturned-away-from-shelters-at-height-of-storm

Chathukulam, J., & John, M. S. (2006). Issues in Tribal development: The recent experience of Kerala. In C. R. Govinda (Ed.), *Tribal development in India: The contemporary debate* (pp. 182–202). Sage Publication.

Chauhan, R. (2019). Climate change: An issue of equity, justice and human rights. *ILI Law Review, 2.* Retrieved March 29, 2021, from https://www.ili.ac.in/pdf/rch.pdf

Chittibabu, P., Dube, S., Macnabb, J., Murty, T., Rao, A., Mohanty, U., & Sinha, P. (2004). Mitigation of flooding and cyclone hazard in Orissa, India. *Natural Hazards, 31*(2), 455–485. https://doi.org/10.1023/b:nhaz.0000023362.26409.22

Climate Action Network South Asia. (2017). *Climate resilient Kerala. Stakeholder recommendations for Kerala SAPCC.* Climate Action Network South Asia. Retrieved May 28, 2021, from https://www.cansouthasia.net/wp-content/uploads/Kerala-SAPCC-Review.pdf

Devika, J. (2010). Egalitarianism, developmentalism, communist mobilization, and the question of caste in Kerala State, India. *The Journal of Asian Studies, 69*(3), 799–820. https://doi.org/10.1017/S0021911810001506

Devika, J. (2016). The 'Kudumbashree Woman' and the Kerala model woman: Women and politics in contemporary Kerala. *Indian Journal of Gender Studies, 23*(3), 393–414. https://doi.org/10.1177/0971521516656077

Dryzek, J. S., Norgaard, R. B., & Schlosberg, D. (2012). Climate change and society: Approaches and responses. In J. S. Dryzek, R. B. Norgaard, & D. Schlosberg (Eds.), *The Oxford handbook of climate change and society* (pp. 1–11). https://doi.org/10.1093/oxfordhb/9780199566600.003.0001

Dubash, N. K., & Jogesh, A. (2014). *From margins to mainstream? State climate change planning in India as a 'door opener' to a sustainable future.* Centre for Policy Research. Retrieved April 3, 2021, from https://www.cprindia.org/system/tdf/policy-briefs/From%20Margins%20to%20Mainstream%209.7.14_1.pdf?file=1&type=node&id=3556&force=1

Dubash, N. K. (2017). Safeguarding development and limiting vulnerability: India's stake in the Paris agreement. *WIREs Climate Change, 1–10.* https://doi.org/10.1002/wcc.444

Dubash, N., Khosla, R., Kelkar, U., & Lele, S. (2018). India and climate change: Evolving ideas and increasing policy engagement. *Annual Review of Environment and Resources, 43*(1), 395–424. https://doi.org/10.1146/annurev-environ-102017-025809

Dubash, N. K., Raghunandan, N., Sant, G., & Sreenivas, A. (2013). Indian climate change policy: Exploring a co-benefits based approach. *Economic and Political Weekly, 48*(22), 47–61.

Eckstein, D., Künzel, V., & Schäfer, L. (2017). *Global climate risk index 2018. Who suffers most from extreme weather events? Weather-related loss events in 2016 and 1997 to 2016.* Briefing paper. German Watch. Retrieved June 13, 2021, from https://germanwatch.org/sites/default/files/publication/20432.pdf

EJnet. (2002). *Bali principles of climate justice.* EJnet.org: Web Resources for Environmental Justice Activists. Retrieved March 28, 2021, from https://www.ejnet.org/ej/bali.pdf

ENVIS Centre: Kerala. (2021, March 10). *Environment: Physiography.* ENVIS Centre: Kerala State of Environment and Related Issues Retrieved March 10, 2021, from http://www.kerenvis.nic.in/Database/ENVIRONMENT_824.aspx

EPW. (2019). Caste in the midst of Cyclone Fani natural disasters have no control over social discrimination. *Economic & Political Weekly, 54*(20). Retrieved April 19, 2019, from https://www.epw.in/journal/2019/20/editorials/caste-midst-cyclone-fani.html

The New Indian Express. (2021, May 16). Cyclone Tauktae: '1128 shifted to relief camps', says Thiruvananthapuram collector Navjot Khosa. *The New Indian Express.* https://www.newindianexpress.com/cities/thiruvananthapuram/2021/may/16/cyclone-tauktae-1128-shifted-to-relief-camps-says-thiruvananthapuramcollector-navjot-khosa-2303122.html

Galloway, G. (2009). Reacting to climate change, floods and uncertainty. *Natural Hazards Observer, 33*(6), 1–25. https://hazards.colorado.edu/uploads/observer/2009/july_observerweb.pdf

George, S. (2006). Local governance and development: The Kerala experience. *Journal of the Development and Research Organisation for Nature, Arts, and Heritage, 3*(2), 55–60.

Global warming of 1.5°C. An IPCC special report on the impacts of global warming of 1.5°C above pre-industrial levels and related global greenhouse gas emission pathways, in the context of strengthening the global response to the threat of climate change, sustainable development, and efforts to eradicate poverty (IPCC, 2018a, b).

Gogoi, E. (2017). *India's state action plans on climate change: Towards meaningful action. In depth series.* Oxford Policy Management. Retrieved May 19, 2021, from https://www.opml.co.uk/files/Publications/corporate-publications/briefing-notes/id-state-action-plan-climate-india.pdf?noredirect=1

Government of India. (2005). *The disaster management act 2005.* Ministry of Law and Justice, Government of India. Retrieved on April 6, 2021, from https://legislative.gov.in/actsofparliamentfromtheyear/disaster-management-act-2005

Government of India. (2008). *National action plan on climate change.* Prime Minister's Council on Climate Change, Government of India. Retrieved March 26, 2021, from https://archivepmo.nic.in/drmanmohansingh/climate_change_english.pdf

Government of Orissa. (2010). *Orissa climate change action plan 2010–2015. Draft copy.* Government of Orissa. Retrieved April 15, 2021, from http://www.indiaenvironmentportal.org.in/files/CAP_Report_Draft.pdf

Government of India. (2011). *Report of the Western Ghats ecology expert panel Part I.* Submitted to The Ministry of Environment and Forests, Government of India. Retrieved March 25, 2021, from https://vdocument.in/report-of-the-western-ghats-ecology-expert-panel.html

Government of Kerala. (2014). *Kerala state action plan on climate change.* Department of Environment and Climate Change, Government of Kerala. Retrieved May 23, 2021, from https://envt.kerala.gov.in/wp-content/uploads/2019/10/Kerala-State-Action-Plan-on-Climate-Change-KSAPCC-2014-August.pdf

Government of Odisha. (2017). *Annual report on natural calamities 2016–17.* Revenue & Disaster Management Department (Disaster Management), Government of Odisha. Retrieved 16 June, 2021, from https://srcodisha.nic.in/annualReport/4s76xHaAAnnual%20Report%20on%20Natural%20Calmities%20for%20the%20year%202016-17.pdf

Government of Odisha. (2018b). *Odisha state action plan on climate change (Phase-II).* Climate change cell. Government of Odisha. Retrieved March 25, 2021, from http://climatechangecellodisha.org/pdf/State%20Action%20Plan%20on%20Climate%20Change%202018a-23.pdf

Government of Odisha. (2018a). *Odisha profile 2018a.* Directorate of Economics & Statistics, Odisha. Retrieved March 28, 2021, from http://www.desorissa.nic.in/pdf/odisha-profile-2018a.pdf

Government of India. (2018). *Study report: Kerala floods of August 2018.* Central Water Commission, Hydrological Studies Organisation, Government of India. Retrieved April 19, 2021, from https://reliefweb.int/sites/reliefweb.int/files/resources/Rev-0.pdf

Government of Kerala. (2018a). *Gender inclusive state action plan for climate change (SAPCC) Kerala.* Directorate of Environment & Climate Change, Government of Kerala. Retrieved June 10, 2021, from http://www.indiaenvironmentportal.org.in/files/file/Gender%20inclusive%20State%20Action%20plan.pdf

Government of Kerala. (2018b). *Soil health status of Kerala in post flood scenario.* Department of Soil Survey and Soil Conservation, Government of Kerala. Retrieved March 29, 2021, from https://sdma.kerala.gov.in/wp-content/uploads/2020/08/Soil-Flood.pdf

Government of Odisha. (2019). *Annual report on natural calamities 2018–2019.* Revenue & Disaster Management Department, Government of Odisha. Retrieved March 14, 2021, from https://srcodisha.nic.in/annualReport/IZQVHTYMAnnual%20Report%20on%20NC%202018-19_compressed.pdf

Government of India. (2021). *Sustainable development and climate change. Economic survey 2020–21,* Government of India. Retrieved May 13, 2021, from https://www.indiabudget.gov.in/economicsurvey/doc/vol2chapter/echap06_vol2.pdf

Gunnell, Y. (1997). Relief and climate in South Asia: The influence of the Western Ghats on the current climate pattern of peninsular India. *International Journal of Climatology, 17*(11), 1169–1182. https://doi.org/10.1002/(SICI)1097-0088(199709)17:11%3c1169::AID-JOC189%3e3.0.CO;2-W

Heyward, C. (2014). Climate change as cultural injustice. In T. Brooks (Ed.), *New waves in global justice* (pp. 149–169). Palgrave Macmillan.

Huang, J. (2017). Climate justice: Climate justice and the Paris agreement. *Journal of Animal & Environmental Law, 9*(1), 23–59. https://doi.org/10.1080/09644016.2017.1287626

Hunt, K. M. R., & Menon, A. (2020). The 2018 Kerala floods: A climate change perspective. *Climate Dynamics, 54,* 2433–2446. https://doi.org/10.1007/s00382-020-05123-7

ICSF. (2016). *Towards the implementation of voluntary guidelines for securing sustainable small-scale fisheries in the context of food security and poverty eradication SSF guidelines.* International Collective in Support of Fishworkers (ICSF). Retrieved June 29, 2021, from http://ict4fisheries.org/wp-content/uploads/2016/10/Voluntary_guidelines_klar-1.pdf

ILO. (2019). *Working on a warmer planet: The impact of heat stress on labour productivity and decent work.* Retrieved March 27, 2021, from https://www.ilo.org/wcmsp5/groups/public/---dgreports/---dcomm/---publ/documents/publication/wcms_711919.pdf

IPCC. (2007). *Climate change 2007: Synthesis report. Contribution of working groups I, II and III to the fourth assessment report of the intergovernmental panel on climate change* (p. 104). Core Writing Team, R.K. Pachauri, A, Reisinger (Eds.), Geneva, Switzerland: IPCC. Retrieved May 6, 2021, from https://www.ipcc.ch/report/ar4/syr/

IPCC. (2018a). Masson-Delmotte, V., P. Zhai, H. -O. Pörtner, D. Roberts, J. Skea, P. R. Shukla, A. Pirani, W. Moufouma-Okia, C. Péan, R. Pidcock, S. Connors, J. B. R. Matthews, Y. Chen, X. Zhou, M. I. Gomis, E. Lonnoy, T. Maycock, M. Tignor, & T. Waterfield (Eds.), In Press.

IPCC. (2018b). Masson-Delmotte, V., P. Zhai, H. -O. Pörtner, D. Roberts, J. Skea, P. R. Shukla, A. Pirani, W. Moufouma-Okia, C. Péan, R. Pidcock, S. Connors, J. B. R. Matthews, Y. Chen, X. Zhou, M. I. Gomis, E. Lonnoy, T. Maycock, M. Tignor, & T. Waterfield (Eds.), In Press.

Islam, S. N., & Winkel, J. (2017). *Climate change and social inequality.* Department of Economic & Social Affairs, United Nations. Retrieved March 27, 2021, from https://www.un.org/esa/desa/papers/2017/wp152_2017.pdf

Jaman, T., Dharanirajan, K., & Shivaprasad Sharma, S. (2021). Assessment of impact of cyclone hazard on social vulnerability of Bhadrak District of Odisha State during Phailin Cyclone in 2013 and Titli Cyclone in 2018 using multi-criteria analysis and geospatial techniques. *International Journal of Disaster Risk Reduction, 53,* 101997. https://doi.org/10.1016/j.ijdrr.2020.101997

Jean-Baptiste, R., Abate, R. S., Tigre, M., Ferreira, P., & Burns, W. (2017). Recent developments in climate justice. *Environmental Law Reporter News & Analysis, 47*(12). Retrieved April 4, 2021, from https://commons.law.famu.edu/cgi/viewcontent.cgi?article=1251&context=faculty-research

Jena, J. K., & George, G. (2018). Small-scale fisheries in India: An appraisal. In S. S. Giri (Ed.), *Small-scale fisheries in South Asia* (pp. 15–41). SAARC Agriculture Centre.

Jisha, A. S. (n.d). *Wayanad: A case of Kerala's environmental degradation.* Climate South Asia Network. Retrieved March 12, 2021, from http://climatesouthasia.org/wayanad-a-case-of-ker alas-environmental-degradation/

Jogesh, A., & Dubash, N. K. (2014). *Mainstreaming climate change in state develop-ment planning an analysis of the Odisha climate change action plan.* Retrieved May 28, 2021, from https://cprindia.org/sites/default/files/working_papers/jogesh_dubash_mainst reaming_climate_in_state_planning_odisha_climate_plan_feb_2014.pdf

Kannan, K. P., & Vijayamohanan Pillai N. (2004). Development as a right to Freedom: An inter-pretation of 'Kerala Model.' In: *Working Paper Series No. 361.* Thiruvannathapuram: Centre for Development Studies.

Kapur, D., Bhanu, P., & Koshla, R. (2009). Climate change: India's options. *Economic & Political Weekly, 44*(31). Retrieved April 13, 2021, from https://www.epw.in/journal/2009/31/climate-cha nge-negotiations-special-issues-specials/climate-change-indias-options

KIRTADS. (n.d). *Tribals in Kerala.* Kerala Institute for Research Training & Development Studies of Scheduled Castes and Scheduled Tribes. Retrieved June 10, 2021, from https://kirtads.kerala. gov.in/tribals-in-kerala/

Korakandy, R. (2000). State of the environment in Kerala: What price the development model? *Economic and Political Weekly, 35*(21/22), 1801–1804.

Koubi, V. (2019). Climate change and conflict. *Annual Review of Political Science, 22*(1), 343–360. https://doi.org/10.1146/annurev-polisci-050317-070830

Krishnan, R., Sanjay, J., Gnanaseelan, C., Mujumdar, M., Kulkarni, A., & Chakraborty, S. (2020). *Assessment of climate change over the Indian region: A report of the Ministry of Earth Sciences (MoES), Government of India.* Springer.

KSCSTE. (2007). *State of environment report—Kerala 2007 Vol-II natural hazards.* Kerala State Council for Science, Technology and Environment, Government of Kerala.

Kumar, T. S., Mahendra, R. S., Nayak, S., Radhakrishnan, K., & Sahu, K. C. (2010). Coastal vulner-ability assessment for Orissa State, east coast of India. *Journal of Coastal Research, 26*(3(263)), 523–534. https://doi.org/10.2112/09-1186.1

Kumar, P., & Naik, A. (2019). India's domestic climate policy is fragmented and lacks clarity. *Economic and Political Weekly, 54*(7). Retrieved May 20, 2021, from https://www.epw.in/eng age/article/indias-domestic-climate-policy-fragmented-lacks-clarity

Kumar, V. (2005). Situating Dalits in Indian sociology. *Sociological Bulletin, 54*(3), 514–532.

Labour Bureau Government of India. (n.d). *Chapter I introduction.* Labour Bureau Government of India. Retrieved October 1, 2021, from http://labourbureau.gov.in/SE_GUJARAT%2006-07_ CHAPTER%20I.pdf

LASU-LAWS Environmental Blog. (2012, July 12). *Indira Gandhi's Speech at the Stockholm Conference in 1972. Man and Environment.* Environmental Law Class of the Lagos State Univer-sity (LASU). Retrieved May 29, 2021, from http://lasulawsenvironmental.blogspot.com/2012/ 07/indira-gandhis-speech-at-stockholm.html

Mangala, P. (2014, July 17). Disastrous Dalit-ness. *Savari.* Retrieved April 20, 2021, from https:// www.dalitweb.org/?p=2630

Mehta, L., Srivastava, S., Adam, H., Alankar, Bose, S., Ghosh, U., & Kumar, V. (2019). Climate change and uncertainty from 'above' and 'below': perspectives from India. *Regional Environmental Change, 19*(6), 1533–1547. https://doi.org/10.1007/s10113-019-01479-7

International Organization for Migration IOM. (2008). *Migration and climate change No. 31.* IOM Migration Research Series. Retrieved May 28, 2021, from https://olibrown.org/wp-content/upl oads/2019/01/2008-Migration-and-Climate-Change-IOM.pdf

Mills-Novoa, M., & Liverman, D. M. (2019). Nationally determined contributions: Material climate commitments and discursive positioning in the NDCs. *Wires Climate Change, 10*(5), 1–15. https:// doi.org/10.1002/wcc.589

Ministry of Environment, Forest and Climate Change, Government of India. (2018). *National REDD+ Strategy India*. REDD+ United Nations Framework Convention on Climate Change. Retrieved September 19, 2021, from https://redd.unfccc.int/files/india_national_redd__strategy.pdf

Mishra, V., Aaadhar, S., Shah, H., Kumar, R., Pattanaik, D. R., & Tiwari, A. D. (2018) The Kerala flood of 2018: combined impact of extreme rainfall and reservoir storage. *Hydrology and Earth System Sciences Discussions* (September), 1–13. https://doi.org/10.5194/hess-2018-480

Mohanty, D. (2013, November 10). *Month after cyclone Phailin, Odisha looking at devastation on the scale of 1999*. The Indian Express. Retrieved March 18, 2021, from https://indianexpress.com/article/news-archive/web/month-after-cyclone-phailin-odisha-looking-at-devastation-on-the-scale-of-1999/

Mohanty, A. (2020). *Preparing India for extreme climate events: Mapping hotspots and response mechanisms*. Council on Energy, Environment and Water. Retrieved June 1, 2021, from https://www.ceew.in/sites/default/files/CEEW-Preparing-India-for-extreme-climate-events-10Dec20_1.pdf

Mukherjee, S., Aadhar, S., Stone, D., & Mishra, V. (2018). Increase in extreme precipitation events under anthropogenic warming in India. *Weather and Climate Extremes, 20*, 45–53. https://doi.org/10.1016/j.wace.2018.03.005

Mukhopadhyay, S., Soonee, S. K., Agrawal, V. K., Narasimhan, S. R., & Saxena, S. C. (2014). Impact of super-cyclone Phailin on power system operation—Defense mechanism and lesson learned. In *IEEE PES General Meeting Conference & Exposition* (pp. 1–5). https://doi.org/10.1109/PESGM.2014.6939338

Münster, D., & Münster, U. (2012). Consuming the forest in an environment of crisis: Nature tourism, forest conservation and neoliberal agriculture in South India. *Development and Change, 43*(1), 205–227. https://doi.org/10.1111/j.1467-7660.2012.01754.x

National Disaster Management Authority. (2009). *National policy on disaster management*. Ministry of Home Affairs, Government of India. Retrieved May 29, 2021, from https://ndma.gov.in/sites/default/files/PDF/national-dm-policy2009.pdf

National Commission for Scheduled Castes Government of India. (n.d). *Chapter II. Special constitutional provisions for protection and development of the scheduled castes and the scheduled tribes*. Retrieved October 2, 2021, from http://ncsc.nic.in/files/Chapter%202.pdf

Nayak, A. N. (2010). Primitive tribal groups of Orissa: An evaluation of census data. *Orissa Review* (Census Special), 202–205.

OrrisaPost. (2017, June 1). Tribals chained to misery as lack of bridge compounds woes. *OrrisaPost*. Retrieved March 20, 2021, from https://www.orissapost.com/tribals-chained-to-misery-as-lack-of-bridge-compounds-woes/

Padhi, R., & Sadangi, N. (2020). *Resisting dispossession The Odisha story*. Palgrave Macmillan.

Panda, A. (2009). Assessing vulnerability to climate change in India. *Economic and Political Weekly, 44*(16), 105–107.

Pandve, H. T. (2009). India's national action plan on climate change. *Indian Journal of Occupational and Environmental Medicine, 13*(1), 17–19.

Patnaik, P. (1995). The international context and the "Kerala Model." *Social Scientist, 23*(1/3), 37. https://doi.org/10.2307/3517890

Patnaik, U., Das, P. K., & Bahinipati, C. S. (2013). Analysing vulnerability to climate variability and extremes in the coastal districts of Odisha, India. *Review of Development and Change, 18*(2), 173–189. https://doi.org/10.1177/0972266120130206

Pattnaik, S. (2019). Multipurpose cyclone shelters and caste discrimination. *Economic & Political Weekly, 54*(21). Retrieved 19 April 2019. https://www.epw.in/journal/2019/21/commentary/multipurpose-cyclone-shelters-and-caste.html

Paul, S., Ghosh, S., Rajendran, K., & Murtugudde, R. (2018). Moisture supply from the Western Ghats forests to water deficit East Coast of India. *Geophysical Research Letters, 45*(9), 4337–4344. https://doi.org/10.1029/2018gl078198

Pearl, M. A. (2018). Human rights, indigenous peoples and the global climate crisis. *Wake Forest Law Review, 53*(4), 713–738. https://papers.ssrn.com/sol3/papers.cfm?abstract_id=3328592

Pillai, A. V., & Dubash N. K. (2021). *Building a climate—Ready Indian state: Institutions and governance for transforming law—Carbon development.* Centre for Policy Research. Retrieved September 12, 2021, from https://cprindia.org/news/9862

National Disaster Management Plan. (2016). *A publication of the national disaster management authority.* New Delhi: Government of India. May 2016, Retrieved May 29, 2021, from https://www.mha.gov.in/sites/default/files/National%20Disaster%20Management%20Plan%20May%202016.pdf

Pujari, N. K. (2014, February 13). Phailin victims still in crying need of aid. *The Pioneer.* Retrieved March 18, 2021, from https://www.dailypioneer.com/2014/state-editions/phailin-victims-still-in-crying-need-of-aid.html

Rajamani, L. (2015). *Differentiation in 2015 climate agreement.* Center for climate and energy solutions. Retrieved May 25, 2021, from https://www.c2es.org/site/assets/uploads/2015/06/differentiation-2015-climate-agreement.pdf

Rajesh, K., & Chandran, V. S. (2018). Impact on indigenous populations. In M. Thummarukudy, & B. Peter (Eds.), *Leaving no one behind: Lessons from the Kerala disasters* (pp. 85–96). Mathrubhumi Books.

Ramachandra, T., & Bharath, S. (2019). Carbon Sequestration potential of the forest ecosystems in the Western Ghats, a global biodiversity hotspot. *Natural Resources Research, 29*(4), 2753–2771. https://doi.org/10.1007/s11053-019-09588-0

Ramasamy, S. M., Gunasekaran, S., Rajagopal, N., Saravanavel, J., & Kumanan, C. J. (2019). Flood 2018 and the status of reservoir-induced seismicity in Kerala, India. *Natural Hazards, 99*, 307–319. https://doi.org/10.1007/s11069-019-03741-x

Rattani, V. (2018). *Coping with climate change: An analysis of India's national action plan on climate change.* Centre for Science and Environment, New Delhi. Retrieved May 3, 2021, from http://www.indiaenvironmentportal.org.in/files/file/coping-climate-change-NAPCC.pdf

Ravi Raman, K. (2010). *Development, democracy and the state: Critiquing the Kerala model of development.* Routledge.

Ray-Bennett, N. (2009). The influence of caste, class and gender in surviving multiple disasters: a case study from Orissa, India. *Environment Hazards—Human and Policy Dimensions, 8*(1), 5–22. https://doi.org/10.3763/ehaz.2009.0001

Reserve Bank of India. (2020). *State finances a study of budgets of 2020–21.* Reserve Bank of India. Retrieved June 14, 2021, from https://rbidocs.rbi.org.in/rdocs/Publications/PDFs/0SF_271020FCF77451F1DF744B2B244875C785B8EF3.PDF

RGIDS. (2018). *A report on Kerala flood 2018 the disaster of the century.* Rajiv Gandhi Institute of Development Studies (RGIDS). Retrieved May 15, 2021, from https://sdma.kerala.gov.in/wp-content/uploads/2020/08/Rajeev-Gandhi-Centre-Kerala-flood-2018-The-disaster-of-the-century.pdf

United Nations Conference on Environment and Development. (1992). *Rio declaration on environment and development.* United Nations. Retrieved on April 3, 2021, from https://www.un.org/en/development/desa/population/migration/generalassembly/docs/globalcompact/A_CONF.151_26_Vol.I_Declaration.pdf

Rosencranz, A., Singh, D., & Pais, J. G. (2010). Climate change adaptation, policies, and measures in India. *Georgetown International Environmental Law Review, 22*(3), 575–590.

Roy, B. C., Mruthyunjaya, S. S., & Selvarajan, S. (2002). Vulnerability to climate induced natural disasters with special emphasis on coping strategies of the rural poor in coastal Orissa, India. In *Draft Prepared for UNFCCC COP 8 Conference*, New Delhi, India. Retrieved April 02, 2021, from https://unfccc.int/cop8/se/se_pres/isdr_pap_cop8.pdf

Salagrama, V. (2012). *Climate change and fisheries perspectives from small scale fishing communities in India on measures to protect life and livelihood.* Samundra Monograph, International Collective in Support of Fish Workers. Retrieved June 10, 2021, from http://aquaticcommons.org/11190/1/Climate_Change_Full.pdf

Saran, S., & Mishra, V. (2015). *Climate change and human rights: Securing the right to life.* Observer Research Foundation. Retrieved June 14, 2021, from https://www.orfonline.org/research/climate-change-and-human-rights-securing-the-right-to-life/

Saran, S., & Jones, A. (2017). *India's climate change identity: Between reality and perception.* Palgrave Macmillan.

Saraswat, C., & Kumar, P. (2016). Climate justice in lieu of climate change: A sustainable approach to respond to the climate change injustice and an awakening of the environmental movement. *Energy, Ecology and Environment, 1*(2), 67–74. https://doi.org/10.1007/s40974-015-0001-8

Sarkar, S., & Sarma, A. (2006). Disaster management act, 2005: A disaster in waiting? *Economic and Political Weekly, 41*(35), 3760–3763.

Schneider, S. H., & Lane, J. (2006) An overview of dangerous climate change. In H. J. Schellnhuber., W. Cramer., N. Nakicenovic., T. Wigley., & G. Yohe. (Eds.), *Avoiding dangerous climate change.* Cambridge University Press.

Senapati, A. (2013, October 11). Mass evacuation on in coastal districts. *Down to Earth.* http://www.downtoearth.org.in/content/mass-evacuation-coastal-districts

Sengupta, S. (2019). India's engagement in global climate negotiations from Rio to Paris. In N. K. Dubash (Ed.), *India in a warming world: Integrating climate change and development.* Oxford University Press.

Shiva, V. (2008). *Soil not oil: Climate change.* Zed Books.

Singh, D., & Jeffries, A. (2013). *Cyclone Phailin in Odisha, October 2013: Rapid damage and needs assessment report.* Government of Odisha. Retrieved March 25, 2021, from https://openknowledge.worldbank.org/bitstream/handle/10986/17608/838860WP0P14880 Box0382116B00PUBLIC0.pdf?sequence=1&isAllowed=y

Singh, J. (2013, October 15). How Phailin was different from super cyclone 1999. *Down to Earth.* http://www.downtoearth.org.in/content/how-phailin-was-different-super-cyclone-1999

Sivakumar, M. V. K., & Stefanski, R. (2011), Climate Change in South Asia. In R. Lal., M.V.K. Sivakumar., S.M.A. Faiz., A.H.M. Mustafizur Rahman., & K.R. Islam. (Eds.), *Climate change and food security in South Asia* (pp. 13–30). Springer.

Sohn, L. B. (1973). The Stockholm declaration on the human environment. *The Harvard International Law Journal, 14*(3). Retrieved April 3, 2021, from https://stg-wedocs.unep.org/bitstream/handle/20.500.11822/28247/Stkhm_DcltnHE.pdf?sequence=1&isAllowed=y

Stocker, T. F., Qin, D., Plattner, G-K., Alexander, L.V., Allen, S.K., Bindoff, N. L., Bréon, F-M., Church, J. A., Cubasch, U., Emori, S., Forster, P., Friedlingstein, P., Gillett, N., Gregory, J. M., Hartmann, D. L., Jansen , E., Kirtman, B., Knutti, R., Krishna, K. K., et al. (Eds.) *Climate change 2013: the physical science basis. Contribution of working group I to the fifth assessment report of the intergovernmental panel on climate.* IPCC, Cambridge University Press.

Surya, J. (2021, May 20). Cyclone Tauktae is just the latest disaster to hit fisher folks in Kerala. *The News Minute.* https://www.thenewsminute.com/article/cyclone-tauktae-just-latest-disaster-hit-fisherfolk-kerala-149212

Tayal, S. (2019). *Climate change impacts on Himalayan glaciers and implications on energy security of India.* TERI Discussion Paper. New Delhi: The Energy and Resources Institute. Retrieved March 18, 2021, from https://www.teriin.org/sites/default/files/2019-11/cc-impact-himalayan-glacier.pdf

Thakur, P. (2021, May 30). UN praises Odisha CM Naveen Patnaik for disaster management. *The Times of India.* https://timesofindia.indiatimes.com/india/un-praises-odisha-cm-naveen-patnaik-for-disaster-management/articleshow/83078672.cms

Tharamangalam, J. (1998). The perils of social development without economic growth: The development debacle of Kerala, India. *Bulletin of Concerned Asian Scholars, 30*(1), 23–34. https://doi.org/10.1080/14672715.1998.10411031

The Hindu. (2016, October 18). Phailin victims yet to get houses. *The Hindu.* https://www.thehindu.com/news/national/other-states/Phailin-victims-yet-to-get-houses/article16074496.ece

The World Bank. (2013). *4 °C turn down the heat: Climate extremes, regional impacts, and the case for resilience.* A Report for the World Bank by the Potsdam Institute for Climate Impact

Research and Climate Analytics. International Bank for Reconstruction and Development/The World Bank.

Thomas, K., Hardy, R. H., Lazrus, H., Mendez, M., Orlove, B., Rivera-Collazo, I., Roberts, T., Rockman, M., Warner, B. P. (2018). Explaining differential vulnerability to climate change: a social science review. *WIREs Climate Change, 10*(2). https://doi.org/10.1002/wcc.565

Thummarukudy. T. & Peter, B. (Eds.). (2018). *Leaving no one behind: Lessons from the Kerala disasters.* Mathrubhumi Books.

UN (2021, February 23). *Climate change 'Biggest Threat Modern Humans Have Ever Faced', World-renowned naturalist tells security council, calls for greater global cooperation.* Press release: Security Council. Retrieved June 14, 2021, from https://www.un.org/press/en/2021/sc14445.doc.htm

UNDP. (2011). *Human development report 2011—Sustainability and equity: A better future for all.* United Nations Development Programme. Retrieved May 25, 2021, from http://hdr.undp.org/sites/default/files/reports/271/hdr_2011_en_complete.pdf

UNEP-GEAS. (2013). *Thematic focus: Environmental governance, Disasters and conflicts cyclone Phailin in India: Early warning and timely actions saved lives.* United Nations Environment Programme. Retrieved March 18, 2021, from https://na.unep.net/geas/getUNEPPageWithArticleIDScript.php?article_id=106

UNFCCC. (2015a). Nationally determined contribution. United Nations Framework Convention on Climate Change. United Nations Framework Convention on Climate Change. Retrieved March 30, 2021, from https://unfccc.int/process-and-meetings/the-paris-agreement/nationally-determined-contributions-ndcs/nationally-determined-contributions-ndcs

UNFCCC. (2015b). *Understanding human rights and climate change.* Office of the High Commissioner for Human Rights. United Nations Framework Convention on Climate Change. Retrieved May 28, 2021, from https://www.ohchr.org/Documents/Issues/ClimateChange/COP21.pdf

UNFCCC. (2017). *Local communities and indigenous peoples platform: proposals on operationalization based on the open multistakeholder dialogue and submission.* United Nations. Retrieved May 30, 2021, from https://unfccc.int/sites/default/files/resource/docs/2017/sbsta/eng/06.pdf

United Nations. (2013). *Warsaw framework for REDD+. United nations climate change.* Retrieved September 30, 2021, from https://unfccc.int/topics/land-use/resources/warsaw-framework-for-redd-plus

United Nations Committee for Development Policy. (2018). *Leaving no one behind.* Department of Economic and Social Affairs Sustainable Development, United Nations. Retrieved May 18. 2021, from https://sustainabledevelopment.un.org/content/documents/2754713_July_PM_2._Leaving_no_one_behind_Summary_from_UN_Committee_for_Development_Policy.pdf

UN Women. (2017). *First-ever gender action plan to support gender-responsive climate action adopted.* Un Women. Retrieved 30 May, 2021, from https://www.unwomen.org/en/news/stories/2017/11/announcement-first-ever-gender-action-plan-on-climate-action-adopted

Van Oldenborgh, G., Philip, S., Kew, S., van Weele, M., Uhe, P., Otto, F., et al. (2018). Extreme heat in India and anthropogenic climate change. *Natural Hazards and Earth System Sciences, 18*(1), 365–381. https://doi.org/10.5194/nhess-18-365-2018

National Dalit Watch—National Campaign on Dalit Human Rights. (2019). *The extent of inclusion of Dalit and Adivasi communities in the post disaster response in Kerala.* National Dalit Watch—National Campaign on Dalit Human Rights. Retrieved April 21, 2021, from http://www.ncdhr.org.in/wp-content/uploads/2019/05/KERALA-INCLUSION-REPORT.pdf

Webster, J. C. B. (1999). Who is a Dalit? In S.M. Michael (Ed), *Dalits in modern India vision and values* (pp. 76–90). SAGE.

Wester, P., Mishra, A., Mukherji, A., & Shrestha, A. B. E. (2019). *The Hindu Kush Himalaya assessment: Mountains, climate change, sustainability and people.* Springer.

World Bank Group. (2017). *Kerala social inclusion.* Retrieved April 10, 2021 from https://documents1.worldbank.org/curated/en/947421504170192386/pdf/119249-BRI-P157572-Kerala-Social.pdf

World Social Report. (2020). *Inequity in a rapidly changing world.* United Nations. Retrieved March 27, 2021, from https://www.un.org/development/desa/dspd/wp-content/uploads/sites/22/2020/02/World-Social-Report-2020-Chapter-3.pdf

Youdon, C. (2020). *Impact of climate change on coastal cities: An 'Integrated Adaptation' approach part I.* National Maritime Foundation. Retrieved May 3, 2021, from https://maritimeindia.org/impact-of-climate-change-on-coastal-cities-an-integrated-adaptation-approach-part-i/

Litigating for Climate Justice–Chasing a Chimera?

M. K. Ramesh and Vidya Ann Jacob

1 Introduction

The global climate change community has identified climate change policy as a "super wicked" problem for policymakers (Lazarus, 2009). It is termed "super wicked" as it is difficult to reduce greenhouse emissions in an era of hyper-industrialization characterized by the global race to development at the cost of the environment. This poses a threat to stabilizing emissions to the desired level and holding parties liable for emissions (Lazarus, 2009). The United Nations Environment Programme, 2017, argues that the main challenges for the policymakers include difficulty in tracking greenhouse gas emissions over time, ensuring active participation and initiative by stakeholders responsible for climate emission, and the lack of a legal body to enforce the regulation of climate emissions at the international level. Such policy complications at the international level have resulted in widening inequities between communities at national and international levels, as comprehensive and effective mitigation and adaptation measures remain incomplete (United Nations Environment Programme, 2017). Litigation has allowed vulnerable communities to address their concerns and direct policymakers and actors to take practical climate actions (Corfee-Morlot. et al., 2009). Globally, climate litigation has emerged as a tool used to influence policymakers and stakeholders to address climate challenges (Peel & Osofsky 2015). In addition, climate litigation has been considered a "multidimensional system of climate governance" (Osofsky, 2010). In recent decades, across the world, there has been an increase in climate litigation as a means to ensure climate justice, as countries were unable to voluntarily reach a consensus on reducing emissions at the international level.

M. K. Ramesh
National Law School of India University, Bengaluru, India

V. A. Jacob (✉)
School of Law, Christ University, Bangalore, Karnataka, India
e-mail: vidya.jacob@christuniversity.in

© The Author(s), under exclusive license to Springer Nature Singapore Pte Ltd. 2022
D. Madhanagopal et al. (eds.), *Environment, Climate, and Social Justice*,
https://doi.org/10.1007/978-981-19-1987-9_10

Climate Justice is the desired goal, as claimed in every conceivable international effort in designing and developing a frame of law on climate change. The 1992 United Nations Framework Convention on Climate Change has justice as its foundation and the 2015 Paris Agreement further embedded its principles into an international agreement. The parties to the negotiations have, time and again, reiterated their commitment to reaching this goal. Indian legal ordering is no exception to this. However, in the articulation and the realization of climate justice, there is a huge chasm between the prescription and practice, in the global approach, as well as in the Indian response. The effects of climatic conditions are made more excruciating owing to the prevalent pandemic of COVID 19, the litigation strategies adopted in different national systems, appear to be a silver lining, especially in fixing "climate liability" and enforcing penal action. This chapter explores the scope for seeking and securing climate justice in the Indian legal system. Climate litigation can be like chasing a chimera, if the adjudicating body in a country is not adequately equipped with knowledge, skill, and application to render climate justice.

The chapter examines the opportunities and limitations of litigation as a strategy for securing climate justice. This is especially so when legislations at the domestic level and legal arrangements at the international level have failed to address the issues of liability and its enforcement to ameliorate the adverse effects of climate impacts. The chapter demonstrates the role of the judiciary in climate litigation in India and the challenges faced in the justice delivery system. In addition, an analysis of climate cases in various legal systems, namely the United States, the United Kingdom, the Netherlands, the Philippines, South Africa, and Pakistan, is examined to highlight judicial innovations in securing climate-related justice. The role played by the courts in different jurisdictions in performing their assigned functions under the law and the skill displayed by them in finding the legal space to take climate cases to their logical end, notwithstanding the vacuum created by the lawmaker, is also discussed here. We conclude by providing possible steps the Indian Judiciary can take in developing and enhancing justice dispensation in the area of climate change.

2 Climate Justice

Conceptualizing Climate Justice and its theoretical moorings: Climate impacts on vulnerable communities have raised concerns about inequity and justice (UN Framework Convention on Climate Change, 2015). Generally, prior to the Paris Agreement in 2015, developing economies, including India prioritized issues of poverty alleviation and economic growth, whereas many developed economies have been focusing on mitigating emissions and taking action against climate crises (Lawrence, 2014). In 2015, countries came together for the first time with a common objective to address climate actions in a sustainable and equitable manner (Gonzalez, 2019). The member countries of the Paris Agreement aim to ensure a climate-just policy framework at both national and international levels, besides reducing the global emission levels.

Climate Justice is a combination of principles, strategies, and goals. The principles of "common but differentiated responsibilities" and "equity" are its anchors (UN Framework Convention on Climate Change, 1992). The strategies include the stabilization of global temperatures, mitigation of adverse impacts, and building and enhancing capacities in nations and communities in adapting to climate change. The goal is to remove inequities by reckoning countries to clear their "ecological debt" for historic emissions by making sufficient contribution to climate finance, and extending technical assistance to ensure environmentally sustainable development for all.

One of the major concerns of climate change policy has been the problem of balancing sustainable and just living (Elliott & Cook, 2016). The developmental choices made by countries at individual and collective levels in both the present and future have the potential to intensify the impacts of the climate crises resulting in injustices to communities. (Elliott & Cook, 2016). When policy frameworks empower already-advantaged communities in a country and ignore the vulnerable communities that are impacted, there is no justice delivered (Elliott & Cook, 2016). Various scholars have defined climate justice by including religious, philosophical, and political arguments, but the commonality is to ensure the problems of the vulnerable climate-impacted communities be redressed in an equitable and just manner (Elliott & Cook, 2016; Sustainable Development Goal 2019; Caney, 2020). Given the ever-growing body of research and policy discussions for understanding "climate justice," in this chapter, we utilize the definition of the Mary Robinson Foundation which states, "climate justice links human rights and development to achieve a human-centred approach, safeguarding the right of the most vulnerable and sharing the burdens and benefits of climate change and its resolution equitably and fairly" (Mary Robinson Foundation, 2015).

Climate Litigation: Climate litigation has been an essential instrument in protecting climate impacted communities and people (Averill, 2009). Any claim brought before a judicial authority on matters relating to climate change is termed "climate litigation"(Averill, 2009). Climate claims have been an important instrument in protecting human rights violations caused due to climate impacts (Averill, 2009). The importance of linking human rights and climate change to render climate justice was reiterated by the Office of the High Commissioner for Human Rights in 2015 (UN Framework Convention on Climate Change, 2015). Litigations have also been used to protect specific communities, to facilitate rehabilitation and compensate for loss, and to provide support to adapt to future climate crises (Averill, 2009).

3 International Concern and Legal Frame for Climate Law and Justice

Before the 1990s, climate change was considered a scientific and environmental concern (Adams & Luchsinger, 2009). Since the climate negotiations in 1992, climate change has become a global concern, and the international community has been taking steps to ensure equitable and effective steps to address climate challenges (Adams & Luchsinger, 2009). Some of the main concerns that have evolved during international climate negotiations include addressing concerns of the vulnerable communities (Adams & Luchsinger, 2009). As outlined above, the climate justice approach is built on the principles of equity, where meaningful participation of all communities in climate negotiation is important. This includes civil society, outside of formal UN negotiations. Article 18 of the Bali Principle of Climate Justice emphasizes that "climate justice affirms the rights of communities that are dependent on natural resources for their livelihood, and whose cultural practices are opposed to the commodification of nature and its resources" (Bali Principles of Climate Justice, 2002). Thus, climate justice helps in framing global warming issues with respect to ethics and politics rather than viewing it as a mere environmental concern. Climate justice mainly proposes that countries should address climate crises from a forward-looking, pragmatic perspective. The principle where the rich countries merely bear the economic burden of any climate change agreement is not considered climate justice by scholars (Posner & Weisbach, 2010). An agreement that looks into the requirement of every nation and their vulnerable communities to ensure sustainable development while also delivering equity ensures a climate justice approach.

Climate impacts on vulnerable communities have raised concerns about inequity and justice (UN Framework Convention on Climate Change, 1992). Developing economies, including India, have been giving importance to concerns of poverty and economic growth when compared to developing countries (Lawrence, 2014). In 2015, countries came together for the first time with a common objective to address climate actions sustainably and equitably (Gonzalez, 2019). The member countries including Ethiopia, Fiji, Haiti, Nigeria, and Sri Lanka of the Paris Agreement aim to ensure a climate-just policy framework at national and international levels.

4 Climate Litigation in Different Legal Systems

The majority of climate litigations filed to date have been in the United States, where the adjudication body has addressed complex and novel claims. In the United States, litigation has a more significant influence in achieving policy goals when compared to the implementation of government agencies (Komesar, 1994). The United States has been leading in the number of climate litigation adjudicated to address climate challenges for a very long time (Peel & Osofsky, 2015). Followed by Australia and the United Kingdom (United Nations Environment Program, 2020). Climate litigations in the United States, the United Kingdom, and the Netherlands have been chosen indiscriminately in this chapter to understand the different approaches courts have taken in addressing climate claims in developed countries.

4.1 Climate Justice Litigation in the United States

The United States has been impacted by climate change since 1950 (NASA Earth Observatory, 2014). In 1970, President Richard Nixon signed environmental statutes that included the National Environmental Policy and the Clean Air Act (Gerrard, 2016) however, none of the environmental regulations encompassed climate actions or regulations. The National Climate Program Act was introduced by President Jimmy Carter in 1978, when the Department of Commerce was given the power to conduct studies on climate change. Since the 1970s the United States has been undertaking initiatives on climate change. However, due to changes in administrative leadership, addressing climate concerns in a comprehensive manner has been inconsistent (National Research Council, 2010). The country's uneven governmental responses to climate actions make it difficult at the national level to formulate comprehensive climate legislation (Peel & Osofsky, 2015), which has spurred various climate legal claims over the past decade. Climate change litigation claims in the United States are brought under statutory or common-law claims (Hester, 2012).

Climate-related claims in the United States can be traced back to the 1990s when states and environmental groups compelled agencies through litigation to reduce greenhouse gases and pay damages for the harm caused (Wold et al., 2013). Suits against agencies were brought under the federal environmental statutes. In addition, suits against emitters of climate change were brought under tort law or civil wrongs. The federal and state courts have faced challenges in incorporating climate change claims within the statutory framework and common-law doctrines despite the prevalence of successful environmental suits in the United States (Wold et al., 2013). However, the existing environmental law provides a platform for parties to address climate claims. The cases of Massachusetts versus Environment Protection Agency (2007) and Friends of Earth versus Spinelli (2002) provide statutory rights to citizens under the United States Clean Air Act of 1970 and the National Environment Policy Act of 1969 to bring claims against statutory violations relating to climate change. The United States Supreme Court, in the decision of Massachusetts versus Environment Protection Agency (2007), paved the way for the government agency to regulate greenhouse gases from vehicles that were harmful to human beings and the environment.

In the United States, the Supreme Court has also addressed specific adaptive claims for vulnerable communities threatened by climate change (Native Village of Kivalina and City of Kivalina v. Exxon Mobil Corp. et al., 2008). By establishing a relationship between human rights and climate change the courts have, in some respects, rendered climate justice. In addition, the literature describes how integrating human rights to climate change and other legal frameworks "contribute[s] substantially in building policy and legal coherence between the fields of international law—an outcome that is important for sustainable development generally and for international responses to climate change more specifically" (Averill, 2009, p. 146).

The United States District Court for the District of Oregon had admitted climate claims on the ground that climate change violates the constitutional rights of the citizens (Kelsey Cascadia Rose Juliana et al. vs. the United States, 2016). However, the Court of Appeals in 2020 struck down the claim because the court was not equipped "to order, design, supervise, or implement" the plaintiffs' requested remedial plan in. The plaintiffs have further appealed to the courts to seek justice. The federal court for the District of Montana has also taken active steps in protecting the environment from climate impacts due to fossil fuel extraction, where the government was directed to revisit the lease agreement and comply with the environmental assessment regulations (WildEarth Guardians vs. U.S. Bureau of Land Mgmt, 2020). In addition, the federal district for the District of Colorado in 2017 for the first time admitted a case pertaining to the Colorado River Ecosystem and declaring it as a "person" with "rights to exist, flourish, regenerate, be restored, and naturally evolve." The complainants also alleged that climate change was also causing threats to the river. The federal district court dismissed the case on the grounds of lack of legal standing (Colorado River Ecosystem vs. the State of Colorado, 2017). Climate litigation has also seen claimants seeking legal status to nature to protect it from climate impacts.

The above case analysis provides an understanding of how the Federal, State, and District courts are dealing and can deal with climate litigation. The Federal, State, and District courts have paved the way in climate litigation not just in the United States, but also globally. New cases on climate change can be unique and can include claims from areas relating to "pre and post-disaster, consumer and investor fraud, increased attention to climate attributes" and involving "international adjudicatory bodies" (United Nations Environment Program, 2020). Courts in the United States have been leading in a number of cases pertaining to climate claims for two decades in the absence of a comprehensive legal framework at the federal level.

4.2 Climate Justice Litigation in the United Kingdom:

In the United Kingdom, the evolution of climate-related cases began in the 1990s, when the first dispute was about government regulations establishing renewable energy farms and the harmful impacts on the ecology. In this case, the Planning Inspector weighed the effects of establishing the renewable farm and the adverse impact on the environment (*City* of Bradford Metropolitan Council vs. Gillson & Sons, 1995). The England and Wales High Court, concluded that there was no harm to the environment. In 2008, the Climate Change Act was introduced, stating that "it is widely accepted that urgent action is required to address the causes and consequences of climate change" (Climate Change Act, 2008 explanatory notes, para 4), and it laid down goals for the United Kingdom to achieve its objectives within a stipulated time period. Climate litigation in the United Kingdom has been used as an instrument to ensure government obligations towards climate change are met. The three main categories of cases addressed by adjudicating bodies in the United Kingdom are administrative law claims against the government, claims to seek "transition to a low carbon society," and litigation relating to protests against climate change (Ohdedar & McNab, 2021).

In 2007, the importance of climate crises and their impact with respect to establishing wind turbines was brought before the planning inspector, who acknowledged the importance of addressing climate mitigation measures (Bradford vs. West Devon BC, 2007). In Plan B Earth and Others versus Secretary of State for Business, Energy and Industrial Strategy (2018) case, the petition was brought before the High Court of Justice Administrative Court on the duty of the Secretary of State to revise the country's target post-Paris Agreement 2015. The England and Wales High Court in 2019 emphasized the importance of considering climate change as an important policy matter when it stated, the United Kingdom's policy provided, "positive contribution that could be made to climate change by even small-scale renewable energy schemes" (R vs. Medway Council, 2019). These directions facilitate in also protecting the environment and human health from climate impacts to a large extent.

We refer to the second category of cases as "moving away from carbon usage." The United Kingdom has introduced various schemes to transition towards low-carbon energy, which claimants were challenging for not being effectively implemented (Secretary of State for Energy and Climate Change vs. Friends of the Earth, 2012; The Department of Energy and Climate Change vs. Breyer Group PLC and Others, 2015). In one case, the government policy on fracking was challenged due to its contribution to climate impacts. The Administrative Court of the Queen's Bench Division of the High Court stated that the Government needed to undertake studies that include the latest climate science and policy before allowing fracking (Claire Stephenson vs. Secretary of State for Housing and Communities and Local Government, 2019). This decision had an important influence on the 2019 parliamentary elections, where policymakers reconsidered the regulations on fracking and considered its adverse impact on climate change. Another important decision before the court was to expand an airport under the Airport National Policy Statement (ANPS) without considering the country's climate change policy (R vs. Secretary of State for Transport, 2020). The Court of Appeal laid down: "We have not found that a national policy statement supporting this project is necessarily incompatible with the United Kingdom's commitment to reducing carbon emissions and mitigating climate change under the Paris Agreement, or with any other policy the Government may adopt or international obligation it may undertake."

An important category of climate litigation in the courts in the United Kingdom has been the criminal action charges against the protests of climate activists (Ohdedar & McNab, 2021). In 2008, climate activists were charged with criminal damage caused to a coal plant (R vs. Hawke [Maidstone Country Court], 2008). This case received broad attention in the United Kingdom as it was considered a "novel use of climate change as a legal defense for protest to block fossil fuel generating activity." Climate protests leading to criminal charges are rising, especially when there are protests that are violent (Baroness Jenny Jones vs. Commissioner for Metropolitan Police, 2019).

Courts in the United Kingdom have evolved jurisprudence in climate change by addressing different facets to ensure climate justice, including matters of environment degradation, development needs, and human rights violations. The above case analyses show that climate litigation has been an important tool to achieve targets and government policies to address climate actions in the United Kingdom. As Banda and Fulton (2017) argue, climate litigation on the grounds of adaptation is yet to be seen in the courts, but there is growing scope for climate claims to render justice in the future. The judiciary has been on the frontline at national and international levels to address climate change. After the Paris Agreement came into force; national courts have been called upon to frame policy and assist with guidelines on climate change by relying on national and international principles by claimants.

One of the significant features of the European Environmental Justice Delivery system which includes the United Kingdom is that it has assigned liability for corporate culpable acts and enforced them. The latest decision in 2021 by the Dutch Supreme Court, in fixing climate liability on the Shell Company and ordering for payment of a huge compensation amount (Business Standard, 2021), is illustrative of this.

4.3 Climate Litigation in the Philippines, South Africa, and Pakistan

Climate litigation has been developing rapidly in developing countries over the past few years (Setzer & Benjamin, 2020). Despite climate change policy and resource constraints, the courts of the developing world have been supportive of addressing climate claims (Setzer & Benjamin, 2020). Developing countries grapple largely with concerns of human rights violations due to the impact of climate crises (Kotze, 2015). Moreover, the human rights approach with regard to climate change has been a challenge for courts in developing countries (Olawuyi, 2015). This is because human rights have different dimensions in climate-vulnerable countries, where grave climate injustices are prevalent due to a lack of legislative and policy framework to address the challenges of the vulnerable communities (Olawuyi, 2015). Despite these challenges, the courts have been proactive in linking human rights and climate change to ensure climate justice. This has been reflected in the claims brought before various jurisdictions in developing countries that are discussed in this section. We examine selected cases from the Philippines, South Africa, and Pakistan, to explore the role of courts in directing government authorities and corporates in meeting their climate goals.

In the case of Ashgar Leghari versus Federation of Pakistan (2015), the Pakistan Court directed the government to issue immediate guidelines on climate change to ensure the prevention of further human rights violations. The first case brought before the court in the Philippines was based on human rights violations caused by the biggest emitters to the people of the Philippines (Global Legal Action on Climate vs. the Philippines Government, 2010). In 2015, the Commission of Human Rights approached the Philippines' court seeking an investigation on the responsibility of "carbon major" companies (including Shell, Chevron, and BHP Billiton) on the violation of human rights (In Re: Greenpeace South East, Commission of Human Rights, 2015). Leghari versus Federation of Pakistan of 2015, is a good example to show how courts have been pioneering climate justice within their limited jurisdiction, where the courts directed the government to implement the country's climate policy to address climate challenges faced by the petitioner who was a farmer. In addition, the courts have allowed climate claims under broader legal frameworks, including constitutional rights, natural resource conservation, and environmental protection (Peel & Lin, 2019). This has been illustrated in the case of EarthLife Africa Johannesburg versus Minister of Environmental Affairs and Others (2017a, b), where the South African High Court decided that it was important to evaluate the climate impacts for setting up a new coal plant under the environmental assessment process.

In addition, the Supreme Court of Pakistan recently emphasized the protection of the rights of nature by providing that "the environment needs to be protected in its own rights" and "[m]an and his environment each need to compromise for the better of both and this peaceful co-existence requires that the law treats environment objects as holders of legal rights" (G.Khan Cement Company vs. Government of Pakistan, 2021). This suggests that there is a growing trend in litigations concerning the right of nature and protection against climate impacts, which is an important aspect of ensuring climate justice.

Many developing nations prioritize poverty alleviation and basic development needs, along with climate change. These nations emphasize other important environmental threats that include protection from impacts of hazardous wastes and access to safe drinking water for all. This is because environmental challenges are interlinked with economic concerns (Atapattu & Gonzalez, 2015). In addition, many conservation-based environmental issues have been construed as a luxurious policy frame in low-income countries, where achieving reduction of poverty and economic development itself has been a hurdle (Gordon, 2015). A lack of financial and skilled human resources has also posed challenges to the developing countries to achieve various international environmental reporting standards (Nanda, 2015). Thus, providing financial aid, technological transfer, and capacity building to supplement policy implementation and effective adjudicatory mechanisms have been important to address various environmental issues, including climate change.

The nations with comprehensive environmental legal frameworks have witnessed the challenge that their policymakers face in implementing environmental regulations in an effective manner. This is largely due to the under-skilled, and understaffed offices, lack of political will, fragmented institutions, or other factors (Blackman, 2008). For example, in South Africa, the apartheid legacy and the inequities caused have positioned the government to create policies that ensure cheap energy and access for all, resulting in heavy reliance on fossil fuel energy sources (Bazilian et al., 2011).

Nevertheless, judicial organs of developing nations have taken steps to ensure climate justice by expanding legal interpretations within their limited jurisdictions. These examples are instrumental to enhance the climate litigation mechanism in India.

4.4 Climate Litigation in India

Arguably, climate justice, as an aspect of broader environmental justice, owes its genesis within India to the Indian justice system. Much before the higher judiciary in India could take it up, the Primary Judiciary in India sowed the seeds of environmental justice when environmental law was in its infancy worldwide. The year was 1984 and in the early morning hours of December 3, a disaster of unprecedented proportion descended on the unsuspecting population of Bhopal. What unfolded in the Bhopal gas tragedy was one of the worst and the most devastating environmental disasters humanity has ever witnessed. While the entire administration and the legal system watched helplessly, a judge of the Bhopal District Court—Justice Deo, exercised his powers under the Civil Procedure Code (ss.94 and 151) to issue an interlocutory order, placing a judgement on the Union Carbide Corporation of 3500 million Rupees as the interim relief for the damage caused. In another action under the Criminal Law Process, he ordered the arrest and detention of Warren Anderson, the CEO of the parent company, immediately on his arrival from the United States. In issuing these orders, he interpreted the role of a judge as not merely that of an umpire, but as someone with the solemn duty to find truth and do justice according to the law (Edwards, 2014).

Ironically, the entire effort came to naught when the Indian political leadership ensured the release of the CEO and provided state protection for his safe return to the United States. Environmental justice was deeply buried in the contaminated site. Forty six years after the tragedy, environmental justice is still a mirage for the victims. In some ways, it is a bigger irony that while the Indian system hardly found effective solutions for this, in some ways the United States system took this as a wake-up call, to set its house order and the Reagan administration initiated a slew of policy and legislative measures under its Super Fund Programme to effectively deal with industrial hazards. Nonetheless, it is the Indian higher judiciary that has, over time, developed a robust jurisprudence, creating space for accessing, seeking, and securing environmental justice. Post-1990s, India addressed climate change concerns.

The term "global warming" was first used in an environmental suit in India in the 1990s, though the courts did not give directions regarding the impact of climate change (Environmental and Ecological Protection Samithy vs. Executive Engineer and Ors., 1991). Claims relating to climate change have been of recent origin in India, where concerns of violations of rights caused by climate change, global warming, and international negotiations are being brought (Ghosh, 2020). Examining the litigation in India, the literature to date has broadly classified climate claims under four main categories, namely suits challenging government decisions, failure of government to meet policy targets, direction to enhance policy to meet climate challenges, and failure of government to perform their duty to prevent climate impacts (Ghosh, 2020).

The Indian judiciary has been playing a pivotal role in evolving environmental jurisprudence since the 1980s (Basu, 2011). The Supreme Court of India has been instrumental in widening the scope of Article 21 of the Constitution to include the "right to the wholesome environment" and the right to enjoy a pollution-free environment (Subash Kumar vs. the State of Bihar, 1991). In addition, the court has also applied international principles, including the polluter pays principle (India Council for Enviro-legal Action vs. Union of India (Bichhri Case), 1993), the intergenerational principle on equity (State of Himachal Pradesh vs. Ganesh Wood Products, 1995) and the sustainable development principle (M. C. Mehta vs. Union of India, 1997) in directing the state to preserve the environment as a trustee of natural resources (M. C. Mehta vs. Kamal Nath, 1997). Moreover, in India the National Green Tribunal (NGT), a judicial forum to address disputes pertaining to "substantial question relating to the environment (including enforcement of any legal right relating to the environment)" has been established under s. 4, National Green Tribunal of 2010. The National Green Tribunal Act provides for the adjudicating body to base the decision on "principles of sustainable development, the precautionary principle, and the polluter pay principle" (s. 20, National Green Tribunal). In addition, the Supreme Court has addressed climate claims by directing authorities to comply with environmental assessment in public projects (Karnataka Industrial Areas Development Board vs. Sri C. Kenchappa, 2006) and also to comply with international standards on climate change (Manushi Sangthan, Delhi vs. Govt. of Delhi, 2010). This shows that the judiciary steps in to protect the rights of the citizens when the government policies and laws are inadequate. In 2017, the Uttarakhand high court declared legal rights to the river Ganga and the Yamuna to protect the rivers from being polluted and duty was cast upon the state to protect the rivers from any further degradation (Safi, 2017). In the near future, the Indian courts can anticipate claims with respect to the protection of rights of nature from the adverse impact of climate change caused by corporations.

Om Dutt Singh versus State of Utter Pradesh (2015), the government scheme for setting up an irrigation project that would increase greenhouse gas emissions was being challenged. The NGT has played an important role in approving the setting up of a waste treatment plant that would help reduce greenhouse gases in a society (Sukhdev Vihar Residents Welfare Association vs. Union of India, 2017). The adjudicating body has been crucial in directing the government in following international standards while providing notifications (Society for Protection of Environment and Biodiversity vs. Union of India, 2017). The NGT also directed the state to control illicit deforestation by analysing localised climate change implications of indiscriminate tree-felling (Yogendra Mohan Sengupta and Others vs. UoI and Others, 2017).

The next cluster of cases that have come before the courts have been claims seeking direction from the government to implement laws or policies in an effective manner (Ghosh, 2020). In Gaurav Bansal versus UoI (2015) case, the claim brought before the adjudication body was to order the central and state governments to produce substantial reports regarding implementing the 2008 National Action Plan on Climate Change (NAPCC). Though the judiciary did not direct the governments to produce the report, it ordered the states that have not submitted their state action plans to submit it at the earliest. The NGT, for the first time in Ratandeep Rangari versus State of Maharashtra and Others (2015), issued an order to the Ministry of Environment Forest and Climate Change (MoEFCC) to formulate a monitoring system that would apply to all coal-based plants, where the plant was to use coal or as that was less than 34 percent. The NGT provided that the order was passed based on the "important co-benefit of such [a]n initiative would be lesser GHG emissions-i.e. lesser carbon footprint in thermal power generation." The Supreme Court has also been active in issuing directions to the government to comply with statutory provisions regarding the construction of an airport (Hanuman Laxman Aroskar vs. UoI and Others, 2019).

The third category of cases deals with the claims of creating new and effective policies to deal with climate change and its impacts (Ghosh, 2020). The applicant brought before the court a "deep-water container port project" and the policy guideline in setting the project in an ecologically sensitive area; the applicant wanted an order that protected "areas likely to be inundated due to rise in seal level consequent upon global warming" (Wilfred J vs Ministry of Env't and Forests, App., 2016). The NGT, after analysing the case, observed that the project was very vital to the community (Wilfred J vs. Ministry of Env't & Forests, 2016). In another case brought before the NGT by a minor, the applicant wanted the tribunal to issue direction to the Union Government of India to take "effective, science-based action to reduce and minimize the adverse impacts of climate change in the country based on international principles and standards" (Ridhima Pandey vs. UoI, 2019). The NGT provided that "no reason to presume that the Paris Agreement and other international protocols are not reflected in the policies of the Government of India or are not taken into consideration in granting environment clearances."

The final category of cases provides defense by the State and Union Governments on their climate change policy decisions (Ghosh, 2020). One of the important cases brought before the Supreme Court was an application challenging mandatory energy purchase from renewable energy sources for companies as per the State Electricity Regulatory Commission (Hindustan Zinc Ltd. v. Rajasthan Electricity Regulatory Commission, 2015). The Supreme Court of India directed that the government regulations on renewable energy sources have been made in the larger public interest to reduce pollution and emission of greenhouse gases emissions.

None of the cases discussed in this section have brought a link between human rights and climate change to the direction of the courts. The Indian judiciary is known for evolving the public trust doctrine with regard to environmental jurisprudence; however, this is yet to be reflected in climate-related decisions relating to climate change. To ensure climate justice litigation, it is important to equip the judiciary to view cases from a rights-based approach rather than a mere statutory compliance concern. In view of India's climate-vulnerable position, parties and the judiciary must consider climate change as an important concern (Ghosh, 2020). The Indian judiciary must anticipate claims pertaining to human rights violations of internally displaced people due to climate change and climate refugees, which are likely to come before the bench in the coming years. As reiterated by Flavia Pansieri, United Nations Deputy High Commissioner for Human Rights in 2015,

> Climate change, human-induced climate change, is obviously an assault on the ecosystem that we all share, but it also has the added features of undercutting rights, important rights like the right to health, the right to food, to water and sanitation, to adequate housing, and, in a number of small island states and coastal communities, the very right to self-determination and existence.

5 Conclusions

As the world faces several climate-related challenges, codification of international and national responses has become of utmost importance. The lacuna in the existing environmental laws has brought about an entirely new dimension of "climate litigation." Even though the concept of climate litigation is still new in most developing nations. Lawyers bear the responsibility of making their clients aware of how climate change may affect their rights. In India, climate litigation is still evolving (Rajamani, 2013). India has an engaging and proactive civil society, an activist judiciary, a progressive body of enviro-legal jurisprudence, and a culture of public interest litigation (Rajamani, 2013). Though several specific laws cover multiple environmental aspects, a more holistic approach is required. In recent times, the NGT has begun to play a more definitive role. The NGT has succeeded in strengthening ties between the judiciary and "climate litigation" as a concept. The tribunal, though functional and active, is limited by its provisions, as discussed in the chapter. Although several provisions prevent the misuse and damage to the environment and the climate, there are no comprehensive legal provisions to cover those affected by the same.

India has strong reasons to be concerned about climate change. A vast population depends on climate-sensitive sectors like agriculture, forestry, and fishery for livelihood in the country (Gupta, 2005) and the country has already witnessed the growing brunt and intensity of extreme events in recent decades (Mohanty, 2020). Capacity building and equipping the NGT and the courts in India are crucial to addressing climate litigation more comprehensively and effectively. Capacity building includes training programs for judicial authorities on the scientific knowledge and application of climate challenges. As the situation is deteriorating, there is a growing recognition of the importance and urgency of the climate challenge and various climate policies and initiatives at the national and state levels (Rajamani, 2013). For a country like India, apart from stringent policies, well-equipped courts are highly important with respect to climate litigation. Many developed and developing nations have already begun to make a unified attempt to address these climate crises and the resulting litigations.

Climate litigation has been prevalent in developed nations including the United States and the United Kingdom for over two decades. Climate emergencies have turned litigation into an important mechanism to address climate crises. In developing nations, including the Philippines, South Africa, and Pakistan, although there have been constraints on litigation concerning climate change, the judiciary has played an important role in ensuring climate-related human rights violations, environmental degradation, and unsustainable development are prevented. This shows that the judiciary has been playing an active role in rendering climate justice in different jurisdictions, where climate change laws are not comprehensive.

As it is crucial and complex to link climate change and human rights, the Indian judiciary must be equipped to evolve a robust climate jurisprudence for the country. India has not viewed climate change as a huge threat yet. The government has been strategizing ways to eradicate poverty and ensure immediate economic and energy needs (Mertz et al., 2009). As climate litigation is increasing, courts must provide decisions that ensure "climate-related accountability, enable resiliency, and contributing to a sustainable future" (Banda & Fulton, 2017). Thus, equipping the Supreme Court, High Court, and NGT with capacity building mechanisms to address climate justice litigation are crucial.

Climate Justice is a value choice that the global community overwhelmingly adopted through UNFCCC,1992. Every meeting of the conference of parties under it, including the Paris Agreement, derives their legitimacy by repeated reference to this as the cornerstone of their efforts. The Solar Alliance shepherded by India and the consequential international organisation that resulted from it has this as its foundation. The Solar Alliance was introduced with an aim to promote clean energy in a collective manner by countries to tackle both national and international challenges of climate change by incorporating the principles of climate justice. This sublime thought is getting lost in translation from an idea into action and results. While this is the fate of it under international negotiations, it is in no way better, as observed above, in the domestic arena. The Action Plans and Policy pronouncements, both at the national and at the state levels, derive their source of energy from this, with little to show, where it matters most, for doing justice to the victims—human and nature. Against this adverse climate, climate litigation and evolving strategies to equip the most affected appear to be the only hope and beacon of light.

Acknowledgment The authors would like to thank *Mr. Vikas Gahlot* [Teaching Associate, Centre for Environmental Law, Education, Research, and Advocacy CEERA, National Law School of India University, Bengaluru] for his assistance with technical aspects of the draft.

Conflict of Interest No potential conflict of interest was reported by the author(s).

References

Adams, B., & Luchsinger, G. (2009). *Climate justice for changing planet: a primer for policy makers and NGOs*. https://unctad.org/system/files/official-document/ngls20092_en.pdf.

Ashgar Leghari v. Federation of Pakistan, Case No. 25501/2015 (Lahore High Court, 2015). http://www.lse.ac.uk/GranthamInstitute/litigation/ashgar-leghari-v-federation-of-pakistan-lah ore-high-court-green-bench-2015.

Atapattu, S., & Gonzalez, C.G. (2015), The North-South Divide in International Environmental Law: Framing Issues. In Alam, S., Atapattu, S., Gonzalez, C.G., & Razzaque, J. (Eds.). *International Law and The Global South.*

Averill, M. (2009). Linking climate litigation and Human rights. *Review of European Comparative & International Environmental Law, 18*(2), 139–147. https://doi.org/10.1111/j.1467-9388.2009.006 36.x.

Banda, M. L., & Fulton, S. (2017). Litigating climate change in national courts: Recent trends and developments in global climate law. *Environmental Law Reporter, 47*(2), 10121–10134. https://www.eli.org/sites/default/files/elr/featuredarticles/47.10121.pdf.

Baroness Jenny Jones v. Commissioner for Metropolitan Police, EWHC 2957 (Queen's Bench High Court, 2019). https://www.judiciary.uk/wp-content/uploads/2019/11/Jones-Ors-v-Comm-of-Pol ice-Approved-judgment.pdf.

Basu, A. (2011). Climate change litigation in India: Seeking new approach through the application of common law principles. *Environmental Law and Practice Review, 1*, 35–51. http://www.com monlii.org/in/journals/NALSAREnvLawPRw/2011/3.html.

Bazilian, M., Hobbs, B. F., Blyth, W., MacGill, I., & Howells, M. (2011). Interactions between energy security and climate change: A focus on developing countries. *Energy Policy, 39*(6), 3750–3756. https://doi.org/10.1016/j.enpol.2011.04.003.

Blackman, A. (2008). Can Voluntary environment regulation work in developing countries? Lesson from case studies. *The Policy Studies Journal, 36*(1), 119–141. https://doi.org/10.1111/j.1541-0072.2007.00256.x.

Bradford v. West Devon BC, P.A.D 45 (2007). http://climatecasechart.com/climate-change-litiga tion/non-us-case/bradford-v-west-devon-bc/.

Business Standard. (2021, May 26). *Court orders Royal Dutch Shell to cut net carbon emissions by 45%*. Retrieved June 3, 2021, https://www.business-standard.com/article/international/court-ord ers-royal-dutch-shell-to-cut-net-carbon-emissions-by-45-121052601281_1.html.

Caney, S. (2020). *Climate justice. The Stanford encyclopaedia of philosophy*. Stanford Encyclopedia of Philosophy. https://plato.stanford.edu/cgi-bin/encyclopedia/archinfo.cgi?entry=justice-climate.

City of Bradford Metropolitan Council v. Gillson & Sons, 10 P.A.D. 255. (1995). http://climateca sechart.com/climate-change-litigation/non-us-case/city-of-bradford-metropolitan-council-v-gil lson-and-sons/.

Claire Stephenson v. Secretary of State for Housing and Communities and Local Government, EWHC 519. (2019). http://climatecasechart.com/climate-change-litigation/non-us-case/claire-stephenson-v-secretary-of-state-for-housing-and-communities-and-local-government/.

Colorado River Ecosystem v. State of Colorado, Case 1:17-cv-02316-NYW. (USDC Colorado, 2017). http://climatecasechart.com/case/colorado-river-ecosystem-v-state-colorado/.

Corfee-Morlot, J., Kamal-Chaoui, L., Donovan, M. G., Cochran, I., Robert, A., & Teasdale, P. J. (2009). *Cities, climate change and multilevel governance*. OECD Environmental Working Paper No. 14. https://www.oecd.org/env/cc/44242293.pdf.

Earthlife Africa Johannesburg v. Minister of Environmental Affairs & Others, Case No. 65662/16 (High Court, 2017a). http://www.lse.ac.uk/GranthamInstitute/litigation/earthlife-africa-johann esburg-v-minister-of-environmental-affairs-others.

Earthlife Africa Johannesburg v. Minister of Environmental Affairs & Others, Case No. 65662/16 (High Court, 2017b). http://www.lse.ac.uk/GranthamInstitute/litigation/earthlife-africa-johann esburg-v-minister-of-environmental-affairs-others.

Edwards, T. (2014). Criminal failure and "The Chilling Effect": A short history of the Bhopal criminal persecutions. *Social Justice, 41*(1/2), 53–79.

Elliott, D. & Cook, L. F. (2016). *Climate justice and the use of human rights law in reducing greenhouse gas emissions*. Quaker United Nations Office. https://quno.org/sites/default/files/resources/Climate%20Justice_August_2016.pdf.

Environmental and Ecological Protection Samithy v. Executive Engineer and Ors., [1991] 2 KLT 493 (Kerala High Court 1991). https://www.casemine.com/judgement/in/56e66b05607dba6b534373f4.

Friends of Earth v. Spinelli, Civ. No. 02–4106 (ND Cal).

G. Khan Cement Company v. Government of Pakistan (Supreme Court of Pakistan, 2021). http://climatecasechart.com/climate-change-litigation/wp-content/uploads/sites/16/non-us-case-documents/2021/20210415_13410_judgment.pdf.

Gaurav Bansal v. Union of India, App. No. 498/2014 (Supreme Court of India, 2015). https://www.casemine.com/judgement/in/582dfd84bc41687dbcd4ba24.

Gerrard, M. G. (2016). United States Climate Change Law. In Carlarne, C. P., Gray, K. R., & Tarasofsky, R. (Eds.), *The Oxford handbook of international climate change law*. Oxford University Press.

Ghosh, S. (2020). Litigating climate claims in India. *American Journal of International Law, 114*, 45–50. https://doi.org/10.1017/aju.2020.5.

Global Legal Action on Climate v. the Philippines Government. (2010). https://climate-laws.org/geographies/philippines/litigation_cases/global-legal-action-on-climate-change-v-the-philippines-government.

Gonzalez, C. G. (2019). Climate justice and climate displacement: evaluating the emerging legal and policy responses. *Wisconsin International Law Journal, 36*, 366–395. https://wilj.law.wisc.edu/wp-content/uploads/sites/1270/2020/01/36.2_366-396_Gonzalez.pdf.

Gordon, R. (2015). Unsustainable development. In Alam, S., Atapatty, S., Gonzalez. C. G., & Razzaque, J. (Eds.), *International environmental law and the global south*. Cambridge University Press.

Gupta, V. (2005). Climate change and domestic mitigation efforts. *Economic and Political Weekly, 40*(1), 981–987. https://doi.org/10.2307/4416308.

Hanuman Laxman Aroskar v. Union of India & Others, MANU/SC/0444/2019 (Supreme Court of India, 2019).

Hester, T. D. (2012). A new front blowing in: State law and the future of climate change public nuisance litigation. *Stanford Environmental Law Journal, 31*(49), 49–89.

Hindustan Zinc Ltd. v. Rajasthan Electricity Regulatory Commission, [2015] 12 SCC 611 (Supreme Court of India, 2015). https://www.recregistryindia.nic.in/pdf/REC_Regulation/Supreme_Court_Judgement_regarding_RPO_Compliance.pdf.

In Re: Greenpeace South East, Commission of Human Rights, Case No. CHR-NI-2016-0001 (2015). http://climatecasechart.com/climate-change-litigation/non-us-case/in-re-greenpeace-southeast-asia-et-al/.

India Council for Enviro-legal Action v. Union of India (Bichhri Case), [1993] 3 SCC 212 (Supreme Court of India). http://www.indiaenvironmentportal.org.in/files/Bichri%20Case%202011.pdf.

International Climate Justice Network. (2002, August 28). *Bali principles of climate justice*. https://corpwatch.org/article/bali-principles-climate-justice.

Karnataka Industrial Areas Development Board v. Sri C. Kenchappa, [2006] 6 SCC 371 (Supreme Court of India). https://www.informea.org/sites/default/files/court-decisions/COU-156136.pdf.

Kelsey Cascadia Rose Juliana, et al. v. United States of America, 217 F. Supp. 3d (USDC, D Oregon, 2016). https://casetext.com/case/juliana-v-united-states-3.

Komesar, N. K. (1994). *Imperfect alternative: Choosing institutions in law, economics, and public policy*. Chicago University Press.

Kotze, L. (2015). Human rights, the environment and the global south. In Alam, S., Atapatty, S., Gonzalez. C. G., & Razzaque, J. (Eds.), *International environmental law and the global south*. Cambridge University Press.

Lawrence, P. (2014). *Justice for future generations: climate change and international law*. Edward Elgar.

Lazarus, R. J. (2009). Super wicked problems and climate change: Restraining the present to liberate the future. *Cornell Law Review, 94*, 1153–1160.

Mary Robinson Foundation Climate Justice. Retrieved 25 March 2021. https://www.mrfcj.org/wp-content/uploads/2015/09/Principles-of-Climate-Justice.pdf.

M. C. Mehta v. Kamal Nath, [1997] 1 SCC 288 (Supreme Court of India).

M. C. Mehta v. Union of India, [1997] 2 SCC 353 (Supreme Court of India). https://www.casemine.com/judgement/in/581180092713e1794796f915.

Manushi Sangthan, Delhi v. Govt. of Delhi, [2010] DLT 168 (Delhi High Court).

Mary Robinson Foundation-Climate Justice. (n.d.). *Principles of Climate Justice*. Retrieved March 25, 2021, from https://www.mrfcj.org/wp-content/uploads/2015/09/Principles-of-Climate-Justice.pdf.

Massachusetts v. Environment Protection Agency, 549 US 497 [2007] (US Court of Appeals, Columbia 2007). https://projects.ncsu.edu/cals/course/are309/cases/massachusettsedited.pdf.

Mertz, O., Halsnaes, K., & Olesen, J. E. (2009). Adaptation to climate change in developing countries. *Environmental Management, 43*(5), 743–752. https://doi.org/10.1007/s00267-008-9259-3.

Mohanty, A. (2020). *Preparing India for extreme climate events: Mapping hotspots and response mechanisms*. Council on Energy, Environment and Water. https://www.ceew.in/publications/preparing-india-extreme-climate-events.

Nandan, V. P. (2015). Global environmental governance and the south. In Alam, S., Atapatty, S., Gonzalez. C. G. & Razzaque, J. (Eds.), *international environmental law and the global south*. Cambridge University Press.

NASA Earth Observatory (2014). *Climate changes in the United States*. https://earthobservatory.nasa.gov/images/83624/climate-changes-in-the-united-states.

National Research Council. (2010). *Informing an effective response to climate change*. The National Academies Press.

Native Village of Kivalina and City of Kivalina v. Exxonm Mobil Corp. et al., Civ. No. CV 08 1138 [ND Cal., 2008]). http://climatecasechart.com/climate-change-litigation/case/native-village-of-kivalina-v-exxonmobil-corp/.

Ohdedar, B.. & SMcNab, S. (2021). climate litigation in the United Kingdom. In Kahl, W., & Marc-Philippe Weller, M.P. (Eds.), *Climate change litigation: A handbook*. Hart Publishing.

Olawuyi, D. S. (2015). advancing climate justice in national climate actions: The promise and limitations of the United Nations human rights-based approaches. *Florida A & M University Law Review, 11*(1), 103–124. http://commons.law.famu.edu/famulawreview/vol11/iss1/3.

Om Dutt Singh v. State of Utter Pradesh, App No. 521/2014 (NGT, 2015). https://www.casemine.com/judgement/in/5de6518a46571b2fd68a43d5.

Osofsky, H. M. (2010). The continuing importance of climate change litigation. *Climate Law, 1*(1), 3–29. https://doi.org/10.1163/CL-2010-002.

Peel, A., & Osofsky, H. M. (2015). *climate change litigation: Regulatory pathways to cleaner energy*. Cambridge University Press.

Peel, J., & Lin, J. (2019). Transnational climate litigation: The contribution of the global south. *American Journal of International Law, 113*(4), 679–726. https://doi.org/10.1017/ajil.2019.48.

Plan B Earth and Others v. Secretary of State for Business, Energy and Industrial Strategy, [2018] EWHC 1892. http://climatecasechart.com/climate-change-litigation/non-us-case/plan-b-earth-others-v-secretary-state-business-energy-industrial-strategy/.

Posner, E. A., & Weisbach, D. (2010). *Climate change justice*. Princeton University Press.

R v. Hewke, No. T20080116 (Maidstone County Court, UK, 2008).

R v. Medway Council, [2019] EWHC 1739 (Queen's Bench Division, 2019). http://climatecasechart.com/climate-change-litigation/non-us-case/r-on-the-application-of-mclennan-v-medway-council/.

R v. Secretary of State for Transport, [2020] EWCA Civ. 285 (England and Wales Court of Appeal, 2020). https://www.casemine.com/judgement/uk/5e5caf2f2c94e00dac31b1b8.

Rajamani, L. (2013). *Rights Based Climate Litigation in the Indian Courts: Potential, Prospects & Problems.* Centre for Policy Research Climate Initiative Working Paper 2013/1. https://cprindia.org/sites/default/files/working_papers/Working%20paper%202013_LRajamani_Climate%20Litigation_5.pdf.

Ratandeep Rangari v. State of Maharashtra & Others, App. No. 19/2014 (WZ) (NGT, 2015). http://www.indiaenvironmentportal.org.in/files/coal%20based%20thermal%20power%20plant%20Vidarbha.pdf.

Ridhima Pandey v. Union of India, App. No. 187/2017 (NGT, 2019). https://www.casemine.com/judgement/in/5de5cb7146571b2fd68a3f39.

Safi, M. (2017, March 21). *Ganges and Yamuna Rivers Granted Same Legal Rights as Human Beings,* The Guardian. https://www.theguardian.com/world/2017/mar/21/ganges-and-yamuna-rivers-granted-same-legal-rights-as-human-beings.

Secretary of State for Energy and Climate Change v. Friends of the Earth, [2012] EWCA Civ. 28 (Court of Appeals, Queen's Bench, 2012). http://climatecasechart.com/climate-change-litigation/non-us-case/secretary-of-state-for-energy-and-climate-change-v-friends-of-the-earth/.

Setzer, J., & Benjamin, L. (2020). Climate litigation in the global south: Constrains and innovations. *Transnational Environmental Law, 9*(1), 77–101. https://doi.org/10.1017/S2047102519000268.

Society for Protection of Environment and Biodiversity v. Union of India, App No. 677/2016 (NGT, 2017). https://www.casemine.com/judgement/in/5b17d5604a9326780100622a.

State of Himachal Pradesh v. Ganesh Wood Products, [1995] 6 SCC 363 (Supreme Court of India). https://leap.unep.org/sites/default/files/court-case/COU-143787E.pdf.

Subash Kumar v. State of Bihar, [1991] 1 SCC 598 (Supreme Court of India). http://www.globalhealthrights.org/asia/subhash-kumar-v-state-of-bihar-ors/.

Sukhdev Vihar Residents' Welfare Association v. Union of India, App. No. 22 (THC)/2013. (NGT, 2017). https://www.casemine.com/judgement/in/5c060d44b338d16e11efe632.

Sustainable Development Goals (2019). *Climate Justice.* UN. Retrieved 20 April, 2021h https://www.un.org/sustainabledevelopment/blog/2019/05/climate-justice/.

The Department of Energy and Climate Change v. Breyer Group PLC and Others, [2015] EWCA Civ 408 (Supreme Court of Appeals, 2015). https://www.bailii.org/ew/cases/EWCA/Civ/2015/408.html.

U.S. Climate Change Litigation (n.d). Retrieved March 30, 2021, from, http://climatecasechart.com/us-climate-change-litigation/.

UNEP. (2017). The Status of Climate Change Litigation: A Global Review. http://columbiaclimatelaw.com/files/2017/05/Burger-Gundlach-2017-05-UN-Envt-CC-Litigation.pdf.

UNEP. (2020). *Global Climate Litigation Report 2020 Status Review.* https://reliefweb.int/sites/reliefweb.int/files/resources/GCLR_0.pdf.

UN Framework Convention on Climate Change (1992). Retrieved on 10 April 2022, https://unfccc.int/resource/docs/convkp/conveng.pdf.

UN Framework Convention on Climate Change (2015). Paris Agreement. Retrieved on 10 April 2022, https://unfccc.int/sites/default/files/english_paris_agreement.pdf.

WildEarth Guardians v. U.S. Bureau of Land Mgmt, No 4:18-cv-00073, 2020 WL 2104740, (USDC. Mont. 2020). http://climatecasechart.com/climate-change-litigation/case/wildearth-guardians-v-us-bureau-of-land-management/.

Wilfred J v. Ministry of Env't & Forests, App. No. 74/ 2014 (NGT 2016). https://www.casemine.com/judgement/in/5c060e00b338d16e11efe646.

Wold, C., Hunter, D. & Powers, M. (2013). *Climate Change and the Law.* Carolina Academic Press.

Yogendra Mohan Segupta & Others v. UoI & Others, App. No. 121/2014 (NGT, 2017). https://www.casemine.com/judgement/in/5c060b3eb338d16e11efe601.

Protected Areas as a Catalyst for Environmental Sustainability, Social Justice, and Human Development: Lessons from South Africa

André J. Pelser

1 Introduction

The past one hundred years have seen a dramatic increase in the number of officially protected areas worldwide, moving from fewer than 600 by the end of World War II (Pelser & Sempe, 2003) to an estimated 9214 in 1962 and more than 209,000 by 2014 (Kernan, 2016). In many cases, especially in developing countries, this rapid swell in protected areas went hand in hand with the forced relocation of local communities and a disruption of their livelihoods. Parks and reserves were fenced off and local communities were prevented from utilizing or harvesting any resources inside the perimeters of the newly proclaimed protected area. This "fortress" policy of exclusion of local communities often resulted in increased poverty and further environmental degradation. For many years, however, the impact of this marked expansion of protected areas on the livelihoods of local communities was largely ignored by conservation authorities (Pelser et al., 2011), but in the past few decades, the interdependent relationship between the conservation of natural resources and the sustainable development of the rural poor has been strongly accentuated (Kernan, 2016). This also applies to South Africa, where conservation policy in the post-1994 political dispensation is seen as an attempt to address some of the socio-economic injustices and ills that became associated with conservation practices during the apartheid era.

Since the 1980s, there has been a growing recognition by international agencies such as the World Wide Fund for Nature, The World Conservation Union, USAID, and several United Nations agencies that national parks and other protected areas cannot be managed successfully without consideration for a socially responsible model that allows for benefits from conservation to be channelled to historically disadvantaged groups. For instance, Sect. 15.6 of Goal 15 of the 2030 Agenda for

---

A. J. Pelser (✉)
Department of Sociology, University of the Free State, Bloemfontein 9300, South Africa
e-mail: pelseraj@ufs.ac.za

© The Author(s), under exclusive license to Springer Nature Singapore Pte Ltd. 2022
D. Madhanagopal et al. (eds.), *Environment, Climate, and Social Justice*,
https://doi.org/10.1007/978-981-19-1987-9_11

Sustainable Development pertinently stresses the need to "promote fair and equitable sharing of the benefits arising from the utilization of genetic resources and promote appropriate access to such resources …" (United Nations, 2015). That said, more and more conservation agencies have been urged to adjust their goals suitably to not only allow for the protection of resources, but also for the fair distribution of benefits to local communities as part of a more comprehensive philosophy of people-centred conservation that, amongst others, aims to address the social injustices caused by previous policies of exclusion and expropriation. In many cases, embracing this new approach of inclusion rather than exclusion of neighbouring communities has become necessary for the survival and continued existence of protected areas (Pelser et al., 2011; Swemmer et al., 2015; Wells, 1996). Now the official policy of many conservation agencies in Africa and elsewhere, people-centred conservation has promised to alleviate poverty among deprived rural communities on the outskirts of protected areas by, amongst others, making provision for increased access to resources within such protected areas.

In many African countries, the conventional "fortress" approach to conservation had its roots in the colonial era and continued after independence in the 1960s. This often resulted in the proclamation of parks surrounded by relocated communities that were showing sentiments of hostility towards the protected area as a result of the injustices they had to endure in the name of conservation, and the little, if any, benefits they derived from the protected area (Wells, 1996). The growing concerns over climate-change-related impacts and the realization to balance conservation interests with socio-economic development needs warranted the need for integrated conservation and development approaches that will restore the socio-economic injustices associated with the "fortress" approach. As outlined later in this chapter, in South Africa too, the proclamation of many protected areas and national parks has been strongly associated with colonial and apartheid policies that subject these communities to exclusionary practices and social injustices. In fact, current efforts in South Africa to reconcile social justice and conservation cannot be appreciated without a brief outline of the historical context of nature conservation and national parks in the country and a brief outline of the theoretical debate on the link between conservation and development.

2 Integrating Conservation and Development: A Theoretical Construct

The international debate on the links between human development and the environment, and specifically the dynamics between conservation and poverty, has grown in intensity and volume since the 1972 Stockholm Conference on the Human Environment (Andam et al., 2010; De Sherbinin, 2008; Fisher et al., 2020; Upton et al., 2008). Central to this debate is an exploration of the interface between protected areas (and national parks in particular) and the development of local rural communities, more particularly the socio-economic role of protected areas in the mitigation of rural poverty (Roe et al., 2013; Simpson, 2009; Spenceley, 2008). The growing need to recognize and consider the development needs of local communities in conservation approaches had given rise to a number of people-centered conservation approaches that allow for the social and economic needs of local communities to be addressed in biodiversity conservation and management of protected areas. The philosophy underpinning these approaches is embedded in the postulation that community involvement in conservation programmes translates into tangible social and economic benefits for local communities, strengthens the sense of ownership, and contributes to positive attitudes towards conservation (Simpson, 2009). This is particularly important in developing countries such as South Africa, where the proclamation and management of protected areas in the past often clashed with the economic interests of the local population, thus creating sentiments of hostility towards conservation and violating the environmental and social rights of communities. In many developing regions, poor rural communities adjacent to protected areas may potentially benefit significantly from either direct or indirect conservation incentives in the form of sustainable resource utilization, employment opportunities, skills development, conservation levies and revenues, training programmes, and development opportunities for small business enterprises (Brooks et al., 2013). Many examples of such integrated conservation and development initiatives are found in the developing regions of southern and central Africa, as well as south and southeast Asia. While such initiatives can be seen as medium-term solutions to clashes between biodiversity conservation and the natural resource needs of local communities in rural areas of high ecological importance (Nyhus, 2016), in the case of South Africa it also serves as a vehicle to address and restore social injustices of the past that were committed under the banner of conservation.

Despite their strong common motivator, people-centered conservation initiatives do not represent a homogenous or blueprint approach that is suitable for all conditions and communities. This can be clearly seen from the many descriptions that are attached to conservation approaches of this kind: Labels such as *grassroots conservation, community-based conservation, community-based natural resource management, community wildlife management, sustainable development and resource use projects, collaborative management models,* and *community-based natural resource management* are commonly used to describe initiatives of an integrated people and conservation kind (Chapin, 2004; Pelser et al., 2011). The collective term "integrated conservation and development programme(s)" (ICDP), as proposed by Wells and McShane (2004), could arguably be accepted as a suitable umbrella for biodiversity conservation initiatives that also incorporate social and economic development goals that target marginalized and vulnerable segments of local communities. Under the ICDP umbrella, we can distinguish between three typologies of ICDP approaches (Barrow & Murphree, 2001): *Protected area outreach* programmes aim to promote the biodiversity of protected areas by channelling direct and indirect economic benefits to neighbouring communities and running environmental education programmes in these communities; *collaborative management* programmes allow for representatives of conservation agencies and local communities to come to a mutual agreement on the utilization of natural resources inside protected areas under the supervision of a management committee or monitoring authority consisting of members of all parties to the agreement; and *community-based conservation* that aims to put the sustainable management of natural resources under the control of community structures. Although this threefold categorization of ICDP approaches provides a useful theoretical construct, it is not mutually exclusive and still remains a simplification of the various ICDP typologies. In practice, therefore, most conservation programmes and policies in Southern Africa allow for the incorporation of one or more elements of the aforementioned approaches, yet they all endorse the philosophy of integrated conservation management with benefits to local populations.

3 Conservation and Social (In)Justice in South Africa: A Paradoxical History of Protected Areas, Exclusions, and Inequalities

South Africa counts amongst one of the wealthiest countries in the world when it comes to biodiversity. Often referred to as the third most biodiverse country on the planet (Pelser, 2012), South Africa is home to an estimated 10% of the world's flora and fauna, and is custodian to approximately 80% of vascular plant species not to be found anywhere else in the world (Pelser et al., 2011). The country has a total of 19 national parks, ranging from as small as 50 km^2 in the case of the Bontebok National Park to an extensive 20,000 km^2 of the world-renowned Kruger National Park (Vermeulen et al., 2019; see Fig. 1). All national parks are managed by the country's official conservation agency, South African National Parks (SANParks). The parks are widely diverse when it comes to their biodiversity, historical context, and the size of their neighbouring communities.

To combat the loss of biodiversity and rapid deterioration of habitats, in the 1930s, South Africa adopted the then internationally dominant "fortress" or protectionist conservation paradigm. The predecessor of SANParks, the National Parks Board (established in 1926), enforced the protectionist management paradigm until the dawn of democracy in 1994. From the 1930s until the early 1990s, conservation and the proclamation of many protected areas in South Africa became synonymous with dispossession, forced removal of communities, persecution, the exclusion of black communities from national parks, and a ban on the use of resources inside protected areas (Meskell, 2012; Wells, 1996). With the institutional enforcement of apartheid policies in 1948, a series of disempowering and racist legislation followed to ensure the exclusion of black South Africans from national parks and intensify environmental injustices (Leonard, 2013). Sanctioned by the political ideology of apartheid, thousands of people were forcefully evicted from their land to enable the proclamation of national parks (Kruger, 2015). Well-known examples of such evictions include

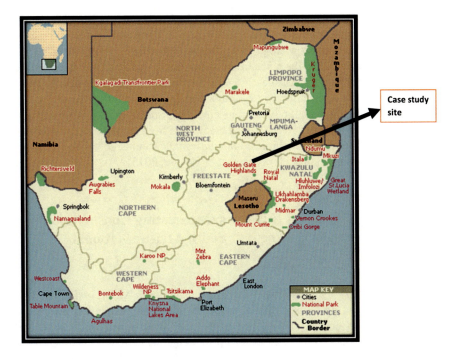

Fig. 1 National Parks of South Africa. Reproduced from TourSA (2021), with amendments

the forced relocation of the San communities to facilitate the proclamation of the Kalahari Gemsbok National Park in 1931 (now known as the Kgalagadi Transfrontier Park) and the displacement of the Makuleke community from the Pafuri region in 1969 in order to incorporate this area into the larger Kruger National Park. As an extension of the apartheid ideology, this protectionist conservation policy endorsed by the then National Parks Board strictly prohibited the majority of South Africans from entering the protected areas as consumers of the parks' educational, recreational, and resource use opportunities, and also excluded them from any decision-making regarding the operation of these parks (Kernan, 2016). In many ways, the "fortress" conservation policy in South Africa in turn fuelled many local communities' resentment towards conservation and amplified social conflict, which also resulted in the accelerated degradation of the environment, as they were often relocated to areas that did not match the carrying capacity of their previous land in terms of size, resources or distance from work and family/friends. Moreover, this approach had a devastating effect on poverty levels among affected communities, which rose rapidly following the implementation and execution of the protectionist conservation policy (Pelser et al., 2011). Despite successes gained in conserving biodiversity and establishing an impressive network of protected areas, this came at a price of much human misery and community hostility towards conservation (Anthony, 2007). Not only did this conservation practice further augment inequality amongst affected local communities on the boundaries of national parks, but it also served to reinforce the perception among communities that environmental conservation was an unjust and enforced practice wherein wildlife and nature were prioritized over human well-being. Social justice was thus trampled upon in the name of conservation, as marginalized and deprived communities often had to bear the costs of conservation. However, with the dawn of a new political dispensation in 1994, the "fortress" policy of conservation was no longer reconcilable with the goals of a democratic South Africa. Unsurprisingly, therefore, by 2007, an estimated 122 land claims had been lodged against protected areas by historically disenfranchised communities (De Koning, 2009)—a figure that increased to 150 land claims a few years later (Kruger, 2015).

4 Restoring Historical Injustices: Integrating Conservation with Human Development at South African National Parks

The early 1990s saw the transition to majority rule in South Africa, and in line with the growing global discourses on and trends in environmental sustainability that gained momentum since the 1980s, the newly elected government clearly stated that the environmental inequalities and social injustices inflicted upon communities in the previous political dispensation would be addressed as an integral part of a new conservation philosophy and the right to "ecological sustainable development" (Meskell, 2012). Subsequently, a series of new laws and policies followed, aiming to support and promote the principles of social justice, participation, equity, environmental sustainability, and transparency. To give the necessary organizational impetus to the new policy framework as enshrined in the Constitution, in 1997 the National Parks Board changed its name to South African National Parks (SANParks). The political, economic, and social realities of the new political dispensation were reflected in major policy changes in conservation philosophy and organizational structure to accommodate a shift towards integrating conservation interests with the socio-economic needs of communities adjacent to national parks (Anthony, 2007). A Social Ecology Unit that was established in 1994 was tasked with the implementation of the new policy of integrated conservation and development, and to improve the strained relationships between parks and their neighbouring communities. The *People and Parks* Programme of SANParks which was launched in the early 1990s was a direct response to a call at the World Parks Congress (2003) that protected areas should play a role in the mitigation of poverty among neighbouring communities. The revised conservation policy also made provision for parks to channel socio-economic benefits to surrounding communities as part of a more holistic approach to sustainable development and the sustainable utilization of resources (Department of Environmental Affairs, 2009). In 2003, the Social Ecology unit was transformed and renamed the People and Conservation Directorate (Van Damme & Meskell, 2009) to oversee the role SANParks has to play in terms of sustainable socio-economic development and benefit-sharing of conservation initiatives with neighbouring communities.

5 Benefit-sharing from Conservation and the Promotion of Environmental and Social Justice in South Africa

Protected areas, and particularly national parks in the case of South Africa, are part of a wider socio-ecological system that supports communities by means of several ecosystem services or benefits that people derive from the natural environment (Swemmer & Taljaard, 2011). The ability to access such ecosystem services impacts directly on the livelihoods and quality of life of those living within the system. In South Africa, benefit-sharing through the conservation of biodiversity has become increasingly important for the survival of protected areas, bearing in mind the history of environmental and social injustices that formed part of the proclamation of many such areas. In the post-1994 dispensation, the challenge for many national parks is to extend benefit-sharing beyond the limitations of employment opportunities and recreation.

Notwithstanding a lack of international consensus on what "benefit-sharing" specifically means and entails in the context of protected areas (Swemmer et al., 2015), it is nevertheless accepted that not only does a sound policy and practice of benefit-sharing promote environmental justice, but it may also serve to strengthen the message of conservation and help to restore negative attitudes towards protected areas amongst deprived rural communities, who had to bear the cost of conservation in the past. Swemmer et al. (2017) describe benefits as "impacts that make a positive contribution to human well-being," and can differ in terms of type, value, and nature. Ultimately, however, benefits that stem from national parks, whether of an ecological or non-ecological type, aim to mitigate the conservation-related impacts on the well-being of affected communities. The Millennium Ecosystem Assessment (MEA, 2005) defines ecological benefits as those direct positive services that flow from the ecosystem within and around protected areas, and include freshwater, food, building material, medicine, and livestock fodder. Also falling under the ecological benefits of national parks are cultural services such as ecotourism, spiritual enrichment, wilderness experience, etc. On the other hand, non-ecological benefits of national parks refer to benefits such as environmental education and awareness, direct and indirect employment, and the multiplier economic impact of opportunities offered by a specific park (MEA, 2005). All benefits, however, regardless of whether they are ecological, economic, social, cultural, or political, eventually contribute to people's quality of life and well-being. In the context of national parks in South Africa, the net outcome of fair benefit-sharing should, therefore, result in broader societal support for conservation, mitigation of poverty amongst rural communities adjacent to protected areas, and (at least partial) redress of environmental and social injustices of the past.

One possible way of providing conservation benefits to neighbouring communities of national parks is by means of resource harvesting and utilization.

6 Harvesting Resources in Protected Areas

With biodiversity that is increasingly threatened outside national parks as a result of climate change and population pressure, the resources within such protected areas are becoming more and more important (Vermeulen et al., 2019). This is not only applicable to conservation, but also to the livelihoods and social and cultural needs of neighbouring communities who, in many cases, are resentful of the lack of access to resources that they experience as a result of historical injustices in the implementation of past conservation policies. In an attempt therefore to address some of the social inequalities in access brought about by previous conservation policies and to improve community perceptions of conservation in general, SANParks is promoting the use of natural resources in national parks as part of a comprehensive drive to benefit poor rural populations living on the boundaries of parks (Swemmer et al., 2015).

The harvesting and use of resources in national parks are directed by the SANParks Resource Use Policy (SANParks, 2010) and the *National Environmental Management: Protected Areas Act* (Act No. 57 of 2003) (RSA, 2004). The SANParks policy on resource use aims to facilitate and monitor access to the harvesting of selected natural resources inside the boundaries of national parks and to reduce the illegal use and harvesting of such resources, wherever possible (Swemmer et al., 2015). A recent study by Van Wilgen and McGeoch (2015) shows that there is a huge demand for access to a diversity of resources within national parks across South Africa, with an estimated 340 species involved. Most of these species are in demand for sources of food and medicine (Van Wilgen & McGeoch, 2015), but there are numerous examples of resource use and harvesting involving a wide range of biodiversity in many of the national parks across the country. Examples of resources within national parks that are harvested for subsistence, as well as traditional and commercial purposes, include: sour figs in the Agulhas National Park, medicinal plant harvesting in the Garden Route National Park, Kruger National Park, and Kgalagadi Transfrontier Park, indigenous timber harvesting in the Garden Route National Park, forest fern harvesting in the Tsitsikamma National Park, and the harvesting of Mopani worms and grass in the Kruger National Park (SANParks, 2021).

The SANParks Resource Use Policy (SANParks, 2010) is based on a systems approach to sustainable resource use with various ecological and socio-economic drivers that link national parks as protected areas to their surrounding environment (Scheepers et al., 2011). Resource users are not limited to members of neighbouring communities though, as the concept is extended to include stakeholder groups such as staff, researchers, local entrepreneurs, small business owners, and the public. This complex network between parks and their socio-economic environment and multiple stakeholders is clearly illustrated in the case of grass harvesting at the Golden Gate Highlands National Park, as discussed in the next session.

7 Case Study: Grass Harvesting at the Golden Gate Highlands National Park

The Golden Gate Highlands National Park (GGHNP), located in the eastern Free State province of South Africa (see Fig. 1), is the only national park in the country that has been proclaimed for the protection of the all-important Afromontane grassland species found in the park. The grasslands outside the park are either degraded or have been lost to erosion and overgrazing. To appreciate the grass-harvesting project in the park and its impact on poverty mitigation, it is necessary to understand the role and function of grassland ecosystems.

8 A Note on Grassland Ecosystems

With approximately 40% of the planet's surface covered by grasslands, an estimated 800 million to 1 billion people worldwide depend on grassland ecosystems for their livelihoods (Leisher et al., 2011; Pelser et al., 2015). Approximately, one-third of South Africa is covered by the grassland biome—the largest of the country's nine biomes—that includes, amongst others, 42 river systems, 5 Ramsar wetlands, and 3 World Heritage Sites (Kernan, 2016). However, less than 2% of grasslands in South Africa are officially protected, and the South African montane grasslands, such as those found in the Golden Gate Highlands National Park, are listed as critically endangered (Leisher et al., 2011). Apart from being a habitat to many species and its vital role in freshwater production, grasslands also provide a wide range of essential ecosystem services such as grazing for cattle and wildlife, flood attenuation, wetland functioning, thatch for dwellings, grass for weaving and medicinal plants—all services that are of great importance for human health and well-being (Pelser et al., 2015). The grassland biome in South Africa is increasingly threatened by human population growth, mining activities, commercial and subsistence agriculture, urbanization, and climate change. More than one-third of the grassland biome has already been irreversibly transformed (Pelser et al., 2015), and climate change is set to excel in this process—especially in cases where climate change is interlocking with rural poverty (Rudi et al., 2012).

The current and projected future state of degradation of South African grasslands means that human well-being is threatened to such an extent that the National Biodiversity and Action Plan identified the grassland biome as a conservation priority for the country (DEAT, 2005). Climate change in particular holds a major threat to grasslands all over the world, including South African grasslands. Gibson and Newman (2019), for instance, point out that global warming will lead to increased surface water losses, more intense droughts, more frequent heatwaves and heat stress, desertification, and higher frequencies of wildfires. Higher temperatures may also result in a loss of habitat for temperature-vulnerable grassland species. Because of the link between climate change and poverty (Rudi et al., 2012), efforts towards sustainable development will become increasingly difficult as a result of the devastating impact of climate change on poor rural populations surrounding national parks.

9 About GGHNP as Protected Area

The GGHNP, at the foothills of the Maloti-Drakensberg mountains, was proclaimed in 1963 and to date, it is still the only national park in the Free State province of South Africa (SANParks, 2020). The park is more than 32,000 ha in size and, apart from its striking sandstone formations, also serves as a habitat for a large variety of antelope, mammals and bird species. GGHNP is also well renowned for important paleontological discoveries such as the world's oldest fossilized dinosaur nesting sites that date back to the upper Triassic Age (200–230 million years) (Kernan, 2016; SANParks, 2012). The discovery of the initial nesting site in 1973 that contained the remains of *Massospondylus embryos* was later followed by several discoveries of dinosaur footprints and skeletons in the park and mapped the greater GGHNP area as one of the most prominent dinosaur fossil sites in the world.

The park is located in one of the most important water catchment regions in the country and more than 50% of South Africa's freshwater supply comes from the larger Golden Gate Highlands area, while up to 30% of the total freshwater supply of Southern Africa has its origin in the Golden Gate catchment basin (SANParks, 2020). The park is home to 52 small and 58 large mammal species. Also found in the park are 22 amphibian species, 3 fish species, more than 250 bird species (including the highly endangered grass owl, bearded vulture, and bald ibis), 20 reptile species, and 117 invertebrates (SANParks, 2020). Currently GGHNP forms part of the Maloti-Drakensberg Transfrontier Conservation and Development Area following a bilateral treaty between South Africa and Lesotho. The wetlands in GGHNP are very important but became degraded as a result of commercial farming practices prior to the proclamation of the park. The rehabilitation of these wetlands—a project that involves the neighbouring communities—is of great importance for the water catchment systems in the area, and eventually for water security in the country.

More than 60 grass species are found in the park, attracting nearby communities who depend on this and other resources in the park for their livelihoods. As a result, the park faces several threats, ranging from invasive plant species, wildfires, and poaching of the game to overharvesting of medicinal plants (Leonard, 2013). Sporadic conflicts between park management and local communities stem from demands for resource use, land claims, and land-use practices. Some park inhabitants as well as members of the neighbouring community are related to farmworkers, who had once occupied the land before the commercial farms were purchased by government, merged, and converted into the GGHNP during the early 1960s (Leonard, 2013). Some of the community members still use parts of the park for communal grazing—a practice that is often the source of conflict between the park and local communities. Taru et al. (2013), for instance, report huge resistance from park inhabitants who refuse to be relocated as they cannot leave the graves of their ancestors and family members. The conflict between the park and communities partly stems from the fact that the farm labourers of that time were never compensated when the commercial farms were incorporated into the park. Some of these workers remained behind and stayed in the park, and in terms of South African legislation of the post-1994 era, these workers and their offspring may not be relocated or evicted unless a suitable alternative can be found to accommodate them (Leonard, 2013).

The rising demands on ecosystem services in GGHNP and other national parks in the country are increasingly influencing ecosystems as climate change increases with rising population needs and consumption. Managing and protecting these supporting ecosystem services have therefore become of paramount importance to ensure the sustainability of these services and their contribution to human needs and well-being. In the South African context, such conservation efforts inevitably mean restoring environmental and social injustices of the past by sharing the benefits of conservation with neighbouring communities.

10 The Neighbouring Communities of the Park

GGHNP falls within the Thabo Mofutsanyana District Municipality in the Free State province—a municipality with a total population of 762 075 in 2018 (SAIRR, 2019). It is one of five district municipalities in the Free State province and one of the most impoverished regions in the country (Kernan, 2016), with many households relying on one or more social grants as the only source of income for the family (Tau et al., 2013). The average household income is approximately 50% of the comparative amount for the rest of the Free State province. In 2019, the lower-bound poverty rate for the municipality was 52.1% (DCGTA, 2020), which means that more than half of the population fell below the upper-bound poverty line of ZAR1 138 (SAIRR, 2019), or approximately US$78 per person per month, based on the average rand/dollar exchange rate for 2019. The park's neighbouring population is predominantly a young one: Almost 69% is younger than 34 years (SAIRR, 2019), but the high unemployment rate of 32%—increasing to 39% among females—is driving young men out of the region in search of job opportunities elsewhere (DCGTA, 2020; Pelser et al., 2011). Consequently, the sex ratio in the municipality is quite skewed: 53.3% females versus 46.7% males, giving rise to a high proportion of female-headed households that are trapped in poverty.

The above socio-economic conditions have resulted in a poor quality of life and low levels of human development that hamstring the district's population. These conditions are also driving activities such as poaching and the illegal harvesting of plant material inside GGHNP. Maintaining the ecological integrity of GGHNP, therefore, requires park management to reach out to the local community as part of SANParks' philosophy of integrated conservation and development. As in the case of many other national parks in South Africa, GGHNP too has potentially an important role to play in the mitigation of rural poverty. Since 2002 various programmes have been implemented with the purpose of creating conservation-based employment opportunities for members of the local community. More than ZAR78 million (approximately $5.3 million) has been spent on wetland and ecosystem rehabilitation and fire prevention programmes between 2002 and 2020, reaching a total of 1 441 direct beneficiaries in the form of job opportunities (SANParks, 2020). These programmes, albeit of a temporary nature, are an important source of income for poor households that often lack education and skills. The grass-harvesting programme in the park is one example of how the park's management attempts to reconcile conservation concerns with sustainable human development. The GGHNP initiative, in fact, serves as a good example of the characteristics of an outreach programme implemented in a protected area, thereby corresponding with the ICDP typologies alluded to earlier in this chapter.

11 The Grass-Harvesting Programme in GGHNP

Following the switch to a policy of integrated conservation and development programmes adopted by SANParks in the new political dispensation, the management of GGHNP started to reach out to the park's neighbouring communities with the purpose of channelling some of the benefits of conservation to communities in the surrounding areas and thereby to address at least some of their socio-economic needs. The park embarked on several initiatives in this regard, one of which being the issue of commercial access permits to selected members of the local community that allow them to harvest grass in the park. This is one of several projects guided by SANParks' Resource Use Policy.

For many decades, the larger Golden Gate Highlands area was a rich source of harvestable grass for the local population. Once harvested, the grass was used in the manufacturing of hats, floormats, brooms, and baskets (Pelser et al., 2015). Another important use for the grass was for roof thatching. With the proclamation of GGHNP in 1963, the harvesting of resources inside the park was prohibited in accordance with national legislation. Consequently, the neighbouring community was cut off from the use of this natural resource, but upon approval of the SANParks Resource Use Policy in 2010, the park started with an outreach initiative that allowed the neighbouring community access to the park to harvest grass under controlled and regulated circumstances. Programme beneficiaries are recruited from neighbouring communities as well as neighbouring farms. In order to ensure that programme benefits reach the most vulnerable sectors of the community, those on the programme are mainly women who, in many cases, come from female-headed households. Community members also serve on an advisory committee and assist in identifying previously disadvantaged people who might qualify for selection to enter the programme. Areas inside the park were identified where two of the popular grasses that are commonly used for thatching, namely the *Hyparrhenia cf. Hirta* and the *Hyparrhenia cf. dregeana* species, are abundant. Harvesting quotas per person are strictly limited to the identified areas and no harvesting outside these areas is allowed in order to reduce any risk of overharvesting. Park rangers need to monitor the harvesting and enforce the regulations.

A total of 46 community members were initially granted harvesting permits and formed the target population for a programme evaluation conducted in 2014. The research design was both exploratory and evaluative in nature using a predominantly qualitative approach to ascertain the success of the grass-harvesting programme, its impact on the well-being of beneficiaries and obstacles faced in the implementation of the programme. Samples were drawn and data collected among 34 direct programme beneficiaries, two park officials directly responsible for the administration of the programme, as well as representatives of two commercial companies that purchase the thatch after each harvest. Data was collected by means of focus group sessions, personal interviews and telephonic interviews (Kernan, 2016; Pelser et al., 2015). Most of the beneficiaries indicated that, prior to joining the programme, their lives were hard and difficult due to their deprived socio-economic circumstances, but that their lives had improved as a result of their participation in the harvesting programme. Almost all the beneficiaries reported that during the harvesting season they sell their thatch bundles of grass to a harvesting coordinator on either a daily or a weekly basis. The harvesting coordinator in turn sells the thatch bundles to commercial thatching companies. A small portion of the harvested grass is used for the manufacturing of carpets and brooms that are sold in the local community and to tourists. Only two beneficiaries do not feed their harvested thatch into the economic supply chain consisting of harvesters, the harvesting coordinator, and the commercial companies, but either use the thatch themselves or sell it directly to members of their communities for roof repairs (Kernan, 2016). From these options and choices, it transpires that the beneficiaries seem to favour immediate or short-term solutions to meet their basic needs, but in the process their long-term well-being does not improve much. Notwithstanding, the greatest impact of this programme is probably the fact that it has granted community members access to resources that they desperately rely on, and in doing so the programme has managed to bridge the historical divide between the park and the community and promotes environmental justice, especially where the proclamation of GGHNP in the 1960s deprived the community of access to the resource. Apart from being able to meet their basic needs, the direct beneficiaries of this programme, as well as their dependents, also experience immediate relief from abject poverty, and also benefit from other positive impacts such as improved nutritional status, better health and an increased ability to pay their children's school fees (Pelser et al., 2015). High levels of poverty nevertheless remain a harsh reality for the majority of the neighbouring population, thus emphasizing the need for continued benefit-sharing between parks and their communities as part of a more coherent attempt to redress the environmental and social injustices inflicted upon communities by previous conservation philosophies and practices. Although only a very small proportion of the neighbouring population benefits directly from their participation in the programme, the impact on the well-being and livelihoods of this group and their dependents is significant when seen in the wider context of the harsh socio-economic conditions in the area.

12 Restoring Social Injustices of the Past: Lessons Learned from New Conservation Initiatives by National Parks

Integrated conservation and development experiences in post-apartheid South Africa clearly show that such programmes and agreements are only the first mile in a long journey towards a redress of environmental and social injustices committed in the name of conservation. As illustrated in the case of the grass-harvesting programme at GGHNP, an efficient institutional structure is an important condition for the success of these kinds of programmes. For any such programme to maximize its impact, it is important to target and recruit the neediest and vulnerable segments of the neighbouring population, and a supportive institutional structure consisting of all relevant stakeholders can play an important role here. To change negative sentiments towards protected areas and restore some of the environmental injustices of the past (such as a restriction on access to resources inside protected areas), any representative institutional structure should ensure that the outreach programme responds to the socio-economic needs of the neighbouring community, and not only to issues that are of concern to conservation authorities. Without the involvement of and commitment from stakeholders in the political, economic and environmental sectors, there is little chance of the long-term sustainability of these types of initiatives.

A key lesson for conservation authorities and policymakers is that the implementation of a community outreach programme that acknowledges historical wrongs and aims to redress past practices of injustice in conservation management does not imply that social justice will automatically be achieved once a system of benefit-sharing has been put in place. The GGHNP case study further shows that communities require institutional support to reclaim their rights, which implies a process of capacity building, where needed, in order to ensure sustainable development and long-term improvement in well-being and curbing of poverty rates. Programmes that only focus on immediate gratification or short-term benefits will not pass the test of sustainability, and for that reason an improvement in education levels and literacy is equally important for communities to participate effectively in the benefits of national parks and other protected areas (Wells, 1996). The strengthening of human resources is therefore a crucial precondition in the process to restore historical injustices in conservation practices: Unless communities are capacitated to enter into new relationships with protected areas from a position of strength, they will not be able to make informed decisions in their own best interest in the long run. To reclaim their environmental rights, impoverished communities as neighbours of protected areas need to move from a position of passive receivers of short-term benefits to active participants in sustainable benefit-sharing.

South Africa has a long and deep-rooted history of environmental and social injustice to poor, rural communities—an injustice that is tightly intertwined with the country's political and conservation history. Attempts by SANParks to restore (some of) these injustices by means of integrated conservation and development programmes do not mean that national parks should suddenly be seen as a key solution to widespread poverty in rural areas. Both conservation authorities and local communities should, therefore, guard against unrealistic expectations on the part of neighbouring communities, as benefit-sharing from national parks and demands for access to resources inside such areas in many cases outweigh reasonable possibilities of sustainable benefits that can be channelled to communities on a wide-reaching scale (Swemmer & Taljaard, 2011). In the future, increasing population numbers that will interlock with the consequences of climate change in rural areas will see more and more people flocking to protected areas in search of access to resources, and conservation managers will face a tough task to differentiate between neighbouring populations (as victims of past injustices) and other opportunistic groups also demanding access to the same resources. Unabated expectations and demands for access to resources within protected areas pose a huge threat to integrated conservation and development programmes, not only in South Africa but also in many other developing countries too. As Simelane et al. (2006) point out, communities next to protected areas such as GGHNP, Mountain Zebra National Park, Karoo National Park and Addo Elephant National Park often have limited ecological knowledge and a poor understanding of sustainability levels of resources within the park. Differences in cultural backgrounds, historical links with the park, aged groups and education level all lead to different expectations. Any attempt to restore past injustices by means of outreach programmes and benefit-sharing initiatives should therefore take into consideration the heterogeneous nature of neighbouring communities to ensure that such programmes target the neediest segments of the population and those that have truly fallen victim to past conservation practices and policies that had a negative impact on their livelihoods and well-being.

13 Conclusion

As protected areas in developing nations continue to expand and consequently infringe upon the environmental and social rights of poor rural communities, the debate around the impact of protected areas on local populations is likely to intensify. Given South Africa's turbulent political and socio-economic history, restoring the environmental and social injustices of the apartheid era—including injustices committed under the banner of conservation—has become an important point on the post-apartheid agenda. As shown in the GGHNP study, a carefully planned and well-managed outreach programme focusing on benefit-sharing from sustainable resource use can indeed make an important contribution to the livelihoods of communities living next to protected areas. There is, however, no one-size-fits-all approach when it comes to integrated conservation and development programmes as a mechanism to restore historical injustices, which means that such programmes are likely to vary considerably between different protected areas. A number of factors may interlock to determine the outcome and impact of any outreach initiative: the specific park's historical context, the size of the local population and number of beneficiaries, the socio-economic profile of the neighbouring community, mediation of inter- and intra-community conflicts, community participation in the planning of the programme, the identification and recruitment of beneficiaries, the ecological viability of resource harvesting, the efficiency of institutional support, the implementation of a monitoring programme, etc.

The role of protected areas, and national parks in particular, as potential catalysts for social justice and sustainable human development should not be romanticized or seen as the ultimate solution to rural poverty. No protected area can be a substitute for government responsibilities and human development programmes; at its best, it can only supplement national initiatives. Economic and demographic realities dictate that even in the best-case scenarios, only a small proportion of the neighbouring population will potentially benefit from an integrated conservation and development initiative. Arguably the biggest challenge facing any community outreach initiative is to plan a programme that is fair, equitable, and ecologically sustainable. Community needs and demands, however, are often driven by the poor, with the unemployed and environmental justice groups placing an emphasis on access to resources, while conservation groups argue for the protection of the very same resources and caution against habitat destruction and species loss (Simon, 2016). The demands or expectations for benefits from the protected area often exceed the capacity of the protected area to meet those demands in a sustainable and ecologically responsible way—something that can easily lead to increased sentiments of disillusionment, frustration, and even confrontation. Fuelling this situation is the fact that integrated conservation and development initiatives are often hampered by limited networking between conservation managers and environmental justice groups (Leonard, 2013). Even within the ranks of SANParks some conservation groups do not accept development programmes as part of a more elaborate conservation agenda in the post-apartheid dispensation, and therefore view environmental justice as falling outside their expertise and responsibility, which is the protection and management of biodiversity (Swemmer et al., 2011). Striking a balance, therefore, between the two polarized interests of conservation and development groups is perhaps one of the greatest impediments in implementing any benefit-sharing programme and supporting the livelihoods of neighbouring communities in an environmentally sustainable way.

References

Andam, K. S., Ferraro, P. J., Sims, K. R. E., Healy, A., & Holland, M. B. (2010). Protected areas reduced poverty in Costa Rica and Thailand. *PNAS, 107*(22), 9996–10001. https://doi.org/10.1073/pnas.0914177107

Anthony, B. (2007). The dual nature of parks: Attitudes of neighbouring communities towards Kruger National Park South Africa. *Environmental Conservation, 34* (3), 236–245. https://doi.org/10.1017/S0376892907004018

Barrow, E., & Murphree, M. (2001). Community conservation: From concept to practice. In D. Hulme & M. Murphree (Eds.), *African wildlife & livelihoods* (pp. 9–23). David Philip.

Brooks, J., Waylen, K .A., & Mulder, M. B. (2013). Assessing community-based conservation projects: A systematic review and multilevel analysis of attitudinal, behavioral, ecological, and economic outcomes. *Environmental Evidence, 2* (2), 1–34. https://doi.org/10.1186/2047-2382-2-2

Protected Areas as a Catalyst for Environmental Sustainability … 223

Chapin, M. (2004). A challenge to conservationists. *World Watch, 17*(6), 17–31. https://redd-mon itor.org/wp-content/uploads/2019/03/WorldWatch-Chapin.pdf

DCGTA (Department of Cooperative Governance & Traditional Affairs). (2020). *Thabo Mofutsanyana District municipality: District development model.* DCGTA. Retrieved April 2, 2021, from https://www.cogta.gov.za/ddm/wp-content/uploads/2020/08/DistrictProfile_THABO MOFUTSANYANA0807-2.pdf

DEAT (Department of Environment and Tourism). (2005). *South Africa's national biodiversity strategy and action plan.* DEAT. Retrieved March 17, 2021, from https://www.environment.gov.za/sites/default/files/docs/nationalbiodiversit_stractandactionplan.pdf

De Koning, M. (2009). Co-management and its options in protected areas of South Africa. *Africanus, 39*(2), 5–17.

Department of Environmental Affairs. (2009). *Conservation for the people with the people.* Department of Environmental Affairs. Retrieved April 14, 2021, from https://www.environment.gov.za/mediastatement/fourthpeople_parksconference_closing

De Sherbinin, A. (2008). Is poverty more acute near parks? An assessment of infant mortality rates around protected areas in developing countries. *Oryx, 42*(1), 26–35.

Fisher, J. A., Dhungana, H., Duffy, J., He, J., Inturias, M., Lehmann, I., Martin, A., Mwayafu, D. M., Rodríguez, I., & Schneider, H. (2020). Conservationists' perspectives on poverty: An empirical study. *People and Nature, 2*(3), 678–692. https://doi.org/10.1002/pan3.10098

Gibson, D. J. & Newman, J. A. (2019). *Grasslands and climate change.* Cambridge University Press. https://doi.org/10.1017/9781108163941.003

Kernan, A. M. (2016). *Assessment of the thatch harvesting programme at Golden Gate Highlands National Park* (MA dissertation). University of the Free State.

Krüger, R., Cundill, G., & Thondhlana, G. (2015). A case study of the opportunities and trade-offs associated with deproclamation of a protected area following a land claim in South Africa. *Local Environment, 21*(9), 1047–1062. https://doi.org/10.1080/13549839.2015.1065804

Leisher, C., Brouwer, R., Boucher, T. M., Vogelij, R., Bainbridge, W. R., & Sanjayan, M. (2011). Striking a balance: Socioeconomic development and conservation in grassland through community-based zoning. *PLoS ONE, 6* (12), 1–10. Article e28807. https://doi.org/10.1371/journal.pone.0028807

Leonard, L. (2013). The relationship between the conservation agenda and environmental justice in post-apartheid South Africa: An analysis of Wessa KwaZulu-Natal and environmental justice advocates. *South African Review of Sociology, 44*(3), 2–21. https://www.researchgate.net/deref/http%3A%2F%2Fdx.doi.org%2F10.1080%2F21528586.2013.817059

MEA (Millennium Ecosystem Assessment). (2005). *Ecosystems and human well-being: Synthesis.* Island Press. Retrieved March 9, 2021, from https://www.millenniumassessment.org/documents/document.356.aspx.pdf

Meskell, L. (2012). *The nature of heritage: The new South Africa.* Wiley-Blackwell.

Nyhus, P. J. (2016). Human-wildlife conflict and coexistence. *Annual Review of Environment and Resources, 41*(1), 143–171. https://doi.org/10.1146/annurev-environ-110615-085634

Pelser, A. J. (2012). The health, environment and development nexus in South Africa. In H. C. J. van Rensburg (Ed.), *Health and health care in South Africa* (2nd ed., pp. 189–236). Van Schaik.

Pelser, A. J., Redelinghuys, N., & Kernan, A. M. (2015). Protected areas and ecosystem services—Integrating grassland conservation with human well-being in South Africa. In Y. Lo, J. A. Blanco, & S. Roy (Eds.), *Biodiversity in ecosystems: Linking structure and function* (pp. 597–626). InTech.

Pelser, A. J., Redelinghuys, N., & Velelo, N. (2011). People, parks and poverty: Integrated conservation and development initiatives in the Free State Province of South Africa. In O. Grillo & G. Venora (Eds.), *Biological diversity and sustainable resources use* (pp. 35–62). InTech.

Pelser, A. J., & Sempe, A. (2003). Omgewingsbewaring in'n nuwe era:'n Nis vir die geestes-en sosiale wetenskappe. *Tydskrif vir Geesteswetenskappe, 43* (3/4), 164–176.

Roe, D., Elliott,. J, Sandbrook, C., & Walpole,. M. (2013). *Biodiversity conservation and poverty alleviation: Exploring the evidence for a link.* Wiley-Blackwell.

RSA (Republic of South Africa). (2004). *National environmental management: Protected areas act* (Act No. 57 of 2003). *Government Gazette* 464 (26025). https://www.gov.za/sites/default/files/gcis_document/201409/a57-03.pdf

Rudi, A., Azadi, H., & Witlox, F. (2012). Reconcilability of socio-economic development and environmental conservation in Sub-Saharan Africa. *Global and Planetary Change, 86–87*, 1–10. https://doi.org/10.1016/j.gloplacha.2011.12.004

SAIRR (South African Institute of Race Relations). South Africa Survey 2019. SAIRR.

SANParks (South African National Parks). (2010). *SANParks resource use policy*, Ref. 17/P—CSD/pol/resource use/03-10/vs 1. SANParks.

SANParks (South African National Parks. (2012, January 24). *Media release: Ancient Dinosaur nursery—The oldest nesting site ever found.* SANParks. Retrieved March 8, 2021, from https://www.sanparks.org/about/news/?id=1797

SANParks (South African National Parks). (2020). *Golden gate highlands national park management plan 2020–2029.* SANParks. Retrieved March 14, 2021, from https://www.sanparks.org/assets/docs/conservation/park_man/gghnp_approved_plan.pdf

SANParks (South African National Parks). (2021). *Overview of programmes.* SANParks. Retrieved April 8, 2021, from https://www.sanparks.org/about/connecting_to_society/

Scheepers, K., Swemmer, L., & Vermeulen, W. J. (2011). Applying adaptive management in resource use in South African National Parks: A case study approach. *Koedoe 53*(2), 144–157. Article 999. http://www.scielo.org.za/pdf/koedoe/v53n2/v53n2a14.pdf

Simelane, T. S., Kerley, G. I. H., & Knight, M. H. (2006). Reflections on the relationships between communities and conservation areas of South Africa: The case of five South African national parks. *Koedoe, 49*(2), 85–102.

Simon, H. R. (2016). Understanding the polarisation of environmental and social activism in South Africa. *South African Journal of Science, 112*(11/12), Article a0180. http://dx.doi.org/https://doi.org/10.17159/sajs.2016/a0180

Simpson, M. (2009). An integrated approach to assess the impacts of tourism on community development and sustainable livelihoods. *Community Development Journal, 44*(2), 186–208. Retrieved September 3, 2021, from http://www.jstor.org/stable/44259104

Spenceley, A. (2008). Responsible tourism in Southern Africa. In A. Spenceley (Ed.), *Responsible tourism: Critical issues for conservation and development* (pp. 1–24). Earthscan. Retrieved March 31, 2021, from https://books.google.co.za/books?hl=en&lr=&id=wmKsBwAAQBAJ&oi=fnd&pg=PR3&dq=Responsible+tourism:+critical+issues+for+conservation+and+development,&ots=FVkcsWySDc&sig=OoFcIYqxD9dGs2iVIWRg6QDfGGA#v=onepage&q=Responsible%20tourism%3A%20critical%20issues%20for%20conservation%20and%20development%2C&f=false

Swemmer, L. K., & Taljaard, S. (2011). SANParks, people and adaptive management: Understanding a diverse field of practice during changing times. *Koedoe, 53*(2), Article 1017. http://dx.doi.org/https://doi.org/10.4102/koedoe.v53i2.1017

Swemmer, L., Grant, R., Annecke, W., & Freitag-Ronaldson, S. (2015). Toward more effective benefit sharing in South African National Parks. *Society & Natural Resources: An International Journal, 28*(1), 4–20. https://doi.org/10.1080/08941920.2014.945055

Swemmer, L., Mmethi, H., & Twine, W. (2017). Tracing the cost/benefit pathway of protected areas: A case study of the Kruger National Park, South Africa. *Ecosystem Services, 28*. https://doi.org/10.1016/j.ecoser.2017.09.002

Taru, P., Mukwada, G., Somerai, P., & Chingombe, W. (2013). QwaQwa community perceptions on the proposed dinosaur museum in the Golden Gate Highlands National Park, South Africa. *African Journal for Physical, Health Education, Recreation and Dance* (Supplement 2), 187–198. https://www.researchgate.net/publication/257869599_QwaQwa_community_perceptions_on_the_proposed_dinosaur_museum_in_the_Golden_Gate_Highlands_National_Park_South_Africa

Tour, S. A. (2021). *Map of South African National Parks.* Preprint retrieved from http://saparks.co.za/resources/map_sa-parks.htm

Protected Areas as a Catalyst for Environmental Sustainability ...

United Nations. (2015). *Transforming our world: The 2030 agenda for sustainable development.* Retrieved March 16, 2021, from https://sustainabledevelopment.un.org/content/documents/212 52030%20Agenda%20for%20Sustainable%20Development%20web.pdf

Upton, C., Ladle, R., Hulme, D., Jiang, T., Brockington, D., & Adams, W. M. (2008). Are poverty and protected area establishment linked at a national scale? *Oryx, 42*(1), 19–25. https://doi.org/10.1017/S0030605307001044

Van Damme, L. S. M., & Meskell, L. (2009). Producing conservation and community in South Africa. *Ethics, Place and Environment, 12*(1), 69–89. https://doi.org/10.1080/136687909027 53088

Van Wilgen, N. J., & McGeoch, M. A. (2015). Balancing effective conservation with sustainable resource use in protected areas: Precluded by knowledge gaps. *Environmental Conservation, 42*(3), 246–255. https://doi.org/10.1017/S0376892914000320.

Vermeulen, W., Van Wilgen, N., Smith, K., Dopolo, M., Swemmer, L., Annecke, W. Bezuidenhout, H., Durrheim, G., Hanekom, N., Hendricks, H., McGeoch, M., Ngubeni, N., & Symonds, A. (2019). Monitoring consumptive resource use in South African national parks. *Koedoe, 61*(1), Article a1516. https://doi.org/10.4102/koedoe.v61i1.1516

Wells, M. P. (1996). The social role of protected areas in the new South Africa. *Environmental Conservation, 23*(4), 322–331.

Wells, M.P., & McShane, T. (2004). Integrating protected area management with local needs and aspirations. *Ambio, 33*(8), 513–519. http://www.jstor.org/stable/4315540

Critical and Social Movement Perspectives
from the Global South

Indigenous Environmental Movements of Eastern India: Seeing Through Henri Lefebvre's Spatial Lens

Tanaya Mohanty and Devendraraj Madhanagopal

1 Introduction

A strong consensus exists among a great deal of research that an intimate historical relationship exists between indigenous communities and their environment (Turner, 1979; Salmón, 2000; Singhal et al., 2021). Similarly, a large and growing body of scholarship on environmental movements confirms that indigenous populations fight fiercely in multiple ways to claim or maintain their rights and protect the ecosystems where they live (Arenas, 2007; Borde & Bluemling, 2021; Dove, 2006). Indigenous communities draw their cultural forms, livelihood practices, assets, and resources from their physical environment (Jena, 2013; Sahu, 2008). Displacement and dislocation from their native physical space or disturbances within those spaces dislocate them from their social, cultural, and religious identities (Andersson, 2005; ILO, 2009; UN, 2009) and as well as their livelihood mechanisms (UN, 2009). In most cases, the socio-cultural systems of the indigenous populations historically revolve around a direct relationship with nature, and their dependence and relationship with nature are unique and different from the non-tribal groups. In fact, the forests that are managed and governed by the indigenous communities are more protected and preserved from "external pressures" (FAO & FILAC, 2021).

Across Asia, there has been a growing number of environmental movements of marginalized people (Lee & So, 1999; Kalland & Persoon, 1999; Nayak, 2015; Swain, 2015). In recent decades, India has witnessed an emerging number of cases and lawsuits claiming the indigenous populations' land rights—a prominent example

---

T. Mohanty (✉)
Department of Sociology, Utkal University, Bhubaneswar, Odisha, India
e-mail: tanaya.mohanty309@gmail.com

D. Madhanagopal
School of Sustainability, XIM University, Odisha, India

© The Author(s), under exclusive license to Springer Nature Singapore Pte Ltd. 2022
D. Madhanagopal et al. (eds.), *Environment, Climate, and Social Justice*,
https://doi.org/10.1007/978-981-19-1987-9_12

is the case of the Niyamgiri (Krishnan & Naga, 2017). In 2015, according to Environmental Justice Atlas, India has the highest number of cases of social and environmental conflicts and environmental injustices[1] (Das, 2015). Indigenous people, commonly known as Adivasis in India, historically belong to India's eastern regions, including Odisha, Jharkhand, and Chhattisgarh, and Southern states as Andhra Pradesh and Telangana (Ministry of Tribal Affairs, 2018; Srivastava, 2021). The regions they reside in contain some of the world's most lucrative natural resources, such as iron ore, bauxite, copper, coal, mica, manganese, and many others (ENVIS, 2017). The resistance movements of the tribal communities of India have largely been examined by scholars from the perspectives of marginalization, exploitation, resistance to change, and reaffirming their tribal identity (Boal, 1978; Malik, 2020; Pattnaik, 2013; Prabhu, 1998). The literature that discusses the theoretical constructions of "space" and "spatial relations" has largely been limited.

2 Methodological and Theoretical Framework

The methodology that this chapter adopts is based on the application of theory to case studies illuminated through primary and secondary sources. We have made our arguments by looking at two cases of indigenous movements in the Eastern parts of India, analyzed through Henri Lefebvre's spatial lens. The arguments have been corroborated with primary documents made available by national and international bodies. Here we would like to emphasize that French sociologist Henri Lefebvre is known as a Marxist who has immensely contributed to the field of Urban Studies. In the present context, we tend to apply his ideas in the rural context for understanding the contestation over space between the indigenous communities and the State–Capitalist pair. We perceive Lefebvre as a postmodern thinker who has challenged the idea of space as a fixed entity. Here we would draw from Stuart Hall's notion of identity, where the latter refers to shifting identities leading to fragmented subjects in present postmodern globalized era. The idea of identity as a fixed homogenous historical subject has been challenged (Hall, 1992). We see such issues of fluid identity in terms of nationality, gender, and sexuality, to name a few. Here we argue that Lefebvre posits a challenge to the metanarrative of space being a fixed physical homogenous entity, though the idea of homogeneity is attributed by capitalism according to Lefebvre. We analyze the indigenous environmental movements as postmodern movements. First, we emphasize the idea of fluidity of space. Second, we highlight the deconstructionist approach of Lefebvre to dismantle the logocentrism associated with space, especially the space created by capitalists. Third, we see the indigenous resistances as a form of micro-politics emerging in the postmodern context. The strategies adopted

---

[1] It is also to be noted that this database is not comprehensive as there are chances of "non" or underreporting of environmental injustice cases that might have happened due to non-representation. Despite its limitations, it is one of the widely acclaimed databases worldwide to know environmental injustice cases.

by the indigenous communities have the essence of resistance in their everyday lives. Fourth, we see Lefebvre's concept of the "second nature" as a capitalist creation of a homogenizing process. The struggle posed by the community is a resistance to this process that goes on to celebrate difference and heterogeneous local narratives associated with space.

Understanding indigenous movements from a broader perspective of the political economy like the world systems theory, modernization, or development of underdevelopment framework for looking at rising issues like development induced displacement or people's movement has been already recognized. We assert that we are not just giving the framework of political economy a spatial dimension. We aim at arriving at a discourse on space and community. Even as far as social movements are concerned, it has been examined from the perspective of marginalization, relative deprivation, or resource mobilization lens, but here in the present context, we see a complex narrative emerging on issues related to livelihood, identity, and other socio-cultural and political dimensions which are spatial in nature. The nature of the space determines not only economic activities but also socio-cultural practices, and there, the resistances and contestations are about what form of space they want for themselves. The nature of resistances was also unique in its spatial locales giving rise to the local narrative of resistances which are postmodern in nature.

As we noted earlier, in this chapter, we examine indigenous movements through a spatial lens by looking deeply at two cases. The two movements come from the Indian states of Jharkhand and Odisha, where indigenous communities predominantly reside. We discuss how the resistance movements of the indigenous populations of these states are tuned against the transformative quality of capitalism that can convert space in any form into a revenue-generating site and also discuss the long history of indigenous resistance movements against the structures of dominations. We believe that Henri Lefebvre's[2] works are of immense relevance here because any form of resistance movement among the indigenous community in Eastern India in the recent decades have been either directed against the state or the corporate sectors/private business interests. In particular, the resistance movements of these indigenous populations have attempted transformations in those spaces and their relationship with their surrounding environment. There is a clash in the interest of the contending parties, namely the community and the State–Capitalist duo. While the indigenous community wants to retain the available space in its present form, what Lefebvre would refer to as Absolute Space, the state or/and corporate actors/interests would like to engage in the transformative nature of capitalism in the form of abstract space (Lefebvre, 1991; Leferebvre, 2009). Looking at indigenous environment movements through Lefebvre's spatial lens contributes to the existing literature in a novel way. Drawing from Lefebvre's works, this chapter discusses the contesting discourses and struggles between the State–Capitalist and the indigenous tribes.

---

[2] Henri Lefebvre, a French Marxist Philosopher and Sociologist, argued that capitalism could transform spaces to a great extent. He explored space and its dimensions in the modern context. We discuss the thoughts and contributions of Lefebvre in the upcoming sections.

In the following section, we discuss Lefebvre's idea of space and its multiple dimensions. In doing so, we engage in a debate on the role of capitalism in the transformation of space. Here, we discuss the social space that capitalism transforms. This social space is not just the lived space that shifts from one form to another with the pursuit of capitalism. As we will discuss further, capitalism transforms the public spaces with advanced technology, apt knowledge infrastructure, and private everyday life. These private residual spaces act as spaces of resistance in their everyday ways. These everyday practices trigger the inception of new social movements that are looked at from a postmodern framework. Following our examination of Lefebvre's conception of space, we examine the etymological meaning and the connotations that term like indigenous, tribal, and Adivasi offer in different contexts.

We discuss how structural changes emerging during colonial times ended up being present-day structural strains. As a social structure, we argue that ecology causes strains when human beings' relationship with nature gets disturbed through spatial re-location and structural re-arrangement. We conducted two case studies of indigenous environmental movements analyzed from a Lefebvreian spatial lens to justify our argument.

3 Lefebvre's Conception of Space

According to Lefebvre, space is not just a physical setting. It is socially constructed and continuously re-constituted in society. Multiple forces act upon this process of constitution and re-constitution of space. In the interplay of interested parties in the process of creating space, we can witness the whole power of such processes. Lefebvre treats space as an economic entity that can be and is produced socially. Space, in his opinion, possesses three dimensions: 1. The perceived; 2. The conceived; and 3. The representational space or the lived space. The perceived space pertains to the physical material category that can be measured, observed, and treaded. The conceived space is formulated by the discourse on space created by policymakers and architects. It is manifested in the form of maps, plans, and blueprints. The representational space or the lived space is carved out of the negotiated perception of the above two spaces (Lefebvre, 1991). Lefebvre seeks to understand space as a structure, a product, a means of production, a means of consumption, and a political instrument that perpetuates capitalism and has saved the latter from extinction (Lefebvre, 1991, 2009). When explaining social space and relations, he noted:

> There is one question which has remained open in the past because it has never been asked: what exactly is the mode of existence of social relationships? Are they substantial? natural? or formally abstract? The study of space offers an answer according to which the social relations of production have a social existence to the extent that they have a spatial existence; they project themselves into a space, becoming inscribed there, and in the process producing that space itself .... Space itself at once a product of the capitalist mode of production and an economico-political instrument of the bourgeoisie, will now be seen to embody its own contradictions. The dialectic thus emerges from time and actualizes itself, operating now, in an unforeseen manner, in space. The contradictions of space, without abolishing

Indigenous Environmental Movements of Eastern India: Seeing ...

> the contradictions which arise from historical time, leave history behind and transport those old contradictions, in a worldwide simultaneity, onto a higher level; there some of them are blunted, others exacerbated, as this contradictory whole takes on a new meaning and comes to designate 'something else'—another mode of production (Lefebvre, 1991, p. 129)

Space comprises human interactions, power dynamics, conflict, and social practices. It acts as a site of resistance that challenges the dominant discourses on space and substitutes it with a new meaning. It acts as a site for the counter-hegemonic version of space (Wrede, 2015). Lefebvre looks at the physical spaces in terms of dichotomies of being "natural or artificial," "natural or cultural," "work versus product," whether it belongs to the realm of nature or labor (Lefebvre, 1991, p. 332). His argument is posited on the grounds that capitalism transforms space and traverses a journey from one dichotomous position to another, as mentioned above. This negotiation takes place in the lived space. Space is *"endowed with exchange value"* (Lefebvre, 1991, p. 337). The tussle between use-value and exchange value is embodied in this transformation of space. So, the transformation of the inaccessible wild patch of space into a production site, culture, leisure unleashes some signs—*"signs of status, happiness, and lifestyle"* (Lefebvre, 1991, p. 339).

Lefebvre conceptualizes two different forms of space: abstract space and absolute space (Lefebvre, 1991). As Lefebvre explains, the absolute space signifies the use-value, and it is embedded in nature which satiates the common man's needs. There is mysticism associated with this space. The abstract space is produced through a nexus between capitalism and the state. With its intervening technology and mediated practice, capitalism carves out a closed space controlled and shaped by a massive infrastructural network of business, statecraft mechanisms, and other politico-economic structures. It is a space that is used to create surplus value. Soon it becomes a "policed space" (Lefebvre, 2009, p. 188). This space has the dual support of legitimate political patronage emanating from the state and, at the same time, a robust economic infrastructure endorsed by the corporate power. The economic and political power converge to transform this absolute space into a hegemonic site. In his words on abstract space:

> Formal boundaries are gone between town and country, between centre and periphery, between suburbs and city centres, between the domain of automobiles and the domain of people. Between happiness and unhappiness, for that matter. And yet everything ('public facilities', blocks of flats, 'environments for living') is separated, assigned in isolated fashion to unconnected 'sites' and 'tracts'; the spaces themselves are specialized just as operations are in the social and technical division of labour. (Lefebvre, 1991, p. 98)

Such spaces created and shaped by capitalism can act as a "political instrument" for control. (Lefebvre, 2009, p. 188). Space has become, for the state, a political instrument of primary importance. The state uses space to ensure its control of places, its strict hierarchy, the homogeneity of the whole, and the segregation of the parts. It is thus an administratively controlled and even a policed space. The hierarchy of spaces corresponds to that of social classes, and if there exist ghettos for all classes, those of the working class are more isolated than those of the others (Lefebvre, 2009). Lefebvre further notes in his work how capitalism has penetrated our everyday lives resulting in heightened alienation. This residual, personal realm was colonized by capitalism (Lefebvre, 1971, 2002). Lefebvre notes that there is a confrontation between the public and the private. Lefebvre defines the private life as the one with "the individual distinguishing himself from the social, without as such the individual separating from the society" (Lefebvre, 2003a, 2003b, p. 84. Translation work from Lefebvre, 1961). Public life speaks of the citizen who belongs to social groups, the political state, and a historical being.

> Everyday life emerges as a sociological point of feed-back, his crucial yet much disparaged point has a dual character; it is residuum (of all possible specific and specialized activities outside social experience) and the product of society in general; it is the point of delicate balance and that where imbalance threatens. A revolution takes place when and only when, in such a society, people can no longer lead their ordinary lives; so long as they can live their ordinary lives relations are constantly re-established. (Lefebvre, 1971, p. 32)

This every day belongs to the realm of passivity. This passivity is seen in family, leisure, and the private sphere, marked with consumption. The residual private life drenched with passivity has also been shaped by capitalism. Though it apparently seems that private life lies outside the domains of the public sphere like politics and the economy, Lefebvre sees a continuity in both these realms with the private running into the public and vice-versa. He argues that the public sphere is not the only space where one offers resistance against the State and the Capitalist organizations (Lefebvre, 2002). They emerge from every day though every day is also laced with aspects of public life. Yet, one sees a dilemma with every day resisting the public within the private domain. Lefebvre's idea of every day as a space of resistance would have taken the form of new social movements like feminism, ecological struggles, and human rights issues of the 1970s. In fact, "every day" holds the key to the postmodern politics of recent times (Poster, 2002). Here, we refer to Lefebvre's every day as a forum for resistance by the indigenous community, which entails small micro struggles against the State–Capitalist enterprises.

4 Defining Tribal Communities in the Indian Context: A Short Historical Overview

When the British colonial government attempted to write the history of modern India, the term "tribes" was generally understood in more than one common parlance. First, "tribes" referred to a group of people claiming common descent from a common ancestor. Second, "tribes" were perceived as people who lived in primitive conditions and possessed barbaric "animist" features. Though the first sense of understanding of tribes has always been in usage and has a longer history than the second sense of understanding, the second one occupied an ample space in the anthropological writings of the British. Hence, we can understand that the "animism" feature attributed to the tribals was the product of early British colonial writings, which gradually changed in due course of history. In 1921 and 1931, some crucial breakthroughs happened under the head of Mr. J. T. Marten and Mr. J. H. Hutton, the then census commissioners of British India, respectively. They started using the term "tribal religion" instead of the term "animism," where they categorized the tribes based on the religion that they practice. Though the usage of the term "animism" was avoided to define tribals, the efforts to categorize them prevailed, and it was implicit. In the early decades of post-independent India, tribal communities were considered a part of the Hindu society, but in the "backward strata" of the society (Xaxa, 1999, p. 1520).

A prolonged conceptual crisis, contestation, and ambiguities existed to define "tribes" in British India, and it continued in the post-independent period (Atal, 2016). The constitution of India defines "Scheduled Tribes" as such "tribes or tribal communities or parts of or groups within such tribes or tribal communities as are deemed under article 342 to be Scheduled Tribes for the purposes of this Constitution" [Article 366 (25)] (Government of India, n.d). As we see, this definition does not provide the characteristic features and other details to define "tribals." To have a better and shared understanding of the tribal communities of India, we prefer to use the insights suggested by Virginius Xaxa, a notable scholar of tribal communities in contemporary India. Xaxa (1999) argues that in India the tribal communities are vastly diverse and heterogeneous, lacking the traits of modernity. They are the ones who lived in the given territory long before colonization or conquest by a group from another geographical territory; later, they became marginalized after colonization. In contemporary India, the tribal communities lead their lives in accordance with their own cultural and institutional practices, and they are different from the dominant community of the region. The dominant community members have always been seen as "outsiders" by tribal members. Such typical characteristic features are visible in the tribal communities of northeast India and Jharkhand. In scholarships, the tribes have often been referred to as "indigenous people." One critical aspect of the concept of "indigenous" is the idea of marginalization, domination, and subjugation (Xaxa, 1999).

At the global level, the reports of ILO (Indigenous and Tribal Populations Convention, 1957) have broadly categorized indigenous characteristics as 1. Possessing a strong attachment for geographical territories; 2. Maintaining cultural, geographical, and institutional distinctions attempting resistance to assimilation with other national communities; 3. Preserving their distinct socio-cultural and economic practices and customs; 4. Identifying themselves as "indigenous" or "tribal" (FAO, 2009).

Again, in the Indian context, the term "Adivasi"[3] is used in various Indian languages to denote indigenous people. Other terms such as "*autochthonous*" have also been used to refer to the tribes. This term was used to show a mark of identification or differentiation of a group of people than "others" in terms of physical features, language, religion, customs, social organization, and so on. G.S. Ghurye, a renowned Indian Sociologist and tribal scholar, found the term, "Adivasi problematic when in a documented internal history of movement of people within India unavailable to us" (Ghurye, 1963 cited in Xaxa, 1999). Xaxa provides a detailed outline of the

---

[3] It means original inhabitants or indigenous peoples. However, not all original inhabitants are known as indigenous peoples. We provide a brief conceptual clarity in the above paragraphs.

arguments that stood for and against the usage of this term "Adivasi." He notes that the term Adivasi cuts across different dialects to render an identity beyond particular groups and communities (Xaxa, 1999). Though we are aware of the different etymological and ideological references that each of these terms carries, throughout this chapter, we use the terms indigenous, tribes, and Adivasi interchangeably[4] in our argument as we draw references from diverse works from scholars who have used each of these terms to refer to this category of people as a form of the marginalized group with a distinct identity.

5 Structural Change as Structural Strain During Colonial Period

The Indian nationalist movement was not a coherent, unified movement. Across the Indian subcontinent, the tribal communities and peasants resisted against their immediate oppressors. They were also brought under the aegis of the Indian freedom struggle. Such freedom struggles can also be seen as a fight over one's right to nature and natural resources (Sarkar, 1983). The major structural changes introduced by the British were based on the idea of denial of one's right over natural resources, which was one of the fundamental tenets of colonialism around the world. Colonialism re-defined human beings' relationship with nature. For example, in 1864, the British Imperialist Government established the Forest Department in Pre-independent India that regulated and controlled the community's rights over forests. It barred local and indigenous communities from grazing cattle, hunting, collecting forest-based products, or felling trees and even banned shifting cultivation, which formed the livelihood for most tribal communities. There were many instances of punishments on the part of the colonial authority on the local communities for infringing the Forest Act in the late nineteenth century (Mallick, 2012). With their loss of access to forests and their resources, the lives and livelihoods of forest-dependent communities were destabilized. In the process, some communities were declared Criminal Tribes, and others lost their livelihood and identity. Here, reference can be drawn to the Phasepardhis hunting–gathering tribe, where farmers engaged to snare the Blackbuck and other animals who gazed into their fields. The tribe took to stealing after the declaration of hunting as illegal (Gadgil & Malhotra, 2006). This resulted from a structural change arising because of disequilibrium in a community's relationship with nature. In the contemporary era, we largely look at the fractured instances of resistance against the structural changes arising from colonialism from the lens of a dominant discourse on the nationalist freedom movement. To some extent, those acts of resistance and collective resistance movements asserted the right over nature and natural resources. The historic rebellion launched by Birsa Munda in 1894 against

---

[4] Similar to this, we interchangeably use the following words throughout our chapter: Indigenous movements, Tribal movements, Adivasi movements, Indigenous resistance movements, and Tribal resistance movements according to the context.

the structural change introduced by the British by converting tribal agrarian lands into feudal states would be a case in point (Sharma, 1976).

6 Ecology as a Social Structure

As Guha (2006) points out, sociologists tend to divide society into four bands, the economy, the polity, social structure, and culture. The fifth category is the ecological infrastructure, where he looks into the interaction and reciprocal relationship between ecological infrastructures with the other four categories. He refers to it as social ecology. Scholars have highlighted resource allocation and resource partitioning as a distinct identity marker and livelihood option for caste and tribal communities habituating a single ecological space (Gadgil, 1985; Gadgil & Malhotra, 2006). Here it is essential to understand that space is not just a location that holds an event or a phenomenon. Space acts as a social structure as well. For instance, the tribal village as a spatial, geographical, and social category draws meaning from certain social and spatial references. The tribe as a community may be a reality in certain hamlets in urban India, but the category draws meaning within a certain spatial context that shapes their social systems. For instance, a tribal hamlet within the interior jungles gives different levels of signification in understanding the category and their society. The tribal community is marked with certain practices that exercise itself within a spatial category to some extent. The community uses those territories in a unique way for their economic, social, and cultural purpose. Dislocating them from those spaces disrupts these activities. Thus, the struggles in Odisha involving the tribes in Kalinganagar, Kashipur, Narayanpatna, and Niyamgiri have so far been understood as anti-displacement and anti-industrial struggles (Ambagudia, 2010; Das, 2001; Krishna, 2015; Kumar, 2014; Kumbhar, 2010). The resistance movements of indigenous populations and marginal people in eastern India, like Niyamgiri and Chilika Bachao Andolan, align with many of the concepts and concerns of environmental movements (Kumar, 2014; Nanda, 2012).

These struggles and resistance movements indicated a strong emergence in spatial politics among the indigenous communities and State-Capitalist duo. In this context, it is essential to understand Lefebvre's ideas on space to comprehend the current scenario in Eastern India as it offers novel insights.

7 Environmental Movements of the Indigenous Populations for Claiming Their "space": Two Cases from Jharkhand and Odisha

The indigenous struggles in Eastern India have resulted from the interference of the Capitalist–State in the tribal regions. Applying Lefebvre's lens, these tribal sites can be designated as the lived space. In the contemporary period, those "spaces" have turned out to be sites of resistances and contestations, which is a definitive trait of this lived space. The tribes of Eastern India sit on the rich mineral reserves of the nation. The nation needs "development" by extracting out these hidden reserves. With its Capitalist collaborator, the state marches toward the transformation of these community-based absolute spaces into an abstract space. As mentioned earlier, this is a spatial, historical journey. Every space awaits this transformation for the survival and perpetuation of capitalism. Capitalism, with its violent and penetrative strategies, pushes unprecedented uneven growth. Lefebvre points out, Space as a market has "saved capitalism from extinction" (Lefebvre, 1991, p. 346). This growth entails the loss of livelihood, non-accessibility to forest-based resources, landlessness, degradation of the environment, and denial of basic rights for the tribes. This results in a clash of interest between the indigenous communities and the State–Capitalist pair. Lefebvre writes,

> Class struggle intervenes in the production of space today more than ever. Only class conflict can prevent abstract space from spreading across the planet and erasing all spatial differences. (Lefebvre, 2009, p. 188)

The class struggle that unleashes here takes the form of contention over the meaning associated with those spaces. The dominant hegemonic discourse led by the State–Capitalist partnership attempts to form the abstract space against the counter-hegemonic definition of that same space propagated by the indigenous communities supported by civil society organizations to save the absolute space. The lived space provides the platform for the conflict between the hegemonic and the counter-hegemonic. Below, we further clarify the space contestations with the examples of two cases from eastern India.

7.1 Case 1: Niyamgiri Movement in Odisha

The Niyamgiri movement's history is one of the most widely discussed cases of environmental justice movements in India in recent years. It is a classic example of the association of indigenous people with their "living spaces." It exemplifies their grass-roots fights against the powerful state–corporate partnership to claim their "living spaces" and protect nature. The word "Niyamgiri" denotes the hill range located in Odisha, one of the mineral-resources-rich states situated in the eastern fringe of Peninsular India (Government of Odisha, 2011). This state is endowed with a large share of chromite, nickel, bauxite, iron ore, and coal resources (Government of Odisha [erstwhile Orissa], 2009). This state is also home to 62 different scheduled tribe communities (Indigenous communities); they are distributed in all the thirty districts of the state with varying numbers.

According to the Government Census 2011, the total tribal population of the state is around 9.59 million, which constitutes 22.8% of the state's population and 9.17% of the entire indigenous people of the country. More than 90% of the tribal populations live in rural areas of the country. With social and cultural distinctiveness in their social organization, traditions, language, dialects, dress, and ornaments, the tribes of Odisha possess a rich historical background. The tribes of Odisha have faced isolation, neglect, and deprivation for centuries (Government of India, 2011; SCSTRTI & Academy of Tribal Languages and Culture, 2018). Though poverty in Odisha as a whole has declined dramatically, the tribals continue to live in abject poverty, inequality, hunger, and food insecurity (Panda & Padhi, 2020; The Hindu, 2020). Ironically, a large portion of the mineral reserves is available in the forest regions where the tribes of Odisha historically reside. In post-independent Odisha, to fasten the state's development and build employment opportunities, the elected governments continued to encourage industrial investment in the state at a large scale. However, those industrial investments and the establishment of the development projects have had drastic effects on the state's forestry resources.

Consequently, it did severe damages to the living spaces of the tribal people. For example, from independence in 1947 until 1999, Odisha had set up 190 development projects (including irrigation, mining, roads, and housing, railways, defense, and industry), and 24,124 hectares of land have been deforested. The tribal populations of this state bore a large proportion of these damages; however, the impacts were never accounted for (Padhi & Panigrahi, 2011).

Among the 62 tribal groups of Odisha, 13 groups have been identified as Particularly Vulnerable Tribal Groups (PVTGs) as they are more isolated, deprived, vulnerable, and are in very impoverished conditions (SCSTRTI & Academy of Tribal Languages and Culture, 2018). Dongaria Kondhas are one among those 13 PVTGs. Dongaria Kondha[5] reside in the hills and valleys of Niyamgiri hill range in Southwestern Odisha. These hills stretch across Kalahandi and Rayagada districts. Both the districts are undeveloped districts; they historically comprise a substantial proportion of tribal populations in the entire state of Odisha. However, these districts have a rich forest containing products like Kendu, timber, bamboo, and mineral resources, especially bauxite. They form a part of the old KBK (Koraput Bolangir, Kalahandi) districts that stands for backwardness. In fact, Kalahandi had become a symbol of Odisha's poverty and starvation for a very long period, owing to frequent droughts and famine in the region during the colonial times and post-independent India, especially in the 1980s (Krishna, 2015).

---

[5] Dongaria Kondhas consider themselves as the descendants of Niyam Raja, the legendary ancestral king of that land. They are the primitive sub-group of Kondhs, and are one of the vulnerable tribal groups. The name "Dongaria Kondhas" denotes a primitive hill-dwelling people [Dongar—High hill land]. They exclusively reside in the Niyamgiri hill range. Compared to other tribal groups, they possess expertise in horticulture. Their livelihoods are primarily based on non-timber forest products and podu cultivation. Dongaria Kondhas, a sub-group of Kondhas, have distinct features from their "Kuvi" dialect, colorful dress, traditional ornaments, agroforestry expertise, social, cultural, and religious practices. They continue to live in an isolated hill plateau largely inaccessible [Bulliyya, 2010; KBK (Government of Odisha)]. The official census conducted by the Government of India notes that around 7900 Dongaria Kondhas live in the villages and the entire nearby regions. However, as Pandey (2018) claims, there is no such reliable contemporary data of the populations of these tribes, and it should be somewhere around 15,000.

Apart from having a rich forest reserve with various endangered wildlife species, the Niyamgiri hills are the source of the Vamsadhara River. The Dongaria Kondha have historically shared a unique and intimate relationship with nature. Their social structure, livelihoods, cultural and religious systems have been directly intertwined with the forests and the hills. The absolute space belongs to the realm of the sacred, subjected to divine mythical forces. According to Lefebvre, it is the site where the social and the natural converge to form a unified whole. Niyamgiri would be a glowing example of such a space. The hills and the forest are divine and sacred for the Dongaria Kondha tribes. The mountains happened to be the seat of the Lord Niyam Raja, for tribes. They have referred to him as "Niyam Raja Penu, a male deity" (Sahu, 2008, p. 19). The Dongaria Kondha tribes continue to believe that he, the male deity, protects their sacred forests, the source of their livelihood and life. The mountains and the jungle within its wilderness have been touched and shaped by the community. They draw a symbolic meaning from those natural terrains. Their practices, religious, economic, and social, have been tuned with nature, making it an absolute space. A mysticism shrouds those spaces. This space is "real and surreal" at the same time. It is embedded both "socially and mentally" (Lefebvre, 1991, p. 251).

Capitalism made its way through the interiors of this region with its vast infrastructure of knowledge, finance, technology, and most important ally, legitimate political support. In 2003, Vedanta Mining Corporation, a London-based multinational company, with its subsidiary Indian firm Sterlite Industries Limited signed a memorandum of understanding with the State Government of Odisha to set up a refinery at Langigarh, in the foothills of the mountains (Krishna, 2015). This gave the company the power to take over the forest, the hills, land, and water. This came as a violation of the rights of the Dongaria Kondha tribes over the land and resources that they have been using for 200 hundred years (Sahu, 2008). This powerful Diku,[6] in the form of a Capitalist–State nexus, was determined to change the terrains of those spaces forever. The corporate–state partnership looks at those hills and the forests as the prosperous prospect for earning revenue—a capitalistic opportunity for mining ores with a high market value. The State–Capitalist duo concerns the topographical and geological terrains and a logistic plan for access into those spaces with their dominant development ideas.

As the tagline on the billboards of Vedanta reads, "Creating Happiness," they move with a hegemonic discourse on development and on creating opportunity with their massive infrastructures. The narratives of the hegemonic discourse portrayed the ideology of State–Capitalist perspective on development through their promises of quality life, employment generation with billboards of smiling rural tribal people.

---

[6] Roughly, the word "Diku" denotes the "oppressor" by the Tribals. All the oppressors who were introduced by the British are broadly known as "Diku" by the Tribals. They could be the local moneylender who exploits them, the migrant trader, the corporate capitalist, the forest officer who denies them entry into those forest spaces that they have used for generations as a source of life and livelihood. The structural changes in their societies have been perceptible with the presence of a Diku. Diku is symbolic of the strains in their society. Scholarship on tribal movements has been looked at from the lens of the anti-colonial movement, anti-industrial movement, or anti-displacement movements, to name a few.

Even the media bought their hegemonic discourse on development by presenting the ideology of development through mining. It must be taken into consideration that any space is never a neutral or an objective entity. It indulges in ideology and is never far from politics. It has evolved strategies that make it appear apolitical. It is etched out of the natural material elements to fit well into its politicized agenda. Lefebvre argues nature becomes politicized (Lefebvre, 1991). This politicization is just a strategy for transforming the absolute into the abstract. The politicization ensues with such hegemonic discourses put forth by the combined effort of the State and Capitalist who controls media as well. The indigenous community put forth their counter-hegemonic discourse within the same lived space to retain the absolute space with their counter-discourse on the divinity of nature and their natural rights that they draw from nature, vocalizing the sacredness and surrealism of those spaces. These counter-hegemonic practices and ideologies were popularized with the help of NGOs and alternative forms of media, which narrated the activities on the part of the State–Capitalist duo as painful and a violation of human rights. The strong note on the environmental and human impact of mining and industries was popularized as a form of a counter-hegemonic narrative. Even the locals exhibit their relationship with nature and the surrounding environment in their socio-cultural practices. Some noted acts of resistance in the everyday practices, in terms of their ritual and cultural practices, strengthened the counter-hegemonic discourse like the Maria festival of the Dongria Kondh in Niyamgiri which caught the attention of the media.

7.2 Case 2: Koel–Karo Movement in Jharkhand

Jharkhand, a state located in east-central India, was created from the erstwhile state of Bihar in 2000 after the long-standing struggles of the movement for the separate state of Jharkhand. As per the census of 2011, Jharkhand's population is 3.29 crore, and it is the 13th most populated state of India. The state is 79,714 Square Kilometers, and it is one of the most mineral-rich zones, not just in India but also in the world.

Around 40% of India's mineral reserves including coal, bauxite, iron ore, kyanite, copper, uranium, etc., and 20% of India's coal reserves are found in Jharkhand (Government of India, 2011; IBEF, 2017). In addition, around 29% of the area of Jharkhand is recorded as forest regions. Jharkhand is home to 32 different tribal groups; they comprise about 26% of the total population, and a large proportion of them are dependent on forest and forest-based livelihoods. However, Jharkhand is one of the least developed states in India, and around half of the total population of this state lives below the poverty line. In particular, around 60% of the scheduled castes and tribes face acute poverty and hunger, and economic-related troubles more than non-scheduled caste populations. This is because their livelihoods are largely dependent on subsistence farming and forest-based livelihoods without any secondary sources of income (Government of Jharkhand, 2021; Singh et al., 2012).

Though there are various tribal groups in Jharkhand, there is a strong sense of unity among them, unique in tribal-dominated states. For example, in Northeastern

India, it is difficult to see such a collective sense of integrity among the tribal groups. One apparent reason has been that the tribes of Jharkhand have had a long history of conducting struggles against exploitation. At the beginning of the twentieth century, they protested against colonial exploiters. During the post-colonial periods, their struggles and movements have centered on the claims for a separate state, land rights, and against capitalist extractivism. Their continuous struggles against the establishment to claim their rights have made them unite against exploitation (Xaxa, 2008).

The customs, traditions, social norms, gender norms of the tribal communities of India are diverse and heterogeneous, and it varies enormously across and even within regions and states. Despite their heterogeneity in nature, tribals have primarily identified themselves and are seen by others as outsiders of the dominant regional community (Bosu Mullick, 2003). In the present east-central region of India, including the regions that cover the contemporary Jharkhand, the tribals had started facing pressures from the outsiders even in the fourth century. Initially, the non-tribals started infiltrating and acquiring the native lands of Adivasis from the local kingdoms. Then, in the later period, they had faced land alienation and exploitation from the Mughals, mercenaries, and the colonial hegemony. The mercenaries and the colonial domination introduced the idea of transferring the native tribal lands to the "outsiders" (non-tribal communities); it made the tribal communities pay rents for their native lands to the diku (outsiders) landlords. Over the period, the tribal communities of Jharkhand collectively organized themselves and protested against the diku migrants and the colonial powers. The tribal uprisings against "dikus" were witnessed across the region throughout the nineteenth century. Hence, initially, the word "diku" denoted "outsiders." Over the period, after seeing continuous attacks and exploitation against native tribal lands, the term "diku" underwent changes, and it is now understood as "exploiters" of the tribals (Ghosh, 1991, 2016). In the contemporary period, only the scheduled tribes are known as the Adivasis. All others are known as "dikus." However, in this context, it is essential to note that the meaning of diku (exploiters) is not necessarily applicable to all non-tribal communities who migrated to the Adivasi lands, mainly, who belong to peasants and other artisan castes of the yesteryears and the migrant and industrial working-class communities of the contemporary period as they are not the real exploiters or oppressors of the tribals. In many cases, the tribals of these regions mutually coexist with these people. The term "diku" has symbolic representation, and sometimes, it is also used to represent not only landowners and land grabbers of Adivasis but also to denote government officials, teachers, and all others who have had the motivation to grab the lands of Adivasis and alienate them (Sengupta, 1980).

Such centuries-long oppression and increasing marginalization in control over land, water, forests, and other resources also shaped such a strict sense of identity among Jharkhand's tribals against non-tribals. In the contemporary period, such classification also makes them engage in intense competition to claim their rights over their native lands and autonomy and invariably classify such outsiders as oppressors and exploiters (Xaxa, 2008). From 1907 to the 1990s, the tribal communities of Jharkhand lost thousands of acres of their native lands. They were displaced to other regions due to the continuous proliferation of development-related projects, and the magnitude of displacement is continued even in the contemporary period (Fernandes, 1991, 2006; Lahiri-Dutt et al., 2014; Singh, 2021).

After independence in 1952, the erstwhile Bihar government started implementing the 1947 Zamindari Abolition Bill (land reform measures). It abolished all intermediaries, including Zamindars, estate managers, and village headmen. These land reform measures profoundly impacted the land rights of the scheduled tribes, scheduled castes, and backward castes populations of Jharkhand (Hill, 2014; Jharkhand State Team, 2014). In the post-independence period, the official development policies of the state by and large started displacing the tribal communities and scheduled caste communities of Jharkhand. For example, the public sector projects of the first of three five-year plans displaced more than 50,000 scheduled tribes and 10,000 scheduled caste families from their native land destroying their livelihoods and cultural roots (Xaxa, 2008).

In Jharkhand, the resistance against such projects increasingly started among tribals in the 1970s. A classic example of tribal movements of Jharkhand was the Koel-Karo People's Movement against the hydroelectric project. It took place in the cluster of valleys in the hilly regions of the undivided state of Bihar. The democratic long-standing anti-dam movement of the tribal communities of this Chhotanagpur Plateau is a classic case of the environmental movement for identity, justice, and place (Escobar et al., 2002). Koel and Karo are the tributaries of the river Brahmani in Jharkhand [Earlier, in the undivided Bihar] (SANDRP, 2014). This region has been the home to Adivasi communities, Munda and Oraon, also called Kurukh. Munda communities speak Munda languages, belong to Austro–Asiatic lineage, and Oraon communities speak a Dravidian language similar to Gondi and other tribal languages of central India (Brittanica, n.d). The Koel–Karo hydroelectric project was conceptualized in 1955, and the Bihar electricity board did the initial surveys in the subsequent years. Then the land acquisition was begun in 1972 and 1973 after having completed the final report. The project aimed to construct two dams at Basia on the South Koel River and Lohajimi on the North Karo River.

It was estimated that this project would create 710 megawatts of electricity. However, there were enormous contradictions between the estimates of official numbers and the community on the affected villages and victims. For example, the 1973 official project report stated that around 125 villages would have to face the impacts of this project. Whereas locals indicated that it would be 256 villages affected. Similarly, locals estimated that around 150,000 to 200,000 people would have to be displaced to construct these dams. Whereas, the officials noted that only around 7,063 families from 112 villages would have to bear the impacts. In addition, the local tribals claimed that around 66,000 acres of land would be inundated. Of which, 33,000 acres of land are under cultivation, and the remaining ones are forest lands where the tribal communities have traditional rights toward that land. Hence, this project created significant negative consequences for the local tribal communities (EPW, 2001; Escobar et al., 2002; PUCL, 2002 [cited in SANDRP, 2014]; Mathews, 2011; Environmental Justice Atlas, 2014).

Initially, in the 1970s, the local tribals were largely kept in the dark by the officers, and they were largely unaware of the project's developments. The project authorities constructed the offices and the roads without the knowledge and consultation of the local tribals. After some point in time, when the land acquisition of the local tribal communities began by the officers, they realized the real impact and corruption (SANDRP, 2014) and launched Satyagraha (non-violent active resistance) at the dam site to show their protest. To protect their space and identity against external threats, the tribal communities came together in an organization known as the *Koel–Karo Jan Sangathan* (KKJS, the Koel-Karo People's Organization). Under the spearhead of this KKJS, the tribal communities conducted many peaceful protests against displacement and dams' construction; the famous, powerful slogan of tribals was "we will give our life but not the land" (Escobar et al., 2002). The tribal women also joined in the protests with their local communities. From the end of the 1970s to the mid-1980s, the tribals successfully halted the project through various non-violent agitations.

Meanwhile, this project came under the control of the National Hydroelectric Power Corporation from the electricity board of the state of Bihar. It was a setback to the local tribal leaders, including the KKJS, as the new authority was far less accessible than the old one. In 1984, the Supreme Court took the issue by the local activists, and the Supreme Court ruled against the forceful acquisition of the land from the tribal communities. It was a massive setback to the armed forces of the state authorities as they had no option other than stopping forceful acquisition. In 1986, the project came to a halt for ten years. However, after almost a decade, the protests, and the resistance movements of the tribals intensified as the government announced that the then Prime Minister of India would lay the foundation of the project in July of 1995. This announcement was met with a massive resistance of the tribals through solidarity marches and demonstrations; the intensity of the protests was vigorous, so the Prime Minister had to cancel the ground-breaking event of the project. Given this, the then Chief Minister of Bihar (undivided) came forward to inaugurate the event. He had also faced intense resistance and protest from the tribals, and he also had to cancel the event. The continuous cancellation of the event by the then Prime Minister of India and the Chief Minister of Bihar garnered media attention in India and throughout the world (Escobar et al., 2002; Mathews, 2011; SANDRP, 2014).

In late 2000, within a short span of time in the aftermath of the formation of the new state, Jharkhand, attempts were made by the state to revive this project, and those attempts were met with intense resistance by the tribal communities. On February 1, 2001, armed troops removed a barricade that the KKJS had erected. The tribals considered the barricade an important symbol of their protest and resistance movements. Hence, its removal sparked further action by the tribal communities, and they decided to sit in on the site, Tapkara. Some negotiations were also going on between the local tribal leaders and the state; however, armed forces opened fire against the peaceful crowd following the sequence of events. Eight people were killed, and around 30 people were injured.

Even after this violence, the tribes continued their peaceful protests against the state. No doubt, these protests were again a mark of resistance against transforming the lived space of these tribes. These lived spaces meant the absolute space for these tribes was marked with their *sasans* (burial stones of ancestors) and *sarnas* (sacred groves). Their defiance to the state and their resistance to retain those spaces were embedded in the everyday customary practices of these tribes. They strategized their everyday ways to protest against the state (Chandra, 2013). In the aftermath of this lethal incident, the tribals changed their slogan to *"we will give neither our lives nor our lands but we will stop the dam."*

The tribals stopped the government officials from the forest department to defecate in the forest spaces with the alibi that they would be defiling their sacred *sarnas* (Chandra, 2013). They would grow corn around the government officials' camps, forcing them to remain confined to the camp only. The tribes would bargain for compensation if they happened to step on their crops. These officials were forced to cook, eat, sleep, and attend the call of nature inside the camps, and soon they had to leave it in the middle of the night (Chandra, 2013). This is an example of acts of everyday protests that took an organized form. Soma Munda, leader of the KKJS, avoided officials, non-tribal acquaintances, and even tribal educated leaders in his everyday conversation to avoid commitment toward displacement with excuses like the drunkenness of tribes for which they don't need money or sometimes in the name of respect for their traditions (Chandra, 2013; Ghosh, 2006). Hence, the everyday routine acts became the chief weapon for these tribes to mold the everyday spaces into spaces of resistance against the powerful hegemonic state. These micro-mobilizing acts of protest could prevent the penetrative abstract space from taking over their absolute space.

In August 2003, the then Chief Minister of the state finally announced the termination of this project. This project was shelved in 2007; finally, in July 2010, the Governor of Jharkhand announced the complete closure of this project (Escobar et al., 2002; Down to Earth, 2003; Ray & Patra, 2009; Mathews, 2011; SANDRP, 2014). The Koel–Karo movement is one of the examples of the solidarity and resistance movements of the tribals (or indigenous populations) to protect their identity, culture, space, environment, and livelihoods against external forces. This protest was not only a struggle against the attempted transformations of the absolute into the abstract space. Many acts of protest every day were evident in this struggle. Koel–Karo movement was a long-sustained resistance movement that went for more than two decades.

The case of Koel–Karo is a rare example of a long 30-year-old indigenous movement, which was not mediated by any civil society organization nor had a middle-class spokesperson to speak on behalf of the Munda tribal community (Ghosh, 2006). It was fought and negotiated entirely by these tribes, who had a different perception of development. As the famous slogan from the movement states, *"bijli batti kabua, dibri batti abua,"* meaning we don't need electric lamps; we are content with our kerosene lamps (Gautam, 2020, p. 2). This is an example of the self-organization capacity of the tribals to protest against the powerful state and capitalist market actors through non-violent means.

8 Conclusion

Our attempt in this chapter has been to examine the present ongoing scenario involving indigenous communities' resistances with the help of the above-cited case studies. However, we do not intend generalization as far as other cases are concerned. The three dimensions of Lefebvreian notion of space are physical, mental, and social (Gottdiener, 1997). The social space is created out of the everyday lived experience. Lefebvre's notion of everyday life embedded in the social space as a part of the private and personal "residual space" loaded with passivity and stands out as a site of resistance (Lefebvre, 1971, 2002). Individuals attempt to transform or retain the desired spaces, whether one belongs to the absolute or abstract spaces. As the indigenous intends to preserve its absolute space, the one in charge of heralding the abstract still has its control in everyday ways.

> Persons working from the model of the abstract space continually try to reign and control the social space of everyday life with its constant changes, whereas social space always transcends conceived boundaries and regulated forms. (Gottdiener, 1993, p. 131)

The "ways of every day" focus on looking at social movements from a postmodern perspective. The everyday resistance practices have emerged as subaltern forms (Singh, 2001). Everyday life registers many acts of resistance that go unnoticed and social scientists believe these micro-sociological instances of resistances are worth studying (Oommen, 1990; Scott, 1985, 1990). These individual micro-mobilizations and symbolic resistances are acts against the larger structures of domination. But these small instances of every day make their mark a form shared by the class and communities. "The everyday resistance may or may not lead to collective action, but all collective action is bound to have a history of resistance" (Singh, 2001, p. 226). Here in these transforming fluid spaces, we notice acts of resistance by the indigenous communities. The dialectics work not only between the different forms of spaces but also acts within these spaces.

The lived space has two facets: Space, with the help of Capitalism, traverses from the realm of absolute space to abstract space. (Lefebvre, 1991) Stuart Elden has argued that abstract space was once produced and regulated by the modern state (Brenner & Elden, 2009). The absolute space is the natural space that stands for use-value in Marxian terminology.

The result of state power extended to the capitalist, who transforms the absolute space with its massive financial, technological, and knowledge infrastructures (Lefebvre, 1991, 2009). "The abstract space destroys it (historical conditions), its internal differences and any (emergent differences) to impose an abstract homogeneity" (Lefebvre cited in Brenner & Elden, 2009, p. 358). Speaking about abstract space, Brenner & Elden (2009) remark that it is inherently political. Second, it sets up practices and institutional arrangements that unravel new ways of imagining, conceiving, and representing space in everyday life, capital accumulation, and state actions. Third, abstract space is violent and geographically expansive. It provides a framework for interlinking economic, bureaucratic, and military forms of strategic interventions (Brenner & Elden, 2009, p. 359). The struggle emerges in these lived spaces with attempts and resistances to those attempts on spatial transformation. Social relations are always contextualized and shaped from a spatial point of reference. "*Social relations are also spatial relations*" (Gottendiener, 1993, p. 131). Here, the Capitalist–State dyad looks for opportunities to convert the absolute into the abstract that becomes a hegemonic site for power and surveillance (Lefebvre, 2009). They legitimize their attempts with a dominant discourse on development. The indigenous community, on the other hand, to retain the absolute, unleashes a counter-hegemonic discourse that delves with the sacredness of nature and their natural rights. This space becomes a setting for everyday resistance on the part of both parties.

Lefebvre notes that natural space was shrinking at a rapid rate. In simple words, we tried to hint at the capitalists' play on space (Lefebvre, 1991, 2009, 2003a, 2003b). Lefebvre extends the Marxist debates on Capitalism over space (Lefebvre, 1991, 2009). He puts forth a reincarnated Marxism that addresses issues of contemporary times. His central thesis on "production of space" provides a novel way of understanding Capitalism and its intimate relationship with space. He gives a new lens for looking at space itself (Lefebvre, 1991). This lens is posited in the postmodern framework. Here, we would underscore two critical themes from his work. First, that space is socially created out of human practices and desires. Second, every space takes up a journey for its transformation. Capitalism and the State shapes this journey (Lefebvre, 1991). The politicized space is the territory, according to Brennan and Elden (2009). Citing Agnew's ideas on the territorial trap, it comprises with it three geographical assumptions. First, the idea of state sovereignty that encompasses the economic processes. Second, political and economic aspects are separating the domestic from the international. Third, the notion of economy and society is also defined by state boundaries (Agnew, 1994; Brennan & Elden, 2009, p. 354). These ideas create a taken-for-granted notion of the hegemonic territorial expansiveness and political, the economic process of the state. The quintessence of Lefebvreian thought is based upon those ideas. Lefebvre introduces a counter-hegemonic space that belongs to the community, unaware of the politicized military strategy of the state. This is an essentially new way of looking at spatiality as it snaps off the idea of the fixity of space. It introduces us to the notion that space is fluid, which is triggered by this contestation. The utility of material resources, contours, landscapes, infrastructure, technology, power dynamics, habitat, livelihood, social practices changes from time to time. Primarily this change is driven by a State–Capitalist endeavor.

Lefebvre rightly remarks, "The problematic of space…has displaced the problematic of industrialization" (1991). *The space market* is more profitable than any other sector, and capitalism survives on space for its growth and perpetuation. He believed that the Marxist tenet of the inherent contradictions in Capitalism that leads to the destruction of Capitalism itself might not hold (Lefebvre, 1991). This new spatial order would control the contradictions for the benefit of the dominant class (Lefebvre, 2009). Thus, the rising sun for Capitalism would never set as long as the "*space circuits*" are available (Lefebvre, 1991). The State–Capitalist duo seizes the absolute space to transform it into an *abstract space* with immense market value. Here, we would like to draw attention to the fact that Lefebvre has propounded his theory in the context of urban studies only. Most scholars have applied it to urban planning and expansive urbanization processes (Bower, 2016; Gottdiener, 1997; McCann, 2002; Roy, 2012; Stanek, 2008; Walks, 2013). He had minimal contribution as far as rural life was concerned (Unwin, 2000). In this chapter, we attempt to apply his perspective on rural spaces because the resistance movements of the indigenous tribes that we have focused on are located in these "spaces." Here we would argue that the transformation of the absolute into the abstract is not the end of the tale. The shifting meanings of those spaces are always in a process. We have entered an age of un-fixity of space. We see Lefebvre as a postmodernist as he deconstructs the logocentric nature of the space, talking about its different realms and forms. "Space possessed its own dialectical moment" (Gottdiener, 1993, p. 130).

Here we would like to emphasize that the border between the *absolute* and the *abstract* is negotiable. The demarcating line is blurry. The conflict always persists. We believe the *absolute space* is always an ideal space. There will always be a conflict over the definition of *absolute space*. Under capitalism, the *abstract* attempts to take over.

Nevertheless, the *abstract space* will not be a struggle-free site. The longing for the *absolute* would always remain. There is a dialectical relation between the *abstract* and the *absolute*. The synthesis would always be a synthesis emerging out of the *absolute* and *abstract space*. This evolved form would maintain a higher level of abstraction. This space would change the lives of its inhabitants forever. We call it the *negotiated space*. However, again, this negotiated *space* would have a stipulated life expectancy. It will soon face its doomsday. It would again take the form of an *absolute* in the collective memory of the society. A new venture would be taken up in those spaces to create yet another *abstract space*. For example, industrial towns like Chowdwar in the Cuttack District of Odisha, an erstwhile industrial hub, lies in a dilapidated state and seems like a natural part of the semi-urban landscape. We believe the everyday acts of resistance often contribute to the future of spatiality. The everyday acts of protests or controls can, to an extent, decide the nature of space.

Furthermore, the dialectics goes on. In the case of the Niyamgiri movement, the struggle by the Dongaria Kondhas against State–Capitalist power reached a new height. The indigenous community received the support of Amnesty International, an organization with global reach that fights for human rights. The issue of the Niyamgiri resistance movement received a global platform. Researchers, human rights activists, documentary filmmakers across the globe started thronging in. There was immense pressure on the state and the Capitalist organizations. The Supreme Court decision went in favor of the Dongaria Kondhas. Vedanta has stopped its activity. It seems the battle for the indigenous communities has been won. But the absolute spaces of Niyamgiri have been compromised. This transformed space may not be the result of the State–Capitalist attempts to make it an abstract space. However, some level of abstraction has been achieved with international exposure to this region. The presence of foreign scholars studying the tribal protests and activists from civil society organizations from across the globe contribute to it. In Lefebvre's words, he would refer to it as the Urban Society. Here the idea of the urban fabric has a vast

Indigenous Environmental Movements of Eastern India: Seeing … 249

dimension. For example, a vacation house in the remote hinterlands may not make the region an urban space but contributes to the Urban fabric. He writes,

> The Urban fabric grows, extends is borders, corrodes the residue of agrarian life. This expression Urban Fabric does not narrowly define the built world of the cities but all manifestations of the dominance of the city over the country. In this sense, a vacation house, a highway, a supermarket in the country-side are all part of the urban fabric. Of varying thickness and activity, the only regions untouched by it are those that are stagnant or dying, those that are given over to nature. (Lefebvre, 2003a, 2003b, p. 4)

It would be interesting to witness if the indigenous movements we discussed, be it Niyamgiri or Koel–Karo, have entered the "urban fabric" that Lefebvre referred to in his work, *The Urban Revolution* (2003). There has been a negotiation between the absolute and the abstract. It is less of an absolute than its original version before the advent of Vedanta, now in the case of Niyamgiri. For example, at the foothills of the Niyamgiri hills, the State Administration has a setup in 2018, a center for interpreting and illustrating tribal culture. It also serves as a sales center for tribal products. The visitors are reported as saying that the Centre is also a place of accommodation for guests for visiting Niyamgiri.

> In space needs and desires as such informing both the acts of producing and its products. There still exists and there may exist in the future—spaces for play and spaces for enjoyment…In by means of space, the work may shine through the product, use value may gain the upper hand over exchange value: appropriation turning the world upon its head may virtually achieve dominion over domination as the imagery and the utopian incorporate the real. What we have called a second nature may replace the first, standing in for it or superimposing itself upon it without wrecking self-destruction will be imminent threats. (Lefebvre, 1991, p. 348)

Now the tribes of Niyamgiri are conscious of their identity with the constant presence of outsiders (dikus). This time the dikus may not just be a hostile enemy only. Different actors would be seen treading those spaces. It could be a researcher or a representative of the civil society organization, a company staff, a government employee, a foreign national. The changing ideas of space and the dikus in those realms reinforce the volatility of absolute space. This threatens the pristineness of absolute space. The meaning of the absolute space keeps changing to shift little toward the abstract. The so-called abstract space moves to a higher level of abstraction, and the erstwhile abstract once again becomes absolute. Thus, space remains fluid in the context of the indigenous environmental movement. Within these realms of shifting spaces, one finds acts of resistance in everyday life on the part of the indigenous communities. For instance, the celebration of *Maria festival* by Dongaria Kondha protects their village, environment, and family in the hills. That it received good media coverage can also be taken as an act of everyday resistance taking a collective form.

Here, we need to ponder that in both cases, the capitalist endeavor for dams and industries was put to a halt with everyday life protests that ultimately took an organized form. Both isn't it still the case of a "second nature" replacing the first? (Lefebvre, 1991), and the "spaces of consumption" has become "consumption of spaces as in tourism industry" (Gottdiener, 1993, p. 133). Similarly, in the case of Koel–Karo, everyday attempts of resistance against the state and the informal conversations in his everyday life by Soma Munda, the leader of KKJS, to shrug off the persuasion on the part of the state officials or other dikus (Chandra, 2013; Ghosh, 2006) represented the silent, subtle forms of resistance. The Koel–Karo project was scrapped by Jharkhand state. But interestingly, the state of Jharkhand possesses 37% of the entire nation's mineral reserves (Sundar, 2005). Within the first eight years of this inception, the state of Jharkhand that won its distinct provincial status based on flaunting a separate tribal identity, had signed 112 MOUs with different multinational companies as far as mining and extraction were concerned (Basu, 2008). Its long historical contestations for land rights and tribal identity have captured a new imagination of modernity. In this conflict between the absolute and abstract, the dialectics does flow but is the tribal identity searching for second nature in Jharkhand as well?

References

Agnew, J. (1994). The territorial trap: The geographical assumptions of international relations theory. *Review of International Political Economy, 1*(1), 53–80. https://www.jstor.org/stable/417 7090

Ambagudia, J. (2010). Tribal Rights, Dispossession and the State in Orissa. *Economic and Political Weekly, 45*(33), 60–67. Retrieved May 24, 2021, from http://www.jstor.org/stable/25741972.

Andersson, V. (2005*). Indigenous people—territory and identity: The case of Bolivia.* Paper presented at Transforming Landscapes of Poverty, Ås, Norway. Retrieved May 24, 2021, from https://vbn.aau.dk/ws/portalfiles/portal/6277040/indigenous_people_territory_and_identity.pdf.

Arenas, L. C. (2007). The U'wa community's battle against the oil companies: A local struggle turned global. In: B. de Sousa Santos. (Ed.). *Another knowledge is possible: Beyond northern epistemologies* (pp. 120–147). Verso.

Basu, M. (2008) Arcelor-Mittal in Jharkhand. *Economic & Political Weekly, 43*(48). Retrieved May 24, 2021, from http://www.indiaenvironmentportal.org.in/files/Arcelor-Mittal%20in%20J harkhand.pdf.

Boal, B. M. (1978). Centuries of change and resistance to change among the Khonds of Orissa. In R. R. Moser., & M. K. Gautam (Eds.), *Aspects of tribal life in South Asia I: strategy and survival* (pp. 135–151). Studia Ethnologica Bernensia.

Borde, R., & Bluemling, B. (2021). Representing indigenous sacred land: The case of the Niyamgiri movement in India. *Capitalism Nature Socialism, 32*(1), 68–87. https://doi.org/10.1080/104 55752.2020.1730417.

Bosu Mullick, S. (2003). Jharkhand movement: A historical analysis. In R. D. Munda & S. Bosu Mullick (Ed.), *The Jharkhand movement: Indigenous people's struggles for autonomy in India.* Copenhagen: International Work Group for Indigenous Affairs.

Bower, R. (2016). Who decides and who provides? The anarchistic housing practices of John Turner as realizations of Henri Lefebvre's autogestive Space. *Alternatives: Global, Local, Political, 41(2),* 83–97. Retrieved June 18, 2021, from http://www.jstor.org/stable/26386308.

Brennan, N., & Elden, S. (2009). Henri Lefebvre on state, space, territory. *International Political Sociology, 3*, 353–377.

Brittanica. (n.d.). *Oraon people.* Retrieved May 19, 2021, from https://www.britannica.com/topic/Oraon.

Indigenous Environmental Movements of Eastern India: Seeing … 251

Bulliyya, G. (2010). Ethnographic and health profile of the Dongria Kondhs: A primitive tribal group of Niyamgiri hills in Eastern Ghats of Odisha. *Afro Asian Journal of Anthropology and Social Policy, 1*(1), 11–25.

Chandra, U. (2013). Beyond subalternity: Land, community, and the state in contemporary Jharkhand. *Contemporary South Asia, 21*(1), 52–61. https://doi.org/10.1080/09584935.2012.757579.

Das, A. K. (2015). Environmental justice atlas (EJAtlas.org): India reaches the top while mapping the ecological conflicts and environmental injustices. *Current Science, 109*(12), 2176–2177.

Das, V. (2001). Mining Bauxite, maiming people. *Economic and Political Weekly, 36*(28), 2612–2614. Retrieved May 24, 2021, from http://www.jstor.org/stable/4410849.

Dove, M. (2006). Indigenous people and environmental politics. *Annual Review of Anthropology, 35*(1), 191–208. https://doi.org/10.1146/annurev.anthro.35.081705.123235.

Down to Earth. (2003, July 31). *Koel-Karo: Jharkhand.* Retrieved May 25, 2021, from https://www.downtoearth.org.in/coverage/koelkaro-jharkhand-13200.

Environmental Justice Atlas (2014). *Koel-Karo project, India.* Environmental Justice Atlas. Retrieved May 25, 2021, from https://ejatlas.org/conflict/koel-karo-project-india.

ENVIS (2017). *Mineral distribution in India.* ENVIS Centre on Environmental Problems of Mining, Government of India. Retrieved June 10, 2021, from http://ismenvis.nic.in/KidsCentre/Mineral_Distribution_in_India_13948.aspx.

EPW. (2001). *Massacres of Adivasis: A preliminary report source, 36*(9), 717–721.

Escobar, A., Rocheleau, D., & Kothari, S. (2002). Environmental social movements and the politics of place. *Development, 45*(1), 28–36. https://doi.org/10.1057/palgrave.development.1110314.

FAO and FILAC. (2021). *Forest governance by indigenous and tribal peoples. An opportunity for climate action in Latin America and the Caribbean.* Santiago. https://doi.org/10.4060/cb2953en.

FAO. (2009). *Indigenous and tribal people: Building on biological and cultural diversity for food and livelihood security.* FAO. Retrieved 14 May 2021, http://www.fao.org/3/i0838e/i0838e.pdf.

Fernandes, W. (1991). Power and powerlessness: Development projects and displacement of tribals. *Social Action, 41*(3), 243–270.

Fernandes, W. (2006). Liberalisation and development-induced displacement. *Social Change, 36*(1), 109–123.

Gadgil, M., & Malhotra, K. C. (2006). The ecological significance of caste ecology. In R. Guha (Ed.), *Social ecology.* (6th ed., pp. 27–41). Oxford University Press.

Gadgil, M. (1985). Towards an ecological History of India. *Economic and Political Weekly, 20*(45/47), 1909–1918. Retrieved May 24, 2021, from http://www.jstor.org/stable/4375012.

Gautam, A. (2020). Developmental policy and social unrest in Jharkhand: An anthropological analysis. *Anthropology, 8*(210). https://doi.org/10.35248/2332-0915.20.8.210.

Ghosh, A. (1991). Probing the Jharkhand question. *Economic and Political Weekly, 26*(18), 1173–1181.

Ghosh, K. (2006). Between global flows and local dams: Indigenousness, locality, and the transnational sphere in Jharkhand, India. *Cultural Anthropology, 21*(4), 501–534. Retrieved June 19, 2021, from http://www.jstor.org/stable/4124721.

Ghosh, P. (2016). Political identities and dilemma in Jharkhand Movement, India: Question of 'environmental revivalism' and its consequences. *SOCRATES: An International, Multi-lingual, Multi-disciplinary, 4*(2), 27–55.

Ghurye, G. S. (1963). *The scheduled tribes.* Popular Prakashan.

Gottdiener, M. (1993). A Marx for our time: Henri Lefebvre and the production of space. *Sociological Theory, 11*(1), 129–134. https://doi.org/10.2307/201984.

Government of India. (2011). *Executive summary.* Census 2011, Government of India. Retrieved May 20, 2021, from https://censusindia.gov.in/2011census/PCA/PCA_Highlights/pca_highlights_file/Odisha/Executive_Summary.pdf.

Government of Jharkhand. (2021). Jharkhand Economic Survey 2020–21. Centre for Fiscal Studies, Planning-cum-Finance Department, Government of Jharkhand. Retrieved October

01, 2021, from https://finance.jharkhand.gov.in/pdf/Economic_Survey_2020_21/Jharkhand_Eco
nomic_Survey_2020_21.pdf.

Government of Odisha. (2011). *Odisha reference manual 2011 Geology and mineral resources of Odisha.* Retrieved 13 June, 2021, from http://magazines.odisha.gov.in/orissaannualreference/ORA-2011/pdf/27-28.pdf.

Government of Orrisa. (2009). *Compendium of mineral resources of Odisha.* Department of Steel and Mines, Government of Orrisa. Retrieved 15 June, 2021, from https://www.odishaminerals.gov.in/sites/Download/Compendium_of_Mineral_Resources_in_Odisha.pdf.

Guha, R. (2006). *Social ecology (6th ed.).* Oxford University Press.

Hall, S. (1992). The question of cultural identity. In S. Hall., D. Held, & T. Mc Grew (Eds.), *Modernity and its futures.* Polity Press.

Hill, J. K. W. (2014). Agriculture irrigation and ecology in Adivasi villages in Jharkhand: Why control and ownership over natural resources matter. *Journal of Adivasi and Indigenous Studies (JAIS), 1*(1), 43–61.

IBEF. (2017). *Jharkhand: The Mining Base of India. India Brand Equity Foundation (IBEF).* Retrieved March 20, 2021, from https://www.ibef.org/download/Jharkhand-July-2017.pdf.

ILO (2009). *Indigenous & tribal peoples' rights in practice: A guide to ILO Convention No. 169. Programme to promote ILO Convention No. 169* (PRO 169), International Labour Standards Department, Retrieved May 25, 2021, from https://www.ilo.org/wcmsp5/groups/public/---ed_norm/---normes/documents/publication/wcms_106474.pdf.

Jena, M. (2013). Voices from Niyamgiri. *Economic and Political Weekly, 48(36),* 14–16. Retrieved June 18, 2021, from http://www.jstor.org/stable/23528364.

Jharkhand State Team. (2014). *Report on land governance assessment framework, Jharkhand.* Jharkhand State Team & National University of Study and Research in Law, Ranchi. Retrieved March, 14, 2021, from https://documents1.worldbank.org/curated/en/620621504863280205/pdf/119608-WP-P095390-PUBLIC-7-9-2017-10-6-10-JHARKHANDFinalReport.pdf.

Kalland, A. & Persoon, G. (Eds.). (1999) *Environmental movements in Asia.* Routledge.

KBK Government of Odisha. (n.d.). *Tribes of Kalahandi: Dongaria Kondha.* KBK Districts. Retrieved May 18, 2021, from http://kbk.nic.in/koraputtribes/kalDongria.htm.

Krishna, S. (2015). Colonial legacies and contemporary destitution: Law, race, and human security. *Alternatives: Global, Local, Political, 40(2),* 85–101. Retrieved May 24, 2021, from http://www.jstor.org/stable/24569425.

Krishnan, R., & Naga, R. (2017). 'Ecological Warriors' versus 'Indigenous Performers': Understanding state responses to resistance movements in Jagatsinghpur and Niyamgiri in Odisha. *South Asia: Journal of South Asian Studies, 40*(4), 878–894. https://doi.org/10.1080/00856401.2017.1375730.

Kumar, K. (2014). The sacred mountain: Confronting global capital at Niyamgiri. *Geoforum, 54,* 196–206. https://doi.org/10.1016/j.geoforum.2013.11.008.

Kumbhar, S. (2010). The political economy of mining-mediated development and the livelihood movements against mining in Orissa. *The Indian Journal of Political Science, 71*(4), 1213–1222. Retrieved May 24, 2021, from http://www.jstor.org/stable/42748948.

Lahiri-Dutt, K., Krishnan, R., & Ahmad, N. (2014). 'Captive' coal mining in Jharkhand: Taking land from indigenous communites. In K. Lahiri-Dutt (Ed.), *The coal nation: Histories, ecologies and politics of coal in India* (pp. 165–182). Ashgate Publishing.

Lee, Y. F., & So, A. Y. (Eds.). (1999). *Asia's environmental movements Comparative Perspectives.* Routledge.

Lefebvre, H. (1991). *The production of space.* Blackwell.

Lefebvre, H. (1971). *The everyday life in the modern world.* Harper Torchbooks.

Lefebvre, H. (2002). *The critique of everyday life.* Verso.

Lefebvre, H. (2003a). *The Urban Revolution.* University of Minnesota Press.

Lefebvre, H. (2003b). Elucidation. In S. Elden., E. Lebas, & E. Kofman (Eds.), *Henri Lefebvre: Key writings.* Continuum. (Translation work) From Lefebvre, H. (1961). *Critique de la vie quotidienne. 2, Fondements d'une sociologie de la quotidienneté.* L'Arche.

Lefebvre, H. (2009). *State, space, world*. University of Minnesota Press.

Malik, S. K. (2020). *Land alienation and politics of tribal exploitation in India Special focus on tribal movement in Koraput district of Odisha*. Springer Singapore.

Mallick, A. (2012). Encroachment on the Rights of the Adivasis: Colonial forest policy in 19th century Chota Nagpur and Santal Parganas. *Proceedings of the Indian History Congress, 73*, 747–755. Retrieved May 24, 2021, from http://www.jstor.org/stable/44156270.

Mathews, R. D. (2011). *The Koel-Karo People's movement in Eastern India*. Ritimo. Retrieved May 27, 2021, from https://www.ritimo.org/The-Koel-Karo-People-s-Movement-in-Eastern-India.

McCann, E. (2002). Space, citizenship, and the right to the city: A brief overview. *GeoJournal, 58*(2/3), 77–79. http://www.jstor.org/stable/41147753.

Ministry of Tribal Affairs. (2018). Annual report 2017–18. Ministry of Tribal Affairs, Government of India. Retrieved May 15, 2021, from https://tribal.nic.in/writereaddata/AnnualReport/AR2 017-18.pdf.

Nanda, C. (2012). Dislocated by development: Discourse on development and people's movement in post-colonial Odisha. *Proceedings of the Indian History Congress, 73*, 1357–1365. Retrieved May 23, 2021, from http://www.jstor.org/stable/44156338.

Nayak, A. (2015). Environmental movements in India. *Journal of Developing Societies, 31*(2), 249–280. https://doi.org/10.1177/0169796x15576172.

Oommen, T. K. (1990). *Protest and change: Studies in social Movements*. SAGE.

Padhi, S., & Panigrahi, N. (2011). *Tribal movements and Livelihoods: Recent developments in Orissa*. Working Paper 51, Chronic Poverty Research Center, IIPA, Delhi.

Panda, S., & Padhi, B. (2020). Poverty and inequality in Odisha, India. *Journal of Public Affairs, 21*(2). https://doi.org/10.1002/pa.2220.

Pandey, A. D. (2018). Kondhs' Resistance movement to save sacred Niyamgiri, Odisha. In J. Liljeblad., & B. Verschuuren (Eds.), *Indigenous perspectives on sacred natural sites culture, governance and conservation* (pp. 61–89). Routledge.

Pattnaik, B. (2013). Tribal resistance movements and the politics of development-induced displacement in contemporary Orissa. *Social Change, 43*(1), 53–78. https://doi.org/10.1177/004908571 3475727.

Poster, M. (2002). Everyday (virtual) life. *New Literary History, 33*(4), 743–760. Retrieved June 18, 2021, from http://www.jstor.org/stable/20057754.

Prabhu, P. (1998). Tribal movements: Resistance to resurgence. *Journal of Social Work, 59*(1). Retrieved June 10, 2021, from http://ijsw.tiss.edu/greenstone/collect/ijsw/index/assoc/HASHa7dc/915bdb20.dir/doc.pdf.

PUCL. (2002, September). *The Adivasi struggle for land rights at Koel-Karo: Jharkhand PUCL Report on killing of eight tribal villagers police firing at Tapkara Jharkhand on 02.02.2001*. PUCL Bulletin. PUCL (People's Union for Civil Liberties).

Ray, S., & Patra, S. (2009). Evolution of the political economy of land acquisition. In *India infrastructure report 2009 land—A critical resource for infrastructure*. Oxford University Press. Retrieved June 09, 2021, from http://www.indiaenvironmentportal.org.in/files/IIR2009.pdf.

Roy, A. (2011). Urbanisms, worlding practices and the theory of planning. *Planning Theory, 10*(1), 6–15. Retrieved June 18, 2021, from http://www.jstor.org/stable/26165893.

Sahu, G. (2008). Mining in the Niyamgiri hills and tribal rights. *Economic and political weekly, 43*(15), 19–21. Retrieved May 24, 2021, from http://www.jstor.org/stable/40277331.

Salmón, E. (2000). Kincentric ecology: Indigenous perceptions of the human-nature relationship. *Ecological Applications, 10*(5), 1327–1332. https://doi.org/10.1890/1051-0761(2000)010[1327:KEIPOT]2.0.CO;2.

SANDRP. (2014). *Celebrating the story of Koel-Karo resistance: KKJS gets Bhigirath Prayas Samman at first India Rivers Week*. SANDRP, South Asia Network on Dams, Rivers and People. Retrieved 19 May 2021. https://sandrp.in/2014/11/24/celebrating-the-story-of-koel-karo-resist ance-kkjs-gets-bhigirath-prayas-samman-at-first-india-rivers-week/.

Sarkar, S. (1983). *Modern India: 1885–1947*. Macmillan India Ltd.

Scott, J. C. (1985). *Weapons of the weak: Everyday forms of peasant resistance.* Yale University Press.

Scott, J. C. (1990). *Domination and arts of resistance: Hidden transcripts:* Yale University Press.

SCSTRTI & Academy of Tribal Languages and Culture. (2018). *Tribal atlas of Odisha.* Academy of Tribal Languages and Culture & Scheduled Castes & Scheduled Tribes Research and Training Institute ST & SC Development Department, Government of Odisha. Retrieved 20 May 2021. https://repository.tribal.gov.in/bitstream/123456789/74411/1/SCST_2018_book_0322.pdf.

Sengupta, N. (1980) Class and tribe in Jharkhand. *Economic and Political Weekly, 15*(14), 664–671. https://www.jstor.org/stable/4368541.

Sharma, K. (1976). Jharkhand Movement in Bihar. *Economic and Political Weekly, 11*(1/2), 37–43. http://www.jstor.org/stable/4364310.

Singh, A. K. (2021). Endangered tribals of India: Booby trap of development. In V. K. Srivastava (Ed.), *India's tribes: Unfolding realities.* SAGE Publications.

Singh, K. M., Meena, M. S., Singh, R. K. P., Kumar, A., & Kumar, A. (2012). Rural poverty in Jharkhand, India: An empirical study based on panel data. *Munich Personal RePEc Archive.* Retrieved March 13, 2021, from https://mpra.ub.uni-muenchen.de/45258/1/MPRA_paper_45258.pdf.

Singh, R. (2001). *Social Movements, Old and New: A postmodern critique.* Sage Publications.

Singhal, V., Ghosh, J., & Bhat, S. (2021). Role of religious beliefs of tribal communities from Jharkhand (India) in biodiversity conservation. *Journal of Environmental Planning and Management,* 1–23. https://doi.org/10.1080/09640568.2020.1861587.

Srivastava, V. K. (Ed.). (2021). *India's tribes: Unfolding realities.* Sage Publications.

Stanek, L. (2008). Lessons from Nanterre. *Log, (13/14),* 59–67. http://www.jstor.org/stable/41765230

Sundar, N. (2005). Laws, policies and practices in Jharkhand. *Economic and Political Weekly,* 40(41), 4459–4462. http://www.jstor.org/stable/4417266.

Swain, A. (2015). *When state decides not to listen: The emerging new phase of environmental movements in India.* Paper Presented at the International Seminar on Perspectives on Contemporary India Leiden, Netherlands, 16–17 Apr 2015.

The Hindu. (2020, January 1). Odisha tribals still suffering from hunger, malnutrition. *The Hindu.* Retrieved 15 May 2021, https://www.thehindu.com/news/national/other-states/odisha-tribals-still-suffering-from-hunger-malnutrition/article30447339.ece.

Turner, T. S. (1979). Anthropology and the politics of indigenous people's struggles. *The Cambridge Journal of Anthropology, 5*(1), 1–43.

UN. (2009). *State of the world's indigenous peoples. Department of Economic and Social Affairs, Division for Social Policy and Development Secretariat of the Permanent Forum on Indigenous Issues.* United Nations. Retrieved 21 May 2021, from https://www.un.org/esa/socdev/unpfii/documents/SOWIP/en/SOWIP_web.pdf.

Walks, A. (2013). Suburbanism as a way of life, slight return. *Urban Studies, 50*(8), 1471–1488. http://www.jstor.org/stable/26144304.

Wrede, T. (2015). Introduction to Special Issue "Theorizing Space and Gender in the 21st Century". *Rocky Mountain Review, 69*(1), 10–17. Retrieved May 24, 2021, from http://www.jstor.org/stable/24372860.

Xaxa, V. (1999). Tribes as indigenous people of India. *Economic and Political Weekly, 34*(51), 3589–3595. Retrieved June 19, 2021, from http://www.jstor.org/stable/4408738.

Xaxa, V. (2008). *State, society, and tribes: Issues in post-colonial India.* Dorling Kindersley (India) Pvt. Ltd.

Can the Global South Count on the U.S. Climate Movement? Support for Compensatory Climate Justice Among U.S. Climate Change Protesters

Christopher Todd Beer

The climate justice movement, civil society organizations, and some governments from the Global South have called for wealthier, heavily industrialized nations of the Global North to contribute billions of dollars to nations that are more vulnerable to the destructive forces of climate change, lack the resources to adapt to a rapidly changing climate, lack the technology to sufficiently mitigate climate emission, and historically have contributed very little to the cause of climate change. Related academic research focuses on the ethical debates of climate justice from a philosophical lens (Gardiner & Weisbach, 2016; Meyer & Sanklecha, 2017; Shue, 2014), the geopolitical and policy debates of climate justice (Bond, 2014; Roberts & Parks, 2006), or the emergence and activism of climate justice movement organizations (Bond, 2012; Tokar, 2010). This chapter fills a gap in the literature by empirically examining the support among U.S. climate change protestors for a particular aspect of climate justice, financial compensation to nations of the Global South. Do participants in mass-mobilized climate change protest events support climate justice? Can those in the Global South concerned with climate justice count on the U.S. climate change movement to support calls for transnational compensatory climate justice? What individual characteristics of U.S. protestors predict support for compensation from the Global North to the Global South for climate change? Using original survey data from the two largest climate change protest mobilizations in the last decade within the U.S., this chapter examines levels of support for transnational climate justice among U.S. climate change protest participants. Below, I begin by examining the concept of compensatory justice within climate justice and look at some demands made by the Global South. This is followed by the focus of the chapter, an extensive

---

A portion of these findings was presented at the 2019 World Forum on Climate Justice, Glasgow, Scotland. I have no conflicts of interest to disclose. Correspondence regarding this article should be addressed to Christopher Todd Beer, 555 N. Sheridan Rd., Lake Forest, IL 60045, United States.

C. T. Beer (✉)
Department of Sociology and Anthropology, Lake Forest College, Lake Forest, IL, USA
e-mail: beer@lakeforest.edu

© The Author(s), under exclusive license to Springer Nature Singapore Pte Ltd. 2022
D. Madhanagopal et al. (eds.), *Environment, Climate, and Social Justice*,
https://doi.org/10.1007/978-981-19-1987-9_13

analysis of the levels of support for compensatory climate justice within the U.S. climate movement and individual-level predictors of that support.

1 Compensatory Climate Justice

One of the many fundamental principles of climate justice, really justice of any kind, is that those who cause harm to others shall be held responsible (for a broad review of climate justice principles, see Bond, 2014; Shue, 2014). This is clear when considering justice for personal crimes such as assault or theft. Many legal systems attempt to hold people (and other entities such as corporations) responsible for the harm done to others. Punishment may take the form of a prison sentence, an individual fine, or a significant financial settlement. In environmental justice arguments, the compensatory justice principle is often framed as "polluter pays" (Jamieson, 2001; Pedersen, 2010; Schwartz, 2010). Quite simply, it is that those that do the polluting should be the ones to pay for cleaning up the pollution and for the damage done to others' bodies, property, communities, and/or ecosystems. When the principle of justice is applied to the geopolitical context of global climate change, it is an effort to hold accountable those who benefitted from and disproportionally caused climate change for the harm that it has done and will do to others (Roser & Seidel, 2016; Shue, 2014).

Western, advanced industrialized nations have historically contributed a disproportionate proportion of greenhouse gas (GHG) emissions through the burning of fossil fuels for electricity production, transportation, industrial production, and mass consumption. At the same time, nations that have contributed fewer emissions, often drastically fewer historical emissions, are much more vulnerable to the damages and harm of climate change now and in the future (Althor et al., 2016). Climate justice perspectives argue that this imbalance in the causes and consequences of climate change needs to be at the forefront of every effort to address climate change. Climate justice asks, "Who is responsible for the harm caused to others, and how shall they be held responsible?" The responsibility for climate change among nation-states comes in many forms, from the responsibility to reduce emissions to the responsibility to compensate victims. These arguments are generally rooted in ethical questions of fairness. Scientists, policymakers, and journalists that are concerned with anthropogenic climate change often use language referring to a collective "we." While this is not a wholly inaccurate representation, it misses essential complexity and inequality. Subgroups of the collective human population (currently and in the past) have dramatically different responsibilities for causing climate change.

While it is the financially wealthier nations that have contributed a disproportionate share to the causes of climate change, it is the lower income, developing nations of the Global South that are not only more vulnerable to the harms of climate change but also have the fewest financial resources to assist in adaption, that is altering livelihoods in an effort to shield societies and households from harm (Roberts & Parks, 2006). The nations of the Global South are the ones that have contributed the least to the causes of climate change. Efforts to quantify the current and future negative impacts to society for each ton of greenhouse gas emissions are known as the social cost of carbon (dioxide). While there remains debate about the construction of complex models, recent research puts the social cost of carbon as high as $300 USD per ton (Kikstra et al., 2021). Previous formulas have underestimated the persistent damages to regions of the Global South.

Principles of climate justice ask policymakers to account for highly industrialized nations' disproportionate responsibilities for anthropogenic climate change emissions in a fair and just manner. The discourse and arguments of climate justice "offers an interpretative frame for the climate crisis that *foregrounds the stratification of cause and effect*" (Goodman, 2009, p. 509). In addition to compensatory climate justice, analysis of numerous climate justice movement declarations by Warlenius (2018) distinguishes a pattern of claims, including: acknowledging the climate debt that the Global North owes the Global South; "decolonizing" the atmosphere through nations of the North making the most drastic and rapid emissions reductions proportional to their historical contributions; and situating climate justice (debt) in a broader context of ecological debt.

Compensatory justice is an ethical argument that people should not benefit from harming others, and under such circumstances, the victims of the harm should be compensated, most often financially. Calls for compensation have been explicitly rejected by then U.S. Special Envoy for Climate Change, Todd Stern, who led the U.S. climate change delegation to numerous UNFCCC Conference of Party (COP) meetings. During the contentious COP 15 negotiations in Copenhagen, Stern responded to a reporter's question about climate debt and reparations with, "I actually completely reject the notion of a debt or reparations or anything of the like" (U.S. Mission Geneva, 2009). In one of the earliest formulations of climate justice principles from a network of environmental, indigenous, and globalization activists, the 2002 Bali Principles of Climate Justice makes a claim of compensatory justice as such, "Affirming the principle of Ecological debt, Climate Justice protects the rights of victims of climate change and associated injustices to receive full compensation, restoration, and reparation for the loss of land, livelihood and other damages" (International Climate Justice Network, 2002). The Bali Principles of Climate Justice also note that the decreased carbon-absorptive capacity of the atmosphere has now severely limited under-developed nations' ability to follow the path of development taken by wealthy nations. This limitation on their development demands compensation. This is a direct call for compensation based on what is owed ("debt") based on people's rights and the losses they have incurred. Similarly, a 2007 statement by Climate Justice Now! demands, "huge financial transfers from the North to the South based on historical responsibility and ecological debt for adaptation and mitigations costs paid for by redirecting military budgets, innovative taxes, and debt cancellation" (Climate Justice Now!, 2009, p. 154). This statement does not mince words when calling for significant financial compensation to the Global South.

In 2012, UNFCCC's COP 19 agreement formalized the parties' recognition of "loss and damage" caused by climate change, especially loss and damage in developing countries. The debate about loss and damage emerged as far back as 2007 in UNFCCC negotiations (see the Bali Action Plan). Loss and damage are distinguished from adaptation in that adaptation focuses more on the actions and efforts necessary to try and prevent loss and damage. Importantly, the UNFCCC text fails to indicate who is liable for compensation despite the agreement to address loss and damage. In fact, the Paris Agreement (Article 8, Paragraph 52) explicitly states that parties' recognition of loss and damage "does not involve or provide a basis for any liability or compensation" (UNFCCC, 2015). Additionally, like every aspect of the Paris Agreement, efforts to address loss and damage are voluntary and rely on the political goodwill of each nation.

Looking at the African continent as an example, in 2009, the "Nairobi Declaration on the African Process for Combating Climate Change" emerged as the shared negotiating position for African nations at the time. Among other things, it called for the compensation of African nations for environmental, social, and economic losses and for such finance to be new, additional, adequate, predictable, sustainable, and provided primarily in the form of grants. African Environmental Ministers collectively encouraged a common African position that "gives Africa an opportunity to demand compensation for damages caused by global warming" (African Union, 2009, p. 1). Also, in 2009, the Conference of African Heads of State and Government on Climate Change (CAHOSCC) called for developing nations to receive at least $267 billion a year by 2020 to support adaptation and mitigation efforts. The final AU position called for financial support to developing nations equivalent to 1.5% of the GDP of developed nations. For a more complete review of the African perspective and demands for climate debt payments, see Bond (2012).

As recently as April of 2021, African leaders called for mobilizing $25 billion over the next four years. Quoted in an Associated Press article covering the event, called The Leaders' Dialogue on the Africa Covid-Climate Emergency, Akinwumi A. Adesina, President of the African Development Bank Group, argued that "'Ten of the top 12 countries most at risk of drought are in Africa. He said that eight out of the top 12 countries affected by agricultural risks are also in Africa. 'Yet Africa does not get the resources it needs to adapt to climate change. Globally, only 10% of climate finance goes into adaptation, and Africa has received only three percent of global climate finance'" (Petesch, 2021).

Compensation for loss and damage from climate change is certainly not the only demand of climate justice organizations within the global movement. Climate justice movements in the US and around the world also reject carbon markets such as cap and trade schemes, geoengineering, the over-touted abilities of carbon capture, nuclear power, and corporate-led biodiesel (Tokar, 2014). Compensation to nations of the Global South without high-emitting nations of the Global North, the global elite, and transnational corporations also rapidly and drastically mitigating their climate change emissions is seen by some as a form of bribery to ignore their demise in a warming planet (Mwenda & Bond, 2020, pp. 109–110).

Not all climate change social movements or civil society organizations embrace the principles of climate justice. Even within the Global South, calls for compensation as part of climate justice are not uniformly embraced. For example, some Kenyan environmental civil society leaders do not support calls for compensation because they believe it would be misused by their governments or used ineffectively by others (Beer, 2014). In Zimbabwe, the Centre for Natural Resource Governance called for payments to victims of climate-change-fueled Cyclone Idai to be made from the Global North directly to trusted civil society organizations or, bypassing the state, directly to people in need (Centre for Natural Resource Governance, 2019). The expansive global climate movement advocates for a diversity of solutions through numerous perspectives and political lenses. The perspectives within the entirety of the climate justice movement range from developing new technological solutions and policy reforms within the current social and political systems to dismantling existing structures in favor of more just and sustainable systems. It is not a unified, singular global movement. While many climate movements today include at least a semantic reference to climate justice, not all make it their primary and foundational focus, and there remains a risk that the concepts of climate justice are already or will soon become either watered down or co-opted (Dietz, 2014a, pp. 298–299).

Divisions within the climate movement are not unheard of. In the lead up to, during, and in the aftermath of the UNFCCC's COP 15 in Copenhagen, two significant international-level climate change movement networks critically diverged (Chatterton et al., 2013; Hadden, 2015). One network remained focused on working within the system of global negotiations and framing the issue of climate change as one rooted in science and new regulatory policy initiatives, the other network focused on achieving the goals of climate justice through more wholistic and deep systemic change. There is a division within the climate change movement among those that advocate for and those that oppose "green capitalism" (Dietz, 2014a); that is capitalism which more efficiently uses natural resources and reduces waste through a "cradle-to-cradle" use of materials (also see della Porta and Parks, 2014). For an analysis of support of more radical shifts away from capitalism among US climate protestors, see Beer (2020).

2 Data and Methods

To measure the support for compensatory climate justice for the Global South among the climate movement in the U.S., I collected survey data from individuals that were in attendance at the two largest single-day climate change mobilizations in the U.S.—the People's Climate March in New York City in late 2014 and the March for Jobs, Justice, and the Climate in Washington, DC, and Chicago in the spring of 2017. While these two events are not a random sample of the broad climate change movement in the U.S., they are arguably representative of the more dedicated adherents—those that overcome the time and risk barriers to attend protest events rather than just donate money, sign petitions, or write letters to politicians. Both protest events were held in two of the most diverse cities in the U.S, and organizers arranged for busses to help transport participants from other states and distant cities. Organizers and the mainstream press estimated 400,000 attendees in New York City and 200,000 in Washington, DC.

2017 March for Climate, Jobs, and Justice in Washington, DC, USA. Photo by the author.

Both events were organized by the leadership of a broad coalition of organizations, including large environmental groups like 350.org and the Sierra Club, labor unions such as the Service Employees International (SEIU) union, and labor advocacy organizations such as BlueGreen Alliance, as well the social advocacy group Avaaz. In 2014, the theme of the march was, "To change everything, we need everyone." The demands were equally broad, demanding simply that world leaders take action on climate change. Rather than a, this "big tent" approach was designed to draw as many as possible to attend. The People's Climate March in New York City in 2014 reported over 1500 participating organizations. The official platform of the 2017 march in Washington, D.C. included shifting to 100% renewable energy, and increased economic opportunity for everyone. In addition to a rapid and just transition to 100% clean energy, the demands from the march organizers included union wages that could support families, pollution-free communities and workplaces, and support for workers displaced by a shift to clean energy. The DC march was planned to coincide with President Trump's 100th day in office.

The data was gathered from in-person, pen, and paper surveys administered at the respective marches. The resulting valid sample contains 1889 respondents split nearly equally among the two events. All of the analyses reported below is conducted using the full sample of 1889 respondents. In order to obtain such a large sample, over a dozen trained undergraduate and graduate research assistants from New York University, Columbia University, and Lake Forest College assisted the author in the data collection. Surveys were administered throughout the day at each protest event.

To ensure greater randomness in the sample, research assistants were assigned specific starting points along the area where protest participants lined up in preparation for each protest march. At each event, within the recruitment material online, protest organizers asked participants to line up at particular starting points (street intersections or locations within a park indicated on a map) according to their interest or identity, such as youth, labor, and frontline communities. This organization of the marchers by interest, when combined with the research team being spread out in accordance with the organizer's maps published prior to the events, allowed for a stratified random sample covering the entire crowd. Additional methods that were taken to ensure greater randomness of the sample were replicated from other research on mass protest events (Heaney & Rojas, 2007). Data collectors visually identified someone in the crowd (person A), then counted five people in the crowd from person A and approached that person for recruitment into the study. This helps to limit the unconscious biases of the survey team, as the data collectors may otherwise be initially but unintentionally drawn to subjects in the crowd that share their gender, age, or racial identities. The process was repeated after recruiting a subject, avoiding recruiting additional subjects in the immediate group that may have come to the march together and are more likely to share beliefs and opinions. Much of the data collection occurred as people gathered in preparation for the event. As the march began, data collectors moved with their assigned section of the crowd and continued survey recruitment as described above.

Surveys were completed by the subjects without individual identifying information, ensuring the subjects' anonymity. The response rate was 93.7% across both events. There was no gender or race/ethnicity pattern that distinguished the non-respondents from the respondents. In order to ensure higher participation and response rates in the midst of an active protest march, the paper survey form was a single page and took only a few minutes to complete. All responses were close-ended questions, allowing subjects to complete the survey, even while marching. In addition to the focus of this chapter, questions also asked about their support for a radical shift away from capitalism to address climate change (see Beer, 2020).

The dependent variable was measured with a Likert-scale (*strongly disagree* to *strongly agree*) response options for the statement, "The US owes developing countries millions of dollars to help them adapt to climate change." Due to the time limits of collecting survey data among protest participants, this research focused on one aspect of international climate justice, compensatory justice from the US to nations of the Global South. Additionally, because data was collected in the midst of a march, which makes it difficult for people to write sentences compared to ticking a box, no open-ended questions were included in the survey instrument.

Independent variables included self-identified gender, race, and ethnicity, educational attainment, political ideology, income, and event (NYC 2014 or DC 2017). For analysis, measures of gender were analyzed as male and female/other due to the small percentage of people in the sample that identified as neither male nor female (1.1%). Also, for analysis, the full range of race and ethnicity measures collected in the survey was narrowed to white and non-white due to the smaller percentage of Blacks, Asians, Hispanics, and other racial and ethnic minorities in the sample. Measures of household income were gathered and analyzed based on income quintile for the respective years of each event. The survey instrument indicated the income range while the analysis uses corresponding quintile categories (lowest to highest).

Education was measured and analyzed by the highest attainment of major milestones ranging from less than secondary to earning an advanced degree such as an MA or Ph.D. Political ideology was measured using a five-point scale ranging from extremely liberal to extremely conservative which was appropriate for a US context.

Analysis of the ordinal dependent variable was conducted using Stata 13 statistical software. Interpretation of the results is aided by reporting predicted probabilities presented in figures. This allows for analysis of the variation in the probabilities across the response categories of the outcome variable as well as the discrete change in those probabilities (Long & Freese, 2014).

3   Analysis and Discussion

The sample, representative of the U.S. climate change protest participants, is more female (56%) than male, predominantly white (73%), has a disproportionally high level of educational attainment (43% reported a graduate degree), is skewed toward the top two income quintiles (50.5%), and is predominantly liberal in their political ideology (84.2% somewhat or extremely liberal). Compared to the U.S. general population, the climate change protestors sampled here are slightly less diverse in their racial and ethnic identities (more white), substantially more educated, have higher incomes, and are far more liberal in their political ideology. Table 1 reports the descriptive statistics of the independent and dependent variables. Table 2 reports the distributions of independent variable responses.

A strong majority (66.7%) of respondents in the sample of US climate change protest participants agreed or strongly agreed with the statement that the U.S. owes developing countries millions of dollars to help them adapt to climate change (see Fig. 1). Only 10.5% disagreed or strongly disagreed with providing millions of dollars in compensatory climate justice. Over a fifth (22.8%) neither agreed nor disagreed with the statement. Collectively, U.S. climate change protestors report high levels of support for international compensatory climate justice.

What predicts the variation in the levels of support? Statistically significant variables predicting support for compensatory climate justice include gender, race/ethnicity, educational attainment, political ideology, and event/year (see Table 3). Income does not gain statistical significance at the 0.05 level. Ordered logit is appropriate for the analysis of ordinal level outcome variables, in this case, the Likert-scale response choice indicates levels of agreement with compensatory climate justice (Long, 1997). In order to better interpret the results of the ordered logit, I report predicted probabilities across each of the categories of the independent and dependent variables.

Can the Global South Count on the U.S. Climate Movement? …   263

Table 1 Descriptive statistics of independent and dependent variables

	Mean	Standard deviation	Min	Max
Independent variables				
Gender				
Female/other = 1 male = 0	0.56	0.53	0	1
Race/ethnicity				
White = 1 All other races and ethnicities = 0	0.73	0.44	0	1
Educational attainment				
Less than secondary = 0 up to graduate degree = 5	4.17	0.88	1	5
Income				
Quintiles corresponding to U.S. income distribution	3.32	1.37	1	5
Political ideology				
Extremely liberal (1) to extremely conservative (5)	1.75	0.78	1	5
NYC PCM 2014				
NYC = 1 DC 2017 = 0	0.48	0.49	0	1
Dependent variable				
The US owes developing countries millions of dollars to help them adapt to climate change				
Strongly disagree (1) to strongly agree (5)	3.81	1.00	1	5

3.1 Gender

Females and those that did not identify as either male or female made up a majority of the participants (56%) at the protest events (see Table 1). A majority of both men (69.4%) and women (64.1%) either agreed or strongly agreed that the US owed countries of the Global South for damage caused by climate change. However, examining Fig. 2, the predicted probabilities of support for compensatory climate justice by gender, males and females were nearly equally likely to "agree" (0.43 vs. 0.42), but men were more likely to "strongly agree" (0.28 vs. 0.23). It is the degree or strength of agreement where gender becomes a differentiating variable. Among US climate change movement's protest participants, males, report a slightly stronger commitment to their support for compensatory climate justice to developing nations of the Global South.

Table 2 Distribution of independent variables

Variable	Percent
Gender	
Female	55.5
Male	45.5
Race/ethnicity	
White	73.0
All other races and ethnicities	27.0
Education	
Less than high school/secondary	0.3
High school/secondary	4.9
Some college/tertiary	15.7
College/tertiary degree	35.6
Advanced college/tertiary degree (MA, Ph.D., etc.)	43.1
Income	
Lowest income quintile	14.2
Second income quintile	15.6
Middle-income quintile	19.6
Fourth income quintile	25.5
Top income quintile	25.0
Political ideology	
Extremely conservative	0.4
Somewhat conservative	1.3
Moderate	14.1
Somewhat liberal	40.7
Extremely liberal	43.5
Protest event	
NYC 2014	47.7
DC/Chicago 2017	52.3

3.2 Race and Ethnicity

A similar pattern as that which is evident in the analysis of gender appears in the analysis of race and ethnicity (see Fig. 3). White protest participants were nearly as likely as non-white participants to agree with compensatory justice with a predicted probability of "agree" at 0.42 versus 0.43, but those that identified as a race/ethnic other than white were more likely to "strongly agree" compared to whites with a predicted probability of 0.30 versus 0.24. In a society where a socially constructed racial and ethnic hierarchy continues to benefit whites, it is likely that the discriminatory experiences of other races and ethnicities contribute to their greater strength of agreement in support for compensatory climate justice from the US to the largely black and

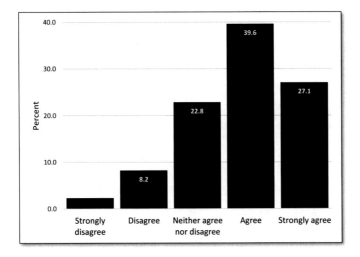

Fig. 1 The US owes developing countries millions of dollars to help them adapt to climate change

Table 3 Ordered logit model for support for compensatory climate justice

Gender (Female)	−0.287**
	(0.092)
Race/ethnicity (White)	−0.309**
	(0.107)
Education	0.111*
	(0.054)
Political ideology	−0.652***
	(0.061)
Income quintile	−0.057
	(0.035)
New York City 2014	0.397***
	(0.091)

Note Standard errors are in parentheses. * $p < 0.05$. ** $p < 0.01$. *** $p < 0.001$

brown populations of the Global South. That being said, the high level of support for climate justice within the U.S. climate movement should not be overlooked but rather seen as an opportunity to build alliances. Additionally, black and brown communities in the U.S. are more likely to be victims of environmental inequality in the form of exposure to toxins, waste sites, and other environmental hazards (Taylor, 2014). Therefore, they are likely primed to see environmental issues through a justice lens, compared to whites.

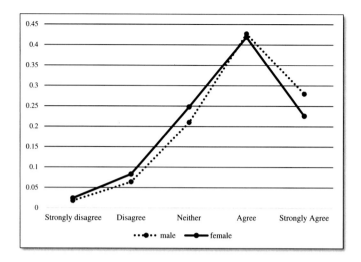

Fig. 2 Predicted probabilities of support for compensatory climate justice by gender

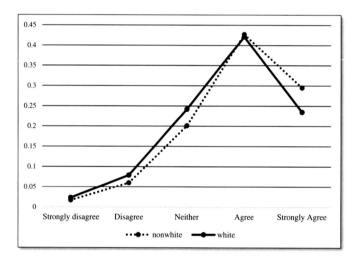

Fig. 3 Predicted probabilities of support for compensatory climate justice by race/ethnicity

3.3 Income

Participants in these two major U.S. climate change protest events were disproportionally from the highest two income quintiles. While the top quintile agreed or strongly agreed with compensatory climate justice at a slightly lower rate, across every income quintile, a majority "agreed" or "strongly agreed" that the US owed developing nations millions of dollars to help them adapt to climate change. The

Can the Global South Count on the U.S. Climate Movement? ... 267

Table 4 Crosstabulation of support for compensatory justice by income quintile

	Lowest	Second	Middle	Fourth	Top	Total
Strongly disagree	6	2	5	12	18	43
	2.4%	0.7%	1.5%	2.6%	4.0%	2.4%
Disagree	17	26	25	34	43	145
	6.8%	9.6%	7.2%	7.4%	9.6%	8.2%
Neither disagree nor	57	57	89	105	97	405
	22.8%	21.1%	25.7%	23.0%	21.8%	22.9%
Agree	102	104	128	187	180	701
	40.8%	38.5%	37.0%	40.9%	40.4%	39.6%
Strongly agree	68	81	99	119	108	475
	27.2%	30.0%	28.6%	26.0%	24.2%	26.9%
Total	250	270	346	457	446	1,769
	100%	100%	100%	100%	100%	100%

coefficient from the ordinal logit analysis is negative (see Table 2) but not statistically significant at the 0.05-level ($p = 0.102$). The income quintile is not a predictor of the variation of support for compensatory climate justice among participants in climate change protest events in the U.S (Table 4).

3.4 Education

Similar to the other independent variables examined thus far, the majority across every level of education agreed or strongly agreed that the U.S. owed developing countries millions of dollars to help them adapt to climate change. Every level of education reported similar levels of "agree," but those with advanced degrees (more than a bachelors) were more likely to "strongly agree" with the need for the U.S. to provide compensatory climate justice. In Fig. 4, only the high and low ends of the range of education levels are shown for clarity of the figure. The other educational categories follow in order with greater education yielding higher levels of "strongly agree" at each increment of attainment.

There is a possibility that, in the U.S., those with more educational attainment are more likely to have been exposed to and continue to follow global geopolitics more than those with less access to education. Knowledge of historical and ongoing inequalities generated by direct and indirect imperialism and political power would imaginably contribute to a greater understanding of how the consequences of climate change will be unjustly distributed onto those with less capacity to avert them while the causes of anthropogenic climate change have been historically centered in the heavily industrialized nations of the Global North.

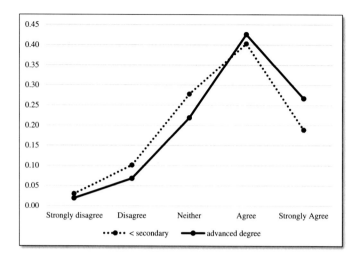

Fig. 4 Predicted probabilities of support for compensatory climate justice by education

3.5 Political Ideology

Unlike the other independent variables, not every category of political ideology reported a majority of agreeing or strongly agreeing with compensatory climate justice. Only 37.6% of those that identified as somewhat conservative agreed or strongly agreed, and 50% of those that identified as extremely conservative agree or strongly agree. However, due to the extremely low number of self-identifying conservatives in the sample, these results should be interpreted with great caution when being applied to conservatives. As it is evident in Fig. 5, among the sample of climate change protestors, those that identified as extremely conservative had a higher probability of reporting strong disagreement, disagreement, or neither agreeing nor disagreeing with compensatory climate justice. The probability that someone who identified as strongly conservative would also strongly agree with compensatory climate justice is only 0.038 compared to 0.35 for someone that identified as strongly liberal. The higher the degree of association with liberal political ideology, the higher the probability of support for the idea that the US owes millions of dollars to developing countries to help adapt to climate change. Unsurprisingly, when climate change has become such a polarized partisan political issue between the dominant political ideologies and parties (Dunlap & McCright, 2008), a similar division is highly evident in support for compensatory climate justice even among participants in a climate change protest event.

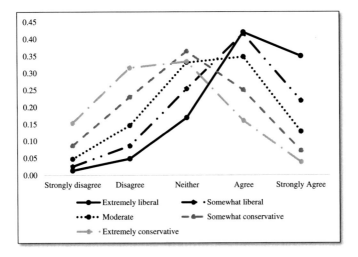

Fig. 5 Predicted probabilities of support for compensatory climate justice by political ideology

3.6 NYC 2014 Versus DC 2017

I also tested for any differences between the two years/events. They occurred two and a half years apart. The first event was when Barrack Obama was president and the second protest was not only after the 2015 adoption of the UNFCCC Paris Agreement but also after Donald Trump had taken office as the president of the U.S. in the 2016 elections. The ordered logit regression showed that there were statistically significant ($p < 0.001$) differences between the two events. Figure 6 illustrates that across both events, the overall probability was higher than respondents would report that they agree or strongly agree, but at the 2014 People's Climate March in New York City, respondents were more likely to strongly agree with compensatory climate justice compared to the 2017 protest in Washington, DC.

Other research also points to a slight decrease in the "radicalness" of the views of the two protest crowds. Compared to the 2014 protesters, the 2017 protest participants were less likely to support a radical shift away from capitalism to address climate change (Beer, 2020). While speculative in its explanatory power, the difference between the political context of the two events is worth considering. In 2014, then-President Obama had at least signaled a desire to begin to address climate change, and protesters may have been focused on pushing him much further. The 2017 protest event was held on then-President Trump's 100th day in office. He had already indicated his intention to withdraw the U.S. from the Paris climate agreement, and a few months later, he would state this intention again during a national press conference. In 2017, U.S. climate change protest participants may have moderated their hopes for achieving meaningful and necessary climate policy and scaled back their enthusiasm for climate justice policies under a Trump administration that

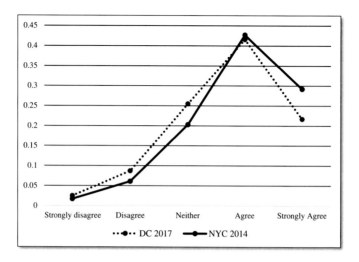

Fig. 6 Predicted probabilities of support for compensatory climate justice by protest event

was hostile to even actively reducing emissions and openly expressed opposition to compensatory climate justice policies.

4 Conclusion

Overall, mainstream protest participants from the U.S. climate change movement report high levels of support for compensatory climate justice, specifically when asked directly about the transfer of millions of dollars from the U.S. to developing nations for climate change adaptation. Their focus on climate justice is not limited to domestic inequalities in the causes and consequences of anthropogenic climate change. While skeptics of U.S. social movement support may argue that it is one thing to report support for such policies on a survey in the midst of a protest, it is another to do the work to help make global climate justice policies a reality. However, this data is drawn from a sample of people who actively participated in a protest. These are not passive supporters of the climate movement. They were mobilized and overcame the personal costs of and barriers (time, money, effort) to engage in protest participation.

Since 2009, the year of the failed (from the lens of climate justice) COP 15 in Copenhagen, climate justice framing has expanded among INGOs and climate change social movements, and a recognition of climate justice issues was included in several aspects of the Paris Agreement, including the preamble; the number of mentions of unequal vulnerability; language tying it to gender equality, indigenous right, and human rights; and commitments in principle to address loss and damage (Gach, 2019). However, the full implementation of sufficient financial pledges of new and additional grants to nations of the Global South has yet to be fulfilled. Possibly, with more cross-national coordination by INGOs or social movement networks, participants in the U.S. climate change movement will contribute to and generate the political will within the U.S. to help deliver this important aspect of global climate justice. A revival of the organizational network Climate Justice Now! (see Dietz, 2014b) or something similar could amplify the collective voice and global coalitions for climate justice. The existing global infrastructure of anti-war, global justice, and other movements can serve as a pathway to a climate justice coalition that can "find avenues and mechanisms for more frequent forums and mobilizations that can maintain and accelerate the momentum of a truly planetary movement" (Almeida, 2019, p. 976). Global coalitions of environmental movements (especially those focused on environmental racism and injustice), humanitarian INGOs (like ActionAid), human rights organizations, women's rights organizations, legal and ethical scholars, indigenous rights organizations, and liberal political parties have the potential to collectively move powerful nation-states toward greater global climate justice. It is arguably these very types of coalitions working with vulnerable communities and a justice frame that contributed to the eventual inclusion of loss and damage into the UNFCCC agreements (Allan & Hadden, 2017). Senator Bernie Sanders is the most prominent U.S. politician to propose a substantial financial commitment, $200 billion, to the global Green Climate Fund (Sanders, N.D.). ActionAid has called for reparations of $100 billion a year on top of $800 billion upfront for climate justice to developing countries (Action Aid, 2021). Other U.S. civil society organizations that support ActionAid's call include Care About Climate, Center for Biological Diversity, Center for International Environmental Law, Corporate Accountability International, EcoEquity, Food and Water Watch, Friends of the Earth U.S., Gulf Coast Center on Law and Policy, Oil Change International, Sunrise Movement, SustainUS, Women's Environment and Development Organization (WEDO), and 350.org.

Future research should examine greater complexities of support for global compensatory climate justice among U.S. climate activists. Experimental research designs may be able to isolate the influence of different regions on people's support for compensatory climate justice. For example, do U.S. climate activists express greater support for nations in African regions compared to various regions within Asia or small island nations? Is there a perceived development threshold at which U.S. climate movement participants no longer support compensation? Future studies could make variables of support for international compensation more concrete by measuring the tax implications for individuals in the U.S. more broadly and within the climate movement in particular. Mixed methods research could follow-up quantitative measures of support, as I measured here, with richer qualitative explanations of the rationale of those within the movement that support or reject compensatory climate justice.

References

Action Aid. (2021). *G7: Climate finance must be about justice and reparations.* Retrieved September 17, 2021, from https://www.actionaidusa.org/news/g7-climate-finance-must-be-about-justice-and-reparations/

African Union. (2009, 2010, July 2). *Concept note for the first meeting of the conference of African heads of state and government on climate change and African lead experts on climate change.* Retrieved March 3, 2010, from http://www.africa-union.org/root/ua/Conferences/2009/aout/SUMMIT/24aout/Concept%20Note%20-%20CONFERENCE%20OF%20AFRICAN%20H EADS%20OF%20STATE%20AND%20GOVERNMENT%20ON%20CLIMATE%20CHAN GE.DOC

Allan, J. I., & Hadden, J. (2017). Exploring the framing power of NGOs in global climate politics. *Environmental Politics, 26*(4), 600–620. https://doi.org/10.1080/09644016.2017.1319017

Almeida, P. (2019). Climate justice and sustained transnational mobilization. *Globalizations, 16*(7), 973–979. https://doi.org/10.1080/14747731.2019.1651518

Althor, G., Watson, J. E., & Fuller, R. A. (2016). Global mismatch between greenhouse gas emissions and the burden of climate change. *Scientific Reports, 6*(1), 1–6. https://doi.org/10.1038/srep20281

Beer, C. T. (2014). Climate justice, the global south, and policy preferences of Kenyan environmental NGOs. *The Global South, 8*(2), 84–100. https://doi.org/10.2979/globalsouth.8.2.84

Beer, C. T. (2020). "Systems change not climate change": Support for a radical shift away from capitalism at mainstream US climate change protest events. *The Sociological Quarterly*, 1–24. https://doi.org/10.1080/00380253.2020.1842141

Bond, P. (2012). *Politics of climate justice: Paralysis above, movement below.* University of Kwa Zulu Natal Press.

Bond, P. (2014). Climate Justice in, by, and for Africa. In M. Dietz & H. Garrelts (Eds.), *Routledge handbook of the climate change movement* (pp. 205–221). Routledge.

Centre for Natural Resource Governance. (2019). *Cyclone Idai: Time the rich countries compensate victims of climate change disasters.* Retrieved September 17, 2021, from https://www.cnrgzim.org/cyclone-idai-time-the-rich-countries-compensate-victims-of-climate-change-disasters/

Chatterton, P., Featherstone, D., & Routledge, P. (2013). Articulating climate justice in Copenhagen: Antagonism, the commons, and solidarity. *Antipode, 45*(3), 602–620. https://doi.org/10.1111/j.1467-8330.2012.01025.x

Climate Justice Now! (2009). What's missing from the climate talks? Justice! In I. Angus (Ed.), *The global fight for climate justice: Anticapitalist responses to global warming and environmental destruction* (pp. 154–155). Resistance Books.

della Porta, D., & Parks, L. (2014). In M. Dietz & H. Garrelts (Eds.), *Routledge handbook of the climate change movement* (pp. 19–30). Routledge.

Dietz, M. (2014a). Debates and conflicts in the climate movement. In M. Dietz & H. Garrelts (Eds.), *Routledge handbook of the climate change movement* (pp. 292–307). Routledge.

Dietz, M. (2014b). Organizational profile—Climate justice now! In M. Dietz & H. Garrelts (Eds.), *Routledge handbook of the climate change movement* (pp. 240–242). Routledge.

Dunlap, R. E., & McCright, A. M. (2008). A widening gap: Republican and democratic views on climate change. *Environment: Science and Policy for Sustainable Development, 50*(5), 26–35. https://doi.org/10.3200/ENVT.50.5.26-35

Gach, E. (2019). Normative shifts in the global conception of climate change: The growth of climate justice. *Social Sciences, 8*(1), 24. https://doi.org/10.3390/socsci8010024

Gardiner, S. M., & Weisbach, D. A. (2016). *Debating climate ethics*: Oxford University Press.

Goodman, J. (2009). From global justice to climate justice? Justice ecologism in an era of global warming. *New Political Science, 31*(4), 499–514. https://doi.org/10.1080/07393140903322570

Hadden, J. (2015). *Networks in contention: The divisive politics of climate change.* Cambridge University Press.

Heaney, M. T., & Rojas, F. (2007). Partisans, nonpartisans, and the antiwar movement in the United States. *American Politics Research, 35*(4), 431–464. https://doi.org/10.1177/1532673X07300763

International Climate Justice Network. (2002). *Bali principles of climate justice*. Retrieved October 12, 2009, from https://www.iicat.org/wp-content/uploads/2012/03/Bali-Princioples-of-Climate-Justice.pdf

Jamieson, D. (2001). Climate change and global environmental justice. In C. A. Miller & P. N. Edwards (Eds.), *Changing the atmosphere: Expert knowledge and global environmental governance* (pp. 287–30). MIT Press. https://doi.org/10.7551/mitpress/1789.001.0001

Kikstra, J., Waidelich, P., Rising, J., Yumashev, D., Hope, C., & Brierley, C. (2021). The social cost of carbon dioxide under climate-economy feedbacks and temperature variability. *Preprint at* https://www.researchgate.net/publication/350443280_The_social_cost_of_carbon_dioxide_under_climate-economy_feedbacks_and_temperature_variability.

Long, J. S. (1997). *Regression models for categorical and limited dependent variables*. Sage.

Long, J. S., & Freese, J. (2014). *Regression models for categorical dependent variables using Stata* (3rd edn.). Stata Press.

Meyer, L. H., & Sanklecha, P. (2017). Climate justice and historical emissions. *Cambridge University Press*. https://doi.org/10.1017/9781107706835

Mwenda, M., & Bond, P. (2020). African climate justice: Articulations and activism. In B. Tokar & T. Gilbertson (Eds.), *Climate justice and community renewal: Resistance and grassroots solutions* (pp. 108–127). Routledge.

Pedersen, O. W. (2010). Environmental principles and environmental justice. *Environmental Law Review, 12*(1), 26–49. https://doi.org/10.1350/enlr.2010.12.1.074

Petesch, C. (2021). African leaders call for climate financing acceleration. *Associated Press*. Retrieved May 20, 2021, 2021, from https://apnews.com/article/africa-climate-summits-climate-change-senegal-f1d6e002bfa064e7f2d22b9f46ffd4a3

Roberts, J. T., & Parks, B. C. (2006). *A climate of injustice: Global inequality, north-south politics, and climate policy*. The MIT Press.

Roser, D., & Seidel, C. (2016). *Climate justice: An introduction*. Taylor & Francis.

Sanders, B. (N.D.). *The green new deal*. Retrieved September 17, 2021, from https://berniesanders.com/issues/green-new-deal/

Schwartz, P. (2010). The polluter-pays principle. In M. Fitzmaurice, D. M. Ong, & P. Merkouris (Eds.), *Research handbook on international environmental law*. Edward Elgar Publishing. https://doi.org/10.4337/9781849807265

Shue, H. (2014). *Climate justice: Vulnerability and protection*. Oxford University Press.

Taylor, D. (2014). *Toxic communities: Environmental racism, industrial pollution, and residential mobility*. NYU Press.

Tokar, B. (2014). U.S. and worldwide climate justice movements. In M. Dietz & H. Garrelts (Eds.), *Routledge handbook of the climate change movement* (pp. 131–146). Routledge.

Tokar, B. (2010). *Towards climate justice: Perspectives on the climate crisis and social change*. Communalism Press.

U.S. Mission Geneva. (2009). Todd Stern, special envoy for climate change—Press Briefing.

UNFCCC. (2015). *The Paris outcome on loss and damage*. Retrieved May 1, 2021, 2021, from https://unfccc.int/files/adaptation/groups_committees/loss_and_damage_executive_committee/application/pdf/ref_8_decision_xcp.21.pdf

Warlenius, R. (2018). Decolonizing the atmosphere: The climate justice movement on climate debt. *The Journal of Environment & Development, 27*(2), 131–155. https://doi.org/10.1177/1070496517744593

Eco-Feminisms in Theory and Practice in the Global South: India, South Africa, and Ecuador

Devendraraj Madhanagopal, Patrick Bond, and Manuel Bayón Jiménez

1 Introduction

In India, South Africa, and Ecuador, where eco-feminist political activism and analysis are well-grounded and powerful, we pay tribute to the importance of a body of thought and practice that is confronting the power of both capitalism and patriarchy as well as their inter-relationships. The combination of fields of inquiry we find vital for today's world—critical political ecology, social reproduction, and political economy—allows for breakthrough ideas. We recognize the tendency of one lineage of eco-feminists, who sometimes inappropriately naturalize social relations, just as we recognize the converse danger within ecological modernization, to reduce all-natural and social life to versions of "capital." Thus, it is in search of a critique of contemporary climate policy that we aim to use all the available analytical perspectives: gender, race, class, anti-imperial, and generational (where in the latter category, youth and women relate so much more strongly to stewardship than do current generations of men).

Maria Mies and Vandana Shiva stressed how women across the world possess certain unique relationships with nature due to a shared historical background (Mies & Shiva, 1993), and hence, as argued by Bina Agarwal, they have more responsibilities, natural qualities, and stakes in not only environmental conservation but environmental justice (Agarwal, 1998). In this spirit, Janis Birkeland defined eco-feminism as

---

D. Madhanagopal
School of Sustainability, XIM University, Odisha, India

P. Bond (✉)
Department of Sociology, University of Johannesburg, Johannesburg, South Africa
e-mail: pbond@mail.ngo.za

M. B. Jiménez
University of Leipzig, Leipzig, Germany

© The Author(s), under exclusive license to Springer Nature Singapore Pte Ltd. 2022
D. Madhanagopal et al. (eds.), *Environment, Climate, and Social Justice*,
https://doi.org/10.1007/978-981-19-1987-9_14

A value system, a social movement, and a practice, but it also offers a political analysis that explores the links between androcentrism and environmental destruction. It is 'an awareness' that begins with the realization that the exploitation of nature is intimately linked to Western Man's attitude toward women and tribal cultures (Birkeland, 1993. p. 18).

Feminists targeting capitalism—such as Ariel Salleh (1997), Mies (1986), Mies and Shiva (1993), Sylvia Federici (2004), and Shiva (2008)—considered the mode of production a formidable barrier to liberation both at home and in the environment. In parallel to eco-feminist scholarship, there has been a burgeoning literature addressing environmental justice, and both academic and movement-generated forms of knowledge have emerged across the globe (Martinez-Alier, 2002; Roberts & Parks, 2006; Walker, 2012; Ako, 2013; Leonard, 2013; Harris, 2016). Environmental justice movements of the Global South have been active since at least the epochs of slavery and colonialism, responding to threats posed to society by unsustainable, patriarchal power relations that were stamped upon landscapes of agriculture, water management, and mineral extraction. In modern academia, a breakthrough point came with Robert Bullard's documentation of racial biases associated with what he termed *"Dumping in Dixie"* (Bullard, 1990).

Subsequently, environmental justice scholarship has become influential in focusing recognition of environmental pollution and conflicts associated with resource politics. Within this tradition, scholarship on climate justice emerged and is increasingly relevant, incorporating activist demands for equitable development, social justice, human rights, ecological reparations, critique of corporate climate strategies, and the need for greater political voice from oppressed peoples, regions, and nations—especially the voice of women.

Since the late 1990s, the cutting-edge environmental justice movements have demonstrated a clear understanding of climate change (Atapattu, 2016; Beer, 2016; Bond, 2012, 2018; Derman, 2020; Harris, 2019; Jafry, 2019; Moss & Umbers, 2020; Page, 2006; Schlosberg & Collins, 2014). However, the scholarly literature has been concentrated on the geographic North (including its own Global South sites of struggle), with less attention paid to densely populated, ecologically vulnerable nations of the South. Likewise, the divisions of labor that arise in academia mean that between the Global South and Global North, knowledge production takes on a class, race, and sometimes gendered bias. One result is a limited understanding of how to apply theoretical insights to climate justice movements, especially those originating within the Global South (Bond, 2018). Sometimes, scholars in the latter sites do not have access to the latest scholarly output given the commodification of ideas. In an era with a noticeable inter and intranational digital divide, far too much of the analysis that would be helpful in the Global South remains locked up in high-priced journals, book publications, or academic-conferencing opportunities, even when the Covid-19 crisis compelled online access.

This bias is visibly striking in the unsatisfactory way environmental justice analysis is incorporated within and across social sciences disciplines in the case study sites of India, South Africa, and Ecuador. Even though environmental and climate

Eco-Feminisms in Theory and Practice in the Global South ...   277

injustices are more common, and even though feminist practical analysis is of enormous importance, there are far fewer scholarly contributions that relate to women's agency against climate change and associated risks (Perkins, 2014).

Climate vulnerability and the need for adaptation, two of the most obvious features of the crisis, are not gender neutral (Goh, 2012; Lambrou & Paina, 2006; Moosa, & Tuana, 2014; Otzelberger, 2011; Nellemann et al., 2011; UNDP, 2013). Popular (often masculinist) discourses typically exclude women's views and indeed their grassroots leadership problems also reflected in the significant research gaps that can be identified across regions (MacGregor, 2010). As Rebecca Pearse argued, scholars' limited understanding of gendered aspects of environment and social reproduction challenge us to consider women's agency more forthrightly, especially in the context of climate justice (Pearse, 2016). The same goes for activists, especially men, who need to establish eco-feminist values more firmly within environmental organizations. This chapter, focusing on India, South Africa, and Ecuador, explores how eco-feminism enriches climate justice activism both in theory and practice.

2 Eco-Feminist Scholarship and Activism

The roots of eco-feminism go back to the 1974 book by Françoise d'Eaubonne *Le feminisme ou la mort* (d'Eaubonne, 1974). The dominance of masculine powers over women's reproductive functions (and birth control) was reflected within patriarchy's command over urbanized technocratic society. Women's resistance entailed saving themselves from patriarchal domination, including protecting the Earth from the clutches of masculine-centered society. In a 1978 book, *Ecologie feminisme: Revolution ou mutation?* D'Eaubonne developed the overlap between feminism and ecology, although she avoided Marxist framings when advancing her analysis (Gates, 1996). Instead, her analysis hinged on blaming patriarchy for resource extraction and unsustainable population growth that generated ecological crises. D'Eaubonne argued that the prior era of socialist revolutions failed to acknowledge the battle between the sexes and their environmental relevance. But features of contemporary capitalism, she recognized, harmed both women and the planet through "dominance, aggressiveness, competitiveness, and absolutism" (d'Eaubonne, 1978, 1999).

These would only disappear through the formation of an ecological, feminist strategy to reconcile production and consumption systems in ways that ensure equality between the sexes and offer equal spaces to the proliferation of all species with the environment. In foregrounding subsequent literature on social reproduction, d'Eaubonne argued that the liberation of procreation from patriarchal domination is one of the critical components of eco-feminism. This would allow women to take control of population growth and, likewise, address fundamental flaws in consumption-production relations, which lead to ecological crises. Women, as procreators, have more intrinsic concern—and different solutions—in reclaiming ecological sustainability and ensuring the future of humanity (d'Eaubonne, 1978, 1999).

This spirit could, from the 1970s, be found in peace movements, environmental protests, anti-nuclear struggles, labor movements, conservation, natural resource politics, animal liberation movements, and youth politics. Eco-feminists drew insights from ecology, feminism, and socialism, acknowledging that structures of race, class, and physical disabilities have oppressed women throughout history, and also contributed to the debates in political ecology and environmental philosophy (Plumwood, 1993). Critically, the parallel modes of oppression within society are at the root of man's oppression of nature (Gaard, 1993; Warren & Cheney, 1991; Warren, 1991a, 1991b).

Nevertheless, Catriona Sandilands (Sandilands, 1999. p. xi) raised concerns over "motherhood environmentalism," as an Ontario Advisory Council expressed it: "Because we have traditionally been mother, nurse, and guardian for the home and community, women have been quick to perceive the threat to the health and lives of our families and neighbors that are posed by nuclear power proliferation, polluted waters, and toxic chemicals." From there, debate arose over whether, as Pat Brewer put it, "in one prominent eco-feminist strand, there is universalism and potential biological determinism," and hence "exhortations to intrinsic feminine morality or sensibility based on reproductive experience are more likely to bolster the strategies of the traditionalist and religious right." (Brewer, 2001).

Quoting Audre Lorde, Salleh (2005, p. 11) advocates for an even broader critique of capitalist patriarchy: *"the master's tools will never dismantle the master's house."* For socialists, the capitalist class, along with government cronies and lifestyle hangers-on, are the masters, and their house is the global public sphere. For radical eco-feminists, this is certainly acknowledged, but another master—patriarchy—is named within private power relations that govern everyday life for women at home, at work, and in scholarship. Therefore, the double construct of capitalist-patriarchal societies is used, whereby capitalism denotes only the latest historical form of economic and social domination by men over women. This double term integrates the two dimensions of power by recognizing patriarchal energetics as a priori to capitalism. As reflexive eco-socialists know: the psychology of masculinity is actively rewarded by the capitalist system, thereby keeping that economy intact.

In addition to historically contextualizing the critique of capitalism, eco-feminists also address additional burdens of racism on the well-being of women. Indeed, because the eco-feminist framework addresses how the oppression of women and nature intersects with sexism, racism, classism, speciesism, and naturism, it is critical to building coalition strategies to liberate women and protect the earth, rather than address women's problems and the environment as a 'single issue' (Abzug, 1991; Gaard, 1993; Shiva, 1988, 1989). In capturing these multiple intersections of struggle, Birkeland (1993) argued for reconstructing value systems—and in the process, emulating bio-centric perspectives—to achieve environmental holism. She rejects the idea of making merely superficial changes in power relationships among individuals and likewise of misconceiving women as a homogenous without considering the differences among women in terms of race, ethnicity, class, and nation when addressing environmental crises.

Eco-feminists have articulated how industrial capitalism caused the excessive exploitation of natural resources, undermining women's rights and, indeed, creating widespread social inequality (Federici and Linebaugh, 2018; Perkins, 2019; Shiva, 1988, 1989) and intensified environmental injustices at multiple levels (Shiva, 2008). One illustrative example of resistance grounded in the spirit and vision of eco-feminism from the Global South was Berta Cáceres, a Honduran indigenous leader popularly known for her fight against destructive megaprojects, including a destructive dam on the Gualcarce River (Del Rio Gabiola, 2020). Cáceres coordinated the Consejo Cívico de Organizaciones Populares e Indígenas de Honduras (Civic Council of Grassroots and Indigenous Organizations in Honduras). The movement advances the social, political, economic, environmental, and cultural rights of Honduras' indigenous people. When Cáceres was awarded the Goldman Environmental Prize for grassroots activism, she grassroots activism, she urged:

> Let us wake up, humankind! We're out of time. We must shake our conscience free of the rapacious capitalism, racism and patriarchy that will only assure our own self-destruction. The Gualcarque River has called upon us, as have other gravely threatened rivers. We must answer their call. Our Mother Earth – militarized, fenced-in, poisoned, a place where basic rights are systematically violated – demands that we take action (Cáceres, 2015).

In 2016, Cáceres was assassinated by the dam-builders, who in 2021 finally stood trial, with one conviction. Her movement continues, in part through the eloquence her daughter Bertha Zúñiga Cáceres learned in the same struggle. In this particular case, resistances are as vibrant as the evils of rapacious capitalism are visible, and indeed in many such cases, they are instant and intense.

However, another feature of eco-feminism is its longer term perspective on living systems. This is vital in addressing the climate crisis because it is a complicated, slow-onset form of disaster. As Germanwatch (2021) explains, such disasters take place gradually over a prolonged period, in which there is no clear-cut beginning or end, such as sea-level rise, ocean acidification, and land and forest degradation. Species extinction is another slow-onset process, although the demise of thousands of life forms can appear suddenly as a catastrophe, for example, when pollination grinds to a halt. Sea-level rise, which is one slow-onset disaster symptom of climate change, can have both momentary catastrophic manifestations—such as more damaging storm surges or ocean intrusion into coastline buildings (such as in Miami, Florida—and longer term implications, such as loss of territory and cultural identity, e.g., with island nations' submergence (IPCC, 2018, 2019; Germanwatch, 2021). Slow-onset climate-crisis processes typically exacerbate the existing gendered, social, economic, political, racial, and cultural inequalities, and not coincidentally, push women to live in a more vulnerable condition.

Climate justice movements should lead by and with greater participation of women (UN Women, 2021). Global Greengrants Fund (2015) compiled case studies of how women community leaders and their organizations in Papua New Guinea, Indonesia, Vietnam, South Africa reacted to multiple environmental and climate injustices, including climate change-induced migration and territory loss, deforestation by extractive industries, hydroelectric power threats, and urban industrial emissions.

For instance, Ursula Rakova from Carteret Islands, Papua New Guinea, allied with elders and chiefs from the mainland of Bougainville to innovate adaptation solutions when faced with rising sea levels.

During the 1990 and 2000s, environment and climate justice movements emerged in the Global South, particularly among indigenous communities of Latin American countries against rampant resource extractivism, in the interests of upholding national sovereignty and indigenous community integrity. For example, Nicole Fabricant described how Bolivia's indigenous climate justice activists mobilized, pushed forward an Andean indigenous vision for resource reclamation, and proposed alternative strategies to the capitalist mode of development (Fabricant, 2013).

If nevertheless, adequate vision and strategies to confront both rapid and slow-onset processes of climate change have been lacking, it may be because eco-feminist theory and analysis have not been sufficiently generalized, particularly because the success of women sometimes threatens men. MenEngage Alliance emphasizes the need to pursue feminist perspectives on climate justice:

> Through the lens of the long-standing eco-feminist analysis of climate change as rooted in histories of colonial resource extraction and capitalist industrial production, which themselves are shaped and legitimated by patriarchal logic of domination and exploitation, we understand the critical need to politicize the work to transform patriarchal masculinities towards climate justice (MenEngage Alliance, 2021).

In recent years, several international organizations have initiated global and regional level projects to integrate gender justice into international climate politics, including within climate activist movements. Strengths and weaknesses of putting gender at the forefront of climate activism can be seen in case studies from India, South Africa, and Ecuador. These sites help us comprehend the very different levels of engagement eco-feminists have initiated in tackling the multiple forms of ecological destruction under patriarchal capitalism, with all its variations in terms of race, ethnicity, and North–South power relations.

3 Eco-Feminism in India

As Porselvi (2016) argued, the metaphor of "Mother Earth" is at the core of eco-feminism theory. India possesses a long history of women's participation in ecological movements from the colonial to the contemporary periods. The Chipko movement, Narmada Bachao Andolan (which helped launch Medha Patkar's leadership of the National Alliance of People's Movements), and Silent Valley movements are classic cases of women-led grassroots environmentalism in contemporary India, asserting values and visions of Mother Earth. The celebrated author Arundhati Roy has also written about India's environmental justice movements in various terrains, especially where their struggles overlap with peasant rebellions, battles over megadams, toxic pollution, extractive industries, and nuclear politics. Another Indian environmentalist is Sunita Narrain, the head of the Centre for Science and Environment based in New Delhi, has fought many battles, including against pesticides,

Eco-Feminisms in Theory and Practice in the Global South ...

unsafe consumer products, and water pollution. These cases have generated not only lessons but debates over eco-feminist principles, analyses, strategies, tactics, and alliances that engaged radical and cultural feminists of the Global North.

In India, the majority religion, Hinduism, historically claimed a vision that recognized the whole universe as a single-family. The worship of "Mother Nature" is deeply ingrained in Hinduism, so it is integral to the large masses of Hindu believers and is part of the general everyday discourse of Indians, including non-Hindus.

Shiva continues to act as one of the important eco-feminist thinkers in India. Since 1980s, she has been advocating eco-feminist practices and scholarship. She has argued that women are "naturally" closer to nature not just because of their biological status but also due to historical and cultural forces. By pointing out the historical character of women's role in reproducing life under conditions of patriarchy, she interconnects the subjugation of women with capitalism. The colonial arrival of Western values did not transcend patriarchy, and indeed she criticizes modern science, development projects, and environmentalism within the Western paradigm for their historical and ideological gender bias. Shiva even suggests that Western concepts of women's liberation risk falling into the trap of "masculinization of the female" (Shiva, 1989).

In short, a merely tokenistic commitment would neither liberate women nor protect the environment. As early as 1988, Shiva insisted on advancing the critique of the eco-modernist scientific and developmental paradigms of the West far beyond prevailing "dependency theory" or "World Systems" analysis of global capitalism:

> Within the western paradigm, the environmental movement is separate from the women's movement. As long as this paradigm with its assumptions of linear progress prevails, 'environmentalism' and 'feminism' independently ask only for concessions *within* maldevelopment because, in the absence of oppositional categories, that is the only 'development' that is conceivable. Environmentalism then becomes a new patriarchal project of technological fixes and political oppression. It generates a new subjugation of ecological movements and fails to make any progress towards sustainability and equity. While including a few women as tokens in 'women and environment,' it excludes the feminine visions of survival that women have conserved. (Shiva, 1989, p. 48).

With an even further-reaching critical approach, Bina Agarwal tackles weaknesses in those more limited versions of eco-feminism, which focus directly on women and the environment without the bigger picture and thus fail to provide an adequate challenge to deep-seated structural inequalities. Indeed, a limited version of eco-feminism "unwittingly provides scope for strengthening them" (Agarwal, 1998). Agarwal (1992) lists three fundamental analytical flaws in even Shiva's eco-feminist theory and activism.

- First, eco-feminism analysis sometimes oversimplifies complicated lifestyles, and the social and cultural histories of third-world women by creating a single reality, overlooking in the process differences of class, caste, ethnicity, and race, living locations, geography, generation, and other factors.
- Second, with Shiva's overemphasis on Hinduism as an ideological and religious prism through which to analyze gender and natural systems in India, the Indian

subcontinent's multicultural and multiethnic backgrounds are evaporated (for even Hinduism has had different schools of thought and social practices based on various factors, including caste and regions).

- Third, Shiva's focus on the impacts of British colonialism is necessary yet underplays the specific socio-economic base and pre-colonial history of the Indian subcontinent, including the Mughal realms and their impact on natural resources.

Another component of Indian eco-feminism is the translation of experience into the production of knowledge. For example, women and children are frontline victims of environmental disasters and hazards, both during and long after. The 2004 Indian Ocean Tsunami is a classic example of the vulnerability that characterizes women's lives, livelihoods, and well-being, both in the short and long term, unequally. The Tsunami disproportionately affected women, with death tolls about three to four times higher than for men in Indonesia, Sri Lanka, Thailand, and India. Although states, international organizations, and donors supported the Tsunami-hit regions, the post-Tsunami difficulties Indian women faced transcended the material damage and included a rise in domestic violence, breakdown of marriages, increasing work-burdens in-home care and community mutual aid, systematic exclusion from political participation, and the denial of post-Tsunami relief measures and old-age pensions (Hines, 2007; MacDonald, 2005; Pincha, 2008). Tamil Nadu, the southernmost state of India, was hit hard by the Tsunami, and already-existing patriarchal social and gender norms of the state and society were amplified during and after the disaster. Gender-insensitive disaster management (knowledge production) meant there was inadequate attention to the needs, livelihood problems, and productive capabilities of women, increasing their vulnerability in multiple dimensions (Juran, 2012; Pincha, 2008).

The greatest threat in recent decades has been climate change. The associated risks are greater for already vulnerable sections of society along the lines of caste, class, power, race, living locations, generation, and especially gender. India is one of the nations most affected by climate change. A Germanwatch report counts India as the seventh most-affected nation in 2019. India faced eight tropical cyclones of unusual strength in 2019 alone. Around 11.8 million people were affected by 2019s severe monsoons and flood events, which displaced 1.8 million people (Eckstein et al., 2021). Most at stake are the well-being of millions of women (Akhtar, 2007; Sorensen et al., 2018; Yadav & Lal, 2018). Linkages between gender and the climate crisis in eco-feminist writings have not yet affected public policy, which remains primarily driven by technology and science.

Gonda (2019) argued that prevailing narratives that victimize women—especially rural, peasant, Dalit, and Tribal women—are not useful in dealing with climate change, in part because they stand in contrast to women leaders of grassroots ecological movements which in the earlier period were considered saviors of nature, acting as an inspiration for global environmental activists. Why is there a drastic change in portraying the victimization of tribal and peasant women in the contemporary period without considering their potential to adapt, offer each other mutual aid, and lead the world in resilience? One potential explanation is that notwithstanding the profile of the likes of Shiva, Patkar, Roy, and Narrain, more Eurocentric feminists and politicians have greater influence in Indian academia and policy circles than do the country's organic intellectuals and organizers. One way to overcome this bias is to consider a broad set of proposals that fight against climate injustice, and in the process, celebrate and protect Mother Earth's rights by learning lessons from women caught up in the extreme weather events that portend climate crisis.

4 Eco-Feminist Groundings in South Africa

The vibrant field of eco-feminism in South Africa contributes to the analysis of climate policy with several critical factors, including intra-continental networking, the "Ubuntu" philosophy of mutual aid, contestation of extractive industries, and the complexity of relations between social reproduction and forces of production (especially in agriculture).

Given South African capitalism's ecologically destructive reach up-continent (Bond, 2013). African-wide eco-feminist agency is vital in these respects, in sites rife with socio-economic and political–ecological exploitation of the most intense character found anywhere on earth in a non-war setting. South Africa is particularly vulnerable to fusions of corporate and state power with entrenched residual patriarchy, as witnessed repeatedly in anti-extractive industry battles with communities.

One group where coordinated struggle and the fusion of eco-feminist visions is increasingly explicit is the Johannesburg-based network, African Women Unite Against Destructive Resource Extraction (WoMin, 2019). Parallel to long-standing efforts of radical feminist ecologists Acción Ecológica (working from Ecuador across Latin America), the network links most of the continent's leading struggles against extractivism waged by community-based women's groups.

At the grassroots level, these struggles inexorably address contradictions in society/nature, in male/female, and—evoking Rosa Luxemburg's (1913) spirit of considering Africa's subordinate role within imperialism (Bond, 2019, 2021)— in capital/non-capitalist power relations. Assessing the ideological glue in diverse settings, WoMin founder Samantha Hargreaves (Hargreaves, 2020) suggests the importance of interlocking approaches to resistance: the commons, Ubuntu, and progressive Pan-Africanism. The first recognizes the (non-capitalist) integrity of "large swathes of the continent held under common or communal property systems" at their finest—where matriarchy and inter-generational stewardship successfully contest patriarchy—typically entail de-commodifying principles." The balance of forces will determine, for example, whether women-led commoning defeats entrenched residual patriarchy, as Hargreaves (2020) argued:

- Those who dwell on the land are the keepers/carers/custodians for generations to come.
- Land cannot be owned as private property and may not be disposed of on the open market. Having said that, rights to communal land are strong, can be bequeathed within the family (variously to the oldest or youngest male child as a commonplace practice), and can only be alienated by collective decision upon serious violation of communal rules.
- Decisions about the use of land must be made collectively by the group/tribe/community.
- Representatives/leaders of the group are required to facilitate collective decisions of the group and represent these to outsiders.
- Land rights and the strength of tenure security generally determines membership of the group and rights to participate in and influence decision-making at a collective level.
- There are strict rules for the entry of outsiders to the group to preserve the integrity and common rules of the collective. (Hargreaves, 2020)

Second, the tradition of what might be termed pre-capitalist land management within hybrid forms of both ownership relations and social reproduction—with migrant labor increasingly common—occurs in the context of a much less alienated form of human relations under the mutual aid rubric of Ubuntu: "I am because we are." For WoMin, the feminist Ubuntu "values care, love, empathy, respect, and common interest over individualism, which few in progressive social movements would argue does not represent, in part, the type of society, community, Africa and the world we strive for" (Hargreaves, 2020).

Third, WoMin's Pan-Africanism is undergoing redefinition and revitalization because of the truncated character of the continent-wide elite-political coordination that officially began in 1963 through the Organization of African Unity (OAU). But the OAU was not, ultimately, the United States of Africa desired by a founder, Ghanaian leader Kwame Nkrumah. Instead, due to ethnicist, nationalist, and imperialist influences, the OAU quickly suffered debilitating neo-colonial penetration and internal divisions. Efforts by the likes of Nkrumah, Julius Nyerere, Sékou Touré, Modibo Keita, and Kenneth Kaunda in subsequent years "failed to bring down imposed national boundaries, deconstruct nationalities, and create a unified African sovereignty," according to WoMin (Hargreaves, 2020). More recently, since 2002, when the OAU was renamed, two other continental institutions rose, yet, as WoMin continues,

> The Pan-African Parliament and African Union have replicated the same disappointments and failed to offer up a transformative vision of the continent. Instead, states continue to compete for elusive foreign investment, trade deals, and loans, in this way facilitating the continued plunder of Africa's resources on highly unjust terms and perpetuating Africa's highly marginalized geopolitical positioning (Hargreaves, 2020).

The African Continental Free Trade Area that began in 2021 will probably exacerbate the sub-imperial power of both productive and mercantilist capital and neo-colonial infrastructural and transport arrangements that it is meant to resist. However,

Eco-Feminisms in Theory and Practice in the Global South … 285

such top-down approaches might, one day be replaced with a bottom-up strategy, according to WoMin:

> While the formal institutionalization of Pan-Africanism has not yielded what the continent and its peoples need for genuine socio-economic, political, and cultural liberation (the guiding elements of Pan-Africanism), Pan-African civil society activism and solidarity across the boundaries of the nation-state is vibrant. This organizing has taken different forms and assumed different politics and includes networking and activism targeting the sub-regional blocs, solidarity campaigns, alliance building within linguistic blocs, and genuine attempts at building Pan-African organizations. This informs a new imagination about Africa's people's needs, drawing from an abundant living praxis and informed by a rich history of African philosophy, spirituality, and movement. A revitalized Pan-Africanism must be built from below by African citizens, wedded in demand and solidarity across nations, and rooted in their daily practices and relations with each other and Mother Nature. The solidarity of African women across the continent to stop mega projects condemn repression and violence, and demand climate justice must be our lodestar, building on and drawing from a long tradition of progressive Pan-Africanism (Hargreaves, 2020).

There are many instances where South African eco-feminist theorists and practitioners have generated path-breaking work, including broad-based environmental justice and climate politics. WoMin remains perhaps the most explicitly committed eco-feminist civil society organization. The most prolific analyst has been Johannesburg-based sociologist Jacklyn, whose range of research includes local-level problems that most adversely affect women—toxicities in the air and land, water degradation and river conservation, coal mining and coal-fired power plant pollution and solid waste—as well as broader concerns associated with climate crisis and eco-socialism. Khayaat Fakier and Cock (2018) argue that in "trying to develop grassroots eco-feminist solidarity among black women in contemporary South Africa," it is useful to draw on "the Marxist feminist notion of social reproduction, i.e., the unpaid care work which these women do outside the market, both in their households and in their communities" (p. 1). In community food sovereignty struggles, for example, Darlene Miller (2020, 110) harked back to the most famous instance of women's leadership: the "cattle-killing" episode in which the prophesies of the young woman, Nongqawuse, were held responsible for the starvation of Xhosa people. The tale is also linked to the loss of women's power and their confinement to private spaces, while men were left to dominate public spaces. Colonialism therefore had to destroy women's power to make men dependent on colonial markets for survival (e.g., working in the mines and for white farmers).

Likewise, eco-feminist insights into waste recycling by Melanie Samson (2009) include innovative analysis, drawing in part upon the Marian concept of valorization and devalorization—to which she adds revalorization—as well in assessing how, under conditions of privatized municipal waste removal, "because of the gender division of labor at work and at home, and because women waste management workers employed by private companies are largely left out of collective bargaining agreements, it is women workers who suffer most" (Samson & Hurt, 2003). Samson along with Francie Lund and Caroline Skinner made strong advances in this micro-labor analysis—including occupational health and safety, which in turn draws upon environmental justice struggles—in part through the international network Women in Informal Employment: Globalizing and Organizing (WIEGO). Rural women's land rights feature strongly in this literature, led by Aninka Claassens (2013). Two recent doctoral theses by black feminists—Ayanda Benya's (2016) study of "socially embedded processes of labor incorporation, allocation, control and reproduction" of women in mining, and Donna Andrews' (2018) study, "Capitalism and Nature in South Africa: Racial Dispossession, Liberation Ideology and Ecological Crisis"—link class, race, gender, and ecology. A scholar-activist journal, *Agenda*, often features environmental justice campaigning.

In the practical world of eco-feminist activism, the most effective organizers include national leaders such as Mercia Andrews (Rural Women's Assembly) and Makoma Lekalakala (Earthlife Africa), Liziwe McDaid (Green Connection), as well as a world-renowned anti-extractivism activist: Nonhle Mbuthuma (Amadiba Crisis Committee). At the renowned South Durban Community Environmental Alliance, since 1995 women have been core organizers opposing the air pollution especially damaging to women's and children's lungs. Two other celebrated women leaders who lost their lives in 2020 were anti-coal campaigner Fikile Ntshangase (assassinated by men threatened by her successes), and Sizani Ngubane (National Movement of Rural Women). One heroine associated with a global struggle against carbon trading ("the privatization of the air," she called it) was Durban resident Sajida Khan, who fought a neighboring (cancer-causing) landfill's expansion from 1994 until her death (due to cancer) in 2007. One other activist making the climate links to LGBTQIA + movements—particularly where violence was amplified by climate crisis—is Orthalia Kunene (2021). Another grassroots network that connects the dots between local, national, and indeed global sources of environmental oppression is Women Affected by Mining United in Action, which generally advances not the standard NGO mining-reform agenda but a "Right to Say No!" perspective. Reflecting the principles and concrete campaigning associated with feminist anti-extractivism, several other women won the Goldman Environmental Prize for their successful activism, including Lekalakala and McDaid in an anti-nuclear battle. Feminist lawyers in civil society (e.g., at the Centre for Environmental Rights (see Centre for Environmental Rights, n.d), Legal Resources Centre, Wits Centre for Applied Legal Studies, Women's Legal Centre and ProBono.org) are often decisive. (One late-2021 example was the way Wilmien Wicomb and Mbuthuma joined other lawyers and communities on the Wild Coast to at least temporarily repel Shell and Impact Africa's seismic drilling for gas in a High Court interdict, in part because of the threat to the Xhosa people's traditions and spiritual practices (Crouth & Sgqolana, 2021)). Typically, the state Gender Commission, prosecutors, officials, and politicians (especially several national environment ministers) fail in their duties since the Minerals-Energy Complex is often not only economically but also patriarchally powerful.

Finally, the most critical aspect of eco-socialist organizing applied to climate catastrophe is integrating the next and future generations' interests. For example, South Africa's best-known young feminist climate activist, Ayakha Melithafa (2020), speaks colloquially, but she nevertheless clearly sets, as her aim, to target the system of capitalism. But we know that capitalism disguises itself. We know that it has been running over and over and that the rich get richer and the poor get poorer. And that's quite grueling. And I feel like we know that the working class has the power to change that. Because if a worker says no, the employer has to do something because they don't want to lose their workers. But the problem is that our unemployment rate is so high, and we know that our workers are disposable. So that's taking quite time for us to move to a greener, sustainable future – it's because we can't take down the system of capitalism. We realize that the power is in our hands and that we have the power as civil society, as just people on the ground, the working class. If we can actually stand together and sacrifice what we can, we will be able to change our society and live for a better future. We see youth are standing up all over the world, in Nigeria against SARS [the most repressive arm of the police], and in Liberia and so many African countries. We are saying "No!" as the youth. And it's so important for us to move forward in the correct and direct way (Melithafa, 2020).

5 Ecuadorian Eco-Feminism Sets Global Trends

In the Andes mountains of South America, eco-feminisms have taken different views and approaches and attracted critiques from other feminisms. In the case of Ecuador, there have been three political practices that have been in dialogue: feminist theologies, decolonial feminisms, and community feminisms. We briefly consider each of these trends as a starting point to assess the political work carried out by feminist organizations, including humanizing men who are committed environmentalists but who need to become more aware of their own male privileges and combat these, especially in vital sites of struggle.

First, feminist theologians such as Ivonne Gebara have played a decisive role in generating reflections within the Catholic Church on what patriarchal and colonial extractivism has caused in the region. Latin American liberation theology sometimes assumes a link between extractivist capitalism and the destruction of nature (which we can see explicitly in Pope Francis' Encyclical Laudato Sí). In the case of feminist liberation theologians, they reinforce this link by emphasizing women's bodies and patriarchal violence (Gebara, 2000). In the case of Ecuador, the social movement Acción Ecológica represents this tradition, especially in alliance with indigenous and peasant communities against mining. It has long had a membership in the Latin American Network of Women Defenders of Social and Environmental Rights and works with the Pan-Amazonian Ecclesial Network (REPAM).

Second, decolonial feminists emphasize the conditions in which patriarchy was functional to colonization, and still today, patriarchy entails the racialization of bodies. At the Latin American level, this perspective has been positioned by feminists such as Rita Segato and María Lugones, who have shown how the extractivist advance of colonization and land usurpation made women's bodies an explicit objective of the war against indigenous people and the peasantry (Segato, 2016). In Ecuador, this perspective has been an axis of work for feminist organizations such as Mujeres de Frente or the Assembly of Popular and Diverse Women. Over several decades, there have been exchanges and cross-reflections between the more autonomous feminist movement and indigenous and popular organizations, creating this current of eco-feminism.

Third, community feminisms, which indigenous women are formulating, have participated in this configuration of Eco-feminism in Ecuador. At the regional level, the contributions of Julieta Paredes (Paredes, 2008) and Lorena Cabnal have been fundamental, denouncing how patriarchy and colonization have formed a whole in the configuration of exploitable and sexed indigenous bodies. This current formulates how the domination of bodies, territory, and landform is a part of a whole. This allows a more unified front in the struggle against extractivism (Cabnal, 2010). In Ecuador, this perspective had a high profile in the Amazonian women's march in 2013 and reflected the growing strength of female leadership within the indigenous movement (CMCTF, 2014).

This review shows different positions in simultaneous dialogue and tension. In dialogue through many forums, meetings, and publications over the last decade, it has made it possible to generate a joint, feminist-rooted common sense, namely that extractivism has an inescapable patriarchal character. But tensions are also present, generating a dialogue in which these currents' intersectionality allows eco-feminists to better position themselves against machismo and patriarchy.

One way this manifest is in the external and internal patriarchal violence experienced by eco-feminists in the ecological spaces they are constructing. For example, the plural and multiple eco-feminisms have a strong position against the patriarchy implied by extractivist structures. In the face of oil or mining megaprojects, there have been essential alliances in which eco-feminisms have been a source of political training, political support among indigenous women, feminists, environmentalists, and sorority cases of criminalization or difficulties eco-feminists face when they exercise leadership. Mining and oil companies have (re)patriarchalized the territory wherever they have settled. They have tried to stigmatize anti-extractivist women. The state has deployed different forms of patriarchal violence against them (CMCTF, 2018). The governments were functional first to colonialism and capitalism with extractivism, thus the struggle of indigenous community feminisms is against both: the global neoliberalism including the destruction of their territory.

Eco-feminisms have succeeded in shaping a new form of resistance to extractive megaprojects based on a union of diverse women that has greatly removed and hindered the implementation of such projects. At the scale of the state, it has also made it possible to confront patriarchal strategies that impose megaprojects from a paternalistic perspective. In many cases, the president decides without regard to the views of indigenous nationalities, and especially to the experience of women's care for the territory (Coba & Bayón, 2020).

At the same time, eco-feminisms have also managed to generate changes in the "common sense" of society, and also within environmental and indigenous organizations regarding the role of women. The macho violence that occurs within environmental collectives and indigenous organizations has been made visible and denaturalized. Patriarchal structures or macho aggressions have been denounced. In the indigenous movement, women are demanding parity in the composition of their leaderships.

To illustrate, the Confederation of Indigenous Nationalities of Ecuador (CONAIE) became part of the March 8, 2012 mobilizations against a Chinese mining project endorsed by then-President Rafael Correa. As another example, the indigenous movement opposed the criminalization of abortion as a crucial reflection of its respect for the sanctity of women's bodies (despite strong Catholic Church support). At a more local level, important women leaders have emerged in the territories where extractive companies operate. In the environmental movement, organizations have come to call themselves feminist in a more explicit way. Women's environmentalist organizations such as YASunidos[1] offer leadership within the young, urban Ecuadorian environmentalist collective fighting against oil exploitation in the Yasuní National Park (Moreno et al., 2019).

In these struggles, patriarchal violence that is condensed in sexual aggressions is now a denounced practice. At the community level, women who form part of political leaderships or articulations with other women have begun to make visible the violence they suffer, fostering collective work against macho violence. The new generations of women environmentalists have put the brakes on violence suffered by women in mixed urban collectives, where male violence was traditionally covered up. Some sites where this featured in the struggles included sexual aggression in oil pollution verification inspections, male anger when enforcing collective decision-making, the patriarchal notion of leisure space through macho humor, or men's irresponsibility in caring for children and families.

The personal is political, so these organizational and practical roles—in which women achieve justice—are vital to the broader agenda of social change and ecological protection. At the same time, these intra-organizational feminist transformations force us to ask, what kind of men are part of the environmental movements, given that they too have been shaped by capitalist, patriarchal, and colonial systems? Men face challenges in allying with eco-feminisms to advance the anti-extractivist struggles and make their own organizational spaces more feminist. First of all, men need to verbalize their part of an oppressive history, and this includes recognizing, denaturalizing, and abandoning the violence that men have been the protagonists of. Within these organizations, men allied with eco-feminists attempt to make visible how males monopolize resources. Part of this requires recognizing the privileges that allow men to assume the productive and recognized part of the struggle—but not the reproductive and invisible part. This requires reexamining the archetype role of the good militant, who is sacrificing everything for the sake of advancing social and environmental progress—all the while neglecting the relational and nurturing spheres. Finally, men's obligation is to openly condemn the objectification of female activists that leads to so many cases of sexual harassment and aggression.

Eco-feminisms' different currents place before us the mirror of patriarchal violence, colonial violence, and capitalist violence that male ecologists—with differences of class, race, sexuality, ability, etc. —deploy in collective spaces. It is evident

---

[1] YASunidos is one of the most organized youth groups in Ecuador. They actively defend Yasuni River and its despite stifling opposition. For more details about YASunidos: YASunidos (2014). https://sitio.yasunidos.org/.

that men are a serious obstacle to making environmental justice organizations and struggles stronger. Eco-feminism generates a root criticism of the power structures that have led our world to environmental degradation and violence unparalleled in the history of humanity, from the scale of the local organization's functioning to halting destructive capitalist projects, to changing national environmental policies to addressing the global climate crisis.

The struggles discussed above are not easy because, faced with the changes proposed by Ecuador's strong tradition of eco-feminists, there are very reactionary, defensive positions taken by some male activists, who consider the arrival of feminism within environmentalism as a barrier to exercising their own personal power. However, the upheaval that eco-feminism has generated in Ecuador opens the door to rethinking the ways of being men—and being men allied with women, within environmentalism within a threatened world where raising the power of women is increasingly vital to planetary and community survival.

6 Conclusion

In this chapter we have seen how the eco-feminisms of three countries in the Global South, with very different processes and background politics, offer examples for analysis, debate, encounters, and radical social change. Especially with respect to climate politics, and whether in the Global North or South, eco-feminisms remain under construction. The cases of India, South Africa, and Ecuador reveal different tensions and priorities, with some eco-feminists drawing on either the opportunities for assimilation or for asserting an essentialist analysis, but with others advocating eco-socialist, decolonial, indigenous community or theological versions in which alliances with other climate justice forces are more common. The complexities are as profound as the intersections of gendered human life and the rest of the natural world.

Consider, in conclusion, a few instances of how these different traditions generate constructive conflict over principles, analyses, strategies, tactics, and alliances. Partly thanks to Vandana Shiva's influence, the Global North's eco-feminists have sometimes portrayed third-world indigenous women, particularly the grassroots peasant women who participated in the Chipko movement in the Garhwal Hills of India, as "*Ultimate Eco-feminists,*" to quote Noël Sturgeon (1999). The peasant and the tribal women of India have emerged as the key spokespersons for environmental protection and conservation, and Shiva's network is one among the leading networks in safeguarding traditional seeds, opposing genetic modification, protecting water from privatization and opposing the ecological modernization "Green Revolution" strategies adopted by the Bill and Melinda Gates Foundation and similar institutions. But unlike Shiva who fuses theory and practice in an epistemology that often draws sustenance from conflict, Sturgeon (1999) differentiates between academic discourses of eco-feminism and activist arenas. Acknowledging critiques of essentialist constructions, Sturgeon nevertheless insists that such narratives create new opportunities for less powerful groups, resulting in strategic coalitions of thinkers and activists (Sturgeon, 1997, 1999):

> The eco-feminist intervention into international political arenas, in uneven and unsatisfactory ways, perhaps, can create a network, a space for debate, a mechanism not just for the intervention of feminism, environmentalism, and anti-colonial scholarship into policy-making, but also for strategic coalitions to take place among disempowered people and between privileged and underprivileged people in one political collectivity (Sturgeon, 1999, p. 274).

The path has not been easy, with some feminists downplaying essentialist associations between women and nature as they reject insinuations of "womanliness." With the most advanced forms of eco-feminism now possessing greater transcultural sensibility and a desire to cultivate a global ecological movement far more expansive than the single-identity politics of liberal feminists, a search arose for alliances to facilitate internationalism. As a result, because the vision and the practice of worshipping "Mother Earth" lies at the core of many indigenous belief systems and the worldviews of many cultures, there was a natural alliance of eco-feminism and first nations.

Bolivian climate leader Pablo Sólon (2018) explains that from the Andean indigenous standpoint, "Mother Nature" encompasses everything in the universe, and in April 2010, at what was the largest climate justice gathering to date (in the wake of the failed Copenhagen United Nations climate summit), a major commitment was made in the city of Cochabamba—at a conference of 35,000 attendees—to the "Universal Rights of Mother Earth" (GARN, n.d; The Guardian, 2010).

For Salleh (1997), "seeking to build a global eco-feminist politics based on multicultural alliances among women" remains crucial. And climate crisis is one of the universalizing processes that makes this increasingly possible and necessary, especially because eco-feminist theory and practice are endowed with an inherent plurality in contrast to the other masculinist theories.

With this chapter, by three men who have observed, learned, and received great inspiration from companions in the struggle for eco-feminism, at least a rudimentary statement is possible about how eco-feminist visions could affect our ways of being and organizing. More sustainable social reproduction within families and communities—and especially in ecological organisations—require men to more actively consider how to contribute to ending patriarchy, at the same time as ending the Anthropocene's degradation of the cycles of life, driven by both men in the search for power, and by the arrangement of society to interact primarily to satisfy the profit motive in the capitalist mode of production.

We hope that this contribution will generate debates among those men for whom the eco-feminism influence has not yet been welcomed or has been considered secondarily as only a women's issue. We therefore emphasize the importance of links between ecologically destructive capitalism and patriarchy in maintaining a system intrinsically violent toward life to the point planetary sustainability is profoundly threatened. Without this openness, the possibilities are truncated for women's full liberation, and in the process for masculinist ecologists to likewise be liberated from a relative form of privilege that is in fact toxic. For this reason, it is essential to think how to best generate dialogues with diverse peoples who experience different forms of extractivist violence and climate crisis, always bearing in mind the many lessons we gain from the eco-feminist standpoint.

References

Abzug, B. (1991). Women and the fate of the earth. *Woman of Power, 20,* 26–30.
Agarwal, B. (1992). The gender and environment debate: Lessons from India. *Feminist Studies, 18*(1), 119. https://doi.org/10.2307/3178217
Agarwal, B. (1998). Environmental management, equity and eco-feminism: Debating India's experience. *Journal of Peasant Studies, 25*(4), 55–95. https://doi.org/10.1080/030661598084 38684
Akhtar, R. (2007). Climate change and health and heat wave mortality in India. *Global Environmental Research, 11*(1), 51–57.
Ako, R. (2013). *Environmental justice in developing countries.* Routledge.
Andrews, D. (2018). *Capitalism and nature in South Africa* (Ph.D. thesis). Department of Politics, University of Cape Town. https://open.uct.ac.za/bitstream/handle/11427/27891/thesis_hum_2018_an-drews_donna.pdf?sequence=1
Atapattu, S. (2016). *Human rights approaches to climate change challenges and opportunities.* Routledge.
Beer, C. T. (2016). Expansive and complex pathways to world society: the global connections of Kenyan environmental organizations and their support for climate change scripts. *Sociological Perspectives, 59*(2), 419–440. https://doi.org/10.1177/0731121415587116
Benya, A. (2016). *Women in mining* (Ph.D. thesis). Department of Sociology, University of the Witwatersrand. http://wiredspace.wits.ac.za/handle/10539/7191
Birkeland, J. (1993). Eco-feminism: Linking theory and practice. In G. Gaard (Ed.), *Eco-feminism: women, animals, nature* (pp. 13–59). Temple University Press.
Bond, P. (2012). *Politics of climate justice paralysis above.* University of KwaZulu-Natal Press.
Bond, P. (2013). Climate justice in, by and for Africa. In M. Dietz & H. Garreltz (Eds.), *Routledge handbook of the climate change movement* (pp. 205–221). Routledge.
Bond, P. (2018). Social movements for climate justice, from international NGOs to local communities. In S. Lele, E. Brondizio, J. Byrne, G.M. Mace, J. Martinez-Alier (Eds.), *Rethinking environmentalism: Linking justice, sustainability, and diversity* (pp. 153–182). Massachusetts Institute of Technology Press.
Bond, P. (2019). Luxemburg's critique of capital accumulation, reapplied in Africa. *Journal für Entwicklungspolitik (Austrian Journal of Development Studies), 35*(1), 92–118. https://www.mat tersburgerkreis.at/site/de/shop/jepartikel/shop.item/1909.html
Bond, P. (2021). Luxemburg's resonances in South Africa: Capital's renewed super-exploitation of people and nature. In D. Cornell & J. Gordon (Eds.), *Creolizing Luxemburg* (pp. 287–316). Rowman & Littlefield International.
Brewer, P. (2001). Nature, development and inequality: are women the last colony? *LINKS International Journal of Socialist Renewal.* Retrieved on 25 June 2021. http://links.org.au/node/109
Bullard, R. D. (1990). *Dumping in Dixie: Race.* Westview Press.
Cabnal, L. (2010). Acercamiento A La Construcción De La Propuesta De Pensamiento Epistémico De Las Mujeres Indígenas Feministas Comunitarias De Abya Yala. En *Feminismos Diversos: El Feminismo Comunitario.* Guatemala: Acsur
Cáceres, B. (2015). *Berta Cáceres acceptance speech, 2015 Goldman Prize ceremony* [Speech translated from Spanish]. Retrieved May 20, 2021, from https://course-building.s3-us-west-2.ama zonaws.com/Public_Speaking/transcripts/BertaCaceresAcceptanceSpeech2015_transcript.txt

Centre for Environmental Rights, (n.d). NGO LINKS—Centre for Environmental Rights. Retrieved July 17, 2021, from https://probono.org.za/ngo-links-centre-for-environmental-rights/

Claassens, A. (2013). Recent changes in women's land rights and contested customary law. *Journal of Agrarian Change, 13*(1), 71–92. https://doi.org/10.1111/joac.12007

CMCTF (2014). *El crudo bajo tierra y la vida en el centro: El Yasuní en clave feminista.* Acción Ecológica, Colectivo Miradas Críticas del Territorio desde el Feminismo.

CMCTF. (2018). (Re)patriarcalización de los territorios y lucha de las mujeres en América Latina. *Revista Ecología Política, 54.* Colectivo Miradas Críticas del Territorio desde el Feminismo. Retrieved April 15, 2021, from https://www.ecologiapolitica.info/?p=10169

Coba, L., & Bayón, M. (2020). Kawsak Sacha: La organizacion de las mujeres en la traduccion política de la selva amazónica en el Ecuador. *En Cuerpos, Territorios y Feminismos* (Cruz Hernández y Bayón). Abya Yala.

Cock, J. (2016a). Radical Agendas #5: An eco-socialist order in South Africa. *Review of African Political Economy.* Retrieved June 18, 2021, from https://roape.net/2016a/01/18/radical-agendas-5-an-eco-socialist-order-in-south-africa/

Cock, J. (2016b). A feminist response to the food crisis in contemporary South Africa. *Agenda, 30*(1), 121–132. https://doi.org/10.1080/10130950.2016.1196983

Cock, J. (2018). The climate crisis and a 'just transition' in South Africa: An eco-feminist-socialist perspective. In V. Satgar (Ed.), *The climate crisis: South African and global democratic eco-socialist alternatives* (pp. 210–230). Wits University Press. https://doi.org/10.18772/220180205 41.15

Crouth, G., & Sgqolana, T. (2021, December 28). Take that, Shell! Locals hail victory over 'bullies' after court halts Wild Coast blasting. *Daily Maverick.* https://www.dailymaverick.co.za/art icle/2021-12-28-take-that-shell-locals-hail-victory-over-bullies-after-court-halts-wild-coast-bla sting/.

d´Eaubonne, F. (1974). *Le Feminisme ou la mort (Feminism or Death).* Pierre Horay.

d'Eaubonne, F. (1978). *Écologie, féminisme : révolution ou mutation?* Éditions A.T.P.

d'Eaubonne, F. (1999). What could an eco-femEco-feminist society be? *Ethics and the Environment, 4*(2), 179–184. https://doi.org/10.1016/s1085-6633(00)88419-3

Del Rio Gabiola, I. (2020). "Berta vive": Solidaridades transnacionales y luchas interseccionales en Honduras. *Middle Atlantic Review of Latin American Studies, 4*(1), 103. https://doi.org/10. 23870/marlas.293

Derman, B. (2020). *Struggles for climate justice uneven geographies and the politics of connection.* Palgrave Macmillan.

Eckstein, D., Künzel, V., & Schäfer, L. (2021). In: E. Opfer & R. Schwarz (Eds.), *Global climate risk index 2021.* Germanwatch. Retrieved on 10 June 2021. https://germanwatch.org/sites/def ault/files/Global%20Climate%20Risk%20Index%202021_2.pdf

Fabricant, N. (2013). Good living for whom? Bolivia's climate justice movement and the limitations of indigenous cosmovisions. *Latin American and Caribbean Ethnic Studies, 8*(2), 159–178. https://doi.org/10.1080/17442222.2013.805618

Fakier, K., & Cock, J. (2018). Eco-feminist organizing in South Africa: reflections on the feminist table. *Capitalism Nature Socialism, 29*(1), 40–57. https://doi.org/10.1080/10455752.2017.142 1980

Federici, S. (2004). Women, land-struggles and globalization: An International perspective. *Journal of Asian and African Studies, 39*(1–2), 47–62. 10.1177%2F0021909604048250

Federici, S., & Linebaugh, P. (2018). *Re-enchanting the world: Feminism and the politics of the commons.* PM Press.

Gaard, G. (Ed.). (1993) *Eco-feminism: Women, animals, nature.* Temple University Press.

GARN. (n.d). *People's Conference on Climate Change and the Rights of Mother Earth. Global Alliance for the Rights of Nature.* GARN Global Alliance for the Rights of Nature. Retrieved on 15 May 2021. https://www.therightsofnature.org/cochabama-rights/

Gates, B. T. (1996). A root of eco-feminism: Ecoféminisme. *ISLE Interdisciplinary Studies in Literature and Environment, 3*(1), 7–16. https://doi.org/10.1093/isle/3.1.7

Gebara, I. (2000). *Intuiciones eco-femeco-feministas: Ensayo para repensar el conocimiento y la religión*. Trotta.

Germanwatch. (2021). *Slow-onset processes and resulting loss and damage—An introduction. Publication series: Addressing loss and damage from slow-onset processes*. Germanwatch. Retrieved June 05, 2021, from https://germanwatch.org/sites/default/files/FINAL_Slow-onset%20paper%20Teil%201_20.01.pdf

Global Greengrants Fund, The International Network of Women's Funds and the Alliance of Funds. (2015). *Climate justice and women's rights: A guide to supporting grassroots women's action*. Retrieved June 27, 2021, from https://www.greengrants.org/wp-content/uploads/2017/10/Climate-Justice-and-Womens-Rights-Guide1.pdf

Goh, A. (2012). *A literature review of the gender-differentiated impacts of climate change on women's and men's assets and well-being in developing countries (CAPRi Working Paper No. 106)*. Washington, DC: CGIAR Systemwide Program on Collective Action and Property Rights (CAPRi). Retrieved May 25, 2021, from https://www.worldagroforestry.org/sites/default/files/4.pdf

Gonda, N. (2019). Re-politicizing the gender and climate change debate: The potential of feminist political ecology to engage with power in action in adaptation policies and projects in Nicaragua. *Geoforum, 106*, 87–96. https://doi.org/10.1016/j.geoforum.2019.07.020

Hargreaves, S. (2020). *Crises, dreaming, and (re)building on African terms. Women in mining position paper for the South African climate justice charter* (Unpublished paper) Johannesburg.

Harris, P. G. (2016). *Ethics*. Edward Elgar Publishing.

Harris, P. G. (2019). *A research agenda for climate justice*. Edward Elgar Publishing.

Hines, R. I. (2007). Natural disasters and gender inequalities: The 2004 tsunami and the case of India. *Race, Gender & Class, 4*(1), 60–68.

IPCC. (2018). Global warming of 1.5 °C. An IPCC Special Report on the impacts of global warming of 1.5 °C above pre-industrial levels and related global greenhouse gas emission pathways, in the context of strengthening the global response to the threat of climate change, sustainable development, and efforts to eradicate poverty. In: V. Masson-Delmotte, P. Zhai, H.-O. Pörtner, D. Roberts, J. Skea, P.R. Shukla, A. Pirani, W. Moufouma-Okia, C. Péan, R. Pidcock, S. Connors, J.B.R. Matthews, Y. Chen, X. Zhou, M.I. Gomis, E. Lonnoy, T. Maycock, M. Tignor, T. Waterfield (Eds.) In Press. Retrieved June 05, 2021, from https://www.ipcc.ch/site/assets/uploads/sites/2/2019/06/SR15_Full_Report_High_Res.pdf

IPCC. (2019). *IPCC Special Report on the Ocean and cryosphere in a changing climate*. In: H.-O. Pörtner, D.C. Roberts, V. Masson-Delmotte, P. Zhai, M. Tignor, E. Poloczanska, K. Mintenbeck, A. Alegría, M. Nicolai, A. Okem, J. Petzold, B. Rama, N.M. Weyer (Eds.), *Intergovernmental panel on climate change* (In press). Retrieved June 05, 2021, from https://www.ipcc.ch/site/assets/uploads/sites/3/2019/12/SROCC_FullReport_FINAL.pdf

Jafry, T. (2019). *Routledge handbook of climate justice*. Routledge.

Juran, L. (2012). The gendered nature of disasters. *Indian Journal of Gender Studies, 19*(1), 1–29. https://doi.org/10.1177/097152151101900101

Kunene, O. (2021 July 6). Let Africa's queer voices speak in the movement for climate justice. *People and Nature*. https://peopleandnature.wordpress.com/2021/07/06/let-africas-queer-voices-speak-in-the-movement-for-climate-justice/

Lambrou, Y., & Paina, G. (2006). *Gender: The missing component of the response to climate change*. Rome: Food and Agriculture Organization of the United Nations (FAO). Retrieved 13 April, 2021. https://biblioteca.semarnat.gob.mx/janium/recursos/224844/Contenido/K%20documentos%20de%20analisis/44%20Gender%20the%20Missing.pdf

Leonard, L. (2013). The relationship between the conservation agenda and environmental justice in post-apartheid South Africa: An analysis of Wessa KwaZulu-Natal and environmental justice advocates. *South African Review of Sociology, 44*(3), 2–21. https://doi.org/10.1080/21528586.2013.817059

Luxemburg, R. (1913). *The accumulation of capital*.

MacDonald, R. (2005). How women were affected by the Tsunami: A perspective from Oxfam. *PLoS Medicine, 2*(6), e178. https://doi.org/10.1371/journal.pmed.0020178

MacGregor, S. (2010). 'Gender and climate change': From impacts to discourses. *Journal of the Indian Ocean Region, 6*(2), 223–238. https://doi.org/10.1080/19480881.2010.536669

Martinez-Alier, J. (2002). *The environmentalism of the poor a study of ecological conflicts and valuation.* Edward Elgar Publishing.

Melithafa, A. (2020 December 4). *Sharpening the spear of climate justice.* Cape Town: European Film Festival Panel Input. https://youtu.be/f1aILK0EDzk?t=2864

MenEngage Alliance. (2021). *Policy agenda: Generation Equality Fora (GEF) feminist action for climate justice AC MenEngage alliance joint recommendations for action coalition leaders.* MenEngage Alliance. Retrieved May 20, 2021, from http://menengage.org/wp-content/uploads/2021/03/Feminist-action-for-climate-justice.pdf

Mies, M (1986). *Patriarchy and accumulation on a world scale.* Zed Books Ltd

Mies, M., & Shiva, V. (1993). *Eco-feminism.* Zed Books.

Miller, D. (2020). Enchanted gardeners in urban food gardens. In E. Bell, S. Gog, A. Simionca, & S. Taylor (Eds.), *Spirituality, organization and neoliberalism* (pp. 106–124). Edward Elgar. https://www.elgaronline.com/view/edcoll/9781788973298/9781788973298.xml

Moreno, M., Vázquez, E., Torres, S., Calle, A., & García, S. (2019 August 28). YASunidas, el activismo diverso que liberó la consulta popular por el Yasuní. *Ctxt Contexto Y Accion.* Retrieved May 10, 2021, from https://ctxt.es/es/20190828/Firmas/27976/YaSunidas-Ecuador-Yasuni-eco logismo-feminismo.htm

Moosa, C., & Tuana, N. (2014). Mapping a research agenda concerning gender and climate change: A review of the literature. *Hypatia, 29*(3), 677–694. https://doi.org/10.1111/hypa.12085

Moss, J., & Umbers, L. (2020). *Climate justice and non-state actors corporations, regions, cities, and individuals.* Routledge.

Nellemann, C., Verma, R., & Hislop, L. (2011). *Women at the frontline of climate change: Gender risks and hopes: A rapid response assessment.* United Nations Environment Program, GRID-Arendal. Retrieved October 15, 2021, from https://gridarendal-website-live.s3.amazonaws.com/production/documents/:s_document/165/original/rra_gender_screen.pdf?1484143050

Otzelberger A. (2011). *Gender-responsive strategies on climate change: recent progress and ways forward for donors.* United Kingdom: Institute for Development Studies. Retrieved 15 May 2021. https://wedo.org/wp-content/uploads/2011/07/Gender-responsive-strategies-on-climate-change_progress-and-ways-forward-for-donors.pdf

Page, E. A. (2006). *Climate change.* Edward Elgar Publishing.

Paredes, J. (2008). *Hilando fino desde el feminismo comunitario.* El Rebozo México.

Pearse, R. (2016). Gender and climate change. *Wires Climate Change, 8*(2). https://doi.org/10.1002/wcc.451

Perkins, P. E. (2014, June 27–29) *Climate justice and gender justice: building women's political agency in times of climate change* [Paper presentation]. International Association for Feminist Economics (IAFFE) Conference, Accra, 27–29 June Retrieved on 12 April 2021. https://yor kspace.library.yorku.ca/xmlui/bitstream/handle/10315/37135/Gender%20Justice%20and%20C limate%20Justice%3B%20Building%20women%27s%20economijc%20and%20political%20a gency%20in%20times%20of%20climate%20change.pdf?sequence=1&isAllowed=y

Perkins, P. E. E. (2019). Climate justice, commons, and degrowth. *Ecological Economics, 160*, 183–190. https://doi.org/10.1016/j.ecolecon.2019.02.005

Pincha, C. (2008). *Indian Ocean Tsunami through the gender lens. Oxfam America & NANBAN Trust.* eldis. Retrieved May 15, 2021, from https://www.eldis.org/document/A58483

Plumwood, V. (1993). *Feminism and the mastery of nature.* Routledge.

Porselvi, P. M. V. (2016). *Nature, culture and gender: Re-reading the Folktale.* Routledge.

Roberts, J. T., & Parks, B. (2006). *A climate of injustice global inequality, North-South politics, and climate policy.* MIT Press.

Salleh, A. (1997). *Eco-feminism as politics.* Zed Press.

Salleh, A. (2005). Moving to an embodied materialism. *Capitalism Nature Socialism, 16*(2), 9–14. https://doi.org/10.1080/10455750500108195

Sólon, P. (2018). The rights of Mother Earth. In V. Satgar (Ed.), *The climate crisis: South African and global democratic eco-socialist alternatives* (pp. 107–130). Wits University Press. Retrieved May 20, 2021, from https://doi.org/10.18772/22018020541.10

Samson, M. (Ed.). (2009). *Refusing to be cast aside: Waste pickers organising around the world.* Women in informal employment: Globalizing and organizing (WIEGO). Boston. Retrieved October 10, 2021, from https://www.wiego.org/sites/default/files/publications/files/Samson-Ref using-to-be-Cast-Aside-Wastepickers-Wiego-publication-English.pdf

Samson, M., & Hurt, K. (2003). *Dumping on women: Gender and privatisation of waste management.* Johannesburg: South African Municipal Workers' Union. IDRC CRDI. Retrieved on 10 March 2021. http://hdl.handle.net/10625/48879

Sandilands, C. (1999). *The good-natured feminist—Eco-feminism and the quest for democracy.* University of Minnesota Press.

Schlosberg, D., & Collins, L. B. (2014). From environmental to climate justice: Climate change and the discourse of environmental justice. *Wires Climate Change, 5*, 359–374. https://doi.org/10.1002/wcc.275

Segato, R. L. (2016). *La guerra contra las mujeres.* Traficantes de Sueños.

Shiva, V. (1988). *Staying alive: Women, ecology and survival in India.* Kali for Women.

Shiva, V. (1989). *Staying alive: Women.* Zed Books.

Shiva, V. (2008). *Soil not oil: Environmental justice in an age of climate crisis.* Zed Books.

Sorensen, C., Saunik, S., Sehgal, M., Tewary, A., Govindan, M., Lemery, J., & Balbus, J. (2018). Climate change and Women's health: Impacts and opportunities in India. *Geohealth, 2*(10), 283–297. https://doi.org/10.1029/2018gh000163

Sturgeon, N. (1997). *Eco-feminist natures: race, gender, feminist theory, and political action.* Routledge.

Sturgeon, N. (1999). Ecofeminist appropriations and transnational environmentalisms. *Identities: Global Studies in Culture and Power, 6*(2–3), 255–279. https://doi.org/10.1080/1070289X.1999.9962645

The Guardian. (2010 April 23). Grassroots summit calls for international climate court (Andres Schipani). *The Guardian.* https://www.theguardian.com/environment/2010/apr/23/cochabamba-climate-court

UNDP. (2013). *Overview of linkages between gender and climate change.* Gender and Climate Change, UNDP Policy Brief. Retrieved on 10 May 2021. https://www.undp.org/content/dam/undp/library/gender/Gender%20and%20Environment/PB1-AP-Overview-Gender-and-climate-change.pdf

UN WOMEN (2021, June 5). *Statement: Women and girls must be at the heart of the fight for climate justice.* UN WOMEN. Retrieved September 10, 2021, from https://www.unwomen.org/en/news/stories/2021/6/statement-ed-phumzile-world-environment-day

Walker, G. (2012). *Environmental justice: Concepts.* Routledge.

Warren, K. (1991a). Toward a feminist peace politics. *Journal of Peace and Justice Studies, 3*(1), 87–102. https://doi.org/10.5840/peacejustice19913114

Warren, K. J. (1991b). Feminism and the environment: An overview of the issues. *APA Newsletter on Feminism and Philosophy, 90*(3), 108–116.

Warren, K. J., & Cheney, J. (1991). Eco-feminism and ecosystem ecology. *Hypatia, 6*(1), 179–197. https://doi.org/10.1111/j.1527-2001.1991.tb00216.x

WoMin. (2019). *WoMin five year strategy (2020–2024)* (Unpublished) Johannesburg.

Yadav, S., & Lal, R. (2018). Vulnerability of women to climate change in arid and semi-arid regions: The case of India and South Asia. *Journal of Arid Environments, 149*, 4–17. https://doi.org/10.1016/j.jaridenv.2017.08.001

YASunidos. (2014). *YASunidos.* Retrieved on 18 June 2021. https://sitio.yasunidos.org/

Hydraulic Fracturing as an Environmental and Social Justice Issue in South Africa

Wade Goodrick and Nola Redelinghuys

1 Introduction and Background

After almost three decades of democracy in South Africa, deep-rooted socio-economic inequalities that diverge along racial[1] and geo-spatial lines still pose challenges to the country's population. South Africa is widely regarded as one of the most unequal societies in the world, with a Gini Coefficient of 0.65 in 2015 (StatsSA, 2019a). More than half of the country's population (55.5%) find themselves in varying degrees of poverty, and the unemployment rate has been hovering around 30% for some time. While some gains toward poverty reduction and increased employment were made between 1994 and 2010, for the past decade, there seems to have been a reversal of this trend (World Bank Group, 2020).

To improve the plight of its poverty-stricken population, the South African national government formulated an ambitious socio-economic development agenda, the National Development Plan (NDP), in 2011 (NPC, 2011). The NDP envisions the elimination of poverty and the sharp reduction of socio-economic inequality by 2030. To achieve the goals of the NDP, widespread job creation in various labor-absorbing economic sectors such as mining, agri-processing, and manufacturing is needed (Kariem & Hoskins, 2016).

The country's development agenda is inextricably linked to future energy planning since affordable and reliable energy provision is vital for industrialization and

---

[1] Population group/ race is an essential determinant of socio-economic development status, especially in a country such as South Africa due to its past exclusionary political system of Apartheid (1948–1994). Statistics South Africa (StatsSA), the official statistical agency of South Africa, uses the following categorization: Black African, Colored, Asian/Indian, and White. For comparative purposes, this chapter adopted this categorization.

W. Goodrick (✉) · N. Redelinghuys
Department of Sociology, University of the Free State (UFS), 205 Nelson Mandela Drive, Park West, Bloemfontein, South Africa
e-mail: goodrickwf@ufs.ac.za

© The Author(s), under exclusive license to Springer Nature Singapore Pte Ltd. 2022
D. Madhanagopal et al. (eds.), *Environment, Climate, and Social Justice*,
https://doi.org/10.1007/978-981-19-1987-9_15

growing domestic energy requirements. Natural gas is explicitly included in future energy and socio-economic development planning. The National Development Plan (NDP), the Integrated Energy Plan (IEP), and the Integrated Resources Plan (IRP) all specifically include natural gas, either imported or to be sold as part of South Africa's energy mix in the future (Scholes et al., 2016).

Some conventional gas resources are currently being extracted offshore for gas-to-liquid fuel production, and some gas is imported from Mozambique to process coal-to-liquid fuel. However, attention is focused on extracting domestic unconventional oil and gas resources for large-scale energy needs. These resources are mainly contained in shale gas[2] formations in the central part of the country, in an area known as the Karoo (Esterhuyse, 2020).

Shale gas development may assist in the diversification of South Africa's energy mix, a critical measure for future economic and social development (Ndlovu & Inglesi-Lotz, 2019). Ageing energy infrastructure, dwindling coal supplies, and increased energy demands of the growing number of households, industries, and businesses pose serious energy challenges to the country considering its current energy mix. While the country's energy system is reasonably self-sufficient, with less than 20% of energy needs supplied by imported sources, the system is heavily reliant on coal. Some 90% of the electricity generated in South Africa is generated from coal, and less than 2% of the country's energy needs are currently met through natural gas (Wright et al., 2016). Another consideration for exploring unconventional gas resources is the reduced carbon emissions associated with natural gas compared to coal. Natural gas may therefore allow South Africa to meet its development needs without compromising its ability to meet its commitments under the Paris Climate Accord (Murcott & Webster, 2020).

South Africa is at present so dependent on coal as an energy resource that it has become the highest CO_2 emitter in Africa and the 14th largest CO_2 emitter in the world (Wakeford, 2016). From a social justice perspective, climate change impacts, such as increased droughts, disproportionally affect poorer sectors of society and populations that rely more directly on the environment for subsistence. Therefore, investing in energy sources with potentially lower emissions is considered important (Barbier & Hochard, 2018).

Apart from these macro-level socio-economic considerations, the government is also seeking a means to establish an industry that can stimulate economic growth and socio-economic opportunities in the Karoo, a marginalized and vulnerable rural region[3] that stretches across the country's Eastern Cape, Northern Cape,

---

[2] Found in shale rock, shale gas is a natural gas that is a hydrocarbon and can be utilized as a fuel source.

[3] A rural area may be defined as such based on a number of indicators such as land use, population density, and remoteness (Kepe, 2016). For the purposes of this chapter, rural areas refer to areas of low population density where livelihoods are largely dependent on agriculture, even though these areas may include small towns, settlements, and villages.

and Western Cape provinces.[4] The FAO (2015) emphasizes that investing in rural development and improving rural livelihoods are critical for achieving inclusive and equitable economic growth and dealing with the root causes of poverty and hunger in these areas. The NDP places specific emphasis on developing an inclusive rural economy, allowing rural communities more opportunities to participate in the country's economy and be more integrated into the socio-political area of the country (NPC, 2011; Partridge et al., 2018). Shale gas development and hydraulic fracturing have been hailed as means to improve the lives of the marginalized communities situated in the areas earmarked for these developments.

This chapter will seek to critically interrogate proposed shale gas development and hydraulic fracturing in South Africa through a social justice lens. Shale gas development and hydraulic fracturing can potentially transform the country, and the affected region, for the better or worse. This chapter specifically focuses on the potential transformation of the Karoo region by shale gas development and extraction in such ways that threaten environmental, social, and energy justice of local communities and natural environments. The discussion first explores how hydraulic fracturing is conceived as a social and environmental justice issue, then provides context to such development and extraction in South Africa and the Karoo. The bulk of the discussion following this uses an energy justice framework to discuss and describe potential procedural, distributional, and recognition injustices caused by decision-making, development practices, and the implications of hydraulic fracturing in South Africa. The discussion concludes with the outline of recommendations to achieve a more just and fair experience in planning for and initiating shale gas development and hydraulic fracturing in the Karoo region of South Africa.

This chapter presents a primarily descriptive discussion conceived by using findings from a wide range of previous studies concerned with the topic of interest. Secondary sources concerned with the impact and planning of shale gas development and hydraulic fracturing in South Africa published between 2010 and 2021 were analyzed using secondary analysis. The chapter further relies on primary data collected from a range of local key stakeholders in the Karoo region in a study by Goodrick (2020) that explored stakeholders' perceptions of risk associated with shale gas development and hydraulic fracturing. This chapter's findings were reviewed and organized according to the tenets of the energy justice framework mentioned earlier.

2 Hydraulic Fracturing as an Environmental and Social Justice Issue

A significant criticism of unconventional gas extraction worldwide is the chosen technique of hydraulic fracturing, also known as fracking. Fracking involves the use

---

[4] In terms of political-administrative areas, South Africa is divided into nine provinces: Western Cape, Eastern Cape, Northern Cape, Free State, KwaZulu Natal, North West, Gauteng, and Mpumalanga and Limpopo. Provinces, in turn, are subdivided into districts and local municipalities.

of a large amount of liquid substances made up of water, sand, and chemicals that are injected at high pressure into the earth's surface. The liquid substance fractures the underground rock, creating openings for natural gas to flow out of and toward the surface (Anderson & Theodori, 2009). Fracking is considered a controversial technology due to the wide array of benefits and burdens that can result from its use and may result in injustices that threaten the tenets and principles emphasized in maintaining a socially and environmentally just relationship between society and nature (Glazewski & Esterhuyse, 2016).

Past research and experience have shown that developmental, industrial, and energy projects are often conceptualized as more technical and economic concerns. However, the process of initiating and engaging in an energy development like that of hydraulic fracturing is very much a social project. Projects of this nature require society to invest its time and manpower into realizing such projects' goals and manage and mitigate potentially harmful implications that communities and nature may face as a result (Lee & Byrne, 2019; Whitton et al., 2017).

In realizing that such an energy project may potentially threaten the social fabric of communities and transform the nature of the relationship between communities and their natural environment, socially responsible stakeholders have noted that the tenets of social justice (such as access; equity; diversity; participation; and human rights) may be harmed or lost as a result of initiating fracking (Atkinson, 2018; Goodrick, 2020; Ingle & Atkinson, 2015).

When exploring social justice and injustice issues concerning fracking, there are key principles that a socially just system requires to be upheld. This includes equal access to resources and outcomes; the provision of equitable resources and outcomes; the acknowledgment of different people's needs and consideration of their diversity; the provision of opportunities for all persons to participate without exclusion in decision-making; and the upholding of human rights for all human beings as manifested in law (Harper & Snowden, 2017). In a socially just society, all persons, irrespective of their race, class, background, or social status, have fair access to both the benefits and a fair distribution of harmful aspects associated with an energy development such as fracking, without certain persons or groups benefiting disproportionally. In contrast, others suffer more as a result of the extraction technique (Thompson, 2016).

This chapter ascribes to the argument that due to the structural, technical, and ideological nature of energy projects and developments, such projects can, directly and indirectly, produce social, environmental, and energy injustice. Energy justice is a research agenda and framework that applies principles of justice to decision-making, thinking, projects, and events within energy systems and its efforts to produce energy for societal consumption (Jenkins et al., 2016). Such an agenda and framework attempt to understand how an energy project such as shale gas extraction by means of hydraulic fracturing in South Africa may result in significant social and environmental injustices. To do this, three core principles or tenets, namely distributive, procedural, and recognition justice, are used to evaluate energy projects in the context of their location and setting (Jenkins et al., 2016; Lee & Byrne, 2019).

Distributional justice involves establishing and maintaining the fair and equitable distribution and sharing of benefits and burdens created by energy developments and projects (Taylor, 2017; Thompson, 2016; Whitton et al., 2017). *Procedural justice* involves the fair and equitable inclusion of all stakeholders in decision-making, participation, and consultation activities of the energy project (Lee & Byrne, 2019). *Recognition justice* involves procedures and practices that respect and consider the characteristics, needs, status, and vulnerabilities of the natural environment, communities, and societies that may potentially be affected by the impacts and consequences of energy developments and projects (Lee & Byrne, 2019). In attempts to achieve recognition justice, efforts are made to establish a thorough understanding of the potentially affected stakeholders, with consideration of their characteristics, needs, status, and vulnerabilities (Hull & Evensen, 2020; Lee & Byrne, 2019; Marlin-Tackie et al., 2020).

Lee and Byrne's (2019) framework for understanding the production of energy injustices outlines the changing nature of society–nature relations as the result of the commodification of nature and its ties to, and implications for, local communities and greater society. As a result of the normalization of pollution, technocratic authoritarianism, and the rise of the Anthropocene, society–nature relations have become conducive for systemic energy injustice. Structurally, energy developments and projects generate injustices by maintaining a preference for large-scale technical systems that are remotely distanced from local decision-making processes; through the centralization of energy production and the distancing of supply from energy users; and as a result of the propensity for energy developers to take "necessary risks" as a price-to-pay for social progress and development.

Additionally, economic, political, and technical ideologies combine to produce injustices by enabling authoritarian, top-down decision-making systems, promoting dominant specialized and technical understandings of sustainability and fairness; and enduring systematic policy that confine decisions and behaviors to past preferences of conduct (Lee & Byrne, 2019).

Ideological and structural properties of energy developments and projects combine to result in an array of distributional, procedural, and recognition injustices. For example, exclusion, inequality, and the violation of human rights can occur as a result of distributional, procedural, and recognition injustices (Taylor, 2017). The nature of societal–nature relations in the Karoo region may be affected as a result of the regions' context and setting being compounded by the systematic, technical, and ideological issues associated with fracking in such a vulnerable place.

3 Contextualizing Shale Gas Development and Hydraulic Fracturing in South Africa

Historically, the exploration of unconventional gas resources in South Africa has occurred intermittently since the 1940s. Notably, in the 1960s, the Southern African

Oil Corporation (SOEKOR) discovered oil and gas resources in shale formations in the Karoo Basin. As was the case in other countries with potentially recoverable unconventional oil and gas resources, technological constraints prevented any further developments at that time. With the development of hydraulic fracturing technology, it was only later that the extraction of such resources became possible, heralding a new era in resource extraction worldwide (Esterhuyse, 2020).

By the beginning of the twenty-first century, exuberant efforts by the oil and gas industry to utilize this new technology in the United States of America (USA) started to bear fruit and contributed to increased energy self-sufficiency for this country. The potential implications of unconventional gas for energy security and economic growth soon captured the attention of other nations with potentially recoverable unconventional gas resources. For South Africa, the implications of unconventional gas resources to strengthen socio-economic development efforts re-ignited interest to explore its own potential resources (Clark et al., 2021; Scholes et al., 2016).

South Africa has an estimated 390tcf[5] of technically recoverable shale gas, but there is a high level of uncertainty associated with this estimate (Wakeford, 2016). Recent studies by the Department of Energy put the potential for shale gas at around 120tcf, of which 9tcf seems to be economically recoverable (Wright et al., 2016). The South African national government has noted the uncertainty and questions of concern surrounding the extraction technique and its consequences for local communities and the natural environment (Glazewski & Esterhuyse, 2016). However, the government hopes to emulate the economic successes of fracking in nations such as the USA while avoiding their mistakes. Some such mistakes revolve around social and environmental injustices caused by the decision-making, processes, and implications associated with fracking.

Despite the uncertainty and potential risks to vulnerable populations associated with shale gas development in South Africa, initial excitement over the amount of technically recoverable gas paved the way for the Petroleum Agency of South Africa (PASA) to issue exploration licenses to a number of oil and gas companies in 2010 to explore the country's potential unconventional shale gas resources.

The decision was met with strong opposition from stakeholders in affected areas, resulting in a temporary moratorium on further exploration. The moratorium was subsequently lifted, and after facing prolonged legal challenges over legislation and regulations, the government is currently still in the process of establishing legislation and regulations for exploration to commence. Currently, only three oil and gas companies are still showing an interest in exploring unconventional gas resources, namely Royal Dutch Shell, Bundu Oil and Gas, and Falcon Oil and Gas (Atkinson, 2018; Clark et al., 2021).

Current applications for exploration of shale gas reserves cover approximately 125,000 km^2 of the land surface area of South Africa in the Karoo Geological Basin. This area is showing the greatest potential to extract economically feasible sources of shale gas in the country (Atkinson, 2018). A large part of the area targeted for shale gas exploration falls (see Fig. 1) within the boundaries of the Eastern Cape,

---

[5] Tcf—Trillion cubic feet is used to measure large volumes of gas.

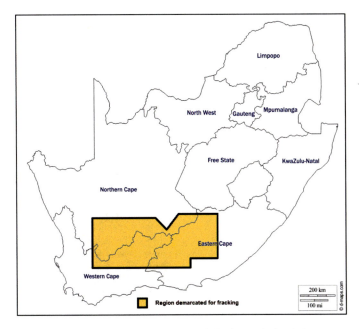

Fig. 1 Fracking in the Karoo. *Source* Goodrick & Redelinghuys (Authors)

Northern Cape, and Western Cape provinces, with the largest area situated within the borders of the more rural Eastern Cape and Northern Cape provinces (Ingle & Atkinson, 2015; Redelinghuys, 2016; Toerien, 2018).

The discussion now turns to how hydraulic fracturing in the Karoo region of South Africa may result in social and environmental injustices. Table 1 highlights the potential injustices associated with hydraulic fracturing in the Karoo region:

4 The Recognition Injustices Associated with Hydraulic Fracturing in South Africa

Recognition injustices may occur as a result of the failure to consider and understand the context and setting where energy projects are taking place, as well as the character and concerns of stakeholders associated with the project and development (Clough, 2018; Martin et al., 2016; Schweiger, 2019). Such injustice results in uncertainty and misunderstanding and may contribute to both distributional and procedural injustices (Clough, 2018; Lee & Byrne, 2019). Thus, recognition injustice is probable if the following characteristics of the region are not considered in assessments and decision-making concerning fracking in the Karoo.

Geographically, the Karoo covers the largest part of the interior plateau of the country, occupying some 30–40% of the surface area. The region is considered an

Table 1 Potential recognition, procedural and distributional injustices caused by hydraulic fracturing in the Karoo region of South Africa

1. Recognition injustices associated with fracking in South Africa	**(a) The failure to recognize that the Karoo region is an ecologically and socially sensitive area**
	The region is largely dependent on limited surface and underground water resources, along with low-annual rainfall. This is compounded by the region's low bio-productivity and complex geological makeup, all of which can influence the outcomes of fracking
	(b) The failure to recognize the Karoo region's small and isolated population
	The region has a low population density where most of the population lives in few urban settlements. The majority of the rural community lives in small settlements scattered across the region with large distances. Such characteristics may impact the population's ability to interact with the planning and initiation of fracking and how such a population can receive benefits and manage harmful impacts of fracking
	(c) The failure to recognize that the Karoo region lacks infrastructure and skills for fossil fuel extraction
2. Procedural injustices associated with fracking in South Africa	The Karoo region's population primarily focuses on agricultural practices, livestock farming, conservation, and the tourism industry. With little fossil fuel extraction experience, the region would require significant capital and infrastructure developments to allow for shale gas development and extraction at an economically feasible level
	(d) The failure to recognize that the local Karoo population are largely socially and economically vulnerable
	Having significant poverty, especially in rural areas, the region is characterized by a high dependence on social welfare grants for survival. As a result, the region is considered an epicenter of social unrest largely spurred by poverty. The nature of economic opportunities provided by fracking may not serve to increase employment among the existing population, as occupations created by fracking target skilled and experienced workers that are not present in the region
	(e) The failure to recognize patterns of rural de-agrarianization across the Karoo

(continued)

Table 1 (continued)

	Patterns of rural de-agrarianization where rural Karoo households are turning from agriculture as sources of livelihood to other alternative economic opportunities are evident. Fracking may serve to undermine the existing agriculture sector further as workers look to employment opportunities provided by fracking over previously popular agriculture-based occupations
	Various stakeholders are not adequately presented with knowledge and data that can allow them to engage in informed decision-making, resulting in uncertainty and misunderstandings of the planning, process, and outcomes of the fracking project
	(d) Undermining and inconsideration of human and legal rights
	Isolated, vulnerable, and uninformed groups lack resources to access legal representation and protection necessary when faced with harmful impacts of fracking that may jeopardize their rights to access environmental resources such as water
3. Distributional injustices associated with fracking in South Africa	**(a) Unjust distribution of job creation**
	Many occupations associated with fracking require skills and knowledge not actively available in the potentially affected region, thus requiring outsiders to fill such positions. At the same time, locals mostly occupy low-paying and low-skilled positions
	(b) Unjust distribution of environmental burdens, harm, and degradation of natural resources
	Fracking generates various forms of pollution, environmental degradation, and loss of biodiversity while exacerbating the usage of rare resources such as water. This may result in less resources for other industries and farming in the fracking region and harm local livelihoods tied to such resources
	(c) Unjust distribution of the benefits of energy security

(continued)

Table 1 (continued)

	Energy resources provided from fracking are set to flow into the South African national grid. Energy security benefits from such extraction are shared across the country with no explicit energy security benefits, primarily targeting local communities in the fracking region
	(d) Unjust distribution of social change
	Fracking may force local communities to change their social and spatial identity from a rural to industrial one as shale gas development is initiated and developed over time, potentially affecting local spaces' social cohesion and structure. This may require affected communities to actively use their limited resources to manage and mitigate the harmful impacts of fracking
	(e) Unjust effect of fracking hindering efforts toward managing climate change
	Fracking continues the development of a carbon economy, contributing to climate change through the high volumes of methane in shale gas. This may bolster climate change impacts on temperature and rainfall in the fracking region. At the same time, fracking developments also redirect attention away from existing and proposed renewable energy efforts and developments in the region

Source Goodrick & Redelinghuys (Authors)

ecologically and socially sensitive area, highly dependent on limited water resources, and has a complex geological makeup (Esterhuyse et al., 2017). Bio-regionally, the area spans two of the nine biomes in the country, namely the succulent Karoo and the Nama Karoo biomes.

The succulent Karoo biome in the south-west lies in an arid winter rainfall region and is credited with the highest diversity of succulent plants worldwide, while the Nama Karoo is situated in an arid, summer-rainfall area in the western part of the Karoo (Murcott & Webster, 2020; Skowno et al., 2019). The area is characterized by low-annual rainfall of less than 400 mm per annum, with some parts receiving less than 250 mm per annum (Toerien, 2018).

Surface water resources are scarce and water scarcity, incidentally, resulted in settlements first developing close to surface water resources. Only after groundwater resources were located did populations settle in areas further away from surface water resources. The aridity and low bio-productivity of the region place ecological limitations on agricultural and economic activity (Walker et al., 2018).

Less than 2% of South Africa's 59.6 million people reside in the Karoo. While the population density is low (less than 2 people per square km over most of the region), at least 75% of the people in this area live in urban settlements of varying sizes. Comparatively, 67% of South Africa's population is urbanized (Population Reference Bureau, 2020). The 60–100 settlements, villages, and small towns in the Karoo are interspersed with livestock and game farming units and conservation areas (Redelinghuys, 2016). Settlements, towns, and villages are small, with even the largest Karoo towns, such as Graaff Reinet, having populations of less than 50 000 people (Nel & Hill, 2008; Nel et al., 2011; Walker et al., 2018).

Economic activity during the colonial period until the mid-twentieth century mainly became centered around livestock farming (Chinigò, 2019; Toerien, 2018). The Karoo currently supports around 30 different types of agricultural practices, with wool (sheep and goat) and sheep farming for meat production still being the dominant agricultural activities. In some areas, cattle and dairy farming are practiced, while there is also some maize and wheat and fruit crop production. Livestock farming remains a major contributor to the livelihoods of the people in the Karoo. Agricultural activities provide employment for around 100,000 people in the larger Karoo, while agricultural production is the main source of income for some 38,000 people in the area earmarked for shale gas extraction (Murcott & Webster, 2020; Oettle et al., 2016).

Despite these economic activities, the Karoo is sometimes viewed as a vast, expansive, sparsely inhabited place with limited development opportunities due to its aridity and low population density. However, for the people living there, the Karoo already supports their livelihoods, is a place of rest, restoration, and creativity, and holds untold botanical, paleontological, and archaeological treasures to be explored and enjoyed (Seeliger et al., 2016). The spaciousness, low population density, low levels of air and light pollution, and low radio interference also elevated the Karoo to the status of an astronomy hotspot, adding another development dimension that in some respects stands in conflict with shale gas development (Chinigò, 2019).

However, the Karoo is also a place of hardship, economic exclusion, and marginalization that national and provincial governments largely neglect regarding socio-economic development (Kepe, 2016; Murcott & Webster, 2020; Walker et al., 2018).

To highlight the plight of the people of the Karoo, the high dependence on social welfare grants is telling. Social grants are the second most important source of income for households in South Africa, after salaries, with 30% of the South African population being beneficiaries of social grants and 45.5% households receiving at least one type of social grant. Dissecting the distribution of grants along geo-spatial lines reveals that poverty is more deeply felt among rural populations (Kariem & Hoskins, 2016; StatsSA 2019a, b, 2020a).

More than two thirds (66.6%) of households in the Eastern Cape and 55.9% of households in the Northern Cape, two provinces with large rural populations, and the two provinces with the largest share of the land area targeted for shale gas exploration, receive at least one social grant, compared to 35.8% of households in the Western Cape, and 31.5% of households in Gauteng, the two more urbanized provinces.

High grant dependence is an important reason why rural towns in the Karoo have not experienced outmigration to the extent that other countries such as Australia and the USA have witnessed in the face of declining agricultural employment opportunities. In the case of South Africa, rural households tend to move away from agriculture as their main source of livelihood, often in the absence of viable alternative economic opportunities in a phenomenon termed "rural de-agrarianization" (Partridge et al., 2018; Pereira & Drimie, 2016). Environmental decline, the consolidation of farming units into larger units, land-use changes that include the conversion of livestock farms to game farms, redundancy of the agricultural workforce due to labor-saving technologies, and changes in labor legislation all contribute to the phenomenon of de-agrarianization applicable to the Karoo (Toerien, 2018).

The loss of agricultural employment results in high levels of vulnerability for agricultural workers who lose their livelihoods and their tenure rights on the farms where they were employed (Kepe, 2016). As a result of this trend, small towns in the Karoo have become important centers for collecting social welfare grants that sustain households in the absence of alternative employment opportunities (Pereira & Drimie, 2016; Redelinghuys, 2016). Many former agricultural workers that end up in these towns are constrained by joblessness, landlessness, and poorer access to education, health care, and basic service delivery and are unable to break the intergenerational cycle of poverty (Nel & Hill, 2008; Pereira & Drimie, 2016).

Therefore, it is not surprising that rural towns in South Africa have become epicenters of social unrest spurred by poverty and poor access to basic services such as water and sanitation. While advances have been made in terms of housing, electrification, and water and sanitation provision over the past 30 years, rural areas have been lagging urban areas in terms of service delivery, leading to frustration among residents of rural towns. Additionally, poor households are often unable to pay for services rendered and experience the services delivered as poor, thus fueling tensions in poorer communities (Kariem & Hoskins, 2016). Issues with service delivery, particularly in respect of access to water, are experienced in Karoo towns, and these issues may be amplified in the face of added pressure from fracking on the institutional capacity of municipalities that are already under pressure (Atkinson et al., 2016).

The scourge of poverty and joblessness also impacts school dropout rates, poor educational attainment, and skills development that in turn exacerbates poverty and unemployment. More than half of South Africa's population (54%) is younger than 30 years, while 28.6% of the population is younger than 14 years, and 9.1% is older than 60 (StatsSA, 2020b). In Karoo municipalities potentially affected by shale gas development and fracking, the proportion of the population under the age of 14 ranges between 25 and 35%. Youth age dependency ratios are on average more than 60%, while overall age dependency ratios are more than 70% (StatsSA, 2020a). With limited economic prospects and limited access to skills development and training, youth in these towns are unable to benefit from economic opportunities, such as those potentially offered by shale gas development and fracking.

5 The Procedural Injustices Caused by Hydraulic Fracturing in South Africa

Procedural injustices involve the mechanisms that revolve around decision-making and communication concerning the initiation, experience, and consequences, in this case, of energy developments and projects that do not allow for the fair and just inclusion, participation, and understanding of all stakeholders, while also failing to uphold stakeholders' rights (Jenkins et al., 2016; Marlin-Tackie et al., 2020). The following sections discuss the array of procedural injustices potentially caused by fracking in the Karoo region.

5.1 The Lack of Rigorous Exploration and Testing Processes

A common theme in research and media coverage of the proposed shale gas development in South Africa has been the concern surrounding the lack of rigorous exploration and testing of the extraction technique and its potential implications (Glazewski & Esterhuyse, 2016; Goodrick, 2020). Exploration and testing are required to generate data and information that can be used to make informed and empirically supported decisions while also allowing for all stakeholders to be aware of the array of benefits and burdens that may in reality impact on the Karoo region and South Africa as a whole (Esterhuyse et al., 2017; Scholes et al., 2016).

The quality of existing data on the availability of natural gas for extraction and the degree of risk and severity that could impact the region are two themes causing much uncertainty among stakeholders (Goodrick, 2020). Stakeholders have criticized the way that exploration and testing have been handled, noting that the impacts of fracking in South Africa have been based on limited and potentially outdated data sets; the experiences of fracking elsewhere in the world that are dissimilar to the South African region's context and setting; as well as perceived political agendas among stakeholders that are driving developments toward a more pro-fracking direction (Glazewski & Esterhuyse, 2016; Goodrick, 2020; Scholes et al., 2016).

Concerns with exploration and testing can have grave implications for the perception and understanding of the extraction technique and its implications. The existing data has been further criticized for not being easily approached and understood by persons lacking more technical and scientific background and knowledge. Local communities in the Karoo have noted their dissatisfaction in this, stating that they are still uncertain of the nature of fracking and struggle to develop opinions on whether the development will be largely positive or largely negative for the people of the Karoo and the environment (Goodrick, 2020).

If not effectively managed, such uncertainty has the potential to lead to expectations of the energy project that are unrealistic or incorrect. An increasingly identified theme in the literature of perceptions of fracking has been the perceived degree of communities' desires to frack where they live (Goodrick, 2020; Yao et al., 2020).

Some opposition leaders who oppose fracking have noted that local communities have not been adequately examined on their actual willingness and desire to see fracking take place and argue that without a confirmed desire of the majority of the Karoo population, the South African national government does a disservice to the people it represents and serves (Goodrick, 2020).

5.2 The Lack of Active and Just Public Participation and Consultation in Decision-Making

A core tenet of procedural justice requires active participation and consultation of public stakeholders when assessing and examining the implications of an energy project such as fracking (Evensen, 2016). This requires that the public be actively involved in decision-making processes and consulted on how they perceive, experience, understand, and respond to the consequences of fracking.

Various bodies and organizations of stakeholders are part of the decision-making processes concerning fracking in the Karoo. There has, however, been concern about the handling of the representation process and the ways in which the public has been included in consultation and participatory processes (Goodrick, 2020; Walker et al., 2018).

The first issue pertains to the active participation of public stakeholders. Local communities of the region have tended to be represented by elected officials and community leaders, with the wider public only being directly involved when invited to community gatherings and meetings with industry and government officials. However, some stakeholders criticize these sessions as not being widely advertised and focusing on the participation and consultation of specific stakeholders over the general population (Goodrick, 2020). As a large proportion of the Karoo population is spread out across large, vast spaces, in small communities, they tend to be isolated from the spaces where much of the nation's protests and opposition to fracking has taken place (Atkinson, 2018; Glazewski & Esterhuyse, 2016). As a result, consultation sessions and meetings have come to be seen by some stakeholders as being dominated by the voices of more wealthy landowners and farm owners, who are mostly made up of middle-income and higher income white South Africans (Augustine, 2018; Goodrick, 2020).

Such perceptions have resulted in white South African commercial farmers and landowners being accused of having been given greater consideration in consultation and participatory activities than poorer, landless, Black, and Colored South Africans in the same region. Skewed inclusion of stakeholders was also a concern in other developmental projects in the region, such as the Square Kilometer Array (SKA). The persistent concern is that wealthier landowners' concerns drown out concerns of the poor and marginalized inhabitants in the area (Atkinson, 2018; Augustine, 2018). This tension exacerbates the existing divisions of class, race, and economical means within the stratified Karoo population still bearing the structural and economic scars left from the nation's segregated past.

The content and process of conducting consultation and participation with the public have also come under scrutiny. For the better part of the past decade, the content presented at such meetings was often criticized as being challenging to understand due to it being presented technically and scientifically incomprehensible to an average South African, with the result that it had limited use in informing the public opinion. Secondly, language barriers excluded many participants in these meetings from the discourse, as many of these sessions have been conducted in English, a language that is not widely spoken in the region (Walker et al., 2018). This situation compounds uncertainty, distrust, and feelings of lacking control among stakeholders, thus undermining the participation and consultations process (Goodrick, 2020).

5.3 The Lack of Access to and Provision of Information and Knowledge of Fracking in South Africa for All Stakeholders

A common theme in stakeholder's perceptions and reviews of knowledge and understanding of fracking and its potential benefits and burdens is that of a lack of access to information and knowledge on fracking in the Karoo region (Glazewski & Esterhuyse, 2016; Goodrick, 2020; Walker et al., 2018).

Persons who have inadequate resources and infrastructure to allow them access to knowledge and information aside from word of mouth may find it challenging to inform themselves of the many intricate and varied impacts of fracking in the region. A lack of an easily accessible, sufficient, and informative central body of knowledge and information database that all stakeholders can access to observe and consult on information pertaining to fracking and its potential benefits and burdens, as well as its related activities in South Africa, has been highlighted as an important issue in the Karoo (Esterhuyse et al., 2017; Goodrick, 2020; Walker et al., 2018).

Considering the region's many isolated communities and settlements, a significant proportion of the Karoo's population face a dearth of information, forcing such persons to look to their leaders and communities for knowledge and insight into the matter (Glazewski & Esterhuyse, 2016; Roberts, 2013; Willems, 2015).

Ultimately, a lack of reliable and comprehensive data and information may further hinder the participation and consultation process, resulting in stakeholders not viewing the issue in as comprehensive a manner as they would prefer. In addition, stakeholders have shown differences in their understanding of the nature and outcomes of shale gas development and fracking. This has been noted as resulting in further conflict between stakeholders (Goodrick, 2020).

5.4 The Undermining and Inconsideration of Human and Legal Rights

A less frequently identified theme in studies of the potential implications of hydraulic fracturing, the impact of hydraulic fracturing on undermining human and legal rights, is a necessary concern, especially in regions where socio-economic inequality is prevalent (Evensen, 2016; Omidire, 2020). The South African population is guaranteed human and legal rights that have legal backing. However, the process of activating such backing and ceasing of any opportunities to harm one's legal and human rights are challenging for poorer South Africans living in marginalized and isolated locales (Glazewski & Esterhuyse, 2016; Omidire, 2020).

Rights to environmental resources such as water and natural vegetation, freedom of choice, equality, and private property rights stand to be impacted by the various distributional and procedural injustices caused by fracking and its associated developments in the Karoo region (Evensen, 2016). For Omidire (2020), the poorer population of the region are likely to have the fracking process infringe upon their human and legal rights as a result of their lack of funds to access representation, as well as them lacking knowledge of the country's court system and the manner in how their rights are enforced. Furthermore, the lack of legal practitioners relative to the population in the region may further hinder their ability to successfully allow them access to representation and protection under the law (Augustine, 2018; Omidire, 2020).

Augustine (2018) identifies several cases where major infringements on human and legal rights in South Africa by energy projects and their impacts were at their core a result of the lack of community and public participation and consultation in the planning of such projects.

Protection of the rights of the Karoo population and their natural environment may come to be undermined even with existing legal protections if socio-economic characteristics and procedural injustices are allowed to hinder both the community and environment's ability for achieving legal protection (Augustine, 2018; Glazewski & Esterhuyse, 2016).

6 The Distributional Injustices Caused by Hydraulic Fracturing in South Africa

Distributional injustices involve the unfair and inequitable distribution and sharing of benefits and burdens that are, in this case, created by energy developments and projects (Evensen, 2016; Lee & Byrne, 2019; Marlin-Tackie et al., 2020). With regards to fracking in South Africa, the various distributional injustices that may potentially occur are likely to originate from combinations of flawed procedure and ill-recognized, as well as unrecognized contextual characteristics (Glazewski &

Esterhuyse, 2016; Goodrick, 2020; Taylor, 2017). The following sections discuss the array of distributional injustices potentially caused by fracking in the Karoo region.

6.1 The Unjust Distribution of Job Creation

As highlighted by a variety of studies (Anderson & Theodori, 2009; Rijsdijk, 2016; Sovacool, 2014), fracking has the ability to create numerous job opportunities due to the need for a wide variety of positions, such as drillers, engineers, and truck drivers, required to make possible the initiation, exploration, development, and extraction stages of fracking. The creation of such opportunities can significantly impact stimulating economic prosperity, improving household income, and reducing unemployment (Scholes et al., 2016; Sovacool, 2014).

Proponents of fracking in South Africa hope to emulate such an experience in the Karoo region. In a highly productive scenario, it is expected that less than 4000 jobs could be created for this region within the first decade of activity (Scholes et al., 2016). However, the nature and provision of jobs may not always significantly benefit regions where fracking occurs, especially in the long term. Researchers note the potential of fracking to create jobs, but many of these jobs require skills and knowledge not readily available in places such as the Karoo (Esterhuyse et al., 2017; Glazewski & Esterhuyse, 2016).

Therefore, energy companies and industries choose to source workers outside the affected regions. The opportunities created by fracking that are readily available and suited for local communities often fall within less-skilled and lower-paid occupations, for example, security and construction work. Even if locals can acquire the necessary training and skills for high-skilled positions, energy companies may still use workers from outside the area. If a project is only going to be economically viable for several months or a few years, the costs to train local personnel may be considered too expensive and not worthwhile in the long term (Goodrick, 2020).

Furthermore, the wealth generated from incomes paid to workers may not actually go toward benefiting people living in the affected regions. There is concern that many of the jobs that local people will occupy will only exist for a few years and not offer employment security in the long term. In a worst-case scenario, locals employed in such positions will experience temporary reprieve before struggling with unemployment again once the energy project has come to mature or concluded altogether (Scholes et al., 2016).

The job opportunities created by shale gas development may occur at the expense of jobs in other prominent economic sectors in the region. Esterhuyse et al. (2017) and Walker et al. (2018) note that the region's tourism, conservation, and agricultural sectors may lose workers due to the attractions presented by newly created fracking-related jobs. Jobs being diverted away from already existing employment sectors may undermine existing development plans that rely on a relatively small population from which to draw people from and target long-term goals that fracking projects may not allow for (Scholes et al., 2016). Promises of jobs for a largely vulnerable and poverty-stricken population are necessary for such an energy project to be considered worthwhile, but the potential for such positions to not primarily benefit or even harm existing opportunities for that population is a distributional concern and potential injustice (Goodrick, 2020).

6.2 The Unjust Distribution of Environmental Burdens, Harm, and Degradation of Natural Resources

Coupled with its development process, hydraulic fracturing has been found to result in a wide array of environmental burdens, harm, and degradation of natural resources (Esterhuyse et al., 2017; Kondash et al., 2018; Scholes et al., 2016). Fracking and its associated processes have the ability to generate various forms of pollution, environmental degradation, and loss of biodiversity. However, it is the usage of water and its contamination by the leakage of chemical substances in fracking liquids that have received notable concern in South Africa (Esterhuyse et al., 2017; Fakir & Davies, 2016).

As noted earlier in the chapter, the Karoo region has little water to spare and is heavily reliant on the few perennial rivers and permanent springs in the area (Walker et al., 2018). Groundwater and surface water are integral to the success of the region's farming and conservation sectors and are too scarce to allow for additional usage in other burgeoning sectors (Esterhuyse et al., 2017; Scholes et al., 2016).

Fracking requires extraordinary levels of water to extract available unconventional gas and has been found to require increasing amounts overtime to maintain sufficient levels of extraction (Kondash et al., 2018). Fracking's ability to exacerbate the use and pollution of water resources can disrupt the Karoo's social and natural ecosystems and negatively impact the health and habitats of living organisms in the region (Esterhuyse et al., 2017; Scholes et al., 2016; Todd et al., 2016).

From a distributional justice standpoint, the rural Karoo population that is reliant on crop production and livestock farming may be disproportionally affected by the impacts of fracking on environmental resources such as water. Livestock farming, for example, largely relies on reservoirs by which water is brought to the surface via windmills. The contamination of this groundwater by fracking would not allow for such ranching to be possible (Walker et al., 2018).

Furthermore, this vulnerable population may lack the resources and skills to handle the social and environmental burdens they are forced to face as a result of the impacts of gas development on the natural environment. This applies especially to the changing character of the region from a rural, pastoral space to industrial spaces (Du Plessis, 2016; Goodrick, 2020; Scholes et al., 2016).

The inability to farm effectively could motivate movements of workers from sectors reliant on water to other existent ones, further undermining the farming sector. However, such a transition is made difficult by the large distances between isolated towns and dwellings of the region and may result in heightened transport costs and necessitate further development of migratory infrastructure (Butler-Adam, 2016; Scholes et al., 2016).

Overall, the isolated and vulnerable local communities reliant on farming practices may stand to lose their basic access to sufficient and usable water resources, as well as their capabilities to work and earn a living if fracking were to take place in the region. The disproportional distribution of such social and environmental burdens brought on by fracking may further generate inequalities between those persons living in isolated rural areas and those persons in more developed urban spaces (Goodrick, 2020; Thompson, 2016).

6.3 The Unjust Distribution of the Benefits of Energy Security

South Africa's energy mix, security, and ability to provide adequate power have come under much pressure over the past decade, with the nation regularly engaging in significant mass power cuts in order to save up power for peak periods (Goldberg, 2015). Fracking has the potential to transform the distribution and availability of energy in South Africa (Scholes et al., 2016).

However, the energy generated by it may not actually necessarily benefit local residents in close proximity to the fracking operations (Scholes et al., 2016; Walker et al., 2018). This is a result of the energy and power generated by energy projects flowing into the country's national grid. Local residents of the Karoo have been told on numerous occasions that they should expect to receive cheaper power as a result of residing in the fracking-affected region. However, according to energy specialists, this is not certain and would require explicit measures set in place by various governmental and state offices (Goodrick, 2020).

Unfortunately, such promises by some community leaders and industry operatives do not guarantee that local communities will ultimately benefit from receiving more affordable energy. The population of the Karoo region could thus be under a false impression of receiving benefits above that of the energy project's burdens. However, those benefits may never transpire and leave the population disillusioned, sandbagged, and victimized.

6.4 The Unjust Distribution of Social Change

Fracking in the Karoo region may drive significant transformation in the region's socio-economic character and natural environment, which may affect how individuals and communities interact with one another, satisfy their needs, and navigate challenges they face (Redelinghuys, 2016; Scholes et al., 2016).

With regards to the disproportional distribution of fracking's benefits and burdens, such injustices may come to affect the Karoo region's social cohesion and structure. Experiences outside of South Africa illustrate that communities may feel that they are increasingly unable to manage and adapt to change brought about by the developments, especially when past and existing social and economic issues become compounded by those brought on by fracking projects (Evensen, 2016; Jacquet, 2014).

Some community leaders in the Karoo have revealed that even in the case that the benefits of fracking are sufficient to bolster the local population's economic prosperity, the poorer proportion may spend their newly received resources to manage and mitigate burdens brought on by fracking. These burdens include handling health issues brought on by pollution, the loss of sense of place, and the changing nature of the local environment (Goodrick, 2020). Thus, the benefits may not actually be effectively significant to produce long-term positive change and are offset by disturbed communities that increasingly feel unstable and vulnerable (Glazewski & Esterhuyse, 2016).

6.5 The Unjust Effect of Fracking Hindering Efforts Toward Managing Climate Change

As stipulated in the nation's *National Climate Change Response White Paper* and its *National Development Plan,* South Africa is committed to transitioning toward a climate-resilient society and lower carbon economy (Department of Environmental Affairs, 2017). This requires the nation to balance efforts of economic growth and transformation with that of more sustainable use of its natural resources, which include natural gas.

Efforts to transition to less carbon-intensive or renewable energy resources are seen as an utmost necessity. The costs and time associated with establishing a renewable energy sector, in conjunction with dwindling local non-renewable energy resources, are making unconventional shale gas extraction appealing as a means to bridge the gap between an energy sector that is primarily driven by non-renewable sources to one that is largely driven by renewable sources (Glazewski & Esterhuyse, 2016). Furthermore, while shale gas is still a carbon-intensive resource, it is regarded as a cleaner energy source in comparison to other fossil fuels (Scholes et al., 2016).

Despite these benefits associated with the extraction and usage of shale gas, there is an array of harmful implications tied to climate change and its associated socio-economic impacts. For example, extracted shale gas contains large volumes of methane, a hydrocarbon that contributes to greenhouse gas emissions (Howarth, 2019).

Looking at climate change impacts specifically applicable to the Karoo, current trends of erratic and variable rainfall are expected to persist and become more extreme over time (Conradie et al., 2019; Walker et al., 2018). Alongside this, the Karoo has increasingly been experiencing higher average temperatures across all seasons of the year (Walker et al., 2018). The result of this is an increasingly drier climate for increasingly longer periods of time. With less rain and higher temperatures, drought and lack of water resources are expected to produce an unbearable environment that will be detrimental to local livelihoods and the natural environment (Esterhuyse et al., 2017; Glazewski & Esterhuyse, 2016).

Importantly, a focus on shale gas extraction may threaten and divert the opportunities for investment and action in initiating renewable energy resources in the region. Fracking may thus be a hindrance to the residents of the Karoo in their being able to engage in climate-friendly energy practices, such as the Perdekraal East Wind Farm and the Oya Energy Hybrid Projects that are being developed there. Unfortunately, fracking continues an already existing trend of developing non-renewable fossil fuels that further carbonize the region's climate.

7 Conclusion and the Way Forward

With consideration of the potential environmental and social injustices caused by fracking in the region, the following measures are deemed necessary to develop a just and fair experience for planning and managing fracking and its impacts.

Firstly, clarity on social and environmental protection policies and strategies must be provided by the South African government. At present, the specifics on which state departments and divisions are responsible for the management and regulation of fracking remain unclear and problematic (Esterhuyse, 2020; Omidire, 2020). Detailed provisions of how the management and regulation processes will take place in the case of fracking must be effectively disclosed, starting with the procedures being followed in the planning phase that fracking is currently within. In the mind of this, efforts to establish community and environmental sustainability must be made a priority, and thereby inform the other developmental stages of fracking in the Karoo (Marlin-Tackie et al., 2020; Walker et al., 2018).

Secondly, in attempts to achieve distributional justice in the region, efforts should be made to establish and maintain the fair and equitable distribution and sharing of benefits and costs that are created by energy developments and projects (Taylor, 2017; Thompson, 2016; Whitton et al., 2017). This requires an enhanced understanding of the extraction technique and its potential impacts. Thus, more comprehensive exploration and testing of fracking, as well as consultation with the public and other stakeholders, must be a priority in the planning stage.

Furthermore, in efforts to achieve a more informed and shared understanding of fracking and its potential impacts in the region, stakeholders, government, and industry must take proactive efforts to establish a centralized database that records and presents useful information on the status, process, and findings on fracking in the Karoo (Esterhuyse, 2020; Esterhuyse et al., 2017; Walker et al., 2018). Importantly, such a database needs to be mindful of the population who will access such information. Thus, data and information should be made available in languages to best cover the region where fracking is to take place, English, Afrikaans, and isiXhosa in the case of the Karoo, while also being presented in such a way that a wide array of stakeholders and interested persons can understand it, and not only a specialized minority of scientists and academics (Goodrick, 2020; Walker et al., 2018). Different notions and understandings of shale gas development and extraction's nature and outcomes will need to be incorporated and considered for this to be worthwhile in establishing epistemic justice, where decision-making and initiatives are aware and considerate of stakeholder's cultural values and goals (Goodrick, 2020; Osborne & Shapiro-Garza, 2017). Also, the processes on how to report infractions, injustices, and concerns related to fracking should be clearly provided.

Across studies of fracking in South Africa, as well as elsewhere in the world, researchers and stakeholders have requested and noted the importance of establishing local task teams that can collectively identify, monitor, and recommend solutions concerning the impacts of fracking (Glazewski & Esterhuyse, 2016; Scholes et al., 2016). Such task teams must involve a variety of stakeholders from varied backgrounds, locations, and disciplines to best allow for a wide variety of variables and impacts to be assessed while monitoring the probability of distributional, procedural, and recognition injustices taking place. Ideally, persons and parties in opposition to such development and extraction can be more closely involved in collaboration efforts between developers and opposition, thus allowing for enhanced planning and management of the coming energy project, which invokes a sense of responsibility among all manner of stakeholders (Johnston et al., 2020; Temper, 2018).

Also, efforts to establish more comprehensive and available legal aid must be made with a focus on meeting the needs of disadvantaged and vulnerable persons in the region. Ideally, all persons in the Karoo should be able to identify legal aid and engage with the South African courts in order to enforce and assert their legal and human rights (Augustine, 2018; Omidire, 2020).

In reaction and response to concerns of potential procedural injustice, the process surrounding hydraulic fracturing, its decision-making, its stages, and its implications must attempt to establish fair processes of conduct and decision-making that legitimize authorities, stakeholders, and decisions by aiming for fairness in all aspects of it. Without question, fair rules and regulations are required that are able to be effectively accepted and approved by a wide array of stakeholders, and not just specialized authorities. Additionally, in the case that stakeholders do have concerns, fair mediation and negotiation are essential, which make an attempt to remain unbiased and fair.

Additionally, an essential element to establishing a just and fair experience of fracking in South Africa requires restorative justice to be invoked. This requires interaction between stakeholders, industry, and government where issues are identified, solutions are determined and developed, and behaviors are transformed and adjusted to effectively manage and mitigate burdens and disproportionally distributed benefits. Ideally, efforts of such justice allow for the maximization of benefits while minimizing burdens in a social and environmentally responsible manner.

Lastly, active community participation in decision-making and policy drafting is necessary for the recognition, procedural and distributional justice with regards to fracking in the Karoo. To invoke a justice-defined system that effectively incorporates the local communities surrounding and within the energy project, the initiative and process of fracking should be one where the community is considered a defining mechanism of the project's entire process from beginning to end (Goodrick, 2020; Marlin-Tackie et al., 2020).

Ideally, a community-led and defining approach would make progress in developing trust, respect, and relationships between various stakeholders and the community as the community have an inclusive part in such development and collective agency (Whitton et al., 2017). Communication between different groups of stakeholders should be presented on an open, reflective, and interactive platform that feels meaningful and responsive, allowing for trust to be built between stakeholders in a collaborative effort.

This chapter has explored how fracking in the Karoo region of South Africa has the potential to transform the area for better and worse. Unfortunately, a host of structural, technical, and ideological issues in the country may enhance the probability of distributional, procedural, and recognition injustices experienced as a result of fracking. Without consideration of such issues and the provision of effective and realistic solutions, fracking may further compound existing socio-economic inequalities and environmental degradation in this already vulnerable and marginalized region.

References

Anderson, B. J., & Theodori, G. L. (2009). Local leaders' perceptions of energy development in the Barnett Shale. *Southern Rural Sociology, 24*(1), 113–129.

Atkinson, D. (2018). Fracking in a fractured environment: Shale gas mining and institutional dynamics in South Africa's young democracy. *The Extractive Industries and Society, 5*(2018), 441–452. https://doi.org/10.1016/j.exis.2018.09.013

Atkinson, D., Schenk, R., Matebesi, Z., Badenhorst, K., Umejesi, I., & Pretorius, L. (2016). Impacts on the social fabric. In R. Scholes, P. Lochner, G. Schreiner, G., L. Snyman-Van der Walt, & M. de Jager (Eds.), *Shale gas development in the central Karoo: a scientific assessment of the opportunities and risk.* Pretoria: CSIR.

Augustine, M. (2018). *Fracking in the Karoo: An environmental justice perspective* (Mini-dissertation) Johannesburg: University of the Witwatersrand.

Barbier, E. B., & Hochard, J. P. (2018). The impacts of climate change on the poor in disadvantaged regions. *Review of Environmental Economics and Policy, 12*(1), 26–47. https://doi.org/10.1093/reep/rex023

Butler-Adam, J. (2016). Resolving fractured debates about fracking? The shale gas industry in South Africa. *South African Journal of Science, 112*(11). https://doi.org/10.17159/sajs.2016/90186

Chinigò, D. (2019). From the 'Merino Revolution' to the 'Astronomy Revolution.' *Journal of Southern African Studies, 45*(4), 749–766. https://doi.org/10.1080/03057070.2019.1642028

Clark, S. R., van Niekerk, J. L., Petrie, J., & Fakir, S. (2021). South African shale gas economics: Analysis of the breakeven shale gas price required to develop the industry. *Journal of Energy in Southern Africa, 32*(1), 83–96. https://doi.org/10.17159/2413-3051/2021/v32i1a8362

Clough, E. (2018). Environmental justice and fracking: A review. *Current Opinion in Environmental Science & Health, 3*(2018), 14–18. https://doi.org/10.1016/j.coesh.2018.02.005

Conradie, B., Piesse, J., & Stephens, J. (2019). The changing environment: Efficiency, vulnerability and changes in land use in the South African Karoo. *Environmental Development, 32*(2019). https://doi.org/10.1016/j.envdev.2019.07.003

Department of Environmental Affairs. (2017). *South Africa's 2nd Annual Climate Change Report.* Pretoria: Department of Environmental Affairs.

Du Plessis, A. (2016). The governance of hydraulic fracturing in the Karoo: A local government perspective. In J. Glazewski, & S. Esterhuyse (Eds.), *Hydraulic fracturing in the Karoo: Critical legal and environmental perspectives.* Cape Town: Juta.

Esterhuyse, S., Sokolic, F., Redelinghuys, N., Avenant, M., Kijko, A., Glazewski, J., Plit, L., Kemp, M., Smit, A., Vos, T., & von Maltitz, M. (2017). Vulnerability mapping as a tool to manage the environmental impacts of oil and gas extraction. *Royal Society of Open Science, 4*, 171044. https://doi.org/10.1098/rsos.171044

Esterhuyse, S. (2020). *Towards a regulatory framework to protect groundwater resources during and as a result of unconventional oil and gas extraction* (Doctoral thesis). Bloemfontein: University of the Free State.

Evensen, D. (2016). Ethics and 'fracking': A review of (the limited) moral thought on shale gas development. *Wires Water, 3*(4), 575–586. https://doi.org/10.1002/wat2.1152

Fakir, S., & Davies, E. (2016). The economics of shale gas fracking in the Karoo: What can the American experience teach us? In J. Glazewski, S. Esterhuyse (Eds.), *Hydraulic fracturing in the Karoo: Critical legal and environmental perspectives.* Cape Town: Juta.

FAO. (2015). *FAO and the 17 sustainable development goals.* FAO.

Glazewski, J., & Esterhuyse, S. (2016). *Hydraulic fracturing in the Karoo: Critical legal and environmental perspectives.* Cape Town: Juta.

Goldberg, A. (2015). *The economic impact of load shedding: The case of South African retailers* (Mini-dissertation). University of Pretoria.

Goodrick, W. F. (2020). *The social construction of the perception of risk associated with unconventional gas development in South Africa* (Doctoral thesis). Bloemfontein: University of the Free State.

Harper, C., & Snowden, M. (2017). *Environment and society: Human perspectives on environmental issues* (6th ed.). Routledge.

Howarth, R. W. (2019). Ideas and perspectives: Is shale gas a major driver of the recent increase in global atmospheric methane? *Biogeosciences, 16*(15), 3033–3046. 10.519/bg-16-3033-2019

Hull, E., & Evensen, D. (2020). Just environmental governance for shale gas? Transitioning towards sustainable local regulation of fracking in Spain. *Energy Research & Social Science, 59*, 101307. https://doi.org/10.1016/j.erss.2019.101307

Ingle, M., & Atkinson, D. (2015). Can the circle be squared? An enquiry into shale gas mining in South Africa's Karoo. *Development Southern Africa, 32*(5), 539–554. https://doi.org/10.1080/0376835x.2015.1044076

Jacquet, J. B. (2014). Review of risks to communities from shale energy development. *Environmental Science & Technology, 48*(1), 8321–8333. https://doi.org/10.1021/es404647x

Jenkins, K., McCauley, D., Heffron, R., Stephan, H., & Rehner, R. (2016). Energy justice: A conceptual review. *Energy Research & Social Science, 11*(2016), 174–182. https://doi.org/10.1016/j.erss.2015.10.004

Johnston, R. J., Blakemore, R., & Bell, R. (2020). *The role of oil and gas companies in the energy transition.* Atlantic Council: Global Energy Center.

Kariem, A., & Hoskins, M. (2016). From the RDP to the NDP: A critical appraisal of the developmental state, land reform, and rural development in South Africa. *Politikon, 43*(3), 325–343. https://doi.org/10.1080/02589346.2016.1160858

Kepe, T. (2016). Rural geography research in post-apartheid South Africa: Patterns and opportunities. *South African Geographical Journal, 98*(3), 495–504. https://doi.org/10.1080/03736245.2016.1212731

Kondash, A. J., Lauer, N. E., & Vengosh, A. (2018). The intensification of the water footprint of hydraulic fracturing. *Science Advances, 4*(8), 1–8. https://doi.org/10.1126/sciadu.aar5982

Lee, J., & Byrne, J. (2019). Expanding the conceptual and analytical basis of energy justice: Beyond the three-tenet framework. *Frontiers Energy Research, 7*(99). https://doi.org/10.3389/fenrg.2019.00099

Marlin-Tackie, F. A., Polunci, S. A., & Smith, J. M. (2020). Fracking controversies: Enhancing public trust in local government through energy justice. *Energy Research & Social Science, 65*(2020), 101440. https://doi.org/10.1016/j.erss.2020.101440

Martin, A., Coolsaet, B., Corbera, E., Dawson, N., Fraser, J., Lehmann, I., & Rodriguez, I. (2016). Justice and conservation: The need to incorporate recognition. *Biological Conservation, 197*(2016), 254–261. https://doi.org/10.1016/j.biocon.2016.03.021

Murcott, M., & Webster, E. (2020). Litigation and regulatory governance in the age of the Anthropocene: The case of fracking in the Karoo. *Transnational Legal Theory, 11*(1–2), 144–164. https://doi.org/10.1080/20414005.2020.1777037

Ndlovu, V., & Inglesi-Lotz, R. (2019). Positioning South Africa's energy supply mix internationally: Comparative and policy review analysis. *Journal of Energy in Southern Africa, 30*(2), 14–27. https://doi.org/10.17159/2413-3051/2019/v30i2a5409

Nel, E., & Hill, T. (2008). Marginalisation and demographic change in the semi-arid Karoo, South Africa. *Journal of Arid Environments, 72*, 1164–2274. https://doi.org/10.1016/j.jaridenv.2008.07.015

Nel, E., Taylor, B., Hill, T., & Atkinson, D. (2011). Demographic and economic changes in small towns in South Africa's Karoo: Looking from the inside out. *Urban Forum, 22*, 395–410. https://doi.org/10.1007/s12132-011-9131-z

NPC. (2011). *National development plan 2030: Our future—Make it work (Executive summary)*. Pretoria: The Presidency, RSA.

Oettle, N., Lindeque, L., du Toit, J., Samuels, I., Osler, A., Vetter, S., & van Garderen, EA. (2016). Impacts on Agriculture. In R. Scholes, P. Lochner, G. Schreiner, L. Snyman-Van der Walt, L., M. de Jager (Eds.), *Shale gas development in the central karoo: A scientific assessment of the opportunities and risks*. Pretoria: CSIR.

Omidire, K. (2020). Access to courts by vulnerable persons in relation to hydraulic fracturing in South Africa. *Commonwealth Law Bulletin, 46*(4), 662–688. https://doi.org/10.1080/03050718.2020.1795898

Osborne, T., & Shapiro-Garza, E. (2017). Embedding carbon markets: Complicating commodification of ecosystem services in Mexico's forests. *Annal's of the American Association of Geographers*. https://doi.org/10.1080/24694452.2017.1343657

Partridge, A., Daniels, R., Kekana, D., & Musundwa, S. (2018). South Africa's rural livelihood dynamics. In *56th Annual Conference of the Agricultural Economics Association of South Africa*. Somerset West: Agricultural Economics Association of South Africa.

Pereira, L., & Drimie, S. (2016). Governance arrangements for the future food system: Addressing complexity in South Africa. *Environment, 58*(4), 18–31. https://doi.org/10.1080/00139157.2016.1186438

Population Reference Bureau. (2020). *World population data sheet, 2020*. PRB.

Redelinghuys, N. (2016). Effects on communities: The social fabric, local livelihoods and the social psyche. In J. Glazewski & S. Esterhuyse (Eds.), *Hydraulic fracturing in the Karoo: Critical legal and environmental perspectives*. Cape Town: Juta.

Rijsdijk, I. (2016). The scripto-visual rhetoric of fracking in South Africa. In J. Glazewski, S. Esterhuyse (Eds.), *Hydraulic fracturing in the Karoo: Critical legal and environmental perspectives*. Cape Town: Juta.

Roberts, J. A. (2013). *A comparative analysis of shale gas extraction policy: Potential lessons for South Africa* (Masters dissertation). Stellenbosch: Stellenbosch University.

Scholes, R., Lochner, P., Schreiner, G., Snyman-Van der Walt, L., & de Jager, M. (2016). *Shale gas development in the Central Karoo: A scientific assessment of the opportunities and risks*. Stellenbosch: CSIR.

Schweiger, G. (2019). Recognition, misrecognition and justice. *Ethics & Global Politics, 12*(4). https://doi.org/10.1080/16544951.2019.1693870

Seeliger, L., de Jongh, M., Morris, D., Atkinson, D., du Toit, K., & Minnaar, J. (2016). Impacts on sense of place. In R. Scholes, R., P. Lochner, G. Schreiner, L. Snyman-Van der Walt, & M. de Jager (2016). *Shale gas development in the central karoo: A scientific assessment of the opportunities and risks.* Pretoria: CSIR.

Skowno, A. L., Poole, C. J., Raimondo, D. C., Sink, K. J., Van Deventer, H., Van Niekerk, L., & Driver, A. (2019). *National biodiversity assessment 2018: The status of South Africa's ecosystems and biodiversity. Synthesis report.* Pretoria: SANBI.

Sovacool, B. J. (2014). Cornucopia or curse? Reviewing the costs and benefits of shale gas hydraulic fracturing (fracking). *Renewable and Sustainable Energy Reviews, 37*(1), 249–264. https://doi.org/10.1016/j.rser.2014.04.068

StatsSA. (2019a). *Inequality trends in South Africa: A multidimensional diagnostic of inequality.* Pretoria: Statistics South Africa.

StatsSA. (2019b). *Quarterly labour force survey, Statistical Release: P0211.* Pretoria: StatsSA.

StatsSA. (2020a). *General household survey, 2019.* Pretoria: Statistics South Africa.

StatsSA. (2020b). *Mid-year population estimates, 2020b.* Pretoria: Statistics South Africa.

Taylor, T. (2017). *Land, race and the environment: Fracking in South Africa.* Retrieved from: http://www.rosalux.co.za. Accessed January 03, 2021.

Temper, L. (2018). Blocking pipelines, unsettling environmental justice: From rights of nature to responsibility to territory. *Local Environment, 24*(2), 94–112. https://doi.org/10.1080/13549839.2018.1536698

Thompson, G. (2016). The double-edged sword of sovereignty by the barrel: How native nations can wield environmental justice in the fight against the harms of fracking. *UCLA Law Review, 1818*(2016).

Todd, S. W., Hoffman, M. T., Henschel, J. R., Cardoso, A. W., Brooks, M., & Underhill, L. G. (2016). The potential impacts of fracking on biodiversity of the Karoo basin, South Africa. In J. Glazewski, S. Esterhuyse (Eds.), *Hydraulic fracturing in the Karoo: Critical legal and environmental perspectives.* Cape Town: Juta.

Toerien, D. F. (2018). The 'Small Town Paradox' and towns of the Eastern Cape Karoo, South Africa. *Journal of Arid Environments, 154*(2018), 89–98. https://doi.org/10.1016/j.jaridenv.2018.04.001

Walker, C., Milton, S. J., O'Connor, T. G., Maguire, J. M., & Dean, W. R. J. (2018). Drivers and trajectories of social and ecological change in the Karoo, South Africa. *African Journal of Range & Forage Science, 35*(3–4), 157–177. https://doi.org/10.2989/10220119.2018.1518263

Wakeford, J. (2016). The South African energy context. In J. Glazewski, S. Esterhuyse (Eds.), *Hydraulic fracturing in the Karoo: Critical legal and environmental perspectives.* Cape Town: Juta.

Whitton, J., Brasier, K., Charnley-Parry, I., & Cotton, M. (2017). Shale gas governance in the United Kingdom and the United States: Opportunities for public participation and the implications for social justice. *Energy Research & Social Science, 26*(2017), 11–22. https://doi.org/10.1016/j.erss.2017.01.015

Willems, M. (2015). *Health risk perception of Karoo residents related to fracking, South Africa* (Masters dissertation). Cape Town: University of Cape Town.

World Bank Group. (2020). *Poverty & equity brief, Sub-Saharan Africa–South Africa: April 2020.* Retrieved from www.worldbank.org/poverty. Accessed January 03, 2021.

Wright, J., Bischof-Niemz, T., Carter-Brown, C., & Zinamen, O. (2016). Effects on national energy planning and energy security. In R. Scholes, P. Lochner, P., G. Schreiner, L. Snyman-Van der Walt, M. de Jager (Eds.), *Shale gas development in the central karoo: A scientific assessment of the opportunities and risks.* Pretoria: CSIR.

Yao, L., Zang, Q., Lai, K., & Cao, X. (2020). Explaining local residents' attitudes toward shale gas exploitation: The mediating roles of risk and benefit perceptions. *International Journal of Environmental Research and Public Health, 17*(2020), 7268. https://doi.org/10.3390/ijerph17197268

Land Acquisition and a Question of "Justice": Voices of the Unheard Marginal Groups in the Interior Odisha, India

Mohon Kumar Naik and Devendraraj Madhanagopal

1 Introduction

Over the past few decades, there have been several incidences of the complications of rehabilitating the development-induced displaced people, particularly in the underdeveloped and the developing world (Einbinder, 2017; Parasuraman, 1999; Rojas & Litzinger, 2016). In most cases, the Development-Induced Displacement and Resettlement (DIDR) has resulted in intensifying inequality in the society where a vast majority of displaced people are forced to live in substandard conditions (McDowell, 1996; Satiroglu & Choi, 2015). Fernandes (2001) has provided an estimate from the "displacement" data that from 1951 to 1990, at least 21.3 million people had

---

[1] The direct meaning of the term "Dalit" is Downtrodden or Oppressed. It widely came into use in the 1930s after the translation of the Marathi word "Depressed classes" (Omvedt, 2012). As Shah (2002) has explained, in general, the term "Dalit" denotes all the downtrodden people of the Hindu society, including Scheduled Caste, Scheduled Tribes, and other backward communities. But, in everyday political discourse, the word "Dalit" denotes the Scheduled Caste people. The term "Dalit" became more popularized in the 1960s, when Marathi-speaking intellectuals, including neo-Buddhists started using the word "Dalit" in their literary works instead of M.K. Gandhi's favorite term "Harijan (The Man of God) to denote "Scheduled Caste" people. The term "Dalit" does not denote any caste. In modern parlance, the term "Dalit" also denotes revolution and the symbol of change. It is to be noted that the architect of the constitution of India also opposed the usage of the term "Harijan" to denote untouchables of the Hindu society. As Omvedt (2012) has noted, the term "Scheduled Caste" is a legal and neutral term. Though we agree with Shah (2002) and Omvedt (2012), in this chapter, we prefer to largely use the term "Dalits" to denote "Scheduled Caste" people. We use the terms "Dalits" and "Scheduled Caste" according to the contexts and interchangeably.

M. K. Naik
Department of Humanities and Social Sciences, Indian Institute of Technology Bombay, Mumbai, India

D. Madhanagopal (✉)
School of Sustainability, XIM University, Odisha, India
e-mail: devendraraj.mm@gmail.com

© The Author(s), under exclusive license to Springer Nature Singapore Pte Ltd. 2022
D. Madhanagopal et al. (eds.), *Environment, Climate, and Social Justice*,
https://doi.org/10.1007/978-981-19-1987-9_16

been displaced by development-related projects in India. These numbers might have crossed 30 million in 2001. Marginal groups are the most affected ones due to these development projects. For example, Dalits[1] constitute 20%, and tribals constitute 40% among the project-affected and displaced people (Fernandes, 2001). This estimate shows a clear picture of how "development" projects unequally had hit the assetless poor and marginal groups, including Dalits and tribals, over the last decades.

In India, there has been an integral and complicated relationship among common property resources (CPR),[2] equity, and social justice since CPRs play central roles in the socioeconomic systems of the marginal people, including the Dalits and tribals. It contributes to their sustainable livelihoods systems and plays a major role in reducing their poverty, economic inequality, and food insecurity crisis (Beck & Ghosh, 2000; Jodha, 1990; Narayan, 2021). But there has been a burgeoning literature focusing on India discusses the complications of the neoliberal economy of the state since the 1990s and demonstrates how it unequally helped the privileged groups of the society to grow richer and how it intensified the expropriation of the lands, including CPRs of the rural poor and tribals[3] (Kothari, 1996; Das, 2001; Sarangi, 2002; Patnaik, 2007; Walker, 2008; Prasad et al., 2012).

In the post-1991 economic reform[4] period, across India, large industrial projects, including mining projects, have created large-scale displacement of marginal people and caused environmental destruction (Siddiqui, 2012; Jena, 2014). A few prime reasons for such large-scale displacement have been the relaxation of investment rules, capital ownership regulations, expatriation of profits, and the relaxation and modifications of leasing policies of minerals by the state. The accumulation of private capital has started replacing state projects, and it has been one of the significant drivers of enclosures, displacement, and environmental destruction (Kumar, 2014). Such liberalized policies and the resulting extractive capitals are continued to impact

---

[2] We have a vast literature focusing on CPRs. In this chapter, to understand CPRs, we use the explanation given by N.S. Jodha, one of the influential "commons" scholars in India. He describes CPRs as the resources that are accessible to the entire community of a village or region, without exclusive individual ownership or access rights (Jodha, 1986).

[3] According to Article 366 of the Constitution of India, "the STs are such tribes or tribal communities or part of or groups within such tribal or tribal communities as are deemed under Article 342 to be Scheduled Tribes for this constitution" (For more details, Government of India. (n.d.)). The Government of India adopts five criteria to categorize the STs, which are as follows: (i) Primitive traits, (ii) Distinctive culture, (iii) Geographical isolation (iv) The shyness of the community to communicate with other communities, and (v) Socioeconomic backwardness (National Commission for STs, 2017. For more details: Government of India (2017). Throughout this chapter, we interchangeably use the terms "tribals," and "indigenous communities" as substantial literature uses the term "indigenous communities" to denote the "tribals." To avoid conceptual complications, we largely use the term "tribals" to denote Scheduled Tribes and use the term "indigenous" according to the contexts.

[4] In the early 1990s, India had severe economic crises due to multiple economic and political factors. To meet the challenges of the crises, the then Union government of India under the leadership of the Prime Minister P. V. Narasimha Rao initiated major economic reforms, including the abolition of License-Permit Raj and promoted investor-friendly trade policy reforms. Dr. Manmohan Singh, the then Finance Minister of the Union government of India played a major role in these economic and trade policy reforms (Wadhva, 2000).

the resources-rich rural and hilly regions of Odisha, formerly called Orissa, a state that is in the eastern part of the Indian peninsula. A good proportion of Southern and Northern Odisha come under the category of the "Fifth Schedule".[5] In Odisha, these regions historically predominately resided by the Scheduled Tribes (ST), including primitive vulnerable tribal groups (PVTGs). Besides that, these regions comprise a significant proportion of Scheduled Caste (SC) and other backward caste communities. Overall, many of them are landless and marginal landholders, and their sole survival depends on CPRs such as forest, forest land, water bodies, wastelands, grazing land, and other common places (Barik, 2006). The aftermath of the execution of the neoliberal economic policy, their source of survival and their customary rights, and indigenous management over such resources have largely been ignored. However, the roots of such indiscriminate acquisition of CPRs of the marginal groups by the state and other private interests lie in the administration of the colonial state by British Imperialism. The Land Acquisition Act (LAA), 1894 of the colonial state justifies the displacement by the power of "eminent domain," and it does not recognize the importance of CPRs of the dependent communities. It allows an alienation that negatively impacts the marginal and vulnerable communities (Fernandes, 2009). This Act and its underpinned rules and regulations continued to govern the land acquisition processes of postindependent India until it was replaced by the Right to Fair Compensation and Transparency in Land Acquisition, Rehabilitation, and Resettlement Act, 2013, which we will discuss in the forthcoming section (Wahi, 2013: 52–53).

To show the brunt of land acquisition processes of the last decades through the LAA 1894, we show the estimate made by Kumar (2014) in the state of Odisha. By referring to the Comptroller and Auditor General of India report, Kumar (2014) pointed out that the state government of Odisha allotted around 50,276 acres of land to industrial projects. Almost two-thirds of these lands were private lands and were acquired using the Land Acquisition Act, 2011. About 0.25 million acres of the lands of Odisha were allocated under mining leases; a large majority of them are in the tribal-dominated regions of the state. In Odisha, such massive investments in the mining sector are largely capital intensive; it has generated minimal new employment opportunities for the local and project-affected people. Such extractive capitalism has had substantial adverse effects on inducing displacement of the marginal groups and environmental disruption in the respective regions and caused extensive social and environmental injustices to those marginal groups.

In this chapter, we first briefly review and discuss the land acquisition and forest acts of India and discuss how they are inadequate to provide "justice" to the already marginal groups across India and Odisha. After that, we introduce our case, focusing on the selected villages of Rayagada district of Odisha, and discuss how the land acquisition process had happened for the establishment of the alumina refinery plant

---

[5] The fifth schedule of the constitution of India deals with the administration of the scheduled areas where the tribal communities predominately reside. For details about the list of scheduled castes and the list of fifth schedule areas in Odisha: ST & SC Development, Minorities, & Backward Classes Welfare Department, Government of Odisha (2020); NITI Aayog (n.d.).

of Utkal Alumina International Ltd., (UAIL) in the 1990s, and how it has continued to affect them in multiple dimensions, resulting in social and environmental injustices of the marginal communities across these regions. This region in the South of Odisha is one of the most backward regions not just in the State of Odisha but also in the entire Indian subcontinent. After that, we present selected field insights from the intensive fieldwork conducted in the study villages. The chapter concludes by suggesting some policy recommendations for ensuring transformative changes in the lives of marginal people of the research region and as well as in the entire Indian subcontinent. The scope of this chapter lies in hearing the unheard voices of the marginal groups of the interior Odisha, India, and to show that the "development" needs of the state hit the most marginal groups of India. Hence, this chapter does not intend to provide theoretical debates on development, social, and environmental [in] justices. Instead, it highlights the narratives of the marginal groups straightforwardly and offers some immediate and long-term policy-oriented suggestions.

2   The Land Acquisition Acts of India—A Brief Overview

In preindependent India, the British colonial state introduced, adopted, and experimented with acquiring lands (including private lands and CPRs) through the LAA, 1894 (Wahi et al., 2017). It came into implementation on 1 March 1894 (Government of Meghalaya, n.d.). It continued to govern the land policy and acquisition processes in the postcolonial state of India until the replacement of this act by the new law, which is the Right to Fair Compensation and Transparency in Land Acquisition, Rehabilitation, and Resettlement Act, 2013 (Varshney, 2019). Hence, for this chapter, it is essential to discuss the LAA, 1894, as the land acquisition processes had happened in our research region by adopting this law.

As Ramanathan (2011) has described, this LAA, 1894 provided expansive power to the state to take over the common and private lands. Through this *"eminent domain"*[6] doctrine of this act, the state gets the power to *"institutionalize involuntary acquisition"* (Nair, 2016: 33–34; Ramanathan, 2011: 10;). As Setalvad (1971) has observed, the principle of eminent domain empowers the state to compel the owner/s to sell their lands to the state (or the private agency authorized by the state) with or without their consent. This law also recommends that the state provide compensation to the landowner/s. Hence, this act interferes with the rights of the private individuals to sell or not to sell their lands, and it is justified on the grounds of the *good for the greater number—community as a whole*—in short, for public purpose. As Desai (2011) has described, this law is essentially used against private landowners who are unwilling to sell their lands to the state, or the private entity authorized by the state.

---

[6] The origins of the term "Eminent Domain" go back to 1625 when it was first used by the Dutch jurist Hugo Grotius in the legal treatise *De Jure Belli et Pacis,* written in 1625. The term "Eminent Domain" denotes *"ominium eminens"* (in Latin: It means supreme lordship). For more: Grotius and Kelsey (1925).

He has listed that this law has three major components, which are as follows: (i) It provides power to the state to take over the lands of the private owners. (ii) The power of the state to take over the private lands has to be exercised for public purposes. (iii) The state has the responsibility to provide compensation to the private landowners whose lands are taken over.

Though some provisions of this act sound fair, in postindependent India, it largely affected the marginal people, particularly the tribals, other traditional forest dwellers[7] (hereafter, OTFDs), and Dalits. Around 40–50% of the displaced people in postindependent India are tribals. Among them, not more than 25% of the displaced tribal people were resettled (Lobo, 2014), meaning a large majority of them were forced to live in deprived conditions. This act was also used to acquire the CPRs resources owned and managed by the village community through their "customary norms" and traditional arrangements at the local levels. The state machinery directly kept an authorization with the CPRs by using this act. As Nielsen and Nilsen (2015) have noted, this LAA of 1894 recognized the individual rights of the private owners, but not the community rights. Hence, it provided no rehabilitation to the community who lost their "commons" under this act. It also offered no compensation to the private owners who do not own legal title (or documents) to claim their lands. The people who lost their community-owned lands and other CPRs, including losing their traditional livelihood systems, were not compensated. Hence, the roots of these conflicts are deep, and they go back to the colonial LAA, 1894. This act legitimized acquiring both private and shared lands from the public in the name of "public purposes."

However, the new land law, which is the Right to Fair Compensation and Transparency in Land Acquisition, Rehabilitation, and Resettlement Act, 2013 (hereafter LAA, 2013), has several provisions that address the complications of the LAA, 1984. The LAA, 2013 provides a "fair" scale of compensation to landowners and landless and other project-affected persons (Jenkins, 2014; Neilsen & Nilsen, 2015; Pal, 2018).

Nielsen and Nilsen (2015) has critically discussed the bills (which, later become the Land Acquisition Act, 2009 following the revisions) became proposed by the then Government of India (United Progressive Alliance) in 2009. Among the two bills, as they noted, the Resettlement and Rehabilitation Bill contains certain progressive elements that provide social and economic justice to the displaced and project-affected people. It considers the interest of the landowners and recommends that the state receive the consent of landowners for land acquisition. It provides considerable protection to the land rights of the landowners where the private sectors are engaged. Besides that, certain clauses of the bill recognize the rights of the landless and artisans and direct the state to provide "fair" compensation to them as well, not just the landowners. The compensation that is suggested by this bill is a fairer amount than the old law; hence, this is undoubtedly a significant improvement to ensure

---

[7] According to the Forest Rights Act (2006), "other traditional forest dweller" means *any member or community who has for at least three generations prior to the 13th day of December, 2005 primarily resided in and who depend on the forest or forests land for bona fide livelihood needs* (Government of India, 2014: 03). For details: Government of India (2014).

"justice" to them. This bill directs the state to undertake a social impact assessment before beginning the project to identify whether the proposed project serves "public purpose." Also, it directs the state to analyze the social costs, and adverse social impacts outweigh the benefits of the project. Perhaps, if the adverse social effects outweigh the benefits, the particular project has to be abandoned. Given these critical provisions and considerable protection to the project-affected people, this bill is certainly a mile ahead of the centuries-old land law. The drafts of these bills underwent several revisions, and finally, the new law-the Right to Fair Compensation and Transparency in Land Acquisition, Rehabilitation and Resettlement Bill, 2013 was enacted by the state, and it came into effect on 1st January 2014 (Nielsen & Nilsen, 2015; Pal, 2018). In this context, it is essential to note that this LAA, 2013 also underwent certain amendments, including the provision of social impact assessment in the later years. Some exemptions have been granted by passing the new amendment bill in 2015, which is the Right to Fair Compensation and Transparency in Land Acquisition, Rehabilitation, and Resettlement (Second Amendment) Bill, 2015 (Government of India, 2015; Hoda, 2018; Nair, 2016; PRS India, 2015). In recent years, the loopholes and the complications of the Land Acquisition Act, 2013 has widely been reported in the news outlets and reports; again, the victims of such loopholes are marginal people, including Dalits and the tribals (Ghatak & Ghosh, 2013; Krishnan, 2017; Sonak, 2018).

3 The Marginalization of the Already Marginal Groups of Odisha: Interlinks Among Mining, Land Alienation, and the Denial of Community Rights

In India, one of the prime causes of ecological degradation has been the unequal structure of Indian society (Development Alternatives Group, 2017). Indian elites have pursued a form of development that intensifies resource extraction at the expense of the environment and the subaltern classes that depend on subsistence. Thus, the concept "environmentalism of the poor" (Martinez-Alier, 2014:239) focuses on social justice to defend land rights, and preserve livelihoods against mining, dams, land grabs, oil and gas exploitation of the poor, marginal, and the impoverished (Gadgil & Guha, 1994; Guha & Martinez-Alier, 1997; Martinez-Alier, 2002). The environmental agenda in modern India comprises two broad streams. The first focuses on protected areas and largely relies on the bureaucracy. Ironically, the bureaucracy often misuses its powers against the communities that live close to nature. The second focuses on protecting nature to safeguarding the livelihoods and health of the people. The environmental agenda should focus on the reassertion of people's rights over natural resources. It should be coupled with an action-oriented promotion of nature-friendly cooperative enterprises, including quarrying, mineral, and sand mining (Gadgil, 2016). The case that this chapter addresses the social and environmental justice concerns of the marginals through the "environmentalism of the poor."

Odisha, a mineral-rich state, is located along the east coast of India. Along with mineral resources, this State is endowed with diverse natural resources, including wetlands, 480 km of resources-rich coastal zones, and different big and small rivers (Government of Orissa, 2009; Pati, 2010) with a rich historical significance. Due to the geographical and resource-rich value, public and private industries have predominately occupied the mineral-rich regions of the State. These industries are continued to extract and export the minerals to international markets. Mining industries in Odisha contribute a large proportion to the State's economy and labor market (Adduci, 2017); Dash, 2007a, b; Jena, 2014). Particularly, in the postliberalization period, the export and consumption of minerals have largely intensified. The investors have started receiving several relaxations on expatriation of profit and leasing of mineral resources by the State (Dash, 2007a, b; Jena, 2014; Panda, 2014). National Aluminium Company (NALCO), UAIL, Vedanta, and Larsen & Toubro (L&T) are some of the influential companies operating in Odisha (Khatua & Stanley, 2006). Iron ore and manganese mining are the most common industrial projects in north Odisha, especially in Sundargarh and Keonjhar districts (Government of Odisha, n.d. (b)). Most mining companies in Odisha follow opencast mining systems and there has been a gross range of environmental violations observed. The mining sector in Odisha is continued to have several health-related complications on the marginal groups,[8] including tribals and Dalits, who predominately reside in the fifth schedule areas. It has led to their displacement, and finally, they have ended up in deprived living conditions (Amnesty International, 2016; Hota & Behera, 2016; Jena, 2014; Paltasingh & Satapathy, 2021; Ray & Saini, 2011; Sahu & Kumbhar, 2020). Research shows that opencast mining has damaged the green ecological systems and creates environmental pollution in the Koraput region of Odisha, the neighboring district of Rayagada (Debasree, 2015).

In the southern areas of Odisha, apart from land acquisition for various development projects, the tribal lands are continued to pass into the hands of non-tribals. The alienation of the lands of the tribals was much rigorous and massive in the tribal-dominated district, Koraput of Odisha. By the end of December 1999, about 841,916.50 acres of tribal land were acquired, which were the highest in the Koraput district (28,901.55 acres), and the next was Kandhamal district (15,864.55 acres) of Odisha (Malik, 2020, pp. 157–186). Hence, land alienation has been an important factor in the impoverishment and dispossession of tribals in Odisha.

The customary land governance patterns of the tribals of scheduled areas of Odisha were largely ignored both in colonial and postcolonial states, and it has had continuous repercussions on the land alienation of the tribals of Odisha. In the scheduled areas of Odisha, about 74% of the land is categorized as state-owned lands. Among

---

[8] Throughout the following portions of this chapter, we use the term "marginal groups" as an umbrella term to denote Dalits, tribals, and other backward communities reside across the study region, Rayagada district of Odisha.

this, 74% of the state-owned lands, 48% is forest land, and 26% is non-forest land. The state owns about three-fourth of the lands of the tribal-dominated districts of Odisha (as we noted earlier, it comes under the fifth schedule). It should be mentioned that a large proportion of the tribals of these districts are either come under the category of marginal landowners and landless tribals, and their livelihoods are largely dependent on subsistence agriculture-based on forest land, common land, forest, water bodies, grazing land and nonagricultural activities (Fernandes, 2009; Kumar et al., 2011).

The Indian Parliament enacted the Scheduled Tribes and Other Traditional Forest Dwellers (Recognition of Forest Rights) Act, 2006—popularly known as Forest Rights Act (FRA), 2006—to compensate for the historical injustices that have been faced by the tribals and other traditional forest dwellers and provide them legal rights over their traditional lands (Rights and Resources Initiative with Vasundhara, and Natural Resources Management Consultants, 2015; Amnesty International, 2016). Despite various progressive elements in this act to protect the rights of the tribals and other traditional forest dwellers, the implementation has largely been poor. Around just 1.6% of the lands that come under the category of community forest resources rights have legally been recognized. It must be noted that at least half of the forests of India come under community forest rights, and hence, they fall under the purview of the FRA. Accordingly, under the law, the respective villages have the right to govern and manage these forest lands. However, very little has been done so far (Rights and Resources Initiative with Vasundhara and Natural Resources Management Consultants, 2015). Hence, needless to say, the marginal groups of Odisha, including tribals and Dalits, who are largely dependent on CPRs, were affected by the LAA, 1894; however, a large majority of them have not been compensated under the FRA, 2006. The assessment report conducted by Rights and Resources Initiative with Vasundhara and Natural Resources Management Consultants (2015) has noted that about 32,711 villages of Odisha are eligible for community forest resources rights and a large majority of these villages are located in the tribals and upland districts of Odisha. Around 2360 villages of Rayagada have the potential to claim community forest rights. This is the region that this chapter focuses on. About 84% of the forest regions of the Rayagada district are eligible for Community Forest Resources rights recognition.

4   Research Sites and Methodology

Odisha has the fourth-largest bauxite reserve in the entire world, and it is the largest bauxite mineral producer in India. It has 59% of India's total bauxite deposits (Environmental Justice Atlas, 2019; Outlook, 2010). The research region of this study, the Kashipur block of the Rayagada district, is rich in bauxite minerals, which is one of the high qualities in the world (The Bastion, 2017). The minerals are deposited in different mountains (locally known as *malis,* such as Baphlimali, Patarmali, Sasubhumali, Kutrumali, Kodingamali, and Sijimali) across the Eastern Ghats of Odisha (Government of Orissa, 2010). Historically, these mountains and the surrounding forests are the sources of survival and habitat for the tribal communities, including Pengo Kondh, Kondh, Jhodia Paroja, and Lohara. Dom,[9] Medri, and Ghasi belonging to the SC category (Dalits) reside in these regions. For local people, these mountains and forests, including other CPRs, are not just livelihoods sources, but are also sacred, particularly for the tribal communities. According to the cosmology of the tribal communities, the hilltops are sacred. For example, the Baphlimali hill located in the Kashipur block of the Rayagada district is a scared deity to the tribal communities of these regions. They believe that their Goddess, *"Baphalai Budhi,"* resides here (Kumar, 2014; Mohanty, 2016; The Bastion, 2017).

The mineral-rich mountains have attracted the influential aluminium industries in the Rayagada district, including UAIL, NALCO, Vedanta, and L&T. The study villages that we covered for our study have been hit by UAIL; hence, our focus on this chapter is on UAIL. Utkal Alumina International Limited[10] was a consortium of four international companies, including TATA Group, Norsk Hydro of Norway, ALCAN of Canada, and INDAL of India. In 1993, UAIL made an undertaking with the state Government of Odisha for bauxite mining by setting up opencast mining plants in the Rayagada district of Odisha (including the hills) and planned to build a 100% export-oriented mining industry. However, this project had faced severe opposition and protests from the local people, including tribals and Dalits, resulting in the prolonged delay in the operationalization of the plants (Shome, 2020).

However, the state government was determined to continue to operate the mining plants in these regions. After the series of developments, setbacks, dissent, and protests, one of the peak moments was reached on 16 December 2000, when three peaceful protestors (tribals) against mining plants in this region were killed by police firing and around 30 people (mostly tribals) were severely injured in the Maikanch village of Kashipur block. However, the mining continued to operate (Satya, n.d; The Bastion, 2017). Kashipur anti-bauxite movement is one of the long and famous environmental justice movements of the marginal groups in the entire India (Das & Das, 2006; Environmental Justice Atlas, 2019; Kashipur Solidarity Tripod, n.d; Shome, 2020). Kashipur Solidarity Tripod provides extensive information about the sequence of events that had happened in the Kashipur anti-bauxite movement (For details: Kashipur Solidarity Tripod, n.d). As Manjit (2006) has observed, after all the series of resistance events, the state government of Odisha started providing more support

---

[9] The Scheduled Castes, Dom, Dombo, Duria Dom, Adhuria Dom, Adhuria Domb, are grouped together in the list of Scheduled Castes of the ST & SC Development, Minorities & Backward Classes of the Welfare Department of the Government of Odisha. For details: ST & SC Development, Minorities & Backward Classes, Welfare Department, Government of Odisha (2020). : https://stsc. odisha.gov.in/sites/default/files/2020-02/ScheduledCast_List.pdf.

As per the census special of Orrisa review (2010), the Scheduled Caste populations of the Rayagada district of Odisha come around 13.9%. Among them, the Dom caste has a large proportion (of about 76.1%). For details, Rayagada district, Orissa Review Census Special (2010). http://mag azines.odisha.gov.in/Orissareview/2010/December/engpdf/176-179.pdf.

[10] The recent website details of UAIL show that this limited is a 100% subsidiary of Aditya Birla Group company Hindalco, which is engaged in alumina refining (Utkal Alumina International Limited, n.d. https://www.adityabirla.com/businesses/companies/utkal-alumina-internati onal-limited).

to these multinational companies, resulting in the crush of protest movements and the mining plants of these regions continued to operationalize.

Against this backdrop, and for purposes of this chapter, we selectively focus on two villages of the Kashipur block of Rayagada district and discuss the social and environmental injustices that the marginal groups of these regions have been facing for the last two decades. After a rigorous pilot survey, the villages of Karanjakupakhal and Dimundi were chosen to conduct this research. These two villages fall under the Kashipur block of Rayagada district in Odisha. Kashipur block is a part of the KBK[11] region of Odisha (For details of the villages in Kashipur Block, Kashipur Block. (n.d.): http://kbk.nic.in/rayagadavillages/kashipurblock.pdf. These two study villages have been inhabited by Pengo Kondh, Kondh, Jhodia Paroja, and Dom communities for generations. Mostly, these communities consist of landless and marginal farmers, so their day-to-day life depend on CPRs, including common lands, rivers, villages' forests, sharecropping, and other nonagricultural activities. Their production and consumption activities are based on subsistence and barter systems (Sahu, 2019). In the study regions, we observed that Pengo Kondh, Kondh, and Jhodia Paroja are more dependent on CPRs than Dom communities.

From the pilot survey, it was observed that the communities of both the villages have largely been affected along with the neighboring villages. The Karanjakupakhal village is located foot area of the Baphlimali hill, where the UAIL was extracting bauxite, and the Dimundi is almost close to the Alumina refinery plant of UAIL. Such nearby locations with the plant have made the communities of both villages more vulnerable than the other nearby villages.

The fieldwork[12] was conducted in different phases during May 2018, June, and July 2019, and again the final fieldwork was conducted from October to November 2020 to complement our field findings. Given the aims and scope, we adopted qualitative techniques such as non-participant observations, open-ended interviews, and focus-group discussions (FGDs). Open interviews with eleven social activists of this region and seven academicians based in Odisha were conducted separately during

---

[11] In Odisha, the old districts of Koraput, Balangir, and Kalahandi are popularly known as KBK districts. Since 1992–1993, these KBK districts have been further divided into eight districts, which are as follows: Koraput, Malkangiri, Nabarangpur, Rayagada, Balangir, Subarnapur, Kalahandi, and Nuapada. These eight districts consist of several subdivisions, tahsils, and community development blocks. Our study region, the Kashipur block of Rayagada district, is a part of the KBK district. For more details: KBK district. (2010). http://www.kbk.nic.in/ These districts are one of the most backward regions of India in terms of health, education, chronic poverty, communication, and natural resources degradation. Along with that, social exclusion also prevails in these districts (Government of India, 2017; Dash, 2007a, b; Parida, 2008). Given this backwardness, the state and the union governments have emphasized these districts and provided special funds (Dash, 2007a, b). In recent years, the poverty range in the KBK regions are in the declined stage; however, it has been very slow (Parida, 2012).

[12] The first author of this chapter entirely conducted the fieldwork. The selection of the study villages, respondents, including key informants, was done completely by him. He conducted the interviews and focus-group discussions with the respondents in the state language, Odia. The native language of the first author of this chapter is Odia. Hence, the data collection did not face any language-related barriers.

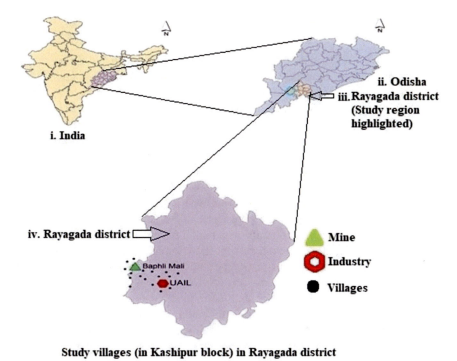

Fig. 1 Map showing study location. *Source* The first author. [Map is only for illustrative purpose; not to scale]

this period. All in all the sample population of this study totaled 171.[13] Out of the total respondents, 98 respondents were males, and 73 were females. Almost two-thirds (65%) of the respondents belonged to Scheduled Tribes (Pengo Kondh, Kondh, and Jhodia Paroja), 22% were Dalits (Scheduled Caste: Dom), and the remaining people belong to other backward castes (Gouda). A few respondents belong to general caste category (mostly, key informants).

Purposive sampling methods drove the selection of the respondents. To begin with, the first author explained the purpose and scope of the study to the respondents and received their oral consent to participate in the research. In some cases, the first author met with the respondents through the local village leader (informal), and he referred the potential respondents to him. Only those who gave their oral consent to participate in the research were included in the study (Fig. 1).

---

[13] The focus that this chapter covers essentially spans around development-induced displacement, CPRs, and environmental issues in the aftermath of the operation of the mining plant. Whereas our data collection also covered gender, culture, and other social aspects of the people, this chapter selectively provides the field findings, field insights, and field narratives along the lines of scope and relevance.

5 A Brief Profile of the Study Villages and Respondents

Karanjakupakhal is located at the foot area of the Baphlimali hill range of the Kashipur block. This village does not have proper infrastructure and public transportation facilities. The quality of the public healthcare and education facilities of this region is poor. Dimundi is located near to UAIL plant, and it is about 18 km away from the hills range. According to the local villagers, the quality of healthcare and education facilities of this village are relatively better than those of Karanjakupakhal, but nevertheless inadequate and of a low quality. This village also suffers from a lack of proper infrastructure and public transportation facilities.

The age group of all our respondents was 18 to 65. The key informants of our study had fair literacy levels, and some were well-educated (seven academicians). In contrast, a large majority of the population of Karanjakupakhal and Dimundi were either less or not educated at all. Although a few respondents had secondary school education and higher secondary education, the remaining respondents were low educated. As we noted earlier, across the study region, we could find five native tribal communities, which as follows: Pengo Kondh, Kondh, Jhodia Paroja, Dom, and Gouda. Among them, Pengo Kondh, Kondh, Jhodia Paroja are tribes (Scheduled Tribes), Dom (Dalit: Scheduled Caste), and Gouda (other backward class community). Despite the prevalence of caste bias, different caste groups across the research region had amicably been living without any conflicts. They mutually participate in local developmental activities and related decision-making processes. From the fieldwork, overall, we found that there were around 300 households in both villages and the total population was approximately 1800. About 60% of the people belonged to Scheduled Tribes, 35% belonged to SC, and the remaining 5% were other backward caste categories, that is, Gouda. Given this, both the study villages were home to marginal populations, and their livelihoods were entirely based on natural resources.

6 Findings and Discussions

The local people across the study region, irrespective of their caste backgrounds, considered themselves as "natives" and the original inhabitants of these lands (regions). Their villages, settlements, and CPRs had clearly defined boundaries based on customary arrangements, norms, and traditions. They shared and managed the existing CPRs through their traditional setups (primarily based on informal rules and customs). Since 1993, people belonging to both the study villages actively participated and organized the "people movement" against land acquisition and the construction of mining plants. Despite their protests and agitations, the land acquisition was made by the State Government of Odisha in these two villages from 1995 to 1997 by adopting the LAA, 1894. In Dimundi, the state acquired about 60 acres of common lands (public lands including public spaces of the villages) and about 484 acres of private lands/Patta lands. In Karanjakupakhal, the villagers lost their common lands of approximately 23 acres (Source: Field survey, July 2019). Even after allotting the lands for the UAIL, these regions had witnessed a series of protests and resistance from the local villagers. In the fieldwork, the respondents noted that they (including Dalit and tribal women) were registered under fabricated cases and jailed for some months. Similar incidents were also reported in the nearby villages. The police raided the village and chased the village men (protestors), and they hid in the nearby hills. Sarangi et al. (2005) elaborately discuss the plight of the marginal groups across Kashipur block in the second phase of repression by the state who stood against bauxite mining in their region. The accounts of the local respondents of the two villages on state-sponsored repression against them and the protested villages across the Kashipur block reflected the picture described by Sarangi et al. (2005) and Sahu (2019).

All the households of both study villages lost access to their common lands (including public spaces) and other CPRs that played an essential role in their lives and livelihoods. For decades, in the aftermath of the land acquisition, they have been facing several challenges to earn adequate income to manage their livelihoods. Landless and marginal adult villagers work as daily wage laborers in the construction sector in the local regions, and they earn a meager amount. In recent years, seasonal migration toward urban centers is gradually becoming high among them, particularly among the Dalits and the Other Backward Classes (OBC), due to ecological degradation and food insecurity crises. This phenomenon is increasingly being witnessed across Odisha (OTELP, 2007; Sharma et al., 2014). The tribals of these villages, other than the Dalits, are mainly reliant on agriculture and agriculture-related activities for their livelihoods. Currently, most families of these two villages are either landless or marginal landholders. Hence, they mainly depend on commons for their subsistence-based economy. A good proportion of them engage in nonagricultural activities, including livestock.

7 Continued Distress and Despair

The local respondents, irrespective of their socioeconomic backgrounds, shared their distressful experiences in losing livelihoods and facing displacement from their ancestral lands. Respondents shared their experiences of hearing the traumatic experiences from the marginal people of their neighboring district, Koraput. In the early 1980s, NALCO established three operations (including a bauxite mining project and the construction of the alumina refinery complex) in the Koraput district by acquiring thousands of acres of lands of the marginal people. This triggered a series of consequences including land, social, health, resettlement, rehabilitation, and psychological issues (Jena, 2015; Stanley, 1996). The people of these two affected villages did not receive proper compensation from the mining plant or the state, and it has pushed them to live in distressful situations. By stating this, a few respondents, particularly, elderly respondents noted that the distressful situations they have been facing are nothing less than the distressful lives of the Koraput marginal people. The local respondents of Dimundi village stated that they had already lost their grazing lands, traditional roads, cremation grounds, sacred spaces, water resources (from the nearby stream), and vegetation due to land acquisition. In a similar vein, Karanjakuphakal respondents noted that they too had lost access to nearby forests and lost their grazing lands, common places, sacred spaces, and vegetation lands. Almost all of them shared the fear of losing their homes, agriculture fields, temples, deities, schools, *Dhangadabosa*, and *Dhangdibosa* (dormitories of boys and girls) in the future and expressed their precarious life (Naik, 2021). They had already experienced that displacement inevitably breaks their close kinship relations and community ties. The fear of further losing their sacred spaces and deities are high among the tribal community people, particularly elderly tribal women.

A female respondent, aged around 55 and a member of the Pengo Kondh community, said the following:

> Our Baphlibudhi (deity) has been facing threats from this extractive plant on the Baphlimali hill. Since time immemorial, the deity is continued to live on this hill range, blessing us by giving us resources (including crops, water, and so on) and keeping us safe from natural disasters and other anti-social elements. We regularly worship our beloved deity every January. Everyone in our community is aware that our faith and traditional practices have been facing destruction in recent decades. The outsiders (indicating the state, officers, and the private sectors) do not understand our relationship with the hill and deity. Who can understand us? Who will protect us and our generations and all our resources? (Village: Karanjakupakhal. Data collection: July 2019).

8 The Question of Social Justice to the Marginal Groups

The discussions with the tribals and the Dalits across the study regions clearly show that they are continued to face the brunt of land acquisition in multiple aspects. In the words of a Pengo Kondh tribal woman aged around forty is of the following:

> When I was an adolescent girl, my social life in this village was quite good. We used to play in these lands with our community song and share small stories amongst us. Our parents used to collect different minor forest produces for family maintenance from the Baphlimali hill. After the operation of this mining company, we have been banned and restricted by the company's security guard. In recent years, we have largely lost our social lives (Place: Karanjakupakhal, Data collection: July 2019).

The interviews and discussions with the tribal and Dalit respondents across the study regions show their strong and special connections with the "place" and the surrounding environments. The identity, culture, and livelihoods of the local villagers, irrespective of their caste backgrounds, are intimately associated with the "place," including land, forest, and water bodies. According to them, alienating them from this "place" is the worst form of injustice against them.

For example, a middle-aged Dalit respondent explained his association with his village and the CPRs, and how injustice was meted out to them in the name of "development":

Initially, the corporation provided us with three months of semi-skilled training. Around May 2009, after the training, I got a job offer letter from the company office. However, up until now, I have not received any such employment-related hearings from the company. As you can see, it mainly offers jobs to the outsiders, not to the local people. We, the native people, are the ones who have given the price to such 'development' by losing our common and private lands (Village: Dimundi, Data collection: June 2019).

A few households that few households that belong to the OBC (Other Backward Classes) communities across the two study villages have also raised such concerns. For example, a respondent who belongs to the Gouda community aged around 40 stated the following:

We OBC (Other Backward Classes) community people have already lost good income that we used to earn in the last decades since we lost our CPRs as a part of land acquisition processes. It is not an easy task to get job opportunities from the mining plant. Only those who have a 'strong' voice and 'networks' can get it. In recent years, the income that we earn is meagre. As you can see, there are no such alternative livelihoods opportunities in this region other than entirely dependent on the lands and CPRs left by the mining plant. Our lives are full of uncertainties, and so our children lives are (Place: Karanjakupakhal, Data collection: October 2020).

9 Alienation of Women from CPRs and Social Injustice

In rural India, the women traditionally lack private ownership of their family-owned lands. Due to this, the women have largely been dependent on CPRs for their everyday activities to manage their families and herself. The loss of CPRs has led to the peasant, tribal, Dalit women's impoverishment and the women belonging to other tribal forest-dependent communities (Agarwal, 1998). Chinara (2013) has argued that the loss and degradation of CPRs lead to the complications of gender relations, resulting in the increased work burden to women. Such an increase in the work burden of women is visible across our study regions. This is exceptionally higher among the tribal women than the Dalit women.

In tribal households, traditionally women play the leading role in collecting edible leaves and other related materials from CPRs; also, they play equal roles and labor in agriculture. In the riverbeds, the tribal women of our study villages collect *kochida sag*,[14] *gad gonga, modreng, lebuka, hatrenga, elmiti, joba,* and *mutmuli sag.* In the forests, they collect *vorda sag, and chil.* In the plain regions, they collect *ghurdi sag, kangi, kochida, kena,* and *chakunda sag.* The *kuchida sag* is available in both riverbed and plain regions. They also collect roots such as *kulikanda, chergakanda, pit kanda, mugakanda,* and *solpakanda* for their food. Both tribal men and women share almost equal roles and responsibilities in collecting the edible roots; however, the women spend extra time in preparing the food. They noted that many such roots, leaves, and wild vegetables (that we noted earlier), which are a part of their traditional food sources, have gradually disappeared after the operation of mining activities. In

---

[14] The italicized words of this paragraph indicate the local names of edible roots, lentils, and green leaves. Tribal communities across these regions traditionally eat this, and they consider that these are rich in nutrients.

the contemporary period, they rarely get such edible roots, leaves, and vegetables, which directly and indirectly has increased their work burden, expenses, and reduced their nutrients intake. These findings also reflect the discussions of Naik (2012) on the impoverishment of tribal women in the Kashipur block.

In this context, it is noteworthy to highlight that the Union government of India and the State government of Odisha have been implementing several tribal welfare schemes[15] and providing special attention to the tribal-dominated districts of Odisha since independence. Nevertheless, the development schemes have failed to offer a balanced diet and to meet the demands of the basic necessities of the tribals (Rath, 2006:15–62).

10   The Question of Environmental Justice of the Marginal People

Before the 1990s, the landless and marginal farmers (belonging to Dalit and other backward caste households) across the study regions used to do shifting cultivation in the foot of the hill range. They also used to catch fish and crabs in the nearby water bodies. Apart from that, CPRs also provided them with edible leaves, flowers, fruits, and other non-timber forest products, and supported them in agriculture and agriculture-related activities and livestock. That was highly beneficial to them in multiple ways to have nature-based sustainable living, and it ensured their food security. For this, their common lands and CPRs acted as a pillar to support their everyday livelihoods. Before the land acquisition, the local people produced 30–40 bags of paddy in an acre of land; after land acquisition, it went down to 10–15 bags. The land-owned households of the villages gradually avoided paddy cultivation due to the threat of siltation. A respondent told us that they could not cultivate over the last three years due to siltation. The opencast mining plant regularly releases harmful solid effluents, such as red mud, and it has caused severe damages to their fertile lands. The formation of "red mud" due to the bauxite mining activity in the Karanjakupakhal of Kashipur block has recently been reported in the news outlet by highlighting similar local voices (Mohanty, 2017). The women across the study regions shared their other issues along with environmental pollution and ecological degradation that are visible. A Dalit woman aged around 45 of the Dimundi village expressed her despair:

> The plant is located very close to us and regularly discharges chemical dust; in recent years, we are periodically getting health-related issues, and it has become a common incident. The women's workloads have vastly increased after the loss of our CPRs (Place: Dimundi, Data collection: June 2019).

---

[15] A few examples of the micro project agencies that work for the development of the Scheduled Tribes of Odisha: Juang Development Agency (JDA), Bonda Development Agency (BDA), and Dongria Kondh Development Agency (DKDA).

Land Acquisition and a Question of "Justice": Voices ...

In June 2019, while conducting the focus-group discussions with the villagers of Karanjakupakhal, a huge amount of dust emerged from the hill, and it slowly spreads down in the village regions. One elderly respondent of Karanjakupakhal village has narrated the problems in the following words:

> It happens almost every day on the hill, and just after the blasting, the tremendous dust it produces goes across the hill, and then it spreads here (pointing the village), [into the] water bodies, and across all of our CPRs. In the beginning, we were alienated from our lands and CPRs. After facing such alienation from our resources, we have started facing air and water pollution that gives a big threat to our very existence in this land (Place: Karanjakupakhal, Data collection: June 2019).

Both the study villages have been severely affected by air and water pollution, which has had adverse effects on their everyday lives. The issues of Karanjakupakhal village are different from Dimundi. The mining plant removes the topsoil before extracting bauxite and dumps it at the hill's edge. During monsoons, the dumped soil mixes with rainwater and runs downhill over the landscape. Karanjakupakhal is located at the foot of the hill area; it has siltation at its bathing ghats, agricultural fields, and public spaces. Due to unplanned dumping, it damages their streams and has caused ecological degradation and water pollution. The villagers used to get small fish and crabs in the perennial stream; it was their prime source to combat hunger, and it provided nutrition support to their entire households. The local respondents of Karanjakupakhal said old fishing practices no more exist after dumping the soil at the edge of the Baphlimali hill (Fig. 2).

According to accounts of local respondents of both the villages, such blasting activities are prime sources of dust and air pollution across their regions. Due to chemical contamination, they frequently get itching problems and other health ailments, including breathing issues and eye pain. The elderly respondents of Dimundi village highlighted the untimed death of their fellow villagers. As he pointed out, from 2013 to 2017, seven local villagers aged 19–40 died untimely. Indicating their untimely death, the respondent linked it to growing air and water pollution of their regions. Further, the respondent stated they had already complained to the responsible government offices; however, the state took no proper actions.

Along with air and water pollution, the respondents shared their worries about noise pollution, and it has had far-reaching effects on their everyday lives. Expressing her concerns, a tribal woman of Dimundi village noted the following:

> As you can see, the distance between our houses and the mining refinery plant is not too far. Due to this, noise pollution has become a part of our lives. It is particularly affecting our children; many of us, middle-aged and elderly women have already had complaints about the growing loss of our hearing capacity. It also affects our cattle in multiple ways (Place: Dimundi. Data collection: July 2019).

Fig. 2 The topsoil of the Baphlimali hill is dumped on the hill's edge, which is located upstream of the Karanjakupakhal village[16]

11 Conclusion

The acquisition of the native lands and CPRs of the marginal communities by the state and other actors through forceful ways is a global issue, particularly in the global south. Over the past few decades, their respective governments have forcefully displaced the marginal communities of the global south for various development-related projects, including urban development projects, hydroelectricity projects, mining, proclamation of protected areas, and highway constructions (Cernea, 2000; Ribeiro, 2015; Thomas, 2002). Hence, the alienation of the marginal groups from their ancestral lands is not something that is confined only to the Indian subcontinent and to the state of Odisha. Over the past few decades, there has been a growing body of literature related to issues such as land alienation, land grabbing, and complications in land access across the developing and underdeveloped world, including various regions of India (Rao et al., 2006; Cotula et al., 2008; Abbink, 2011; German et al., 2013; Olanya, 2013; Aha & Ayitey, 2017). The land acquisition processes across the tribal-dominated regions of India have had long-lasting adverse effects on the lives of the marginal groups. According to Martinez Alier (2014), the massive protests

---

[16] This is unplanned dumping and lack of treatment of topsoil as a part of the mining activities of UAIL. During rainy days, the dumbed soil mixes with rainwater and causes severe pollution on the lands and water bodies of the village. *Source*: The first author collected the information while conducting the field survey in July 2019 at Karanjakupakhal village.

of the poor and indigenous communities are not just in terms of their economic and livelihoods interests, but also to protect their territorial rights and cultural and religious symbols.

Though this chapter provides shallow theoretical debates on social justice, environmentalism, and environmental justice, the case study that we presented here, focusing on the Kashipur block of Odisha, provides certain essential insights and revelations of the land acquisition processes that happened in recent decades across Odisha (and also in other regions of India) and the continuing cascading effects on the "justice" of the marginal groups across these regions. The land acquisition processes in the Kashipur block of Odisha started by subverting the flawed (colonial) land acquisition act and forest policies. The state and the transnational corporations, directly and indirectly, are responsible for the past complications. But it was implemented in the garb of "development" and "public purpose."

On the one hand, it is easy to make the state and the transnational corporations the scapegoat for all these past and ongoing social and environmental injustices and complications. However, the reality is far more complicated. The deeper we delve into this, the more it becomes complicated and strange. The developmental policies of Odisha are in line with the national policy, which is growth-oriented development rather than distributive justice. Hence, the economic growth of Odisha is largely biased toward urban centers and it is dependent on primary sectors, including mining (Panda, 2017).

The industrial policies of Odisha in 1996 and 2001 were biased toward higher private investments. The state systematically simplified the procedures through the policies by forming new governmental institutions to clear the fast-track projects (industrial projects including mining) through a single-window system. These institutions were given authority to deal with land acquisition and other related procedures, including sharing information and so on. The state policy believes that the increased investment in the mining sector would generate more employment opportunities and overall economic growth. With glaring disparities across regions and communities, the increase in the state's overall economic growth has seemed genuine in the past decades. For example, the recent Odisha economic survey 2020–2021 shows that the revenue collection from the mining sectors in 2019–2021 was around INR 1102 million. This is a massive growth of 90% when compared with the period 2015–2016. However, we should also note that it comes with a price. The same report says that during 2019–2020, around 3008 hectares of forest land were diverted for 22 developmental projects, including eight mining projects (Government of Odisha, 2021; Vasundhara, 2005). In this context, it is also essential to highlight that, with every rise in investment and production in the mining sector, there has been a decline in the percentage of employment generations. For example, the mineral production in the mining sector of the year 1991–1992 was 372 lakh tons, and it provided employment to 68,886 persons; whereas, the year 2001–2002 witnessed the production of minerals in 749.79 lakh tons, but it employed 45,135 persons, which reveals the myth of employment generations from large-scale projects (Vasundhara, 2005). Odisha is continued to remain low in the human development index. However, it made a big jump in the overall economic growth in the post-reform period and is doing relatively better in the human development index range compared to the past decades. The primary sector, including mining and quarrying, contributes much to the economic development, and it has witnessed high growth after 2003–2004. In contrast, its contribution to eliminating inequality in the state is declining (Sahoo & Paltasingh, 2019).

The Kashipur case that this chapter focuses on shows that the "development model" propagated by the state has least contributed to the well-being, employment opportunities, and the overall local development of the region. However, we do not mean to suggest a "radical change" that is far from reality. It is undeniable that the less economically developed states of India certainly require overall economic growth; the mining sector has largely contributed to it. However, it has to be coupled with the sustainability, social, and environmental justice of the marginal people. The field insights coupled with narratives highlight the distressing lives of the marginal groups across the region, and they hear the word "development" with fear and suspicion, which is certainly not a good indication in the long run, not just for this state, but also for the entire nation. Mainly, Odisha, one of the states that has a large proportion (around 40%) of the depressed population (SC and ST) to the total population. About 83% of the people are based on rural, hilly, and coastal regions where natural resources are central to their lives, livelihoods, culture, and traditions. The development model of the state and nation needs to be reconceptualized on the lines of individual and community rights of the locals. There is a strong need to perform credible land reforms for the masses of depressed and marginal groups of the state to manage their self-sustained lives. This is also applicable to all the regions of India that fall under the fifth schedule category.

Acknowledgments The first author of this chapter, Mohon Kumar Naik, wish to thank his doctoral supervisor, Prof. Sarmistha Pattanaik [Associate Professor, Department of HSS, Indian Institute of Technology Bombay] for her support. He also wishes to thank the villagers of Karanjakupakhal and Dimundi for their interest and cooperation in participating in this study.

References

Abbink, J. (2011). 'Land to the foreigners': Economic, legal, and sociocultural aspects of new land acquisition schemes in Ethiopia. *Journal of Contemporary African Studies, 29*(4), 513–535. https://doi.org/10.1080/02589001.2011.603213

Adduci, M. (2017). Neo-liberalism, mining and labour in the Indian state of Odisha: Outlining a political economy analysis. *Journal of Contemporary Asia, 47*(4), 596–614. https://doi.org/10.1080/00472336.2016.1277252

Agarwal, B. (1998). Environmental management, equity and ecofeminism: Debating India's experience. *Journal of Peasant Studies, 25*(4), 55–95. https://doi.org/10.1080/03066159808438684

Aha, B., & Ayitey, J. Z. (2017). Biofuels and the hazards of land grabbing: Tenure (in) security and indigenous farmers' investment decisions in Ghana. *Land Use Policy, 60*, 48–59. https://doi.org/10.1016/j.landusepol.2016.10.012

Land Acquisition and a Question of "Justice": Voices ...

Amnesty International (2016). *India: "When land is lost, do we eat coal"? Coal mining and violations of adivasi rights in India.* Amnesty International. Retrieved November 28, 2020, from https://www.amnesty.org/en/documents/asa20/4391/2016/en/

Barik, R. K. (2006). Faculty planning in a tribal region: The Dandakranya development authority. In G. C. Rath (Ed.), *Tribal development in India, the contemporary debate* (pp. 112–132). SAGE.

Beck, T., & Ghosh, M. G. (2000). Common property resources and the poor: Findings from West Bengal. *Economic and Political Weekly, 35*(3), 147–153. https://www.jstor.org/stable/4408824

Cernea, M. M. (2000). Risk, safeguards and reconstruction: A model for population displacement and resettlement. *Economic and Political Weekly, 35*(41), 3659–3678. https://www.jstor.org/stable/4409836

Chinara, M. (2013). The new land acquisition bill, 2011: A historical and gender perspective. *Orissa Economic Journal, 45*(1&2), 73–83. http://www.orissaeconomicjournal.in/Journal/Journal_2013.pdf

Cotula, L., Dyer, N., & Vermeulen. S. (2008). *Fuelling exclusion? The biofuels boom and poor people's access to land.* International Institute for Environment and Development and Food and Agriculture Organization of the United Nations. Retrieved April 10, 2021, from http://www.indiaenvironmentportal.org.in/files/12551IIED.pdf

Das, A., & Das, V. (2006). *Chronicle of a struggle and other writings. Agragamee Kashipur: Agragamee publication.* Agragamee Publication. Retrieved December 30, 2020, from http://sanhati.com/wp-content/uploads/2007/08/kashipur_chronicle.pdf

Das, V. (2001). Mining Bauxite, Maiming people. *Economic and Political Weekly, 36*(28), 2612–2614. https://www.jstor.org/stable/4410849?seq=1#metadata_info_tab_contents

Dash, L. N. (2007a). Economics of mining in Orissa review. *Orissa Review.* Retrieved February 14, 2021, from http://magazines.odisha.gov.in/Orissareview/nov-2007a/engpdf/Pages69-76.pdf

Dash, S.P. (2007b). Development and poverty in an Indian state: A study of KBK districts of Orissa. *Social Change, 37*(2), 76–98. https://doi.org/10.1177/004908570703700206

Debasree, D. (2015). Development-induced displacement: Impact on Adivasi women of Odisha. *Community Development Journal, 50*(3), 448–462. https://doi.org/10.1093/cdj/bsu053

Desai, M. (2011, June 25-July 8). Land acquisition law and the proposed changes. *Economic and Political Weekly, 46*(26/27), 95–100. https://www.jstor.org/stable/pdf/23018639.pdf

Development Alternatives Group (2017). *Addressing inequalities and environmental degradation in the Indian economy exploring policy implications for achieving the SDGs.* Retrieved December 30, 2020, from https://www.devalt.org/images/L2_ProjectPdfs/IndiaCaseStudy.pdf?Tid=177

Einbinder, N. (2017). *Dams, displacement and development. perspectives from Rio Negro, Guatemala.* Springer.

Environmental Justice Atlas. (2019, March 24). *Kashipur anti-bauxite mining movement, India.* Retrieved January 13, 2021, from https://ejatlas.org/conflict/human-rights-and-environmental-violation-for-bauxite-mining-in-the-baphlimali-hills-of-kashipur-rayagada-district-odisha

Fernandes, W. (2001). Development-induced displacement and sustainable development. *Social Change, 3*(1), 87–103. http://citeseerx.ist.psu.edu/viewdoc/download?doi=10.1.1.932.8648&rep=rep1&type=pdf

Fernandes, W. (2009). Displacement and alienation from common property resources. In L. Mehta (Ed.), *Displacement by development confronting marginalisation and gender injustice* (pp. 105–132). Sage. https://www.nesrc.org/Studies/05_Lyla_Mehta_Ch-05.pdf

Gadgil, M., & Guha, R. (1994). Ecological conflicts and the environmental movement in India. *Development and Change, 25*(1), 101–136. https://doi.org/10.1111/j.1467-7660.1994.tb00511.x

Gadgil, M. (2016). Today's environmentalism time for constructive cooperative action. *Economic and Political Weekly, 51*(46), 57–61. https://www.researchgate.net/publication/310619587_Today's_environmentalism_Time_for_constructive_cooperative_action

German, L., Schoneveld, G., & Mwangi, G. (2013). Contemporary processes of large-scale land acquisition in Sub-Saharan Africa: Legal deficiency or elite capture of the rule of law? *World Development, 48*, 1–18. https://doi.org/10.1016/j.worlddev.2013.03.006

Ghatak, M., & Ghosh, P. (2013). *The land acquisition Act is deeply flowed.* Ideas for India. Retrieved January 27, 2021, from https://www.ideasforindia.in/topics/macroeconomics/the-land-acquisition-act-is-deeply-flawed.html

Government of India. (2014). *Forest Rights Act, 2006, Act rules and guidelines.* Ministry of Tribal Affairs, Government of India. Retrieved February 3, 2021, from https://tribal.nic.in/FRA/data/FRARulesBook.pdf

Government of India. (2015, May 30). *The Right to Fair Compensation and Transparency in Land Acquisition, Rehabilitation and Resettlement (Second Amendment) Bill, 2015.* Department of Land Resources, Government of India. Retrieved June 10, 2021, from https://dolr.gov.in/sites/default/files/RFCTLARR%20Act%20%28Amendment%29%20Second%20Ordinance%2C%202015.pdf

Government of India. (2017). *National Commission for Scheduled Tribes. No. 18/1/2017-coord.* Government of India National Commission for Scheduled Tribes. Retrieved January 21, 2021, from https://ncst.nic.in/sites/default/files/2017/Office_Order/798.pdf

Government of India. (n.d.). *II provisions relating to STs- ministry of tribal affairs.* Ministry of Tribal Affairs, Government of India. Retrieved January 23, 2021, from https://tribal.nic.in/download/CLM/CLM_Const/2.pdf

Government of Meghalaya. (n.d.). *The Land Acquisition Act, 1894.* Revenue and Disaster Management Department, Government of Meghalaya. Retrieved November 19, 2021, from https://meg revenuedm.gov.in/acts/land-aquisition-act-1894.pdf.

Government of Odisha (n.d. (a)). ST & SC Development, Minorities & Backward classes Welfare Department, Government of Odisha. Retrieved January 21, 2021, from http://stscodisha.gov.in/Aboutus.asp?GL=abt&PL=1

Government of Odisha. (n.d. (b)). *Mineral based industries.* Department of Steel & Mines, Government of Odisha. Retrieved January 3, 2021, from https://odishaminerals.gov.in/MiningInOdisha/MineralBasedIndustries

Government of Orissa. (2009). *Compendium of mineral resources of Orissa.* Department of Steel and Mines, Government Orissa. Retrieved December 30, 2020, from https://www.odishaminerals.gov.in/sites/Download/Compendium_of_Mineral_Resources_in_Odisha.pdf

Government of Orrisa. (2010). *Bauxite resources in Orissa.* Directorate of Geology, Department of Steel and Mines, Government of Orissa. Retrieved December 30, 2020, from https://www.odisha minerals.gov.in/sites/Download/BauxiteResources_Orissa.pdf

Government of Odisha. (2021, February). Odisha economic survey 2020–21. Planning and Convergence Department, Directorate of Economics and Statistics, Government of Odisha. Retrieved March 15, 2021, from http://www.desorissa.nic.in/pdf/Odisha%20Economic%20Survey%202020-21-1.pdf

Grotius, H., & Kelsey, F.W. (1925). *De jure belli ac pacis libri tres. Vol. 2, The translation.* Clarendon Press. Retrieved January 3, 2021, from https://www.worldcat.org/title/de-jure-belli-ac-pacis-libri-tres-vol-2-the-translation/oclc/25387916

Guha, R., & Martinez-Alier. J. (1997). *Varieties of environmentalism: Essays north and south.* Oxford University Press.

Hoda, A. (2018). *Land use and land acquisition laws in India.* Working paper No. 361. Indian Council for Research on International Economic. Relations. Retrieved December 14, 2020, from https://icrier.org/pdf/Working_Paper_361.pdf

Hota, B., & Behera, B. (2016). Opencast coal mining and sustainable local livelihoods in Odisha, India. *Mineral Economics, 29,* 1–3. https://doi.org/10.1007/s13563-016-0082-7

Jena, D. (2014). Mining and the economy: An empirical inquest with special reference to Odisha. *Orissa Economic Journal, 46*(1&2), 108–123. http://www.orissaea.in/Journal/Journal_2014.pdf#page=108

Jena, S. K. (2015). A multi-dimensional contemplation into mining induced displacement and resettlement (MIDR)—A case study of NALCO, Damanjodi, In A. K. Mohapatra, K. C. Das., & S. K. Jena (Eds.), *Good governance and economic growth publisher* (pp. 1–23). Regal publications.

Jenkins, R. (2014). India's SEZ policy: The political implications of 'permanent reform.' In R. Jenkins, L. Kennedy, & P. Mukhopadhyay (Eds.), *Power, policy and protest: The politics of India's special economic zones* (pp. 39–71). Oxford University Press.

Jodha, N. (1986). Common property resources and rural poor in dry regions of India. *Economic and Political Weekly, 21*(27), 1169–1181. https://www.jstor.org/stable/4375858

Jodha, N. S. (1990, Jun 30). Rural common property resources: Contributions and crisis. *Economic and Political Weekly, 25*(26). A65–A78. https://www.jstor.org/stable/pdf/4396434.pdf

Kashipur Block. (n.d.). *Name of the block: Kashipur.* KBK Districts. Retrieved February 15, 2021, from http://kbk.nic.in/rayagadavillages/kashipurblock.pdf

Kashipur Solidarity Tripod (n.d). Kashipur Solidarity. Retrieved December 27, 2020, from https://kashipursolidarity.tripod.com/index.html

KBK district. (n.d.). *Koraput, Malkangiri, Nabarangpur, Balangir, Subaranpur, Kalahandi, & Nuapada.* KBK Districts. Retrieved February 15, 2021, from http://www.kbk.nic.in/

Khatua, S. & Stanley, W. (2006). Ecological debt: A case study from Orissa, India. In A.K. Peralta (Ed.), *Ecological debt the peoples of the South are the creditors, cases from Ecuador, Mozambique, Brazil, and India.* Troika Press. Retrieved January 16, 2021, from http://www.deudaecologica.org/publicaciones/Chapter5%28125-168%29.pdf

Kothari, S. (1996). Whose nation? The displaced as victims of development. *Economic and Political Weekly, 31*(24), 1476–1485. http://www.jstor.org/stable/4404269

Krishnan, V. (2017). Land acquisition against the violation of 'development'. *Frontline India's National Magazine.* Retrieved December 18, 2020, from https://frontline.thehindu.com/social-issues/against-the-violence-of-development/article9834760.ece

Kumar, K., Choudhury, P. R., Sarangi, S., Mishra, P., & Behera, S., (2011). *A status of adivasis/indigenous people land series-2, Orissa.* Aakar Books. Retrieved December 23, 2020, from https://www.researchgate.net/publication/232062516_Status_of_AdivasisIndigenous_Peoples_Land_Series_-_Orissa

Kumar, K. (2014). Confronting extractive capital: Social and environmental movements in Odisha. *Economic and Political Weekly, 49*(14), 66–73. https://www.jstor.org/stable/24479385

Lobo, L. (2014). Land acquisition and displacement among tribals, 1947–2004. In A. Shah & J. Pathak (Eds.), *Tribal development in western India* (pp. 285–309). Routledge.

Malik, S. K. (2020). *Land acquisition and politics of tribal exploitation in India: Special focus on tribal movement in Koraput district of Odisha.* Springer Nature Singapore

Manjit, D. (2006). The peoples' movement in Kashipur. *Revolutionary Democracy,* 12,2. Retrieved January 17, 2021, from https://revolutionarydemocracy.org/rdv12n2/kashipur.htm

Martinez-Alier, J. (2002). *Environmentalism of the poor: A study of ecological conflicts and valuation.* Edward Elgar.

Martinez-Alier, J. (2014). The environmentalism of the poor (Critical review). *Geoforum, 54,* 239–241. https://doi.org/10.1016/j.geoforum.2013.04.019

McDowell, C. (1996). *Understanding impoverishment. The consequences of development-induced displacement.* Berghahn.

Mohanty, A. (2016). In Odisha, more tribal voices against mining. *India Together.* Retrieved January 13, 2021, from https://www.indiatogether.org/in-odisha-more-tribal-voices-against-mining-environment

Mohanty, A. (2017). Photo essay: Bauxite mining a curse for adivasis in Odisha's Baphlimali. *The Wire.* Retrieved January 27, 2021, from https://thewire.in/rights/photo-essay-bauxite-mining-curse-adivasis-odishas-baphlimali

Naik, I. C. (2012). Tribal women and environmental movement in India: A study of Kashipur block of Odisha. *Voice of Dalit, 5*(2), 153–161. https://doi.org/10.1177/0974354520120202

Naik, M. K. (2021). Interface of gender and caste in the resettlement and rehabilitation of displaced women in the Rayagada district of Odisha. *The Oriental Anthropologist, 21*(2), 311–328. https://doi.org/10.1177/0972558X211032369

Nair, R. (2016, March). Judicial interpretation of the land acquisition Act in India: LAA, 1894 to RFCTLARR Act, 2013. *ASCI Journal of Management, 45*(1), 17–44. http://asci.org.in/wp-con tent/uploads/2020/07/AJoM_45-1-Mar-2016.pdf#page=23

Narayanan, S. (2021). Food security from free collection of foods: Evidence from India. *Food Policy, 100*(101998), 1–13. https://doi.org/10.1016/j.foodpol.2020.101998

Nielsen, K. B., & Nilsen, A. G. (2015). Law struggles and hegemonic processes in neoliberal India: Gramscian reflection on land acquisition legislation. *Globalization, 12*(2), 203–216. https://doi.org/10.1080/14747731.2014.937084

NITI Aayog. (n.d.). Fifth schedule areas. NITI Aayog. Retreived November 15, 2021, from https://niti.gov.in/planningcommission.gov.in/docs/sectors/sj/List%20of%20Fifth%20Scheduled%20Area.doc.

Olanya, D. R. (2013). Indigenous peoples and customary land rights: Public policy discourse of large-scale land acquisitions in East Africa. *US–China Law Review, 10*(6), 620.

Omvedt, G. (2012, July). *Dalit or Scheduled Caste: A terminological choice. Seeking Begumpura— a blog by Gail Omvedt.* Retrieved January 13, 2021, from https://seekingbegumpura.wordpress.com/2012/07/08/dalit-or-scheduled-caste-a-terminological-choice/

OTELP. (2007). *Orissa tribal empowerment and livelihoods programme: Assessment survey for designing comprehensive livelihoods strategy.* KCD, Bhubaneswar; Knowledge trust Bhubaneswar; NRMC New Delhi. Odisha Tribal Empowerment & Livelihoods Programme (OTELP). Retrieved January 23, 2021, from http://otelp.org/downloads/implementation_process/strategy_papers/livelihoods_strategy_manual.pdf

Outlook. (2010, August 25). Orissa has 4th largest bauxite reserve in the world. *Outlook.* Retrieved March 5, 2021, from https://www.outlookindia.com/newswire/story/orissa-has-4th-largest-bauxite-reserve-in-the-world/691504

Pal, M. (2018). Land acquisition and "fair compensation" of the "project affected" scrutiny of the law and its interpretation. In A.P. D'Costa, and A. Chakraborty (Eds.), *The Land Question in India: State, Dispossession, and Capitalist Transition* (pp. 151–175). Oxford University Press.

Paltasingh, T., & Satapathy, J. (2021). Unbridled coal extraction and concerns for livelihood: Evidences from Odisha, India. *Mineral Economics, 34,* 491–503. https://doi.org/10.1007/s13563-021-00272-5

Panda, H. (2017). Development challenges and prospects in Odisha. *Centurion Journal of Multidisciplinary Research, 2*(1), 47–59.

Panda, S. C. (2014, January-June & July-December). How is Odisha doing? A critical assessment of economic performance of the state in the last two decades. *Orissa Economic Journal, 46*(1&2), 14–27. http://www.orissaea.in/Journal/Journal_2014.pdf#page=108

Parasuraman, S. (1999). *The development dilemma displacement in India.* Macmillan Press Ltd.

Parida, N. (2008). *Chronic poverty and hunger in KBK region of Orissa: Identifying causes in the perspective of a case study in watershed development project in Nabarangpur district.* Institute of Social Studies.

Parida, S. P. (2012). Poverty and inequality of KBK region of rural Odisha: A comparative analysis. *International Journal of Social Science Tomorrow, 1*(4), 1–8. Retrieved August 12, 2021, from https://www.researchgate.net/publication/239937668_Poverty_and_Inequality_of_KBK_Region_of_Rural_Odisha_A_Comparative_Analysis

Pati, B. K. (2010). *Water resources of Odisha issues and challenges.* Regional Centre for Development Cooperation. Retrieved February 12, 2021, from https://rcdcindia.org/PbDocument/8adc57865d55134-7374-401a-97b4-118393445fd2Water%20Resource%20Booklet%20FINAL.pdf

Patnaik, S. (2007). Neoliberalism and rural poverty in India. *Economic and Political Weekly, 42*(30), 3132–3150. https://www.jstor.org/stable/4419844

Prasad, N. P., Vakulabharanam, V., Laxminarayanan, K., & Kilaru, S. (2012). Tragedy of the Commons Revisited (II) mining in tribal habitats of Araku valley. *Economic and Political Weekly, 47*(42), 14–17. https://www.jstor.org/stable/41720260

Land Acquisition and a Question of "Justice": Voices … 347

PRS India. (2015). *Land acquisition: An overview of proposed amendments to the law.* PRS Legislative Research. Retrieved January 21, 2021, from https://prsindia.org/theprsblog/land-acquisition-an-overview-of-proposed-amendments-to-the-law

Ramanathan, U. (2011). Land acquisition, eminent domain and the 2001 Bill. *Economic and Political Weekly, 46*(44/45), 10–14. https://www.jstor.org/stable/23047379

Rao, S. L., Deshingkar, P., & Farrinton, J. (2006, December 30–2007, January 5). Tribal land alienation in Andhra Pradesh: Processes, impacts and policy concerns. *Economic and Political Weekly, 41*(52), 5401–5407. https://www.jstor.org/stable/4419086

Rath, G. C. (Ed.). (2006). *Tribal development in India, the contemporary debate.* SAGE.

Ray, S., & Saini, S. (2011). Development and displacement: The case of an opencast coal mining project in Orissa. *Sociological Bulletin, 60*(1), 45–64. https://www.jstor.org/stable/23620995?seq=1#metadata_info_tab_contents

Rayagada district, Orissa Review Census Special. (2010). Retrieved January 30, 2021, from http://magazines.odisha.gov.in/Orissareview/2010/December/engpdf/176-179.pdf

Ribeiro, L. (2015). Development projects, violation of human rights, and the silence of archaeology in Brazil. *International Journal of Historical Archaeology, 19*(4), 810–821. https://www.jstor.org/stable/24572818

Rights and Resources Initiative with Vasundhara, and Natural Resources Management Consultants. (2015). *Potential for recognition of community forest resource rights under India's Forest Rights Act.* Rights and Resources Initiative. Retrieved March 3, 2021, from https://rightsandresources.org/wp-content/uploads/CommunityForest_July-20.pdf

Rojas, C., & Litzinger, R. A. (2016). *Ghost protocol: Development and displacement in Global China.* Duke University Press.

Sahoo, P., & Paltasingh, K. R. (2019). Examining growth–inequality nexus in post-reform Odisha: A sectoral decomposition analysis. *Journal of Development Policy and Practice, 4*(1), 12–34. https://doi.org/10.1177/2455133318812988

Sahu, S. (2019). The rhetoric of development and resistance by tribal women in Kashipur. *Social Change, 49*(1), 61–77. https://doi.org/10.1177/0049085718821503

Sahu, S., & Kumbhar, R. K. (2020). Coal mining-induced dispalcment and its impact on human development, a study on selected tribal households in Odisha. In S.I. Rajan., & D. Baral (Eds.), *Development, environment and migration lessons for sustainability* (pp. 38–56). Routledge.

Sarangi, D. R. (2002). In surviving against odds case of Kashipur. *Economic and Political Weekly, 37*(31), 3239–3241. https://www.jstor.org/stable/4412437

Sarangi, D., Pradhan, R., & Mohanty, S. (2005). State repression in Kashipur. *Economic and Political Weekly, 26*(3), 1312–1314.

Satiroglu, I., & Choi. N. (2015). *Development-induced displacement and resettlement new perspectives on persisting problems.* Routledge.

Satya, (n.d.). *Kashipur solidarity; why does Kashipur burn?* Kashipur Solidarity. Retrieved November 29, 2020, from https://kashipursolidarity.tripod.com/id17.html

Setalved, A. M. (1971). A study into certain aspects of the land acquisition Act, 1894. *Journal of the Indian Law Institute, 13*(1), 1–69. https://www.jstor.org/stable/43950105?seq=1#metadata_info_tab_contents

Shah, G. (2002). *Dalits and the state* (Ed.), Concept Publishing Company.

Sharma, A., Ali, Z., Vidyarthi, A., Daniel, U., Poonia, S., Jha. A., Jhnson, J., & Daspattanayak, B. (2014). *Studies, stories and a canvas: Seasonal labor migration and migrant workers from Odisha.* Center for Migration and Solutions: Aajeevika Bureau. Retrieved January 22, 2021, from https://www.humandignity.foundation/wp-content/uploads/2018/11/Odisha-State-Migration-Profile-Report.pdf

Shome, S. (2020). Environmental justice movement and ecological conflicts in India. *Environment, Technology and Social Change, Indian Journal of Law and Justice, 11*(1) (Part III), 204–214. https://ir.nbu.ac.in/bitstream/123456789/4015/1/IJLJ%20-%20Vol.%2011%20No.%201%20%28Part%20III%29%20Article%20No%2015.pdf

Siddiqui, K. (2012, May). Development and displacement in India: Reforming the economy towards sustainability. *Journal of Physics: Conference Series, 364*(1), 012108. IOP Publishing. Chicago. https://doi.org/10.1088/1742-6596/364/1/012108.

Sonak, I. (2018). State govts acquire land by subverting rights and bending the law. *Down-ToEarth*. Retrieved December 29, 2020, from https://www.downtoearth.org.in/news/agriculture/-state-govts-acquire-land-by-subverting-rights-and-bending-the-law--62463

ST & SC Development, Minorities & Backward Classes Welfare Department, Government of Odisha. (2020). *Odisha—List of scheduled castes*. Retrieved January 28, 2021, from https://stsc.odisha.gov.in/sites/default/files/2020-02/ScheduledCast_List.pdf

Stanley, W. (1996). Machkund, upper Kolab and NALCO projects in Koraput district, Orissa. *Economic and Political Weekly 31*(24), 1533–1538. https://www.jstor.org/stable/pdf/4404278.pdf?refreqid=excelsior%3A8ad960797eb10465541397d54f11bb11

The Bastion (2017). *Jal, jangal, zameen; adivasis amidst bauxite mining in Rayagada, Odisha*. The Bastion Development in Depth. Retrieved February 13, 2021, from https://thebastion.co.in/politics-and/environment/adivasis-amidst-bauxite-mining-in-rayagada-odisha/

Thomas, K. J. A. (2002). Development projects and involuntary population displacement: The World Bank's attempts to correct past failures. *Population Research and Policy Review, 21*(4), 339–349. https://www.jstor.org/stable/40230792

Utkal Alumina International Ltd. (n.d.). Retrieved January 18, 2021, from https://www.adityabirla.com/businesses/companies/utkal-alumina-international-limited

Varshney, A. (2019). *Despite new Land Acquisition Act, farmers remain vulnerable to poor compensation as many states dilute law for several sectors*. Retrieved January 10, 2021, from https://www.firstpost.com/india/despite-new-land-acquisition-act-farmers-remain-vulnerable-to-poor-compensation-as-many-states-dilute-law-for-several-sectors-7241221.html

Vasundhara, (2005). *Development policies and rural poverty in Orissa: Macro analysis and case studies*. Retrieved March 13, 2021, from https://niti.gov.in/planningcommission.gov.in/docs/reports/sereport/ser/stdy_dvpov.pdf

Wadhva, C. D. (2000). Political economy of post-1991 economic reforms in India. *South Asia: Journal of South Asian Studies, 23*, 207–220. https://doi.org/10.1080/00856400008723409

Wahi, N., Bhatia, A., Shukla, P., Gandhi, D., Jain, S., & Chauhan, U. (2017). *Land acquisition in India: A review of Supreme Court cases (1950–2016)*. Centre for Policy Research. Retrieved December 11, 2020, from https://www.cprindia.org/research/reports/land-acquision-india-review-supreme-court-cases-1950-2016

Wahi, N. (2013, February). Land acquisition, development and the constitution. *Seminar Magazine*. Retrieved January, 20, 2021, from https://papers.ssrn.com/sol3/papers.cfm?abstract_id=2222321

Walker, K. L. M. (2008). Neoliberalism on the ground in rural India: Predatory growth, agrarian crisis, internal colonization and the intensification of class struggle. *The Journal of Peasant Studies, 35*(4), 557–620. https://doi.org/10.1080/03066150802681963

Climate Change, Conflict, and Prosocial Behavior in Southwestern Bangladesh: Implications for Environmental Justice

Tuhin Roy, Md Kamrul Hasan, and M. M. Abdullah Al Mamun Sony

1 Introduction

Globally, climate change has become a matter of debate, policy concern, and political activism. Over the past few decades, world leaders and various stakeholders including nongovernment organizations (NGOs), policymakers, academics, students, and the media have paid considerable attention to the problem. They have debated issues such as climate change adaptation and mitigation strategies to tackle the harmful effects of extreme natural events. The Intergovernmental Panel on Climate Change (IPCC) published a series of powerful reports such as *Global Warming of 1.5 ºC* (Masson-Delmotte et al., 2018) and *Climate Change and Land* (Shukla et al., 2019) showing that climate change is a consequence of human actions. Furthermore, climate change has resulted in increasing global warming, sea-level rise, and increasing natural calamities such as floods, infrequent rainfall, cyclones, tornadoes, hurricanes, salinity, drought, and so forth. The Paris Agreement reflects the global commitment to reduce climate change emissions in an effort to keep global temperatures below 2 °C compared to preindustrial levels (Dimitrov, 2016).

Historically, richer and industrialized western countries contributed disproportionately to the contemporary global climate crisis by emitting pollutants such as carbon dioxide into the atmosphere largely through the consumption of fossil fuels. The USA and European Union (EU) countries have contributed more to climate

---

T. Roy
Khulna University, Khulna, Bangladesh

M. K. Hasan
Western Sydney University, Sydney, Australia

Bangladesh Institute of Social Research Trust, Dhaka, Bangladesh

M. M. A. A. M. Sony (✉)
University of Debrecen, Debrecen, Hungary
e-mail: abdullahsony.as@mailbox.unideb.hu

© The Author(s), under exclusive license to Springer Nature Singapore Pte Ltd. 2022
D. Madhanagopal et al. (eds.), *Environment, Climate, and Social Justice*,
https://doi.org/10.1007/978-981-19-1987-9_17

change through the process of industrialization. In contrast, the Global South sits on the receiving end of the harms produced by climate change. More recently, China and India have been increasing their carbon emissions although their per capita contribution is much lower than their Western counterparts (Swim & Bloodhart, 2018). Even within a nation, richer populations who consume more fossil fuel, travel by airplanes, and drive cars emit more carbon dioxide and other greenhouse gases into the atmosphere than their poor counterparts (Swim & Bloodhart, 2018). On the other hand, the poor and the lower classes, who contribute less to climate change, are disproportionately impacted by the negative consequences of climatic variations (Pearson & Schuldt, 2018; Swim & Bloodhart, 2018). It is likely that these marginalized and vulnerable groups bear an unequal share of the risks linked to climate change without being responsible for contributing to the climate change problem in the first place. This raises questions about climate justice. Since all countries, groups, and classes do not contribute equally to climate change and do not receive the harms of climate change proportionately, the issue of climate justice is crucially important (Nielsen et al., 2021).

The idea of environmental justice originated in the 1980s to address environmental racism in the United States and to promote the equitable treatment and distribution of environmental resources and risks (Mohai et al., 2009; Schlosberg & Collins, 2014). This multidisciplinary term overlaps with two other key social science concepts such as climate justice and social justice which, broadly speaking, refer to ensuring a fair distribution of risks and resources such as forests, land, air, water, and social opportunities irrespective of race, color, ethnicity, class, and so forth (Mohai et al., 2009).

In Bangladesh, located in South Asia, climate change has created multifaceted social, economic, environmental, and political problems. Climate change is now a reality in this rapidly growing and promising country, and the effects of climate variation have recently become manifest in recurrent disasters, abnormal weather conditions, higher-than-average temperatures, cyclones, sea-level rise, and the displacement of people. It is predicted that sea-level rise and inundation in Bangladesh would displace about 0.9 million people by 2050 and up to 2.1 million people by 2100, especially in the low-lying coastal regions in the southern parts of the country (Davis et al., 2018), which is the focus of this chapter. As discussed below, the southern coastal region is a suitable site for understanding the effects of climate change and climate justice from a southern perspective.

Strong social bonds and networks are crucially important to build harmony and peace in societies. On the one hand, social bonds and networks foster social capital formation (Bourdieu, 1986) and on the other hand, they enhance happiness. Unity and harmony among social groups, communities, friends, and relatives help to respond to emergencies and collectively solve problems such as climate change. When individuals, communities, and others help each other, such helping behaviors are defined as prosocial behaviors. To understand prosocial behaviors, the conceptualization of Hirschi's (1969) delinquent behavior is useful. Hirschi (1969) introduced four elements of social bonding such as attachment, commitment, involvement, and beliefs. Hirschi (1969) stated that, on an affective level, an individual who has a strong and stable attachment to others within society may not violate societal norms. Similarly, at the cognitive level, such social commitment results in the investment of an individual's time, energy, and resources to pursue a social goal (Hirschi, 2017). The third element related to the behavioral level is "involvement." Hirschi (1969) defines this as time spent in collective (e.g., school extracurricular activities and engagement with peer groups) activities. Hirschi's (1969) last element of social bonding at the individual level is beliefs which provide moral guidelines to individuals in society. Certainly, these psychosocial elements generally develop prosocial and proenvironmental behaviors.

Research in the field of climate change is multidisciplinary with contributions not only from atmospheric and other natural sciences, but also mathematics, economics, statistics, political studies, psychology, sociology, geography, and others. A large body of this research aims at predicting the effects of climate change on sea-level rise, migration, food security, and so on. Less research to date has been conducted from a sociological perspective, especially in Bangladesh, that focuses on the intergroup and social-relational consequences of climate change. Rather less is known about the implications of these social relations for environmental justice. Social psychological and sociological research can elucidate group dynamics associated with climate change.

A modest and growing body of international research on climate change has indicated that climate change may generate social conflicts (Djebou & Singh, 2016; Niemeyer et al., 2005; van Lange et al., 2018). Research has suggested that social-ecological changes produce stresses and conflicts among groups who depend on environmental resources for their livelihood (Pearson & Schuldt, 2018; Spijkers & Boonstra, 2017). Burke et al. (2015) predict that increasing temperature and precipitation will increase conflict risks and the possibility of violence, riots, and war. For example, the increase in the mackerel stock in the North Atlantic waters has triggered an interstate conflict over fishing quotas between the EU, Norway, Iceland, and the Faroe Islands (Spijkers & Boonstra, 2017). Research predicts ocean warming would cause a change in the distribution and quantity of marine resources, which would, in turn, trigger conflict between countries (Spijkers & Boonstra, 2017).

However, the relationship between climate change and conflict, aggression, and violence is not direct and clear-cut (Fritsche et al., 2018; Gilmore, 2017; Koubi, 2019). There are certain pathways through which climatic variability may contribute to conflicts. Some literature has suggested that a low level of economic development, political marginalization, especially in agricultural settings can generate climate-induced conflicts (Koubi, 2019). Furthermore, environmental change does not necessarily result in social conflict, but the nexus is mediated by other factors such as political power, institutions (rules, treaties, laws and procedures, etc.), and control over knowledge. Pearson and Schuldt (2018) have argued that climate change contributes at least indirectly to social conflict by exacerbating drivers of conflict including poverty, unemployment, reduced productivity, and increased food insecurity.

A modest body of literature has emerged linking climate change to its societal consequences in the context of Bangladesh. Roy et al. (2020) have shown how interpersonal conflict and intergroup conflict rose due to salinity intrusion in the southwest coastal areas of Bangladesh. They have also found that certain social customs relating to marriage and divorce may have changed indirectly due to increasing salinity (Roy et al., 2020). Such evidence indicates that climate change impacts the social realm. Roy and Sony (2019) presented a social structural analysis of climate change in southwest coastal Bangladesh after the cyclone Aila struck the region in 2009. They suggest that conflict and competition grew among various interest groups over the control of relief and development aid. A similar scenario of the impact of climate change has been also observed in Pakistan where the whole ecosystem was restructured due to the impacts of climate change (Hussain et al., 2019). Research has further shown that conflict grew between shrimp and paddy farmers in southwestern Bangladesh due to climate change (Haider & Akter, 2018). According to Haider and Akter (2018), shrimp cultivation has evolved as a profitable agricultural business in place of traditional rice paddy cultivation which was negatively affected due to increasing salinity after the 1980s. Over the past few years, the local people wanted to reengage in the traditional paddy cultivation because shrimp cultivation was found unsustainable, giving rise to conflicts between the supporters of paddy cultivators and shrimp farmers (Abdullah et al., 2017; Haider & Akter, 2018; Hossain et al., 2013). Likewise, a political–ecological analysis of the climate change adaptation programs in Bangladesh shows that powerful groups including politicians, government officers, and criminal gangs captured public lands and encroached upon forests, village property, and farms (Sovacool, 2018). This conflict arising between the victims of climate change and the powerful sections of the society who have contributed more to climate change, raises intranational climate justice issues. Nevertheless, this literature has largely failed to address the consequences of climate change on intergroup relationships and behaviors from a critical perspective.

Against the backdrop outlined above, further research on the effects of climate change on human relationships, as well as prosocial behavior, is needed. However, enough empirical evidence is still not available to fully grasp the effects of climatic variations on complex patterns of relationships at the social level. To bridge this gap, this chapter foregrounds some of the effects of climate change on social behaviors and specifically explores how climate change in southwest coastal Bangladesh has shaped interpersonal and intergroup relationships. Further, it explains why such changes have occurred at the individual and community levels. Finally, it examines some of the implications of the changes in intergroup relations for prosocial and proenvironmental actions which are essential for promoting environmental justice.

2 Methodology

2.1 Study Context and Locations

To understand how prosocial behaviors such as intergroup, intragroup, and personal social relationships can be shaped by climate change and by disasters that are linked to climate variability, we used qualitative methods. The researchers chose two disaster-prone southwest coastal villages under *Sreenagar* village of *Kamarkhola* union and *Kalabogi* village of *Suterkhali* union of Dacope Upazila (subdistrict) of Bangladesh (Fig. 1), as these two unions have frequently been struck by natural catastrophes such as cyclones, tidal surges, and slow onset events such as increasing salinity (Dasgupta et al., 2015). The geographical setting of these two villages is 63 km. north from the coast of the Bay of Bengal; and 33 km. South from Khulna city, and about half a kilometer away from the Sundarbans (Kabir et al., 2016). Frequent natural events like cyclone Aila (2009), Mahasen (2013), Amphan (2020), Yaas (2021) are still fresh in the memories of people inhabiting these areas.

Increasing salinity due to sea-level rise was an important concern of the people living in this region (Roy et al., 2020). These remote villages are separated from the mainland by polders and embankments. Several structural changes, both in economic and cultural terms, have occurred in these areas because of the natural events. Roy and Sony (2019) observed that disasters broke down the economic structure of the affected areas and this grabbed the attention of development agencies. Development NGOs and the government have implemented a series of programs in the area and they have also delivered relief and aid in the post-disaster period. We chose these villages to understand whether and how climate change was impacting prosocial behaviors in the communities.

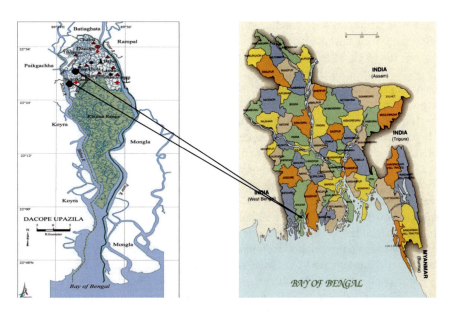

Fig. 1 Study location in southwestern coastal Bangladesh: *Sreenagar* village (black dot) of Kamarkhola union and *Kalabogi* village (Black dot) of Suterkhali union of Dacope Upazila (subdistrict) of Bangladesh (Maps of the World 2016)

2.2 Study Tools and Techniques

To explore the changes in social relationships, a loosely structured research design involving in-depth interviews (IDI), focus group discussion (FGD), and key informant interview (KII) was utilized to collect primary data between April 2019 and September 2021. Interviews were conducted for about 25 days over this period. A total of 12 IDIs, four FGDs, and four KIIs were conducted. In the four FGDs, a total of 27 community members participated. Of the 12 who had participated in IDIs, 6 were men and 6 were women. To understand different perspectives, the researchers collected IDI data from both senior and young adults. The participants ranged in age from 25 to 65 years. The two most commonly practised religions in the study areas are Hinduism and Islam.

Concurrently, to capture community perceptions, four FGDs were conducted. Of these, two FGDs were conducted with men and two with women. Except for one, there were seven participants in each FGD. The most common occupational groups were farmers, shopkeepers, fishermen, housewives, teachers, students, day laborers, businessmen, NGO workers, woodcutters, and the unemployed. While some respondents (e.g., students) did not have an income of their own, the day laborers or workers earned about 400–500 Bangladeshi Taka daily. NGO workers, teachers, and shopkeepers earned approximately twice this income.

To organize the FGDs, the researcher received assistance from a local volunteer. The FGDs with men were conducted in local tea stalls in the two villages and the FGDs with women were organized in two separate houses in each of the two villages. Further, four KIIs were also conducted in the study areas. As key informants, two school teachers from each of the two villages were selected since they were also local people, and both graduated from a college in Dacope. Of the other two KII respondents, one was a Union Parishad (a local government body) chairman and local political representative, and the other was a female Union Parishad member. The KII participants had comprehensive knowledge about intergroup and interpersonal relationships because they regularly engaged with the people.

Local people who had been living within this study area for more than 20 years prior to interviews and had experienced at least two notable climate change-related events in their life were purposively selected as respondents. All of them were informed of the study aims before data collection and oral consent was obtained from all respondents. The respondents agreed to give data on the condition that the researchers would not disclose their names and identity. In line with ethical research guidelines, the researchers used pseudonyms for both individuals and communities.

Participants were asked to share their experiences and life stories about key issues and problems relating to climate change and its effects on community relationships. For instance, they were asked: Over the past few years, due to climate change, what kind of changes have you observed in your social relations as well as your surroundings and how? They were then probed to elicit details about changes in social relationships at various levels such as the individual level, family level, and community level. All interviews were audio-recorded and later transcribed. Since all of the interviews were conducted in the local (Bengali) language, they were translated into English before coding. In addition, the researcher coded all of the transcripts to generate themes related to the study objectives stated above. Overall findings of this study were organized under three subthemes which include: (1) individual level; (2) family level; and (3) community level.

3 Findings: Climate Change and Social Relationships in Southwestern Bangladesh

Bangladesh is a kinship-based, family-oriented society in which collectivism has historically shaped patterns of social relationships. More recently, however, globalization, increasing urbanization, and industrialization have been altering the older forms of social relationships. These processes are linked to modern or postmodern individuality which promotes "fragmented" or more individualized identities, as is seen throughout the "late" modern Western world (Giddens, 1991). Findings from this study reveal that climate change-related disasters that occurred across the research regions influenced social and community relations in multiple ways. These can be clustered under the three main categories: (i) the development of individual self-identity, (ii) increased conflicts among groups, and (iii) the lack of cooperation in multiple social realms. In what follows, social–relational changes that may be at least indirectly linked to climate change and that are occurring at various levels of society are discussed along with explanations for these changes based on the study findings.

3.1 Disaster and Intergroup Relationships

The findings of this study show that in the aftermath of cyclone Aila (a cyclone that struck the region in 2009), the older forms of close individual-level relationships changed to more calculative relationships. Most respondents started maintaining their peer groups based on age instead of caste/class. Importantly, many more friendships grew among people in the same village, compared to relationships with people living in another village. A respondent said:

> Before Aila, I was a fisherman, but I'd a friend who was a businessman, another one was a shopkeeper and the other was a primary school teacher. We used to gather in this tea stall almost every day and chat for a long time. (Shabuddin,[1] 38 years, fisherman, Sreenagar village, IDI-1)

Similarly, another respondent added:

> ...though I'd a good connection with other villagers, most of my friends with whom I used to spend most of my leisure time belonged to this village. We've grown up together

---

[1] Pseudonyms have been used throughout the paper.

> like brothers…if necessary, we could sacrifice our lives for each other. (Muktar, 44 years, boatman, Kalabogi village, IDI-7)

The findings indicate that in the predisaster period, visiting friends and chatting were forms of entertainment at each level which has now relatively reduced among the young respondents. Instead of chatting, most of the young respondents mentioned that they were taking part in income-generating activities, skill development activities, and/or social media like Facebook. After Aila, many people migrated to nearby cities and lost their connection to their villages. The strong collectivist mindset that existed was crucial to taking climate action. However, it appears that disaster-related stresses, marginalization, and dislocation weakened the social fabric. This is not conducive to taking collective action against climate change. A participant described how dislocation due to unexpected and heavy rainfall affected his relationships with a cousin and their families:

> Last year I lost my crops due to heavy rainfall. Therefore, I've failed to pay off the instalments of my bank loan. I've asked my cousin who was working in Dhaka to give me some money, but he's refused to give me money…It hurts because I'd helped him several times whenever he wanted. Even, after Aila, he'd taken shelter for two years in my house. You'd be surprised to know that each year he used to visit us. But from the last year, he hasn't visited us. (Moti, 51 years, farmer, Kalabogi village, IDI-8)

It is noticeable from the above quote that since Moti lost his crop due to rainfall, his cousin refused to lend him money because the cousin anticipated that the farmer would not be able to pay back the money due to crop failures. Similarly, women participants narrated that before Aila, they had had a strong interpersonal relationship with their neighbors. Almost every evening they used to gather in their front yards and spent their time gossiping, laughing, and chatting. However, this form of social bonding can no longer be seen in the study area. Now, most women are involved in different types of income-generating activities such as cattle farming, poultry farming, tailoring, and so on. In this regard, a female respondent said:

> Before Aila, there's a good relationship with our neighbors there [pointing to a corner]. We met here every evening and everyone tried to bring some food and share. We shared our joys and sorrows… but now we meet each other maybe once a week or sometimes we don't meet at all. (Kobita, 47 years, homemaker, Sreenagar village, IDI-3)

Likewise, another respondent stated:

> Now most of us are involved in different jobs… after Aila I've received training from BRAC on hand-stitching… most of the time I'm involved in this activity. Therefore, I've no time to spend gossiping. (Ruksana, 36 years, tailor, Kalabogi village, IDI-11)

Findings such as these show a reduced frequency of community meetings, indicating poorer and weaker social bonds. These suggest that in the post-disaster period, NGOs such as BRAC provided training to build local capacity. Women, who were adversely affected by Aila got involved in income-generating activities which left them little time to engage in community activities. Thus, disaster was indirectly linked to changes in social relationships.

Climate Change, Conflict, and Prosocial Behavior ... 357

Findings also show that prior to Aila, each of the respondents had their own peer groups and the connection to these peer groups was strong. They shared a strong sense of belongingness to their local community and cooperated without thinking about personal self-interests. These relationships were weakened as a result of the hardship generated by Aila. A small businessman recounted:

> One of my friends was a shrimp cultivator, and during the harvesting time, along with other friends, we used to go to his *gher* [special pond to cultivate shrimp] and we used to catch shrimp together. Instead of taking remuneration, we used to have a party at night. Similarly, he also assisted us in our business and when I made some profits ..., I'd call all of my friends and had party ...over the past few years, I've not done such activities...as I've no money to spend ...I think, I've lost my value to them. (Ashik, 39 years, shopkeeper, Sreenagar village, IDI-2)

Thus, after Aila, members of peer groups got separated and became calculative. Some respondents mentioned that members of their previous peer group were reluctant to meet them. These evidences indicate poorer social bonds during the post-disaster period. This might occur due to economic and social vulnerability, and stresses that are associated with disasters.

3.2 Explanations for Changes in Intergroup Relationships

Participants offered several explanations for the changing pattern of intergroup relationships. Our findings show that cyclone Aila and increasing salinity altered the traditional economic structure, which mostly consisted of fishing, farming, honey collecting, and woodcutting. Most of the respondents said that after the loss of their properties such as houses, land, and crops, there was no longer any difference between the upper classes and lower classes. Most of the respondents indicated that immediately after the disaster, individuals endeavored to cope with their mental stresses and anxieties in their own ways resulting in the old close relationships being replaced by relationships based on calculative choices. Thus, instead of protecting peer groups' interests, individual interests were prioritized. For example, one participant explained how disaster-induced stresses affected community-level relationships:

> The shock of Aila forced people to maintain a formal relationship with each other among the villagers because the main concern of the villagers was to earn money and get their families through the aftershocks of the disaster, so they'd spend less time gossiping and chatting. (Pritom Roy, 34 years, school teacher, KII-1)

Increasing salinity due to upstream water flow was cited as a problem in the study areas. Since saline water is negatively associated with agriculture, a lack of opportunity to work in traditional occupations such as farming and job insecurity forced male members of the community to migrate out of their villages. Therefore, many agricultural workers were displaced because work was not available as cultivable lands became scarce due to saltwater intrusion. For this reason, landless people and unemployed agricultural workers migrated to nearby districts to find work. Having limited employment opportunities, many local people made new occupation-based peer groups within the same village or neighboring villages. It is likely that these occupational interest groups can be mobilized to take climate actions because they are more adversely affected by the impacts of climate change.

Some participants observed that the deterioration in the social relationship was not a sudden process, rather it was a slow process. A boatman observed how, after a disaster, people can become selfish gradually:

> Immediately after the disaster, we're sharing our food and water, but day by day to accumulate more relief and resources, our cooperative mindset has become more self-centric. Everyone tried to maintain a friendly relation with local elites and political leaders because those who had strong connections with local leaders generally received much more relief than others. (Muktar, 44 years, boatman, Kalabogi village, IDI-7)

The above quotation suggests that there was a competition among people to get post-disaster relief provided through local government and politicians. Muktar also complained about nepotism in the distribution of post-disaster relief which created conflict between those who received and those who did not receive these resources. Similarly, most of the respondents said that individuals were divided into several groups based on the receipt of relief. Divisiveness among these groups would undercut their capacity to advocate for proenvironmental action which is needed to promote the climate justice agenda. First, one group of people started following local political elites to get many more facilities from the government. Second, another group of people attempted to develop a connection with NGO workers. A participant explained this point by saying:

> …I've seen that the religious leaders motivated a few people and tried to develop relations with religion-based development organizations. Whereas the politically active guys have raised a new group of followers and similarly, some educated people established a good relationship with NGOs. (Karim Molla, 57 years, UP chairman, KII-3)

Third, another group of individuals failed to build connections with these two groups and moved outside of the community as seasonal workers. Fourth, the other group of individuals ignoring all relationships migrated to nearby cities or towns. This displaced group of people are generally the most vulnerable and are sometimes called "climate refugee." Most of the respondents considered this fourth group of individuals "deviant" because they did not fit in with other social groups.

The findings revealed that the relationship among women had been changed, as these did for their male counterparts. For instance, after Aila, several NGOs have been working to empower women in the study area. After receiving aid in the form of microcredit, cash, or training, most of the active women got themselves engaged in income-generating activities. As one respondent said:

> After Aila, instead of wasting my time, I worked in embankment construction. By doing this, I used to earn a good amount of money and could support my family well enough… saving money from those activities I started a business. (Ayasha Banu, 42 years, shopkeeper, Kalabogi village, IDI-5)

Similarly, another respondent stated:

In 2012 along with some neighbors I had received three months of tailoring training from an NGO. And after this training, I got a sewing machine as a gift for my good performance in the post-training test. The organizers had given ten sewing machines to the top ten performers like me...You will be glad to know that my tailoring work is popular in my neighborhood...through this, I am contributing to my family. (Supti, 36 years, tailor, Sreenagar village, FGD-03)

In line with above quotations, Shilpa Banu, a 41 years old Union Parishad member, mentioned that in the post-Aila period, women's engagement in income-generating activities became a common phenomenon which was rare in the pre-Aila times. Thus, the findings of this study have shown that many more female members of the study areas were attempting to be engaged in income-generating activities after disasters.

3.3 Changes in Family and Kinship Relationships

As a traditionally collectivist society, familial bonds have long been strong in Bangladesh society. People lived in close-knit large or extended families in villages and small towns. Increasing urbanization and migration are eroding the strong family bonds in the country. Before Aila, most of the families in the study areas were extended, but now most of the respondent's families are nuclear. As evidence of the extended family/clan bond, the name of the neighborhood one originated from was also recognized according to family lineage. For instance, a respondent from *Sreenagar* village mentioned,

You can find the name of our *Para* [neighborhood] like *Gazi Para, Shakh Para* and so on. Because most of the people are from the Gazi clan, and hold Gazi surname. (Mostofa Gazi, 37 years, businessman, Sreenagar village, FGD-01)

A similar scenario was found in Kalabogi village:

...Yes, most of the *para* in our village is recognized by the clan's surname and you can find blood relations among families in each *para*. This way these clans had grown powerful. (Minu, 47 years, seasonal shrimp fry cultivator, Kalabogi village, FGD-4)

Apart from this, findings of this study have shown that before Aila the hierarchy of the family was demonstrated by the older members being respected by the younger ones, but this has changed since Aila. As the disaster had disrupted their education, younger people had leisure time in which they engaged in delinquent activities. According to most of the respondents, the important decision of the family had always been taken by the elderly, although they had no economic power. Most of the respondents stated that they had maintained a traditional, committed relationship. One of the respondents said,

The very common family cycle was like, the young son with their wife and children live with fathers' family. After the father's death, a few families broke into the nuclear family initially. Next, it also took the shape of an extended family. The bonding between the brothers was strong. If one brother faced any problem, the other brother or sister would invariably come to assist each other... (Karim Molla, 57 years, UP chairman, KII-3)

The findings suggest that the traditional chain of command among the family had been weakening in the context of the rise of individuality, self-interest, and competition for scarce relief and other benefits offered by various stakeholders in a post-disaster setting. Most of the respondents stated that their important family decisions were taken based on mutual understanding between husbands and wives. They added that the elder members of the family are now receiving tokenistic respect. The traditional intimacy between the brothers' families also weakened due to increased tensions in the post-disaster phase. Some participants said that people in the study areas were less likely to share their emotions and feelings with others because of the rise of individualism. Thus, rising individualism in place of collectivism in disaster-affected communities could become a barrier to take collective proenvironmental action. The findings also show that sometimes marital bonds were formed with a prospective marital partner living in a less disaster-prone area with the hope of getting support from their relatives during an emergency such as a cyclone and floods. A participant explained:

> I've arranged my son's marriage with someone living in Kolapara [a village which was about 60 km away from the study areas and not a cyclone vulnerable area]. Thus, after a massive disaster, my son and grandchild can receive the necessary support from them. (Lutfor, 63 years, unemployed, Kalabogi village, IDI-8)

Such evidence indicates that susceptibility to climate-related disasters influenced marital decisions, as the above case suggests. There was a shift from in-group to out-group marital relationships. According to the findings, the traditional trend of marriage within the *Sreenagar* village and the neighboring villages, was shifting to distant areas for some. At the same time, most respondents agreed that over the past seven years, child marriages and early marriages have increased dramatically in the study areas. Poorer families marry off their daughters to cope with economic hardships produced by disasters.

Older respondents reported that after Aila local people were attempting to ignore their ascribed status and were trying to move up the social ladder based on achieved status. Therefore, the traditional power structure has changed. Though most of the senior respondents of this study were satisfied with their ascribed status, the young respondents were not satisfied with the traditional form of status ascription. Subsequently, a psycho-social conflict between two age groups was observed in the study areas. A participant observed:

> I'm surprised that the young people aren't willing to hold on to their traditional occupation as well as status. They thought that earning more money and getting a job will change their traditional identity. For example, [pointing to a house] the member of that family was our family's servant traditionally, but when his boy went to the city after Aila, their attitude has changed. Now, Kaisha [mocking] becomes Kisor Shaheb [Mr. Kisor] …Aila changed our society. (Lutfor, 63 years, unemployed, Kalabogi village, IDI-8)

Thus, as the above quotation suggests, migration influenced the traditional social hierarchy in the study villages. As some groups climbed up the social ladder, other groups became jealous and conflict arose between the opposing groups. This is evinced by Lutfor's mocking behaviors against his neighbors who moved up the social hierarchy after migrating to the city.

It was also found that, in order to strengthen their family ties, exchanging gifts was a common practice. These gifts consisted of seasonal fruits, new paddy, rice cakes, desserts, and so on. According to Hasibur, one of the second FGD respondents, in order to build a strong connection with local elites and government officers, the local people gave their seasonal fruits, new paddy, rice cakes, and so on which were previously exchanged between families and relatives. In addition, some of the respondents recounted that before Aila they used to invite their daughter's family with grandchildren to celebrate different ceremonies, but they could not do so after Aila. A participant recalled:

> In *Jyôishṭhô* [the Bengali month from 15 May to 15 June in the English calendar] when different fruits used to grow here, most of our relatives used to visit us…throughout the year. We're waiting for it. Aila induced a tidal surge to bring saline water into this area and killed those old fruit trees. Now there are no trees and no relatives. (Karimon, 48 years, homemaker, Kalabogi village, IDI-6)

As the above quotation suggests, crop failures attributable to increasing salinity and land degradation may indirectly influence relationships with relatives. However, some social relationships were altered in a way that strengthened ties. For instance, according to the respondents, in case of the death of any neighbors, other neighbors mourned. This hints at the possibility of restrengthening community ties that had existed prior to disasters.

Pritom added that before Aila out-migration was comparatively rare in the study villages. Only educated men migrated to the nearby Khulna city, but they maintained a connection with their relatives. However, climate change-induced out-migration disconnected them from their places of origin, as the following quotation suggests:

> Over the past few decades, several people have migrated to nearby cities. Most of the time, we send our children to get a higher education and after that, they take up jobs in different organizations, and don't return to this village…why would they come? What do we have here? … Due to increasing salinity and heavy rainfall, we're failing to grow crops and even the drinking water shortage is also increasing day by day. There is no money and no jobs. It is a challenge to live here. (Rohomotulla, 61 years, farmer, Sreenagar village, IDI-10)

Participants added that out-migration had become a common scenario in this study area. Most of the respondents agreed that along with educated people, the non-formally educated men were also migrating seasonally to nearby districts during the harvesting period. A participant explained this phenomenon in detail:

> Once, I used to grow paddy on my lands and during the season I used to go to the forest (Sundarbans) to collect honey with my group. However, after Aila, my land become barren due to saltwater and so, I failed to grow paddy in my land. Therefore, to find an alternative means of livelihood, I have chosen to go to Bagerhat [a district which was about 400-km away from the respondent's village] to work in farmland until April [generally the honey collecting season begins at this time]. (Moti, 51 years, farmer, Kalabogi village, IDI-08)

Thus, Moti explained how land salinization created economic insecurity for him and forced him to migrate to a town to find an alternative job. Such dislocation will likely create new demands for alternative jobs in urban areas. This may also trigger competition and tensions within the urban settings of Bangladesh in the future.

3.4 Explanations for Changes in Family and Kinship Relationships

The findings show that several external initiatives were the primary reasons for poor family relationships. According to the respondents, post-disaster relief and aid were generally provided according to a household's needs based on four members. Therefore, in order to get relief after the super cyclone Aila, people wanted to split up their families into smaller units. Many respondents mentioned that the development organizations preferred to provide aid to smaller family units. Such social behavior later gave rise to a self-centric attitude among the family members. To explain how, after Aila, the traditional large family structure was breaking down, a respondent said:

> Generally, the government and the NGOs provided 250 to 300 sq. feet house as rehabilitation where only 4 or 5 members can live. And to be able to stay in that type of housing, we'd to raise a nuclear family. (Mohit Ghosh, 53 years, grocer, Sreenagar village, IDI-02)

The findings also indicated that another reason for the breakdown of old extended family ties was the growing scarcity of wealth and resources. Increasing salinity made land barren and therefore, young sons were less likely to depend on their fathers' cultivable land and tried to look for alternative economic activities. However, there were not enough employment opportunities in their impoverished villages. Given the high unemployment rates among the young people in Bangladesh, it was challenging for them. This suggests that climate-related vulnerability would exacerbate employment prospects and create more demands for jobs. This may create frictions within family relationships in the future. The lack of employment opportunities in the post-disaster period pushed many local people to migrate. A participant made it clear by saying:

> After Aila, lots of people who've lost their cropland and those who wanted to take care of their wives and children migrated to the nearby cities and the capital city. Some of them also cut off connection with the village that they'd left. (Pintu, 34 years, bike driver, Kalabogi village, FGD-03)

The findings also indicate that because of the rehabilitation programs, neighbors relocated to new areas and became disconnected. This changed the patterns of neighborhood relationships because people from distant areas became new neighbors, transforming the intergroup and intragroup relationships. A participant explained this phenomenon when he said:

> Now if you go to the Gazi Para. You may find very few people who hold the Gazi surname. After the rehabilitation program, members of different communities are now living in this area. (Pritom Roy, 34 years, school teacher, KII-1)

Climate Change, Conflict, and Prosocial Behavior ...   363

Thus, out-migration and in-migration that are connected to some of the impacts of climate change influenced intergroup and neighborhood relationships in the study villages.

3.5 Changes in Community Relationships

Changes in social relationships at the community level were much more visible than at any other levels in the study areas. According to respondents, before Aila, the local people of the study area shared a strong sense of belongingness. All the villagers had held a common identity. Likewise, they had followed traditional norms and values. To explain this, a respondent said:

> We're the people of Kamarkhola – this was our common value and we will live together and we die together. (Kholis, 51 years, businessman, Sreenagar village, FGD-01)

Such common feelings were also noticeable in the accounts of other respondents. Religious sentiments also bound people together in the study villages. Notwithstanding that, many participants in the study areas were attempting to form new relationships with people living in less disaster-prone areas. Moreover, most of the respondents mentioned that once the community people practised and celebrated different types of ceremonies together which included marriage, national, and religious ceremonies. A participant reported:

> Before Aila, most of the villagers received invitations if any marriage ceremony took place in our village, but now if any marriage ceremony has taken place even in the next door, people do not hear any noise. (Sokhina, 57 years, homemaker, Sreenagar village, IDI-04)

This quote indicates worsening community relationships in the wake of the conflict between various groups. Despite this, participants talked about some local coping activities that assisted them to cope with disasters. A participant stated:

> In our area every male child must learn swimming, climbing, catching fish and so on. Similarly, female children have to learn cooking, sewing, maintaining family, and so on. Over a period of time, that way we developed our own coping strategy to combat any natural events. Before Aila, this knowledge had been transmitted from one generation to another. (Shilpa Banu, 41 years, Union Parishad member, KII-4)

In addition, some respondents reported conflict between supporters of traditional medicine and those of modern allopathic medicine. After Aila, most of the respondents depended on modern allopathic medicine because several governmental and NGOs set up medical camps and community clinics in the study area where they could easily access proper treatment and medicine for free. Before Aila, most people had depended on the traditional treatment and often it had worked well. Generally, these traditional treatments were provided by nonprofessional midwives, *kabiraj* (traditional healers), and/or religious leaders who were also members of the community. Since many people were not willing to accept traditional treatment after Aila, the value of these traditional medical practitioners decreased. Subsequently, there were two opposing interest groups.

3.6 Explanations for Change in Community Relationships

Findings show a change in interpersonal relationships due to the cyclone Aila and increasing salinity. According to some respondents, such a competitive mindset has generated conflicts between families and community members which provoked individuals to ignore traditional norms and values and thus promoted deviant behaviors. According to the respondents, such a social attitude created a weak sense of belonging among the community members.

Some respondents also believed that because of government and nongovernment interventions, traditional knowledge was not valued any longer as people relied on modern scientific knowledge. Therefore, socialization was happening more through the formal education systems than traditional education. A participant said:

> We want to educate our children because education is the only way to maintain sustainable livelihood patterns. There is no security in our lives and we are here because we have no formal education. (Karim Molla, 57 years, UP chairman, KII-3)

According to most of the respondents, the availability of climate change-related adaptive mechanisms like ICT caused a cultural clash between young people's way of living and elder people's lifestyles in their community. For instance, instead of emphasizing traditional climate-associated knowledge, most of the young respondents had been relying on modern scientific knowledge which they can easily access through various social media. Since faith in traditional knowledge was growing weak, the importance of elder members, who were considered wise people among their community, decreased.

In addition, some people converted to a different religion after being influenced by relief and assistance from other religious communities. Moreover, all respondents mentioned that the relief and aid controlled by local leaders was a source of conflict. This cultivated a sense of self-interest and individualism among community members. A respondent said:

> Seventy-eight edible oil cans [each can contain eight-litres of oil] was recovered from the house of a female UP member. (Misu, 28 years, NGO worker, Kalabogi village, IDI-6)

Another participant added:

> We'd to pay 20 to 40 percent of the cash to local representatives to get the cheque that came from the government to construct a new home. (Kobita, 47 years, homemaker, Sreenagar village, IDI-03)

Thus, participants talked about how the conflict arose over the control of the financial assistance program launched by the government in the post-disaster period. Lastly, most of the respondents were concerned about the rising anti-social behavior and conflicts.

4 Discussion

This study aimed to examine the consequences of climate change for interpersonal and intergroup relationships from a sociological perspective in Bangladesh. To achieve this aim, a qualitative study was designed with some marginalized social groups located in disaster-affected southwestern Bangladesh. The marginalized groups were at risk of climate change without contributing much to its production. Beck (1992) has suggested that environmental risks are experienced on a global scale in the late modern era. Bangladesh, as a Southern country connected to the global economy, has started to experience the risks and vulnerabilities of climate change produced mainly by wealthier and industrialized nations, as well as by the richer population within Bangladesh. In this sense, this is a crucially important environmental justice issue. The cyclone Aila and the increasing salinity in the study locations are closely linked to climate change. The findings of this study show that the sudden scarcity of resources and loss of traditional occupations increased competition and conflicts. This triggered stresses and anxiety for many participants who lived in close-knit rural communities. These, in turn, resulted in poor interpersonal relationships and often weakened traditional cooperative relationships in the southwestern coastal areas of Bangladesh. Thus, the consequences produced by climate change arguably influenced inter-group and personal relationships at least indirectly at various levels.

It is important to note that Bangladesh is located near the equator where the temperature is higher than the Earth's average. Due to climate change, temperatures are likely to increase and this can become a source of stress and a threat to crops (van Lange et al., 2018). This chapter shows that crop failures left people with limited livelihood options and it led to dislocation. It is also likely that violence and aggression will increase in the future due to stresses linked to climate change because such violence is often rooted in inter-group conflict and is often more likely to occur in regions with warmer climates (van Lange et al., 2018).

However, it has to be noted that the relationship between climate change and intergroup conflict is subject to debate and research to date has remained inconclusive. This study does not show any direct relationship between climate-induced disasters and the development of individuality or conflict. It instead suggests that climate variability may trigger stresses, dislocation, crop failures, unemployment, and interpersonal and group conflicts in agricultural and developing country contexts such as Bangladesh. These findings are in line with other international research (Gilmore, 2017; Koubi, 2019; Pearson & Schuldt, 2018) that has suggested that climate change does not inevitably result in conflict, but instead may indirectly produce conflicts by interacting with other contextual factors. In the context of Bangladesh, these contextual factors include poverty, inequality, social marginalization, class, unemployment, gender, and so forth.

Findings from this study demonstrate that in rural agricultural and coastal settings, natural hazards such as Aila, sea-level rise and inundation produced land degradation, loss of property, salinity, livelihood vulnerabilities, and mental stresses. These, in turn, led to alterations in social relationships and cultivated a sense of self-interest rather than collectivism. It is not that conflict did not exist in rural societies previously, but it appears that disaster-related stresses intensified the conflict as people lost their means of livelihood (for example, agricultural land). Some poor and marginalized groups competed for scarce relief materials and aid for the same reasons in the disaster context such as southwestern Bangladesh. New forms of paternalistic alliances were formed by local poor groups with the government and nongovernment organizations to gain control over relief, rehabilitation services, and development aid, indicating intergroup conflicts. This corroborates some of the previous research findings that have shown that outside interventions not only came with relief but also generated conflict due to the control over the relief (Roy & Sony, 2019). For this reason, corruption in the distribution of relief and development aid must be addressed to minimize conflict and foster harmony. Furthermore, climate-related stresses produced dislocation through neonatal marriage, out-migration, and loss of employment and/or means of subsistence in villages where people lived a simple life for generations. Such dislocation will likely continue and worsen in the future, as predicted by other researchers (e. g., Davis et al., 2018).

Climate change is a multifaceted problem produced collectively and thus requires collective environmental action. Responses to an environmental crisis such as climate change are shaped by group identity processes, cultural norms, and appraisal of environmental risks and opportunities (Fritsche et al., 2018). Jansson and Dorrepaal (2015) have emphasized personal climate change norms to understand environmental justice and they have found climate change has a relationship with personal moral concerns such as harm and fairness. Similarly, Pearson et al. (2021) have shown that families play a significant role shaping climate-related beliefs and policy support. Personal and collective emotions play a vital part in influencing both proenvironmental and prosocial behaviors (Fritsche et al., 2018). According to Nolan and Schultz (2015), prosocial behaviors are needed for climate change adaptation at any community level, which is also important to ensure environmental justice. One example of collective environmental action is school students' climate strike across the globe. Greta Thunberg, a teenage Swedish student, protested in front of the Swedish parliament to take climate change action. She inspired thousands of students across the globe to take action. In other words, the problem cannot be addressed individually.

Findings from this study suggest that climate-induced stresses generated a sense of self-centrism, the prioritization of individual needs over group or collective needs. As a result, the old traditional cooperative value was replaced by a new calculative choice which supports the speculation of Niemeyer et al. (2005) regarding climate change maladaptation. This has implications for climate/or environmental justice because the climate change-affected marginalized communities would not be able to raise collective voices if they embody a fragmented or individualistic identity, which is an aspect of the "late" modern self (Giddens, 1991). This would make climate action difficult. For this reason, it is crucially important to raise further awareness about the impacts of climate change in rural communities and make people aware of the collective benefits of climate action instead of short-term individual gains.

Importantly, findings show that members of the climate change-affected communities developed calculative and individualistic values which provoked them to seek better opportunities beyond the village's horizon. Thus, seasonal and permanent migration took place out of the study areas. Some people were dislocated which disconnected them from their communities. For this reason, people lost their faith in traditional or local coping mechanisms and therefore, the elder members of the community were no longer enjoying the same level of prestige and honor as they did in the past.

According to Hirschi (1969), deviant behavior is the product of weak social elements that includes attachments, commitment, involvement, and beliefs. In line with this view, the results of this study reveal that social relationships became weaker on different levels because of the indirect consequences of climate change. Ultimately, these increased several social problems such as corruption in relief distribution, the conflict between families, breakdown of the old chain of command, deviant activities among the youth, and so on in the southwest coastal areas of Bangladesh. Such problems are not conducive to addressing climate change and promoting justice in the climate risk contexts.

5 Conclusion

In conclusion, it has become clear that climate change is not only impacting natural ecology but also impacting social ecology. The study has shed light on the changing patterns of social relationships as one of the indirect products of climate change. For instance, because of Aila and increasing salinity, the traditional collectivist values gave way, at least to some extent, to a more modernist individualist norm. As a consequence of this kind of change, the local people may lose their collective identity which is crucially important for fighting for environmental justice.

The impacts of climate change on social relationships on various levels raise questions about environmental justice because certain groups are more adversely affected by this change than others. Increased competition, conflict regarding control over scarce resources, and poor relationships would undermine the capacity of local people to fight the impacts of climate change. Strong social relationships result in social capital that is important for sustainable climate change adaptation. However, weakening social and intergroup relationships would undermine efforts to initiate proenvironmental action needed for promoting environmental justice. Therefore, in designing climate change adaptation and mitigation programs, attention needs to be paid to how climate change affects social relationships. Prosocial behavior enhancing programs such as community meetings and events can be organized by governmental bodies, youth groups, charities, religious groups, students, nongovernment organizations, and other stakeholders to improve intergroup, intragroup, and personal social relationships in the disaster-affected areas. Collective prosocial/proenvironmental behaviors are essential for promoting environmental justice.

References

Abdullah, A. N., Myers, B., Stacey, N., Zander, K. K., & Garnett, S. T. (2017). The impact of the expansion of shrimp aquaculture on livelihoods in coastal Bangladesh. *Environment, Development, Sustainability, 19*(5), 2093–2114. https://doi.org/10.1007/s10668-016-9824-5

Beck, U. (1992). *Risk society. Towards a new modernity.* Sage.

Bourdieu, P. (1986). The forms of capital. In J. G. Richardson (Ed.), *Handbook of theory and research for the sociology of education* (pp. 241–258). Greenwood Press.

Burke, M., Hsiang, S. M., & Miguel, E. (2015). Climate and conflict. *Annual Review of Economics, 7*(1), 577–617. https://doi.org/10.1146/annurev-economics-080614-115430

Dasgupta, S., Akther Kamal, F., Huque Khan, Z., Choudhury, S., & Nishat, A. (2015). River salinity and climate change: Evidence from coastal Bangladesh. In *World scientific reference on Asia and the world economy* (pp. 205–242). World Scientific. https://doi.org/10.1142/9789814578622_0031

Davis, K. F., Bhattachan, A., D'Odorico, P., & Suweis, S. (2018). A universal model for predicting human migration under climate change: Examining future sea-level rise in Bangladesh. *Environmental Research Letters, 13*(6), 1–11. https://doi.org/10.1088/1748-9326/aac4d4

Dakope Upazila.jpg (2021). Dhaka, *Banglapedia.* https://en.banglapedia.org/index.php/DacopeUpazila#/media/File:DakopeUpazila.jpg

Djebou, D. S., & Singh, V. (2016). Impact of climate change on the hydrologic cycle and implications for society. *Environment Social Psychology, 1*(1), 36–49. https://doi.org/10.18063/ESP.2016.01.002

Dimitrov, R. S. (2016). The Paris agreement on climate change: Behind closed doors. *Global Environmental Politics, 16*(3), 1–11. https://doi.org/10.1162/GLEPa00361

Fritsche, I., Barth, M., Jugert, P., Masson, T., & Reese, G. (2018). A social identity model of pro-environmental action (SIMPEA). *Psychological Review, 125*(2), 245–269. https://doi.org/10.1037/rev0000090

Giddens, Anthony. (1991). *Modernity and self-identity: Self and society in the late modern age*: Stanford University Press.

Gilmore, E. A. (2017). Introduction to special issue: Disciplinary perspectives on climate change and conflict. *Current Climate Change Reports, 3*(4), 193–199. https://doi.org/10.1007/s40641-017-0081-y

Haider, M. Z., & Akter, R. (2018). Shrimp paddy conflict in the South-West coastal region of Bangladesh. *International Journal of Agricultural Economics, 3*(1), 9–13. https://doi.org/10.11648/j.ijae.20180301.12

Hirschi, T. (1969). *Key idea: Hirschi's social bond/social control theory* (pp. 55–69). University of California Press.

Hirschi, T. (2017). On the compatibility of rational choice and social control theories of crime. In *The reasoning criminal* (pp. 105–118). Routledge.

Hossain, M., Uddin, M., & Fakhruddin, A. (2013). Impacts of shrimp farming on the coastal environment of Bangladesh and approach for management. *Reviews in Environmental Science Bio/technology, 12*(3), 313–332. https://doi.org/10.1007/s11157-013-9311-5

Hussain, M., Butt, A. R., Uzma, F., Ahmed, R., Irshad, S., Rehman, A., & Yousaf, B. (2019). A comprehensive review of climate change impacts, adaptation, and mitigation on environmental and natural calamities in Pakistan. *Environmental Monitoring and Assessment, 192*(1), 1–20. https://doi.org/10.1007/s10661-019-7956-4

Jansson, J., & Dorrepaal, E. (2015). Personal norms for dealing with climate change: Results from a survey using moral foundations theory. *Sustainable Devlopment, 23*(6), 381–395. https://doi.org/10.1002/sd.1598

Kabir, R., Khan, H. T., Ball, E., & Caldwell, K. (2016). Climate change impact: The experience of the coastal areas of Bangladesh affected by cyclones Sidr and Aila. *Journal of Environmental and Public Health, 2016*, 1–10. https://doi.org/10.1155/2016/9654753

Koubi, V. (2019). Climate change and conflict. *Annual Review of Political Science, 22*, 343–360. https://doi.org/10.1146/annurev-polisci-050317-070830

Maps of the World. (2016). *Maps of Bangladesh. [Map]*. Small administrative map of Bangladesh. http://www.maps-of-the-world.net/maps-of-asia/maps-of-bangladesh/

Masson-Delmotte, V., Zhai, P., Pörtner, H.-O., Roberts, D., Skea, J., Shukla, P. R., et al. (2018). Global warming of 1.5 °C (Global Warming of 1.5 °C. An IPCC Special Report on the impacts of global warming of 1.5 °C above pre-industrial levels and related global greenhouse gas emission pathways, in the context of strengthening the global response to the threat of climate change, sustainable development, and efforts to eradicate poverty, Issue. https://www.ipcc.ch/site/assets/uploads/sites/2/2019/06/SR15FullReportLowRes.pdf

Mohai, P., Pellow, D., & Roberts, J. T. (2009). Environmental justice. *Annual Review of Environment Resources, 34*, 405–430. https://doi.org/10.1146/annurev-environ-082508-094348

Nielsen, K. S., Clayton, S., Stern, P. C., Dietz, T., Capstick, S., & Whitmarsh, L. (2021). How psychology can help limit climate change. *American Psychologist, 76*(1), 130. https://doi.org/10.1037/amp0000624

Niemeyer, S., Petts, J., & Hobson, K. (2005). Rapid climate change and society: Assessing responses and thresholds. *Risk Analysis, 25*(6), 1443–1456. https://doi.org/10.1111/j.1539-6924.2005.00691.x

Nolan, J. M., & Schultz, P. W. (2015). Prosocial behavior and environmental action. In *The Oxford handbook of prosocial behavior.* (pp. 626–652). Oxford University Press.

Pearson, A. R., & Schuldt, J. P. (2018). Climate change and intergroup relations: Psychological insights, synergies, and future prospects. *Group Processes & Intergroup Relations, 21*(3), 373–388. https://doi.org/10.1177/1368430217747750

Pearson, A. R., Bacio, G. A., Naiman, S., Romero-Canyas, R., & Schuldt, J. P. (2021). Cultural determinants of climate change opinion: Familism predicts climate beliefs and policy support among US Latinos. *Climatic Change, 167*(1), 1–8. https://doi.org/10.1007/s10584-021-03165-2

Roy, T., Chandra, D., Sony, M. A. A. M., & Rahman, M. S. (2020). Impact of salinity intrusion on (sic) health of coastal people: Reflections from Dacope upazila of Khulna district, Bangladesh. *Khulna University Studies, 17*(1&2), 57–66.

Roy, T., & Sony, M. M. A. A. M. (2019). Social structural changes in post-disaster area from marxist point of view: Reflections from Dacope, Khulna, Bangladesh. *NIU International Journal of Human Rights, 6*(1), 3–13.

Schlosberg, D., & Collins, L. B. (2014). From environmental to climate justice: Climate change and the discourse of environmental justice. *Wiley Interdisciplinary Reviews: Climate Change, 5*(3), 359–374. https://doi.org/10.1002/wcc.275

Sovacool, B. K. (2018). Bamboo beating bandits: Conflict, inequality, and vulnerability in the political ecology of climate change adaptation in Bangladesh. *World Development, 102*, 183–194. https://doi.org/10.1016/j.worlddev.2017.10.014

Swim, J. K., & Bloodhart, B. (2018). The intergroup foundations of climate change justice. *Group Processes Intergroup Relations, 21*(3), 472–496. https://doi.org/10.1177/1368430217745366

Spijkers, J., & Boonstra, W. J. (2017). Environmental change and social conflict: The northeast Atlantic mackerel dispute. *Regional Environmental Change, 17*(6), 1835–1851. https://doi.org/10.1007/s10113-017-1150-4

Shukla, P., Skea, J., Calvo Buendia, E., Masson-Delmotte, V., Pörtner, H., Roberts, D., et al. (2019). IPCC, 2019: Climate Change and Land: An IPCC special report on climate change, desertification, land degradation, sustainable land management, food security, and greenhouse gas fluxes in terrestrial ecosystems. https://www.ipcc.ch/srccl/chapter/annex-v-index-3/

van Lange, P. A., Rinderu, M. I., & Bushman, B. J. (2018). CLASH: Climate (change) and cultural evolution of intergroup conflict. *Group Processes & Intergroup Relations, 21*(3), 457–471. https://doi.org/10.1177/1368430217735579

Ecological Justice in Post-COVID-19 Politics: The Role of Affective Ecologies and Amazonian Indigenous Ontologies

Maria Fernanda Gebara

1 Introduction

This chapter highlights the need to rethink human relationships with the rest of nature. It looks at how ecological justice could positively contribute to post-COVID-19 politics being refocused toward affective ecologies and indigenous ontologies. I argue that the purpose of critical post-COVID-19 politics is to investigate an alternate way of conceptualizing social and political relations, starting from human relationships with the ecological world, rather than just thinking in terms of human-state and inter-state relations. The main argument is for a post-COVID-19 politics that fits with a world constructed of the more-than-human and an acknowledgment that humanity is a less than exceptional or necessary species (Haraway, 1991, 2008). Every relationship is embedded in and dependent on nonhuman systems. The concern is not with "nature" itself, but with problematizing its concept when thinking of structuring our relationships with things we designate as being ecological—which I also refer to as "the nonhuman," "the other-than-human," and "the more-than-human." Other-than-human beings, by which I mean other animals, plants, fungi, viruses, parasites, bacteria, rivers, stones, stars, and so many more, have played a fundamental role in the history of humanity. They have been present on Earth long before we were and perhaps long after. In this sense, the way we think about and relate to "nature" both informs and structures the complex and interlocking scientific, political, ethical, and legal issues (Grear, 2015) that underpin post-COVID-19 politics.

To undertake a cultural critique of modern and dominant relationships with "nature," I engage with Amazonian indigenous ontologies. Ontologies shape our values, beliefs, and what we consider possible in a way that is often invisible in everyday lives (Pickering, 2010). However, they are fundamentally interpretive and contestable. I then question our dominant way of belonging to the ecological world

---

M. F. Gebara (✉)
Independent Scholar, London, United Kingdom
e-mail: mfgebara@gmail.com

© The Author(s), under exclusive license to Springer Nature Singapore Pte Ltd. 2022
D. Madhanagopal et al. (eds.), *Environment, Climate, and Social Justice*,
https://doi.org/10.1007/978-981-19-1987-9_18

that surrounds us, the ethical spheres we inhabit, and our place as a species relative to others, especially the other than human. I ask how beginning to think and feel more affectively, meaning the encouragement of an ethos of affect (through care and empathy), might help us reimagine our ways of thinking and living (Ash, 2013), our possibilities of relating to the nonhuman (Singh, 2018) and how to move forward in overcoming the current environmental and health crises.

I am interested in how affect theory and indigenous ontologies can provide practical significance in our understanding and framing of human–nature relationships. Substantially different ways of thinking and being remain today, which are predicated upon different ontologies. Our anthropic relationship to the rest of nature and the objectification and exploitation thereof is considered the basic cause of pandemics such as COVID-19. In such a relationship, nature forms the passive complement to our own activity. The fundamental question is: Is it viable to think and feel affectively and relationally, and follow indigenous cultures' ontologies, to "animate" or "reanimate" the dominant ontology behind modern politics?

Section 1 reviews ideas of ecological justice and political practice. Section 2 examines affect theory and non-dualistic approaches that could help integrate affective ecologies into post-COVID-19 politics. Section 3 outlines indigenous ontologies and political experiences in Brazil, Bolivia, and Ecuador, to provide examples of how to rearticulate the relationships between humans and other beings. The chapter concludes by making a case for using ethics of care to inform our ecological relationships and post-COVID-19 politics.

2 Ecological Justice and Political Practice

Ecological justice is a model that tries to minimize the injustices in human–nature interactions. As such, it represents a turn away from the human/nature dualisms prevalent in Anglo-European political philosophy (Murdoch, 2006; Simonsen, 2013). It suggests a departure from the foundational assumptions of modern culture: in particular, a new way of understanding the human subject in relation to the ecological world.

Ecological justice theory offers a new epistemology and corresponding ethics that is not anthropocentric and therefore not centered in human–nature dualism (Latour, 2004; Murdoch, 2006; Whatmore, 2013). The view of humans as being separate from nature flourished in the Enlightenment (Hatfield, 2007). Since then, the concept of "human" has been reinscribed within categories marked by exclusionary practices. As a consequence, the human subject stands at the center of the juridical order as its only genuine agent and beneficiary, reflecting an anthropocentric political practice with (and mediation of) ecological relationships (Kotze & Calzadilla, 2017). Examples of ecocentric politics, meaning the politics that embraces ecological justice and perceives human beings as an integral part of a much larger whole and as components of an interlinked, and interdependent "web of nature" (Merchant, 1992, p. 86), are a few and far between, but they feature most prominently in the "rights of nature" paradigm.

The "rights of nature" idea subvert claims to unity or universality that leads to an extreme deconstruction of the notion of "human," by bringing "speciesism" (the privilege of some species over others) to its theoretical revision (Agamben, 2004; Derrida, 2002). As argued by Dryzek (1998), we need to be more receptive to other-than-human beings in order to better understand our ecological relationships and be able to include the more-than-human world in political decision-making. This could awaken our capacity to truly perceive the needs of "remote" ecological niches made of other-than-human beings normally left out of political conversations (Plumwood, 2001) and to understand the more-than-human realm as containing a host of political entities (Bennett, 2010).

An ethic of ecological justice is then more democratic and offers an opportunity for receptiveness to a previously unrecognized realm of the "more than human," as argued by Whatmore (2002). Expanding justice to a range of ecological forms is a "politics of sight" (Pachirat, 2013) that brings appreciation and respect to all ecological systems and beings. This brings us to the notion of the multverse, meaning that this universe is one of many (Ferrando, 2013). I prefer to revert to James' (2008) notion of the pluralistic universe, where he defends the mystical and anti-pragmatic view that concepts distort, rather than reveal, reality. Rather than a world of independent units and concepts, pluriversality refers to the entanglement of several connected ontologies.

While "multi-" and "pluriverses" should be at the heart of the development of a post-COVID-19 political society, in practice, implementation of such concepts is still abstract. Human beings (the Western/modern concept of human) and reason remain central within politics; policymakers have used reason to distance human beings from the rest of nature (Cudworth & Hobden, 2015). The increase of philosophical questions about what the interrogation of "the human" and "humanity's" relationship to other beings means for the study and practice of contemporary politics is then welcome (McDonald, 2017). It is important, however, not to become overly embroiled in philosophical arguments that may overshadow important issues of post-COVID-19 political practice, such as the reorientation of social norms and values and the practical emergence of ethics that reflects ecological relations.

Considering the unprecedented environmental change faced by the human species, post-COVID-19 political theorists and practitioners are confronted by two main problems: the way humans perceive the rest of the ecological system and the way we have repressed our own ecological elements. To step outside the human–nature dualism, modern social norms and values need a complete restructuring. COVID-19 does not in itself dictate an appropriate or likely politics of response; however, the ecological, social, and political changes the health crisis has generated should force us to reflect on some key assumptions and guiding principles of modern politics.

For Gruen (2015), our relationships with other-than-human beings should be built on an entwined compassion, basing our assumptions about ethical behavior on principles of "likeness." The author highlights that we have an ethical duty to those with whom we are entangled. The justice that applies to the human community, in this sense, can be extended to other-than-human beings (Kotze & Calzadilla, 2017), as is illustrated in Sect. 3. Haraway (1991) has been key in exploring the porous character of these boundaries on the machine–human-animal–nature continuum. For Haraway (2008), the human–nature relationship is one of direct embodied experience where we "meet" and co-constitute one another.

Thus, instead of striving for a reason, we could strive for feeling, meaning, and relations that enhance our capacity to act and awaken empathy and respect for other-than-human natures (Rocheleau, 2008; Rocheleau & Roth, 2007). This could enhance our natural endeavor for affection and cooperation and a preference for fairness and equity, in opposition to humans as rational, reason-driven individuals (de Waal, 2010). In such a process, non-modern ontologies of affect help us consider the embodiment and otherness that all beings have, awakening a process of "becoming with" the many others with whom we share this planet (Gibson-Graham, 2011; Haraway, 2008). In human–nature studies, engagement with these ideas include a call for ethics and political practice that nurtures the concepts, as Singh (2018, p. 3) argues, of "being-in-common," of "all being(s), human and nonhuman, animate and inanimate, processual and fluid as well as categorical and definite in conception," and models of doing research as a "process of co-transformation that re/constitutes the world" (Gibson-Graham & Roelvink, 2010, p. 320). The following sections look at affect theory and indigenous ontologies in order to illustrate their practical significance in rejecting human/nature dualisms and better integrating affective and relational behaviors into post-COVID-19 politics.

3 Affect Theory and the Emergence of Affective Political Ecology

The context of COVID-19 is a fertile terrain that expands discussions of affect and speculative thought about the challenges of politics and ethics in more-than-human worlds (Singh, 2017). Inspired by the view that affective political ecology can open new ways of thinking, experiencing, and feeling (Singh, 2018), this section asks what it means to encourage an ethos of affect when engaging with sociotechnical relationalities of human and nonhuman beings that defy the traditional ethical boundaries that have marked past eras. While the concept of affect has different interpretations (Gregg & Seigworth, 2010; Massumi, 2002; Thrift, 2008), I follow Singh (2018) and work with an understanding of affect that derives from the Spinoza-Deleuze-Massumi lineage. Here, affect is defined as a dynamic relationship between bodies that enhances or diminishes the capacity of a body to affect and be affected (Deleuze, 1989). In this sense, affect inspires thought about the world in terms of rhizomatic interconnections, assemblages, or a complex "coming together" of things and beings (Singh, 2017, 2018).

Bennett's (2010) argument helps us to think about this embodied cognition and the vivacity and self-organizing aptitude of even apparently inert forms of matter—a rock, for example. According to her (2010, p. 11), things are "alive in their complex interrelationships, entanglements, and propensities for open-ended change" (in Singh, 2018, p. 1). Affection thus reformulates modern notions of agency; in Singh's words, "it helps us to see agency in relationships, and in all that constitutes them" (2018, p. 1). Other authors (Braun, 2008; Ruddick, 2017) suggest that affective ideas might guide our relationships and help us rethink our ways of being human. Also important is the recognition that collaborations and collectivities enhance mutual thriving (Ruddick, 2017). These arguments for alternative socioecological futures are central to "affective political ecology" (Dallman et al., 2013; Hayes-Conroy & Hayes-Conroy, 2013; Sultana, 2015).

I also draw upon feminist thinking to help in the understanding of affect so that it can be practical for politics. Haraway, for example, builds on Latour's (2004) and Stengers's (2010, 2011) etymology of "politics" to highlight its relation to "polite," in addition to "polis." For Haraway (2008, p. 92), hospitality, good behaviors, or politesse, is a cosmopolitical and biopolitical act of "articulating bodies to other bodies with care so that significant others might flourish." Puig de la Bellacasa (2011, p. 89) endorses this view by illustrating the affective senses of the term "concern." As she states, "understood as affective states, concern, and care are…related. Care, however, has stronger affective and ethical connotations. While concern denotes worry and thoughtfulness about an issue as well as the fact of belonging to those 'affected' by it; care adds a strong sense of attachment and commitment to something."

Here I argue that such a view is fundamental when thinking about post-COVID-19 politics because it enables the consideration of the political process as being attuned and open to the transformations that other-than-humans—such as coronavirus—are capable of. In such a perspective, mediations of politics and agency no longer appear as directed by human/social subjects but as coenacted with other-than-humans (Latour, 2004; Puig de la Bellacasa, 2011). To answer the question posed at the beginning of the section, I agree with Von Mossner (2017) that affective ecologies can evoke an embodied cognition, simulated in mind and body as if really experienced, which enables empathy and in turn stimulates care and attention—perhaps even action (Von Mossner, 2017). If we want to build compatible ethics in a post-COVID-19 scenario, we should be able to recognize that agency is indeed distributed among humans and other-than-human beings. Although this may still be difficult to perceive, it became visible with COVID-19 as we were all forced into lockdown by coronavirus, a tiny being that has been deeply affecting our relationships. The next section highlights some examples from indigenous ontologies that may open up our minds to a better understanding of agency distribution between humans and other-than-human beings.

4 Indigenous Ontologies and Post-COVID-19 Politics

What follows provides a sense of different indigenous ontologies and cosmologies still practiced in the Amazon. Such examples offer insights into how to rearticulate relationships between humans and other beings toward affective ecologies, and how we might build a post-COVID-19 attuned politics and ethics.

4.1 *Indigenous Ontologies as a Guide for Post-COVID-19 Relations*

The implicit ontology of Amazonian indigenous cultures locates human beings in larger social environments. People belong not only to a human community, but to a community of all nature. Existence in this larger society, just as in familiar and tribal contexts, means reciprocal responsibilities and mutual obligations between humans and other-than-human beings are taken for granted and assumed without question or reflection (Callicott, 1989, pp. 189–190). This alterity of Amazonian cultures has, not for the first time, inspired intellectual debate that challenges modernist ontology (i.e., Descola, 1992, 2005; Lévi-Strauss, 1971–76; Viveiros de Castro, 2005). This raises questions about possible linkages or conversations to be had across indigenous and modern philosophical traditions about what it means to think affectively and relationally. How might doing so invite us to reflect upon our dominant anthropocentric ways of life and enhance a deeper appreciation of the interconnectedness of all life?

"Perspectivism" or "'multinaturalism," that is, the extension of agency from human to other-than-human beings, is common in Amazonian ontologies; what some call "animism" (Descola, 2005; Escobar, 2016; Kimmerer, 2013; Viveiros de Castro, 2005). Such an extension of agency generates a distinct environmental responsibility to other-than-human beings. Bird-David (1990, 1999), Ingold (2000, 2006) and Hornborg (2006) also stress such relational constitution of beings—both human and other-than-human—which is primarily found among hunter and gatherer societies.

Among the Sateré-Mawé, living in the mid-Amazon River region on the border of Amazonas and Pará in Brazil, the environment is a giving one. Just as Bird-David offers the "root metaphor" of this kind of relationship as "forest as a parent," gatherers and hunters [...] "view their environment as giving; their system is characterized by modes of distribution and property relations, constructed in terms of giving, as within a family, rather than in terms of reciprocity, as between kin" (Bird-David, 1990, p. 189). Trust is the main quality of such a relationship; the Sateré-Mawé trusts the forest as a parent who unconditionally provides for his/her family. They also maintain this non-reciprocal relationship with a person called *miat ehary*, the "mother of animals" (Wright et al., 2012). The animal–mother relationship is affectionate and releasing, whereas any responsibility arising from this relationship may be left open (Hornborg, 2006).

The mother ontology is also present in different indigenous groups in Bolivia, where Pachamama means "Mother Earth." They believe that Pachamama and the people are one. *Aruskipasipxañani* is an indigenous word that means "dialogue among people and parallel worlds" (Belmonte, 2016). This parallel world refers to the cosmos, Pachamama, dead ancestors, and everything that is alive, such as animals, plants, and water. In this indigenous ontology, Pachamama gives humans everything they need to live, so they care for her and offer her tribute in return. Such ontology is common in different indigenous peoples around the world, where the Earth is the provider and everything is seen as "knowledgeable, vital, and interconnected" (Suchet-Pearson et al., 2013). Relationships between humans and Pachamama are based on affect, dialogue, and humility, through which indigenous people have not only enriched their landscapes but have also cultivated cosmological subjectivities that nurture alternative ways of being and relating with parallel worlds and other-than-human natures. Mothers give life, nurture, care, feed, console and raise those who are dependent on them. Mother Earth, a distinctly feminine entity, does the same (Grear, 2007).

Quechua-speaking people in the Amazonian lowlands of Ecuador, can also help to flesh out possibilities for what it might mean to understand oneself as a relationally affectively constituted person, engaging other-than-human beings through what they call becoming *yacharishka*, or "accustomed" to something. As Reddekop (2014, p. 136) observes, "in becoming *yacharishka*, one comes to share a body, and to occupy a shared body with others. This notion of a shared body reflects a basic ontological supposition that relationships and affect come first, positioning the individual as a kind of concrescence or 'fixity' which, nevertheless, always retains a certain transience and mutability that is constantly 'becoming' and requires deliberate work to retain its stability and identity." Lagrou (2000, p. 152) also suggests, with regard to the Kashinawa in western Brazil, that "paths followed, experiences shared, and food eaten mould a being into what it is, an identity that nevertheless has its ephemeral side." All this is associated with affectionate approaches in which humans develop a careful relationship with other-than-human beings.

The care that "glues" relationships together is called, in Quechua, *yakichina* (Reddekop, 2014). Its etymology is derived from the verb *yakina*, "to love," and means "causing another to feel empathy or compassion towards you" (Gow, 2000). *Yakichina,* in this sense, means caring for others, "something one must cultivate as the positive, affective condition of living together with relatives (human and non-human), and which is manifest insofar as co-habitation with others is possible" (Reddekop, 2014, p. 138). Engagement with relatives involves communication of emotion and feeling, and its "causing" in others through *yakichina*; thus, it frequently involves what Brown (1986) termed "technologies of sentiment."

The Yanomami, in North Amazonas, also believe that all beings are interconnected. They see animals (*yaropë*) as part of an ancestral human population that lost its human form when the world was created. They were humanimals who, in Yanomami myths, disrespected the values of their own world and transformed themselves into hunting animals (Kapfhammer, 2012). This human-animal mythical connection is translated in the fact that each Yanomami has a "double animal" (*rixi*), which is at the heart of their soul (Kapfhammer, 2012). It is important to note, however, that this humanification of animals, common in Amerindian cultures, does not denote humanity as a natural species. Rather, they refer to the social condition of 'personhood" (Viveiros de Castro, 1998, p. 476). In an article on "new animism," Harvey (2006) refers to the work of Hallowell (1960) on the Ojibwa, who also linguistically attribute personhood to "other-than-human persons." These persons are a "communicative community" that "places constraints" on each person to become a better person in some way."

Similarly, in Ecuador, the Quechua notion of *Kawsak Sacha,* or "Living Forest," has been voiced in opposition to neoliberal plans for further "development" of the Amazon (Reddekop, 2014). *Kawsak Sacha* (the Living Forest) is a proposal which stems from the millennia-old knowledge of the indigenous peoples who inhabit the rainforest. Whereas modern cultures treat nature as an undemanding source of raw materials destined exclusively for human use, *Kawsak Sacha* recognizes the forest as being constructed of living selves and the communicative relationships they have with each other. These selves, from tiny plants to supreme beings who protect the forest, are persons (*runa*) who inhabit waterfalls, lagoons, swamps, mountains, and rivers, and who collectively form the Living Forest. These persons live together in community (*llakta*) and live their lives in a manner similar to human beings (Gualinga, 2018).

Finally, the *buen vivir* concept, born from indigenous cosmologies in the Amazon and Andes is deeply rooted in indigenous traditions, which affirm the need to live in harmony with "Mother Earth" and all forms of life. *Buen vivir* provides the discursive context for discussions about natural resources, the creation of a plurinational state, cultural decolonization, and the rights of nature (Gudynas, 2013). In Bolivia, *buen vivir* also signifies a radical opposition to the neoliberal growth-without-limits paradigm and "challenges the anthropocentric approach to a civilization based only on the power of markets and financial resources, in which money is what gives life to everything and development is a means without end" (the Plurinational State of Bolivia, 2014). Similarly, the Yawanawá people, living on the borders of Brazil, Bolivia, and Peru, use the word *ikixará* to describe *buen vivir*. For them, *ikixará* means living in "total interconnectedness and integration of all life" as central to the flourishing of life in their ecologies (personal communication, Nani Kateyuve, April 2020).

4.2 Integrating Indigenous Ontologies into Political Enactment

Here, I look at the different experiences of Brazil, Bolivia, and Ecuador to provide insights into how indigenous ontologies could be recognized and integrated as part of political and legal systems. In such countries, legal protection of other-than-human beings is present in juridical systems and public discourses due to the fact that indigenous peoples have been respecting and living in harmony with nature since immemorial times (Petersen, 1990).

Although there are increasing demands to include other-than-human beings in legal systems, only Ecuador has bestowed rights on nature in its constitution. The Ecuadorian Constitution of 2008 proclaims the move from an anthropocentric juridical system to an ecocentric one, recognizing enforceable rights of nature. The election of Rafael Correa to the presidency of Ecuador in 2006 signaled the beginning of a transformative process; his new vision involved "anti-neoliberalism in the service of enhanced equity" (Fitz-Henry, 2014). In the Ecuadorian Constitution, the theoretical notion of the rights of nature and indigenous cosmovisions, which recognize how human and nonhuman beings are inextricably linked, converge in constitutional rights. The Constitution Preamble legitimizes the idea that the relationship between people and nature is ancient and needs to be celebrated, not mired in perpetual conflict, as well as the idea that people and nature are one and must coexist by living well and in collective harmony.

The Constitution, however, does not address a more critical concern—the extent to which environmental care should be prioritized in the application of commercial, agricultural, building, and other non-environmental laws (Kotze & Calzadilla, 2017). The absence of a normative hierarchy within the Constitution itself is supported by the Constitution's provisions on the national "development structure," which establishes the framework within which development must occur in Ecuador. Normative conflicts such as this have their critics, who caution that rights of nature provisions could be "beautiful rhetoric used to entice support for Ecuador from the international community" (Fitz-Henry, 2014, p. 142) and that these provisions effectively greenwash a government's efforts "to prevent any real implementation of the Rights of Nature as it seeks to expand extractive and other industrial development" (Margil, 2014, pp. 149–50).

Another example comes from Bolivia. While the country's 2009 Constitution recognizes the importance of protecting nature, it does not expressly set out a constitutional right for it, like Ecuador's Constitution. The protection of "Mother Earth" rights is rather defined by two legislations: (i) Law 71 of the Rights of Mother Earth of 2010, which entitle different rights to Mother Earth; and (ii) Framework Law 300 of Mother Earth and Integral Development for Living Well of 2012 (Framework Law), which defines how the rights will be put in operation, in the context of the so-called integral development for *Vivir Bien* (based on the *buen vivir* ontology described by Gudynas (2013). This choice to name the law with the words "Mother Earth" rather than "nature" signifies the profound indigenous ontology described above (Zaffaroni, 2011). Mother Earth is referred to by the law as a "dynamic living system comprising an indivisible community of all living systems and organisms, which are interrelated, interdependent and complementary, and which share a common destiny." Even if only on paper, the law represents an attempt to overcome the Cartesian dualism which disassociates people from Mother Earth, as it also recognizes that "the exercise of individual rights is limited by the exercise of collective rights in the living systems of Mother Earth" (Article 6).

Such debates over the rights of Mother Earth and *Vivir Bien* have reinforced the idea that substantial alternatives to modern conceptions of development are soon to be incorporated (Gudynas, 2013). *Vivir Bien (Sumaj Kamaña, Sumaj Kausay, or Yaiko Kavi Päve)* is an alternative vision to neoliberalism. According to the Framework Law, this vision denotes "living in complementarity, in harmony and in balance with Mother Earth and societies, in equality and solidarity and eliminating the inequalities and mechanisms of control and domination." It is not clear in the Framework Law, however, how such relationship between humans and other-than-human beings should be implemented in practice (Kotze & Calzadilla, 2017). The Framework Law institutes different actions with the aim of generating social, spiritual, and material enabling circumstances, aimed at fortifying community principles to achieve *Vivir Bien*, what is reflected in the notion of "integral development." In this sense, as Kotze and Calzadilla (2017, p. 414) state, "integral development is not the end result, but the process leading to *Vivir Bien.*"

Neoliberal politics and discourses, however, show the clear divergences between the idea of *Vivir Bien* and its practice. In Ecuador, this raises the suspicion that the political and legal systems that provide grounds for the rights of Mother Earth are merely attempting to window-dress ongoing environmental destruction and the exploitation of nature and indigenous people (Kotze & Calzadilla, 2017). Although such transformations are only initial steps toward changing the hegemonic political practice, such movements are still hopeful examples of political efforts to turn away from anthropocentric jurisdictions while embracing care for other-than-human beings as an ethical obligation (Kotze & Calzadilla, 2017).

Unfortunately, this attempt to move away from anthropocentric hierarchies is not reflected in Brazil's law and politics. Although the Brazilian 1988 Constitution recognizes different environmental and indigenous rights, it also entrenches the right of human beings (aptly captured in the term "everyone") to benefit from an objectified environment that is removed from them. This environment, in an instrumental way, must promote human health and well-being for those alive today and those assumed to come tomorrow. Thus, the Brazilian constitution still has an anthropocentric background that consolidates efforts to increase access to and expand human exploitation of nature, with a view to ensuring socioeconomic development (Gebara, 2018). It legally elevates, to the highest possible juridical level, nature as an external object that has the potential to be owned, controlled, and exploited for human beings' needs. It evinces the "essentiality of nature to the humanity of man" (Tallacchini, 1997, p. 129). Such a resolutely anthropocentric ideological orientation of rights is still dominant in global politics and requires that we revisit the assumptions and philosophies that have resulted in the situation today.

5   Discussion: The Natural Ethics

The challenge of post-COVID-19 politics is to place the broad context of all ecological beings at the center of our ethical philosophy. This is essentially an ethical–moral responsibility to future generations that could awake respectful, affective conceptions of human and other-than-human relationships. This section argues for the use of an ethics of care to inform how we view other-than-human beings in post-COVID19 politics. This ethics—which I call natural ethics—is attentive to relations between the individual and the universal and recognizes our interconnection with all beings in the experiences and vulnerability of those beyond our immediate horizon.

Section 3 provided empirical examples of the complex horizon of meaning and practice in Amazonian understandings of other-than-human beings. Indigenous practices and ontologies could serve as inspiration to remind us that we are all part of an extensive network of relationships that deepen the various registers and communicative possibilities of one's multiple and relational selfhoods (Smith, 2006; Wilson, 2008). This outlines an outstandingly affective link to what it is "to be" and to care for oneself and others, which is profoundly relational and rooted in empathic collaborations with other-than-human beings (Blackman, 2012). The emergence of natural ethics then requires the enactment of particular affective atmospheres (Ash, 2013), which inevitably include the nonhuman in order to re-discover other possibilities of life. After all, as animals, we co-evolved from bacteria. The evolution of our species was concomitant with the adjustments and changes in their physical bodies as organisms and matter. If we think that bacteria (the first type of life on Earth) is a type of pathogen—like coronavirus—we would maybe have another perception of things. We could even be thankful to pathogens for reproducing their selves, evolving, and allowing us to be here.

A necessary task in such philosophical reckoning involves problematizing or questioning our most fundamental and accustomed assumptions about ourselves and the world, as well as the basic nature and structure of existence itself (Pickering, 1995). It involves troubling assumptions about what "nature" is and how we can/should relate to "it," and about what it means to be human. In short, it is necessary to problematize our dominant ontology. This concern with ontology is both descriptive and normative (Latour, 2005; Pickering, 1995). This "ontological normativity" explores dances of agency to better distribute it and promote practices that move beyond modern separations between humans and other than humans (Pickering, 1995), to enact modes of living that are affective, collaborative, and careful to the more-than-human world. Thus, ontology is not necessarily a way of "explaining" how the world works but a continuous political attempt to transform relationships and practices (Reddekop, 2014).

Ontological concepts are necessary so we can rebuild our relationship with nature and recover the natural togetherness we have with all its beings. Relinquishing the controlling and reasoning powers of binary explanation requires an immersion in the world of affection, emotions, feelings. Becoming "with" other-than-human beings, rather than observing them from afar (Puig de la Bellacasa, 2017), will better guide the realm of post-COVID-19 politics and ethics. There is a pronounced affective underpinning in Amazonian animism that refers to cultures in which people seek to live "respectfully" toward those around them. As Harvey states: "the ethical implication of animist worldviews is that no 'environment' is given to us, or to any other persons and that whatever we need we must seek in the give and take of relationships and actions and in an honest engagement with a diverse community of similarly needy and desiring persons" (Harvey, 2006, p. 12).

Most political systems and the legal structures in which they are entrenched have not embraced such animism meaningfully (Stone, 1972). One reason is that most legal systems have deep anthropocentric ideological commitments and ontological grounding, reinforced by a neoliberal growth-without-limits agenda; they steadfastly block alternative potentialities for politics (Grear, 2007). Modern politics, ethics, and rights focus mostly on the relationship between human and nonhuman beings insofar as nonhuman being able to be owned as objects and used to advance the human project. Inescapably, then, because other-than-human beings are not yet granted singular and intrinsic value, it is challenging to achieve an ethic of ecological justice.

Politics and the creation of rights have been the basis for human domination over the more-than-human, normally seen as external to and removed from the nature of the human being. Because rights protect individual autonomy (an idea established by theorists like Descartes, Locke, and Rousseau) (Gearty, 2010), they may counter efforts to foster ecological justice. As De Lucia (2015, p. 95) highlights, anthropocentrism is not fair to all people equally, but only to "those best approximating to the abstract model of the possessive, rational subject [qualified] as the beneficiaries of current regimes of ecological accumulation, [which exclude] those not conforming to such a model." A post-COVID-19 politics could dissolve this type of hierarchy by providing a more sensible and radical expression of a reevaluated, reenvisioned relationship between humans and other-than-human beings, one that recognizes a broader space of plural subjectivities, each with its own agency and its particular mode of being. Analogous to the behavior of an individual as part of a social community of interdependent parts, Leopold (1949) claimed a "land ethic" should "simply [enlarge] the boundaries of the community to include soils, waters, plants, and animals, or collectively: the land" (1949, p. 239). Thus, the former hierarchical position as a "conqueror" of land would be altered to one of a "member and citizen" thereof (1949, p. 240).

However, the question must be asked: do nature, and other-than-human beings need politics and ethics? Or, once again, are we—humans—trying to incorporate our understanding of ethics into something that is naturally ethical and normally unpredictable, such as relationships that emerge from the natural world? Or should we ask: how can the conception and practice of politics and ethics change as we move away from anthropocentrism? Such interrogations refer to the ethics of our modes of thought and ethos, which in turn will affect the ethics and politics attributed to other-than-human beings. Ways of constructing values, norms, and concepts have ethico-political and affective effects on the perception and reconfiguration of ecological justice and its nature-cultural assemblages (Barad, 2007; Haraway, 1991). The key challenge would be to reconcile affective ecologies and indigenous ontologies with the prevailing, more conventional, and predominantly anthropocentric visions of ethics and justice that form the basis of most political and legal systems the world over.

Although it may appear a utopic task to expect political leaders and practitioners to address this complex reconciliation, it is important to recognize that the countries which have made compelling attempts to integrate indigenous ontologies into their constitutions, such as Ecuador and Bolivia, have done so under governments that—with obvious differences between them—identify themselves as "socialist" or "democratic socialist." The "proper" relationship between socialism and indigenous ontologies has yet to be defined in its full complexity and goes beyond the scope of this chapter. But the analysis made here might point to the possibility of bridges between indigenous and perhaps more socialist interpretations of ontologies.

6 Conclusions

This chapter accepts the diagnosis of various political theorists that part of what is at stake in post-COVID-19 politics is a strong call for a radical change (see Agamben et al., 2020). As such, radical changes manifest precisely as disagreements over the different ontologies that may serve as guidance for post-COVID-19 politics. An important point made here is that indigenous ontologies can be seen to be much more explicitly concerned with ecological justice because they praise relationships with all others that are relational and affective from the beginning. They are also consistent with practices and longstanding relations of interconnectedness with and "taking care" of other-than-human beings. All these are important arguments for an ethical reorientation that may lead to ecological justice in post-COVID-19 politics.

Such an ethical reorientation could steer the broadening of political and legal systems beyond their axiomatic confines now and in the future, acting as a point of departure from which to contemplate a fundamental reordering of social norms and values, the construction of new types of agency, the relationship between human and other-than-human beings and, ultimately, the possible extension of rights to living and nonliving beings in an effort to dissolve interspecies hierarchies. Moreover, indigenous ontologies, as reflected in Ecuador and Bolivia's rights of nature, may have the potential to infiltrate modern liberal constitutional notions and change the ontology of anthropocentrism at its core.

Ultimately, we are all born animists (Hornborg, 2006; Ingold, 2006). Such animistic instinct certainly allows us to investigate the interplay of emotions, care, curiosity, vulnerability, and the more-than-human, drawing attention to the transformative potential of affective ecologies and how these could be absorbed into innovative ethics and politics.

References

Agamben, G. (2004). *The Open: Man and Animal* (trans: Attell, K.). Stanford University Press.

Agamben, G., Žižek, S., Nancy J. L., Berardi, F.B., Petit, S. L., Butler, J., & Badiou, A., et al. (2020). *Sopa de Wuhan*. ASPO: Aislamiento Social Preventivo y Obligatorio.

Ash, J. (2013). Rethinking affective atmospheres: Technology, perturbation and space times of the non-human. *Geoforum, 49*, 20–28. https://doi.org/10.1016/j.geoforum.2013.05.006

Barad, K. (2007). *Meeting the universe halfway: Quantum physics and the entanglement of matter and meaning*. Duke University Press.

Belmonte, F. V., et al. (2016). Right to justice and diversity of the Indigenous Peoples of Bolivia. In H. Devere (Ed.), *Peacebuilding and the rights of indigenous peoples* (pp. 77–85). Springer Nature.

Bennett, J. (2010). *Vibrant matter: A political ecology of things*. Duke University Press.

Bird-David, N. (1990). The giving environment. Another perspective on the economic system of gatherer-hunters. *Current Anthropology, 31*, 183–196. https://doi.org/10.1086/203825

Bird-David, N. (1999). "Animism" revisited. Personhood, environment, and relational epistemology. *Current Anthropology, 40*, S67–S72. https://doi.org/10.1086/200061

Blackman, L. (2012). *Immaterial bodies—affect, embodiment, mediation*. Sage.

Braun, B. (2008). Environmental issues: Inventive life. *Progress in Human Geography, 32*(5), 667–679. https://doi.org/10.1177/0309132507088030

Brown, M. F. (1986). *Tsewa's gift: Magic and meaning in an amazonian society (133)*. Smithsonian Institution Press.

Callicott, J. B. (1989). *In defense of the land ethic: Essays in environmental philosophy*. State University of New York Press. ISBN 0-88706-899-5.

Cudworth, E., & Hobden, S. (2015). *Overcoming the denial of nature: A posthuman perspective*. University of East London. http://www.lse.ac.uk/internationalRelations/Journals/millenn/pdf/conferencePapers/Cudworth-Hobden--Denial-of-Nature---2015-Millennium-Conference.docx. Accessed 1 Jan 2019.

Dallman, S., Ngo, M., Laris, P., & Thien, D. (2013). Political ecology of emotion and sacred space: The Winnemem Wintu struggles with California water policy. *Emotion, Space and Society, 6*, 33–43. https://doi.org/10.4337/9780857936172.00056

De Lucia, V. (2015). Competing narratives and complex genealogies: The ecosystem approach in international environmental law. *Journal of Environmental Law, 27*(1), 91–117. https://doi.org/10.1093/jel/equ031

De Waal, F. (2010). *The age of empathy: Nature's lessons for a kinder society*. Harmony Books.

Deleuze, G. (1989). Qu'est-ce qu'un dispositif? In F. Ewald (Ed.), *Michel foucault philosophe*. Seuil.

Derrida, J. (2002). *The animal that therefore I am*. Fordham University Press.

Descola, P. (1992). Societies of nature and the nature of society. In A. Kuper (Ed.), *Conceptualizing society* (pp. 107–126). Routledge.

Descola, P. (2005). Ecology as cosmological analysis. In: A. Surrallés & P. García Hierro (Eds.), *The land within: Indigenous territory and the perception of the environment* (22–35). International Work Group for Indigenous Affairs (IWGIA).

Escobar, A. (2016). Thinking-feeling with the earth: Territorial struggles and the ontological dimension of the epistemologies of the South. *Revista De Antropología Iberoamericana, 111*, 11–32. https://doi.org/10.11156/aibr.110102e

Ferrando, F. (2013). *The Posthuman: Philosophical Posthumanism and its Others*. Dissertation. Ph.D. in Philosophy and Theory of Human Sciences. Università di Roma Tre. http://dspace-roma3.caspur.it/bitstream/2307/4356/1/TESI_Ferrando_DEF.pdf Accessed 1 Jan 2019.

Fitz-Henry, E. (2014). Decolonizing Personhood. In M. Maloney & P. Burdon (Eds.), *Wild Law – In Practice*. London: Routledge.

Gearty, C. (2010). Do human rights help or hinder environmental protection? *Journal of Human Rights and the Environment, 1*(1), 7–22. https://doi.org/10.4337/jhre.2010.01.01

Gebara, M. F. (2018). Tenure reforms in indigenous lands: Decentralized forest management or illegalism? *Current Opinion in Environmental Sustainability, 32*, 60–67. https://doi.org/10.1016/j.cosust.2018.04.008

Gibson-Graham, J. K. (2011). A feminist project of belonging for the Anthropocene. *Gender, Place and Culture, 181*, 1–21. https://doi.org/10.1080/0966369X.2011.535295

Gibson-Graham, J. K., & Roelvink, G. (2010). An economic ethics for the Anthropocene. *Antipode, 41*(1), 320–346. https://doi.org/10.1111/j.1467-8330.2009.00728.x

Gow, P. (2000). Helpless—the affective preconditions of Piro social life. In J. Overing & A. Passes (Eds.), *The anthropology of love and anger: The aesthetics of conviviality in native amazonia* (pp. 47–51). Routledge.

Grear, A. (2007). Challenging corporate "humanity": Legal disembodiment, embodiment and human rights. *Human Rights Law Review, 7*(3), 511–543. https://doi.org/10.1093/hrlr/ngm013

Grear, A. (2015). Deconstructing anthropos: A critical legal reflection on "Anthropocentric" law and anthropocene "Humanity." *Law and Critique, 26*(3), 225–249. https://doi.org/10.1007/s10978-015-9161-0

Gregg, M., & Seigworth, G. J. (2010). *The affect theory reader*. Duke University Press.

Gruen, L. (2015). *Entangled empathy: An alternative ethic for our relationships with animals.* Lantern Books.

Gualinga, J. (2018). *Kawsak Sacha—Living Forest A proposal of the Kichwa people of Sarayaku for a new protected areas category.* https://wecaninternational.org/uploads/cke_images/2016-kawsak-sacha-proposal-english-1-1-.pdf Accessed 1 Jan 2019.

Gudynas, E. (2013). Development alternatives in Bolivia: The impulse, the resistance, and the restoration. *NACLA Report on the Americas, 46*(1), 22–26. https://doi.org/10.1080/10714839.2013.11722007

Hallowell, I. A. (1960). Ojibwa ontology, behavior and world view. In S. Diamond (Ed.), *Culture in history: Essays in honor of paul radin.* Columbia University Press.

Haraway, D. J. (1991). Situated knowledges: The science question in feminism and the privilege of partial perspective. In C. Simians (Ed.), *Cyborgs and women: The reinvention of nature* (pp. 183–201). Routledge.

Haraway, D. (2008). *When species meet.* University of Minnesota Press.

Harvey, G. (2006). Animals, animists, and academics. *Zygon, 41*(1), 9–19. https://doi.org/10.1111/j.1467-9744.2006.00723.x

Hatfield, G. (2007). The passions of the soul and Descartes's machine psychology. *Studies in History and Philosophy of Science, 38*, 1–35. https://doi.org/10.1016/j.shpsa.2006.12.015

Hayes-Conroy, J., & Hayes-Conroy, A. (2013). Veggies and visceralities: A political ecology of food and feeling. *Emotion, Space & Society, 6*, 81–90. https://doi.org/10.1016/j.emospa.2011.11.003

Hornborg, A. (2006). Animism, fetishism and objectivism as strategies for knowing (or not knowing) the world. *Ethnos, 71*(1), 21–32. https://doi.org/10.1080/00141840600603129

Ingold, T. (2000). *The perception of the environment: Essays in livelihood, dwelling and skill.* Routledge.

Ingold, T. (2006). Rethinking the animate, re-animating thought. *Ethnos, 71*(1), 9–20. https://doi.org/10.1080/00141840600603111

James, W. A. (2008). *Pluralistic Universe.* Cambridge Scholars Publishing.

Kapfhammer, W. (2012). Amazonian pain. Indigenous ontologies and Western eco-spirituality. *Philosophy.*

Kimmerer, R.W. (2013). *Braiding sweetgrass: Indigenous wisdom, scientific knowledge and the teachings of plants.* Milkweed Editions.

Kotze, L. J., & Calzadilla, P. V. (2017). Somewhere between rhetoric and reality: Environmental constitutionalism and the rights of nature in Ecuador. *Transnational Environmental Law, 6*(3), 401–433. https://doi.org/10.1017/S2047102517000061

Lagrou, E. M. (2000). Homesickness and the Cashinahua self. In J. Overing & A. Passes (Eds.), *The Anthropology of love and anger: The aesthetics of conviviality in native amazonia* (pp. 47–51). Routledge.

Latour, B. (2004). *The politics of nature: How to bring sciences into democracy*. MIT Press.

Latour, B. (2005). *Reassembling the social—An introduction to actor-network-theory*. Oxford University Press.

Leopold, A. (1949). *A Sand county almanac, and sketches here and there: With other essays on conservation from Round River*. Oxford University Press.

Lévi-Strauss, C. (1971–1976). *Mythologica*. Suhrkamp.

Margil, M. (2014). Building an international movement for rights of nature. In: M. Maloney & P. Burdon (Eds.), *Wild Law: In Practice* (149–60). Routledge.

Massumi, B. (2002). *Parables for the virtual: Movement, affect, sensation*. Duke University Press.

McDonald, M. (2017). Ecological security. In C. Eroukhmanoff & M. Harker (Eds.), *IR and the anthropocene challenge in reflections on the posthuman in international relations: The anthropocene, security and Ecology*. E-International Relations.

Merchant, C. (1992). *Radical ecology*. Routledge.

Murdoch, J. (2006). *Post-structural geography*. Sage.

Panelli, R. (2010). More-than-human social geographies: Posthuman and other possibilities. *Progress in Human Geography, 34*(1), 79–87. https://doi.org/10.1177/0309132509105007

Pachirat, T. (2013). *Every twelve seconds: Industrialized slaughter and the politics of sight*. Yale University Press.

Petersen, V.S. (1990). Whose Rights? A Critique of the "Givens" in Human Rights Discourse. *Alternatives: Global, Local, Political, 15*(3), 303–344. http://www.jstor.org/stable/40644687

Pickering, A. (1995). *The Mangle of practice—time, agency and science*. Chicago University Press.

Pickering, A. (2010). *The cybernetic brain: Sketches of another future*. University of Chicago Press.

Plumwood, V. (2001). *Environmental Culture: The Ecological Crisis of Reason* (1st ed.). Routledge.

Plurinational State of Bolivia. (2014). *Living well in balance and harmony with mother Earth: A proposal for establishing a new global relationship between human beings and mother earth*. P. 21.

Puig De la Bellacasa, M. (2011). Matters of care in technoscience: Assembling neglected things. *Social Studies of Science, 41*(1), 85–106. https://doi.org/10.1177/0306312710380301

Puig De la Bellacasa, M. (2017). *Matters of care: Speculative ethics in more than human Worlds*. University of Minnesota Press.

Reddekop, J. (2014). *Thinking Across Worlds: Indigenous Thought, Relational Ontology, and the Politics of Nature; Or, If Only Nietzsche Could Meet A Yachaj*. Doctor of Philosophy Thesis, Graduate Program in Theory and Criticism. University of Western Ontario. https://ir.lib.uwo.ca/cgi/viewcontent.cgi?article=3410&context=etd. Accessed 1 Ja 2019.

Rocheleau, D. E. (2008). Political ecology in the key of policy: From chains of explanation to webs of relation. *Geoforum, 39*(2), 716–727. https://doi.org/10.1016/j.geoforum.2007.02.005

Rocheleau, D., & Roth, R. (2007). Rooted networks, relational webs and powers of connection: Rethinking human and political ecologies. *Geoforum, 38*(3), 433–437. https://doi.org/10.1016/j.geoforum.2006.10.003

Ruddick, S. (2017). Rethinking the subject, reimagining worlds. *Dialogues in Human Geography, 7*(2), 119–139. https://doi.org/10.1177/2043820617717847

Simonsen, K. (2013). In quest of a new humanism: Embodiment, experience and phenomenology as critical geography. *Progress in Human Geography, 37*(1), 10–26. https://doi.org/10.1177/0309132512467573

Singh, N. M. (2017). Becoming a commoner: The commons as sites for affective socio-nature encounters and co-becomings. *Ephemera, 17*(4), 751–776.

Singh, N.M. (2018). Introduction: Affective ecologies and conservation. *Conservation and Society, 16*, 1–7. http://www.jstor.org/stable/26380571

Smith, L. T. (2006). Choosing the margins: The role of research in indigenous struggles for social justice. In N. K. Denzin & M. D. Giardina (Eds.), *Qualitative inquiry and the conservative challenge* (pp. 151–174). Left Coast Press.

Stengers, I. (2010). *Cosmopolitics I* (trans: Bononno, R.). University of Minnesota Press.

Stengers, I. (2011). *Cosmopolitics II* (trans: Bononno, R.). University of Minnesota Press.

Stone, C. (1972). Should trees have standing? Towards legal rights for natural objects. *California Law Review, 45*, 450–501.

Suchet-Pearson, S., Wright, S., Lloyd, K., & Burarrwanga, L. (2013). Caring as country: Towards an ontology of co-becoming in natural resource management. *Asia Pacific Viewpoint, 54*(2), 185–197. https://doi.org/10.1111/apv.12018

Sultana, F. (2015). Emotional political ecology. In R. L. Bryant (Ed.), *The international handbook of political ecology* (pp. 633–645). Edward Elgar.

Tallacchini, M. (1997). Human Right to the Environment or Rights of Nature? In R. Martin & G. Sprenger (Eds.), *Rights: Proceedings of the 17th World Congress of the International Association for Philosophy of Law and Social Philosophy*, Vol I. (pp. 125–33). Franz Steiner Verlag.

Thrift, N. (2008). *Non-representational theory: Space, politics, affect*. Routledge.

Viveiros de Castro, E. (1998). Cosmological Deixis and Amerindian Perspectivism. *Journal of the Royal Anthropological Institute, 4*(3), 469–470. https://doi.org/10.2307/3034157

Viveiros de Castro, E. (2005). Perspectivism and multinaturalism in indigenous America. In A. Surrallés & P. García Hierro (Eds.), *The land within: Indigenous territory and the perception of the environment* (pp. 36–74). International Work Group for Indigenous Affairs (IWGIA).

Weik von Mossner, A. (2017). *Affective ecologies: Empathy, emotion, and environmental narrative*. Ohio State University Press.

Whatmore, S. (2002) *Hybrid geographies. Natures cultures spaces*. University of Oxford, Sage Publications.

Whatmore, S. (2013). Earthly powers: Thinking through flooding. *Theory, Culture and Society, 30*, 7–8. https://doi.org/10.1177/0263276413480949

Wilson, S. (2008). *Research is ceremony: Indigenous research methods*. Fernwood.

Wright, R. M., Kapfhammer, W., & Wiik, F. B. (2012). The clash of cosmographies: indigenous societies and project collaboration—three ethnographic cases (Kaingang, Sateré-Mawé, Baniwa). *Vibrant: Virtual Brazilian Anthropology, 9*(1), 382–450. https://doi.org/10.1590/S1809-434120 12000100014.

Zaffaroni E. R. (2011). La Pachamama y el humano. In A. Acosta & E. Martínez (Eds.), *La naturaleza con derechos: de la filosofía a la política* (pp. 25–137). Ediciones Abya Yala.

Printed in the United States
by Baker & Taylor Publisher Services